W9-BJD-756

THE MACARTHUR NEW TESTAMENT COMMENTARY

JOHN 1-11

John MacArthur

MOODY PUBLISHERS/CHICAGO

© 2006 by
JOHN MACARTHUR

All rights reserved. No part of this book may be reproduced in any form without permission in writing from the publisher, except in the case of brief quotations embodied in critical articles or reviews.

All Scripture quotations, unless otherwise indicated, are taken from the *New American Standard Bible®*, Copyright © The Lockman Foundation 1960, 1962, 1963, 1968, 1971, 1972, 1973, 1975, 1977, 1995. Used by permission.

Scripture quotations marked NIV are taken from the *Holy Bible, New International Version®*. NIV®. Copyright © 1973, 1978, 1984 by International Bible Society. Used by permission of Zondervan Publishing House. All rights reserved.

Scripture quotations marked NKJV are taken from the *New King James Version*. Copyright © 1982 by Thomas Nelson, Inc. Used by permission. All rights reserved.

Scripture quotations marked KJV are taken from the King James Version.

The abbreviation LXX denotes the Septuagint, the Greek translation of the Old Testament.

Library of Congress Cataloging-in-Publication Data

MacArthur, John, 1939-
    The MacArthur New Testament commentary : John 1-11 / by John MacArthur.
        p. cm.
    Includes bibliographical references and index.
    ISBN-13: 978-0-8024-0771-9
    1. Bible. N.T. John 1-11—Commentaries. I. Title.

BS2615.53.M33 2006
226.5'077—dc22

2005029226

We hope you enjoy this book from Moody Publishers. Our goal is to provide high-quality, thought-provoking books and products that connect truth to your real needs and challenges. For more information on other books and products written and produced from a biblical perspective, go to www.moodypublishers.com or write to:

Moody Publishers
820 N. LaSalle Boulevard
Chicago, IL 60610

ISBN: 0-8024-0771-4
ISBN-13: 978-0-8024-0771-9

3 5 7 9 10 8 6 4 2

Printed in the United States of America

*Dedicated to
the memory of Jon Campbell,
whose generosity and grace made us all
anticipate the sweetness of the Heaven he now enjoys.*

Contents

Preface

The message of John's gospel is simple. The apostle writes with straightforward clarity and in words that make the truth accessible to every reader. That fact is critical, because this is the saving gospel, written for unbelievers. John said so:

> Many other signs Jesus also performed in the presence of the disciples, which are not written in this book; but these have been written that you may believe that Jesus is the Christ, the Son of God; and that believing you may have life in His name. (John 20:30–31)

I have tried in this commentary to keep verbiage out and say only what is directly helpful to the understanding of the text. There is little digression and no attempt to give embellishing content. This is a departure from the style of my other commentaries, where I often introduce an abundance of related theological and illustrative material. That is not to say there are not glorious themes throughout John that can and should be developed in the process of exposition, and by comparing Scripture with Scripture. But for the most part I have left that task to others this time, in favor of flow and concise adherence to the apostle John's own stated intent. At times I felt I should write more; sometimes less. But my deliberate goal throughout has been to serve the inspired message by restraint, minimizing interruptions, and letting the Word speak without adding anything more than essential explanations, without drifting from the text itself into parallel passages—thus keeping the simplicity and clarity of the Spirit's inspired truth uncluttered. I hope I have done that.

In this profound yet plain account of the coming of the Son of God to redeem sinners is the most needed message anyone will ever hear or understand. With just a little clarification and background, it proclaims to the mind of the willing and humble sinner the truth that transforms eternally.

JOHN MACARTHUR
September 2005

Introduction to John

John is unique among the gospels. The first three, Matthew, Mark, and Luke, are known as the Synoptics (from a Greek word meaning "to see together") because of their similarities to each other. Although each has its own distinctive emphases and themes, the Synoptics have much in common. They follow the same general outline of Christ's life and are similar in contents, structure, and perspective.

But even a cursory reading of John's gospel reveals it to be strikingly different from the first three. All four contain a mixture of narrative history and discourses of Jesus. John's gospel, however, contains a higher proportion of discourse in relation to narrative than do the Synoptics. Unlike the Synoptics, John contains no narrative parables, no eschatological discourses, no accounts of Jesus exorcising demons or healing lepers, no list of the twelve apostles, and no formal institution of the Lord's Supper. John also does not record Jesus' birth, baptism, transfiguration, temptation, agony in Gethsemane, or ascension.

On the other hand, John includes a large amount of material (more than 90 percent of the gospel) not found in the Synoptics, such as the prologue describing Christ's pre-existence and incarnation (1:1–18); Jesus' early ministry in Judea and Samaria (chaps. 2–3); His first miracle (2:1–11); His dialogue with Nicodemus (3:1–21); His encounter with a

Samaritan woman (4:5–42); His healing of a lame man (5:1–15) and a blind man (9:1–41); both at Jerusalem; His Bread of Life discourse (6:22–71); His claim to be the living water (7:37–38); His taking for Himself the name of God (see the discussion of 8:24 in chapter 29 of this volume); His discourse presenting Himself as the Good Shepherd and its aftermath (10:1–39); the resurrection of Lazarus (11:1–46); the washing of the disciples' feet (13:1–15); the Upper Room Discourse (chaps. 13–16); Jesus' High Priestly Prayer (chap. 17); the miraculous catch of fish (21:1–6); and Jesus' recommissioning of Peter and prediction of His martyrdom (21:15–19). John also contains more teaching on the Holy Spirit than is found in the Synoptics.

Two things must be borne in mind concerning the differences between John and the Synoptic Gospels. First, those differences are not contradictions; nothing in John contradicts the Synoptics, and vice versa. Second, the differences between John and the Synoptics must not be exaggerated. Both John and the Synoptics present Jesus Christ as the Son of Man, Israel's Messiah (Mark 2:10; John 1:51), and the Son of God, God in human flesh (Mark 1:1; John 1:34). All four gospels picture Him as the Savior, who came to "save His people from their sins" (Matt. 1:21; cf. John 3:16), died a sacrificial death on the cross, and rose from the dead.

John and the Synoptics were designed by the divine Spirit to supplement each other. They "represent an *interlocking* tradition, that is, . . . they mutually reinforce or explain each other" (D. A. Carson, Douglas J. Moo, and Leon Morris, *An Introduction to the New Testament* [Grand Rapids: Zondervan, 1992], 161. Italics in original.). For example, at His trial (Mark 14:58) and while He was on the cross (Mark 15:29), Jesus' enemies accused Him of having claimed that He would destroy the temple. The Synoptics do not record the basis for that false allegation, but John does (2:19). The Synoptics do not explain why the Jews had to bring Jesus before Pilate; John explains that the Romans had withheld from them the right of capital punishment (18:31). The Synoptics place Peter in the high priest's courtyard (Matt. 26:58; Mark 14:54; Luke 22:54–55); John explains how he gained access (John 18:15–16). The call of Peter, Andrew, James, and John (Matt. 4:18–22) becomes more understandable in light of John 1:35–42, which reveals that they had already spent time with Jesus. The Synoptics record that immediately after the feeding of the five thousand Jesus sent the crowds away (Matt. 14:22; Mark 6:45); John reveals why He did that: They intended to try to make Him king (John 6:15). From John's gospel it is evident that when the Sanhedrin met on Wednesday of Passion Week to plot Jesus' arrest (Mark 14:1–2) they were merely implementing a decision made earlier, after the raising of Lazarus (John 11:47–53).

Not only does John's background information make passages in the Synoptics more understandable; the opposite is also true. John, writing decades after the others, assumed his readers were familiar with the events recorded in the Synoptics. The birth narratives in Matthew and Luke reveal how the eternally preexistent Word (John 1:1) came to have a human family (John 2:12). In 1:40 John introduced Andrew as Peter's brother, although he had not yet mentioned Peter. John's explanatory footnote that "John [the Baptist] had not yet been thrown into prison" (John 3:24) assumes that his readers knew he eventually would be. Yet the gospel of John does not record the Baptist's imprisonment, which is described in the Synoptics (Matt. 4:12; 14:3; Mark 6:17; Luke 3:20). John noted that "Jesus Himself testified that a prophet has no honor in his own country" (John 4:44), yet that statement is not found in his gospel. It is, however, recorded in the Synoptics (Matt. 13:57; Mark 6:4; Luke 4:24). John 6:67, 70–71 refers to the twelve apostles; but as noted above, John's gospel, unlike the Synoptics (Matt. 10:2–4; Mark 3:14–19; Luke 6:13–16), does not have a list of the twelve apostles. From the way they are introduced, John evidently expected his readers to know who Mary and Martha were (11:1), even though he had not previously referred to them. They are, however, mentioned in Luke's gospel (10:38–42). In that same connection, John noted that Mary was the one who anointed the Lord's feet (11:2). He would not relate that story until chapter 12, but assumed his readers would be familiar with it from the synoptic accounts (Matt. 26:6–13; Mark 14:3–9). John's account of Philip's hesitancy to bring the Greeks to Jesus until after he consulted first with Andrew (12:21–22) may have been motivated by the readers' familiarity with Jesus' command, "Do not go in the way of the Gentiles" (Matt. 10:5).

THE AUTHORSHIP OF JOHN'S GOSPEL

Like the other three gospels, the gospel of John does not name its author. But according to the testimony of the early church, the apostle John wrote it. Irenaeus (c. A.D. 130–200) was the first person to explicitly name John as author. In his work *Against Heresies,* written in the last quarter of the second century, Irenaeus testified, "Afterwards [after the Synoptic Gospels were written], John, the disciple of the Lord, who also had leaned upon His breast, did himself publish a Gospel during his residence at Ephesus in Asia" (3.1.1). What makes his witness especially valuable is that Irenaeus was a disciple of Polycarp (Eusebius, *Ecclesiastical History,* 5.20), who was a disciple of the apostle John (Irenaeus, *Against Heresies,* 3.3.4). Thus there was a direct line from Irenaeus to John, with only one intervening link. Theophilus of Antioch, who lived at about the same time as Irenaeus, wrote, "The holy writings teach us, and all the spirit-bearing [inspired] men, one of whom, John, says, 'In the beginning was the Word, and the Word was with God'" (*To Autolycus*, 2.22). The church fathers after Irenaeus consistently held that the apostle John authored this gospel. The Muratorian Canon (a second-century list of New Testament books), Tertullian, Clement of Alexandria, Origen, Dionysius of Alexandria, and Eusebius all cite him as its author.

Earlier writers, while not naming the apostle John as its author, show familiarity with the fourth gospel. Justin Martyr (c. A.D. 100–165) quoted John 3:5 (*First Apology*, 61). That his student Tatian included John in his *Diatessaron* (the earliest known harmony of the gospels) offers further evidence that Justin was familiar with it. Even some outside the church (e.g., Gnostics such as Heracleon, Ptolemaeus, Basilides, and the apocryphal *Gospel of Thomas;* Marcion [who rejected all the gospels except Luke]; and the pagan opponent of Christianity, Celsus), though they rejected it or twisted its truth, acknowledged that the fourth gospel was penned by the apostle John.

The title ("According to John," or "The Gospel According to John") is not part of the original inspired text, but was added in later manuscripts. Nevertheless, no manuscript has ever been found that attributes John's gospel to anyone other than him. Daniel B. Wallace notes that

> the unbroken stream suggests recognition (or at least acknowledgment) of Johannine authorship as early as the first quarter of the second century. Indeed, John's Gospel is unique among the evangelists for two early papyri (p^{66} and p^{75}, dated c. 200) attest to Johannine authorship. Since these two [manuscripts] were not closely related to each other, this common tradition [of Johannine authorship] must precede them by at least three or four generations of copying. ("The Gospel of John: Introduction, Argument, Outline" [Biblical Studies Press: www.bible.org, 1999])

Unlike the canonical gospels, spurious gospels written by forgers invariably claimed to have been authored by a prominent figure in the early church, but could not survive scrutiny externally or internally. On the other hand, the true gospels have always withstood every legitimate examination as to authorship, though the authors' names are not included.

The earliest extant portion of any New Testament book is a tiny fragment (p^{52}) containing a few verses from John 18 and dating from about A.D. 130 (or earlier). (Another early fragment, known as the Egerton Papyrus 2, also quotes portions of John's gospel. Scholars date it no later than the middle of the second century.) Nineteenth-century critics confidently dated the gospel of John in the second half of the second century. The discovery of p^{52} early in the twentieth century sounded the death knell for that view. The fragment was found in a remote region of Egypt. Allowing time for John's gospel to have circulated that far pushes its date of writing back into the first century. In addition to the above-mentioned manuscript fragments, there is some archaeological evidence that also suggests that the gospel of John was known early in the second century (see Leon Morris, *The Gospel According to John,* The New International Commentary on the New Testament [Grand Rapids: Eerdmans, 1979], 28–29).

As well as the external testimony, the internal evidence also points to the apostle John as the author. The nineteenth-century commentator and textual scholar B. F. Westcott summarized that evidence in a series of concentric circles, gradually narrowing the focus down to the apostle John (*The Gospel According to St. John* [Reprint; Grand Rapids: Eerdmans, 1978], v–xxiv). His reasoning is still valid today; "Westcott has not so much been confuted as bypassed. Nobody seems to have dealt adequately with his massive argument (Morris, *John,* 9). His argument may be briefly summarized as follows:

1. *The author was a Jew.* He was familiar with contemporary Jewish opinions about a wide range of topics, including the Messiah (e.g., 1:21, 25; 6:14–15; 7:26–27, 31, 40–42; 12:34), the importance of formal religious training (7:15), the relationship of suffering to personal sin (9:2), and the Jews' attitude toward the Samaritans (4:9), women (4:27), and the Hellenistic Jews of the Diaspora (7:35). He was familiar with Jewish customs, including the necessity of avoiding ceremonial defilement from contact with Gentiles (18:28), the need for purification before celebrating Passover (11:55), as well as wedding (2:1–10) and burial (11:17–44; 19:40) customs. He was familiar with the great Jewish feasts of Passover (2:13; 6:4; 11:55), Tabernacles (Booths; 7:2), and Dedication (Hanukkah; 10:22).

2. *The author was a Palestinian Jew.* He had a detailed knowledge of local places available only to one who had actually lived in Palestine. He distinguished between the Bethany beyond the Jordan (1:28) and the Bethany on the outskirts of Jerusalem (11:1), and he knew the precise distance of the latter from Jerusalem (11:18). He was familiar with Jerusalem, describing at least three sites not mentioned in the Synoptics (the pool of Bethesda [5:2], the pool of Siloam [9:7; though Luke mentions a tower near the pool; Luke 13:4], and the ravine of the Kidron [18:1]). He also had a detailed knowledge of the temple (2:14, 20; 8:20; 10:23).

3. *The author was an eyewitness.* He gave specific details, even when they were not essential to the story. Many of those details could not have come from the Synoptics, which do not record them. They include the name of Judas Iscariot's father (6:71; 13:2, 26), how long Lazarus had

been in the tomb (11:17, 39), how long Jesus stayed in Sychar (4:40, 43), the precise time at which certain events occurred (1:39; 4:6, 52; 19:14; cf. 13:30), and exact numbers (1:35; 2:6; 6:9, 19; 19:23; 21:8, 11). He alone recorded that the loaves the boy had at the feeding of the five thousand were made of barley (6:9), that after Mary poured the perfume on Jesus' feet the house was filled with its fragrance (12:3), that the branches the people lined the road with during the triumphal entry were palm branches (12:13), that Roman soldiers were in the party that accompanied Judas to Gethsemane (18:3, 12), that Jesus' tunic was seamless (19:23), and that His facecloth was separate from the linen wrappings (20:7).

4. *The author was an apostle.* He was intimately acquainted with what the Twelve were thinking and feeling (e.g., 2:11, 17, 22; 4:27; 6:19; 12:16; 13:22, 28; 20:9; 21:12).

5. *The author was the apostle John.* It is remarkable that the apostle John, mentioned some twenty times in the Synoptic Gospels, is not named once in his gospel. Leon Morris observes, "It is not easy to think of a reason why any early Christian, other than John himself, should have completely omitted all mention of such a prominent Apostle" (Morris, *John,* 11). Further, only a preeminent person of unquestioned authority could have written a gospel that differed so markedly from the other three (see the discussion above) and had it universally accepted by the church.

Instead of naming the apostle John as its author, John's gospel claims to have been written by "the disciple whom Jesus loved" (21:20). An analysis of the texts that mention him makes it clear that the beloved disciple is none other than the apostle John. The first clue to his identity is that he was present at the Last Supper (13:23). Since only the Twelve were present at that meal (Matt. 26:20; Mark 14:17–18; Luke 22:14), the beloved disciple had to have been an apostle (which means he cannot have been John Mark, Lazarus, or the rich young ruler [who was not even a believer! (Matt. 19:22)], as some critics have proposed). John 21:2 further narrows his identification to Peter, Thomas, Nathanael, the sons of Zebedee, or two other unnamed disciples. Peter, Thomas, and Nathanael cannot be the beloved disciple, since they are named in the text. (He also cannot be Peter, because they address each other [13:24; 21:7]). The two unnamed disciples can also be ruled out; if one of them was the beloved disciple and hence the author of the fourth gospel, why did he not mention the apostle John by name? Further, his closeness to Jesus ("reclining on Jesus' bosom" [13:23]) at the Last Supper reveals that the beloved disciple was one of the inner circle of the Twelve. Of those three, he cannot, as noted above, have been Peter. Nor could he have been James, because he was martyred too early to have written the gospel of John (Acts 12:2).

By process of elimination, the beloved disciple and author of John (21:24) can only be the apostle John. That identification is further strengthened by the beloved disciple's close association with Peter (13:23–24; 20:2; 21:7), which was true of John (Luke 22:8; Acts 3:1–11; 4:13,19; 8:14; Gal. 2:9).

Despite the powerful external and internal evidence, many critics, as always desperately needing to assault the integrity of Scripture to discredit its truth and authority over their sinful lives, deny that the apostle John wrote the fourth gospel. The arguments they put forth are reflective of unbelief, unconvincing, and often highly subjective. Some argue that John, like his brother James, was martyred too early to have written the gospel of John. But that view is based on a misreading of Mark 10:39, which merely indicates that the two brothers would suffer, not necessarily that they would be martyred.

Others point to a "John the Elder" mentioned (according to Eusebius's interpretation) by Papias. But it is unlikely that such a person even existed, much less wrote anything (D. A. Carson, *The Gospel According to John*, The Pillar New Testament Commentary [Grand Rapids: Eerdmans, 1991], 69–70).

Another baseless argument put forth by the critics is that the Christology of the fourth gospel is too advanced for a first-generation Christian to have written it. But John's Christology was divinely revealed (which critics reject) and is in harmony with that of the rest of the New Testament (cf. Rom. 9:5; Phil. 2:6; Col. 2:9; Titus 2:13; 2 Peter 1:1).

Still other spiritually blind skeptics maintain that an uneducated (Acts 4:13) Galilean fisherman could not have been fluent enough in Greek to have written the fourth gospel. But Acts 4:13 does not mean that John was illiterate, but merely that he had not been trained in the rabbinic schools (cf. John 7:15). Galilee was near the predominantly Gentile region known as the Decapolis, which was east and south of the Sea of Galilee. There is also evidence that Greek was commonly spoken throughout Palestine in the first century (cf. Robert L. Thomas and Stanley N. Gundry, "The Languages Jesus Spoke," in *A Harmony of the Gospels* [Chicago: Moody, 1978], 309–12). In addition, John wrote this gospel after many years of living and ministering among Greek-speaking people in Ephesus (see below). Therefore it is foolish to make dogmatic presumptions regarding his competency in Greek.

A closer look at John reveals that he was the younger of the two sons of Zebedee (James is almost always listed first when the two are mentioned together, suggesting he was the elder brother), who was a prosperous fisherman on the Sea of Galilee and who owned his own boat and hired servants (Mark 1:20). John's mother was Salome (cf. Mark 15:40 with Matt. 27:56), who contributed financially to Jesus' ministry

(Matt. 27:55–56), and who may have been the sister of Mary, the mother of Jesus (John 19:25). If so, John and Jesus would have been cousins.

John first appears in Scripture as a disciple of John the Baptist (John 1:35–40; though characteristically, John did not name himself). When the Baptist pointed out Jesus as the Messiah, the apostle John immediately left him and followed Jesus (1:37). After remaining with Him for a while, John went back to his father's fishing business. Later, he became a permanent disciple of Jesus (Matt. 4:18–22).

Along with his brother, James, and fellow fisherman, Peter, John was one of the three most intimate associates of Jesus (cf. Matt. 17:1; Mark 5:37; Mark 13:3; 14:33). After the ascension, John became one of the leaders of the Jerusalem church (Acts 1:13; 3:1–11; 4:13–21; 8:14; Gal. 2:9). According to tradition, John spent the last decades of his life at Ephesus, overseeing the churches in the surrounding region (Clement of Alexandria, *Who Is the Rich Man That Shall Be Saved?*, 42) and writing his three epistles (c. A.D. 90–95). Toward the end of his life (according to Irenaeus [*Against Heresies*, 3.3.4], John lived until the time of the emperor Trajan [A.D. 98–117]), John was banished to the island of Patmos. It was there that he received and wrote down the visions described in the book of Revelation (c. A.D. 94–96).

Despite his reputation as "the apostle of love," John had a fiery temperament. Jesus named John and James "Sons of Thunder" (Mark 3:17), and the two brothers lived up to that name. Indignant when a Samaritan village refused to receive Jesus and the disciples, and overestimating their apostolic power, they eagerly asked the Lord, "Do You want us to command fire to come down from heaven and consume them?" (Luke 9:54). In the only place recorded in the Synoptic Gospels where John acted and spoke alone, he reveals the same attitude, saying to Jesus, "Master, we saw someone casting out demons in Your name; and we tried to prevent him because he does not follow along with us" (Luke 9:49).

Though he mellowed toward people over time (I trace the development of his spiritual character in my book *Twelve Ordinary Men* [Nashville: W Publishing Group, 2002]), John never lost his passion for the truth. Two vignettes from his years at Ephesus reveal that. According to Polycarp, "John, the disciple of the Lord, going to bathe at Ephesus, and perceiving [the heretic] Cerinthus within, rushed out of the bath-house without bathing, exclaiming, 'Let us fly, lest even the bath-house fall down, because Cerinthus, the enemy of the truth, is within'" (Irenaeus, *Against Heresies*, 3.3.4). Clement of Alexandria relates how John fearlessly entered the camp of a band of robbers whose captain had once professed faith in Christ and led him to true repentance (*Who Is the Rich Man That Shall Be Saved?*, 42).

DATE AND PLACE OF WRITING

There is nothing specific in the gospel itself to indicate when it was written. Dates given by conservative scholars range from before the fall of Jerusalem to the last decade of the first century. (As noted above, a date in the second century is ruled out by the discovery of the papyrus fragments p52 and Egerton Papyrus 2.) Several considerations favor a date toward the end of that range (c. A.D. 80–90). The gospel of John was written long enough after Peter's death (c. A.D. 67–68) for the rumor that John would live to see the second coming to have developed (John 21:22–23). That rumor would have had more plausibility when John was an old man. John does not mention the fall of Jerusalem and the destruction of the temple (A.D. 70). If his gospel were written a decade or more after that event, it may no longer have been an issue to his readers. (The temple's destruction in any case would have been less significant to Gentiles and Jews of the Diaspora than to Palestinian Jews.) Finally, although not dependent on them, John was aware of the Synoptic Gospels. The later date allows time for them to have been written and circulated among John's readers. The testimony of the church fathers further confirms that John was the last of the four gospels to be written (e.g., Irenaeus, *Against Heresies*, 3.1.1; Eusebius, *Ecclesiastical History*, 3.24, 6.14).

According to the uniform tradition of the early church, John wrote his gospel while living in Ephesus.

PURPOSE

John is the only one of the gospels that contains a precise statement of the author's purpose: "But these have been written so that you may believe that Jesus is the Christ, the Son of God; and that believing you may have life in His name" (20:31). John's objective was both apologetic ("that you may believe that Jesus is the Christ, the Son of God") and evangelistic ("and that believing you may have life in His name"). In keeping with his evangelistic purpose, John used the verb "to believe" nearly one hundred times—more than twice as much as the Synoptics, emphasizing that those who savingly believe in Jesus will receive eternal life (3:15–16, 36; 4:14; 5:24, 39–40; 6:27, 33, 35, 40, 47–48, 54, 63, 68; 10:10, 28; 12:50; 14:6; 17:2–3; 20:31).

John's apologetic purpose, which is inseparable from his evangelistic purpose, was to convince his readers of Jesus' true identity. He presents Him as God incarnate (1:1, 14; 8:23, 58; 10:30; 20:28), the Messiah (1:41; 4:25–26), and the Savior of the world (4:42). To that end, John repeatedly stressed Jesus' miraculous signs (e.g., 3:2; 6:2, 14; 7:31; 9:16;

11:47; 12:18; 20:30), including eight specific ones: turning water into wine (2:1–11), healing a royal official's son (4:46–54), healing a lame man at the pool of Bethesda (5:1–18), feeding the five thousand (6:1–15), walking on the Sea of Galilee (6:16–21), healing a man born blind (9:1–41), raising Lazarus from the dead (11:1–45), and providing a miraculous catch of fish (21:6–11). In addition to those signs was the most convincing sign of all—Jesus' own resurrection (20:1–29).

In short, John presents Jesus as the eternal Word, Messiah, and Son of God who, through His death and resurrection, brings the gift of salvation to mankind. People respond by either accepting or rejecting the salvation that comes only through believing in Him.

OUTLINE

  I. The Incarnation of the Son of God (1:1–18)
     A. His Deity (1:1–2)
     B. His Pre-incarnate Work (1:3–5)
     C. His Forerunner (1:6–8)
     D. His Rejection (1:9–11)
     E. His Reception (1:12–13)
     F. His Becoming Flesh (1:14–18)
 II. The Presentation of the Son of God (1:19–4:54)
     A. Presentation by John the Baptist (1:19–34)
        1. To the religious leaders (1:19–28)
        2. At Christ's baptism (1:29–34)
     B. Presentation to His First Disciples (1:35–51)
        1. Andrew and Peter (1:35–42)
        2. Philip and Nathanael (1:43–51)
     C. Presentation in Galilee (2:1–12)
        1. First sign: water to wine (2:1–10)
        2. Disciples believe (2:11–12)
     D. Presentation in Judea (2:13–3:36)
        1. Cleansing the temple (2:13–25)
        2. Teaching Nicodemus (3:1–21)
        3. Preaching by John the Baptist (3:22–36)
     E. Presentation in Samaria (4:1–42)
        1. Witness to the Samaritan woman (4:1–26)
        2. Witness to the disciples (4:27–38)
        3. Witness to the Samaritans (4:39–42)
     F. Presentation in Galilee (4:43–54)
        1. Reception by the Galileans (4:43–45)
        2. Second sign: healing the nobleman's son (4:46–54)

III. The Opposition to the Son of God (5:1–12:50)
    A. Opposition at the Feast in Jerusalem (5:1–47)
        1. Third sign: healing the paralytic (5:1–9)
        2. Rejection by the Jews (5:10–47)
    B. Opposition in Galilee (6:1–71)
        1. Fourth sign: feeding the 5,000 (6:1–14)
        2. Fifth sign: walking on water (6:15–21)
        3. Bread of Life discourse (6:22–71)
    C. Opposition at the Feast of Tabernacles (7:1–10:21)
    D. Opposition at the Feast of Dedication (10:22–42)
    E. Opposition at Bethany (11:1–12:11)
        1. Seventh sign: raising of Lazarus (11:1–44)
        2. The Sanhedrin plots to kill Christ (11:45–57)
        3. Mary anoints Christ (12:1–11)
    F. Opposition in Jerusalem (12:12–50)
        1. The triumphal entry (12:12–22)
        2. The discourse on faith and rejection (12:23–50)
IV. The Preparation of the Disciples by the Son of God (13:1–17:26)
    A. In the Upper Room (13:1–14:31)
        1. Washing feet (13:1–20)
        2. Announcing the betrayal (13:21–30)
        3. Teaching on His departure (13:31–14:31)
    B. On the Way to the Garden (15:1–17:26)
        1. Instructing the disciples (15:1–16:33)
        2. Interceding with the Father (17:1–26)
V. The Execution of the Son of God (18:1–19:37)
    A. The Rejection of Christ (18:1–19:16)
        1. His arrest (18:1–11)
        2. His trials (18:12–19:16)
    B. The Crucifixion of Christ (19:17–37)
VI. The Resurrection of the Son of God (19:38–21:23)
    A. The Burial of Christ (19:38–42)
    B. The Resurrection of Christ (20:1–10)
    C. The Appearances of Christ (20:11–21:23)
        1. To Mary Magdalene (20:11–18)
        2. To the disciples without Thomas (20:19–25)
        3. To the disciples with Thomas (20:26–29)
        4. Parenthesis: John's purpose in writing his gospel (20:30–31)
        5. To the disciples (21:1–23)
VII. Conclusion (21:24–25)

The Divine Word

(John 1:1–5)

In the beginning was the Word, and the Word was with God, and the Word was God. He was in the beginning with God. All things came into being through Him, and apart from Him nothing came into being that has come into being. In Him was life, and the life was the Light of men. The Light shines in the darkness, and the darkness did not comprehend it. (1:1–5)

The opening section of John's gospel expresses the most profound truth in the universe in the clearest terms. Though easily understood by a child, John's Spirit-inspired words convey a truth beyond the ability of the greatest minds in human history to fathom: the eternal, infinite God became a man in the person of the Lord Jesus Christ. The glorious, incontrovertible truth that in Jesus the divine "Word became flesh" (1:14) is the theme of John's gospel.

The deity of the Lord Jesus Christ is an essential, nonnegotiable tenet of the Christian faith. Several lines of biblical evidence flow together to prove conclusively that He is God.

First, the direct statements of Scripture affirm that Jesus is God. In keeping with his emphasis on Christ's deity, John records several of those statements. The opening verse of his gospel declares, "the Word [Jesus] was God" (see the discussion of this verse later in this chapter). In John's gospel Jesus repeatedly assumed for Himself the divine name "I am" (cf. 4:26; 8:24, 28, 58; 13:19: 18:5, 6, 8). In 10:30, He claimed to be one in nature and essence with the Father (that the unbelieving Jews recognized this as a claim to deity is clear from their reaction in v. 33; cf. 5:18). Nor did Jesus correct Thomas when he addressed Him as "My Lord and my God!" (20:28); in fact, He praised him for his faith (v. 29). Jesus' reaction is inexplicable if He were not God.

To the Philippians Paul wrote, "[Jesus] existed in the form of God," possessing absolute "equality with God" (Phil. 2:6). In Colossians 2:9 he declared, "For in Him all the fullness of Deity dwells in bodily form." Romans 9:5 refers to Christ as "God blessed forever"; Titus 2:13 and 2 Peter 1:1 call Him "our God and Savior." God the Father addressed the Son as God in Hebrews 1:8: "Your throne, O God, is forever and ever, and the righteous scepter is the scepter of His kingdom." In his first epistle John referred to Jesus Christ as "the true God" (1 John 5:20).

Second, Jesus Christ receives titles elsewhere in Scripture given to God. As noted above, Jesus took for Himself the divine name "I am." In John 12:40 John quoted Isaiah 6:10, a passage which in Isaiah's vision refers to God (cf. Isa. 6:5). Yet in verse 41 John declared, "These things Isaiah said because he saw His [Christ's; cf. vv. 36, 37, 42] glory, and he spoke of Him." Jeremiah prophesied that the Messiah would be called "The Lord [YHWH] our righteousness" (Jer. 23:6).

God and Jesus are both called Shepherd (Ps. 23:1—John 10:14); Judge (Gen. 18:25—2 Tim. 4:1, 8); Holy One (Isa. 10:20—Ps. 16:10; Acts 2:27; 3:14); First and Last (Isa. 44:6; 48:12—Rev. 1:17; 22:13); Light (Ps. 27:1—John 8:12); Lord of the Sabbath (Ex. 16:23, 29; Lev. 19:3—Matt. 12:8); Savior (Isa. 43:11—Acts 4:12; Titus 2:13); Pierced One (Zech. 12:10—John 19:37); Mighty God (Isa. 10:21—Isa. 9:6); Lord of lords (Deut. 10:17—Rev. 17:14); Alpha and Omega (Rev. 1:8—Rev. 22:13); Lord of Glory (Ps. 24:10—1 Cor. 2:8); and Redeemer (Isa. 41:14; 48:17; 63:16— Eph. 1:7; Heb. 9:12).

Third, Jesus Christ possesses the incommunicable attributes of God, those unique to Him. Scripture reveals Christ to be eternal (Mic. 5:2; Isa. 9:6), omnipresent (Matt. 18:20; 28:20), omniscient (Matt. 11:27; John 16:30; 21:17), omnipotent (Phil. 3:21), immutable (Heb. 13:8), sovereign (Matt. 28:18), and glorious (John 17:5; 1 Cor. 2:8; cf. Isa. 42:8; 48:11, where God states that He will not give His glory to another).

Fourth, Jesus Christ does the works that only God can do. He created all things (John 1:3; Col. 1:16), sustains the creation (Col. 1:17; Heb. 1:3), raises the dead (John 5:21; 11:25–44), forgives sin (Mark 2:10; cf. v. 7), and His word stands forever (Matt. 24:35; cf. Isa. 40:8).

Fifth, Jesus Christ received worship (Matt. 14:33; 28:9; John 9:38;

Phil. 2:10; Heb. 1:6)—even though He taught that only God is to be worshiped (Matt. 4:10). Scripture also records that both holy men (Acts 10:25–26) and holy angels (Rev. 22:8–9) refused worship.

Finally, Jesus Christ received prayer, which is only to be addressed to God (John 14:13–14; Acts 7:59–60; 1 John 5:13–15).

Verses 1–18, the prologue to John's presentation of the deity of Christ, are a synopsis or overview of the entire book. John clearly defined his purpose in writing his gospel in 20:31—that his readers "may believe that Jesus is the Christ, the Son of God; and that believing [they] may have life in His name." John revealed Jesus Christ as "the Son of God," the eternal second person of the Trinity. He became a man, the "Christ" (Messiah), and offered Himself as a sacrifice for sins. Those who put their faith in Him will "have life in His name," while those who reject Him will be judged and sentenced to eternal punishmnt.

The reality that Jesus is God, introduced in the prologue, is expounded throughout the book by John's careful selection of claims and miracles that seal the case. Verses 1–3 of the prologue teach that Jesus is co-equal and co-eternal with the Father; verses 4–5 relate the salvation He brought, which was announced by His herald, John the Baptist (vv. 6–8); verses 9–13 describe the reaction of the human race to Him, either rejection (vv. 10–11) or acceptance (vv. 12–13); verses 14–18 summarize the entire prologue.

The prologue also introduces several key terms that appear throughout the book, including light (3:19–21; 8:12; 9:5; 12:35–36, 46), darkness (3:19; 8:12; 12:35, 46), life (3:15–16, 36; 4:14, 36; 5:21, 24, 26, 39–40; 6:27, 33, 35, 40, 47–48, 51, 53–54, 63, 68; 8:12; 10:10, 28; 11:25; 12:25, 50; 14:6; 17:2, 3; 20:31), witness (or testify; 2:25; 3:11; 5:31, 36, 39; 7:7; 8:14; 10:25; 12:17; 15:26–27; 18:37), glory (2:11; 5:41, 44; 7:18; 8:50, 54; 11:4, 40; 12:41; 17:5, 22, 24), and world (3:16–17, 19; 4:42; 6:14, 33, 51; 7:7; 8:12, 23, 26; 9:5, 39; 10:36; 11:27; 12:19, 31, 46–47; 13:1; 14:17, 19, 22, 27, 30–31; 15:18–19; 16:8, 11, 20, 28, 33; 17:5– 6, 9, 11, 13–16, 18, 21, 23–25; 18:36–37).

From the first five verses of John's gospel prologue flow three evidences of the deity of the incarnate Word, Jesus Christ: His preexistence, His creative power, and His self-existence.

THE PREEXISTENCE OF THE WORD

In the beginning was the Word, and the Word was with God, and the Word was God. He was in the beginning with God. (1:1–2)

Archē (**beginning**) can mean "source," or "origin" (cf. Col. 1:18; Rev. 3:14); or "rule," "authority," "ruler," or "one in authority" (cf. Luke 12:11;

20:20; Rom. 8:38; 1 Cor. 15:24; Eph. 1:21; 3:10; 6:12; Col. 1:16; 2:10, 15; Titus 3:1). Both of those connotations are true of Christ, who is both the Creator of the universe (v. 3; Col. 1:16; Heb. 1:2) and its ruler (Col. 2:10; Eph. 1:20–22; Phil. 2:9–11). But *archē* refers here to the **beginning** of the universe depicted in Genesis 1:1.

Jesus Christ **was** already in existence when the heavens and the earth were created; thus, He is not a created being, but existed from all eternity. (Since time began with the creation of the physical universe, whatever existed before that creation is eternal.) "The Logos [Word] did not then begin to be, but at that point at which all else began to be, He already *was*. In the beginning, place it where you may, the Word already existed. In other words, the Logos is before time, eternal." (Marcus Dods, "John" in W. Robertson Nicoll, ed. *The Expositors' Bible Commentary* [Reprint; Peabody, Mass.: Hendrickson, 2002], 1:683. Emphasis in original.). That truth provides definitive proof of Christ's deity, for only God is eternal.

The imperfect tense of the verb *eimi* (**was**), describing continuing action in the past, further reinforces the eternal preexistence of the Word. It indicates that He was continuously in existence before the beginning. But even more significant is the use of *eimi* instead of *ginomai* ("became"). The latter term refers to things that come into existence (cf. 1:3, 10, 12, 14). Had John used *ginomai*, he would have implied that the Word came into existence at the beginning along with the rest of creation. But *eimi* stresses that the Word always existed; there was never a point when He came into being.

The concept of the **Word** (*logos*) is one imbued with meaning for both Jews and Greeks. To the Greek philosophers, the *logos* was the impersonal, abstract principle of reason and order in the universe. It was in some sense a creative force, and also the source of wisdom. The average Greek may not have fully understood all the nuances of meaning with which the philosophers invested the term *logos*. Yet even to laymen the term would have signified one of the most important principles in the universe.

To the Greeks, then, John presented Jesus as the personification and embodiment of the *logos*. Unlike the Greek concept, however, Jesus was not an impersonal source, force, principle, or emanation. In Him, the true *logos* who was God became a man—a concept foreign to Greek thought.

But *logos* was not just a Greek concept. The word of the Lord was also a significant Old Testament theme, well-known to the Jews. The word of the Lord was the expression of divine power and wisdom. By His word God introduced the Abrahamic covenant (Gen. 15:1), gave Israel the Ten Commandments (Ex. 24:3–4; Deut. 5:5; cf. Ex. 34:28; Deut. 9:10), attended the building of Solomon's temple (1 Kings 6:11–13), revealed God to Samuel (1 Sam. 3:21), pronounced judgment on the house of Eli (1 Kings 2:27), counseled Elijah (1 Kings 19:9ff.), directed Israel through God's spokesmen (cf. 1 Sam. 15:10ff.; 2 Sam. 7:4ff.; 24:11ff.; 1 Kings 16:1–4; 17:2–4., 8ff.; 18:1; 21:17–19; 2 Chron. 11:2–4), was the agent of creation (Ps. 33:6), and revealed Scripture to the prophets (Jer. 1:2; Ezek. 1:3; Dan. 9:2; Hos. 1:1; Joel 1:1; Jonah 1:1; Mic. 1:1; Zeph. 1:1; Hag. 1:1; Zech. 1:1; Mal. 1:1).

John presented Jesus to his Jewish readers as the incarnation of divine power and revelation. He initiated the new covenant (Luke 22:20; Heb. 9:15; 12:24), instructs believers (John 10:27), unites them into a spiritual temple (1 Cor. 3:16–17; 2 Cor. 6:16; Eph. 2:21), revealed God to man (John 1:18; 14:7–9), judges those who reject Him (John 3:18; 5:22), directs the church through those whom He has raised up to lead it (Eph. 4:11–12; 1 Tim. 5:17; Titus 1:5; 1 Peter 5:1–3), was the agent of creation (John 1:3; Col. 1:16; Heb. 1:2), and inspired the Scripture penned by the New Testament writers (John 14:26) through the Holy Spirit whom He sent (John 15:26). As the incarnate Word, Jesus Christ is God's final word to mankind: "God, after He spoke long ago to the fathers in the prophets in many portions and in many ways, in these last days has spoken to us in His Son" (Heb. 1:1–2).

Then John took his argument a step further. In His eternal preexistence **the Word was with God.** The English translation does not bring out the full richness of the Greek expression (*pros ton theon*). That phrase means far more than merely that the Word existed with God; it "[gives] the picture of two personal beings facing one another and engaging in intelligent discourse" (W. Robert Cook, *The Theology of John* [Chicago: Moody, 1979], 49). From all eternity Jesus, as the second person of the trinity, was "with the Father [*pros ton patera*]" (1 John 1:2) in deep, intimate fellowship. Perhaps *pros ton theon* could best be rendered "face-to-face." The Word is a person, not an attribute of God or an emanation from Him. And He is of the same essence as the Father.

Yet in an act of infinite condescension, Jesus left the glory of heaven and the privilege of face-to-face communion with His Father (cf. John 17:5). He willingly "emptied Himself, taking the form of a bondservant, and being made in the likeness of men. . . . He humbled Himself by becoming obedient to the point of death, even death on a cross" (Phil. 2:7–8). Charles Wesley captured some of the wonder of that marvelous truth in the familiar hymn "And Can It Be That I Should Gain?":

> He left His Father's throne above,
> So free, so infinite His grace!
> Emptied Himself of all but love,
> And bled for Adam's helpless race.

Amazing love! How can it be
That Thou, my God, shouldst die for me?
Amazing love! How can it be
That Thou, my God, shouldst die for me?

John's description of the Word reached its pinnacle in the third clause of this opening verse. Not only did the Word exist from all eternity, and have face-to-face fellowship with God the Father, but also **the Word was God.** That simple statement, only four words in both English and Greek (*theos ēn ho logos*), is perhaps the clearest and most direct declaration of the deity of the Lord Jesus Christ to be found anywhere in Scripture.

But despite their clarity, heretical groups almost from the moment John penned these words have twisted their meaning to support their false doctrines concerning the nature of the Lord Jesus Christ. Noting that *theos* (**God**) is anarthrous (not preceded by the definite article), some argue that it is an indefinite noun and mistranslate the phrase, "the Word was divine" (i.e., merely possessing some of the qualities of God) or, even more appalling, "the Word was *a* god."

The absence of the article before *theos*, however, does not make it indefinite. *Logos* (**Word**) has the definite article to show that it is the subject of the sentence (since it is in the same case as *theos*). Thus the rendering "God was the Word" is invalid, because "the Word," not "God," is the subject. It would also be theologically incorrect, because it would equate the Father ("God" whom the Word was with in the preceding clause) with the Word, thus denying that the two are separate persons. The predicate nominative (**God**) describes the nature of the Word, showing that He is of the same essence as the Father (cf. H. E. Dana and Julius R. Mantey, *A Manual Grammar of the Greek New Testament* [Toronto: MacMillan, 1957], 139–40; A. T. Robertson, *The Minister and His Greek New Testament* [Reprint: Grand Rapids: Baker, 1978], 67–68).

According to the rules of Greek grammar, when the predicate nominative (**God** in this clause) precedes the verb, it cannot be considered indefinite (and thus translated "a god" instead of **God**) merely because it does not have the article. That the term **God** is definite and refers to the true God is obvious for several reasons. First, *theos* appears without the definite article four other times in the immediate context (vv. 6, 12, 13, 18; cf. 3:2, 21; 9:16; Matt. 5:9). Not even the Jehovah's Witnesses' distorted translation of the Bible renders the anarthrous *theos* "a god" in those verses. Second, if John's meaning was that the Word was divine, or a god, there were ways he could have phrased it to make that unmistakably clear. For example, if he meant to say that the Word was merely in some sense divine, he could have used the adjective *theios* (cf. 2 Peter

1:4). It must be remembered that, as Robert L. Reymond notes, "No standard Greek lexicon offers 'divine' as one of the meanings of *theos*, nor does the noun become an adjective when it 'sheds' its article" (*Jesus, Divine Messiah* [Phillipsburg, N.J.: Presb. & Ref., 1990], 303). Or if he had wanted to say that the Word was a god, he could have written *ho logos ēn theos*. If John had written *ho theos ēn ho logos*, the two nouns (*theos* and *logos*) would be interchangeable, and God and the Word would be identical. That would have meant that the Father was the Word, which, as noted above, would deny the Trinity. But as Leon Morris asks rhetorically, "How else [other than *theos ēn ho logos*] in Greek would one say, 'the Word was God'?" (*The Gospel According to John*, The New International Commentary on the New Testament [Grand Rapids: Eerdmans, 1979], 77 n. 15).

Under the inspiration of the Holy Spirit, John chose the precise wording that accurately conveys the true nature of the Word, Jesus Christ. "By *theos* without the article, John neither indicates, on the one hand, identity of Person with the Father; nor yet, on the other, any lower nature than that of God Himself" (H. A. W. Meyer, *Critical and Exegetical Handbook to the Gospel of John* [Reprint; Winona Lake, Ind.: Alpha, 1979], 48).

Underscoring their significance, John restated the profound truths of verse 1 in verse 2. He emphasized again the eternity of the Word; **He** already **was** in existence **in the beginning** when everything else was created. As it did in verse 1, the imperfect tense of the verb *eimi* (**was**) describes the Word's continuous existence before **the beginning.** And as John also noted in verse 1, that existence was one of intimate fellowship **with God** the Father.

The truth of Jesus Christ's deity and full equality with the Father is a nonnegotiable element of the Christian faith. In 2 John 10 John warned, "If anyone comes to you and does not bring this teaching [the biblical teaching concerning Christ; cf. vv. 7, 9], do not receive him into your house, and do not give him a greeting." Believers are not to aid heretical false teachers in any way, including giving those who have blasphemed Christ food and lodging, since the one who does so "participates in [their] evil deeds" (v. 11). Such seemingly uncharitable behavior is perfectly justified toward false teachers who deny the deity of our Lord and the gospel, since they are under God's curse:

> There are some who are disturbing you and want to distort the gospel of Christ. But even if we, or an angel from heaven, should preach to you a gospel contrary to what we have preached to you, he is to be accursed! As we have said before, so I say again now, if any man is preaching to you a gospel contrary to what you received, he is to be accursed! (Gal. 1:7–9)

Emphasizing their deadly danger, both Paul (Acts 20:29) and Jesus (Matt. 7:15) described false teachers as wolves in disguise. They are not to be welcomed into the sheepfold, but guarded against and avoided.

Confusion about the deity of Christ is inexcusable, because the biblical teaching regarding it is clear and unmistakable. Jesus Christ is the eternally preexistent Word, who enjoys full face-to-face communion and divine life with the Father, and is Himself God.

THE CREATIVE POWER OF THE WORD

All things came into being through Him, and apart from Him nothing came into being that has come into being. (1:3)

Once again John expressed a profound truth in clear language. Jesus Christ, the eternal Word, created everything that **came into being.** John underscored that truth by repeating it negatively; **apart from Him nothing** (lit., "not even one thing") **came into being that has come into being.**

That Jesus Christ created everything (cf. Col. 1:16; Heb. 1:2) offers two further proofs of His deity. First, the Creator of all things must Himself be uncreated, and only the eternal God is uncreated. The Greek text emphasizes the distinction between the uncreated Word and His creation, since a different verb is used here than the one used in verses 1 and 2. As noted in the previous point, John used a form of the verb *eimi* ("to be"), which denotes a state of being, to describe the Word in verses 1 and 2; here, speaking of the creation of the universe, he used a form of the verb *ginomai* (**came into being**). That Jesus is the Creator also verifies His deity, because God is portrayed throughout the Bible as the Creator (Gen. 1:1; Ps. 102:25; Isa. 40:28; 42:5; 45:18; Mark 13:19; Rom. 1:25; Eph. 3:9; Rev. 4:11).

By stressing the role of the Word in creating the universe, John countered the false teaching that later developed into the dangerous heresy known as Gnosticism. The Gnostics embraced the philosophical dualism common to Greek philosophy that held that spirit was good and matter was evil. They argued that since matter was evil, the good God could not have created the physical universe. Instead, a series of spirit beings emanated from Him until finally one of those descending emanations was evil and foolish enough to create the physical universe. But John rejected that heretical view, strongly affirming that Jesus Christ was the Father's agent in creating everything.

The present world, however, is radically different from God's original good creation (Gen. 1:31). The catastrophic results of the fall not only affected the human race, but also the entire creation. Jesus therefore will one day redeem not only believers, but also the material world as well, as Paul noted in Romans 8:19–21:

> For the anxious longing of the creation waits eagerly for the revealing of the sons of God. For the creation was subjected to futility, not willingly, but because of Him who subjected it, in hope that the creation itself also will be set free from its slavery to corruption into the freedom of the glory of the children of God.

When the curse is lifted during Christ's millennial reign,

> The wolf will dwell with the lamb,
> And the leopard will lie down with the young goat,
> And the calf and the young lion and the fatling together;
> And a little boy will lead them.
> Also the cow and the bear will graze,
> Their young will lie down together,
> And the lion will eat straw like the ox.
> The nursing child will play by the hole of the cobra,
> And the weaned child will put his hand on the viper's den.
> They will not hurt or destroy in all My holy mountain,
> For the earth will be full of the knowledge of the Lord
> As the waters cover the sea. (Isa. 11:6–9)

> The wolf and the lamb will graze together, and the lion will eat straw like the ox; and dust will be the serpent's food. They will do no evil or harm in all My holy mountain, says the Lord. (Isa. 65:25)

THE SELF-EXISTENCE OF THE WORD

In Him was life, and the life was the Light of men. The Light shines in the darkness, and the darkness did not comprehend it. (1:4–5)

Displaying yet again his Spirit-inspired economy of words, John in these two brief verses summarized the incarnation. Christ, the embodiment of **life** and the glorious, eternal **Light** of heaven, entered the sin-darkened world **of men,** and that world reacted in various ways to Him.

As noted earlier in this chapter, the themes **life** and **Light** are common in John's gospel. *Zōē* (**life**) refers to spiritual life as opposed to *bios,* which describes physical life (cf. 1 John 2:16). Here, as in 5:26, it refers primarily to Christ having life in Himself. Theologians refer to that as aseity, or self-existence. It is clear evidence of Christ's deity, since only God is self-existent.

This truth of God's and Christ's self-existence—having life in themselves—is foundational to our faith. All that is created can be said to be "becoming," because nothing created is unchanging. It is essential to understand that permanent, eternal, non-changing being or life is distinct from all that is becoming. "Being" is eternal and the source of life for what is "becoming." That is what distinguishes creatures from the Creator, us from God.

Genesis 1:1 establishes this fundamental reality with the statement, "In the beginning God created the heavens and the earth." Because it is the most important truth in the Bible, it is the one most assaulted. Unbelievers know that to be rid of creation is to be rid of a Creator. And to be rid of God leaves men free to live in whatever way they want, with no judgment.

The whole universe falls into the category of "becoming" because there was a point when it did not exist. Before existence it was the self-existent eternal being—the source of life—God, who is pure, self-existent being, pure life, and never becoming anything. All creation receives its life from outside, from Him, but He derives His life from within Himself, depending on nothing for His life. There was a point when the universe did not exist. There was never a point when God did not exist. He is self-existence, life, "I am who I am" (Ex. 3:14). He is from everlasting to everlasting. Acts 17:28 rightly says: "In Him we live and move and exist." We cannot live or move or be without His life. But He has always lived and moved and been.

This is the purest ontological description of God—and to say Jesus is the **life** is to say the most pure truth about the nature of God that He possesses. And, as in verse 3, He then is the Creator.

While as the Creator Jesus is the source of everything and everyone who lives, the word **life** in John's gospel always translates *zōē*, which John uses for spiritual or eternal life. It is imparted by God's sovereign grace (6:37, 39, 44, 65; cf. Eph. 2:8) to all those who believe savingly in Jesus Christ (1:12; 3:15–16, 36; 6:40, 47; 20:31; cf. Acts 16:31; Rom. 10:9–10; 1 John 5:1, 11–13). It was to impart spiritual life to sinners who "were dead in [their] trespasses and sins" (Eph. 2:1) that Jesus came into the world (10:10; cf. 6:33).

While it is appropriate to make some distinction between life and light, the statement **the life was the Light** halts any disconnect between the two. In reality, John is writing that **life** and **light** cannot be separated. They are essentially the same, with the idea of light emphasizing the manifestation of the divine life. **The life was the Light** is the same construction as "the Word was God" (v. 1). As God is not separate from the Word, but the same in essence, so life and light share the same essential properties.

The light combines with life in a metaphor for the purpose of clarity and contrast. God's life is true and holy. **Light** is that truth and holiness manifest against the darkness of lies and sin. Light and life are linked in this same way in John 8:12, in which Jesus says: "I am the Light of the world; he who follows Me will not walk in the darkness, but will have the Light of life." The connection between light and life is also clearly made in the Old Testament. Psalm 36:9 says: "For with You is the fountain of life; in Your light we see light."

"The light of the gospel of the glory of Christ, who is the image of God" (2 Cor. 4:4) is nothing more than the radiating, manifest life of God shining in His Son. Paul specifically says: "God . . . is the One who has shone in our hearts to give the Light of the knowledge of the glory of God in the face of Christ" (v. 6). So light is God's life manifest in Christ.

In addition to its connection to life, light carries its own significance, as seen in the contrast between light and darkness, which is a common theme in Scripture. Intellectually, light refers to truth (Ps. 119:105; Prov. 6:23; 2 Cor. 4:4) and darkness to falsehood (Rom. 2:19); morally, light refers to holiness (Rom. 13:12; 2 Cor. 6:14; Eph. 5:8; 1 Thess. 5:5) and darkness to sin (Prov. 4:19; Isa. 5:20; Acts 26:18). Satan's kingdom is the "domain of darkness" (Col. 1:13; cf. Luke 22:53; Eph. 6:12), but Jesus is the source of **life** (11:25; 14:6; cf. Acts 3:15; 1 John 1:1) and the **Light** that **shines in the darkness** of the lost world (8:12; 9:5; 12:35–36, 46).

Despite Satan's frantic, furious assaults on the **Light, the darkness did not comprehend it.** *Katalambanō* (**comprehend**) is better translated "overcome." Even a small candle can drive the darkness from a room; the brilliant, glorious **Light** of the Lord Jesus Christ will utterly destroy Satan's realm of darkness. Since He came into the world, "the darkness is passing away and the true Light is already shining" (1 John 2:8).

The thrust of this verse, then, is not that the **darkness** failed to understand the truth about Jesus; on the contrary, the forces of darkness know Him all too well. In Matthew 8:29 some demons "cried out [to Jesus], saying, 'What business do we have with each other, Son of God? Have You come here to torment us before the time?'" In Peter's house in Capernaum, Jesus "cast out many demons; and He was not permitting the demons to speak, because they knew who He was" (Mark 1:34). Luke 4:41 records that "demons also were coming out of many, shouting, 'You are the Son of God!' But rebuking them, He would not allow them to speak, because they knew Him to be the Christ." In Luke 4:34 a terrified demon pleaded, "Let us alone! What business do we have with each other, Jesus of Nazareth? Have You come to destroy us? I know who You are—the Holy One of God!" The demons not only know the truth about Christ, but they also believe it. "You believe that God is one," wrote James, "You do well; the demons also believe, and shudder" (James 2:19).

It is because they understand with total clarity the judgment that awaits them that Satan and the demons have tried desperately throughout history to kill the **life** and extinguish the **Light.** In the Old Testament, Satan tried to destroy Israel, the nation from which the Messiah would come. He also tried to destroy the kingly line from which the Messiah would descend (2 Kings 11:1–2). In the New Testament, he prompted Herod's futile attempt to kill the infant Jesus (Matt. 2:16). At the beginning of His earthly ministry, Satan vainly tried to tempt Jesus to turn aside from the cross (Matt. 4:1–11). Later, he repeated the temptation again through one of His closest followers (Matt. 16:21–23). Even Satan's seeming triumph at the cross in reality marked his ultimate defeat (Col. 2:15; Heb. 2:14; cf. 1 John 3:8).

Similarly, unbelievers are eternally lost not because they do not know the truth, but because they reject it:

> For the wrath of God is revealed from heaven against all ungodliness and unrighteousness of men who suppress the truth in unrighteousness, because that which is known about God is evident within them; for God made it evident to them. For since the creation of the world His invisible attributes, His eternal power and divine nature, have been clearly seen, being understood through what has been made, so that they are without excuse. For even though they knew God, they did not honor Him as God or give thanks, but they became futile in their speculations, and their foolish heart was darkened. (Rom. 1:18–21)

(For a further discussion of this point, see the exposition of 1:9–11 in chapter 2 of this volume.)

No one who rejects Christ's deity can be saved, for He Himself said in John 8:24, "Therefore I said to you that you will die in your sins; for unless you believe that I am He, you will die in your sins." It is fitting, then, that John opens his gospel, which so strongly emphasizes Christ's deity (cf. 8:58; 10:28–30; 20:28), with a powerful affirmation of that essential truth.

Responding to the Incarnate Word (John 1:6–13)

2

There came a man sent from God, whose name was John. He came as a witness, to testify about the Light, so that all might believe through him. He was not the Light, but he came to testify about the Light. There was the true Light which, coming into the world, enlightens every man. He was in the world, and the world was made through Him, and the world did not know Him. He came to His own, and those who were His own did not receive Him. But as many as received Him, to them He gave the right to become children of God, even to those who believe in His name, who were born, not of blood nor of the will of the flesh nor of the will of man, but of God. (1:6–13)

The sinless life (John 8:46; 2 Cor. 5:21), unprecedented words (Matt. 7:29; John 7:46), and astonishing claims (John 4:25–26; 8:58) of Jesus Christ arrested people's attention and forced them to react, which they did in several ways.

Some were superficially drawn to Jesus. Later in his gospel John records that "some were saying [of Jesus], 'He is a good man'" (7:12). Going a step beyond that, others acknowledged Him as a great religious leader; a prophet (Matt. 21:11, 46; Luke 7:16), possibly even "John the

Baptist . . . Elijah . . . Jeremiah, or one of the prophets" (Matt. 16:14). Because of the meal Jesus created for them, the Galilean crowd decided to make Him king by force (John 6:14–15), hoping He would throw off the yoke of the hated Romans and continue to miraculously provide food. But such shallow, material sentiment was fleeting. The same kind of fickle Judean crowd that rejoiced at His triumphal entry into Jerusalem, crying out, "Hosanna to the Son of David; blessed is He who comes in the name of the Lord; hosanna in the highest!" (Matt. 21:9) would a few short days later scream, "Away with Him, away with Him, crucify Him!" (John 19:15).

Some were strongly attracted to Jesus, but unwilling to commit themselves to Him. John 12:42 records that "many even of the rulers believed in Him, but because of the Pharisees they were not confessing Him, for fear that they would be put out of the synagogue." The classic example of one who shrank back from a full commitment to Christ is the rich young ruler:

> As He was setting out on a journey, a man ran up to Him and knelt before Him, and asked Him, "Good Teacher, what shall I do to inherit eternal life?" And Jesus said to him, "Why do you call Me good? No one is good except God alone. You know the commandments, 'Do not murder, do not commit adultery, do not steal, do not bear false witness, do not defraud, honor your father and mother.'" And he said to Him, "Teacher, I have kept all these things from my youth up." Looking at him, Jesus felt a love for him and said to him, "One thing you lack: go and sell all you possess and give to the poor, and you will have treasure in heaven; and come, follow Me." But at these words he was saddened, and he went away grieving, for he was one who owned much property. (Mark 10:17–22)

Still others were openly hostile to Jesus. According to John 7:12 some were claiming, "He leads the people astray." At His trial before Pilate, the Jewish authorities "began to accuse Him, saying, 'We found this man misleading our nation and forbidding to pay taxes to Caesar, and saying that He Himself is Christ, a King'" (Luke 23:2). Even after His death the slanderous accusations about Him continued: "Now on the next day, the day after the preparation, the chief priests and the Pharisees gathered together with Pilate, and said, 'Sir, we remember that when He was still alive that deceiver said, "After three days I am to rise again"'" (Matt. 27:62–63).

To others, Jesus was a madman: either demon possessed, or deranged. John 10:20 records that "many of them were saying, 'He has a demon and is insane. Why do you listen to Him?'" The Jewish leaders asked sarcastically, "Do we not say rightly that You are a Samaritan and have a demon? . . . Now we know that You have a demon" (John 8:48, 52; cf. 7:20; Matt. 9:34; 10:25). Even His own family at one point "went out to take custody of Him; for they were saying, 'He has lost His senses'" (Mark 3:21).

The Pharisees and scribes, unable to deny His supernatural power, and unwilling to attribute it to God, were left with the blasphemous alternative that His power came from Satan himself (Matt. 12:24; Mark 3:22; Luke 11:15). They apparently spread this damning lie throughout Israel, as the event recorded in Matthew and Mark occurred in Galilee and the one described in Luke months later in Judea.

The common theme linking all of those inadequate responses is unbelief—the sin that ultimately damns all those who reject Jesus Christ. John 3:18 says, "He who believes in Him is not judged; he who does not believe has been judged already, because he has not believed in the name of the only begotten Son of God." Jesus repeatedly rebuked those who refused to believe in Him:

> You do not have His word abiding in you, for you do not believe Him whom He sent. (John 5:38)

> I have come in My Father's name, and you do not receive Me; if another comes in his own name, you will receive him. (John 5:43)

> But I said to you that you have seen Me, and yet do not believe. (John 6:36)

> But because I speak the truth, you do not believe Me. (John 8:45)

> Jesus answered them, "I told you, and you do not believe; the works that I do in My Father's name, these testify of Me. But you do not believe because you are not of My sheep." (John 10:25–26)

But in contrast to the unbelief of the lost, those whom the Father gave to Jesus (John 6:37) respond by fully believing in His claims and teaching. They will receive all the blessings of salvation, eternal life, forgiveness of sins, and adoption as children of God:

> Whoever believes will in Him have eternal life. For God so loved the world, that He gave His only begotten Son, that whoever believes in Him shall not perish, but have eternal life. For God did not send the Son into the world to judge the world, but that the world might be saved through Him. (John 3:15–17)

> He who believes in the Son has eternal life; but he who does not obey the Son will not see life, but the wrath of God abides on him. (John 3:36)

> Truly, truly, I say to you, he who hears My word, and believes Him who sent Me, has eternal life, and does not come into judgment, but has passed out of death into life. (John 5:24)

> For this is the will of My Father, that everyone who beholds the Son and believes in Him will have eternal life, and I Myself will raise him up on the last day. (John 6:40)

> Truly, truly, I say to you, he who believes has eternal life. (John 6:47)

> Of Him all the prophets bear witness that through His name everyone who believes in Him receives forgiveness of sins. (Acts 10:43; cf. 13:39)

> For I am not ashamed of the gospel, for it is the power of God for salvation to everyone who believes, to the Jew first and also to the Greek. (Rom. 1:16)

> Whoever believes that Jesus is the Christ is born of God, and whoever loves the Father loves the child born of Him. (1 John 5:1)

The gospels record the belief of Peter (Matt. 16:16), Nathanael (John 1:48–50), the disciples (Matt. 14:33), a Samaritan woman (John 4:28–29) and others from her village (John 4:42), a blind man whom Jesus healed (John 9:35–38), the women who visited the empty tomb (Matt. 28:9), and the former skeptic, Thomas (John 20:28). Acts 1:14 reports that our Lord's brothers had come to believe after the resurrection (cf. John 7:5).

Having established the deity of Jesus Christ in the opening five verses of the prologue, John now turns to the only two possible responses to that reality: unbelief or belief. Before describing those responses, however, John described the one who came to testify of Jesus so that people might believe in Him.

JOHN THE BAPTIST: BELIEVABLE TESTIMONY

There came a man sent from God, whose name was John. He came as a witness, to testify about the Light, so that all might believe through him. He was not the Light, but he came to testify about the Light. (1:6–8)

The abrupt change of subject from the exalted Lord Jesus Christ, the eternal, self-existent creator God (vv. 1–5), to a mere **man sent from God,** is striking. **There came** is actually "there appeared," indicating the shift from the heavenly Word to His earthly herald. After describing the Word who was God, John turned to the one who announced that the Word was God. That herald's **name was John** the Baptist. (John the apostle does not name himself in his gospel, so every time the name John appears, it refers to the Baptist [except for four references to Peter's father; 1:42; 21:15, 16, 17].)

The phrase **sent from God** confirms John's role as herald in several ways. First, the Baptist had a divine commission as the one who fulfilled the Old Testament prophecies regarding Messiah's forerunner. Isaiah predicted him (Isa. 40:3; cf. Matt. 3:3; Mark 1:2–3). The Old Testament closes with Malachi's prophecy of the Elijah-like prophet to come before the Day of the Lord (Mal. 3:1; 4:5–6), which the angel of the Lord told Zacharias referred to John (Luke 1:17). Second, the Baptist was uniquely sent from God because his conception and birth were miraculous, since his parents were old and had never had children (Luke 1:7, 36). Third, the angel of the Lord came from heaven to tell Zacharias that he and Elizabeth would have a son who would be the herald of the Messiah (Luke 1:8–17). Fourth, the Holy Spirit filled Zacharias to prophesy concerning John (Luke 1:67–79). Fifth, the Baptist was sent from the Lord at the divinely appointed time to begin his public ministry (Luke 1:80).

John was the first true prophet (Matt. 14:5; 21:26) to appear in Israel in 400 years, and his bold, confrontive preaching created a sensation. Mark 1:5 describes his enormous impact by reporting how "all the country of Judea was going out to him, and all the people of Jerusalem; and they were being baptized by him in the Jordan River, confessing their sins" (cf. Matt. 3:5–6). He was to prepare the hearts of the people for the Messiah; therefore, he fearlessly confronted sin and called for repentance: "Now in those days John the Baptist came, preaching in the wilderness of Judea, saying, 'Repent, for the kingdom of heaven is at hand'" (Matt. 3:1). John even rebuked Herod, "on account of Herodias, the wife of his brother Philip, because he had married her. For John had been saying to Herod, 'It is not lawful for you to have your brother's wife'" (Mark 6:17–18). Even that godless king acknowledged that John "was a righteous and holy man, . . . and when he heard him, he was very perplexed; but he used to enjoy listening to him" (Mark 6:20). Luke records, however, that Herod had John imprisoned for confronting his sin. Matthew 14:1–12 gives the account of Herod's beheading of John.

Because John's mission was also to herald the Messiah's arrival, "He was preaching, and saying, 'After me One is coming who is mightier than I, and I am not fit to stoop down and untie the thong of His sandals. I baptized you with water; but He will baptize you with the Holy Spirit'" (Mark 1:7–8). Like Herod, the Jewish religious leaders were perplexed about John, and sent a delegation to interrogate him. He reiterated that his mission was to herald Messiah's arrival. The apostle John records his testimony in 1:19–36 (cf. Matt. 3:1–12; Luke 7:18–23).

The Baptist's ministry stirred up such excitement that although he said of himself in relation to Christ, "One is coming who is mightier than I, and I am not fit to untie the thong of His sandals" (Luke 3:16), a cult of devoted followers grew up around him (cf. John 3:25). Sadly, some were devoted to John instead of the Messiah whose arrival he proclaimed. Years later the apostle Paul encountered some of them in Ephesus:

> It happened that while Apollos was at Corinth, Paul passed through the upper country and came to Ephesus, and found some disciples. He said to them, "Did you receive the Holy Spirit when you believed?" And they said to him, "No, we have not even heard whether there is a Holy Spirit." And he said, "Into what then were you baptized?" And they said, "Into John's baptism." Paul said, "John baptized with the baptism of repentance, telling the people to believe in Him who was coming after him, that is, in Jesus." When they heard this, they were baptized in the name of the Lord Jesus. (Acts 19:1–5)

Groups of John the Baptist loyalists persisted into the second century, and hence were still around when John wrote his gospel. Therefore he stressed John the Baptist's inferiority to Christ.

John the Baptist was the greatest man who had ever lived up to his time, as Jesus affirmed: "Truly I say to you, among those born of women there has not arisen anyone greater than John the Baptist!" (Matt. 11:11). He was the greatest man because God chose him to perform the most important task to that point in human history—being the forerunner of the Messiah. He was the first to announce publicly that Jesus was the Savior (John 1:29). Yet despite that, he himself acknowledged: "This was He of whom I said, 'He who comes after me has a higher rank than I, for He existed before me'" (John 1:15). Some of his zealous disciples, concerned for his reputation,

> came to John and said to him, "Rabbi, He who was with you beyond the Jordan, to whom you have testified, behold, He is baptizing and all are coming to Him." John answered and said, "A man can receive nothing unless it has been given him from heaven. You yourselves are my witnesses that I said, 'I am not the Christ,' but, 'I have been sent ahead of Him.' He who has the bride is the bridegroom; but the friend of the bridegroom, who stands and hears him, rejoices greatly because of the bridegroom's voice. So this joy of mine has been made full. He must increase, but I must decrease." (John 3:26–30)

William Hendriksen points out the contrast between John the Baptist and Jesus:

Christ was (*ēn*) from all eternity; John came (*egenetō*).
Christ is *the Word* (*ho logos*); John is a mere man (*anthrōpos*).
Christ is himself God; John is commissioned by God.
Christ is the real light; John came to testify concerning the real light.
Christ is the *object* of trust; John is the *agent* through whose testimony
men come to trust in the real light, even Christ. (*New Testament
Commentary:The Gospel According to John,* Vol. 1 [Grand Rapids: Baker,
1953], 76. Emphasis in original.)

John's mission was not to exalt himself, but to be **a witness**
about Messiah, **to testify about the Light.** He is the first of eight witnesses that appear in John's gospel; the others are the Father (5:37),
Jesus' words (8:18) and works (5:36; 10:25), the Old Testament Scriptures
(5:39), some of those who met Him (4:29), the disciples (15:27; 19:35;
21:24), and the Holy Spirit (15:26). The legal terms **witness** (*marturia*)
and **testify** (*martureō*) are words related to fact, not opinion, as in a
courtroom setting. The terms are used predominantly in the New Testament by the apostle John (77 out of their 113 occurrences are in John's
gospel, epistles, or Revelation).

John is properly called the Baptist because he was sent by God
to baptize repentant sinners in preparation for the Messiah's coming
(1:31). Yet the purpose of all he did was to bear witness to Jesus (1:15, 23,
29, 32, 34, 36; 5:33, 36), so **that all might believe through him.** People
believe in Christ (1:12; 3:18; 6:29) **through** the testimony of witnesses
like John. They are the agents of belief, but Christ is the object of belief.
Salvation, then, as at all times was a matter of faith in God and in what He
said (cf. Rom. 4:1–16).

To counter any false exaltation of John the Baptist, the apostle
John wrote that he **was not the Light, but he came to testify about
the Light.** At first glance, that statement seems to contradict Jesus' statement that John the Baptist "was the lamp that was burning and was shining and you were willing to rejoice for a while in his light" (5:35). Two
different Greek words are used, however. The term **Light** used in this passage to refer to Christ is *phōs,* which refers to the essence of light. In 5:35,
however, Jesus described John as a *luchnos,* which refers to a portable
lamp. Jesus is **the Light;** John merely reflected it (see the discussion of v.
4 in chapter 1 of this volume).

UNBELIEVERS: TESTIMONY REJECTED

**There was the true Light which, coming into the world, enlight-
ens every man. He was in the world, and the world was made**

through Him, and the world did not know Him. He came to His own, and those who were His own did not receive Him. (1:9–11)

That John the Baptist had to point out the **true Light** graphically illustrates the world's blindness, for only blind people cannot see the light. Unbelievers are spiritually blind because, as Paul wrote to the Corinthians, "the god of this world has blinded the minds of the unbelieving so that they might not see the light of the gospel of the glory of Christ, who is the image of God" (2 Cor. 4:4; cf. Isa. 61:1–2; Luke 4:17–18).

The unbelieving world's blindness is inexcusable, because Jesus **was the true Light which, coming into the world, enlightens every man.** *Alēthinos* (**true**) is another distinctly Johannine term; all but five of its twenty-eight uses in the New Testament are in John's writings. It refers to what is real and genuine; according to Thayer's *Greek Lexicon*, *alēthinos* describes "that which has not only the name and semblance, but the real nature corresponding to the name." God's people had seen reflections of the light of His glory, but in Jesus the full "radiance of His glory" (Heb. 1:3) was revealed.

Through His **coming into the world** Jesus **enlightens every man** (cf. Isa. 49:6). There are several possible explanations of that truth; each is taught in the New Testament. It could mean that the Word incarnate is none other than the fullest revelation of God who has already revealed Himself in every human soul, a truth Paul expressed to the Romans:

> For the wrath of God is revealed from heaven against all ungodliness and unrighteousness of men who suppress the truth in unrighteousness, because that which is known about God is evident within them; for God made it evident to them. For since the creation of the world His invisible attributes, His eternal power and divine nature, have been clearly seen, being understood through what has been made, so that they are without excuse. For even though they knew God, they did not honor Him as God or give thanks, but they became futile in their speculations, and their foolish heart was darkened. (Rom. 1:18–21; cf. Eph. 4:18)

The phrase could also mean that Jesus is God's self-disclosure in the most glorious way for every man who has seen Him or heard about Him or read His story. Some would narrow the idea to restrict **every man** to only those who receive Him. The first interpretation seems best in the context, since it refers to those in the world who do not receive Him, as well as those who do. Even those who never become children of God are accountable for the knowledge of God and His light revealed in Christ. Though all men are spiritually dead (Eph. 2:1–3) and blind, they are accountable for the knowledge of God revealed in creation and conscience (Rom. 2:14–15).

The tragic reality is that sinners reject the "Light of the world" (John 8:12):

> This is the judgment, that the Light has come into the world, and men loved the darkness rather than the Light, for their deeds were evil. For everyone who does evil hates the Light, and does not come to the Light for fear that his deeds will be exposed. (John 3:19–20)

People refuse to come to the light of Jesus Christ because they love their sin and do not want it exposed; they are willfully blind. Thus, though Jesus **was in the world, and the world was made through Him,** yet **the world did not know Him.** The Creator of the **world** (1:3) became its Savior (cf. 4:42), but the **world** rejected Him and thus **did not know Him** in a saving way.

Kosmos (**world**) is another term used frequently by John; more than half of its occurrences in the New Testament are in his writings. It describes the physical world (v. 9; 12:25; 16:21, 28; 21:25); humanity in general (3:16; 6:33, 51; 12:19); and, most frequently, the evil system dominated by Satan (3:19; 7:7; 14:17, 30; 15:18–19). It is this third sense of *kosmos* that John had in mind when he wrote that **the world did not know** Christ. Despite its rejection of Him, the unbelieving world will nonetheless one day be forced to acknowledge Jesus as Lord (Phil. 2:9–11) and judge (John 5:22, 27).

As shocking and tragic as the world's rejection of Christ is, John turned to the even greater tragedy of Israel's rejection. That Jesus **came to His own** place can mean the world He created (cf. the second sense of *kosmos* above). It could also mean His particular place, the land of promise given to the Jews through Abraham, including the coming earthly kingdom predicted by the prophets. He came to God's land, to the city of David, the land of the temple. The Jews had waited all through the centuries for the Messiah and Savior to come. Most tragic of all was the sad reality that when He did, **those who were His own** people **did not receive Him.** This second use of **own** refers primarily to the nation of Israel, of whom God said, "You only have I known of all the families of the earth" (Amos 3:2 NKJV). Throughout the Old Testament God referred to the Jewish people as "My people" (e.g., Ex. 3:7, 10; 6:7; Lev. 26:12; 1 Sam. 2:29; 2 Sam. 3:18; 1 Kings 6:13; 2 Kings 20:5; 1 Chron. 11:2; 2 Chron. 1:11; Ps. 50:7; Isa. 1:3; Jer. 2:11; Ezek. 11:20; Hos. 4:6; Joel 3:2; Amos 7:15; Obad. 1:13; Micah 6:3; Zeph. 2:8; Zech. 8:7–8), despite their frequent rebellion against Him.

Like their ancestors, the Israelites of Jesus' day stiffened their necks (Deut. 10:16; 2 Kings 17:14; Neh. 9:29; Jer. 7:26; 17:23) and rejected Him despite the clear testimony of the Old Testament Scriptures (John 5:39). Instead of repenting of their sin and accepting Him as their Messiah, they screamed, "Crucify Him! . . . His blood shall be on us and on our children!" (Matt. 27:23, 25). Israel's rejection and collaboration in the murder of her Messiah was a common theme in apostolic preaching. In the first Christian sermon ever preached, Peter said to the crowds gathered in Jerusalem for the Day of Pentecost,

> Men of Israel, listen to these words: Jesus the Nazarene, a man attested to you by God with miracles and wonders and signs which God performed through Him in your midst, just as you yourselves know—this Man, delivered over by the predetermined plan and foreknowledge of God, you nailed to a cross by the hands of godless men and put Him to death. . . . Therefore let all the house of Israel know for certain that God has made Him both Lord and Christ—this Jesus whom you crucified. (Acts 2:22–23, 36; cf. 3:13–15; 4:10; 5:30; 10:38–39; 13:27–29)

The theme of rejection will be repeated throughout John's gospel.

BELIEVERS: TESTIMONY BELIEVED

But as many as received Him, to them He gave the right to become children of God, even to those who believe in His name, who were born, not of blood nor of the will of the flesh nor of the will of man, but of God. (1:12–13)

The conjunction *de* (**but**) is a small fulcrum that marks a dramatic shift. The world's hatred of God and rejection of Christ in no way overrules or frustrates God's plan, for He makes even the wrath of men praise Him (Ps. 76:10). There will be some who receive Him. Those whom God willed for salvation before the foundation of the world (Eph. 1:4; 2 Tim. 1:9) will in faith embrace Christ. As He declared in John 6:37, "All that the Father gives Me will come to Me, and the one who comes to Me I will certainly not cast out."

Lambanō (**received**) could be translated "take hold of," "obtain," or "grasp." To receive Christ involves more than mere intellectual acknowledgment of His claims. The last clause of verse 12 refers to those who **received** as **those who believe in His name.** The concept of believing in Christ, another important theme for John, will be developed in several passages in his gospel (6:29; 8:30; 9:35–36; 12:36, 44; 14:1; 16:9; 17:20; cf. 1 John 3:23; 5:13). **His name** refers to the totality of Christ's being, all that He is and does. Thus, it is not possible to separate His deity from His humanity, His being Savior from His being Lord, or His person from His redemptive work. Saving faith accepts Jesus Christ in all that Scripture reveals concerning Him.

Though people cannot be saved until they receive and believe in Jesus Christ, salvation is nonetheless a sovereign work of God on the dead and blind sinner. John simply states that no one would come to believe in Jesus unless **He gave** them **the right to become children of God.** They are saved entirely by "grace . . . through faith; and that not of [themselves], it is the gift of God; not as a result of works, so that no one may boast" (Eph. 2:8–9), because "God has chosen [them] from the beginning for salvation" (2 Thess. 2:13). Thus they **were born** again (John 3:3, 7; 1 Pet. 1:3, 23) **not of blood nor of the will of the flesh nor of the will of man, but of God.** Those three negative statements stress the fact that salvation is not obtainable through any racial or ethnic heritage (**blood**), personal desire (**flesh**), or man-made system (**man**). (See also Matt. 8:11–12; Luke 3:8; Gal. 3:28–29.)

The great truth of election and sovereign grace is here introduced appropriately at the very foundation of John's mention of salvation. Our Lord Himself will speak of this truth in 6:36–47; 15:16; 17:6–12.

Because all bear the guilt of unbelief and rejection, the phrase **but of God** means that salvation, that is, receiving and believing in the Lord Jesus Christ, is impossible for any sinner. God must grant the power supernaturally and with it the divine life and light to the lifeless, darkened sinner.

The Glory of the Incarnate Word (John 1:14–18)

3

And the Word became flesh, and dwelt among us, and we saw His glory, glory as of the only begotten from the Father, full of grace and truth. John testified about Him and cried out, saying, "This was He of whom I said, 'He who comes after me has a higher rank than I, for He existed before me.'" For of His fullness we have all received, and grace upon grace. For the Law was given through Moses; grace and truth were realized through Jesus Christ. No one has seen God at any time; the only begotten God who is in the bosom of the Father, He has explained Him. (1:14–18)

For the first five centuries of its existence the early church defended the true doctrine of the Incarnation. During that time many erroneous teachings about the hypostatic union (the union of the divine and human natures in Christ) were put forth, examined, and rejected. For example, some argued that Jesus did not have a human spirit, but rather that His divine spirit united with a human body. That view preserved His deity, but at the expense of denying His full humanity. Others argued that the divine Christ-spirit entered the man Jesus at His baptism, and left Him before His crucifixion. Another false view held by some was that Jesus was a created being, and thus inferior to God the Father. Still others viewed Him as two separate persons, one human and the other divine; according to that teaching Jesus was a man in whom God dwelt.

All of those views (and others as well) erred fatally either by denying Jesus Christ's full deity or His full humanity. The true church rejected them all in favor of the biblical view of Jesus as the God-man. The Council of Chalcedon (A.D. 451) officially declared that truth in one of the most famous and important statements in church history:

> Therefore, following the holy Fathers, we all with one accord teach men to acknowledge one and the same Son, our Lord Jesus Christ, at once complete in Godhead and complete in manhood, truly God and truly man, consisting also of a reasonable soul and body; of one substance [*homoousios*] with the Father as regards his Godhead, and at the same time of one substance with us as regards his manhood; like us in all respects, apart from sin; as regards his Godhead, begotten of the Father before the ages, but yet as regards his manhood begotten, for us men and for our salvation, of Mary the Virgin, the God-bearer (*theotokos*); one and the same Christ, Son, Lord, Only-begotten, recognized in two natures, without confusion, without change, without division, without separation; the distinction of natures being in no way annulled by the union, but rather the characteristics of each nature being preserved and coming together to form one person and subsistence [*hupostasis*], not as parted or separated into two persons, but one and the same Son and Only-begotten God the Word, Lord Jesus Christ; even as the prophets from earliest times spoke of him, and our Lord Jesus Christ himself taught us, and the creed of the Fathers has handed down to us. (cited in Henry Bettenson, ed., *Documents of the Christian Church* [London: Oxford Univ., 1967], 51–52)

The fact that the church invisible has necessarily always held to a true doctrine of the Incarnation, and has at various times reconfirmed Chalcedon's statement, does not mean that this doctrine has ceased to be embattled. It is still a target for false teachers, cults, and false religions. The apostle John was clear in his epistles that a true view of Jesus as divine and human was an essential mark of salvation (cf. 1 John 1:1–3; 2:22–24; 4:1–3, 14; 5:1, 5, 10–12, 20; 2 John 3, 7, 9). Revelation opens with the glory of Christ (1:4–20).

Throughout the prologue to his gospel (1:1–18) John has declared the profound truths of Christ's deity and Incarnation, reaching a powerful crescendo in these last five verses. They summarize the prologue, which in turn summarizes the entire book. In his characteristically simple language, John expressed the glorious reality of the Incarnation by pointing out its nature, witnesses, and impact.

THE NATURE OF THE INCARNATION

And the Word became flesh, and dwelt among us, and we saw His glory, glory as of the only begotten from the Father, full of grace and truth. (1:14)

Verse 14 is the most concise biblical statement of the Incarnation, and therefore one of Scripture's most significant verses. The four words with which it begins, **the Word became flesh,** express the reality that in the Incarnation God took on humanity; the infinite became finite; eternity entered time; the invisible became visible (cf. Col. 1:15); the Creator entered His creation. God revealed Himself to man in the creation (Rom. 1:18–21), the Old Testament Scriptures (2 Tim. 3:16; 2 Peter 1:20–21), and, supremely and most clearly, in Jesus Christ (Heb. 1:1–2). The record of His life and work, and its application and significance for the past, present, and future, is in the New Testament.

As noted in the discussion of 1:1 in chapter 1 of this volume, the concept of the **Word** was one rich in meaning for both Greeks and Jews. John here clearly stated what he implied earlier in the prologue: Jesus Christ, God's final **Word** to mankind (Heb. 1:1–2), **became flesh.** *Sarx* (**flesh**) does not have here the negative moral connotation that it sometimes carries (e.g., Rom. 8:3–9; 13:14; Gal. 5:13, 16–17, 19; Eph. 2:3), but refers to man's physical being (cf. Matt. 16:17; Rom. 1:3; 1 Cor. 1:26; 2 Cor. 5:16; Gal. 1:16; Eph. 5:29; Phil. 1:22). That He actually **became** flesh affirms Jesus' full humanity.

Ginomai (**became**) does not mean that Christ ceased being the eternal Word when He became a man. Though God is immutable, pure eternal "being" and not "becoming" as all His creatures are, in the Incarnation the unchangeable (Heb. 13:8) God did become fully man, yet remained fully God. He entered the realm of those who are time and space creatures and experienced life as it is for those He created. In the words of the fifth-century church father Cyril of Alexandria,

> We do not . . . assert that there was any change in the nature of the Word when it became flesh, or that it was transformed into an entire man, consisting of soul and body; but we say that the Word, in a manner indescribable and inconceivable, united personally . . . to himself flesh animated with a reasonable soul, and thus became man and was called the Son of man. . . . The natures which were brought together to form a true unity were different; but out of both is one Christ and one Son. We do not mean that the difference of the natures is annihilated by reason of this union; but rather that the Deity and Manhood, by their inexpressible and inexplicable concurrence into unity, have produced for us the one Lord and Son Jesus Christ. (cited in Bettenson, *Documents*, 47)

No wonder Paul wrote of the Incarnation,

> By common confession, great is the mystery of godliness:
> He who was revealed in the flesh,
> Was vindicated in the Spirit,
> Seen by angels,
> Proclaimed among the nations,
> Believed on in the world,
> Taken up in glory. (1 Tim. 3:16)

Charles Wesley also captured the wonder of the Incarnation in his majestic hymn "Hark! the Herald Angels Sing":

> Veiled in flesh the Godhead see,
> Hail th' incarnate Deity!
> Pleased as man with men to dwell,
> Jesus, our Emmanuel.

Some found the Incarnation so utterly beyond human reason to comprehend that they refused to accept it. The heretical group known as the Docetists (from *dokeō;* "to seem," or "to appear"), accepting the dualism of matter and spirit so prevalent in Greek philosophy at that time, held that matter was evil, and spirit was good. Accordingly, they argued that Christ could not have had a material (and hence evil) body. They taught instead either that His body was a phantom, or an apparition, or that the divine Christ spirit descended upon the mere man Jesus at His baptism, then left Him before His crucifixion. Cerinthus, John's opponent at Ephesus, was a Docetist. John strongly opposed Docetism, which undermines not only the incarnation of Christ, but also His resurrection and substitutionary atonement. As noted earlier in this chapter, in his first epistle he warned,

> Beloved, do not believe every spirit, but test the spirits to see whether they are from God, because many false prophets have gone out into the world. By this you know the Spirit of God: every spirit that confesses that Jesus Christ has come in the flesh is from God; and every spirit that does not confess Jesus is not from God; this is the spirit of the antichrist, of which you have heard that it is coming, and now it is already in the world. (1 John 4:1–3)

John was so horrified by Cerinthus's heresy that, as the early church historian Eusebius records,

John the apostle once entered a bath to wash; but ascertaining Cerinthus was within, he leaped out of the place, and fled from the door, not enduring to enter under the same roof with him, and exhorted those with him to do the same, saying, "let us flee, lest the bath fall in, as long as Cerinthus, that enemy of the truth, is within." (*Ecclesiastical History,* book III, chap. XXVIII)

The eternal Son not only became man; He also **dwelt among** men for thirty-three years. **Dwelt** translates a form of the verb *skēnoō,* which literally means "to live in a tent." Jesus Christ's humanity was not a mere appearance. He took on all the essential attributes of humanity and was "made in the likeness of men" (Phil. 2:7), "since the children share in flesh and blood, He Himself likewise also partook of the same, that through death He might render powerless him who had the power of death, that is, the devil" (Heb. 2:14). As the writer of Hebrews goes on to explain, "He had to be made like His brethren in all things, so that He might become a merciful and faithful high priest in things pertaining to God, to make propitiation for the sins of the people" (Heb. 2:17). And He pitched His tent **among us.**

In the Old Testament, God tented with Israel through His glorious presence in the tabernacle (Ex. 40:34–35) and later in the temple (1 Kings 8:10–11), and revealed Himself in some pre-incarnate appearances of Christ (e.g., Gen. 16:7–14; Ex. 3:2; Josh. 5:13–15; Judg. 2:1–4; 6:11–24; 13:3–23; Dan. 3:25; 10:5–6; Zech. 1:11–21). Throughout eternity, God will again tent with His redeemed and glorified people:

And I heard a loud voice from the throne, saying, "Behold, the tabernacle of God is among men, and He will dwell [*skēnoō*] among them, and they shall be His people, and God Himself will be among them, and He will wipe away every tear from their eyes; and there will no longer be any death; there will no longer be any mourning, or crying, or pain; the first things have passed away." (Rev. 21:3–4; cf. 12:12; 13:6)

Though Jesus manifested God's divine **glory** during His earthly life with a clarity never before seen, it was still veiled by His human flesh. Peter, James, and John saw a physical manifestation of Jesus' heavenly glory at the transfiguration, when "His face shone like the sun, and His garments became as white as light" (Matt. 17:2; cf. 2 Peter 1:16–18). That was a preview of the unveiled glory to be seen at His return (Matt. 24:29–30; 25:31; Rev. 19:11–16) and the fullness of His heavenly glory as the only Light of the New Jerusalem (Rev. 21:23). But the disciples saw Jesus manifest God's holy nature primarily by displaying divine attributes, such as truth, wisdom, love, grace, knowledge, power, and holiness.

Jesus manifested the same essential **glory** as **the Father,** because as God they possess the same nature (10:30). Despite the claims of false teachers through the centuries, *monogenēs* (**only begotten**) does not imply that Jesus was created by God and thus not eternal. The term does not refer to a person's origin, but describes him as unique, the only one of his kind. Thus Isaac could properly be called Abraham's *monogenēs* (Heb. 11:17) even though Abraham had other sons, because Isaac alone was the son of the covenant. *Monogenēs* distinguishes Christ as the unique Son of God from believers, who are God's sons in a different sense (1 John 3:2). B. F. Westcott writes, "Christ is the One and only Son, the One to whom the title belongs in a sense completely unique and sin-gular, as distinguished from that in which there are many children of God (vv. 12f.)" (*The Gospel According to St. John* [Reprint; Grand Rapids: Eerd-mans, 1978], 12). Jesus' unique relationship to the Father is a major theme of John's gospel (cf. 1:18; 3:35; 5:17-23, 26, 36-37; 6:27, 46, 57; 8:16, 18-19, 28, 38, 42, 54; 10:15, 17, 30, 36-38; 12:49-50; 14:6-13, 20-21, 23, 31; 15:9, 15, 23-24; 16:3, 15, 27-28, 32; 17:5, 21, 24-25; 20:21).

Jesus' manifestation of the divine attributes revealed His essen-tial glory as God's Son, "for in Him all the fullness of Deity dwells in bodily form" (Col. 2:9). The two attributes most closely connected with salvation are **grace and truth.** Scripture teaches that salvation is wholly by be-lieving God's **truth** in the gospel, by which one receives His saving **grace.**

The Jerusalem Council declared, "But we believe that we [Jewish believers] are saved through the grace of the Lord Jesus, in the same way as they [Gentiles] also are" (Acts 15:11). Apollos "greatly helped those who had believed through grace" (Acts 18:27). Paul described the mes-sage he preached as "the gospel of the grace of God" (Acts 20:24). In Romans 3:24 he wrote that believers are "justified as a gift by His grace through the redemption which is in Christ Jesus," while in Ephesians 1:7 he added, "In Him we have redemption through His blood, the forgive-ness of our trespasses, according to the riches of His grace." Later in that same letter, Paul wrote, "For by grace you have been saved through faith; and that not of yourselves, it is the gift of God; not as a result of works, so that no one may boast" (Eph. 2:8-9). He reminded Timothy that God "has saved us and called us with a holy calling, not according to our works, but according to His own purpose and grace which was granted us in Christ Jesus from all eternity" (2 Tim. 1:9). That same "grace of God has appeared, bringing salvation to all men" (Titus 2:11), with the result that believers "being justified by His grace ... would be made heirs according to the hope of eternal life" (Titus 3:7).

There is no salvation grace except to those who believe the **truth** of the gospel message. Paul reminded the Ephesians, "In Him, you also, after listening to the message of truth, the gospel of your salvation—having also believed, you were sealed in Him with the Holy Spirit of promise" (Eph. 1:13). In Colossians 1:5 he defined the gospel as the "word of truth" (cf. James 1:18). Paul expressed to the Thessalonians his thankfulness that "God ha[d] chosen [them] from the beginning for salvation through sanctification by the Spirit and faith in the truth" (2 Thess. 2:13). People are saved when they "come to the knowledge of the truth" (1 Tim. 2:4; cf. 2 Tim. 2:25). On the other hand, "those who perish" will do so "because they did not receive the love of the truth so as to be saved" (2 Thess. 2:10). Everyone will "be judged who did not believe the truth, but took pleasure in wickedness" (2 Thess. 2:12).

Jesus Christ was the **full** expression of God's grace. All the necessary truth to save is available in Him. He was the **full** expression of God's truth, which was only partially revealed in the Old Testament (cf. Col. 2:16–17). What was foreshadowed through prophecy, types, and pictures became substance realized in the person of Christ (cf. Heb. 1:1–2). Therefore He could declare, "I am the way, and the truth, and the life. . . . If you continue in My word, then you are truly disciples of Mine; and you will know the truth, and the truth will make you free" (John 14:6; 8:31–32).

A vague belief in God apart from the truth about Christ will not result in salvation. As Jesus Himself warned, "Unless you believe that I am He, you will die in your sins" (John 8:24). Those who think they are worshiping God, but are ignorant of or reject the fullness of the New Testament teaching about Christ, are deceived, because "he who does not honor the Son does not honor the Father who sent Him" (John 5:23; cf. 15:23). In his first epistle John affirmed that "whoever denies the Son does not have the Father; the one who confesses the Son has the Father also" (1 John 2:23; cf. 2 John 9). Those who reject God's full revelation of Himself in Jesus Christ will be eternally lost.

Summarizing the magnificence of this verse, Gerald L. Borchert writes,

> In analyzing this crucial verse of the Prologue it becomes quickly apparent that this verse is like a great jewel with many facets that spreads it rays of implication into the various dimensions of Christology—the theology of Christ. As a summary of this verse it may be said that the evangelist recognized and bore witness to the fact that *the characteristics ascribed only to God by the Old Testament were present in the incarnate Logos, God's unique messenger to the world, who not only epitomized in person the awesome sense of God's presence in their midst as a pilgrim people but also evidenced those stabilizing divine qualities God's people had experienced repeatedly.* (*John 1–11*, The New American Commentary [Nashville: Broadman & Holman, 2002], 121–22. Italics in original.)

THE WITNESSES TO THE INCARNATION

John testified about Him and cried out, saying, "This was He of whom I said, 'He who comes after me has a higher rank than I, for He existed before me.'" For of His fullness we have all received, and grace upon grace. (1:15–16)

In keeping with his purpose in writing his gospel (20:31), John brought in other witnesses to the truth about the divine, preexistent, incarnate Word, the Lord Jesus Christ. He first called on **John** the Baptist, who also **testified about Him and cried out, saying, "This was He of whom I said, 'He who comes after me has a higher rank than I, for He existed before me.'"** John's testimony will be related in more detail beginning in verse 19. Here the apostle John merely summarizes it. John the Baptist, of course, had died long before this gospel was written. But as noted in chapter 2 of this volume, there was still a John the Baptist cult in existence. So as he did in verse 8, the apostle notes John the Baptist's inferiority to Christ—this time in the Baptist's own words. In contrast to some of his followers, he understood clearly and accepted gladly his subordinate role.

That John **cried out** speaks of the bold, public nature of his witness to Jesus; he was "the voice of one crying in the wilderness, 'Make ready the way of the Lord, make His paths straight!'" (Matt. 3:3). He was the herald, proclaiming the arrival of the Messiah, and calling people to repent and prepare their hearts to receive Him. Acknowledging Jesus' preeminence John **said** of Him, **"He who comes after me has a higher rank than I, for He existed before me."** Jesus, the Expected (lit., "coming") One (Matt. 11:3; Luke 7:19–20; John 6:14) came **after** John in time; He was born six months later (Luke 1:26) and began His public ministry after John began his. Yet, as John acknowledged, Jesus had **a higher rank than** he did, **for He existed before** him. The reference here, as in verses 1 and 2, is to Jesus' eternal preexistence (cf. 8:58).

Then John called on the testimony of believers, including himself and **all** who **have received** the **fullness** of blessing from the one who is "full of grace and truth" (v. 14). Because in Christ "all the fullness of Deity dwells in bodily form" (Col. 2:9), He provides for all His people's needs (Rom. 5:2; Eph. 4:12–13; Col. 1:28; 2:10; 2 Peter 1:3). That abundant supply will never be exhausted or diminished; **grace** will continually follow **grace** in a limitless, never-ending flow (cf. 2 Cor. 12:9; Eph. 2:7).

THE IMPACT OF THE INCARNATION

For the Law was given through Moses; grace and truth were realized through Jesus Christ. No one has seen God at any time; the only begotten God who is in the bosom of the Father, He has explained Him. (1:17–18)

Obviously, the impact was monumental. First, grace triumphed over law. Since the **Law was given** by God **through Moses** (5:45; 9:29; Ex. 31:18; Lev. 26:46; Deut. 4:44; 5.1; Acts 7:37–38), it was imbued with His glory and reflected His holy and righteous character. Therefore Paul could write, "What shall we say then? Is the Law sin? May it never be! . . . The Law is holy, and the commandment is holy and righteous and good" (Rom. 7:7, 12; cf. 2 Cor. 3:7–11). Yet though God was gracious in the Old Testament (e.g., Gen. 6:8; Ezra 9:8; Ps. 84:11; Prov. 3:34; Jer. 31:2; Zech. 4:7), the Law was not an instrument of grace. Rather, God granted grace and forgiveness to repentant sinners who violated His holy law, based on what Christ would do to provide atonement. The **Law** saves no one (Acts 13:38–39; Rom. 3:20–22; 8:3; 10:4; Gal. 2:16; 3:10–12; Phil. 3:9; Heb. 7:18–19; 10:1–4); it merely convicts sinners of their inability to keep perfectly God's righteous standards, and condemns them to the eternal punishment of divine justice; and thus reveals their need for the grace of forgiveness. Paul wrote to the Galatians that "the Law has become our tutor to lead us to Christ, so that we may be justified by faith" (Gal. 3:24).

But as the Son over the house in which Moses was only a servant (Heb. 3:5–6), Jesus Christ brought the full realization of **grace and truth** (cf. the discussion of v. 14 above). God's grace in the Old Testament was applied to the believing penitents in anticipation of the full revelation of His **grace** in Jesus Christ. In Him God's salvation **truth** was fully revealed and accomplished. The "truth is in Jesus" (Eph. 4:21; cf. John 14:6).

Second, God was made visible with a clarity never before seen or known. Not merely because He is a Spirit who is invisible (Col. 1:15; 1 Tim. 1:17; Heb. 11:27), but more important because to do so would bring instant death (Ex. 33:20; cf. Gen. 32:30; Deut. 5:26; Judg. 13:22), **no one has seen God at any time** (John 6:46; 1 Tim. 6:16; 1 John 4:12, 20). It is through Jesus Christ, the "image of the invisible God" (Col. 1:15), that God is revealed.

The NASB follows the reading best attested in the Greek manuscripts, **only begotten God** (instead of the alternate reading, "only begotten Son" found in some English translations). It is a fitting conclusion to the prologue, which has stressed Christ's deity and absolute equality with the Father. The intimate expression **who is in the bosom of the Father** is reminiscent of the phrase *pros ton theon* ("with God") in verse 1 (cf. the discussion in chapter 1 of this volume). It expresses Christ's shared nature with the Father (cf. 17:24).

God, who cannot be known unless He reveals Himself, became most fully known because Jesus **explained Him.** Jesus is the explanation of God. He is the answer to the question, "What is God like?" In John 14:7–9, Jesus declared that truth to His obtuse disciples:

> "If you had known Me, you would have known My Father also; from now on you know Him, and have seen Him." Philip said to Him, "Lord, show us the Father, and it is enough for us." Jesus said to him, "Have I been so long with you, and yet you have not come to know Me, Philip? He who has seen Me has seen the Father; how can you say, 'Show us the Father'?"

Explained translates a form of the verb *exēgeomai,* from which the English word "exegesis" (the method or practice of interpreting Scripture) derives. Jesus is the only one qualified to exegete or interpret God to man, since "no one knows the Son except the Father; nor does anyone know the Father except the Son, and anyone to whom the Son wills to reveal Him" (Matt. 11:27).

The prologue presents an introductory synopsis of John's entire gospel. It introduces themes that will be expanded throughout the rest of the book. None are more important than this: Jesus, who existed in intimate fellowship with the Father from all eternity (v. 1), became flesh (v. 14), brought the full expression of grace and truth to mankind (v. 17), and revealed God to man (v. 18). How He did so will be seen in the remainder of John's gospel.

John the Baptist's Testimony to Christ (John 1:19–37)

4

This is the testimony of John, when the Jews sent to him priests and Levites from Jerusalem to ask him, "Who are you?" And he confessed and did not deny, but confessed, "I am not the Christ." They asked him, "What then? Are you Elijah?" And he said, "I am not." "Are you the Prophet?" And he answered, "No." Then they said to him, "Who are you, so that we may give an answer to those who sent us? What do you say about yourself?" He said, "I am a voice of one crying in the wilderness, 'Make straight the way of the Lord,' as Isaiah the prophet said." Now they had been sent from the Pharisees. They asked him, and said to him, "Why then are you baptizing, if you are not the Christ, nor Elijah, nor the Prophet?" John answered them saying, "I baptize in water, but among you stands One whom you do not know. It is He who comes after me, the thong of whose sandal I am not worthy to untie." These things took place in Bethany beyond the Jordan, where John was baptizing. The next day he saw Jesus coming to him and said, "Behold, the Lamb of God who takes away the sin of the world! This is He on behalf of whom I said, 'After me comes a Man who has a higher rank than I, for He existed before me.' I did not recognize Him, but so that He might be manifested to

Israel, I came baptizing in water." John testified saying, "I have seen the Spirit descending as a dove out of heaven, and He remained upon Him. I did not recognize Him, but He who sent me to baptize in water said to me, 'He upon whom you see the Spirit descending and remaining upon Him, this is the One who baptizes in the Holy Spirit.' I myself have seen, and have testified that this is the Son of God." Again the next day John was standing with two of his disciples, and he looked at Jesus as He walked, and said, "Behold, the Lamb of God!" The two disciples heard him speak, and they followed Jesus. (1:19–37)

The ancient world had seen many great men. It had known feared war leaders, like Alexander the Great; judicious lawgivers, like Hammurabi; profound thinkers, like Socrates; powerful rulers, like Augustus Caesar; wise men, like Solomon; and noble religious leaders, like Abraham, Moses, David, and the judges and prophets of Israel. But the greatest of them all was a most improbable candidate by human standards for that supreme honor. He lived his life in obscurity in the desert, far from society and the seats of power and influence. Nor was he wealthy; by the way he dressed and ate he identified with the poor (Matt. 3:4). Yet he had the most important and elevated task in history: to announce the arrival of the Messiah. This man, John the Baptist, the last of the Old Testament prophets, was introduced in verse 15 where it is recorded that he confessed that Christ was greater than he. Yet Jesus pronounced him greater than any other person who had ever lived before him (Matt. 11:11). He also said that everyone after John in the kingdom was greater than John because they lived in the fullness of all the new covenant work of the Messiah. John died on the other side of the cross and resurrection, though its merits were applied to him as to all Old Testament saints.

As referenced in chapter 2 of this volume, even his birth was totally unexpected, since his mother, Elizabeth, had always been barren, and she and her husband "were both advanced in years" (Luke 1:7) and beyond childbearing times. While his father, Zacharias, a priest (v. 5), was fulfilling his course of ministering in the temple, the angel Gabriel suddenly appeared to him and made a shocking and unexpected announcement: he and Elizabeth were to have a son (vv. 13–17). Though initially terrified (v. 12), Zacharias found it so unlikely that his fear gave way to doubt and he recovered sufficiently to question the veracity of the angel's message (v. 18). While his incredulity is understandable, having used his voice to express that sinful doubt, Zacharias was denied by God the use of it until the birth of his son (v. 20).

In the sixth month of Elizabeth's pregnancy Mary, pregnant with

Jesus, visited her. In keeping with Gabriel's prophecy that John would "be filled with the Holy Spirit while yet in his mother's womb" (1:15), the unborn baby John, prompted by the Spirit, leaped for joy at the sound of Mary's greeting (vv. 41, 44).

The unusual circumstances surrounding John's birth reached a climax at his circumcision. After naming his son John in obedience to Gabriel's command (v. 13), "at once [Zacharias's] mouth was opened and his tongue loosed, and he began to speak in praise of God" (v. 64). No wonder "fear came on all those living around them; and all these matters were being talked about in all the hill country of Judea" (v. 65), and "all who heard them kept them in mind, saying, 'What then will this child turn out to be?' For the hand of the Lord was certainly with him" (v. 66).

Sometime after his remarkable entry into the world, John disappeared into obscurity "in the deserts" until the beginning of his ministry, when he was about twenty-nine or thirty years old (Luke 1:80). When the word of God came to him (Luke 3:2) initiating his prophetic ministry (cf. Jer. 1:2; Ezek. 1:3; Jonah 3:1; Hag. 1:1; Zech. 1:1), he suddenly "appeared in the wilderness preaching a baptism of repentance for the forgiveness of sins" (Mark 1:4). Israel had been waiting for four centuries for God to send them a prophet, so John's dynamic, forceful preaching stirred up an enormous amount of interest. Large crowds from "Jerusalem . . . and all Judea and all the district around the Jordan" (Matt. 3:5) flocked to hear his message. In keeping with his role as the herald of the Messiah (v. 23; Mark 1:2–3), John exhorted his hearers, "Repent, for the kingdom of heaven is at hand" (Matt. 3:2) and baptized those who repented as a symbol of their spiritual cleansing (Mark 1:5; John 1:28; 3:23).

In this passage the apostle John gives examples of the Baptist's witness, alluded to earlier (1:6–8, 15). The events recorded here took place at the peak of his ministry, subsequent to John's baptism of Jesus. While the Lord was in the wilderness being tempted (Matt. 4:1–11; Luke 4:1–13), John continued his ministry of preaching repentance and baptizing. On three successive days, to three different groups, he emphasized three truths about Jesus Christ.

FIRST DAY, FIRST GROUP, FIRST EMPHASIS

This is the testimony of John, when the Jews sent to him priests and Levites from Jerusalem to ask him, "Who are you?" And he confessed and did not deny, but confessed, "I am not the Christ." They asked him, "What then? Are you Elijah?" And he said, "I am not." "Are you the Prophet?" And he answered, "No." Then they said to him, "Who are you, so that we may give an answer to

those who sent us? What do you say about yourself?" He said, "I am a voice of one crying in the wilderness, 'Make straight the way of the Lord,' as Isaiah the prophet said." Now they had been sent from the Pharisees. They asked him, and said to him, "Why then are you baptizing, if you are not the Christ, nor Elijah, nor the Prophet?" John answered them saying, "I baptize in water, but among you stands One whom you do not know. It is He who comes after me, the thong of whose sandal I am not worthy to untie." These things took place in Bethany beyond the Jordan, where John was baptizing. (1:19–28)

The opening phrase, **this is the testimony of John,** introduces all three accounts in verses 19–37. As noted in chapter 1 of this volume, the noun *marturia* (**testimony**) and the related verb *martureō* ("testify") are favorite terms of John's, appearing more than seventy-five times in his writings. John the Baptist was the first witness called by the apostle John to testify to the truth about Jesus Christ.

The term **Jews,** while certainly appropriate for all the people of Israel, is in the majority of its uses in John's gospel restricted especially to the religious authorities (particularly those in Jerusalem) who were hostile to Christ. John alluded to that hostility, a repeated theme, when he wrote, "[Jesus] came to His own, and those who were His own did not receive Him" (1:11). In this verse the term **Jews** likely targets the Sanhedrin, the supreme governing body in Israel (under the ultimate authority of the Romans). John's powerful preaching (including his scathing denunciation of the Jewish religious establishment; cf. Matt. 3:7–10) and widespread popularity prompted them to send a delegation to investigate him. That some were beginning to wonder if he might be the Messiah (Luke 3:15) further alarmed the Jewish authorities. They feared a popular uprising, which would have been brutally suppressed by the Romans (cf. John 11:47–50) and diminished their power. So this strange prophet not only unsettled the Jewish authorities religiously, but politically as well.

The delegation sent to investigate John was composed of **priests and Levites,** at least some of whom were Pharisees (see the discussion of v. 24 below). The **priests** were the human intermediaries between God and man, and officiated at the religious ceremonies (cf. Luke 1:8–9). They were also the theological authorities in Israel. When they were not serving in the temple for their two-week annual duty, they lived throughout the land as local experts on religion. The **Levites** assisted the priests in the temple rituals (cf. Num. 3:6–10; 18:2–4). Since the temple police force was made up of Levites (cf. 7:32; Luke 22:4; Acts 4:1; 5:24), they likely served as a security detachment to protect the priests in the delegation.

The first question posed to John, **"Who are you?"** reflects the Jewish leaders' confusion regarding him (cf. their questions in vv. 21–22), since he did not fit into any of their messianic expectations. The question implied that John might consider himself the Messiah, as his emphatic (cf. his use of the emphatic pronoun *egō*) reply, **"I am not the Christ"** (the Greek word for Messiah) indicates. Messiah had come, John insisted, but he disavowed any thought that he might be Him. In fact, the apostle John's threefold declaration, **he confessed and did not deny, but confessed** emphasizes the vehemence of the Baptist's denial. Unlike some of his followers, he clearly understood his subordinate role as the forerunner of Christ (cf. 3:25–30).

If John were not the Messiah, was there a possibility that he might be another significant figure associated with the end times? Hence the delegation next asked him, **"Are you Elijah?"** Based on the prophecy of Malachi (3:1 and 4:5), the Jews expected Elijah himself to return in bodily form just before Messiah returned to establish His earthly kingdom. Even today many Jewish people leave an empty seat at the table for Elijah when they celebrate their Passover Seder. John's appearance was strikingly similar to Elijah's; according to Mark 1:6, "John was clothed with camel's hair and wore a leather belt around his waist," while 2 Kings 1:8 describes Elijah as "a hairy man with a leather girdle bound about his loins." John's call for repentance (Matt. 3:2) and warning of coming judgment (Matt. 3:10–12) would have further reminded his hearers of Elijah (cf. 1 Kings 18:18, 21; 21:17–24).

But to the question of whether he was Elijah John also replied, **"I am not."** He was not Elijah, at least not in the literal sense that he knew his questioners meant; he was not Elijah returned to earth from heaven where he had gone in a whirlwind (2 Kings 2:11). Yet there was a sense in which John was Elijah, as Jesus explained to His disciples:

> And His disciples asked Him, "Why then do the scribes say that Elijah must come first?" And He answered and said, "Elijah is coming and will restore all things; but I say to you that Elijah already came, and they did not recognize him, but did to him whatever they wished. So also the Son of Man is going to suffer at their hands." Then the disciples understood that He had spoken to them about John the Baptist. (Matt. 17:10–13)

John was not actually Elijah as the Jews expected; instead he was Elijah-like, coming "in the spirit and power of Elijah" (Luke 1:17). As noted above, John preached with the same boldness and power as Elijah did. Had the Jewish people believed his message and accepted Jesus as the Messiah, John would have been the fulfillment of Malachi's prophecy. "If you are willing to accept it," declared Jesus, "John himself is Elijah who was to come" (Matt. 11:14). With those words, Jesus interpreted Malachi's prophecy as referring to one similar to Elijah and not to the prophet himself. John's reply to the delegation may also suggest that he did not understand himself to be Elijah even in the sense that Jesus affirmed he was. Leon Morris notes,

> No man is what he is in his own eyes. He really is only as he is known to God. At a later time Jesus equated John with the Elijah of Malachi's prophecy, but that does not carry with it the implication that John himself was aware of the true position. . . . Jesus confers on John his true significance. No man is what he himself thinks he is. He is only what Jesus knows him to be. (*The Gospel According to John,* The New International Commentary on the New Testament [Grand Rapids: Eerdmans, 1979], 135–36)

The next query, **Are you the Prophet?** came from the prophecy of Moses in Deuteronomy 18:15–18 about a prophet like him who would come and speak the word of God. There was no consensus in first-century Judaism about the precise identity of that **Prophet** (cf. John 6:14; 7:40). Some believed that he, like Elijah, would be a forerunner of the Messiah (possibly Jeremiah or one of the other prophets resurrected; cf. Matt. 16:14); others saw him as the Messiah Himself. The latter view is the correct one, since both Peter (Acts 3:22–23) and Stephen (Acts 7:37) applied Deuteronomy 18:15–18 to Jesus. Thus John denied being that prophet, answering simply, **"No."**

Frustrated by John's string of terse, negative replies and out of obvious options, the exasperated members of the delegation finally **said to him, "Who are you, so that we may give an answer to those who sent us?"** In light of John's popularity (and thus his perceived threat to the authorities), they needed a positive **answer** from him to include in their report **to those who sent** them. Giving up trying to guess who he might be, they demanded, **"What do you say about yourself?"**

John's reply was undoubtedly not what the delegation expected to hear. Rather than claiming to be someone important, he humbly referred to himself merely as **a voice of one crying in the wilderness.** Leon Morris observes,

> "The point of the quotation is that it gives no prominence to the preacher whatever. He is not an important person, like a prophet or the Messiah. He is no more than a voice (contrast the reference to Jesus as 'the Word'). He is a voice, moreover, with but one thing to say. . . . 'Make straight the way of the Lord' is a call to be ready, for the coming of the Messiah is near." (*The Gospel According to John,* 137)

John's self-abasement is reminiscent of Paul, who viewed himself as "the very least of all saints" (Eph. 3:8; cf. 1 Cor. 15:9; 1 Tim. 1:12–16). It is also in keeping with Jesus' admonition, "So you too, when you do all the things which are commanded you, say, 'We are unworthy slaves; we have done only that which we ought to have done'" (Luke 17:10).

But John's response was more than a humble confession; it was an Old Testament prophecy. That text speaks of the coming glory of the kingdom of God and the necessary preparation for it. Understandably, since he is the herald of the king and His kingdom, all four gospels quote Isaiah 40:3 in connection with John the Baptist (cf. Matt. 3:3; Mark 1:3; Luke 3:4). Only here, however, does he actually quote the verse himself. With that quote John both answered the delegation's question as to his identity and shifted the focus away from himself and onto Christ. His (and Isaiah's) message, **"Make straight the way of the Lord,"** was a challenge both to the nation and to his questioners to prepare their hearts for the coming of the Messiah. The analogous imagery is of all barriers being leveled and impediments smoothed out in preparation for the visit of an ancient Eastern king. John and Isaiah likened the hearts of Messiah's people to a desolate wilderness, through which a smooth, level road needed to be prepared for His coming. Once again, John emphasized his humility and subordinate role. He was merely a laborer, preparing the road in advance of the King.

At this point the apostle John said, **Now they had been sent from the Pharisees,** which further clarifies the specific intention of the phrase "the Jews" (v. 19). The Sadducees controlled the temple at this time and were the majority party in the Sanhedrin. But here we learn that the **Pharisees** had **sent** this delegation. Nor is it likely that the Sadducees would have sent a delegation comprised solely of their arch-rivals, the Pharisees. Because the high priest and the chief priests were Sadducees, they would have been concerned about John, since he was from a priestly family. This statement, then, may indicate that the Pharisees prompted the confrontation and were included in the delegation. Not content to let the matter drop, they further questioned John about his authority to baptize—something Pharisees would have been far more concerned about than the more religiously liberal Sadducees. The Pharisees' question, "Why then are you baptizing, if you are not the Christ, nor Elijah, nor the Prophet?" was a further challenge. Since by his own admission John was not one of those figures, what authority did he have to baptize?

John answered them by again directing their attention away from himself and onto Christ. Instead of defending his baptizing ministry, he merely acknowledged its limitations by saying, **"I baptize in water."** He then shifted the discussion back to the **One** to whom he bore witness,

declaring, **"but among you stands One whom you do not know."**
The Old Testament spoke of spiritual cleansing in connection with Messiah's coming (Ezek. 36:25, 33; 37:23; Zech. 13:1). The Jews therefore baptized proselytes, converts to Judaism, but John was baptizing Jews. That shocked the religious leaders, who viewed the Jews as already God's kingdom people and not in need of baptism. But those who submitted to John's baptism thereby acknowledged that their sin had placed them outside God's saving covenant, and they were no better than Gentiles. John then baptized them as a public expression of their repentance (Matt. 3:6, 11), in preparation for Messiah's coming. His baptizing was another feature of his witness to Jesus Christ, the Messiah, who was already **among** the people, though they did **not know** Him and never would (1:10).

John repeated the words attributed to him by the apostle John in the prologue. He identified the Messiah whom they did not recognize as **He who comes after me** because he was born and began his ministry before Jesus. Then, in a stunning expression of humility, the Baptist reaffirmed the truth that Jesus had a higher rank than he did (1:15). Untying **the thong of** his master's **sandal** was the task of the lowliest slave. John did not even consider himself **worthy** to perform that most menial and degrading task—one that Jewish teachers were forbidden to demand of their students.

The exact geography of **Bethany beyond the Jordan,** which John identifies as the location of this dialogue to solidify its historicity, is unknown to us now. Since there was a village named Bethany on the eastern slope of the Mount of Olives, near Jerusalem (Mark 11:1), some scribes mistakenly assumed that the text gives the wrong location for the place **where John was baptizing.** Therefore some manuscripts incorrectly substitute Bethabara for **Bethany.** To avoid any confusion, however, the apostle John added the appellation **beyond the Jordan** to distinguish for the people who knew of both the **Bethany** where John was ministering from the one near Jerusalem. That there would be two cities of the same name in the same region is not unusual.

John's first emphasis was simple, yet urgent: Prepare your hearts, because the Messiah is here. The prophecy of Isaiah six hundred years earlier that the way was to be prepared for Messiah's coming was being fulfilled. And it would not be economic, military, or political. The next conversation proves that it would be a deliverance and a kingdom that was deeply spiritual.

SECOND DAY, SECOND GROUP, SECOND EMPHASIS

The next day he saw Jesus coming to him and said, "Behold, the Lamb of God who takes away the sin of the world! This is He on behalf of whom I said, 'After me comes a Man who has a higher rank than I, for He existed before me.' I did not recognize Him, but so that He might be manifested to Israel, I came baptizing in water." John testified saying, "I have seen the Spirit descending as a dove out of heaven, and He remained upon Him. I did not recognize Him, but He who sent me to baptize in water said to me, 'He upon whom you see the Spirit descending and remaining upon Him, this is the One who baptizes in the Holy Spirit.' I myself have seen, and have testified that this is the Son of God." (1:29–34)

The phrase **the next day** introduces a sequence of days, which continues in verses 35, 43, and 2:1. Apparently, the events from John's interview with the delegation from Jerusalem (vv. 19–28) to the miracle at Cana (2:1–11) spanned one week. On the day after he spoke to the delegation, John **saw Jesus coming to him.** Faithful to his duty as a herald, and defining a momentous redemptive moment, John immediately called the crowd's attention to Him, exclaiming **"Behold, the Lamb of God."** That title, used only in John's writings (cf. v. 36; Rev. 5:6; 6:9; 7:10, 17; 14:4, 10; 15:3; 17:14; 19:9; 21:22–23; 22:1, 3), is the first in a string of titles given to Jesus in the remaining verses of this chapter; the rest include Rabbi (vv. 38, 49), Messiah (v. 41), Son of God (vv. 34, 49), King of Israel (v. 49), Son of Man (v. 51), and "Him of whom Moses in the Law and also the Prophets wrote—Jesus of Nazareth, the son of Joseph" (v. 45). That was not a guess on John's part, but was revelation from God that was absolutely true, as the life, death, and resurrection of Jesus proved.

The concept of a sacrificial **Lamb** was a familiar one to the Jewish people. All through Israel's history God had revealed clearly that sin and separation from Him could be removed only by blood sacrifices (cf. Lev. 17:11). No forgiveness of sin could be granted by God apart from an acceptable substitute dying as a sacrifice. They knew of Abraham's confidence that God would provide a lamb to offer in place of Isaac (Gen. 22:7–8). A lamb was sacrificed at Passover (Ex. 12:1–36; Mark 14:12), in the daily sacrifices in the tabernacle and later in the temple (Ex. 29:38–42), and as a sin offering by individuals (Lev. 5:5–7). God also made it clear that none of those sacrifices were sufficient to take away sin (cf. Isa. 1:11). They were also aware that Isaiah's prophecy likened Messiah to "a lamb that is led to slaughter" (Isa. 53:7; cf. Acts 8:32; 1 Peter 1:19). Though Israel sought a Messiah who would be a prophet, king, and conqueror, God had to send them a **Lamb.** And He did.

The title **Lamb of God** foreshadows Jesus' ultimate sacrifice on the cross for **the sin of the world.** With this brief statement, the prophet John made it clear that the Messiah had come to deal with sin. The Old Testament is filled with the reality that the problem is sin and it is at the very heart of every person (Jer. 17:9). All men, even those who received the revelation of God in Scripture (the Jews), were sinful and incapable of changing the future or the present, or of repaying God for the sins of the past. Paul's familiar indictment of human sinfulness in Romans 3:11–12 is based on Old Testament revelation. As noted in the discussion of 1:9–11 in chapter 2 of this volume, *kosmos* (**world**) has a variety of meanings in the New Testament. Here it refers to humanity in general, to all people without distinction, transcending all national, racial, and ethnic boundaries. The use of the singular term **sin** with the collective noun **world** reveals that as sin is worldwide, so Jesus' sacrifice is sufficient for all people without distinction (cf. 1 John 2:2). But though His sacrificial death is sufficient for the sins of everyone (cf. 3:16; 4:42; 6:51; 1 Tim. 2:6; Heb. 2:9; 1 John 4:14), it is efficacious only for those who savingly believe in Him (3:15–16, 18, 36; 5:24; 6:40; 11:25–26; 20:31; Luke 8:12; Acts 10:43; 13:39; 16:31; Rom. 1:16; 3:21–24; 4:3–5; 10:9–10; 1 Cor. 1:21; Gal. 3:6–9, 22; Eph. 1:13; 1 John 5:1; 10–13). This verse does not teach universalism, the false doctrine that everyone will be saved. That such is not the case is obvious, since the Bible teaches that most people will suffer eternal punishment in hell (Matt. 25:41, 46; 2 Thess. 1:9; Rev. 14:9–11; 20:11–15; cf. Ezek. 18:4, 20; Matt. 7:13–14; Luke 13:23–24; John 8:24), and only a few will be saved (Matt. 7:13–14).

John for the third time (cf. vv. 15, 27) stressed his subordinate role to Jesus, the eternal Word who had become **a Man,** acknowledging, **"This is He on behalf of whom I said, 'After me comes a Man who has a higher rank than I, for He existed before me.'"** John was created. Jesus' **higher rank** was infinite. He was the One who created everything (1:1–3), including John. Though John was actually born before Jesus, Jesus **existed before** him. And though John was a relative of Jesus' (probably His cousin), since their mothers were related (Luke 1:36), he still **did not recognize Him** as the Messiah until he baptized Him, so **that He might be manifested to Israel.** For that most significant of all John's baptisms, he declared, **"I came baptizing in water,"** though he was reluctant to baptize Jesus (Matt. 3:14). It was at Jesus' baptism that God, **who sent** John **to baptize in water,** fully revealed Jesus as the Messiah through a prearranged sign. **John testified saying, "I have seen the Spirit descending as a dove out of heaven, and He remained upon Him"** (cf. Matt. 3:16; Mark 1:10; Luke 3:22). That sign was supernatural proof of Jesus' messiahship, because God had told John, **"He upon whom you see the Spirit descending and remain-**

ing upon Him, this is the One who baptizes in the Holy Spirit."
Like Peter (Matt. 16:17), John understood who Jesus truly was only
through divine revelation. That Jesus is far greater than John is reinforced
in that He **baptizes in the Holy Spirit.**

For the sixth time in his gospel (cf. 1:7, 8, 15, 19, 32), John the
apostle refers to the Baptist's witness to Christ, recording his affirmation, **"I
myself have seen, and have testified that this is the Son of God."**
As noted in chapter 1 of this volume, witness, or testifying, is thematic in
this gospel. John's testimony in verse 34 is a fitting conclusion to this section, as the narrative makes the transition from him to Jesus. Although
believers are in a limited sense children of God (Matt. 5:9; Rom. 8:14, 19;
Gal. 3:26; cf. John 1:12; 11:52; Rom. 8:16, 21; 9:8; Phil. 2:15; 1 John 3:1–2, 10),
Jesus is uniquely **the Son of God** in that He alone shares the same nature
as the Father (1:1; 5:16–30; 10:30–33; 14:9; 17:11; 1 John 5:20).

To his first emphasis—Messiah is here—John added an equally
compelling exhortation: Recognize Him for who He is—the Son of God,
the Messiah, the ultimate sacrificial Lamb for the sin of the world.

THIRD DAY, THIRD GROUP, THIRD EMPHASIS

**Again the next day John was standing with two of his disciples,
and he looked at Jesus as He walked, and said, "Behold, the
Lamb of God!" The two disciples heard him speak, and they followed Jesus.** (1:35–37)

The phrase **the next day** continues the sequence of days discussed above in connection with verse 29. This is now the third day in
the sequence, the second one after John's encounter with the investiga-
tive delegation from Jerusalem. The third group is the smallest one, consisting only of **two of** John's **disciples** (Andrew [v. 40], and John [who
never names himself in his gospel]). John **looked at Jesus as He
walked** nearby and repeated to his **disciples** what he had proclaimed
to the crowds on the previous day, **"Behold, the Lamb of God!"** Having
heard their teacher **speak** again those powerful words, the two disciples
followed Jesus. John's willingness to unhesitatingly hand them over to
Him is further evidence of his self-effacing humility and complete
acceptance of his subordinate role.

That the two disciples **followed** Jesus does not imply that they
became His permanent disciples at this time. It is true that *akoloutheō*
(**followed**) is used in John's gospel to mean "to follow as a disciple"
(e.g., 8:12; 10:27; 12:26; 21:19; cf. Matt. 4:20, 22; 9:9). But it can also be used
in a general sense (e.g., 6:2; 11:31; 18:15; 20:6; 21:20). Andrew and John

here received their first exposure to Jesus. Later, they became His permanent disciples (Matt. 4:18–22).

John's third emphasis follows logically from his first two. Since the Messiah, the Son of God, the Lamb of God, is here, the only proper response is to follow Him.

Having served his purpose as a witness to the true identity of Jesus, John the Baptist now faded from the scene (apart from a brief mention in 3:23ff.). The rest of the gospel focuses on the ministry of Jesus, something the Baptist himself would have approved of. As he said to some of his disciples who were jealous for his reputation,

> A man can receive nothing unless it has been given him from heaven. You yourselves are my witnesses that I said, "I am not the Christ," but, "I have been sent ahead of Him." He who has the bride is the bridegroom; but the friend of the bridegroom, who stands and hears him, rejoices greatly because of the bridegroom's voice. So this joy of mine has been made full. He must increase, but I must decrease. (John 3:27–30)

He did decrease and, while in prison wondering how that imprisonment fit with the anticipated glory of Messiah's kingdom, was hit with doubts about Jesus being Messiah. The Lord graciously dispelled those doubts by reporting the record of His miracles (Matt. 11:2–5; Luke 7:19–22).

The Balance of Salvation (John 1:38–51)

5

And Jesus turned and saw them following, and said to them, "What do you seek?" They said to Him, "Rabbi (which translated means Teacher), where are You staying?" He said to them, "Come, and you will see." So they came and saw where He was staying; and they stayed with Him that day, for it was about the tenth hour. One of the two who heard John speak and followed Him, was Andrew, Simon Peter's brother. He found first his own brother Simon and said to him, "We have found the Messiah" (which translated means Christ). He brought him to Jesus. Jesus looked at him and said, "You are Simon the son of John; you shall be called Cephas" (which is translated Peter). The next day He purposed to go into Galilee, and He found Philip. And Jesus said to him, "Follow Me." Now Philip was from Bethsaida, of the city of Andrew and Peter. Philip found Nathanael and said to him, "We have found Him of whom Moses in the Law and also the Prophets wrote—Jesus of Nazareth, the son of Joseph." Nathanael said to him, "Can any good thing come out of Nazareth?" Philip said to him, "Come and see." Jesus saw Nathanael coming to Him, and said of him, "Behold, an Israelite indeed, in whom there is no deceit!" Nathanael said to Him,

"How do You know me?" Jesus answered and said to him, "Before Philip called you, when you were under the fig tree, I saw you." Nathanael answered Him, "Rabbi, You are the Son of God; You are the King of Israel." Jesus answered and said to him, "Because I said to you that I saw you under the fig tree, do you believe? You will see greater things than these." And He said to him, "Truly, truly, I say to you, you will see the heavens opened and the angels of God ascending and descending on the Son of Man." (John 1:38–51)

The Bible reveals God to be infinitely beyond human understanding. In Isaiah 55:8–9 He said, "'For My thoughts are not your thoughts, nor are your ways My ways,' declares the Lord. 'For as the heavens are higher than the earth, so are My ways higher than your ways and My thoughts than your thoughts.'" "Oh, the depth of the riches both of the wisdom and knowledge of God!" exclaimed Paul in Romans 11:33. "How unsearchable are His judgments and unfathomable His ways!" Job 5:9 describes God as the one "who does great and unsearchable things, wonders without number," while Job 11:7–9 asks rhetorically, "Can you discover the depths of God? Can you discover the limits of the Almighty? They are high as the heavens, what can you do? Deeper than Sheol, what can you know? Its measure is longer than the earth and broader than the sea." Job 37:5 says that God does "great things which we cannot comprehend." David wrote in Psalm 40:5, "Many, O Lord my God, are the wonders which You have done, and Your thoughts toward us; there is none to compare with You. If I would declare and speak of them, they would be too numerous to count."

Not surprisingly, then, the interface of the infinite God's sovereign will and purposes with human actions and responsibility results in a number of apparent paradoxes. For example, Judas's betrayal of Jesus was part of God's predetermined plan (Luke 22:22), as Jesus affirmed: "For the Son of Man is to go just as it is written of Him" (Mark 14:21). But that did not excuse his sin, which he entered into willingly (Matt. 26:14–16; John 12:4), or lessen his guilt. In the second half of Mark 14:21 Jesus went on to say, "Woe to that man by whom the Son of Man is betrayed! It would have been good for that man if he had not been born." Judas was sentenced to eternal hell because of his choice to betray Jesus. The historical record in Exodus also displays the interaction of God's sovereignty and human responsibility, noting ten times that God hardened Pharaoh's heart (4:21; 7:3; 9:12; 10:1, 20, 27; 11:10; 14:4, 8, 17) and ten times that he hardened his own heart (7:13–14, 22; 8:15, 19, 32; 9:7, 34–35; 13:15).

Another apparent paradox involves the authorship of Scripture.

The Bible claims God as its author; "All Scripture is inspired by God" (2 Tim. 3:16), and "no prophecy was ever made by an act of human will" (2 Peter 1:21). Yet Jesus introduced a quote from the Old Testament with the words "Moses said" (Mark 7:10; cf. 10:3; 12:26; Matt. 8:4; 19:8; Luke 5:14; 20:37), and referred to the Old Testament as the writings of Moses and the prophets (Luke 24:27, 44; John 5:45–46; 7:19–23). Peter referred to Paul's writings as Scripture (2 Peter 3:15–16), and noted that in the inspiration process, "Men moved by the Holy Spirit spoke from God" (2 Peter 1:21). Thus the Bible, though written by some forty human authors over a period of approximately 1,500 years, is nevertheless one unified book with one Divine author.

The Bible teaches that it is impossible for believers to live the Christian life on their own. "Are you so foolish?" Paul chided the Galatians. "Having begun by the Spirit, are you now being perfected by the flesh?" (Gal. 3:3). Earlier in that epistle he wrote, "I have been crucified with Christ; and it is no longer I who live, but Christ lives in me; and the life which I now live in the flesh I live by faith in the Son of God, who loved me and gave Himself up for me" (2:20). Yet the same apostle who wrote, "the life which I now live in the flesh I live by faith in the Son of God" also wrote, "Therefore I run in such a way, as not without aim; I box in such a way, as not beating the air; but I discipline my body and make it my slave, so that, after I have preached to others, I myself will not be disqualified" (1 Cor. 9:26–27), and likened the Christian life to a fight (1 Tim. 6:12; 2 Tim. 4:7), a race (1 Cor. 9:24), and labor-intensive farming (2 Tim. 2:6). He also commanded believers, "Therefore do not let sin reign in your mortal body so that you obey its lusts, and do not go on presenting the members of your body to sin as instruments of unrighteousness; but present yourselves to God as those alive from the dead, and your members as instruments of righteousness to God" (Rom. 6:12–13).

Stressing the responsibility of the believer, the New Testament frequently depicts the Christian life as a walk of obedience (Rom. 14:15; 2 Cor. 5:7; Eph. 2:10; 4:1, 17; 5:2, 8, 15; Phil. 3:17; Col. 1:10; 2:6; 1 Thess. 2:12; 4:1; 1 John 1:6–7; 2:6; 2 John 4, 6; 3 John 3–4). Among the many obligations of the Christian walk are prayer (Rom. 12:12; Eph. 6:18; Col. 4:2; 1 Thess. 5:17; 1 Tim. 2:8; James 5:13), reading (1 Tim. 4:13), and studying (Acts 17:11) the Bible, having a reverential fear of God (Acts 9:31; cf. Job 28:28; Ps. 111:10; Prov. 1:7; 3:7; 9:10; 15:33; Mic. 6:9), partaking of the Lord's Supper (1 Cor. 11:23–26), being thankful (Phil. 4:6; Col. 1:12; 3:15–17; 1 Thess. 5:18), being joyful (Rom. 12:12, 15; 14:17; 15:13; 2 Cor. 13:11; Phil. 2:18; 3:1; 4:4; 1 Thess. 1:6; 5:16; 1 Peter 4:13), forgiving one another (Matt. 6:14–15; 18:21–35; Mark 11:25; Luke 17:3–4; Eph. 4:32; Col. 3:13), and turning away from evil (Job 28:28; Pss. 34:14; 37:27; 101:4; Prov. 3:7; 4:27; 16:17; Jer. 18:11; 25:5; 35:15; Ezek. 33:11; 1 Peter 3:11), such as lying (Eph. 4:25;

Col. 3:9), sexual immorality (1 Cor. 6:18; Eph. 5:3; 1 Thess. 4:3, 7), anger (Matt. 5:22; Eph. 4:31; Col. 3:8; James 1:19–20), abusive speech (Eph. 4:29; 5:4; Col. 3:8; James 3:8–10), and covetousness (Ex. 20:17; Mark 7:21–22; Rom. 7:7–8; 13:9).

Paul brought together the human and divine sides of living the Christian life when he commanded the Philippians, "Work out your salvation with fear and trembling; for it is God who is at work in you, both to will and to work for His good pleasure" (Phil. 2:12–13; cf. 4:13). The apostle exemplified that truth; as he wrote to the Colossians, "For this purpose also I labor, striving according to His power, which mightily works within me" (Col. 1:29; cf. 1 Cor. 15:10; 2 Cor. 3:5; Gal. 2:8).

But of all the issues involving the relationship of divine sovereignty to human responsibility, the most basic is that of salvation. The biblical teaching that salvation is a divine act that demands a human response may be likened to a clearly marked, but narrow path between two chasms. To err on either side of that path is to plummet to spiritual ruin.

Scripture clearly reveals that salvation is a divine act. Unbelievers are "dead in [their] trespasses and sins" (Eph. 2:1), "separate from Christ, . . . having no hope and without God in the world" (Eph. 2:12), "alienated and hostile in mind, engaged in evil deeds" (Col. 1:21), enemies of God (Rom. 5:10), hostile to God (Rom. 8:7), unable to please Him (Rom. 8:8), "darkened in their understanding, excluded from the life of God because of the ignorance that is in them, because of the hardness of their heart" (Eph. 4:18), "foolish . . . , disobedient, deceived, enslaved to various lusts and pleasures, spending [their lives] in malice and envy, hateful, hating one another" (Titus 3:3), "pursu[ing] a course of sensuality, lusts, drunkenness, carousing, drinking parties and abominable idolatries" (1 Peter 4:3). Obviously, such people are utterly unable to save themselves.

Given fallen humanity's total depravity, complete helplessness, and utter lack of spiritual resources, there would be no salvation unless God provided it (Gen. 49:18; 1 Sam. 2:1; Pss. 3:8; 21:1; 35:9; 37:39; 98:2; 149:4; Isa. 43:11; 45:21–22; Jonah 2:9; Acts 4:12; Rev. 19:1). Thus, the Bible teaches that salvation is wholly by God's grace and not by human works (cf. Acts 15:11; Rom. 3:20–30; 4:5; 5:1; 6:23; Gal. 2:16; 3:8–14, 24; Eph. 1:7; 2:5, 8–9; Phil. 3:9; Titus 3:5; Rev. 1:5). Further, God Himself chose the redeemed for salvation in eternity past (Acts 11:18; 13:48; Rom. 8:28–30; Eph. 1:4–5; Col. 3:12; 1 Thess. 1:4; 2 Thess. 2:13; 2 Tim. 1:9; Titus 1:1; 1 Peter 1:1–2; 2:9).

But the Bible is equally clear that no one is saved apart from faith in the Lord Jesus Christ. Implicit in the biblical commands that sinners repent (Matt. 3:2; 4:17; Mark 6:12; Luke 5:32; 13:3, 5; 15:7, 10; 24:47; Acts 2:38; 3:19; 17:30; 26:20; 2 Peter 3:9) and believe in Christ (Mark 1:15; Luke

8:12; John 1:12; 3:15–18; 4:39, 53; 5:24; 6:29, 35, 40, 47; 7:38; 9:35–38; 11:25–26; Acts 16:31; Rom. 1:16; 10:9–10; 1 Cor. 1:21; Gal. 3:22; Eph. 1:13; 1 Tim. 1:16; 1 John 3:23; 5:1, 13) is their responsibility to do both. In fact, Scripture condemns sinners for not doing them (Matt. 11:20–21; 12:41; John 3:36; 12:36–40; 2 Thess. 2:12; Jude 5; Rev. 9:20–21; 16:9, 11).

In a passage that perfectly illustrates the biblical balance between divine sovereignty and human responsibility, John records the call of Jesus' first disciples to salvation. We meet first the seeking souls, and then the seeking Savior.

The Seeking Souls

And Jesus turned and saw them following, and said to them, "What do you seek?" They said to Him, "Rabbi (which translated means Teacher), where are You staying?" He said to them, "Come, and you will see." So they came and saw where He was staying; and they stayed with Him that day, for it was about the tenth hour. One of the two who heard John speak and followed Him, was Andrew, Simon Peter's brother. He found first his own brother Simon and said to him, "We have found the Messiah" (which translated means Christ). He brought him to Jesus. Jesus looked at him and said, "You are Simon the son of John; you shall be called Cephas" (which is translated Peter). (1:38–42)

As noted in the previous chapter of this volume, John the Baptist had pointed out Jesus, the Lamb of God, to two of his disciples, Andrew and John (cf. the discussion of v. 40 below), who then followed Him (1:35–37). This section continues the story of their initial encounter with Jesus. As Andrew and John walked after Him, **Jesus turned and saw them following, and said to them, "What do you seek?"** He did not ask that question for His benefit, since in His omniscience He already knew what the two wanted. That they were followers of John the Baptist indicated that they were convicted of their sin and seeking the forgiveness and righteousness Messiah would bring. Instead, the Lord asked the question to challenge them to consider their motives; He did not ask them *whom* they were seeking, but *what* they were seeking. R. C. H. Lenski notes,

> This first word spoken by Jesus [in John's gospel] is a master question. It bids them look searchingly at their inmost longings and desires. . . . A hidden promise lies in the question "What are you seeking?" Jesus has the highest treasure any man can seek, longs to direct our seeking toward that treasure in order that he may bestow it for our everlasting

enrichment. (*The Interpretation of St. John's Gospel* [Reprint; Peabody, Mass.: Hendrickson, 1998], 145–46)

Perhaps intimidated by Jesus' presence, Andrew and John replied not by answering His question directly, but by asking one of their own: **"Rabbi (which translated means Teacher), where are You staying?"** **Rabbi** was a title of respect and honor, **which,** as John **translated** for his Gentile readers (cf. vv. 41, 42; 9:7), **means Teacher.** By asking the question, **where are You staying?** Andrew and John were not merely asking where He was residing. They were courteously requesting an extended private interview with Him. The question also signaled their willingness to become His disciples.

Jesus' immediate response **to them, "Come, and you will see,"** was the invitation Andrew and John were hoping for. But Jesus "is in fact bidding these men do something more than discover where He is staying for the night; He is inviting them to come and gain from Him an insight into the mind and purpose of God Himself" (R. V. G. Tasker, *The Gospel According to St. John*, The Tyndale New Testament Commentaries [Grand Rapids: Eerdmans, 1975], 52). Jesus knew their hearts, that they were honest, sincere seekers. They had already been drawn to Him by the Father (6:44) and convicted of their sin by the Holy Spirit (cf. 16:8). The honest seeker will always find Him (Deut. 4:29; 1 Chron. 28:9; 2 Chron. 15:2; Jer. 29:13) because, as He promised, "If anyone is willing to do His will, he will know of the teaching, whether it is of God or whether I speak from Myself" (John 7:17). On the other hand, Jesus will not commit Himself to the insincere and hypocritical, no matter what their outward profession may be:

> Now when He was in Jerusalem at the Passover, during the feast, many believed in His name, observing His signs which He was doing. But Jesus, on His part, was not entrusting Himself to them, for He knew all men, and because He did not need anyone to testify concerning man, for He Himself knew what was in man. (2:23–25; cf. Matt. 7:21–23; Luke 6:46; 13:25–27)

Jesus never put off the sincere, Spirit-prompted seeker. He was never too busy to show compassion for lost sheep who were seeking a Shepherd (Matt. 9:36). To one so desperate to see Him that he cast aside his dignity and climbed a tree Jesus said, "Zaccheus, hurry and come down, for today I must stay at your house" (Luke 19:5). In response to His invitation, Andrew and John **came and saw where He was staying; and they stayed with Him that day.** For them, like Zaccheus, the day they met Jesus was to be the day of salvation (cf. the discussion of v. 41 below).

So vividly etched in his mind was that life-changing encounter that John recorded the precise time, noting that it was **about the tenth hour.** The day was drawing to a close, and darkness was fast approaching. In an era before electric lighting, this was the time of day when people began wrapping up their outdoor activities, and travelers began seeking shelter for the night. Thus, Andrew and John might have been expected to seek lodging in a nearby village.

But instead of seeking shelter, Andrew and John sought the Savior. As they had hoped He would, Jesus graciously extended to them an invitation to stay with Him for the night, as His statement, **"Come, and you will see,"** implies. John does not record what they discussed that memorable evening, but the Lord undoubtedly "opened their minds to understand the Scriptures" (Luke 24:45) as "He explained to them the things concerning Himself in all the Scriptures" (Luke 24:27). Whatever He said was enough to persuade them that He was indeed Israel's Messiah, as Andrew's excited testimony to his brother Peter the next day indicates (see the discussion of vv. 40–41 below).

The reference to the **tenth hour** is the first mention of time in John's gospel. This detail offers one of the many evidences that its author was an eyewitness to the events he recorded (see the discussion of this point in the Introduction). The truth that the apostles were eyewitnesses to Jesus is one which John stressed in his first epistle: "What we have heard, what we have seen with our eyes, what we have looked at and touched with our hands, concerning the Word of Life . . . what we have seen and heard we proclaim to you also" (1 John 1:1, 3). Because they were "witnesses of all the things [Christ] did both in the land of the Jews and in Jerusalem" (Acts 10:39), the apostles' testimony was unassailable (cf. Luke 24:48; John 15:27; Acts 1:8, 22; 2:32; 3:15; 4:33; 5:32; 10:39–41; 13:31; 2 Peter 1:16). So important was that testimony that when the apostles sought a replacement for Judas Iscariot, they looked for someone who had "accompanied [them] all the time that the Lord Jesus went in and out among [them] beginning with the baptism of John until the day that He was taken up from [them]" (Acts 1:22–23). This incident marked the beginning of John's firsthand observation of Jesus' life and ministry.

Verse 40 names **one of the two who heard John** the Baptist **speak and followed** Jesus as **Andrew.** As noted above, the other disciple was John, who throughout his gospel does not name himself. (For biographical information on John and evidence that he is the unnamed disciple, see the Introduction to this volume.) **Andrew** is identified as **Simon Peter's brother,** since Peter was more widely known than his less prominent brother. Here, as in his other two appearances in John's gospel, Andrew brings someone to meet Christ. In 6:8–9 he brought a young boy with barley loaves and fish to Him before the feeding of the

5,000, while in 12:20–22 he brought some Greeks to meet Him. After spending the rest of the day (and by implication the night) with Jesus (v. 39), Andrew the following day **found first his own brother Simon and said to him, "We have found the Messiah" (which translated means Christ).** (A number of commentators believe the Greek text suggests that John also found his brother James shortly afterward.) The time spent with Jesus had convinced Andrew and John of His true identity. That does not mean, however, that they fully understood the implications of Jesus' messiahship; the disciples' understanding of that would grow over the years they spent with Him.

Messiah transliterates a Hebrew or Aramaic term that, like its Greek equivalent **Christ,** means "anointed one." In the Old Testament it was used of the high priest (Lev. 4:3, 5, 16; 6:22), the king (1 Sam. 12:3, 5; 16:6; 24:6; 26:9; 2 Sam. 1:14; 22:51; 23:1), the patriarchs (Ps. 105:15), and the people of God (Ps. 28:8). But supremely, the term referred to the prophesied (e.g., Dan. 9:25–26) Coming or Expected One (Matt. 11:3), God's anointed Deliverer and King, His Son the Lord Jesus Christ.

Not content with merely delivering the good news that he had found the Messiah, Andrew actually **brought** Peter **to Jesus.** When he arrived, **Jesus looked at him and said, "You are Simon the son of John; you shall be called Cephas" (which is translated Peter).** Jesus' penetrating, omniscient look saw not merely **Simon,** but also the man He would mold him into. Jesus therefore **called** him **Cephas,** the Aramaic word for "rock," **which,** as John again **translated** for his Gentile readers, is rendered **Peter** in Greek. That name would both inform **Simon** of the rock that he was to become, and challenge him to pursue it. Over time, Jesus would transform Simon's character to match the new name He had given him, and use him as the foundational leader in the earliest days of the church (cf. Acts 1:15ff.; 2:14ff.; 3:1ff.; 4:8ff.; 5:1–11, 15, 29; 8:14–24; 9:32–11:18; 12:3–19; 15:7–11).

In my book *Twelve Ordinary Men* I wrote the following concerning the significance of Jesus giving to Simon the name Peter:

> Simon was a very common name. There are at least seven Simons in the Gospel accounts alone. Among the Twelve were two named Simon (Simon Peter and Simon the Zealot). In Matthew 13:55, Jesus' half brothers are listed, and one of them was also named Simon. Judas Iscariot's father was called Simon as well (John 6:71). Matthew 26:6 mentions that Jesus had a meal at the home of a man in Bethany named Simon the leper. Another Simon—a Pharisee—hosted Jesus at a similar meal (Luke 7:36–40). And the man conscripted to carry Jesus' cross partway to Calvary was Simon the Cyrene (Matthew 27:32).
>
> Our Simon's full name at birth was Simon Bar-Jonah (Matthew 16:17), meaning "Simon, son of Jonah" (John 21:15–17). Simon Peter's

father's name, then, was John (sometimes rendered Jonas or Jonah). We know nothing more about his parents.

But notice that the Lord gave him another name. Luke introduces him this way: "Simon, whom He also named Peter" (Luke 6:14). Luke's choice of words here is important. Jesus didn't merely give him a new name to replace the old one. He "also" named him Peter. This disciple was known sometimes as Simon, sometimes as Peter, and sometimes as Simon Peter.

Peter was a sort of nickname. It means "Rock." (*Petros* is the Greek word for "a piece of rock, a stone.") The Aramaic equivalent was *Cephas* (cf. 1 Corinthians 1:12; 3:22; 9:5; 15:5; Galatians 2:9). John 1:42 describes Jesus' first face-to-face meeting with Simon Peter: "Now when Jesus looked at him, He said, 'You are Simon the son of Jonah. You shall be called Cephas' (which is translated, A Stone)." Those were apparently the first words Jesus ever said to Peter. And from then on, "Rock" was his nickname.

Sometimes, however, the Lord continued to refer to him as Simon anyway. When you see that in Scripture, it is often a signal that Peter has done something that needs rebuke or correction.

The nickname was significant, and the Lord had a specific reason for choosing it. By nature Simon was brash, vacillating, and undependable. He tended to make great promises he couldn't follow through with. He was one of those people who appears to lunge wholeheartedly into something but then bails out before finishing. He was usually the first one in; and too often, he was the first one out. When Jesus met him, he fit James's description of a double-minded man, unstable in all his ways (James 1:8). Jesus changed Simon's name, it appears, because He wanted the nickname to be a perpetual reminder to him about who he *should* be. And from that point on, whatever Jesus called him sent a subtle message. If He called him Simon, He was signaling him that he was acting like his old self. If He called him Rock, He was commending him for acting the way he ought to be acting. . . .

This young man named Simon, who would become Peter, was impetuous, impulsive, and overeager. He needed to become like a rock, so that is what Jesus named him. From then on, the Lord could gently chide or commend him just by using one name or the other.

After Christ's first encounter with Simon Peter, we find two distinct contexts in which the name Simon is regularly applied to him. One is a *secular* context. When Scripture refers to his house, for example, it's usually "Simon's house" (Mark 1:29; Luke 4:38). When it speaks of his mother-in-law, it does so in similar terms: "Simon's wife's mother" (Mark 1:30; Luke 4:38). Luke 5, describing the fishing business, mentions "one of the boats, which was Simon's" (v. 3)—and Luke says James and John were "partners with Simon" (v. 10). All of those expressions refer to Simon by his given name in purely secular contexts. When he is called Simon in such a context, the use of his old name usually has nothing to do with his spirituality or his character. That is just the normal way of signifying what pertained to him as a natural man—his work, his home, or his family life. These are called "Simon's" things.

The second category of references where he is called Simon is seen whenever Peter was displaying the characteristics of his unregenerate self—when he was sinning in word, attitude, or action. Whenever he begins to act like his old self, Jesus and the Gospel writers revert to calling him Simon. In Luke 5:5, for example, Luke writes, "Simon answered and said to Him, 'Master, we have toiled all night and caught nothing; nevertheless at Your word I will let down the net.'" That is young Simon the fisherman speaking. He is skeptical and reluctant. But as he obeys and his eyes are opened to who Jesus really is, Luke begins to refer to him by his new name. Verse 8 says, "When Simon Peter saw it, he fell down at Jesus' knees, saying, 'Depart from me, for I am a sinful man, O Lord!'"

We see Jesus calling him Simon in reference to the key failures in his career. In Luke 22:31, foretelling Peter's betrayal, Jesus said, "Simon, Simon! Indeed, Satan has asked for you, that he may sift you as wheat." Later, in the Garden of Gethsemane, when Peter should have been watching and praying with Christ, he fell asleep. Mark writes, "[Jesus] came and found them sleeping, and said to Peter, 'Simon, are you sleeping? Could you not watch one hour? Watch and pray, lest you enter into temptation. The spirit indeed is willing, but the flesh is weak'" (Mark 14:37–38). Thus usually when Peter needed rebuke or admonishment, Jesus referred to him as Simon. It must have reached the point where whenever the Lord said "Simon," Peter cringed. He must have been thinking, *Please call me Rock!* And the Lord might have replied, "I'll call you Rock when you act like a rock."

It is obvious from the Gospel narratives that the apostle John knew Peter very, very well. They were lifelong friends, business associates, and neighbors. Interestingly, in the Gospel of John, John refers to his friend fifteen times as "Simon Peter." Apparently John couldn't make up his mind which name to use, because he saw both sides of Peter constantly. So he simply put both names together. In fact, "Simon Peter" is what Peter calls himself in the address of his second epistle: "Simon Peter, a bondservant and apostle of Jesus Christ" (2 Peter 1:1). In effect, he took Jesus' nickname for him and made it his surname (cf. Acts 10:32).

After the resurrection, Jesus instructed His disciples to return to Galilee, where He planned to appear to them (Matthew 28:7). Impatient Simon apparently got tired of waiting, so he announced that he was going back to fishing (John 21:3). As usual, the other disciples dutifully followed their leader. They got into the boat, fished all night, and caught nothing.

But Jesus met them on the shore the following morning, where He had prepared breakfast for them. The main purpose of the breakfast meeting seemed to be the restoration of Peter (who, of course, had sinned egregiously by denying Christ with curses on the night the Lord was betrayed). Three times Jesus addressed him as Simon and asked, "Simon, son of Jonah, do you love Me?" (John 21:15–17). Three times, Peter affirmed his love.

That was the last time Jesus ever had to call him Simon. A few weeks later, on Pentecost, Peter and the rest of the apostles were filled with the Holy Spirit. It was Peter, the Rock, who stood up and preached that day.

Peter was exactly like most Christians—both carnal and spiritual. He succumbed to the habits of the flesh sometimes; he functioned in the Spirit other times. He was sinful sometimes, but other times he acted the way a righteous man ought to act. This vacillating man— sometimes Simon, sometimes Peter—was the leader of the Twelve. ([Nashville: W Publishing Group, 2002], 33–37. Emphases in original. See this same book for biographical information on the rest of the Twelve.)

Seeking souls will always find Christ receptive; as He later promised: "All that the Father gives Me will come to Me, and the one who comes to Me I will certainly not cast out" (6:37).

THE SEEKING SAVIOR

The next day He purposed to go into Galilee, and He found Philip. And Jesus said to him, "Follow Me." Now Philip was from Bethsaida, of the city of Andrew and Peter. Philip found Nathanael and said to him, "We have found Him of whom Moses in the Law and also the Prophets wrote—Jesus of Nazareth, the son of Joseph." Nathanael said to him, "Can any good thing come out of Nazareth?" Philip said to him, "Come and see." Jesus saw Nathanael coming to Him, and said of him, "Behold, an Israelite indeed, in whom there is no deceit!" Nathanael said to Him, "How do You know me?" Jesus answered and said to him, "Before Philip called you, when you were under the fig tree, I saw you." Nathanael answered Him, "Rabbi, You are the Son of God; You are the King of Israel." Jesus answered and said to him, "Because I said to you that I saw you under the fig tree, do you believe? You will see greater things than these." And He said to him, "Truly, truly, I say to you, you will see the heavens opened and the angels of God ascending and descending on the Son of Man." (1:43–51)

Unlike the first disciples (Andrew, John, Peter, and possibly James), who were introduced to Jesus by another person, Jesus took the initiative in calling Philip. In any case, whoever initiates the contact, those who come to Christ do so only because God first sought them. In John 6:44 Jesus said, "No one can come to Me unless the Father who sent Me draws him," while in 15:16 He added, "You did not choose Me but I chose you, and appointed you." That Jesus **found Philip and . . . said to him, "Follow Me"** established that he was brought by no one, nor did he look for Jesus, but rather the contact was initiated by the Lord Himself. Though this is distinct from the others, their being brought to Jesus by another refers only to the human contact, not the sovereign divine election by God. That is true of everyone who comes savingly to Jesus. Philip's response of faith is not recorded, but it certainly took place.

The phrase **the next day** indicates that it is now the day after Andrew found Peter and brought him to meet Jesus. Jesus **purposed to** leave the section of the Jordan River where John the Baptist was ministering and **go into Galilee.** Where Jesus met **Philip** is not stated, but he, like Andrew, Peter, and John, was a Galilean. He was **from Bethsaida,** a fishing village (its name means "house of fishing," or "house of the fisherman") located on the northeast shore of the Sea of Galilee, not far from Capernaum. **Bethsaida** was also the hometown of **Andrew and Peter** who, though they later moved to Capernaum (Mark 1:21, 29), remained identified with the village where they grew up. In the same way, Jesus was associated with Nazareth (Matt. 26:71; Luke 18:37; Acts 10:38; 26:9), where He grew up, instead of Bethlehem, where He was born (Matt. 2:1), or Capernaum, where He moved to from Nazareth (Matt. 4:13).

Like Andrew, **Philip** could not keep the good news about Jesus to himself, but immediately went and **found** his friend **Nathanael.** "Philip's part in the calling of Nathanael is like that of Andrew in the calling of Peter, and that of Peter and Andrew in his own. One lighted torch serves to light another; thus faith propagates itself" (Frederic Louis Godet, *Commentary on John's Gospel* [Reprint; Grand Rapids: Kregel, 1985], 331–32). **Nathanael** ("God has given") is called Bartholomew in the Synoptic Gospels, which never use the name Nathanael, just as John never uses Bartholomew. Evidently Nathanael was his given name and Bartholomew (Bar-Tolmai; "son of Tolmai") his surname. In the lists of the twelve apostles in the Synoptic Gospels, his name immediately follows Philip's. John's only other mention of him notes that he was from the Galilean village of Cana (21:2).

Having found Nathanael, Philip excitedly **said to him, "We have found Him of whom Moses in the Law and also the Prophets wrote—Jesus of Nazareth, the son of Joseph."** The use of the plural pronoun **we** shows that Philip now included himself as one of Jesus' followers. The **Law and the Prophets** is the common New Testament designation of the Old Testament (Matt. 5:17; 7:12; 11:13; 22:40; Luke 16:16;

Acts 13:15; 24:14; 28:23; Rom. 3:21). Aware of Nathanael's intense love of the Old Testament Scriptures, Philip declared that he had found the One who fulfilled them (cf. 5:39; Deut. 18:15–19; Luke 24:25–27, 44–47; Acts 10:43; 18:28; 26:22–23; Rom. 1:2; 1 Cor. 15:3–4; 1 Peter 1:10–11; Rev. 19:10). As noted in the discussion of verse 45, **Jesus** was often associated with **Nazareth,** where He grew up. Philip's identification of Him as **the son of Joseph** must not be misconstrued as a denial of Christ's virgin birth (as it was by the unbelieving Jews in 6:42). It may suggest, however, that Jesus had not revealed that truth to the disciples during the brief time they had spent with Him. Philip identified Jesus the way people in that day were usually identified, by the name of their father and the village they came from. Thus, Jesus was commonly viewed as Joseph's son (Luke 3:23), which He was legally, though not biologically.

Nathanael's initial skepticism mirrors that of Thomas at the end of John's gospel (20:24–25). His dubious reply to Philip, **"Can any good thing come out of Nazareth?"** reflects his incredulity that the Messiah could come from such an insignificant town, of which Moses and the prophets said nothing (Nazareth is not mentioned in the Old Testament, the Talmud, the Midrash, or any contemporary Gentile writings). It also shows his disdain for the town itself; just as the Judeans looked down on Galileans in general (cf. 7:52; Acts 2:7), so also did the rest of the Galileans look down on the inhabitants of Nazareth. Since Nathanael's hometown of Cana was about ten miles north of Nazareth, his disdain may also reflect a local rivalry between the two towns.

Philip's reply, echoing the Lord's reply to Andrew and John in verse 39, was simple and compelling: **"Come and see."** Idle speculation is no substitute for personally investigating Christ. Philip was certain that his friend's questions would be answered and his doubts satisfied when he met Jesus, just as his had been. Despite his preconceived notions about Nazareth, Nathanael rose above his prejudice and went with Philip to meet Jesus.

As he approached, **Jesus saw Nathanael coming to Him, and said of him, "Behold, an Israelite indeed, in whom there is no deceit!"** From the human perspective, Nathanael came to Jesus through the witness of Philip. But, as his interview with Jesus reveals, he did so only because Jesus had first sought him. Gerald L. Borchert perceptively notes,

> Jesus "finds" . . . Philip (1:43). Philip in turn "finds" Nathanael and reports to Nathanael, "We have found" him (1:45). . . . But it is intriguing to ask the very simple question concerning these stories: *Who really finds whom?* Christians have frequently been known to say that they found Christ or found faith as Andrew and Philip reported, but maybe Jesus' perspective in these stories could profitably alter such a self-centered view of salvation. It was not Jesus who was lost! (*John 1–11,*

The New American Commentary [Nashville: Broadman & Holman, 2002], 146. Italics in original.)

Jesus described Nathanael as **an Israelite indeed, in whom there is no deceit!** His point was that Nathanael's blunt, honest reply to Philip revealed his lack of duplicity and eagerness to examine Jesus' claims for himself. Jesus may have been alluding to Jacob (and by implication the nation descended from him) who, in contrast to Nathanael, was a deceiver (Gen. 27:35; 31:20). But unlike many of his fellow Jews, who were hypocrites (Matt. 6:2, 5, 16; 15:7; 22:18; 23:13ff.; Luke 12:1, 56; 13:15), Nathanael was **an Israelite** indeed. *Alēthōs* (**indeed**) means "genuinely," "in truth," or "actually." Paul pointed out how mere external conformity to the rites, rituals, and observances of Judaism did not make one **an Israelite indeed:**

> For he is not a Jew who is one outwardly, nor is circumcision that which is outward in the flesh. But he is a Jew who is one inwardly; and circumcision is that which is of the heart, by the Spirit, not by the letter; and his praise is not from men, but from God. . . . For they are not all Israel who are descended from Israel; nor are they all children because they are Abraham's descendants. (Rom. 2:28–29; 9:6–7)

It is those who continue in Jesus' word who are His true (*alēthōs*) followers (8:31). Nathanael was a true disciple from the beginning, as his response makes clear.

Taken aback by Jesus' omniscient recognition of him, Nathanael exclaimed, **"How do You know me?"** Jesus' reply was even more shocking: **"Before Philip called you, when you were under the fig tree, I saw you."** Not only did Jesus accurately sum up Nathanael's character without having met him, He also displayed a supernatural knowledge of information known only to him. Most likely **the fig tree** in question was the place where Nathanael studied and meditated on the Old Testament Scriptures. Not only did Jesus supernaturally see Nathanael's physical location, but He also saw into his heart (cf. Ps. 139:1–4).

Whatever happened under the fig tree, Jesus' supernatural knowledge of it removed Nathanael's doubt. Overwhelmed by Jesus' omniscience, he **answered** Him, **"Rabbi, You are the Son of God; You are the King of Israel."** In that outburst of confident faith, Nathanael acknowledged Jesus as the long-awaited Messiah. The two titles are also used of the Messiah in Psalm 2:6–7: "But as for Me, I have installed My King upon Zion, My holy mountain. I will surely tell of the decree of the Lord: He said to Me, 'You are My Son, today I have begotten You.'"

John's purpose in writing his gospel was so people "may believe that Jesus is the Christ, the Son of God" (20:31), who shares the same nature as God (1:1). To the earlier testimony of John the Baptist that Jesus is **the Son of God** (1:34), the apostle added that of Nathanael. The use of the definite article indicates that the title here is used in its fullest sense, affirming Jesus' absolute equality with God. Throughout His earthly ministry, Jesus' followers repeatedly acknowledged that He was the Son of God (cf. 6:69; 11:27; Matt. 14:33; 16:16; cf. Luke 1:32, 35), with a growing understanding of the riches of that marvelous truth.

The Old Testament described the Messiah as the **King of Israel** in such passages as Zephaniah 3:15 ("The Lord has taken away His judgments against you, He has cleared away your enemies. The King of Israel, the Lord, is in your midst; you will fear disaster no more."), Zechariah 9:9 ("Rejoice greatly, O daughter of Zion! Shout in triumph, O daughter of Jerusalem! Behold, your king is coming to you; He is just and endowed with salvation, humble, and mounted on a donkey, even on a colt, the foal of a donkey."), and Micah 5:2 ("But as for you, Bethlehem Ephrathah, too little to be among the clans of Judah, from you One will go forth for Me to be ruler in Israel. His goings forth are from long ago, from the days of eternity."). At the triumphal entry, the crowd "began to shout, 'Hosanna! Blessed is He who comes in the name of the Lord, even the King of Israel" (12:13). By addressing Jesus as **King of Israel,** Nathanael also acknowledged Him as his personal King.

Jesus' reply, **"Because I said to you that I saw you under the fig tree, do you believe?"** should probably be understood not as a question, but as a statement of fact. Thus, Nathanael is the first person in John's gospel reported to have believed in Jesus (though the disciples called earlier had as well). The Lord's display of supernatural knowledge in seeing Nathanael **under the fig tree** was enough to make him a believer, but Jesus promised that he would **see greater things than** that. The first of the thirty-seven miracles of Jesus recorded in the gospels would soon take place in Nathanael's own hometown of Cana (2:1–11). In addition, Nathanael would witness countless other miracles beyond those recorded in Scripture (cf. 21:25).

Speaking specifically of those greater things that Nathanael and the other disciples would see, Jesus solemnly assured him, **"Truly, truly, I say to you, you will see the heavens opened and the angels of God ascending and descending on the Son of Man."** Jesus was probably alluding to Jacob's dream, in which he saw angels ascending and descending from heaven on a ladder (Gen. 28:12). The point of this statement is that Jesus is the link between heaven and earth, the revealer of heavenly truth to men (1:17; 14:6; Eph. 4:21), the "one mediator . . . between God and men" (1 Tim. 2:5), and the mediator of a new (Heb. 9:14; 12:24) and better (Heb. 8:6) covenant. In John 3:13 He declared to Nicodemus, "No one has ascended into heaven, but He who descended from heaven: the Son of Man" (cf. 6:33, 38, 41–42, 50–51, 58, 62; 13:3; 16:28; 17:8). That truth would become increasingly clear to Nathanael and the rest of the disciples as they observed Jesus' life and ministry.

This is the first of thirteen occurrences in John's gospel of the title **Son of Man,** Jesus' favorite way of referring to Himself (He did so about eighty times in the gospels). In John's gospel, it is associated with Jesus' suffering and death (3:14; 8:28; 12:34), His provision of salvation (6:27, 53), and His authority to judge (5:27; 9:35, 39). In the future, the **Son of Man** will receive the kingdom from the Ancient of Days (Dan. 7:13–14). As with His other titles in this section, Nathanael (and the others who were present) did not immediately grasp the full significance of what it meant for Jesus to be the **Son of Man.**

This passage, which records Jesus' call of His first disciples to salvation, pictures the balance of salvation taught throughout Scripture. Salvation takes place when seeking souls come in faith to the Savior who has already sought them.

Christ's First Miracle (John 2:1-11)

6

On the third day there was a wedding in Cana of Galilee, and the mother of Jesus was there; and both Jesus and His disciples were invited to the wedding. When the wine ran out, the mother of Jesus said to Him, "They have no wine." And Jesus said to her, "Woman, what does that have to do with us? My hour has not yet come." His mother said to the servants, "Whatever He says to you, do it." Now there were six stone waterpots set there for the Jewish custom of purification, containing twenty or thirty gallons each. Jesus said to them, "Fill the waterpots with water." So they filled them up to the brim. And He said to them, "Draw some out now and take it to the headwaiter." So they took it to him. When the headwaiter tasted the water which had become wine, and did not know where it came from (but the servants who had drawn the water knew), the headwaiter called the bridegroom, and said to him, "Every man serves the good wine first, and when the people have drunk freely, then he serves the poorer wine; but you have kept the good wine until now." This beginning of His signs Jesus did in Cana of Galilee, and manifested His glory, and His disciples believed in Him. (2:1-11)

Ever since the fall, rebellious sinners have sought autonomy from God, rejecting Him and placing themselves at the center of the universe. At the heart of most humanistic systems of belief is the erroneous, rationalistic belief that people, beginning only from themselves, can construct an adequate worldview. Consequently, if modern man believes in a god at all, it is one of his own creation; as someone wryly observed, God created man in His image, and man has returned the favor. God rebuked such proud, sinful arrogance in Psalm 50:21, declaring, "You thought that I was just like you."

Perhaps nowhere is fallen man's sinful propensity for creating God in his own image more clearly illustrated than in the so-called "quest for the historical Jesus" that dominated nineteenth-century liberal theology. Based on their anti-supernaturalistic presuppositions, the critics

> believed that the real Jesus must have been an ordinary person with nothing supernatural or divine about him. His life must have conformed to ordinary human patterns, and be explicable in purely human categories. For such people the phrase "the historical Jesus" clearly meant a non-supernatural Jesus. They further believed that if the Gospels were examined critically, such a picture of Jesus would emerge from them. (I. Howard Marshall, *I Believe in the Historical Jesus* [Grand Rapids: Eerdmans, 1979], 110–11)

It is hardly surprising that those who begin by assuming the supernatural realm does not exist end up with a purely human Jesus. (Such blasphemous nonsense in the guise of scholarship finds its modern counterpart in the "Jesus Seminar," whose members, like their nineteenth-century forerunners, also attempt to reinvent Jesus to fit their anti-supernatural worldview.) Yet despite the faulty reasoning on which they were based, the nineteenth century saw a seemingly endless parade of "lives" of Jesus—each interpreting Him in keeping with whatever particular worldview the author happened to espouse.

But all attempts to explain Jesus as a mere man fail to explain the facts of His life, death (why anyone would have wanted to crucify the innocuous, politically correct sage invented by the rationalist critics defies explanation), and resurrection. In the Incarnation, God entered the natural realm in a human body. Therefore it is impossible to remove the miraculous elements from Jesus' life, as anti-supernaturalist critics have attempted to do. The historical Jesus of Nazareth and the divine Christ are inseparably linked, for they are one and the same person. Jesus was and is the God-man.

The miracles Jesus performed constitute one of the most powerful and convincing proofs of His deity (3:2; cf. Matt. 11:1–5; Acts 2:22). In keeping with his theme of presenting Jesus as the incarnate God-man, John catalogs eight miraculous signs that He performed. That list is, of course, by no means exhaustive; there were certainly many occasions when He did more than eight miracles in one day. Out of the countless miracles that Christ performed (cf. 20:30; 21:25), John selected these eight as examples that prove His deity. It is not the quantity of miracles that matters, or God would have given that number. It is the quality of every miracle, as a supernatural act, that proves who Jesus is. This passage describes the first of those eight miracles, which was also the first miracle Jesus did at the outset of His public ministry (which John records in chapters 2–12). It may be divided into four points: the scene, the situation, the supply, and the significance.

THE SCENE

On the third day there was a wedding in Cana of Galilee, and the mother of Jesus was there; and both Jesus and His disciples were invited to the wedding. (2:1–2)

The phrase **the third day** refers back to the call of Philip and Nathanael in the previous passage (1:43–51). It is the last in a series of time indicators (cf. 1:29, 35, 43) that suggest the events from John the Baptist's interview with the Jewish authorities (1:19–28) to the **wedding in Cana** took place within the span of one week.

Cana of Galilee is probably to be identified with modern Khirbet Qana, an uninhabited ruin about nine miles north of Nazareth. Jesus and His disciples could have easily reached **Cana** on **the third day** after leaving the vicinity of the Jordan River. Thus, there is no need to speculate, as some have, that the third day indicates **the third day** of the **wedding** feast.

A **wedding** was a major social event in first-century Palestine, and the celebration could last as long as a week. Unlike modern weddings, which are traditionally paid for by the bride's family, the groom was responsible for the expenses of the celebration. The **wedding** marked the culmination of the betrothal period. During that period, which often lasted for several months, the couple was considered legally man and wife (Matt. 1:18–19 refers to Joseph as Mary's husband during their betrothal period), and only a divorce could terminate the betrothal (cf. Matt. 1:19). They did not, however, live together or consummate the marriage during that period (cf. Matt. 1:18). On the night of the ceremony (usually a Wednesday), the groom and his friends would go to the bride's house. They would then escort her and her attendants to the groom's house, where the ceremony and banquet would be held (cf. Matt. 25:1–10). The whole celebration ended with the actual wedding.

The mother of Jesus (John never refers to Mary by name in his gospel) was at this particular wedding. That both she and Jesus attended suggests the wedding involved relatives or friends of the family. That would explain why Mary seems to have been more than just a guest, but apparently had some responsibility for helping the groom's family at the celebration. For example, she was aware of the situation regarding the lack of wine, and took the initiative to solve the serious problem. The different terminology used in regard to Mary (she **was there**) and **Jesus and His disciples** (they **were invited**) also suggests that she had some role in serving at the event. Since Joseph is not mentioned (the last time he appears in the gospels is in the account of the journey to Jerusalem when Jesus was twelve [Luke 2:41–50]), it may be that he was already dead. At the crucifixion Jesus committed Mary into the care of the apostle John (John 19:26–27), so Joseph was certainly dead by then.

How Jesus and the disciples received their invitation is not stated. Some have felt, without evidence, that it could have been delivered by Nathanael, who was from Cana (21:2). More likely, however, Jesus was in Nazareth, and there received the invitation. The disciples were no doubt invited because of their connection with Jesus, since only Nathanael was from the vicinity of Cana.

By attending a wedding and performing His first miracle there, Jesus sanctified both the institution of marriage and the ceremony itself. Marriage is the sacred union of a man and a woman whereby they become one in the sight of God. The ceremony is an essential element of that union, because in it the couple publicly vow to remain faithful to each other. Both the Old Testament (e.g., Gen. 29:20–23; Judg. 14:10; Ruth 4:10–13; Song of Sol. 3:11) and the New Testament (e.g., Matt. 22:2; 25:10; Luke 12:36; 14:8) view the public ceremony as a necessary part of marriage. That Jesus attended the celebration reveals His ministry to be markedly different than that of His forerunner, John the Baptist (Matt. 11:18–19). Instead of being a voice in the wilderness, Jesus had the more difficult task of mingling socially with the people and ministering to them in their daily activities.

THE SITUATION

When the wine ran out, the mother of Jesus said to Him, "They have no wine." And Jesus said to her, "Woman, what does that have to do with us? My hour has not yet come." His mother said to the servants, "Whatever He says to you, do it." (2:3–5)

Wine was the staple drink in the ancient Near East. Due to the warm climate and the lack of any means of refrigeration or purification, fruit juice tended to ferment. The result was an alcoholic beverage with the capability of inducing drunkenness. To help avoid the risk of inebriation, wine was commonly diluted with water to one-third to one-tenth of its strength. Though the Bible does not forbid drinking wine, and in some cases commends it (e.g., Ps. 104:14–15; Prov. 31:6; Jer. 31:12; 1 Tim. 5:23), it strongly condemns drunkenness (Gen. 9:20–27; Deut. 21:20–21; Prov. 20:1; 23:29–35; Rom. 13:13; 1 Cor. 5:11; 6:10; Gal. 5:21; Eph. 5:18; 1 Tim. 3:3, 8; Titus 1:7; 2:3; 1 Peter 4:3).

A major crisis loomed at the wedding celebration **when the wine ran out** because the supply was insufficient. Such an embarrassing faux pas could have stigmatized the couple and their families for the rest of their lives. It could even have left the groom and his family open to a lawsuit by the bride's family for failing to meet their responsibilities. Thus Jesus' turning the water into wine was not a sensational miracle, designed only to amaze His audience with His power. All of His miracles met specific needs, such as opening blind eyes or deaf ears, delivering those oppressed by demons, feeding hungry people, or calming a threatening storm. This miracle met the genuine need of the family and their guests, who otherwise faced a social catastrophe.

As noted above, Mary was apparently helping to oversee the catering of the celebration. Aware of the serious problem that had developed, she anxiously said to Jesus, **"They have no wine."** If she was already a widow, Mary would naturally have learned to depend on her firstborn son. Whether she expected Jesus to perform a miracle is not clear, since He as yet had never done one (v. 11). Yet Mary knew better than anyone who Jesus really was. She was well aware of His miraculous virgin birth and the amazing things said of Him by the angel Gabriel (Luke 1:31–33, 35), the shepherds (Luke 2:8–18), Simeon (Luke 2:25–35), and Anna (Luke 2:36–38), having pondered them in her heart over the years (Luke 2:19). She had experienced His sinless life and its perfection as He had "kept increasing in wisdom and stature, and in favor with God and men" (Luke 2:52). She may also have heard of John the Baptist's recent public testimony about Him (1:26–27, 29–34, 36), confirming what she knew. It may be that she was prompting Jesus to reveal Himself publicly as the Messiah she knew Him to be.

Jesus' abrupt and startling reply, **"Woman, what does that have to do with us?"** signaled a major change in their relationship. **Woman** was a polite, but not intimate, form of address (cf. 4:21; 19:26; 20:13, 15; Matt. 15:28; Luke 13:12), much like the English word "Ma'am." Jesus' reply, **"What does that have to do with us?"** (lit., "What to me and to you?") is an idiomatic expression (cf. Judg. 11:12; 2 Sam. 16:10; 19:22), which asks rhetorically what the two parties in question have in common, and has the effect of distancing them. The statement, coupled with Jesus' addressing Mary as **"Woman"** instead of "Mother," politely but firmly informed her that what they had in common in their relationship was no longer to be what it had been while He was growing up in Nazareth. His public ministry had begun, and earthly relationships would not determine His actions. Mary was to relate to Him no longer as her son, but as her Messiah, the Son of God, and her Savior (cf. Matt. 12:47–50; Mark 3:31–35; Luke 11:27–28).

The phrase **"My hour has not yet come"** refers to Jesus' death and glorification (7:6, 8, 30; 8:20; 12:23, 27; 13:1; 16:32; 17:1; Matt. 26:18, 45; Mark 14:35, 41). This supports the possibility that Mary was knowingly asking Jesus to reveal Himself at that time, since He had for years been in the fullness of mature manhood. Jesus made it clear that He would act according to God's timetable, decreed before the foundation of the world, not hers or any man's (cf. 7:2–8). It was not the appointed time for Jesus' full messianic glory to be revealed; yet the miracle He would perform would make His divine power unmistakable, and preview His glory to come. The dark hour of the cross would precede the full revelation in His glorious messianic kingdom where wine, emblematic of joy and gladness, will abound:

> "Behold, days are coming," declares the Lord, "when the plowman will overtake the reaper and the treader of grapes him who sows seed; when the mountains will drip sweet wine and all the hills will be dissolved. Also I will restore the captivity of My people Israel, and they will rebuild the ruined cities and live in them; they will also plant vineyards and drink their wine, and make gardens and eat their fruit." (Amos 9:13–14; cf. Isa. 25:6; Jer. 31:12; Joel 3:18)

Undeterred by the mild rebuke (cf. Matt. 15:22–28), and aware that He was not saying no to the request, Mary **said to the servants, "Whatever He says to you, do it."** She immediately turned to the servants, anticipating that He would respond. The **servants** were *diakonois* (from which the English word "deacons" [1 Tim. 3:8, 12] derives), not *doulois* ("slaves"), suggesting that they were not slaves or household servants. Most likely they, like Mary, were family and friends helping with the celebration. Her charge to them was necessary, since they might otherwise have hesitated to follow the strange instructions they would receive from a guest.

THE SUPPLY

Now there were six stone waterpots set there for the Jewish custom of purification, containing twenty or thirty gallons each. Jesus said to them, "Fill the waterpots with water." So they filled them up to the brim. And He said to them, "Draw some out now and take it to the headwaiter." So they took it to him. When the headwaiter tasted the water which had become wine, and did not know where it came from (but the servants who had drawn the water knew), the headwaiter called the bridegroom, and said to him, "Every man serves the good wine first, and when the people have drunk freely, then he serves the poorer wine; but you have kept the good wine until now." (2:6–10)

The **stone waterpots** were, as John explained for the benefit of his Gentile readers, used **for the Jewish custom of purification.** Ceremonial washings were an integral part of first-century Judaism:

> The Pharisees and all the Jews do not eat unless they carefully wash their hands, thus observing the traditions of the elders; and when they come from the market place, they do not eat unless they cleanse themselves; and there are many other things which they have received in order to observe, such as the washing of cups and pitchers and copper pots. (Mark 7:3–4)

The Jews used **stone waterpots** to hold the water used for ritual purification because they believed that, unlike earthenware pots (Lev. 11:33), they did not become unclean. Unlike the smaller one used by the Samaritan woman to draw water from a well (4:28), these were large pots, **containing twenty or thirty gallons each.** Such a large amount of water was needed not only to accommodate the guests, but also because the cooking and eating utensils had to be washed (Mark 7:4).

Mary's faith and confidence in her Son were not misplaced. As she had foreseen, He responded by commanding the servants, **"Fill the waterpots with water."** In response, **they filled them up to the brim,** either by topping them off, or by emptying and refilling them. This seemingly insignificant detail, that the water was up to the very top, shows that nothing was added to the water, and that what followed was indeed a transformation miracle. By ordering the jars to be completely filled before He transformed the water in them into wine, Jesus also displayed His magnanimous grace (cf. 1:14, 16–17). Such a large amount of wine (120 to 180 gallons) was more than enough to last for the rest of the celebration. Jesus not only rescued the bride and groom from an embarrassing situation, but the leftover wine also provided them with a generous wedding present.

After the pots were filled, Jesus instructed the servants to **draw some out** and **take** the instantly created wine **to the headwaiter.** Jewish sources do not make clear whether this individual was the head servant, or a guest chosen to preside over the banquet. That he summoned the groom and spoke to him as at least his equal (vv. 9–10) suggests the latter. In either case, he served as the master of ceremonies at the feast. Since he was responsible for making sure that the guests were supplied with food and drink, the servants **took** the wine **to him.**

To make sure it was acceptable, the headwaiter sampled the food and drink before it was served to the guests. Therefore after the servants brought it to him, he **tasted the water which had become wine.** Though he **did not know where it came from** (though of course **the servants who had drawn the water** did), he was astonished at the high quality of this new batch of wine. He **called the bridegroom, and said to him, "Every man serves the good wine first, and when the people have drunk freely, then he serves the poorer wine."** There is some historical evidence that most hosts did, as the headwaiter suggested, serve the best wine first (D. A. Carson, *The Gospel According to John*, The Pillar New Testament Commentary [Grand Rapids: Eerdmans, 1991], 174). In any case, it was only common sense to serve the **good wine first** and save the **poorer wine** for later **when the people** had **drunk freely.** The verb *methuskō* (**drunk freely**) literally means "to become drunk," and is so translated in its only other appearances in the New Testament (Luke 12:45; Eph. 5:18; 1 Thess. 5:7; Rev. 17:2). That does not mean, however, that this particular banquet had become a drunken orgy; the headwaiter was speaking from his own experience. **But** much to his surprise (and no doubt the groom's as well), it seemed that the groom had **kept the good wine until** the last. Surely it was the sweetest, freshest wine ever tasted. This wine did not come from the normal process of fermentation, from grapes, vines, the earth and the sun. The Lord brought it into existence from nothing. Truly this was evidence that He is the Creator (John 1:1–4).

THE SIGNIFICANCE

This beginning of His signs Jesus did in Cana of Galilee, and manifested His glory, and His disciples believed in Him. (2:11)

The result of **this beginning** (or first) of Jesus' **signs** was twofold. First, He **manifested His glory** (cf. 1:14); that is, He put His deity on display. Jesus' **signs** were not simply powerful displays of compassion, but were designed to reveal who He really was, since they unmistakably manifest God at work (cf. 2:23; 3:2; 4:54; 6:2, 14; 7:31; 9:16; 20:30; Acts 2:22). Signs, miracles, and wonders nevertheless do not necessarily convince people to believe in the Lord and the gospel (2:23–25; 12:37; 15:24; Matt. 11:20–24; 13:58; Luke 16:31). There is no record that any of the servants who witnessed Jesus' turning the water into wine followed Him (cf. 2:12). Amazingly, Jesus seems to have left Cana with only the disciples who came there with Him, despite having performed a miracle, the likes of which had not happened since God created flour and oil in the days of Elijah and Elisha (1 Kings 17:8–16; 2 Kings 4:1–7). The obvious deduction that He was the Messiah escaped them; they saw the sign, but missed what it pointed to. As he does with all unbelievers, Satan "blinded [their] minds . . . so that they might not see the light of the gospel of the glory of Christ, who is the image of God" (2 Cor. 4:4). This incident was another tragic illustration of the truth of Jesus' saying, "A prophet has no honor in his own country" (4:44; cf. Matt. 13:58).

His disciples, however, **believed in Him.** Having heard John the Baptist's testimony that Jesus was the Messiah (1:34), having heard Jesus' own words (1:39) and believed in Him (1:41), they now saw first-hand miraculous confirmation of that faith. Many others, reading this gospel of John, would come to believe, as they did. And that was John's purpose in writing not only his account of this miracle, but also his entire gospel: "Therefore many other signs Jesus also performed in the presence of the disciples, which are not written in this book; but these have been written so that you may believe that Jesus is the Christ, the Son of God; and that believing you may have life in His name" (20:30–31).

Jesus Displays His Deity
(John 2:12–25)

7

After this He went down to Capernaum, He and His mother and His brothers and His disciples; and they stayed there a few days. The Passover of the Jews was near, and Jesus went up to Jerusalem. And He found in the temple those who were selling oxen and sheep and doves, and the money changers seated at their tables. And He made a scourge of cords, and drove them all out of the temple, with the sheep and the oxen; and He poured out the coins of the money changers and overturned their tables; and to those who were selling the doves He said, "Take these things away; stop making My Father's house a place of business." His disciples remembered that it was written, "Zeal for Your house will consume me." The Jews then said to Him, "What sign do You show us as Your authority for doing these things?" Jesus answered them, "Destroy this temple, and in three days I will raise it up." The Jews then said, "It took forty-six years to build this temple, and will You raise it up in three days?" But He was speaking of the temple of His body. So when He was raised from the dead, His disciples remembered that He said this; and they believed the Scripture and the word which Jesus had spoken. Now when He was in Jerusalem at the Passover, during the feast,

many believed in His name, observing His signs which He was doing. But Jesus, on His part, was not entrusting Himself to them, for He knew all men, and because He did not need anyone to testify concerning man, for He Himself knew what was in man. (2:12–25)

There is no question more important than, "Who is Jesus Christ?" Its implications are profound and its significance unparalleled. Simply posing it immediately evokes a vast array of emotions—from outright hostility to fervent adoration. Merely contemplating it is not enough—it is a question that must be answered. And answering it incorrectly, no matter what the excuse, ultimately leads to eternal devastation.

Throughout history, that very question has sparked much confusion and debate. Such was even true in Jesus' time. When He asked, "Who do people say that the Son of Man is?" (Matt. 16:13), the disciples listed several popular possibilities: "Some say John the Baptist; and others, Elijah; but still others, Jeremiah, or one of the prophets" (v. 14). There is, however, only one correct answer to Jesus' question, and Peter gave it when he said, "You are the Christ, the Son of the living God" (v. 16).

Scripture abundantly reaffirms Peter's assessment of Christ's true identity. He is called "God" (John 1:1, 18; 20:28; Rom. 9:5; Heb. 1:8; 1 John 5:20), "our great God and Savior" (Titus 2:13; 2 Peter 1:1), the "Mighty God" (Isa. 9:6), the "I AM" (John 8:58; cf. Ex. 3:14), the "first and the last" (Rev. 1:17; 22:13; cf. Isa. 44:6; 48:12), the "Lord of lords" (Rev. 17:14; cf. Deut. 10:17), and the "Alpha and the Omega" (Rev. 22:13; cf. Rev. 1:8). He is one in essence with the Father (John 10:30); He exists in the form of God (Phil. 2:6) and is the "exact representation of His nature" (Heb. 1:3); He is the Creator and Sustainer of the universe (John 1:3; Col. 1:16; Heb. 1:3; cf. Gen. 1:1; Ex. 20:11; Isa. 40:28); and "in Him all the fullness of Deity dwells in bodily form" (Col. 2:9). He is the One who forgives sins (Mark 2:7, 10; cf. Isa. 43:25; Dan. 9:9), raises the dead (John 5:21; 11:25), and receives the worship reserved for God alone (Phil. 2:10 [cf. Isa. 45:23]; Matt. 14:33; cf. Matt. 4:10). Clearly, the biblical evidence leads to only one possible conclusion: Jesus Christ is God.

Despite the unmistakable clarity of Scripture, there are some skeptics who deny those clear claims. In their unbelieving opinions, the Christ of Scripture is a mythical figure, invented by His followers. The "real" or "historical" Jesus of Nazareth, they argue, was a social critic, itinerant cynic philosopher, politically correct sage—but definitely not the Messiah, the Son of God, God incarnate in human flesh. Richard N. Longenecker notes that according to the "Jesus Seminar," for example,

Jesus was a cynic-like Jewish charismatic peasant, whose teaching was witty, clever and counter-cultural, but not eschatological and certainly not focused on himself. All portrayals of Jesus of a messianic, sacrificial, redemptive, or eschatological nature in the Gospels (and in the rest of the New Testament) are the products of later church theology, which grew up around the figure of this Mediterranean cynic-like teacher and turned him into a cult figure. (*The Jesus of History and the Christ of Faith: Some Contemporary Reflections* [www.mcmaster.ca/mjtm/2-51.htm])

In order to reach their conclusions, such skeptics audaciously question either the reliability of the New Testament or the honesty of Jesus' disciples. But the New Testament is the most well-attested document from antiquity. There are far more early manuscripts of the New Testament in existence today than of any other ancient writing, and the time gap between them and the original documents is much shorter. Thus, "to be skeptical of the resultant text of the New Testament books is to allow all of classical antiquity to slip into obscurity, for no documents of the ancient period are as well attested bibliographically as the New Testament" (John Warwick Montgomery, *History and Christianity* [Downers Grove, Ill.: InterVarsity, 1974], 29).

The view that Jesus' followers invented the biblical story of His life also falls far short of credibility. After all, what did they gain from it? The apostles endured arrest, beatings, imprisonment, exile, and martyrdom; and the early church faced bitter opposition punctuated by outbursts of savage persecution. Eusebius, the fourth-century church father, pointed out the absurdity of claiming that the disciples were deceivers:

I would ask, then, where would be the sense in suspecting that hearers of [Jesus' ethical] teaching, who were themselves masters in such instruction, invented their account of their Master's work? How is it possible to think that they were all in agreement to lie? ... No argument can prove that so large a body of men were untrustworthy, who embraced a holy and godly life, regarded their own affairs as of no account ... chose a life of poverty, and carried to all men as from one mouth a consistent account of their Master. ... Come, tell me, if such an enterprise engineered by such men would hold together? ... Whence came, among a crew of so many, a harmony of rogues? Whence their general and consistent evidence about everything, and their agreement even unto death? ... Surely they had all seen the end of their teacher, and the death to which He came. Why then after seeing His miserable end did they stand their ground? Why did they construct a theology about Him when He was dead? Did they desire to share His fate? No one surely on any reasonable ground would choose such a punishment with his eyes open. (*The Proof of the Gospel,* III.5.110, 111.

Eusebius's devastating critique of the view that the disciples were deceivers continues throughout chapter 5 of book III.)

The presence of numerous eyewitnesses to Jesus' life—many of them hostile—would also have made it impossible for His disciples to spread lies about Him. For example, if He had not really risen from the dead as His followers claimed, His enemies could have simply presented His body. Had they done so, the Christian faith would have immediately collapsed (cf. 1 Cor. 15:14). Furthermore, the gospel accounts were finished while many such eyewitnesses were still alive. Had the gospel writers lied about what Jesus said or did, those eyewitnesses could have easily exposed their fabrications.

Other blasphemous views—that Jesus was a liar, a lunatic, or a mystic—fare no better; they utterly fail to explain His noble character as revealed in the New Testament. For instance, church historian Philip Schaff responds to accusations that Jesus was a liar (cf. John 8:46):

How, in the name of logic, common sense, and experience, could an impostor—that is a deceitful, selfish, depraved man—have invented, and consistently maintained from the beginning to end, the purest and noblest character known in history with the most perfect air of truth and reality? How could he have conceived and successfully carried out a plan of unparalleled beneficence, moral magnitude, and sublimity, and sacrificed his own life for it, in the face of the strongest prejudices of his people and ages? (cited in Josh McDowell, *Evidence That Demands a Verdict, Volume 1* [San Bernardino, Calif.: Here's Life, 1986], 106)

C. S. Lewis forcefully dismisses the notion that Jesus was a madman:

The historical difficulty of giving for the life, sayings and influence of Jesus any explanation that is not harder than the Christian explanation, is very great. The discrepancy between the depth and sanity and (let me add) *shrewdness* of His moral teaching and the rampant megalomania which must lie behind His theological teaching unless He is indeed God, has never been satisfactorily got over. Hence the non-Christian hypotheses succeed one another with the restless fertility of bewilderment. (*Miracles* [New York: Macmillan, 1972], 113. Italics in original.)

It is also preposterous to view Jesus as a mystic, whose claim to be God was not remarkable since everyone is God. While such assertions are commonplace in Eastern religions, they would have been utterly foreign to first-century Judaism. Far from welcoming Jesus as an enlightened guru, the Jews were outraged by His claim to deity. As a result, they accused Him of blasphemy (10:33; cf. 5:18) and crucified Him for claiming equality with the one and only God (Matt. 26:65–66).

The only view that adequately explains Jesus' perfect life, profound teaching, sacrificial death, and miraculous resurrection is the biblical one—namely, that Jesus came as God incarnate. All other views utterly collapse under examination.

The apostle John walked with Jesus from the outset of His earthly ministry. He saw His miracles, heard His teaching, and observed His life from an intimate vantage point shared only by Peter and James. Thus, he wrote his gospel so that his readers would understand Jesus' true identity as God the Son in human flesh (20:31).

In this passage, John continues this theme through three vignettes that each illustrate an aspect of Christ's deity. Individually, they show His passion for reverence, His power of resurrection, and His perception of reality. Collectively, they underscore the inscrutable reality of His divine nature.

JESUS' PASSION FOR REVERENCE

After this He went down to Capernaum, He and His mother and His brothers and His disciples; and they stayed there a few days. The Passover of the Jews was near, and Jesus went up to Jerusalem. And He found in the temple those who were selling oxen and sheep and doves, and the money changers seated at their tables. And He made a scourge of cords, and drove them all out of the temple, with the sheep and the oxen; and He poured out the coins of the money changers and overturned their tables; and to those who were selling the doves He said, "Take these things away; stop making My Father's house a place of business." His disciples remembered that it was written, "Zeal for Your house will consume me." (2:12–17)

The Feast of **Passover** commemorated Israel's deliverance from bondage in Egypt—when the Lord killed, by His death angel, the firstborn of the Egyptians but passed over the houses of the Israelites (Ex. 12:23–27). It was celebrated annually on the fourteenth day of Nisan (March/April). On that day, between 3:00 and 6:00 P.M., lambs were slaughtered and the Passover meal eaten. In obedience to Exodus 23:14–17, **Jesus went up to Jerusalem** to observe both the Passover and the Feast of Unleavened Bread which immediately followed (cf. Ezek. 45:21; Luke 22:1; Acts 12:3–4). This is the first of three Passovers mentioned in John's gospel (cf. 6:4; 11:55).

Upon His arrival, Jesus would have found Jerusalem teeming with Jewish pilgrims from all around the Roman world, there to celebrate this foremost of Jewish feasts. Because of the multitudes who came, Passover meant big business for Jerusalem-based merchants. **In the temple** complex, where they had set up shop (probably in the court of the Gentiles), vendors were **selling oxen and sheep and doves, and the money changers seated at their tables.** Since it was impractical for those traveling from distant lands to bring their own animals, the merchants sold them the animals required for the sacrifices—at greatly inflated prices. The **money changers** also provided a necessary service. Every Jewish male twenty years of age or older had to pay the annual temple tax (Ex. 30:13–14; Matt. 17:24–27). But it could be paid only using Jewish or Tyrian coins (because of the purity of their silver content), so foreigners had to exchange their money for acceptable coinage. Because they had a monopoly on the market, the **money changers** charged an exorbitant fee for their services (as high as 12.5 percent [F. F. Bruce, *The Gospel of John* (Grand Rapids: Eerdmans, 1983), 74]).

What had begun as a service to the worshipers had, under the corrupt rule of the chief priests, degenerated into exploitation and usury. Religion had become external, crass, and materialistic; the temple of God had become a "robbers' den" (Matt. 21:13).

As He surveyed the sacred temple grounds now turned into a bazaar, Jesus was appalled and outraged. The worshipful atmosphere that befitted the temple, as the symbol of God's presence, was completely absent. What should have been a place of sacred reverence and adoration had become a place of abusive commerce and excessive overpricing. The sound of heartfelt praise and fervent prayers had been drowned out by the bawling of oxen, the bleating of sheep, the cooing of doves, and the loud haggling of vendors and their customers.

Realizing that the purity of temple worship was a matter of honor to God, Jesus took swift and decisive action. Making **a scourge of cords** (probably from those used to tie the animals), He **drove all** the merchants **out of the temple,** along **with** their **sheep and oxen.** In addition, **He poured out the coins of the money changers and overturned their tables,** an amazing feat for one man in the light of the resistance that must have come.

Jesus' display of force would have immediately created pandemonium in the temple court: the animal sellers frantically chasing their beasts, which were running aimlessly in all directions; the startled money-changers (and, no doubt, some of the bystanders) scrambling desperately on the ground to pick up their coins; **those who were selling the doves** hastily removing their crates as Jesus had commanded them; the temple authorities rushing to see what all the commotion was about. Yet

Jesus was neither cruel to the animals (those who object to His mild use of force on them have never herded animals), nor overly harsh with the men. Apparently the uproar He created was contained enough not to alert the Roman garrison stationed in Fort Antonia, which overlooked the temple grounds. Watching Romans may have found some satisfaction in this assault on the temple system and its leaders, who gave them so much grief.

At the same time, the intensity of His righteous indignation was unmistakable. Christ would not tolerate any mockery of the spirit of true worship. His indignant words **to those who were selling the doves, "Take these things away; stop making My Father's house a place of business,"** applied to all who were polluting the temple and corrupting its intended purpose. Jesus' reference to God as His Father was a reminder both of His deity and His messiahship; He was the loyal Son purging His **Father's** house of its impure worship (an action that prefigures what He will again do at His second coming [Mal. 3:1–3; cf. Zech. 14:20–21]).

Several years later, at the end of His ministry, Christ would again cleanse the temple (Matt. 21:12–16; Mark 11:15–18; Luke 19:45–46). Some commentators assert that John is actually referring here to that later cleansing, having moved the account out of chronological sequence. Instead of correctly putting this story at the end of Jesus' ministry, they argue, John put it here—thus, Jesus cleansed the temple only once, not twice. But their explanations for why John would have misplaced such a significant event are ultimately unconvincing. The cleansing recorded in the Synoptic Gospels took place during Passion Week; the one recorded by John came at the outset of Jesus' public ministry (cf. John 2:11–13).

The details of the two accounts also differ significantly. In the Synoptics, Jesus quotes the Old Testament as His authority (Matt. 21:13; Mark 11:17; Luke 19:46); in John He uses His own words (2:16). Moreover, John does not mention Jesus' prohibition against using the temple as a shortcut (Mark 11:16) nor Jesus' significant judicial statement: "Behold, your house is being left to you desolate!" (Matt. 23:38). And the Synoptics do not mention Jesus' remarkable challenge, "Destroy this temple, and in three days I will raise it up" (John 2:19)—although they do refer to it in the accounts of His trial before the Sanhedrin (Matt. 26:61; Mark 14:58; cf. Matt. 27:39–40; Mark 15:29–30). In light of these differences, it is difficult to see how both the Synoptic writers and John could be referring to the same event. (For a further discussion of Jesus' second temple cleansing, see my comments on Matthew 27:39–40 in *Matthew 24–28*, The MacArthur New Testament Commentary Series [Chicago: Moody, 1989], 258–60).

Watching in amazement as their Master dispersed the temple

merchants, **His disciples remembered that it was written** in Psalm 69:9, **"Zeal for Your house will consume me."** Jesus' resolute passion and unwavering fervor was clear to all who saw Him. His righteous indignation, stemming from an absolute commitment to God's holiness, revealed His true nature as the Judge of all the earth (cf. Gen. 18:25; Heb. 9:27). R. C. H. Lenski notes,

> The stern and holy Christ, the indignant, mighty Messiah, the Messenger of the Covenant of whom it is written: "He shall purify the sons of Levi, and purge them as gold and silver, that they may offer unto the Lord an offering of righteousness," is not agreeable to those who want only a soft and sweet Christ. But John's record here ... portray[s] the fiery zeal of Jesus which came with such sudden and tremendous effectiveness that before this unknown man, who had no further authority than his own person and word, this crowd of traders and changers, who thought they were fully within their rights when conducting their business in the Temple court, fled pell-mell like a lot of naughty boys. (*The Interpretation of St. John's Gospel* [Reprint; Peabody, Mass.: Hendrickson, 1998], 207)

Like David, who penned the messianic Psalm 69, Jesus' zeal for pure worship found expression in His concern for God's house. And also like David, Jesus suffered as a result, personally feeling the pain when His Father was dishonored. The second half of Psalm 69:9 reads, "The reproaches of those who reproach You have fallen on me." The Jewish leaders never forgot Jesus' assault on the heart of their religious enterprise and on the very seat of their power. In fact, Christ's two physical cleansings of the temple, along with His constant verbal assaults on their hypocrisy, were more than enough motivation to cause them to pursue His crucifixion so vehemently. Not surprisingly, His followers were also later accused of threatening the temple (Acts 6:13–14; 21:28; 24:6).

JESUS' POWER OF RESURRECTION

The Jews then said to Him, "What sign do You show us as Your authority for doing these things?" Jesus answered them, "Destroy this temple, and in three days I will raise it up." The Jews then said, "It took forty-six years to build this temple, and will You raise it up in three days?" But He was speaking of the temple of His body. So when He was raised from the dead, His disciples remembered that He said this; and they believed the Scripture and the word which Jesus had spoken. (2:18–22)

The **Jews** who confronted Jesus were probably members of the temple police force (cf. 7:32,45–46; 18:3,12,18,22; 19:6; Acts 5:21–22,26), representatives from the Sanhedrin, or both. Arriving to investigate the commotion in the temple court, they demanded of Him, **"What sign do You show us as Your authority for doing these things?"** Their question was not a request for information, but a challenge to His authority. Jesus had taken it upon Himself to disregard their dominion and regulate the temple activities, and they wanted a miraculous **sign** as proof of His **authority for doing** so.

Interestingly, although they challenged His right to do what He did, the Jewish authorities did not arrest Jesus. Taken aback by His bold display of authority, they may have wondered if He were a prophet, like John the Baptist. Their demand for a sign, however, was foolish; the messianic act of single-handedly cleansing the temple was itself a clear sign that God had a message for them. In their hard-hearted unbelief, the Jewish leaders repeatedly asked for such signs, yet they never accepted the ones they were given. As John later wrote, "But though He had performed so many signs before them, yet they were not believing in Him" (John 12:37). The fact that the temple authorities demanded a sign also exposed the wickedness of their hearts. They knew that their greedy, corrupt commercialization of temple worship was wrong, even though they obstinately refused to admit it.

Jesus' enigmatic reply, **"Destroy this temple, and in three days I will raise it up,"** baffled the Jewish authorities (and, for the time being, His own disciples as well, v. 22). Like His parables (cf. Matt. 13:10–11; Luke 8:10), this veiled statement judicially concealed the truth from hostile unbelievers, whose spiritual blindness resulted from their own unbelief and rebellion against God. (Unbelievers' failure to understand Jesus' message is a theme that runs throughout John's gospel, e.g., 3:3–4; 4:14–15; 6:32–35,51–52; 7:34–36; 8:51–53,56–57; 10:1–6.)

The authorities were astonished by Jesus' reply. Their response betrays a mixture of shock and indignation: **"It took forty-six years to build this temple, and will You raise it up in three days?"** The **temple** of Jesus' day was not Solomon's temple, which the Babylonians had destroyed (Ezra 5:12). Rather, it was the postexilic temple, rebuilt after the Babylonian captivity was over, under the leadership of Zerubbabel, Jeshua, Haggai, and Zechariah (Ezra 1–6). Many centuries later, around 20 B.C., Herod the Great began an extensive reconstruction and expansion of the postexilic temple. Ironically, those reconstruction efforts were not completed until shortly before A.D. 70—when the postexilic temple itself was destroyed by the Romans.

The **Jews** were incredulous; how could Jesus possibly accomplish in three days' work what had already taken **forty-six years** and was still not finished? As the account of His trial a few years later before the Sanhedrin indicates (Matt. 26:61; Mark 14:58), the Jewish authorities completely missed the point of Jesus' statement, incorrectly applying it to the Herodian temple. **But** as John points out, Jesus **was speaking of the temple of His body.** The sign He would give them would be far greater than simply reconstructing a destroyed building:

> An evil and adulterous generation craves for a sign; and yet no sign will be given to it but the sign of Jonah the prophet; for just as Jonah was three days and three nights in the belly of the sea monster, so will the Son of Man be three days and three nights in the heart of the earth. (Matt. 12:39–40; cf. 16:4)

The sign He would give was His own resurrection, which even His disciples did not immediately understand (cf. 12:16). It was not until **He was raised from the dead** that **His disciples remembered that He said this; and they believed the Scripture and the word which Jesus had spoken.** His death as the ultimate sacrificial Lamb would render the Jerusalem temple obsolete (cf. 4:21; Matt. 27:51); and His resurrection as the triumphant Lord would lay the foundation for a new, spiritual temple in its place—namely, the church (1 Cor. 3:16–17; 2 Cor. 6:16; Eph. 2:19–22).

Throughout his gospel, John generally uses the singular **Scripture** to refer to a specific passage (cf. 7:38, 42; 10:35; 13:18; 19:24, 28, 36–37); if that is the case here, he is probably referring to Psalm 16:8–11 (cf. Acts 2:25–28; 13:35). He may, however, be making a general reference (cf. 20:9) to the Old Testament prophecies regarding Christ's death and resurrection (cf. Luke 24:27, 44–47). In any case, it was not until after the resurrection that the disciples understood everything clearly. Only then did they make sense of this prophecy and recognize Jesus' resurrection power as a clear indication of His deity.

JESUS' PERCEPTION OF REALITY

Now when He was in Jerusalem at the Passover, during the feast, many believed in His name, observing His signs which He was doing. But Jesus, on His part, was not entrusting Himself to them, for He knew all men, and because He did not need anyone to testify concerning man, for He Himself knew what was in man. (2:23–25)

These three verses serve as a bridge between the account of the cleansing of the temple and the story of Nicodemus, which immediately follows. Though brief, this section has profound implications concerning the nature of saving faith.

Jesus remained in **Jerusalem** for **Passover** and the Feast of Unleavened Bread that immediately followed. **During** that time, He performed a number of miracles that are not specifically recorded in Scripture (cf. 20:30; 21:25). As a result, **many believed in His name, observing His signs which He was doing.** They thought He might be a prophet (cf. Matt. 21:11; Luke 7:16), or even the conquering Messiah they were expecting (cf. John 6:14–15, 26).

But such faith was shallow, superficial, and disingenuous. It was not true saving faith, as John's play on words indicates. **Believed** in verse 23 and **entrusting** in verse 24 both come from the same Greek verb, *pisteuō*. Though they believed in Jesus, Jesus did not believe in them; He had no faith in their faith. Jesus "regarded all belief in Him as superficial which does not have as its most essential elements the consciousness of the need for forgiveness and the conviction that He alone is the Mediator of that forgiveness" (R. V. G. Tasker, *The Gospel According to St. John*, The Tyndale New Testament Commentaries [Grand Rapids: Eerdmans, 1975], 65).

Although **many** claimed to believe, Jesus knew that mere intellectual assent proves nothing; even the demons have such faith (James 2:19). Like the seed that fell on rocky and thorny ground, those who possess such faith hear the Word, and initially receive it with joy (Matt. 13:20). But because their hearts are never truly changed, they fall away when affliction comes (v. 21), or when worldly riches beckon (v. 22).

Without question, the difference between spurious faith and saving faith is crucial. It is the difference between living faith and dead faith (James 2:17); between the wicked, who "go away into eternal punishment" and "the righteous [who enter] into eternal life" (Matt. 25:46); between those who will hear, "Well done, good and faithful slave. . . . Enter into the joy of your master" (Matt. 25:21) and those who will hear, "I never knew you; depart from Me, you who practice lawlessness" (Matt. 7:23).

Jesus did not embrace the false faith manifested by those who witnessed His signs, because **He knew all men, and** therefore **did not need anyone to testify concerning man, for He Himself knew what was in man.** He knows the true state of every heart. He saw in Nathanael the heart of an honest, true seeker (1:47); He saw in these people a superficial façade—a mere outward attraction to His spectacular signs (cf. 6:2). Genuine saving faith goes far beyond that. It demands wholehearted commitment to Jesus as the Lord of one's life (Matt. 16:24–26; Rom. 10:9). (I discuss the nature of saving faith in my books *The Gospel According to Jesus* [Rev. ed.; Grand Rapids: Zondervan, 1994] and *The Gospel According to the Apostles* [Nashville: Thomas Nelson, 1993].)

Jesus' lordship goes hand in hand with His deity. As the God of the universe, He is worthy to be worshiped and obeyed—reverently adored as the King of kings and the Lord of lords (Rev. 19:6; cf. Phil. 3:10–11). The three vignettes in this passage (vv. 12–25) underscore His deity with unmistakable clarity. As God He single-handedly cleansed the temple with messianic zeal; as God He accurately predicted His own resurrection; and as God He truly knew the contents of men's hearts.

At the same time, these three accounts also picture the process of salvation. The first scene, the cleansing of the temple, graphically depicts God's hatred of sin and impurity. The second scene, the discussion of Jesus' resurrection, reveals that God provides new life in Christ, who "was raised because of our justification" (Rom. 4:25). And the final scene, the shallow belief of the people, reveals that God's provision of salvation comes only through genuine saving faith.

The New Birth
(John 3:1–10)

8

Now there was a man of the Pharisees, named Nicodemus, a ruler of the Jews; this man came to Jesus by night and said to Him, "Rabbi, we know that You have come from God as a teacher; for no one can do these signs that You do unless God is with him." Jesus answered and said to him, "Truly, truly, I say to you, unless one is born again he cannot see the kingdom of God." Nicodemus said to Him, "How can a man be born when he is old? He cannot enter a second time into his mother's womb and be born, can he?" Jesus answered, "Truly, truly, I say to you, unless one is born of water and the Spirit he cannot enter into the kingdom of God. That which is born of the flesh is flesh, and that which is born of the Spirit is spirit. Do not be amazed that I said to you, 'You must be born again.' The wind blows where it wishes and you hear the sound of it, but do not know where it comes from and where it is going; so is everyone who is born of the Spirit." Nicodemus said to Him, "How can these things be?" Jesus answered and said to him, "Are you the teacher of Israel and do not understand these things?" (3:1–10)

"Everybody talkin' about heaven ain't goin' there." This line, from an old spiritual, accurately describes many in the church. Outwardly they identify with Christ, but inwardly they have never been genuinely converted. Because they cling to a false profession, they fool themselves into thinking they are on the narrow path leading to life, when in reality they are on the broad road that leads to destruction. To make matters worse, their self-deception is often reinforced by well-meaning but undiscerning Christians who naively embrace them as true believers. Such confusion stems from the watered-down pseudo-gospels that are propagated from far too many pulpits. Cheap grace, market-driven ministry, emotionalism, subjectivism, and an indiscriminate inclusivism have all infiltrated the church with devastating consequences. As a result, almost any profession of faith is affirmed as genuine—even from those whose lives manifest no signs of true fruit (e.g., Luke 6:43–44). For many, no one's faith is to be questioned. Meanwhile, key New Testament passages regarding the danger of false faith (e.g., James 2:14–26) and the need for self-examination (e.g., 2 Cor. 13:5) go unheeded.

The ministry of our Lord provides a stark contrast to the contemporary evangelical confusion. Christ was not interested in shallow responses or quick pseudo-conversions. He refused to compromise the truth or give anyone false hope. Instead of making it easy for people to believe, Jesus turned away more prospects than He received. The rich young ruler, for example, eagerly sought out Jesus and asked Him sincerely, "Teacher, what good thing shall I do that I may obtain eternal life?" (Matt. 19:16). Yet the Bible says that he went away grieving and unsaved (v. 22). To His shocked disciples Jesus later explained,

> "Truly I say to you, it is hard for a rich man to enter the kingdom of heaven. Again I say to you, it is easier for a camel to go through the eye of a needle, than for a rich man to enter the kingdom of God." When the disciples heard this, they were very astonished and said, "Then who can be saved?" And looking at them Jesus said to them, "With people this is impossible, but with God all things are possible." (vv. 23–26)

As a result of Christ's uncompromising demand for total commitment, "many of His disciples withdrew and were not walking with Him anymore" (John 6:66). He repeatedly warned His followers of the danger of spurious faith, even on the part of those who ministered in His name:

> Not everyone who says to Me, "Lord, Lord," will enter the kingdom of heaven, but he who does the will of My Father who is in heaven will enter. Many will say to Me on that day, "Lord, Lord, did we not prophesy in Your name, and in Your name cast out demons, and in Your name perform many miracles?" And then I will declare to them, "I never knew you; depart from Me, you who practice lawlessness." (Matt. 7:21–23)

Jesus also explained that being His disciple meant dying to self, declaring, "If anyone wishes to come after Me, he must deny himself, and take up his cross daily and follow Me" (Luke 9:23). Such a high cost was often too much for would-be disciples:

> As they were going along the road, someone said to Him, "I will follow You wherever You go." And Jesus said to him, "The foxes have holes and the birds of the air have nests, but the Son of Man has nowhere to lay His head." And He said to another, "Follow Me." But he said, "Lord, permit me first to go and bury my father." But He said to him, "Allow the dead to bury their own dead; but as for you, go and proclaim everywhere the kingdom of God." Another also said, "I will follow You, Lord; but first permit me to say good-bye to those at home." But Jesus said to him, "No one, after putting his hand to the plow and looking back, is fit for the kingdom of God." (Luke 9:57–62)

Clearly, an emphasis on abandoning self and submitting to Him permeated Jesus' evangelistic approach, both in His public ministry and in His private conversations. John 3:1–10 recounts one of those private interactions, a nighttime meeting with the prominent Pharisee Nicodemus. Throughout their conversation, Jesus refused to soften the truth simply to gain the approval of this influential religious leader. Instead, He spoke with clarity and precision—confronting Nicodemus's misconceptions and telling him exactly what he needed to hear. Christ's dialogue with Nicodemus can be discussed under three headings: Nicodemus' inquiry of Jesus, Jesus' insight into Nicodemus, and Jesus' indictment of Nicodemus.

The Inquiry

Now there was a man of the Pharisees, named Nicodemus, a ruler of the Jews; this man came to Jesus by night and said to Him, "Rabbi, we know that You have come from God as a teacher; for no one can do these signs that You do unless God is with him." Jesus answered and said to him, "Truly, truly, I say to you, unless one is born again he cannot see the kingdom of God." (3:1–3)

The placing of the chapter break here is unfortunate, since the story of Jesus' interaction with Nicodemus is logically tied to the previous section (2:23–25). As noted in chapter 7 of this volume, John 2:23–25 described Jesus' refusal to accept shallow, sign-based faith, since in His omniscience, He understood the people's hearts. The story of Nicodemus is a case in point, since Nicodemus himself was one of those superficial believers whose heart He read like an open book. Instead of affirming his profession, the Lord refused to accept Nicodemus's faith, which was solely based on the signs he had witnessed (v. 2). Jesus pointed him to the life-transforming nature of true saving faith.

Nicodemus ("victor over the people") was a Greek name common among the Jews of Jesus' day. Some have identified **Nicodemus** with a wealthy man of that same name mentioned in the Talmud. But since that Nicodemus was still alive when Jerusalem was destroyed in A.D. 70, he would probably have been too young to have been a member of the Sanhedrin during Jesus' ministry four decades earlier (cf. 7:50–51). The implication of verse 4 that Nicodemus was already an old man when he met with Jesus argues further against that identification.

Nicodemus was a member of the elite religious party **the Pharisees.** Their name probably derives from a Hebrew verb meaning "to separate"; they were the "separated ones" in the sense of being zealous for the Mosaic law (and their own oral traditions, which they added to it [cf. Matt. 15:2–6; Mark 7:8–13]). The Pharisees originated during the intertestamental period, likely as an offshoot of the Hasidim ("pious ones"), who opposed the Hellenizing of Jewish culture under the wicked Seleucid king Antiochus Epiphanes. Unlike their archrivals the Sadducees, who tended to be wealthy priests or Levites, the Pharisees generally came from the middle class. Therefore, though few in number (there were about 6,000 at the time of Herod the Great, according to the first-century Jewish historian Josephus), they had great influence with the common people (though, ironically, the Pharisees often viewed some with contempt [cf. 7:49]). Despite being the minority party, their popularity with the people gave them significant influence in the Sanhedrin (cf. Acts 5:34–40).

With the disappearance of the Sadducees in A.D. 70 (after the temple was destroyed) and the Zealots in A.D. 135 (after the Bar Kochba revolt was crushed), the Pharisees became the dominant force in Judaism. In fact, by the end of the second century A.D., with the completion of the Mishnah (the written compilation of the oral law, rituals, and traditions), the Pharisee's teaching became virtually synonymous with Judaism.

Ironically, it was their very zeal for the law that caused the Pharisees to become ritualized and external. Having unchanged hearts, they would only replace true religion with mere behavior modification and ritual. In response to their pseudo-spirituality, Jesus scathingly pointed out: "Woe to you, scribes and Pharisees, hypocrites! For you tithe mint and dill and cummin, and have neglected the weightier provisions of the law: justice and mercy and faithfulness; but these are the things you should have done without neglecting the others" (Matt. 23:23; cf. 6:1–5;

9:14; 12:2; Luke 11:38–39). Even worse, the wide gap between their teaching and their practice led to gross hypocrisy, which both Jesus (e.g., Matt. 23:2–3) and, surprisingly, the Talmud (which lists seven classes of Pharisees, six of which are hypocritical) denounced. As a result, despite their zeal for God's law, they were "blind guides of the blind" (Matt. 15:14), who made their proselytes doubly worthy of the hell to which they themselves were headed (Matt. 23:15). Even if they had not been hypocrites, keeping the law could never have saved them, "because by the works of the Law no flesh will be justified" (Rom. 3:20; cf. 3:28; Gal. 2:16; 3:11, 24; 5:4)—a truth that the zealous Pharisee Saul of Tarsus eventually discovered (Phil. 3:4–11).

But Nicodemus was no run-of-the-mill Pharisee; he was **a ruler of the Jews.** That is, he was a member of the Sanhedrin (cf. 7:50), the governing council of Israel (under the ultimate authority of the Romans). Jewish tradition traced the origin of the Sanhedrin to the seventy elders who assisted Moses (Num. 11:16–17). Ezra, also according to tradition, reorganized that body after the exile (cf. Ezra 5:5, 9; 6:7–8, 14; 10:8). However, the Sanhedrin of New Testament times probably originated during the period of Persian or Greek rule. It consisted of seventy-one members, presided over by the reigning high priest. It included men from the influential priestly families, elders (family and tribal heads), scribes (experts in the law), and any former high priests who were still alive. Under the Romans, the Sanhedrin exercised wide-ranging powers in civil, criminal, and religious matters (though the Romans withheld the power of capital punishment [18:31]). It had the authority both to make arrests (Matt. 26:47; Acts 4:1–3; 5:17–18) and to conduct trials (Matt. 26:57ff.; Acts 5:27ff.). Although its influence extended even to Jews of the Diaspora (cf. Acts 9:1–2; 22:5; 26:12), the Sanhedrin's direct authority seems to have been limited to Judea (it apparently wielded no power over Jesus while He was in Galilee; cf. John 7:1). After the failure of the Jewish revolt (A.D. 66–70), the Sanhedrin was abolished and replaced by the *Beth Din* (Court of Judgment). Unlike the Sanhedrin, however, the *Beth Din* was composed solely of scribes (lawyers), and its decisions were exclusively limited to religious matters.

The fact that Nicodemus was a member of the Sanhedrin probably explains why he **came to Jesus by night.** He might not have wanted his coming to imply the approval of the entire Sanhedrin, nor did he want to risk incurring the disfavor of his fellow members. Nighttime would also have afforded more time for conversation than during the day, when both he and Jesus would be occupied. The important point, however, is not when Nicodemus came, but that he came at all. Though coming to Jesus does not always guarantee salvation (cf. the rich young ruler, Luke 18:18–23), it is a necessary beginning.

By using the respectful term **Rabbi,** Nicodemus, although a member of the Sanhedrin and an eminent teacher (v. 10), addressed Jesus as an equal. He did not share the suspicion and hostility that many of his fellow religious leaders had toward Christ (cf. 7:15, 47–52). Nicodemus, and others like him (cf. the plural, **we know**), accepted **that** Jesus had **come from God as a teacher**—even though He had not received proper rabbinic training (7:15). As Nicodemus acknowledged, **"No one can do these signs that You do unless God is with him."** Like the people in the previous section (2:23), he was impressed with and believed that the undeniable power manifested in Jesus' miracles was divine. Undoubtedly, he was also aware of John the Baptist's testimony about Christ. That, coupled with the evidence of them, may have caused Nicodemus to wonder if Jesus was the Messiah.

But Jesus was not interested in discussing His signs, which had resulted only in superficial faith. Instead, He went straight to the real issue—the transformation of Nicodemus's heart by the new birth. Jesus answered Nicodemus's unasked question (cf. Matt. 19:16) **and said to him, "Truly, truly, I say to you, unless one is born again he cannot see the kingdom of God."** The phrase *amēn amēn* (**truly, truly**) appears in the New Testament only in John's gospel. It solemnly affirms the veracity and significance of what follows. In this instance, Jesus used the phrase to introduce the vitally important truth that there is no entrance into God's kingdom **unless one is born again.** The new birth, or regeneration, is the act of God by which He imparts eternal life to those who are "dead in . . . trespasses and sins" (Eph. 2:1; cf. 2 Cor. 5:17; Titus 3:5; James 1:18; 1 Peter 1:3, 23; 1 John 2:29; 3:9; 4:7; 5:1, 4, 18), thus making them His children (John 1:12–13).

The kingdom of God in its universal aspect refers to God's sovereign rule over all of His creation. In that broadest sense of the term, everyone is part of God's kingdom, since "the Lord has established His throne in the heavens, and His sovereignty rules over all" (Ps. 103:19; cf. 10:16; 29:10; 145:13; 1 Chron. 29:11–12; Jer. 10:10; Lam. 5:19; Dan. 4:17, 25, 32).

But Jesus is not referring here to the universal kingdom. Instead, He is speaking specifically of the kingdom of salvation, the spiritual realm where those who have been born again by divine power through faith now live under the rulership of God mediated through His Son. Nicodemus, like the rest of his fellow Jews, eagerly anticipated that glorious realm. Unfortunately, they thought that being descendants of Abraham, observing the law, and performing external religious rituals (particularly circumcision) would gain them entrance into that kingdom. But in thinking this, they were severely mistaken, as Jesus made clear. No matter how religiously active someone might be, no one can enter the kingdom without experiencing the personal regeneration of the new birth (cf. Matt. 19:28).

The implications of Jesus' words for Nicodemus were staggering. All of his life he had diligently observed the law (cf. Mark 10:20) and the rituals of Judaism (cf. Gal. 1:14). He had joined the ultrareligious Pharisees, and even become a member of the Sanhedrin. Now Jesus called him to forsake all of that and start over; to abandon the entire system of works righteousness in which he had placed his hope; to realize that human effort was powerless to save. Describing the consternation Nicodemus must have felt, R. C. H. Lenski writes:

> Jesus' word regarding the new birth shatters once for all every supposed excellence of man's attainment, all merit of human deeds, all prerogatives of natural birth or station. Spiritual birth is something one undergoes, not something he produces. As our efforts had nothing to do with our natural conception and birth, so in an analogous way but on a far higher plane, regeneration is not a work of ours. What a blow for Nicodemus! His being a Jew gave him no part in the kingdom; his being a Pharisee, esteemed holier than other people, availed him nothing; his membership in the Sanhedrin and his fame as one of its scribes went for nought. This Rabbi from Galilee calmly tells him that he is not yet in the kingdom! All on which he had built his hopes throughout a long arduous life here sank into ruin and became a little worthless heap of ashes. (*The Interpretation of St. John's Gospel* [Reprint; Peabody, Mass.: Hendrickson, 1998], 234–35)

THE INSIGHT

Nicodemus said to Him, "How can a man be born when he is old? He cannot enter a second time into his mother's womb and be born, can he?" Jesus answered, "Truly, truly, I say to you, unless one is born of water and the Spirit he cannot enter into the kingdom of God. That which is born of the flesh is flesh, and that which is born of the Spirit is spirit. Do not be amazed that I said to you, 'You must be born again.' The wind blows where it wishes and you hear the sound of it, but do not know where it comes from and where it is going; so is everyone who is born of the Spirit." (3:4–8)

Jesus' shocking statement was far more than Nicodemus had expected. Incredulous, Nicodemus **said to Him, "How can a man be born when he is old? He cannot enter a second time into his mother's womb and be born, can he?"** Certainly, this highly educated

Pharisee was not so obtuse as to have misinterpreted Jesus' words in a simplistically literal sense. He knew our Lord was not talking about being physically reborn, but he replied in the context of the Lord's analogy. How could he start all over, go back to the beginning? Jesus was telling him that entrance to God's salvation was not a matter of adding something to all his efforts, not topping off his religious devotion, but rather canceling everything and starting all over again. At the same time, he clearly could not grasp the full meaning of what that meant. His questions convey his confusion, as he openly wondered at the impossibility of Christ's statement. Jesus was asking for something that was not humanly possible (to be born again); He was making entrance into the kingdom contingent on something that could not be obtained through human effort. But if that was true, what did it mean for Nicodemus's works-based system? If spiritual rebirth, like physical rebirth, was impossible from a human standpoint, then where did that leave this self-righteous Pharisee?

Far from minimizing the demands of the gospel, Jesus confronted Nicodemus with the most difficult challenge He could make. No wonder Christ would later say to His disciples, "Children, how hard it is to enter the kingdom of God!" (Mark 10:24). By calling him to be born again, Jesus challenged this most religious Jew to admit his spiritual bankruptcy and abandon everything he was trusting in for salvation. That is precisely what Paul did, as he declared in Philippians 3:8–9:

> More than that, I count all things to be loss in view of the surpassing value of knowing Christ Jesus my Lord, for whom I have suffered the loss of all things, and count them but rubbish so that I may gain Christ, and may be found in Him, not having a righteousness of my own derived from the Law, but that which is through faith in Christ, the righteousness which comes from God on the basis of faith.

Jesus answered Nicodemus's confusion by elaborating on the truth He introduced in verse 3: **"Truly, truly, I say to you, unless one is born of water and the Spirit he cannot enter into the kingdom of God."** A number of interpretations have been offered to explain the phrase **born of water.** Some see two births here, one natural, and the other spiritual. Proponents of this view interpret the **water** as the amniotic fluid that flows from the womb just before childbirth. But it is not clear that the ancients described natural birth in that way. Further, the phrase **born of water and the Spirit** parallels the phrase "born again" in verse 3; thus, only one birth is in view. Others see in the phrase **born of water** a reference to baptism, either that of John the Baptist, or Christian baptism. But Nicodemus would not have understood Christian baptism (which did not yet exist) nor misunderstood John the Baptist's baptism. Nor would Jesus have refrained from baptizing people (4:2) if baptism were necessary for salvation. Still others see the phrase as a reference to Jewish ceremonial washings, which being born of the Spirit transcends. However the two terms are not in contrast with each other, but combine to form a parallel with the phrase "born again" in verse 3. (For a careful examination of the various interpretations of **born of water,** see D. A. Carson, *The Gospel According to John,* The Pillar New Testament Commentary [Grand Rapids: Eerdmans, 1991], 191–96.)

Since Jesus expected Nicodemus to understand this truth (v. 10), it must have been something with which he was familiar. **Water** and **Spirit** often refer symbolically in the Old Testament to spiritual renewal and cleansing (cf. Num. 19:17–19; Isa. 4:4; 32:15; 44:3; 55:1; Joel 2:28–29; Zech. 13:1). In one of the most glorious passages in all of Scripture describing Israel's restoration to the Lord by the new covenant, God said through Ezekiel,

> For I will take you from the nations, gather you from all the lands and bring you into your own land. Then I will sprinkle clean water on you, and you will be clean; I will cleanse you from all your filthiness and from all your idols. Moreover, I will give you a new heart and put a new spirit within you; and I will remove the heart of stone from your flesh and give you a heart of flesh. I will put My Spirit within you and cause you to walk in My statutes, and you will be careful to observe My ordinances. (Ezek. 36:24–27)

It was surely this passage that Jesus had in mind, showing regeneration to be an Old Testament truth (cf. Deut. 30:6; Jer. 31:31–34; Ezek. 11:18–20) with which Nicodemus would have been acquainted. Against this Old Testament backdrop, Christ's point was unmistakable: Without the spiritual washing of the soul, a cleansing accomplished only by the Holy Spirit (Titus 3:5) through the Word of God (Eph. 5:26), no one can enter God's kingdom.

Jesus continued by further emphasizing that this spiritual cleansing is wholly a work of God, and not the result of human effort: **"That which is born of the flesh is flesh, and that which is born of the Spirit is spirit."** Just as only human nature can beget human nature, so also only the Holy Spirit can effect spiritual transformation. The term **flesh** (*sarx*) here refers merely to human nature (as it does in 1:13–14); in this context, it does not have the negative moral connotation that it frequently does in Paul's writings (e.g., Rom. 8:1–8, 12–13). Even if a physical rebirth were possible, it would produce only **flesh.** Thus, only the **Spirit** can produce the spiritual birth required for entrance into God's kingdom. Regeneration is entirely His work, unaided by any human effort (cf. Rom. 3:25).

Although Jesus' words were based on Old Testament revelation, they ran completely contrary to everything Nicodemus had been taught. For his entire life he had believed that salvation came through his own external merit. Now he found it exceedingly difficult to think otherwise. Aware of his astonishment, Jesus continued, **"Do not be amazed that I said to you, 'You must be born again.'"** The verb translated **must** is a strong term; John used it elsewhere in his gospel to refer to the necessity of the crucifixion (3:14; 12:34), of John the Baptist's inferiority to Christ (3:30), of the proper method of worshiping God (4:24), of Jesus carrying out His ministry (4:4; 9:4; 10:16), and of the necessity of the resurrection (20:9). It was absolutely necessary for Nicodemus to get over his astonishment at being so wrong about how one is accepted into God's kingdom and seek to be **born again** if he was to enter. And he could never do so based on his own righteous works.

Then the Lord illustrated His point with a familiar example from nature: **"The wind blows where it wishes and you hear the sound of it, but do not know where it comes from and where it is going; so is everyone who is born of the Spirit."** The wind cannot be controlled; it blows **where it wishes.** And though its general direction can be known, **where it comes from and where it is going** cannot be precisely determined. Nevertheless, the wind's effects can be observed. The same is true of the work of the **Spirit.** His sovereign work of regeneration in the human heart can neither be controlled nor predicted. Yet its effects can be seen in the transformed lives of those who are **born of the Spirit.**

THE INDICTMENT

Nicodemus said to Him, "How can these things be?" Jesus answered and said to him, "Are you the teacher of Israel and do not understand these things?" (3:9–10)

Although he was a renowned teacher, Nicodemus proved to be a poor learner. His question, **"How can these things be?"** indicates that he had made little progress since verse 4. Despite Jesus' further clarification in verses 5–8, Nicodemus still could not accept what he was hearing. He could not let go of his legalistic religious system and realize that salvation was a sovereign, gracious work of God's Spirit.

Because of his position as **the teacher of Israel,** Nicodemus could have been expected to **understand** the **things** Jesus had said. His lack of understanding was inexcusable considering his exposure to the Old Testament. The use of the definite article before **teacher** indicates that Nicodemus was a recognized, established teacher in **Israel.** Jesus found it inexcusable that this prominent scholar was not familiar with the foundational new covenant teaching from the Old Testament regarding the only way of salvation (cf. 2 Tim. 3:15). Sadly, Nicodemus serves as a clear example of the numbing effect that external, legalistic religion has on a person's spiritual perception—even to the point of obscuring the revelation of God.

His ignorance also exemplified Israel's spiritual bankruptcy (cf. Rom. 10:2–3). In Paul's words the Jews, failing to recognize "God's righteousness and seeking to establish their own . . . did not subject themselves to the righteousness of God" (Rom. 10:3). Therefore, their "zeal for God [was] not in accordance with knowledge" (Rom. 10:2), meaning that it was all for naught.

Although nothing in this passage suggests Nicodemus was converted that evening (and v. 11 strongly implies that he was not), he never forgot his discussion with Jesus. Later, he boldly defended Him before the Sanhedrin (7:50–51), and helped Joseph of Arimathea prepare His body for burial (19:38–39)—actions that indicate the presence of genuine faith in his life. Sometime after that memorable evening he spent with Jesus but before the crucifixion, Nicodemus came to understand sovereign grace and experience the reality of the new birth.

Responding to the Divine Offer of Salvation
(John 3:11–21)

9

"Truly, truly, I say to you, we speak of what we know and testify of what we have seen, and you do not accept our testimony. If I told you earthly things and you do not believe, how will you believe if I tell you heavenly things? No one has ascended into heaven, but He who descended from heaven: the Son of Man. As Moses lifted up the serpent in the wilderness, even so must the Son of Man be lifted up; so that whoever believes will in Him have eternal life. For God so loved the world, that He gave His only begotten Son, that whoever believes in Him shall not perish, but have eternal life. For God did not send the Son into the world to judge the world, but that the world might be saved through Him. He who believes in Him is not judged; he who does not believe has been judged already, because he has not believed in the name of the only begotten Son of God. This is the judgment, that the Light has come into the world, and men loved the darkness rather than the Light, for their deeds were evil. For everyone who does evil hates the Light, and does not come to the Light for fear that his deeds will be exposed. But he who practices the truth comes to the Light, so that his deeds may be manifested as having been wrought in God." (3:11–21)

Over the last few centuries, life spans have been extended, living conditions improved, and labor made safer and easier. Dreaded diseases that once were widespread, such as smallpox, polio, and various plagues, have been controlled or eliminated. Mechanization (at least in developed countries) has taken the drudgery and danger out of many jobs, and some of the most labor-intensive tasks are now performed entirely by machines. Of course, unsolved problems still remain, including war, poverty, certain incurable diseases, environmental concerns, and new problems raised by the very technology that helped solve the old ones. Yet humanity's faith in progress remains largely unshaken. Many ardently believe that, given enough time, science and technology will one day overcome all of mankind's remaining troubles.

But although man has made great strides in improving his living conditions, his most pressing problem—the one beside which all others pale in comparison—remains forever beyond his ability to solve. It is the same insurmountable issue that confronted Adam and Eve after the fall—namely, that all people, without exception (Rom. 3:10), are guilty sinners (Rom. 5:8) before a holy God, the righteous Judge (Ps. 7:11; 2 Tim. 4:8), who will justly condemn them to eternal punishment in hell (Rev. 20:11–15) for violating His holy law (Gal. 3:10).

Ever since Adam's disobedience plunged the human race into sin (Rom. 5:12–21), Satan has ceaselessly promoted the lie that people can come to God on their own terms. That lie, embraced by all who follow the broad way that leads to destruction (Matt. 7:13), is at the heart of every false religion. But the Bible is clear that unregenerate people cannot save themselves; their condition is utterly hopeless, humanly speaking (Matt. 19:25–26). They are "dead in [their] trespasses and sins" (Eph. 2:1); unable to accept or understand spiritual truth (1 Cor. 2:14) because "the god of this world has blinded the minds of the unbelieving so that they might not see the light of the gospel of the glory of Christ" (2 Cor. 4:4; cf. Eph. 4:18). They are enemies of God (Rom. 5:10; James 4:4); alienated from Him (Eph. 2:19; Col. 1:21; cf. Ps. 58:3); disobedient to Him (Eph. 2:2; Col. 3:6; Titus 3:3; cf. Job 21:15); ignorant of Him (Pss. 10:4; 14:1; 53:1; 2 Thess. 1:8; cf. Job 8:13); hostile to Him (Rom. 8:7; Col. 1:21); unloving toward Him (2 Tim. 3:4); haters of Him (Ps. 81:15; Rom. 1:30); rebellious toward Him (Ps. 5:10; 1 Tim. 1:9); and subject to His wrath (John 3:36; Rom. 1:18; Eph. 5:6). They are on the path to destruction (Matt. 7:13; Phil. 3:19) because they hate the light of spiritual truth (John 3:20) and hence are blind to it (Matt. 15:14). As children of Satan (Matt. 13:38; John 8:44; 1 John 3:10), they live under his control (Eph. 2:2), being members of his kingdom (Matt. 12:26; Col. 1:13) and "by nature children of wrath" (Eph. 2:3). Thus, they are slaves to sin (John 8:34; Rom. 6:17, 20) and corruption (2 Peter 2:19), "vessels of wrath prepared for destruction" (Rom. 9:22).

In light of that, religious rituals, good works, and self-reformation cannot solve the problem of spiritual death (Eph. 2:8–9; 2 Tim. 1:9; Titus 3:5). Only the radical transformation" (2 Cor. 5:17) wrought by God in regeneration can impart spiritual life to the spiritually dead. That was the shocking truth with which Jesus confronted the zealous Pharisee Nicodemus (3:1–10). Although the Lord's teaching on the new birth was solidly grounded in the Old Testament, Nicodemus was incredulous. He struggled to accept that his religious efforts were useless and needed to be abandoned altogether as a means to gain God's kingdom.

Because Nicodemus responded in unbelief, he apparently walked away from his conversation with Jesus unconverted. (He did become a believer later, however, as noted in chapter 8 of this volume.) His initial response typifies those who reject the gospel. Unrepentant unbelief is the sin that ultimately condemns all lost sinners (cf. Matt. 12:31–32), for unless they confess Christ's lordship, and repent of all sin, including the sin of trying to earn heaven, they cannot be saved. In this discourse on the meaning of salvation, Jesus addressed the problem of unbelief, provided the answer for unbelief, and warned of the results of unbelief.

THE PROBLEM OF UNBELIEF

"Truly, truly, I say to you, we speak of what we know and testify of what we have seen, and you do not accept our testimony. If I told you earthly things and you do not believe, how will you believe if I tell you heavenly things?" (3:11–12)

Chapter 3 began by recounting Nicodemus's nighttime interview with Jesus. But after his question in verse 9, the renowned Pharisee added nothing more to the conversation (at least nothing that is recorded), as the dialogue between the two men moved into a discourse by Jesus. Although Nicodemus twice professed ignorance of Jesus' teaching (3:4, 9), his real problem, as noted above, was not a lack of divine revelation. He was highly educated in the Old Testament (3:10) and had just dialogued with the Teacher who was the source of truth. Nicodemus did not **accept** the truth to which Jesus testified, because he refused to **believe** it. Paul wrote, "a natural man does not accept the things of the Spirit of God, for they are foolishness to him; and he cannot understand them, because they are spiritually appraised" (1 Cor. 2:14). Even those who have never heard the gospel are still culpable for their ignorance, because they reject the truth that they do have (Rom. 1:18–21).

In a statement introduced by the solemn declaration **truly,**

truly, I say to you (cf. the discussion of 3:3 in chapter 8 of this volume), Jesus affirmed, **"We speak of what we know and testify of what we have seen, and you do not accept our testimony."** The plurals **we** and **our** encompassed Jesus' disciples and even John the Baptist, who understood and testified to the truth of salvation. They provided a contrast with the "we" in verse 2 (which referred to Nicodemus and his colleagues). The Pharisees and their fellow Jews were ignorant of the new birth, but Jesus and His disciples were certain about regeneration—the truth to which they testified. Moreover, Nicodemus spoke with human authority, but Jesus with heavenly authority (cf. Matt. 7:28–29).

The Lord's use of the plural pronoun **you** indicates that His rebuke went beyond Nicodemus to include the nation of Israel, of which Nicodemus was a representative. The Jewish people did **not accept** the **testimony** of Jesus and His true followers (cf. 1:11); their unbelief was what perpetuated their spiritual ignorance.

Jesus' pointed rebuke, **"If I told you earthly things and you do not believe, how will you believe if I tell you heavenly things?"** shattered Nicodemus's self-righteousness. His shallow profession of faith in Jesus as a teacher sent from God (v. 2) was meaningless, as was his misconstrued understanding of salvation (cf. v. 10). Because of his refusal to **believe,** he could not even fathom the **earthly** truth of the new birth, not to mention profound **heavenly** realities such as the relationship of the Father to the Son (John 1:1; 17:5), God's kingdom (Matt. 25:34), or His eternal plan of redemption (Eph. 1:4; 2 Thess. 2:13; 2 Tim. 1:9).

There were two sides to Nicodemus's unbelief. Intellectually, while he acknowledged Jesus to be a teacher sent from God (3:2), he was unwilling to accept Him as God. Spiritually, he was very reluctant to admit that he himself was a helpless sinner, since that was unthinkable for proud members of the Pharisees, the self-righteous, self-confessed religious elite of Israel. Further, he was a privileged member of the Sanhedrin and thus viewed as a prominent spiritual leader by the people (3:10). To humble himself to admit that he was in spiritual darkness and needed to come to the light of true salvation and righteousness (cf. 3:19–21) would have been to confess his sinfulness and lack of righteousness. Like many who were impressed by Jesus' miracles (2:23–25), Nicodemus refused to commit himself to Christ as Lord and Savior.

THE ANSWER FOR UNBELIEF

"No one has ascended into heaven, but He who descended from heaven: the Son of Man. As Moses lifted up the serpent in the

wilderness, even so must the Son of Man be lifted up; so that whoever believes will in Him have eternal life. For God so loved the world, that He gave His only begotten Son, that whoever believes in Him shall not perish, but have eternal life. For God did not send the Son into the world to judge the world, but that the world might be saved through Him." (3:13–17)

Only someone who has been to heaven can truly know what it is like. Yet human beings, short of death, do not have the ability to visit heaven since they are confined to time and space. Thus Jesus said that **no one has ascended into heaven** (cf. Prov. 30:4) because it is humanly impossible to do so. John declared in the prologue to his gospel, "No one has seen God at any time; the only begotten God who is in the bosom of the Father, He has explained Him" (1:18). "Not that anyone has seen the Father," Jesus agreed, "except the One who is from God; He has seen the Father" (6:46). It may be noted that Lazarus was to return from the dead (11:23–24), and after the crucifixion of our Lord, the graves were opened and some saints returned (Matt. 27:52–53). These rare exceptions prove the rule. The other unique event was the visit of the apostle Paul to "the third heaven" (2 Cor. 12:2).

The only one possessing true knowledge of heavenly reality is **He who descended from heaven: the Son of Man.** God "in these last days has spoken to us in His Son" (Heb. 1:2). He is "the bread of God . . . which comes down out of heaven, and gives life to the world" (John 6:33; cf. 6:51). "I have come down from heaven," He declared in John 6:38, "not to do My own will, but the will of Him who sent Me." In John 6:62 He asked, "What then if you see the Son of Man ascending to where He was before?" In John 8:42 Jesus said to His accusers, "If God were your Father, you would love Me, for I proceeded forth and have come from God, for I have not even come on My own initiative, but He sent Me." John prefaced his account of Jesus' washing the disciples' feet with the statement that Jesus "had come forth from God and was going back to God" (John 13:3). Later that same evening in the Upper Room Jesus told the disciples, "I came forth from the Father and have come into the world; I am leaving the world again and going to the Father" (John 16:28). In His High Priestly Prayer Jesus prayed, "Now, Father, glorify Me together with Yourself, with the glory which I had with You before the world was" (John 17:5). To the Corinthians Paul wrote, "The first man [Adam] is from the earth, earthy; [but] the second man [Jesus] is from heaven" (1 Cor. 15:47).

Beginning in verse 14, Jesus appealed to an Old Testament illustration to make His point, further emphasizing that there was no excuse for Nicodemus, an expert in the Scriptures, to be ignorant of the way of salvation. As a type of His sacrificial death on the cross, the Lord referred to an incident recorded in Numbers 21:5–9:

> The people spoke against God and Moses, "Why have you brought us up out of Egypt to die in the wilderness? For there is no food and no water, and we loathe this miserable food." The Lord sent fiery serpents among the people and they bit the people, so that many people of Israel died. So the people came to Moses and said, "We have sinned, because we have spoken against the Lord and you; intercede with the Lord, that He may remove the serpents from us." And Moses interceded for the people. Then the Lord said to Moses, "Make a fiery serpent, and set it on a standard; and it shall come about, that everyone who is bitten, when he looks at it, he will live." And Moses made a bronze serpent and set it on the standard; and it came about, that if a serpent bit any man, when he looked to the bronze serpent, he lived.

The event took place during Israel's forty years of wilderness wandering before entering the Promised Land. As a judgment upon the people's incessant complaining, the Lord sent venomous snakes to infest their camp. In desperation, the Israelites begged Moses to intercede on their behalf. And Moses' prayerful petition was answered with a display of divine grace, as God showed mercy to His rebellious people. He instructed Moses to make a bronze replica of a snake and raise it above the camp on a pole. Those who were bitten would be healed if they but looked at it, thereby acknowledging their guilt and expressing faith in God's forgiveness and healing power.

The point of Jesus' analogy was that just as **Moses lifted up the serpent in the wilderness, even so must the Son of Man be lifted up** (crucified; cf. 8:28; 12:32, 34). The term **must** emphasizes that Christ's death was a necessary part of God's plan of salvation (cf. Matt. 16:21; Mark 8:31; Luke 9:22; 17:25; 24:7, 26; Acts 2:23; 4:27–28; 17:3). He had to die as a substitute for sinners, because "the wages of sin is death" (Rom. 6:23), and "without shedding of blood there is no forgiveness" (Heb. 9:22). Therefore God, "being rich in mercy, because of His great love with which He loved us" (Eph. 2:4), "sent His only begotten Son into the world so that we might live through Him. In this is love, not that we loved God, but that He loved us and sent His Son to be the propitiation for our sins" (1 John 4:9–10). The stricken Israelites were cured by obediently looking apart from any works or righteousness of their own in hope and dependence on God's word at the elevated bronze serpent. In the same way **whoever** looks in faith alone to the crucified Christ will be cured from sin's deadly bite and **will in Him have eternal life.**

This is the first of fifteen references in John's gospel to the important term **eternal life.** In its essence, **eternal life** is the believer's participation in the blessed, everlasting life of Christ (cf. 1:4) through his or her union with Him (Rom. 5:21; 6:4, 11, 23; 1 Cor. 15:22; 2 Cor. 5:17; Gal. 2:20; Col. 3:3–4; 2 Tim. 1:1, 10; Jude 21). Jesus defined eternal life in His High Priestly Prayer to the Father: "This is eternal life, that they may know You, the only true God, and Jesus Christ whom You have sent" (John 17:3). It is the life of the age to come (Eph. 2:6–7), and believers will most fully experience it in the perfect, unending glory and joy of heaven (Rom. 8:19–23, 29; 1 Cor. 15:49; Phil. 3:20–21; 1 John 3:2).

Verse 16 is undoubtedly the most familiar and beloved verse in all of Scripture. Yet its very familiarity can cause the profound truth it contains to be overlooked. God's motive for giving "His indescribable gift" of Jesus Christ (2 Cor. 9:15) was that He **loved the** evil, sinful **world** of fallen humanity. As noted earlier in this chapter, all humanity is utterly sinful, completely lost, and unable to save itself by any ceremony or effort. Thus, there was nothing in man that attracted God's love. Rather He loved because He sovereignly determined to do so. The plan of salvation flowed from "the kindness of God our Savior and His love for mankind" (Titus 3:4). "God demonstrates His own love toward us," wrote Paul to the Christians in Rome, "in that while we were yet sinners, Christ died for us" (Rom. 5:8). John wrote in his first epistle, "In this is love, not that we loved God, but that He loved us and sent His Son to be the propitiation for our sins. . . . We love, because He first loved us" (1 John 4:10, 19). Such love is so vast, wonderful, and incomprehensible that John, shunning all adjectives, could only write that God so loved the world that He gave His own Beloved Son (cf. 1 John 3:1). **World** is a nonspecific term for humanity in a general sense. The statement in verse 17, "that the world might be saved through Him," proves that it does not mean everyone who has ever lived, since all will not be saved. Verse 16 clearly cannot be teaching universal salvation, since the context promises that unbelievers will perish in eternal judgment (vv. 16–18). Our Lord is saying that for all in the world there is only one Savior (1 John 2:2), but only those who are regenerated by the Spirit and who believe in His gospel will receive salvation and eternal life through Him. (For a more extensive discussion of this point, see my book *The God Who Loves* [Nashville: Word, 2001], especially pp. 99ff.)

Paul in 2 Corinthians 5:19 used the term **world** in a similar way: "God was in Christ reconciling the world to Himself, not counting their trespasses against them, and He has committed to us the word of reconciliation." God was in Christ reconciling the world to Himself, not in the sense of universal salvation, but in the sense that the world has no other reconciler. That not all will believe and be reconciled is clear from the pleading in verse 20: "Therefore, we are ambassadors for Christ, as though God were making an appeal through us; we beg you on behalf of Christ, be reconciled to God." (For a further discussion of those verses, see *2 Corinthians*, The MacArthur New Testament Commentary [Chicago: Moody, 2003]).

There are no words in human language that can adequately express the magnitude of God's saving gift to the world. Even the apostle Paul refused to try, declaring that gift to be "indescribable" (2 Cor. 9:15). The Father **gave His only begotten** (unique; one of a kind; cf. the discussion of 1:14 in chapter 3 of this volume) **Son**—the One of whom He declared, "This is My beloved Son, in whom I am well-pleased" (Matt. 3:17; cf. 12:18; 17:5; 2 Peter 1:17); the One whom He "loves . . . and has given all things into His hand" (John 3:35; cf. 5:20; 15:9; 17:23, 26); the One whom He "highly exalted . . . and bestowed on Him the name which is above every name" (Phil. 2:9); the One with whom He had enjoyed intimate fellowship from all eternity (John 1:1)—to die as a sacrifice on behalf of sinful men. "He made Him who knew no sin to be sin on our behalf," wrote Paul, "so that we might become the righteousness of God in Him" (2 Cor. 5:21). In his majestic prophecy of the Suffering Servant Isaiah declared,

> He was pierced through for our transgressions,
> He was crushed for our iniquities;
> The chastening for our well-being fell upon Him,
> And by His scourging we are healed.
> All of us like sheep have gone astray,
> Each of us has turned to his own way;
> But the Lord has caused the iniquity of us all
> To fall on Him. (Isa. 53:5–6)

By "sending His own Son in the likeness of sinful flesh and as an offering for sin, [God] condemned sin in the flesh" (Rom. 8:3). To the Galatians Paul wrote, "when the fullness of the time came, God sent forth His Son, born of a woman, born under the Law, so that He might redeem those who were under the Law, that we might receive the adoption as sons" (Gal. 4:4–5). Just as the supreme proof of Abraham's love for God was his willingness to sacrifice his son (cf. Gen. 22:12, 16–18), so also, but on a far grander scale, the Father's offering of **His only begotten Son** was the supreme manifestation of His saving love for sinners.

God's gracious gift of salvation is freely and only available (Rom. 5:15–16; 6:23; 1 John 5:11; cf. Isa. 55:1) to **whoever believes in** Christ (Luke 8:12; John 1:12; 3:36; 5:24; 6:40, 47; 8:24; 11:25–26; 12:46; 20:31; Acts 2:44; 4:4; 5:14; 9:42; 10:43; 13:39, 48; 16:31; 18:8; Rom. 3:21–22; 4:3–5; 10:4, 9–10; Gal. 2:16; 3:22; Phil. 1:29; 1 John 3:23; 5:1, 13). The free offer of the gospel is broad enough to encompass the vilest sinner (1 Tim. 1:15), yet narrow enough to exclude all who reject Christ (John 3:18). But to those who come to Him on His terms Jesus gave the marvelous promise,"The one who comes to Me I will certainly not cast out"(John 6:37).

The guarantee given to those who possess eternal life is that they will never **perish.** Genuine salvation can never be lost; true believers will be divinely preserved and will faithfully persevere (Matt. 10:22; 24:13; Luke 8:15; 1 Cor. 1:8; Heb. 3:6, 14; 10:39) because they are kept by God's power (John 5:24; 6:37–40; 10:27–29; Rom. 5:9; 8:29–39; 1 Cor. 1:4–9; Eph. 4:30; Heb. 7:25; 1 Peter 1:4–5; Jude 24).

To **perish** is to receive God's final and eternal judgment. It is true that **God did not send the Son into the world to judge the world;** Jesus Himself declared in John 12:47,"I did not come to judge the world, but to save the world." In Luke 19:10 He said,"The Son of Man has come to seek and to save that which was lost," and Jesus made a similar statement in Luke 5:31–32:"It is not those who are well who need a physician, but those who are sick. I have not come to call the righteous but sinners to repentance." God will judge those who reject His Son (cf. the discussion of v. 18 below); that judgment, however, was not the mission of the Son in His first coming, but the consequence of sinners rejecting Him (John 1:10–12; 5:24, 40).

Jesus' statement in verse 17 also repudiated the popular belief that when Messiah came, he would judge the heathen and the Gentiles—but not the Jews. The prophet Amos had already warned against that foolish misinterpretation of the Day of the Lord:

> Alas, you who are longing for the day of the Lord,
> For what purpose will the day of the Lord be to you?
> It will be darkness and not light;
> As when a man flees from a lion
> And a bear meets him,
> Or goes home, leans his hand against the wall
> And a snake bites him.
> Will not the day of the Lord be darkness instead of light,
> Even gloom with no brightness in it? (Amos 5:18–20)

The point of Jesus' coming was not to redeem Israel and condemn the Gentiles, **but that the world might be saved through Him.** God's gracious offer of salvation extended beyond Israel to all mankind. Once again, Nicodemus (and by extension the Jewish nation he represented) should have known that, for in the Abrahamic covenant God declared,"I will bless those who bless you, and the one who curses you I will curse. And in you all the families of the earth will be blessed" (Gen. 12:3; cf. 18:18; 22:18; Acts 3:25). Gentile salvation was always God's purpose (Isa. 42:6–8; 55:1).

THE RESULTS OF UNBELIEF

"He who believes in Him is not judged; he who does not believe has been judged already, because he has not believed in the name of the only begotten Son of God. This is the judgment, that the Light has come into the world, and men loved the darkness rather than the Light, for their deeds were evil. For everyone who does evil hates the Light, and does not come to the Light for fear that his deeds will be exposed. But he who practices the truth comes to the Light, so that his deeds may be manifested as having been wrought in God." (3:18–21)

Although God graciously has offered the world salvation through the work of Christ, that salvation is not appropriated except by penitent faith. For all who respond to the gospel with unbelief, their final doom is set by divine judgment. Jesus stated that sobering truth to Nicodemus both positively and negatively.

On the other hand, **he who believes in** Christ **is not judged.** Later in John's gospel Jesus declared, "Truly, truly, I say to you, he who hears My word, and believes Him who sent Me, has eternal life, and does not come into judgment, but has passed out of death into life" (5:24). To the Romans Paul wrote triumphantly, "Therefore there is now no condemnation for those who are in Christ Jesus. . . . Who will bring a charge against God's elect? God is the one who justifies; who is the one who condemns? Christ Jesus is He who died, yes, rather who was raised, who is at the right hand of God, who also intercedes for us" (Rom. 8:1, 33–34). David exulted, "How blessed is he whose transgression is forgiven, whose sin is covered! How blessed is the man to whom the Lord does not impute iniquity" (Ps. 32:1–2).

But the one **who does not believe has been judged already, because he has not believed in the name of the only begotten Son of God.** While the final sentencing of those who reject Christ is still future (cf. 5:28–29), their judgment will merely consummate what has already begun. The lost are condemned because they have **not believed** in (lit., "believed into") **the name of the only begotten Son of God.** Saving faith goes beyond mere intellectual assent to the facts of the gospel and includes self-denying trust in and submission to the Lord Jesus Christ (Rom. 10:9; cf. Luke 9:23–25). Only such genuine faith produces the new birth (John 3:7) and its resulting transformed heart and obedient life.

The object of saving faith is the **only begotten** (unique) **Son of God.** He is "the way, and the truth, and the life; no one comes to the Father but through [Him]" (John 14:6), because "there is salvation in no one else; for there is no other name under heaven that has been given among men by which we must be saved" (Acts 4:12), and there is only "one mediator . . . between God and men, the man Christ Jesus" (1 Tim. 2:5).

Jesus described **judgment** using the contrast between light and darkness already introduced in the prologue (1:4–5; cf. 11:9–10; 12:35–36, 46; 1 John 1:5; 2:9–10). **The Light** (Christ; cf. 1:4–9; 8:12; 9:5; 12:35) **has come into the world** and by doing so "enlightens every man" (1:9). But people refused to come to the **Light** because they **loved the darkness rather than the Light, for their deeds were evil.** As noted earlier in this chapter, unbelievers are not ignorant, but willfully reject the truth. Therefore **everyone who does evil hates the Light, and does not come to the Light for fear that his deeds will be exposed.** Unbelievers hate (cf. 7:7; Prov. 1:29) the **Light,** knowing it will reveal their sin (cf. Eph. 5:13; 1 Thess. 5:7). As a result, they seal their own condemnation because they reject the only One who can save them from their spiritual **darkness.**

The one **who practices the truth,** however, willingly **comes to the Light, so that his deeds may be manifested as having been wrought in God.** Believers hate their sin and love righteousness (1 John 2:3–6, 9; 3:6–10). They have nothing to hide, and thus no reason to fear what the light will reveal. Jesus defined the genuine believer as one **who practices the truth,** because true saving faith invariably manifests itself in **deeds . . . wrought in God.** "For we are His workmanship," Paul reminded the Ephesians, "created in Christ Jesus for good works, which God prepared beforehand so that we would walk in them" (Eph. 2:10; cf. Mark 4:20). The redeemed will always "bear fruit in keeping with repentance" (Matt. 3:8); indeed, it is by bearing the fruit of good works that they prove themselves to be Jesus' disciples (John 15:8). On the other hand, "Every tree that does not bear good fruit is cut down and thrown into the fire" (Matt. 7:19).

Though no saving response is indicated here, Nicodemus evidently took Jesus' sobering warning to heart, since John's later references to him imply that he became a true follower of Christ (7:50–51; 19:39). But those who prove "unwilling to come to [Jesus] so that [they] may have life" (5:40) face the certainty of divine judgment, as the writer of Hebrews solemnly warns: "How will we escape if we neglect so great a salvation? . . . See to it that you do not refuse Him who is speaking. For if those did not escape when they refused him who warned them on earth, much less will we escape who turn away from Him who warns from heaven. . . . For our God is a consuming fire" (Heb. 2:3; 12:25, 29).

From John to Jesus
(John 3:22–36)

10

After these things Jesus and His disciples came into the land of Judea, and there He was spending time with them and baptizing. John also was baptizing in Aenon near Salim, because there was much water there; and people were coming and were being baptized—for John had not yet been thrown into prison. Therefore there arose a discussion on the part of John's disciples with a Jew about purification. And they came to John and said to him, "Rabbi, He who was with you beyond the Jordan, to whom you have testified, behold, He is baptizing and all are coming to Him." John answered and said, "A man can receive nothing unless it has been given him from heaven. You yourselves are my witnesses that I said, 'I am not the Christ,' but, 'I have been sent ahead of Him.' He who has the bride is the bridegroom; but the friend of the bridegroom, who stands and hears him, rejoices greatly because of the bridegroom's voice. So this joy of mine has been made full. He must increase, but I must decrease. He who comes from above is above all, he who is of the earth is from the earth and speaks of the earth. He who comes from heaven is above all. What He has seen and heard, of that He testifies; and no one receives His testimony. He who has received His testimony has set

his seal to this, that God is true. For He whom God has sent speaks the words of God; for He gives the Spirit without measure. The Father loves the Son and has given all things into His hand. He who believes in the Son has eternal life; but he who does not obey the Son will not see life, but the wrath of God abides on him." (3:22–36)

For centuries the children of Israel lived under the burdensome covenant God made with their fathers at Mount Sinai. As well as being God's absolute law of righteousness, reflecting His own holy nature, it contained also the unique marks of their national identity as God's chosen people (Deut. 7:6; 14:2). Thus, it set them apart from their pagan neighbors by its detailed social and ceremonial regulations. Yet almost from the beginning they misunderstood and abused the moral and spiritual elements of that covenant. It was meant to reveal their sin and abysmal failure to obey God, but they turned it into a source of arrogant pride, as well as a false hope for salvation. The old covenant's central pillars were holiness and love for God and man (Mark 12:28–31). But by Jesus' day, Israel's adherence to that covenant had degenerated into an external form of superficial morality, mechanical ceremony, legalistic ritualism, and extraneous tradition.

Israel also erred by assuming that the old covenant was the means to salvation, when that was never God's intent. His purpose was to confront sinners with a reflection of His absolute holiness, demand that they keep the law perfectly, and leave them facing their inability to keep it. That would point them to either divine judgment or the opportunity to repent, trust His grace, and receive the forgiveness He offered, provided in the new covenant (Jer. 31:34) to be ratified by the death of Christ. In the words of the apostle Paul, "The Law has become our tutor to lead us to Christ, so that we may be justified by faith" (Gal. 3:24). The old covenant was unable to justify anyone. However, it pointed to the coming Savior, through whom sinners could be "reconciled to God" (Rom. 5:10).

Approximately six hundred years before the Savior came, God told His people about the new covenant through the prophet Jeremiah.

"Behold, days are coming," declares the Lord, "when I will make a new covenant with the house of Israel and with the house of Judah, not like the covenant which I made with their fathers in the day I took them by the hand to bring them out of the land of Egypt, My covenant which they broke, although I was a husband to them," declares the Lord. "But this is the covenant which I will make with the house of Israel after those days," declares the Lord, "I will put My law within them and on their heart I will write it; and I will be their God, and they shall be My people. They will not teach again, each man his neighbor and each man his brother, saying, 'Know the Lord,' for they will all know Me, from the least of them to the greatest of them," declares the Lord, "for I will forgive their iniquity, and their sin I will remember no more." (Jer. 31:31–34)

In promising salvation in the new covenant, God indicated that the old covenant could never be the final hope. Thus, the author of Hebrews explains, "When He said, 'A new covenant,' He has made the first obsolete. But whatever is becoming obsolete and growing old is ready to disappear" (Heb. 8:13).

The old covenant did have a certain glory inherent in it. Isaiah wrote, "The Lord was pleased for His righteousness' sake to make the law great and glorious" (Isa. 42:21). And Paul reminded the Corinthians,

> But if the ministry of death, in letters engraved on stones, came with glory, so that the sons of Israel could not look intently at the face of Moses because of the glory of his face, fading as it was, how will the ministry of the Spirit fail to be even more with glory? For if the ministry of condemnation has glory, much more does the ministry of righteousness abound in glory. For indeed what had glory, in this case has no glory because of the glory that surpasses it. For if that which fades away was with glory, much more that which remains is in glory. (2 Cor. 3:7–11)

Yet, as the apostle noted in verses 7 and 11, the glory of the old covenant was not permanent, but fading; it was intended to give way to the new.

Scripture makes it clear that the new covenant is not merely a revision of the old. Rather, it is something brand-new and completely different, because it alone provides salvation. There is no salvation in the other covenants stated in the Old Testament (Noahic, Abrahamic, Priestly, Davidic, or Mosaic). The writer of Hebrews emphasized its distinctiveness by describing it with the Greek word *kainos*, which refers to something new in kind, not subsequent in time (Heb. 8:13).

As a unique demonstration of divine saving grace, the new covenant's superiority to the old is manifest in a number of ways. For instance, it has a better mediator, the Lord Jesus Christ (Heb. 8:6); it offers a better hope based on better promises, most notably that of complete forgiveness (Jer. 31:34; cf. Heb. 10:4); it grants all believers direct access to God without the need for priests; it is gracious (Heb. 8:9) in that its blessings will never be forfeited by disobedience (though disobedience brings chastening [Heb. 12:4–11]); it is internal, written not on tablets of stone (2 Cor. 3:7; Ex. 31:18), but on the heart (Jer. 31:33; Heb. 8:10); it brings spiritual life, not spiritual death (2 Cor. 3:6; cf. vv. 7, 9; Rom. 8:2–3); it results in righteousness, not condemnation (2 Cor. 3:9); it is clear and straightforward, unlike the old covenant's types, pictures, symbols, and mysteries; and it is energized by the liberating power of the Holy Spirit (2 Cor. 3:17–18). (For Paul's explanation of the uniqueness of the new covenant, see *2 Corinthians,* The MacArthur New Testament Commentary [Chicago: Moody, 2003], chaps. 7–8.)

The transition from John the Baptist's ministry to that of Jesus Christ, which is the theme of this section (cf. v. 30), symbolized the transition from the old covenant to the new. His father, Zacharias, understood the significance of the coming Messiah's relation to the new covenant, as he makes clear in his Spirit-filled prophecy in Luke 1:67–79:

> And his father Zacharias was filled with the Holy Spirit, and prophesied, saying:
> "Blessed be the Lord God of Israel,
> For He has visited us and accomplished redemption for His people,
> And has raised up a horn of salvation for us
> In the house of David His servant—
> As He spoke by the mouth of His holy prophets from of old—
> Salvation from our enemies,
> And from the hand of all who hate us;
> To show mercy toward our fathers,
> And to remember His holy covenant,
> The oath which He swore to Abraham our father,
> To grant us that we, being rescued from the hand of our enemies,
> Might serve Him without fear,
> In holiness and righteousness before Him all our days.
> And you, child, will be called the prophet of the Most High;
> For you will go on before the Lord to prepare His ways;
> To give to His people the knowledge of salvation
> By the forgiveness of their sins,
> Because of the tender mercy of our God,
> With which the Sunrise from on high will visit us,
> To shine upon those who sit in darkness and the shadow of death,
> To guide our feet into the way of peace."

As a priest who knew the Scripture, Zacharias understood the Messiah was coming to fulfill the promise of the new covenant. He was saying that all the promises to David (v. 69) and Abraham (v. 73) depended for their fulfillment on the arrival of Messiah (vv. 77–79). This whole prophecy is based on Old Testament texts regarding the Davidic, Abrahamic, and new covenants (e.g., Isa. 60:1–5, 19–21; 61:1–2, 10; 62:11–12).

John the Baptist was the last prophet under the old covenant (Luke 16:16); Jesus came as the mediator of the new covenant (Heb. 8:6; 12:24), which He ratified by His sacrificial death (Luke 22:20; 1 Cor. 11:25). Up to this point, John had enjoyed tremendous popularity (Matt.

3:4–6; Mark 1:4–5), while Jesus remained in obscurity. Although His cleansing of the temple (John 2:13–22) had broken Him out of that anonymity and created a sensation, Jesus still had only a handful of followers. But that was about to change, as the crowds that had been following John left him and flocked to Jesus. Thus, Christ would move to the forefront, and John would fade from the scene, giving his final testimony to the Messiah.

In God's sovereign plan, John's ministry overlapped that of Jesus. If it had not, there would have been no forerunner to point the nation to the Messiah (Isa. 40:3; cf. Mal. 3:1; John 1:23). It must not be imagined, however, that John and Jesus were ever rivals; John clearly understood and accepted his subservient role (cf. the discussion of this point in chapter 4 of this volume). Yet, despite John's general popularity (Matt. 14:5; Mark 11:32) among the common people (Matt. 3:5–6; Luke 7:29), Israel—under the influence of its religious leaders (Matt. 3:7–10; Luke 7:30)—ultimately rejected his testimony concerning Jesus (Matt. 27:20–25).

The phrase **after these things** indicates that the events recorded in this section followed (after an unspecified interval) the events described in 2:13–3:21 (Jesus' cleansing of the temple, His miraculous signs, and His dialogue with Nicodemus). After the Passover, **Jesus and His disciples came into the land of Judea,** meaning that they left Jerusalem (which is in Judea) for the surrounding Judean countryside (the Greek text literally reads "the Judean land" or "region").

Jesus' purpose in leaving Jerusalem was twofold: **spending time with** His disciples, and inaugurating His preaching that led to His **baptizing** ministry (although Jesus did not personally baptize, only His disciples did; cf. 4:2). **Spending time** translates a form of the verb *diatribō,* which implies that a considerable period of time elapsed (cf. its use in Acts 12:19; 14:3, 28; 15:35; 25:14), probably several months. During this interval, Jesus' disciples were **baptizing** those who came to hear Him preach and heeded His call to repent (cf. Matt. 4:17). Their baptisms foreshadowed Christian baptism, which was not instituted until after Jesus' death and resurrection (of which Christian baptism is a picture; cf. Rom. 6:3–4).

At the same time **John also** continued his **baptizing** ministry **in Aenon near Salim.** Two locations have been proposed for that site, one near Shechem in the hill country and the other near Beth Shean in the Jordan River valley. Both sites were in Samaria, leaving Judea to Jesus while John was ministering to the north. There is abundant water at both locations, in keeping both with the meaning of **Aenon** (a transliterated Aramaic or Hebrew word meaning "springs") and the statement that **there was much water there.** Even as Jesus' ministry was gaining momentum, large crowds of **people were** still **coming** to John **and being baptized.**

The parenthetical note that **John** the Baptist **had not yet been thrown into prison** does more than just state what is self-evident; obviously, John was not in prison, or he could not have been openly preaching and baptizing. The statement informs readers that this incident took place between Jesus' temptation and John's imprisonment, a period of time about which the Synoptic Gospels (Matthew, Mark, and Luke) are silent. The Synoptics begin their account of Jesus' public ministry in Galilee after John is already in prison (Matt. 4:12; Mark 1:14; cf. Luke 3:19–20 with 4:14). The gospel of John supplements them by recording these earlier events from Jesus' ministry, events that were simultaneous with John the Baptist's ministry in Samaria. The apostle John clarifies the timing here so that his readers will not be confused. By the time John penned his gospel, the Synoptics had already been in circulation for many years. This explanatory note makes it clear that John's time frame does not conflict with that of Matthew, Mark, or Luke.

This passage may be divided into two sections: John the Baptist and the end of the old age, followed by Jesus and the beginning of the new age.

JOHN THE BAPTIST AND THE END OF THE OLD AGE

Therefore there arose a discussion on the part of John's disciples with a Jew about purification. And they came to John and said to him, "Rabbi, He who was with you beyond the Jordan, to whom you have testified, behold, He is baptizing and all are coming to Him." John answered and said, "A man can receive nothing unless it has been given him from heaven. You yourselves are my witnesses that I said, 'I am not the Christ,' but, 'I have been sent ahead of Him.' He who has the bride is the bridegroom; but the friend of the bridegroom, who stands and hears him, rejoices greatly because of the bridegroom's voice. So this joy of mine has been made full. He must increase, but I must decrease." (3:25–30)

At some point during the concurrent but separate ministries of John and Jesus **there arose a discussion** between **John's disciples** and **a Jew** (the singular "Jew" is the preferred reading, rather than the plural "Jews," as in the KJV and NKJV) **about** Jewish ritual **purification** (cf. 2:6). Whether or not the **Jew** was a follower of Jesus is unclear. The reaction of John's disciples, however, reveals that they felt a deeper issue was at stake—namely, the relative merits of John's baptism ministry in comparison to that of Jesus.

The dispute surfaced an issue that had no doubt been disturbing John's disciples for some time. During the prolonged time (cf. the discussion of v. 22 above) that John ministered in close proximity to Jesus, John's following had gradually diminished. Troubled by their master's waning popularity (cf. 4:1), which their dispute with the Jew highlighted, John's disciples **came to John and said to him, "Rabbi, He who was with you beyond the Jordan, to whom you have testified, behold, He is baptizing and all are coming to Him."** Apparently unwilling even to name Jesus, John's envious disciples saw Jesus as a competitor, who was gaining popularity at their master's expense (their exaggerated use of **all** reveals the extent of their bias). Incredibly, they also missed the purpose of John's ministry, which was to point the nation to the Messiah (cf. 1:19ff.).

Unlike his overly zealous followers, however, John was not bothered in the least by his declining popularity. Despite his tremendous initial influence, he had always remained focused on the purpose of his ministry that he had probably known from childhood—to testify to Christ (cf. 1:27, 30). Now as his ministry began to wind down, John's purpose did not waver. His humble reply must have startled his disciples: **"A man can receive nothing unless it has been given him from heaven."** In this way, he affirmed and embraced his subordinate role as the herald of the Messiah. God had sovereignly granted him his ministry (cf. Rom. 1:5; 1 Cor. 4:7; 15:10; Eph. 3:7; 1 Tim. 2:7); if God now chose to change or end that ministry, John was content. Everything among God's servants, including popular ministry, is a gracious gift from God, not something to which a person is entitled. Therefore there is no place for jealousy, as John's self-effacing reply indicated (note the opposite reaction by the Pharisees in 12:19).

John's emphatic reminder to his envious disciples, **"You yourselves are my witnesses that I said, 'I am not the Christ'** (cf. 1:8, 20), **but, 'I have been sent ahead of Him'"** (cf. 1:23; Matt. 3:3; Mark 1:3; Luke 1:17, 76; 3:4–6; Acts 19:4), was a rebuke for their obtuseness. Nothing he had said could account for their misunderstanding of his role; on the contrary, he had always maintained that he was the forerunner of the Messiah, not the Messiah Himself. Thus, John saw Jesus' increasing popularity not as a concern, but as the fulfillment of his ministry. Far from upsetting him, it brought him great joy.

The measure of success for any ministry is not how many people follow the minister, but how many people follow Christ through the minister. The factious Corinthians proudly lined up under the banners of their spiritual heroes—Paul, Apollos, Cephas (Peter), and the super pious under Christ (1 Cor. 1:12). Yet in focusing their allegiance on those leaders, they were not fully following the Lord (even the so-called Christ faction was not following Him with a right attitude, but rather from a false sense of spiritual superiority). "Has Christ been divided?" Paul scathingly asked them, "Paul was not crucified for you, was he? Or were you baptized in the name of Paul?" (v. 13). Later in that same epistle he demanded, "When one says, 'I am of Paul,' and another, 'I am of Apollos,' are you not mere men? What then is Apollos? And what is Paul? Servants through whom you believed, even as the Lord gave opportunity to each one. I planted, Apollos watered, but God was causing the growth" (3:4–6). Thus, all genuine ministry is Christ-centered, "for no man can lay a foundation other than the one which is laid, which is Jesus Christ" (v. 11).

John the Baptist illustrated his subservient role using the familiar imagery of a wedding (cf. Matt. 22:2–14; 25:1–13; Mark 2:19–20; Luke 12:36; 14:8–10; Rev. 19:7–9). He cast himself not in the role of the **bridegroom,** but rather as **the friend of the bridegroom,** a position similar to the best man in a modern wedding. The **friend of the bridegroom** oversaw many of the details of the wedding, serving as the master of ceremonies (in a Judean wedding; weddings in Galilee were somewhat different [D. A. Carson, *The Gospel According to John,* The Pillar New Testament Commentary (Grand Rapids: Eerdmans, 1991), 211]). He was even responsible for bringing the bride to the bridegroom to begin the wedding ceremony. Having done that, his task was completed; the focus now rightfully shifted from him to the bridegroom.

There is good evidence that according to ancient Mesopotamian law the friend of the bridegroom was forbidden under any circumstances to marry the bride, even if the bridegroom rejected her (Carson, 212; Homer A. Kent Jr. *Light in the Darkness: Studies in the Gospel of John* [Grand Rapids: Baker, 1974], 67; J. D. Douglas, ed., *The New Bible Dictionary* [Grand Rapids: Eerdmans, 1979], s.v., "Friend of the Bridegroom"). That explains Samson's outrage when his fiancée was given to his companion (Judg. 14:20–15:3). If that were still the case in John's day, his depiction of himself as the friend of the bridegroom reinforced the fact that he did not see himself and Jesus as rivals. Bringing the faithful remnant of Israel (depicted in the Old Testament as the bride of the Lord; cf. Isa. 54:5–6; 62:4–5; Jer. 2:2; 31:32; Hos. 2:16–20) to Christ was the culmination of John's ministry as His forerunner.

Unlike his jealous disciples, John found great joy in phasing out so that Jesus' ministry could receive Israel's full attention. Having brought him the bride, the faithful **friend of the bridegroom . . . rejoices greatly because** he hears **the bridegroom's voice** expressing joy over the bride. **So** John's **joy** was **made full** as he watched the crowds leave him for Jesus: "This is the joy which John claims for himself, the joy of the bridegroom's friend, who arranges the marriage, and this joy is attained in Christ's welcoming to Himself the people whom John has prepared for Him and directed to Him" (Marcus Dods, "John," in W. Robertson Nicoll, ed. *The Expositors' Bible Commentary* [Reprint; Peabody, Mass.: Hendrickson, 2002], 1:720).

John summarized his view of himself in relation to Jesus in perhaps the most humble statement uttered by anyone in Scripture: **He must increase, but I must decrease.** Leon Morris observes, "It is not particularly easy in this world to gather followers about one for a serious purpose. But when they are gathered it is infinitely harder to detach them and firmly insist that they go after another. It is the measure of John's greatness that he did just that" (*The Gospel According to John,* The New International Commentary on the New Testament [Grand Rapids: Eerdmans, 1979], 242).

Must speaks of divine necessity. It was God's will for John to give way to Jesus; there was no reason for the crowds to hang around the herald once the king had arrived. Because he understood this, John the Baptist joyously accepted God's plan for his ministry.

JESUS AND THE BEGINNING OF THE NEW AGE

"He who comes from above is above all, he who is of the earth is from the earth and speaks of the earth. He who comes from heaven is above all. What He has seen and heard, of that He testifies; and no one receives His testimony. He who has received His testimony has set his seal to this, that God is true. For He whom God has sent speaks the words of God; for He gives the Spirit without measure. The Father loves the Son and has given all things into His hand. He who believes in the Son has eternal life; but he who does not obey the Son will not see life, but the wrath of God abides on him." (3:31–36)

Commentators disagree on whether John the Baptist continues to speak in these verses, or whether they are an editorial comment by the apostle John (first-century writers did not use quotation marks). But since there is no indication in the text of a break in thought or continuity, it is best to see these verses as a continuation of John the Baptist's words to his disciples. In his last recorded speech in this gospel, John listed five reasons for his disciples (and, by extension, everyone) to accept the absolute supremacy of Jesus Christ.

CHRIST HAD A HEAVENLY ORIGIN

"He who comes from above is above all, he who is of the earth is from the earth and speaks of the earth. He who comes from heaven is above all." (3:31)

The adverb *anōthen* (**from above**) is the same word translated "born again" in 3:3, 7, where it reflects the heavenly origin of the new birth. Here it refers to Christ as the One "who descended from heaven" (3:13; cf. 6:33, 38, 50–51, 58; 8:42; 13:3; 16:28; 17:8; 1 Cor. 15:47; Eph. 4:10). As such, He is **above all;** Christ is sovereign over the universe in general, and the world of men in particular.

In contrast, John the Baptist declared himself to be **of the earth, from the earth, and** one who **speaks of the earth.** Unlike *kosmos* ("world"), *gē* (**earth**) carries no negative moral implications; it merely refers here to human limitations. John's preaching was bold, powerful, and persuasive, yet he was just a "man sent from God" (1:6). Jesus, in contrast, was God incarnate (1:1, 14), and His testimony to the truth was infinitely greater than John's (cf. 5:33–36). Because of Jesus' heavenly origin, He had to increase while John had to decrease.

CHRIST KNEW THE TRUTH FIRSTHAND

"What He has seen and heard, of that He testifies; and no one receives His testimony." (3:32)

In the old covenant, "God ... spoke long ago to the fathers in the prophets" (Heb. 1:1), the last and greatest of whom was John the Baptist. But in the new covenant God "in these last days has spoken to us in His Son" (v. 2). Jesus' teaching is superior to anyone else's because His knowledge is not secondhand. He is the source of divine revelation. What **He has seen and heard** in the heavenly realm (cf. v. 31), **of that He testifies** with certainty (cf. Matt. 7:28–29; Mark 1:22, 27). "Truly, truly, I say to you," Jesus said to Nicodemus, "we speak of what we know and testify of what we have seen" (3:11). Later He taught, "He who sent Me is true; and the things which I heard from Him, these I speak to the world" (8:26). To His disciples He declared, "All things that I have heard from My Father I have made known to you" (15:15; cf. 8:40). Even Jesus' enemies acknowledged, "Never has a man spoken the way this man speaks" (John 7:46).

Tragically, John lamented, despite Jesus' powerful, authoritative proclamation of the truth, **no one receives His testimony.** Echoing

Jesus' words to that same effect (3:11; cf. 5:43; 12:37), the Baptist's hyperbolic statement emphasized that the world in general rejects Jesus and His teaching. The apostle John noted that rejection in the prologue to his gospel: "[Jesus] was the true Light which, coming into the world, enlightens every man. He was in the world, and the world was made through Him, and the world did not know Him. He came to His own, and those who were His own did not receive Him" (1:9–11). "A natural man does not accept the things of the Spirit of God," Paul wrote to the Corinthians, "for they are foolishness to him; and he cannot understand them, because they are spiritually appraised" (1 Cor. 2:14). It is because they are dead in their trespasses and sins (Eph. 2:1) and blinded by Satan (2 Cor. 4:4) that unbelievers willfully reject Jesus' testimony to the truth.

CHRIST'S TESTIMONY ALWAYS AGREED WITH GOD

"He who has received His testimony has set his seal to this, that God is true." (3:33)

Having stated the general rule, John gave the exception. Although the majority of people reject Jesus' message, not everyone does. There are those who accept **His testimony,** believing in Him for eternal life. In the ancient world, people **set** their **seal** to something (often with a signet ring; Gen. 41:42; Est. 3:10, 12; 8:2, 8, 10; Dan. 6:17) as a sign of complete acceptance and approval. In today's jargon, they signed off on it. Those who have **received** Christ's **testimony** thereby certify their belief that **God is true** when He speaks through His Son, as always (cf. John 17:17; Rom. 3:4; Titus 1:2).

Unlike human teachers, whose words sometimes agree with divine truth and sometimes do not, Jesus always spoke in complete harmony with the Father. Thus, those who profess to believe in God yet reject Jesus Christ are deceived. Jesus is one with the Father (10:30). "He who does not honor the Son does not honor the Father who sent Him" (5:23), and the Father said of Him, "This is My beloved Son, with whom I am well-pleased; listen to Him!" (Matt. 17:5). He is "the way, and the truth, and the life; no one comes to the Father but through [Him]" (14:6). To reject Jesus is to call God a liar (1 John 5:10), and to perish eternally (John 8:24).

CHRIST EXPERIENCED THE POWER OF THE HOLY SPIRIT WITHOUT LIMIT

"For He whom God has sent speaks the words of God; for He gives the Spirit without measure." (3:34)

The prophets of old who spoke for God were led, empowered, and inspired by the Holy Spirit; John the Baptist himself was "filled with the Holy Spirit while yet in his mother's womb" (Luke 1:15). Yet the Spirit's ability to empower them was limited by their sinful, fallen human natures. But Jesus Christ, **He whom God has sent** (3:17; 4:34; 5:24, 30, 36–38; 6:29, 38, 39, 44, 57; 7:16, 28–29, 33; 8:16, 18, 26, 29, 42; 9:4; 10:36; 11:42; 12:44–45, 49; 13:20; 14:24; 15:21; 16:5; 17:3, 8, 18, 21, 23, 25; 20:21; Matt. 10:40; Mark 9:37; Luke 4:18; 10:16), infallibly spoke **the words of God** because God gave the **Spirit** to Him **without measure** (1:32–33; cf. Isa. 11:2; 42:1; 61:1). Since "in Him all the fullness of Deity dwells in bodily form" (Col. 2:9), there were no limits to the Spirit's power working through Him.

CHRIST RECEIVED ALL AUTHORITY FROM THE FATHER

"The Father loves the Son and has given all things into His hand. He who believes in the Son has eternal life; but he who does not obey the Son will not see life, but the wrath of God abides on him." (3:35–36)

This last point explicitly states what the first four imply. Because of His love for **the Son** (cf. 5:20; 15:9; 17:23, 26; Matt. 3:17), **the Father has given** Him supreme authority over **all things** on earth and in heaven (Matt. 11:27; 28:18; 1 Cor. 15:27; Eph. 1:22; Phil. 2:9–11; Heb. 1:2; 1 Peter 3:22). That supremacy is a clear indicator of the Son's deity.

John's affirmation of Jesus' absolute authority demonstrated his humble attitude, even as his heralding ministry faded into the background. Having fulfilled his mission on this earth, John realized that his work would soon be finished. In fact, not long after this, he was arrested and beheaded by Herod Antipas, ruler of Galilee (Matt. 14:3–11).

But before he faded from the scene, John the Baptist gave an invitation and a warning that form a fitting climax, not only to this chapter, but also to his entire ministry. Like Moses (Deut. 11:26–28; 30:15–20), Joshua (Josh. 24:15), Elijah (1 Kings 18:21), and Jesus (John 3:18) before him, he set forth the only two choices available to lost sinners: **"He who believes in the Son has eternal life; but he who does not obey the Son will not see life, but the wrath of God abides on him."**

The blessed truth of salvation is that the one **who believes in the Son has eternal life** as a present possession, not merely as a future hope. Jesus said, "Truly, truly, I say to you, he who hears My word, and believes Him who sent Me, has eternal life, and does not come into judgment, but has passed out of death into life" (5:24; cf. 1:12; 3:15–16; 6:47; 1 John 5:10–13).

But on the other hand, the one **who does not obey the Son will not see life.** The juxtaposition of belief and disobedience is a reminder that the New Testament portrays belief in the gospel as obedience to God, an essential element of saving faith (cf. Acts 6:7; Rom. 1:5; 15:18; 16:26; 2 Thess. 1:8; Heb. 5:9; 1 Peter 1:2; 4:17). The fearful reality is that **the wrath of God** (His settled, holy displeasure against sin) continually **abides on** disobedient sinners who refuse to believe in Jesus Christ. Just as eternal life is the present possession of believers, so also is condemnation the present condition of unbelievers. The idea here is not that God will one day condemn sinners for their disobedient unbelief; they are already in a state of condemnation (3:18; 2 Peter 2:9) from which only saving faith in Jesus Christ can deliver them. The ultimate consequence of refusing to believe will be to experience God's wrath for eternity in the lake of fire (Rev. 20:10–15). But it was to save helpless, doomed sinners from that terrifying fate that God sent His Son to be the Savior of the world (1:29; 3:17; 4:42; Matt. 1:21; Rom. 5:9; 1 Thess. 1:10; 1 John 4:14).

In this way, John the Baptist clearly declared the sovereignty and supremacy of Jesus Christ, emphasizing that He alone is able to save sinful men from the consequences of their disobedience. And what John proclaimed with his lips, he exemplified with his life, actively promoting Jesus' ministry even at the expense of his own. Thus, the weight of John's witness can still be felt today—as a warning to unbelievers, that they must repent and follow Christ, and as an example to believers, that they should seek the Savior's glory rather than their own.

The Living Water
(John 4:1–26)

11

Therefore when the Lord knew that the Pharisees had heard that Jesus was making and baptizing more disciples than John (although Jesus Himself was not baptizing, but His disciples were), He left Judea and went away again into Galilee. And He had to pass through Samaria. So He came to a city of Samaria called Sychar, near the parcel of ground that Jacob gave to his son Joseph; and Jacob's well was there. So Jesus, being wearied from His journey, was sitting thus by the well. It was about the sixth hour. There came a woman of Samaria to draw water. Jesus said to her, "Give Me a drink." For His disciples had gone away into the city to buy food. Therefore the Samaritan woman said to Him, "How is it that You, being a Jew, ask me for a drink since I am a Samaritan woman?" (For Jews have no dealings with Samaritans.) Jesus answered and said to her, "If you knew the gift of God, and who it is who says to you, 'Give Me a drink,' you would have asked Him, and He would have given you living water." She said to Him, "Sir, You have nothing to draw with and the well is deep; where then do You get that living water? You are not greater than our father Jacob, are You, who gave us the well, and drank of it himself and his sons and his cattle?" Jesus answered and said to her, "Everyone who drinks of this water will thirst again; but whoever drinks of the water that I will give him shall never thirst; but the water that I will give him will become in him a well of water springing up to eternal life." The woman said to Him, "Sir, give me this water, so I will not be thirsty nor come all the way here to draw." He said to her, "Go, call your husband and come here." The woman answered and said, "I have no husband." Jesus said to her, "You have correctly said, 'I have no husband'; for you have had five husbands, and the one whom you now have is not your husband; this you have said truly." The woman said to Him, "Sir, I perceive that You are a prophet. "Our fathers worshiped in this mountain, and you people say that in Jerusalem is the place where men ought to worship." Jesus said to her, "Woman, believe Me, an hour is coming when neither in this mountain nor in Jerusalem will you worship the Father. You worship what you do not know; we worship what we know, for salvation is from the Jews. But an hour is coming, and now is, when the true worshipers will worship the Father in spirit and truth; for such people the Father seeks to be His worshipers. God is spirit, and those who worship Him must worship in spirit and truth." The woman said to Him, "I know that Messiah is coming (He who is called Christ); when that One comes, He will declare all things to us." Jesus said to her, "I who speak to you am He." (4:1–26)

The hope of the Messiah lies at the heart of the Old Testament. From the third chapter of Genesis (Gen. 3:15) to the third chapter of Malachi (Mal. 3:1), the Hebrew Scriptures repeatedly proclaim that the Savior is coming. In fact, all three parts of the Old Testament canon—the Law, the Psalms, and the Prophets—make precise predictions about Him and His ministry (cf. Luke 24:25–27, 44–45).

As the generations of Israel became familiar with these passages, they took God's promises to heart. Though they waited eagerly, year after year, for their coming Savior, their sense of expectation only increased as the centuries passed. Thus, by the time of Jesus' birth, anticipation regarding the Messiah had reached an all-time high.

But then the unthinkable happened. The Messiah came, and Israel rejected Him. Under the influence of their religious leaders, the people refused to embrace the One for whom they had been waiting and instead had Him murdered.

It was not that the evidence was unclear. In fact, "the Old Testament, written over a one-thousand-year period, contains nearly three hundred references to the coming Messiah. All of these were fulfilled in

Jesus Christ, and they establish a solid confirmation of His credentials as the Messiah." (Josh McDowell, *The New Evidence That Demands a Verdict* [Nashville: Thomas Nelson, 1999], 164). Instead, it was that Israel's religious establishment felt threatened by Jesus' ministry—He challenged their authority and confronted their hypocrisy.

In response, the Pharisees stubbornly refused to believe the truth about Him (7:48). They openly contradicted His teachings, and scorned any who followed Him. When they heard the astonished crowds wondering about Jesus, "This man cannot be the Son of David [i.e., the Messiah], can he?" (Matt. 12:23), the Pharisees indignantly declared, "This man casts out demons only by Beelzebul the ruler of the demons" (v. 24). The very fact that He cast out demons was powerful evidence of His authenticity. Yet, the religious leaders were so obstinate in their unbelief that they attempted to turn even that against Him.

Eventually, in the most heinous and apostate act in its history, Israel delivered its Messiah into "the hands of godless men and put Him to death" (Acts 2:23):

> But the chief priests and the elders persuaded the crowds to ask for Barabbas and to put Jesus to death. But the governor said to them, "Which of the two do you want me to release for you?" And they said, "Barabbas." Pilate said to them, "Then what shall I do with Jesus who is called Christ?" They all said, "Crucify Him!" And he said, "Why, what evil has He done?" But they kept shouting all the more, saying, "Crucify Him!" When Pilate saw that he was accomplishing nothing, but rather that a riot was starting, he took water and washed his hands in front of the crowd, saying, "I am innocent of this Man's blood; see to that yourselves." And all the people said, "His blood shall be on us and on our children!" (Matt. 27:20–25)

But the crowds were completely wrong about Him. Although dozens of pseudo-messiahs have come and gone, an examination of the Old Testament data points unmistakably to Jesus Christ as the true Messiah.

For instance, the Messiah's ancestry is clearly delineated in the Old Testament. God promised that the coming Savior would be a descendant of Abraham (Gen. 12:7; cf. Gal. 3:16), of Jacob (Deut. 18:18; cf. Acts 3:22–23), of Judah (Gen. 49:10), of Jesse (Isa. 11:1–2; cf. v. 10; Rom. 15:12), and of David (Jer. 23:5–6; cf. 33:15–16; 2 Sam. 7:12–14; Heb. 1:5). Jesus Christ's lineage met every one of these requirements (Matt. 1:1, 5–6; Rom. 9:3–5; Heb. 7:14; cf. Luke 1:32; 3:31–33; Rom. 1:3; 2 Tim. 2:8; Rev. 5:5; 22:16).

Furthermore, the Messiah would have to be descended from not one, but two of David's sons. The kingship was passed down through his son Solomon, who succeeded him on the throne. But one of Solomon's descendants, the wicked king Jeconiah (also called "Coniah" or "Jehoiachin") was cursed by the Lord: "Thus says the Lord, 'Write this man down childless, a man who will not prosper in his days; for no man of his descendants will prosper sitting on the throne of David or ruling again in Judah'" (Jer. 22:30). Jeconiah would be childless, in the sense that none of his descendants would ever sit on Israel's throne. Yet God promised that the Messiah will reign as Israel's king on David's throne (2 Sam. 7:12; Jer. 23:5–6; cf. Luke 1:32). This seeming conundrum was resolved in Jesus Christ. He was descended from the royal, Solomonic line through his legal (though not biological) father, Joseph (Matt. 1:11–12). But His physical descent from David came through another of David's sons, Nathan, the ancestor of His mother, Mary (Luke 3:31). Thus, Jesus' virgin birth allowed Him to be both the legal heir to David's throne and his biological descendant (as God had promised; cf. Acts 13:22–23), while also avoiding the curse on Jeconiah's family line.

The Messiah's identity may be further narrowed by the specific predictions regarding His birth.

First, He had to be born in a specific place: "But as for you, Bethlehem Ephrathah, too little to be among the clans of Judah, from you One will go forth for Me to be ruler in Israel. His goings forth are from long ago, from the days of eternity" (Mic. 5:2; cf. Matt. 2:1–6). The Bible records that "Jesus was born in Bethlehem of Judea" (Matt. 2:1; cf. Luke 2:4–15).

Second, the Messiah had to be born within a specific time frame. Since He was to be from the tribe of Judah (cf. Gen. 49:10), He had to come before the individual tribes lost their identity following the Roman destruction of the temple with all its genealogical records. In fact, Daniel's prophecy of the seventy weeks actually predicted that the Messiah would be killed before the temple was destroyed (Dan. 9:26). That incredible prophecy also singled out the exact day, nearly five centuries in the future, that the Messiah would present Himself to the nation (9:25). On that very day, Jesus entered Jerusalem to the adulation of the crowds hailing Him as the Messiah (Matt. 21:1–11).

Finally, the Messiah would be born under unique and miraculous circumstances to a special person: "Therefore the Lord Himself will give you a sign: Behold, a virgin will be with child and bear a son, and she will call His name Immanuel" (Isa. 7:14). Jesus Christ alone in human history was born of a virgin:

> But when he had considered this, behold, an angel of the Lord appeared to him in a dream, saying, "Joseph, son of David, do not be afraid to take Mary as your wife; for the Child who has been conceived in her is of the Holy Spirit. She will bear a Son; and you shall call His name Jesus, for He will save His people from their sins." Now all this took place to fulfill what was spoken by the Lord through the prophet:

"Behold, the virgin shall be with child and shall bear a son, and they shall call His name Immanuel," which translated means, "God with us." And Joseph awoke from his sleep and did as the angel of the Lord commanded him, and took Mary as his wife, but kept her a virgin until she gave birth to a Son; and he called His name Jesus. (Matt. 1:20–25)

The Old Testament also made specific predictions about the Messiah's earthly ministry. He would be heralded by a forerunner (Isa. 40:3). He would minister in Galilee (9:1–2). He would perform miracles (35:5–6). Again, Jesus met the criteria perfectly (John 1:23; Matt. 4:12–16; 9:35).

The Messiah's death was also foretold in great detail, and Jesus fulfilled every prophecy. The Old Testament predicted that Messiah would be betrayed by someone close to Him. Psalm 41:9 reads, "Even my close friend in whom I trusted, who ate my bread, has lifted up his heel against me." That prophecy was fulfilled by Judas, of whom Jesus declared, "I do not speak of all of you. I know the ones I have chosen; but it is that the Scripture may be fulfilled, 'He who eats my bread has lifted up his heel against Me'" (13:18; cf. Luke 22:3–4). Even the exact amount Judas was paid, thirty pieces of silver (Matt. 26:14–15), was predicted in the Old Testament (Zech. 11:12).

The Old Testament prophesied that the Messiah would be executed with wicked men: "Therefore, I will allot Him a portion with the great, and He will divide the booty with the strong; because He poured out Himself to death, and was numbered with the transgressors; yet He Himself bore the sin of many, and interceded for the transgressors" (Isa. 53:12); when Christ was crucified, "two robbers were crucified with Him, one on the right and one on the left" (Matt. 27:38). Although none of His bones would be broken (Ps. 34:20), the Messiah would be pierced (Zech. 12:10), which was exactly what happened to Jesus (John 19:33–34; 36–37). Finally, the Messiah was to be buried in a rich man's grave (Isa. 53:9), as in fact Jesus was (Matt. 27:57–60).

The evidence, then, unambiguously and overwhelmingly points to Jesus of Nazareth as the Messiah. Only He fulfilled these and all other Old Testament messianic prophecies.

The apostle John obviously understood the weighty evidence that confirmed Jesus' authenticity. In fact, the reason he wrote his gospel was to confirm the obvious—"that Jesus is the Christ, the Son of God" (John 20:31). And it is in keeping with this purpose that John relates the story of Jesus' encounter with a Samaritan woman.

The woman's reaction to Jesus, as related in John's account, strongly suggests that she embraced Him as her Lord and Savior. But her conversion is not the main point of this passage. The central truth of this section is found in Jesus' revelation of Himself as the Messiah (v. 26). He did so here for the first time—and to a most unlikely non-Jew.

But why did He decide not to first declare His messiahship to the most politically correct and influential target—the Jewish religious leaders? Why choose to reveal that monumental truth to an obscure, despised, immoral, Samaritan woman? The answer lies in the sweeping truth that in the matter of salvation, "God is not one to show partiality" (Acts 10:34; cf. Deut. 10:17; 2 Chron. 19:7; Rom. 2:11; 10:12; Gal. 2:6; 3:28; Eph. 6:9; Col. 3:11).

The contrast between the Samaritan woman and Nicodemus, for example, was striking. He was a devoutly religious Jew; she was an immoral Samaritan. He was a learned theologian; she was an uneducated peasant woman. He recognized Jesus as a teacher sent by God; she had no clue who He was. He was wealthy; she was poor. He was a member of the social elite of Israel; she was the dregs of Samaritan society—an outcast among outcasts, since the Jews regarded all Samaritans as unclean pariahs.

Jesus' revelation of Himself to this woman demonstrated that God's saving love knows no limitations; it transcends all barriers of race, gender, ethnicity, and religious tradition. In contrast to human love, divine love is indiscriminate and all-encompassing (cf. 3:16). That Jesus chose to make Himself known first not only to a Samaritan, but also to a woman, was a stinging rebuke to members of Israel's religious elite— who rejected Him even when He did reveal Himself to them.

The story of the Lord's encounter with the woman at the well unfolds in four scenes: the circumstances, the contact, the conviction, and the Christ.

The Circumstances

Therefore when the Lord knew that the Pharisees had heard that Jesus was making and baptizing more disciples than John (although Jesus Himself was not baptizing, but His disciples were), He left Judea and went away again into Galilee. And He had to pass through Samaria. So He came to a city of Samaria called Sychar, near the parcel of ground that Jacob gave to his son Joseph; and Jacob's well was there. So Jesus, being wearied from His journey, was sitting thus by the well. It was about the sixth hour. (4:1–6)

Word of Jesus' growing popularity reached **the Pharisees,** who **heard that** He **was making and baptizing more disciples than**

John. The parenthetical note that **Jesus Himself was not baptizing, but His disciples were** is impossible to reconcile with the doctrine of baptismal regeneration, the false teaching that baptism is necessary for salvation. Surely the Lord Jesus Christ, who came to "seek and to save that which was lost" (Luke 19:10), would Himself have done whatever was necessary to bring sinners to salvation.

As they had done with John (cf. 1:19–25), the Jewish authorities (particularly the **Pharisees;** cf. 1:24–25) viewed Jesus with suspicion. He too proclaimed the kingdom of God, called for repentance (Matt. 4:17), and baptized (through His disciples) those who repented (cf. the discussion of 1:26 in chapter 4 of this volume). As noted in the previous chapter of this volume, some of John the Baptist's disciples were also disturbed by Jesus' growing popularity at their master's expense. Although John confirmed that his ministry was giving way to the ministry of Jesus (3:30), it was not yet time for the forerunner to fade completely from the scene. His work was not done.

Therefore, the Lord **left Judea and went away again into Galilee.** He did not want a public rivalry to develop between His followers and those of John. He also knew that, in His Father's sovereign plan, a public confrontation with the Jewish authorities was still premature (cf. 7:30; 8:20).

On His return to Galilee, Jesus **had to pass through Samaria.** It was not geographic necessity that compelled Him to do so, despite the fact that it was the most direct of several routes. The road through Samaria was shorter than the coastal road or the road on the east side of the Jordan, which is why many Jews traveled on it, especially at the time of the major religious festivals. But so great was their disdain for the Samaritans that the stricter Jews avoided traveling through Samaria altogether. They preferred instead to be defiled by a lesser evil, thus they would cross the Jordan and travel up its east bank through the largely Gentile region of Perea. They would then cross back into Galilee north of Samaria. Jesus could have easily gone that way.

But the Lord was compelled to pass through Samaria and stop in a certain village, not to save time and steps, but because He had a divine appointment there. John frequently used the verb *dei* (**had to**) to speak of Jesus fulfilling the mission given Him by the Father (3:14; 9:4; 10:16; 12:34; 20:9). He was always conscious of doing the Father's will, which was why He came to earth (6:38; cf. 4:34; 5:30; 17:4; Matt. 26:39).

As He traveled north toward Galilee, Jesus **came to a city of Samaria called Sychar** (probably the modern village of Askar), located on the slope of Mount Ebal, opposite Mt. Gerizim (cf. Deut. 11:29; Josh. 8:33). **Samaria** was the capital city of the northern kingdom, called Israel. The nation split in two after Solomon's reign. King Omri named the city the capital of the northern kingdom (1 Kings 16:24). The name came to refer to the whole region and sometimes to the whole northern kingdom, which went into captivity in 722 B.C. (2 Kings 17:1–6) at the hands of the Assyrians. **Sychar,** a town in the district of Samaria, was **near the parcel of ground that Jacob gave to his son Joseph.** When he returned to the land of Canaan after twenty years in Haran (Gen. 27:43; 31:38), Jacob bought a piece of land near the Old Testament city of Shechem (33:18–19), not far from Sychar. Then, shortly before his death, Jacob bequeathed that property to his son Joseph (Gen. 48:22; "portion" [Heb., *shechem*] lit. means "shoulder," or "ridge"). Many years later, Joseph was buried there after Israel conquered the land under Joshua (Josh. 24:32). It was thus a familiar and important site to both Jews and Samaritans.

According to well-attested ancient tradition, **Jacob's well** was about half a mile south of Sychar. The precise location has been well established by tradition, and the well sits today near an unfinished Orthodox church. It was a deep well (approx. 100 feet), fed by a running spring (the word translated "well" in vv. 11–12 refers to a cistern or dugout well, while the word used here denotes a spring or fountain). The **sixth hour,** by Jewish reckoning, would have been the sixth hour after sunrise at about 6:00 A.M.; that is, noon. Jesus, **being wearied from His journey, was sitting thus by the well.** As the incarnate divine Word (1:14) Jesus was without sin (8:46; 2 Cor. 5:21; 1 Peter 2:22; 1 John 3:5). But He was still subject to the physical limitations of His full humanity. As Gerald L. Borchert observes,

> It is absolutely crucial to recognize that all the Gospel writers were fully aware of the humanity of Jesus. The strategic Christian doctrine of the incarnation is not merely a theological assertion about the deity of Jesus; it is equally a theological assertion about his humanity. Heretical tendencies result when either element is omitted or submerged. Jesus was really a mortal who experienced the bodily weaknesses of being human, even though he did not suffer the human curse of sin (cf. Heb. 4:15). (*John 1–11,* The New American Commentary [Nashville: Broadman & Holman, 2002], 201)

The stage was set; Jesus was in the right place at the right time for an encounter in God's will. He was in reality keeping a divine appointment that He Himself had made before the foundation of the world.

THE CONTACT

There came a woman of Samaria to draw water. Jesus said to her, "Give Me a drink." For His disciples had gone away into the city

to buy food. Therefore the Samaritan woman said to Him, "How is it that You, being a Jew, ask me for a drink since I am a Samaritan woman?" (For Jews have no dealings with Samaritans.) Jesus answered and said to her, "If you knew the gift of God, and who it is who says to you, 'Give Me a drink,' you would have asked Him, and He would have given you living water." She said to Him, "Sir, You have nothing to draw with and the well is deep; where then do You get that living water? You are not greater than our father Jacob, are You, who gave us the well, and drank of it himself and his sons and his cattle?" Jesus answered and said to her, "Everyone who drinks of this water will thirst again; but whoever drinks of the water that I will give him shall never thirst; but the water that I will give him will become in him a well of water springing up to eternal life." The woman said to Him, "Sir, give me this water, so I will not be thirsty nor come all the way here to draw." (4:7–15)

As Jesus sat beside the well that evening, tired and thirsty from His journey, **there came a woman of Samaria to draw water.** The cool of the evening was the time when women customarily performed that chore (Gen. 24:11). This woman came at high noon, perhaps because of her desire to avoid public shame. What was also unusual was that this woman came such a long distance to this well when there were other sources of water closer to the village. But she, for reasons that will soon become evident, was an outcast. She would rather walk the extra distance in the hottest time of the day than face the hostility and scorn of the other women at the closer well earlier or later in the day.

The Lord's simple request, **"Give Me a drink,"** was in that culture a shocking breach of social custom. Men did not speak with women in public—not even their wives. Nor did rabbis associate with immoral women (cf. Luke 7:39). Most significant of all in this situation, Jews customarily wanted nothing to do with Samaritans (cf. the discussion of v. 9 below). But Jesus shattered all of those barriers. The parenthetical note that the **disciples had gone away into the city to buy food** explains why Jesus was sitting at the well by Himself. It also indicates that our Lord did not pay attention to the taboos of the strict Jews, who would not eat food handled by Samaritans.

Taken aback that Jesus spoke to her, **the Samaritan woman said** in astonishment, **"How is it that You, being a Jew, ask me for a drink since I am a Samaritan woman?"** As noted above, it was culturally incorrect for a man, especially a rabbi, to speak to any woman, particularly an immoral outcast. But her question reveals that what she found most surprising was that Jesus, **being a Jew,** would speak to her, **a**

Samaritan woman since, as John explained in an understated way, **Jews have no dealings with Samaritans.** Even more astounding was His willingness to ceremonially defile Himself by drinking from her water pot, since He had no vessel of His own from which to drink (v. 11). (The word translated **dealings** in John's explanatory note literally means "to use the same utensils.") But Jesus was the infinitely holy God in human flesh. He could not be defiled by a Samaritan water pot. Whatever He touched—even corpses (Luke 7:12–15) or lepers (Matt. 8:2–3)— did not taint Him, but instead became clean.

The bitter rivalry between the **Jews** and the **Samaritans** had been going on for centuries. After the fall of the northern kingdom to the Assyrians, the ten tribes of

> Israel [were] carried away into exile from their own land to Assyria . . . [and] the king of Assyria brought men from Babylon and from Cuthah and from Avva and from Hamath and Sephar-vaim, and settled them in the cities of Samaria in place of the sons of Israel. So they possessed Samaria and lived in its cities. (2 Kings 17:23–24).

The foreign non-Jews intermarried with the population of Jews who had not been deported, forming a mixed race known as the Samaritans (the name derives from the region and capital city, both called Samaria). The new settlers brought their idolatrous religion with them (2 Kings 17:29–31), which became intermingled with the worship of Yahweh (vv. 25–28, 32–33, 41). In time, however, the Samaritans abandoned their idols and worshiped Yahweh alone, after their own fashion (for example, they accepted only the Pentateuch as canonical Scripture, and worshiped God on Mount Gerizim, not at Jerusalem).

When the Jewish exiles returned to Jerusalem under Ezra and Nehemiah, their first priority was to rebuild the temple. Professing loyalty to Israel's God, the Samaritans offered their assistance (Ezra 4:1–2). The Jews' blunt refusal (Ezra 4:3) enraged the Samaritans, who then became their bitter enemies (Ezra 4:4ff.; Neh. 4:1–3, 7ff.). Rebuffed in their attempt to worship at Jerusalem, the Samaritans built their own temple on Mount Gerizim (c. 400 B.C.). The Jews later destroyed that temple during the intertestamental period, further worsening relations between the two groups.

After centuries of mistrust, there was a deep animosity between the Jews and the Samaritans. The writer of the apocryphal book of Ecclesiasticus expressed the scorn and contempt the Jews felt for the Samaritans. Claiming that God detested the Samaritan people, he derisively referred to them as "the stupid people living at Shechem" (50:25–26). The Jewish leaders of Jesus' day manifested this same prejudice. In fact, when they wanted to insult Jesus, the worst they could do was to call Him a Samaritan (8:48). The Samaritans, of course, reciprocated the Jews' hostility—as was illustrated when one of their villages refused to receive Jesus because He was on His way to Jerusalem (Luke 9:51–53).

In response to the woman's query, **Jesus answered and said to her, "If you knew the gift of God, and who it is who says to you, 'Give Me a drink,' you would have asked Him, and He would have given you living water."** The Lord's reply turned the tables on her. When the conversation began, He was the thirsty one, and she the one with the water. Now He spoke as if she were the thirsty one and He the one with the water. The woman's reply reflected her confusion. Still thinking in terms of physical water she asked, **"Sir, You have nothing to draw with and the well is deep** (cf. the discussion of v. 6 above); **where then do You get that living water?"** She did not understand that Jesus was talking about spiritual realities. The **living water** that He offered her was salvation in all its fullness, including forgiveness of sin and the ability and desire to live an obedient life that glorifies God.

The Old Testament uses the metaphor of living water to describe the spiritual cleansing and new life that comes at salvation through the transforming power of the Holy Spirit. Disobedient Israel was guilty of having foolishly "forsaken [God], the fountain of living waters, to hew for themselves cisterns, broken cisterns that can hold no water" (Jer. 2:13). Later Jeremiah warned that "all who forsake [the Lord] will be put to shame. Those who turn away on earth will be written down, because they have forsaken the fountain of living water, even the Lord" (17:13). Both passages emphasize that God is the only source of salvation; He alone is the "fountain of life" (Ps. 36:9), and in Him the redeemed "will joyously draw water from the springs of salvation" (Isa. 12:3; cf. Isa. 1:16–18). Isaiah 55:1 echoes God's gracious offer of salvation: "Ho! Every one who thirsts, come to the waters," and this invitation is reiterated in the book of Revelation (21:6; 22:17). As God Himself promised regarding the new covenant:

> I will sprinkle clean water on you, and you will be clean; I will cleanse you from all your filthiness and from all your idols. Moreover, I will give you a new heart and put a new spirit within you; and I will remove the heart of stone from your flesh and give you a heart of flesh. I will put My Spirit within you and cause you to walk in My statutes, and you will be careful to observe My ordinances. (Ezek. 36:25–27; cf. Isa. 44:3)

John applies these themes to Jesus as the living water, which symbolizes eternal life (v. 14; 6:35; 7:37–39).

The woman's question, **"You are not greater than our father**

Jacob, are You, who gave us the well, and drank of it himself and his sons and his cattle?" expects a negative answer. She was skeptical of this stranger's ability to provide the living water He offered. Even the revered patriarch **Jacob** could not provide water without expending the effort to dig this well. And in her mind this Jewish traveler certainly was not greater than Jacob. But as D. A. Carson notes, "Misunderstanding combines with irony to make the woman twice wrong: the 'living water' Jesus offers does not come from an ordinary well, and Jesus is in fact far greater than the patriarch Jacob" (*The Gospel According to John,* The Pillar New Testament Commentary [Grand Rapids: Eerdmans, 1991], 219).

Patiently, **Jesus answered** her skeptical question **and said to her, "Everyone who drinks of this water will thirst again; but whoever drinks of the water that I will give him shall never thirst; but the water that I will give him will become in him a well of water springing up to eternal life."** Jacob was rightly accorded a place of honor by both Jews and Samaritans. Yet, as Jesus pointed out, **everyone who** drank **of** the **water** from his well would **thirst again.** It is a measure of Jesus' incomparable greatness that **whoever drinks of the water that** He **will give him shall never thirst; but the water that** He **will give him will become in him a well of water springing up to eternal life** (cf. Isa. 12:3). Here was the living water of spiritual life (cf. 7:38) that her parched soul desperately needed (cf. Ps. 143:6).

Still thinking primarily on the physical level, she replied eagerly, **"Sir, give me this water, so I will not be thirsty nor come all the way here to draw."** Her response parallels that of the Galilean crowd, who responded to Jesus' teaching about the bread from heaven, "Lord, always give us this [physical] bread" (6:34; cf. v. 26). Whatever else the living water did, she was ready to receive it if it would eliminate her daily trip to the well and give her also eternal life.

At this point, the woman does not appear to have been clear on the matter of spiritual transformation. Jesus had spoken to her about the water of eternal life, and she seemed willing to accept it, but no conditions had been stated. As with any lost sinner, this woman needed to understand two crucial issues before she could receive the living water of eternal life—namely, the reality of her sin and His identity as Savior. In these last two points, Jesus addressed both of those issues.

THE CONVICTION

He said to her, "Go, call your husband and come here." The woman answered and said, "I have no husband." Jesus said to her, "You have correctly said, 'I have no husband'; for you have

had five husbands, and the one whom you now have is not your husband; this you have said truiy." The woman said to Him, "Sir, I perceive that You are a prophet. (4:16–19)

Since the woman failed to grasp the nature of the water He spoke of, Jesus moved the conversation to her need for repentance and salvation from sin. His command, **"Go, call your husband and come here,"** exposed the heart of the issue—her sin. Those who truly thirst for the righteousness God provides in salvation will confess and forsake their wicked ways (Isa. 55:6–7). Scripture knows nothing of a salvation without repentance, and that always involves turning from sin (Acts 26:19–20; 1 Thess. 1:9). Jesus did not come to grant sinners perfection in the next life while leaving them to continue in sin in this one (cf. Jer. 7:9–10; Rom. 3:5–8; 6:1–2). On the contrary, He "gave Himself for us to redeem us from every lawless deed, and to purify for Himself a people for His own possession, zealous for good deeds" (Titus 2:14; cf. Acts 3:26; Eph. 5:25–27; Col. 1:20–23). As a result, those who come to Him and truly receive the living water of eternal salvation have "been freed from sin, [and become] slaves of righteousness . . . and enslaved to God" (Rom. 6:18, 22; cf. Eph. 6:6; Col. 3:24; 1 Peter 2:16). Jesus responded to the woman's interest by offering her the opportunity to confess her sins and receive forgiveness to be purified and delivered from iniquity to righteousness.

Shocked and shamed by the unnerving realization that Jesus knew all about her morally debased life, the woman answered evasively, **"I have no husband."** Although she was not lying, she was not telling the whole truth either. But her desperate attempt to conceal her sin from Jesus was futile; His devastating reply forced her to face it: **"You have correctly said, 'I have no husband'; for you have had five husbands, and the one whom you now have is not your husband; this you have said truly."** While commending her for her truthfulness (as far as it went), Jesus nonetheless unmasked her sin. It should also be noted that by refusing to call the man she was currently living with her husband, Jesus rejected the notion that merely living together constitutes marriage. The Bible views marriage as a formal, legal, public covenant between a man and a woman (Matt. 19:5–6).

Shaken by Jesus' amazingly accurate knowledge of her sinful life, the woman said, **"Sir, I perceive that You are a prophet."** By calling Him a **prophet,** she affirmed that His knowledge of her sordid lifestyle was accurate. No longer did she attempt to hide her sin; rather, this statement constituted a confession by which she was turning from her sin, hoping to receive the water of eternal life.

THE CHRIST

"Our fathers worshiped in this mountain, and you people say that in Jerusalem is the place where men ought to worship." Jesus said to her, "Woman, believe Me, an hour is coming when neither in this mountain nor in Jerusalem will you worship the Father. You worship what you do not know; we worship what we know, for salvation is from the Jews. But an hour is coming, and now is, when the true worshipers will worship the Father in spirit and truth; for such people the Father seeks to be His worshipers. God is spirit, and those who worship Him must worship in spirit and truth." The woman said to Him, "I know that Messiah is coming (He who is called Christ); when that One comes, He will declare all things to us." Jesus said to her, "I who speak to you am He." (4:20–26)

Having been convicted of her sin and need for forgiveness, and having repented and agreed with Jesus' indictment, the woman wondered where she should go to meet God and seek His grace and salvation. Since Jesus was obviously a prophet of God, she reasoned that He would know, so she said, **"Our fathers worshiped in this mountain, and you people say that in Jerusalem is the place where men ought to worship."** Her comment highlighted one of the major points of contention between Jews and Samaritans. Both believed that under the old covenant God directed His people to worship Him in a specific location (cf. Deut. 12:5; 16:2; 26:2). The Samaritans, accepting only the Pentateuch as canonical, chose Mount Gerizim. It was at nearby Shechem that Abraham first built an altar to God (Gen. 12:6–7), and it was from Mount Gerizim that the Israelites proclaimed the blessings of obedience to God's commandments (Deut. 11:29). The Jews, accepting the complete Old Testament canon, recognized that God had chosen Jerusalem as the place where He was to be worshiped (2 Chron. 6:6; cf. Pss. 48:1–2; 78:68–69; 132:13).

Jesus' unexpected reply was that the issue would soon be irrelevant. In the near future, true worship would take place **neither in this mountain** (Gerizim) **nor in Jerusalem.** During the Jewish revolt against Rome a few decades later (A.D. 70), the temple at Jerusalem would be destroyed, and thousands of Samaritans would be slaughtered on Mount Gerizim. More significantly, the new covenant renders all external ceremonies and rituals, whether Jewish or Samaritan, obsolete.

However, at the time of Jesus' dialogue with the woman, the Jews were right and the Samaritans wrong since the new covenant had not yet been initiated. Thus Jesus said, **"You worship what you do not know; we worship what we know, for salvation is from the Jews."**

Because they rejected most of the Old Testament, the Samaritans lacked the full revelation that it contained. There is a twofold sense in which **salvation is from the Jews;** first, the revelation of salvation came first to them and then to the rest of the world (Rom. 3:1–2; 9:3–5); and, second, the source of salvation—namely, the Messiah—was Himself a Jew (Rom. 9:5).

Jesus' point was that, under the new covenant, the place of worship will not be an issue, but rather the nature of worship. **"An hour is coming,"** Jesus informed the woman, **'and now is, when the true worshipers will worship the Father in spirit and truth." Spirit** does not refer to the Holy Spirit but the human spirit. Worship must be internal, not external conformity to ceremonies and rituals. It must be from the heart. **Truth** calls for this heart worship to be consistent with what Scripture teaches and centered on the incarnate Word. The worship of neither the Samaritans nor the Jews could be characterized as being **in spirit and truth,** even though the Jews had a more complete understanding of the **truth.** Both groups focused on external factors. They conformed outwardly to regulations, observed rituals, and offered sacrifices. But the time had arrived, since the Messiah had come, when true worshipers would no longer be identified by where they worshiped. True worshipers are those who **worship the Father in spirit and truth.** Paul calls them "the true circumcision, who worship in the Spirit of God and glory in Christ Jesus and put no confidence in the flesh" (Phil. 3:3). It is **such people the Father seeks to be His worshipers** by sovereignly drawing them to Himself (6:44, 65).

The phrase **God is spirit** is the classic biblical definition of the nature of God. Despite the heretical teaching of false cults, God is not an exalted man (Num. 23:19), "for a spirit does not have flesh and bones" (Luke 24:39). He is "the invisible God" (Col. 1:15; cf. 1 Tim. 1:17; Heb. 11:27), who "dwells in unapproachable light [cf. Ps. 104:2], whom no man has seen or can see" (1 Tim. 6:16; cf. Ex. 33:20; John 1:18; 6:46). Had He not revealed Himself in Scripture and in Jesus Christ, God would be utterly incomprehensible.

Because God is spirit, those who would truly worship Him **must worship in spirit and truth.** True worship does not consist of mere outward conformity to religious standards and duties (Isa. 29:13; 48:1; Jer. 12:1–2; Matt. 15:7–9), but emanates from the inner **spirit.** It must also be consistent with the **truth** God has revealed about Himself in His Word. The extremes of dead orthodoxy (truth and no spirit) and zealous heterodoxy (spirit and no truth) must be avoided.

Still unable to fully comprehend what Jesus was telling her, **the woman said to Him, "I know that Messiah is coming (He who is called Christ); when that One comes, He will declare all things to**

us." She was still confused, but expressed her hope that one day the Messiah (whose coming the Samaritans also anticipated, based on Deut. 18:18) would clarify all of these vexing religious questions.

The story reached its powerful, dramatic climax in Jesus' reply, **"I who speak to you am He."** He had avoided such a forthright declaration to the Jewish people (cf. Matt. 16:20), because of the crassly political and militaristic expectations they had for the Messiah; they hoped for someone who would lead a revolt to throw off the yoke of the hated Romans (cf. John 6:15). The faith of this Samaritan woman, on the other hand, was not obstructed by such self-styled misconceptions (as her response in v. 29 indicates). The word **He** is not in the original text. Our Lord actually said, "I who speak to you am." Here is another one of the "I am" statements that are so common in this gospel (cf. 8:58). Twenty-three times our Lord says, "I am," and seven times adds rich metaphors (cf. 6:35, 41, 48, 51; 8:12; 10:7, 9, 11, 14; 11:25; 14:6; 15:1, 5).

Jesus' words must have rocked the woman to the core of her being. The man who just a few minutes earlier had made a simple request for a drink of water now claimed to be the long-awaited Messiah. Unlike Nicodemus, she knew nothing of any signs and miracles Jesus had performed. But merely because of what He knew about her the woman did not doubt the veracity of His claim. That was great, God-given trust. Indeed, she went and proclaimed it in her village, a fact that strongly suggests that she had genuinely come to saving faith.

Jesus' conversation with the woman at the well illustrates three nonnegotiable truths about salvation. First, salvation comes only to those who recognize their desperate need for spiritual life they do not have. Living water will be received only by those who realize that they are spiritually thirsty. Second, salvation comes only to those who confess and repent of their sin and desire forgiveness. Before this promiscuous woman could embrace the Savior, she had to acknowledge the full weight of her iniquity. And, third, salvation comes only to those who embrace Jesus Christ as their Messiah and sin bearer. After all, salvation is found in no one else (cf. 14:6; Acts 4:12).

The Savior of the World
(John 4:27–42)

12

At this point His disciples came, and they were amazed that He had been speaking with a woman, yet no one said, "What do You seek?" or, "Why do You speak with her?" So the woman left her waterpot, and went into the city and said to the men, "Come, see a man who told me all the things that I have done; this is not the Christ, is it?" They went out of the city, and were coming to Him. Meanwhile the disciples were urging Him, saying, "Rabbi, eat." But He said to them, "I have food to eat that you do not know about." So the disciples were saying to one another, "No one brought Him anything to eat, did he?" Jesus said to them, "My food is to do the will of Him who sent Me and to accomplish His work. Do you not say, 'There are yet four months, and then comes the harvest'? Behold, I say to you, lift up your eyes and look on the fields, that they are white for harvest. Already he who reaps is receiving wages and is gathering fruit for life eternal; so that he who sows and he who reaps may rejoice together. For in this case the saying is true, 'One sows and another reaps.' I sent you to reap that for which you have not labored; others have labored and you have entered into their labor." From that city many of the Samaritans believed in Him because of the word of the

woman who testified, "He told me all the things that I have done." So when the Samaritans came to Jesus, they were asking Him to stay with them; and He stayed there two days. Many more believed because of His word; and they were saying to the woman, "It is no longer because of what you said that we believe, for we have heard for ourselves and know that this One is indeed the Savior of the world." (4:27–42)

Israel is a nation uniquely blessed by God. Of no other people did He say, "You only have I chosen among all the families of the earth" (Amos 3:2). Or as Moses reminded the Israelites, "You are a holy people to the Lord your God; the Lord your God has chosen you to be a people for His own possession out of all the peoples who are on the face of the earth" (Deut. 7:6; cf. 10:15; 14:2; 26:18–19; 28:9–10; 32:9; Ex. 19:5–6; Lev. 20:26; Luke 1:54; John 4:22; Rom. 1:16; 3:1–2).

As God's chosen people, the Israelites were granted singular promises and blessings. For example, God assured Abraham that his descendants would become a great nation, and that through them the other "families of the earth will be blessed" (Gen. 12:1–3; cf. Acts 3:25). God also brought them "to a good and spacious land, to a land flowing with milk and honey" (Ex. 3:8; cf. 6:7–8; Gen. 13:14–17; 15:18; 17:8; 35:9–12; Deut. 30:5). The Lord even promised to defend them from their enemies if they faithfully obeyed Him: "Blessed are you, O Israel; who is like you, a people saved by the Lord, Who is the shield of your help and the sword of your majesty! So your enemies will cringe before you, and you will tread upon their high places" (Deut. 33:29; cf. 20:1–4; 23:14; 28:7; Gen. 49:8; Ex. 23:22; Num. 10:9; Josh. 10:24–25).

Sadly, Israel's disobedience caused the nation to be oppressed by its enemies (cf. Lev. 26:15–17; Deut. 4:27; 28:64–66; Judg. 2–16; Isa. 1:7–8; 5:5–7) and eventually conquered and sent into exile (Lev. 26:33–37; Deut. 4:27; 2 Kings 17:6–23; 18:11; 25:21; Ps. 44:11; Jer. 9:16; Lam. 1:3; Ezek. 12:15; 20:23–24; 22:15; 36:19; Amos 5:27; 7:11, 17; Zech. 7:14). Yet God's promises to bless the nation remained in force, even as they do today (Jer. 33:20–26; Rom. 9:4–5; 11:1–26). Despite Israel's continual disobedience and subsequent defeat, God's promise has never wavered:

> Thus says the Lord,
> Who gives the sun for light by day
> And the fixed order of the moon and the stars for light by night,
> Who stirs up the sea so that its waves roar;
> The Lord of hosts is His name:
> "If this fixed order departs
> From before Me," declares the Lord,
> "Then the offspring of Israel also will cease

From being a nation before Me forever."
Thus says the Lord,
"If the heavens above can be measured
And the foundations of the earth searched out below,
Then I will also cast off all the offspring of Israel
For all that they have done," declares the Lord. (Jer. 31:35–37)

As God's chosen people, Israel has every advantage. The apostle Paul, in writing to the Romans, says: "Then what advantage has the Jew? Or what is the benefit of circumcision? Great in every respect. First of all, that they were entrusted with the oracles of God" (Rom. 3:1–2). They are also the ones "to whom belongs the adoption as sons, and the glory and the covenants and the giving of the Law and the temple service and the promises, whose are the fathers, and from whom is the Christ according to the flesh, who is over all, God blessed forever. Amen" (Rom. 9:4–5). In His gracious goodness, God bestowed upon Israel privileges that no other nation has ever enjoyed.

The Lord Jesus Christ summed up the most significant privilege Israel received when He told the Samaritan woman that "salvation is from the Jews" (4:22). As noted in the previous chapter of this volume, that truth has a twofold meaning: that the gospel was preached first to the Jews (Matt. 10:5–7; 15:24; Luke 24:47; Acts 1:8; 3:26; Rom. 1:16), and that the Messiah came from the nation of Israel (Gen. 49:10; Isa. 11:1–5; cf. Matt. 1:1; Rom. 9:5; 2 Tim. 2:8).

But because "God [is not] the God of Jews only, [but] the God of Gentiles also" (Rom. 3:29), the Bible promises salvation to them as well. Isaiah 45:22 records God's gracious invitation, "Turn to Me and be saved, all the ends of the earth; for I am God, and there is no other." Later in Isaiah, God said prophetically to the Messiah: "It is too small a thing that You should be My Servant to raise up the tribes of Jacob and to restore the preserved ones of Israel; I will also make You a light of the nations so that My salvation may reach to the end of the earth" (49:6; cf. 42:6; Luke 2:32). The apostle Paul cited this verse in Acts 13:47 as his mandate for preaching the gospel to the Gentiles. And Jesus Himself, after His resurrection, declared that "repentance for forgiveness of sins would be proclaimed in His name to all the nations, beginning from Jerusalem" (Luke 24:47; cf. Acts 1:8).

As a preview of His plan for global evangelism, Jesus openly revealed Himself as the Messiah to a Samaritan woman whom He met at Jacob's well near the village of Sychar (v. 26). The woman had come to draw physical water from the well, but what she found was far greater—living water from the source of life Himself. Having acknowledged her sin and her need for a Savior, she confirmed the genuineness of her faith by immediately witnessing to others in her village (v. 29).

Verses 27–42 record the events that took place following Jesus' conversation with the woman. This passage is the first recorded instance of cross-cultural evangelism in the New Testament. It foreshadows the later spread of the gospel to the Samaritans and the Gentiles after Israel rejected salvation and the Savior (cf. Matt. 22:1–14; Luke 14:16–24). It was the unbelief and impenitence of the Jews that shut them off from divine blessing in the time of Elijah and Elisha and caused God's power and blessing to go to outcasts (Luke 4:25–30). This same unbelief set them against their only Savior.

The story that unfolds in this section reveals five subtle, yet unmistakable proofs that corroborate Jesus' claim to be the Messiah: His impeccable control of circumstances, His impact on the woman, His intimacy with the Father, His insight into men's souls, and His impression on the Samaritans.

CHRIST'S IMPECCABLE CONTROL OF CIRCUMSTANCES

At this point His disciples came, and they were amazed that He had been speaking with a woman, yet no one said, "What do You seek?" or, "Why do You speak with her?" (4:27)

The Greek phrase *epi toutō* (**at this point;** or "at that very moment") captures Jesus' complete mastery of the situation. The **disciples came** back from buying food in Sychar (v. 8) at the exact moment Jesus revealed His messiahship to the Samaritan woman. Had they returned earlier, they would have interrupted the conversation before it reached its dramatic conclusion; had they returned later, they would have missed hearing Jesus' declaration. Divine providence was at work.

The disciples were **amazed** to see that Jesus **had been speaking with a woman**—a shocking breach of societal norms, as noted in the previous chapter of this volume. In Judaism it was believed that for a rabbi to speak with a woman was at best a waste of time, and at worst a distraction from studying the Torah—which could lead to eternal damnation. That she was a Samaritan made the Lord's action even more astonishing. And had they known the woman's immoral background, the disciples would have been completely stunned. How could their Master have anything to do with such a person? Of all people, why would He choose to reveal His messiahship to her? Nonetheless, their respect for Jesus was such that they knew better than to interrupt the conversation. Therefore, though these were exactly their thoughts, they did not ask the woman, **"What do You seek?"** or ask Jesus, **"Why do You speak with her?"** They had already learned that Jesus was not bound by Jewish expectations, traditions, and prejudices, and that He had good reasons for doing what He did.

There was an important lesson here for the disciples to learn. Although the gospel would be preached first to Israel (Matt. 10:5–6; 15:24), it would not be preached exclusively to Israel (Isa. 59:20–60:3; Rom. 1:16). It would cross all cultural barriers—a concept that was difficult for many Jews to accept. The unforgettable story of Jonah's dramatic refusal to obey when God called him to preach to Nineveh demonstrates the Jews' anti-missionary attitude. In fact, Jonah ran in the opposite direction. His disobedience did not stem from fear for his own safety, but from an unwillingness to see his enemies (the hated Assyrians) experience God's mercy. The prophet himself admitted that this was his motive: "[Jonah] prayed to the Lord and said, 'Please Lord, was not this what I said while I was still in my own country? Therefore in order to forestall this I fled to Tarshish, for I knew that You are a gracious and compassionate God, slow to anger and abundant in lovingkindness, and one who relents concerning calamity'" (Jonah 4:2). Like Jonah, the disciples needed to be shaken out of the rigid provincialism of their cultural prejudice. They needed to recognize that the good news of the gospel is for all people (Rom. 10:12; Gal. 3:28).

As He explained the truth to this woman, the Lord's conversation was not forced, hurried, or manipulative. Instead, Jesus sovereignly orchestrated the timing of events so that the disciples would arrive at the opportune moment. As God in human flesh, Jesus' providential control of the situation comes as no surprise, since God sovereignly orchestrates all events.

History is under God's absolute control, prewritten in eternity past. Paul told the pagan philosophers in Athens that God determined the appointed times of every nation (Acts 17:26; cf. 1:7). Accordingly, Jesus Himself always acted according to the Father's timetable. At the wedding in Cana He told His mother, "My hour has not yet come" (2:4). In 7:6 He said to His skeptical brothers, "My time is not yet here" (cf. v. 8). Verse 30 of that same chapter records that His enemies "were seeking to seize Him; and no man laid his hand on Him, because His hour had not yet come" (cf. 8:20). John prefaced his account of the Upper Room Discourse by noting that Jesus knew "that His hour had come that He would depart out of this world to the Father" (13:1). The Lord began His High Priestly Prayer with the words, "Father, the hour has come; glorify Your Son, that the Son may glorify You" (17:1).

In this situation, at a well in Samaria, as so often in His life, Jesus' sovereign control of the events opens a window through which His deity may be seen.

CHRIST'S IMPACT ON THE WOMAN

So the woman left her waterpot, and went into the city and said to the men, "Come, see a man who told me all the things that I have done; this is not the Christ, is it?" They went out of the city, and were coming to Him. (4:28–30)

Why **the woman left her waterpot** behind is not stated. It may be that in her haste to tell the others about her conversation with Jesus she forgot it. Or she may not have filled it yet, and not wanted to carry the empty pot to the village and back. Or perhaps she had already filled it and left it for Jesus in case He wanted a drink. Whatever the reason, the detail adds a touch of realism, and indicates that the author of this gospel was an eyewitness to this incident.

Leaving her jar at the well, the woman hastened back **into the city** and, gathering a crowd, excitedly **said to the men, "Come, see a man who told me all the things that I have done."** A stranger who knew all about her past was hardly an ordinary man. So profound was Jesus' impact on her that she did not hesitate to share the news about Him—even with those familiar with her sordid reputation. Jesus had read her heart and forced her to face who she really was. She had already recognized her need (4:15), her sin (4:19), her true condition (4:26) and that He was the source of her eternal life. Now she eagerly desired to communicate her discovery to others. Her zeal and enthusiasm provides the clinching piece of evidence that her conversion was genuine.

The woman was wise in not bluntly declaring to the men that Jesus was the Messiah. Homer Kent explains the reason for her more cautious, indirect approach:

> The woman immediately wanted to give testimony to others of what she had found. But she did so with utmost tact. It would have been unseemly, presumptuous, and probably ineffective for this woman to attempt to teach the men of the city regarding spiritual truth. Her background hardly qualified her to speak with authority on religious and spiritual matters. Therefore, her statement to them was phrased in a deliberately cautious way so as not to arouse antagonism. (Homer A. Kent Jr. *Light in the Darkness: Studies in the Gospel of John* [Grand Rapids: Baker, 1974], 79–80)

With prudence and respect, she tactfully asked the men, **"This is not the Christ, is it?"** The Greek construction of that question implies a negative or at least doubtful answer. The woman described her conversation with Jesus and humbly deferred the question of His identity to the men. They were so impressed by her excitement and sincerity that **they**

went out of the city, and were coming (during Jesus' conversation with the disciples in vv. 31–38) to investigate the situation for themselves. Although no specific number is given, the implication is that the woman's testimony had stirred up a sizable group.

CHRIST'S INTIMACY WITH THE FATHER

Meanwhile the disciples were urging Him, saying, "Rabbi, eat." But He said to them, "I have food to eat that you do not know about." So the disciples were saying to one another, "No one brought Him anything to eat, did he?" Jesus said to them, "My food is to do the will of Him who sent Me and to accomplish His work. (4:31–34)

Meanwhile, as the woman went back to the village and returned with the men, **the disciples were urging** Jesus, **saying, "Rabbi, eat."** They had brought food back from Sychar, knowing He would be hungry after His long day's journey. Here again is a glimpse of the Lord's humanity (see the discussion of v. 6 in the previous chapter of this volume).

Up to this point, the disciples' primary interest was food, a concern which they expressed in **urging** Jesus to eat. He, however, had a far higher priority, as His reply to them makes clear, **"I have food to eat that you do not know about."** Like the Samaritan woman (4:11; cf. 2:20–21; 3:4), **the disciples** misunderstood Jesus' words and began **saying** doubtfully (the Greek construction again expects a negative answer) to one another, **"No one brought Him anything to eat, did he?"** They were sure no one had taken Him food.

Jesus responded to their confusion by teaching them a critical spiritual truth. In words reminiscent of Moses' declaration, "man does not live by bread alone, but man lives by everything that proceeds out of the mouth of the Lord" (Deut. 8:3)—words He Himself quoted to Satan during His temptation (Matt. 4:4)—**Jesus said to them, "My food is to do the will of Him who sent Me and to accomplish His work."** Doing God's will (cf. 5:30; 6:38; 8:29; Ps. 40:8; Matt. 26:39; Rom. 15:3) by proclaiming the truth to a lost sinner gave the Lord far more satisfaction (cf. Luke 15:10; 19:10) than any physical food could provide (cf. Job 23:12). Jesus frequently referred to the Father as the One **who sent** Him (5:24, 30; 36–37; 6:38–39, 44, 57; 7:16, 28, 29, 33; 8:16, 18, 26, 29, 42; 9:4; 11:42; 12:44–45, 49; 13:20; 14:24; 15:21; 16:5; 17:8, 18, 21, 23, 25; 20:21; Matt. 10:40; Mark 9:37; Luke 4:18; 9:48; 10:16); His goal during His earthly ministry was **to accomplish His work** (cf. 5:17, 36; 9:4; 10:25, 32, 37–38; 14:10; 17:4) of salvation (6:38–40; Matt. 1:21; Luke 5:31–32; 19:10; 1 John 4:9).

Throughout His ministry, Jesus walked in perfect intimacy with His Father. He lived in complete accordance with the Father's will until His cry of triumph from the cross, "It is finished!" (19:30), marked the accomplishment of His mission on earth. Submitting to the Father was Jesus' constant devotion, consummate joy, and true sustenance.

CHRIST'S INSIGHT INTO MEN'S SOULS

Do you not say, 'There are yet four months, and then comes the harvest'? Behold, I say to you, lift up your eyes and look on the fields, that they are white for harvest. Already he who reaps is receiving wages and is gathering fruit for life eternal; so that he who sows and he who reaps may rejoice together. For in this case the saying is true, 'One sows and another reaps.' I sent you to reap that for which you have not labored; others have labored and you have entered into their labor." (4:35–38)

Some commentators view the opening statement of this section as a first-century proverb. More likely, however, it indicates that the incident at the well took place in December, **four months** before the spring **harvest** in April. No such proverb has been recorded anywhere else, and the normal time between planting and harvest was closer to six months. The adverb *eti* (**yet**) also seems out of place in a proverbial saying, which would more likely have read, "There are four months and then comes the harvest" (cf. William Hendriksen, *New Testament Commentary: The Gospel of John* [Grand Rapids, Baker, 1979], 173).

Using the grain growing in the surrounding fields as an object lesson (cf. the use of similar illustrations in Matt. 9:37–38; 13:3–8, 24–32; Mark 4:26–32), Jesus impressed on the disciples the urgency of reaching the lost. There was no need to wait four months; the spiritual **fields** were already **white for harvest.** The disciples had only to **lift up** their **eyes and look** at the Samaritans coming toward them (v. 30), their white clothing forming a striking contrast against the brilliant green of the ripening grain and looking like white heads on the stalks that indicated the time for harvest.

Although the Samaritans had not yet reached the well, Jesus knew men's hearts and whose was ready for salvation (cf. 1:47–49; 2:24–25; 6:64), just as He had known the unspoken life story of the woman (vv. 16–18). Such supernatural insight was a manifestation of His deity (cf. 1 Sam 16:7; Jer. 17:9–10). By telling the disciples that the one **who reaps is receiving wages and is gathering fruit for life eternal** the Lord highlighted their responsibility to participate in the harvest of souls. They would receive their **wages,** the rewarding joy of gathering **fruit** for eternity (cf. Luke 15:7).

In the agricultural realm the same farmer who sows the seed usually reaps the harvest. But that is often not the case in the spiritual realm. Nevertheless, **he who sows and he who reaps may rejoice together. For in this case the saying is true, 'One sows and another reaps.'** As Paul reminded the Corinthians, "I planted, Apollos watered, but God was causing the growth" (1 Cor. 3:6). Others had sowed the seed in the Samaritans' hearts (e.g., Moses, John the Baptist, and Jesus Himself). Yet the disciples would have the privilege of sharing in the resulting harvest. Although they had played no part in sowing the seed, Jesus **sent** them **to reap that for which** they had **not labored; others** had **labored and** they had **entered into their labor.** It was with prepared hearts in view that Jesus commanded His followers, "Therefore beseech the Lord of the harvest to send out workers into His harvest" (Matt. 9:38).

CHRIST'S IMPRESSION ON THE SAMARITANS

From that city many of the Samaritans believed in Him because of the word of the woman who testified, "He told me all the things that I have done." So when the Samaritans came to Jesus, they were asking Him to stay with them; and He stayed there two days. Many more believed because of His word; and they were saying to the woman, "It is no longer because of what you said that we believe, for we have heard for ourselves and know that this One is indeed the Savior of the world." (4:39–42)

Following the interlude of verses 31–38, the **Samaritans** reenter the narrative as the story builds to a powerful conclusion. Many of the villagers **believed in Him because of the word of the woman who testified, "He told me all the things that I have done."** Surely we can assume that she gave the details of His supernatural knowledge, not just this summary comment. That supernatural knowledge of the details of her past settled for them that He was in fact the Messiah. Therefore when they **came to Jesus** at the well, **they were** continually **asking Him to stay with them; and He stayed there two days.** During that time **many more believed because of His word.** Though they were influenced by the woman's testimony, hearing from Jesus Himself was the clincher. So they were **saying to** her, **"It is no longer because of what you said that we believe, for we have heard for ourselves and know that this One is indeed the Savior of the world."** Such words were not intended to denigrate her testimony, but rather to indicate that their time with Jesus confirmed it.

The Samaritans' confession of Jesus as **the Savior of the world** (cf. 2 Cor. 5:19; 1 John 2:2; 4:14) was especially significant because they were not Jewish. Had He come only to save Israel as the Jews preferred to think (and not the whole world), the Samaritans would have been excluded. But the Lord did not come to save Israel alone. His saving mission extended far beyond the borders of Judea and Galilee, encompassing men and women from every nation on earth.

Through His conversation with a non-Jewish woman, Jesus gave an entire non-Jewish village the opportunity to receive salvation. In so doing, He set the precedent for the worldwide impact of His saving work. As His forerunner John the Baptist had earlier exclaimed, "Behold, the Lamb of God who takes away the sin of the world!" (1:29).

Christ's Response to Unbelief
(John 4:43–54)

13

After the two days He went forth from there into Galilee. For Jesus Himself testified that a prophet has no honor in his own country. So when He came to Galilee, the Galileans received Him, having seen all the things that He did in Jerusalem at the feast; for they themselves also went to the feast. Therefore He came again to Cana of Galilee where He had made the water wine. And there was a royal official whose son was sick at Capernaum. When he heard that Jesus had come out of Judea into Galilee, he went to Him and was imploring Him to come down and heal his son; for he was at the point of death. So Jesus said to him, "Unless you people see signs and wonders, you simply will not believe." The royal official said to Him, "Sir, come down before my child dies." Jesus said to him, "Go; your son lives." The man believed the word that Jesus spoke to him and started off. As he was now going down, his slaves met him, saying that his son was living. So he inquired of them the hour when he began to get better. Then they said to him, "Yesterday at the seventh hour the fever left him." So the father knew that it was at that hour in which Jesus said to him, "Your son lives"; and he himself believed and his whole household. This is again a second

sign that Jesus performed when He had come out of Judea into Galilee. (4:43–54)

John's gospel is preeminently the gospel of belief. He wrote his inspired record so that his readers "may believe that Jesus is the Christ, the Son of God; and that believing [they] may have life in His name" (20:31). The verb *pisteuō* ("believe") appears nearly 100 times in this gospel, and the overwhelming majority of its occurrences refer to believing savingly in the Lord Jesus Christ (e.g., 1:12; 6:29; 8:30; 12:44; 14:1; 17:20). Through believing in Him people become children of God (1:12; 12:36), obtain eternal life (3:15–16, 36; 6:40, 47), avoid judgment (3:18; 5:24), partake in the resurrection of life (11:25; cf. 5:29), possess the indwelling Holy Spirit (7:38–39), are delivered from spiritual darkness (12:46), and find empowerment for spiritual service (14:12).

Furthermore, God commands people to believe in His Son. When asked by the crowd, "What shall we do, so that we may work the works of God?" (John 6:28), Jesus replied, "This is the work of God, that you believe in Him whom He has sent" (v. 29; cf. 3:18; 14:1). But the tragic truth is that most people refuse to believe in Jesus Christ. In the Sermon on the Mount He warned, "The gate is wide and the way is broad that leads to destruction, and there are many who enter through it. For the gate is small and the way is narrow that leads to life, and there are few who find it" (Matt. 7:13–14; cf. Luke 13:23–30). Expressing that same truth from the perspective of divine sovereignty He declared, "For many are called, but few are chosen" (Matt. 22:14; cf. John 10:26). Despite their good deeds or religious zeal, unbelievers can never please God (Rom. 8:8), since "without faith it is impossible to please Him, for he who comes to God must believe that He is and that He is a rewarder of those who seek Him" (Heb. 11:6).

Unbelief is the damning sin. It is the sin for which people are ultimately sentenced to hell, since all other sins are forgiven for those who repent and believe in Christ. Therefore, "he who does not believe [in Christ] has been judged already, because he has not believed in the name of the only begotten Son of God" (John 3:18). In John 16:8–9 Jesus said of the Holy Spirit, "He, when He comes, will convict the world concerning sin and righteousness and judgment; concerning sin, because they do not believe in Me."

An "evil, unbelieving heart" (Heb. 3:12) characterizes unregenerate people —a heart that loves sin's darkness and detests the light of the gospel (John 3:19–20). The heart's unbelief is also compounded by Satan, "the god of this world [who] has blinded the minds of the unbelieving so that they might not see the light of the gospel of the glory of Christ" (2 Cor. 4:4). Sometimes God Himself hardens the hearts of unbelievers as an act of judgment for their stubborn unbelief (John 12:39–40). For example, the Old Testament records that while Pharaoh hardened his heart (Ex. 8:15, 32; 9:34; 1 Sam. 6:6), God also hardened Pharaoh's heart (Ex. 4:21; 7:3; 9:12; 10:1, 20, 27; 11:10; 14:4, 8).

At its core, unbelief is a rejection of the saving truth from God contained in Scripture. Thus Jesus said to the unbelieving Jews, "Because I speak the truth, you do not believe Me. Which one of you convicts Me of sin? If I speak truth, why do you not believe Me?" (John 8:45–46). Unbelief is a rejection of Jesus Christ, who is the truth of God incarnate (John 14:6). "But though He had performed so many signs before them," John noted, "yet they were not believing in Him. This was to fulfill the word of Isaiah the prophet which he spoke: 'Lord, who has believed our report? And to whom has the arm of the Lord been revealed?'" (12:37–38; cf. 5:38; 16:9; Rom. 11:20; Heb. 3:12). The people of Israel rejected Jesus' miraculous signs, just as they had similarly rejected God's mighty works throughout their history (Ps. 78:32; cf. v. 22; Num. 14:11; Deut. 1:32; 9:23; 2 Kings 17:14; Luke 22:67; Acts 14:2; Heb. 3:18–19).

The gospel accounts describe several levels of unbelief. First, there was unbelief due to lack of exposure. This was the unbelief of the prepared and ready heart, just awaiting the revelation of the truth from God. This is the shallowest level of unbelief, requiring only knowledge of the glorious majesty of Christ's person to be overcome. For example, when John the Baptist pointed out Christ to Andrew and John (1:35–37), they immediately followed Him—even though He had not yet even spoken to them. Their knowledge of the Old Testament and their love for God made them ready.

Second, there was unbelief due to lack of information. This type of unbelief required more than mere exposure to the person of Christ; those at this level were less prepared and had to hear His words to be persuaded. The Samaritan woman at the well was not impressed by Jesus' appearance or exposed to any of His miracles; to her He seemed to be just another Jewish rabbi. But after she experienced His supernatural knowledge regarding her sin (4:16–19); His forthright declaration that He was the Messiah (4:26) was convincing. His words also persuaded many of her fellow villagers to believe in Him (4:41–42).

Third, there was unbelief due to a perceived lack of evidence. Those who fall into this category had heard the claims of Christ, but desired evidence that those claims were true. The Gospels describe them as those who need to see the works of Christ. Jesus Himself offered His miracles as proof that He was the Messiah (Luke 7:20–22; John 5:36; 10:25, 37–38; 14:11; cf. Acts 2:22). Although the attesting miracles Christ performed did not bring all who observed them to saving faith (2:23–25; 12:37; cf. Luke 4:23), they did convince some. They were enough to persuade

Nicodemus that Jesus was sent by God (3:2), and start him down the path to saving faith (see chap. 8 of this volume).

But there was a fourth level of unbelief found in the extremely religious and self-righteous—namely, unbelief due to deliberate hardheartedness. Those at this level refused to believe in Christ and the gospel of grace, and no amount of evidence would convince them otherwise. They knew who Jesus was; they understood His teachings; they were aware of the overwhelming evidence; yet they stubbornly rejected His claims. Jesus warned of the consequences of this obstinate unbelief when He said, "Unless you believe that I am He, you will die in your sins" (8:24). The Pharisees exemplified this ultimate level of self-righteous unbelief when they concluded of Jesus, "This man casts out demons only by Beelzebul the ruler of the demons" (Matt. 12:24). They decided, exactly opposite the truth, that Jesus was satanic. Such deliberate unbelief is the most deadly type. Because such people, who think they have achieved righteousness, continually reject all the evidence for the gospel God shows them and hate the reality that they are spiritually poor, blind, enslaved, and oppressed with sin (cf. Luke 4:16–30). Their unbelief will never give way to repentance and saving faith (cf. Matt. 12:31–32; Heb. 6:4–8).

As He began His Galilean ministry, Jesus encountered some people at the third level of unbelief. The Galileans were not impressed by His person or His words; He had grown up among them, and they thought they knew who He was (cf. Matt. 13:54–58). They demanded signs and wonders (vv. 45, 48). This passage tells the story of how Jesus moved one of the Galileans from the third level of unbelief to saving faith.

Although some view this story as a variant account of the healing of the centurion's son (Matt. 8:5–13; Luke 7:2–10), the significant differences between the two stories rule out that possibility. For instance, the man in this story was a royal official, whereas the centurion was a soldier; the official requested healing for his son, whereas the centurion interceded on behalf of his servant; and the official's faith was not commended by Jesus (v. 48), whereas the centurion's faith was (Luke 7:9).

The passage itself may be divided into three sections: unbelief contemplated, unbelief confronted, and unbelief conquered.

UNBELIEF CONTEMPLATED

After the two days He went forth from there into Galilee. For Jesus Himself testified that a prophet has no honor in his own country. So when He came to Galilee, the Galileans received Him, having seen all the things that He did in Jerusalem at the feast; for they themselves also went to the feast. (4:43–45)

After staying **two days** in Sychar at the request of the newly converted Samaritans (4:40), Jesus resumed His journey to **Galilee** (4:3). The Lord's brief ministry in Samaria was a prophetic interlude, foreshadowing the later spread of the gospel to the Samaritans and Gentiles (cf. Acts 1:8). As the Samaritan villagers correctly perceived, He is the "Savior of the world" (4:42). But the good news of the kingdom was to be offered first to Israel (cf. Luke 24:47; Acts 3:26; 13:46; Rom. 1:16). The Jewish people were the primary focus of Jesus' ministry (Matt. 10:5–6; 15:24).

The proverbial statement **a prophet has no honor in his own country** (cf. Luke 4:24) contrasts Jesus' acceptance by the Samaritans with His general rejection by the Jewish people (1:11). It also explains His motive for returning to His home region of Galilee (as the conjunction *gar* [**for**] indicates). At first glance it seems somewhat perplexing that **Jesus** went to Galilee because, as He **Himself testified,** He would receive no honor there. The point, however, is that Jesus was not taken by surprise when many in His home region rejected Him. He went there knowing that He would be given a cold reception, especially at Nazareth, where He had been raised (Luke 4:16ff.). But some in Galilee would believe and, therefore, honor Him.

John's statement, **so when He came to Galilee, the Galileans received Him,** does not mean that they believed savingly in Jesus as the Messiah. *Oun* (**so**) refers back to Jesus' statement in the preceding verse, and confirms that the Galileans did not honor Him for who He really was. On the contrary, having **seen all the things that He did in Jerusalem at the feast** (cf. 2:23), they welcomed Him merely as a miracle worker. They were curiosity seekers, eagerly hoping to see Jesus perform some more sensational feats. Thus the apostle John writes with a sense of irony; the Galileans' reception of Jesus was not genuine, but superficial and shallow.

UNBELIEF CONFRONTED

Therefore He came again to Cana of Galilee where He had made the water wine. And there was a royal official whose son was sick at Capernaum. When he heard that Jesus had come out of Judea into Galilee, he went to Him and was imploring Him to come down and heal his son; for he was at the point of death. So Jesus said to him, "Unless you people see signs and wonders, you simply will not believe." The royal official said to Him, "Sir, come down before my child dies." (4:46–49)

The fact that Jesus encountered a royal official in **Cana of Galilee where He had made the water wine** (cf. 2:1–11) only added to the irony of the situation. This was the very place where Jesus had performed His first miracle. Yet, instead of exhibiting true belief in Him because of His undeniable, supernatural power, the people simply displayed a desire to see more miracles. As this incident demonstrates, the reception of the Galileans, like that of most Judeans (2:23–25), was superficial, curious, thrill-seeking, non-saving, sign-based interest. The conjunction *oun* (**therefore**) introduces the story of the **royal official** and presents him as an example of those Galileans who viewed Jesus not as the Messiah, but only as a miracle worker (cf. the discussion of v. 48 below).

The **royal official** (*basilikos*) was most likely in the service of Herod Antipas, tetrarch of Galilee from 4 B.C. to A.D. 39. (It is unlikely that he was in the service of the emperor, since Galilee was not part of an imperial province.) Antipas was a son of Herod the Great, who ruled Palestine at the time of Christ's birth. After his father's death, Antipas was made ruler of Galilee. Although Rome denied him the formal royal title, Antipas was nonetheless commonly referred to as a king (Matt. 14:9; Mark 6:14). Some have speculated that this **royal official** was "Chuza, Herod's steward" (Luke 8:3), whose wife was one of the women who accompanied Jesus. Others think he might have been the "Manaen who had been brought up with Herod the tetrarch," who was one of Paul's co-pastors at Antioch (Acts 13:1). Such identifications, however, are merely speculative.

Urgent need compelled this man to journey to Christ; his **son was sick at Capernaum,** some sixteen miles away. Having **heard that Jesus had come out of Judea into Galilee, he went to Him.** Perhaps he had heard of the miracle Jesus performed at the wedding at Cana some months earlier (2:1–11). Or he may have witnessed the signs Jesus performed at Jerusalem during Passover, or heard about them from Galilean pilgrims who had been there (2:23–25). Finding Jesus, he began frantically **imploring Him to come down** to Capernaum **and heal his son.** The imperfect tense of the verb *erōtaō* (**was imploring**) indicates that he repeatedly begged Jesus to cure his son's disease. Swallowing his pride, this respected member of Herod's court begged for help from a carpenter's son (cf. Matt. 13:55; Mark 6:3).

At this point, the official's faith was little more than a desperate hope that led him to ask for Jesus' intervention. His anxiety was certainly understandable, since his son **was at the point of death.** But his belief in Jesus was not yet driven by a desire for salvation for his own soul, but by desperation for his son.

The feebleness of his faith in Jesus' ability to heal is underscored by two erroneous assumptions that he made about Him. First, unlike the centurion (Luke 7:6–7) and the Syrophoenician woman (Mark 7:24–30), he assumed Jesus had to be physically present to heal his son. Second, he hoped Jesus had the power to heal his son's illness, but had no hope that He could raise him from the dead. Those two assumptions were behind his insistance that Jesus come at once before it was too late. Unlike the rich young ruler (Mark 10:17–22), he was not seeking spiritual truth, but was instead driven by an overwhelming physical and emotional need. His goal in coming to Jesus was not to obtain eternal salvation for himself, but physical healing for his dying child.

Faced with the royal official's fearful, feeble, imperfect faith and the unbelief of the Galileans in general, Jesus issued a stern rebuke: **"Unless you people see signs and wonders, you simply will not believe."** The NASB rightly adds the italicized word **people,** since the verb translated **see** is plural. Jesus' rebuke encompassed the royal official and all of the Galileans whose flawed faith disregarded His message and mission of salvation and focused instead on the sensational miracles He performed on their behalf.

The royal official ignored Jesus' assessment of him and his fellow Galileans. Single-mindedly, he poured out his heart, exclaiming, **"Sir, come down** to Capernaum **before my child** (a more endearing, affectionate term than "son" [vv. 46–47]) **dies."** Despite His stern rebuke of the kind of faith before Him, the Lord graciously performed the miracle, consequently drawing the official's faith to a higher level. By healing his son physically, the Great Physician moved to heal the father spiritually.

UNBELIEF CONQUERED

Jesus said to him, "Go; your son lives." The man believed the word that Jesus spoke to him and started off. As he was now going down, his slaves met him, saying that his son was living. So he inquired of them the hour when he began to get better. Then they said to him, "Yesterday at the seventh hour the fever left him." So the father knew that it was at that hour in which Jesus said to him, "Your son lives"; and he himself believed and his whole household. This is again a second sign that Jesus performed when He had come out of Judea into Galilee. (4:50–54)

Instead of agreeing to go back to Capernaum with him as the official had begged Him to do, **Jesus** merely **said to him, "Go; your son lives."** At that very instant (vv. 52–53), the boy was healed. Even though he had no confirmation of it, **the man** nevertheless **believed**

the word that Jesus spoke to him. The Lord's words to him had moved him from the third level of unbelief (which needs miracles) to the second (which believes Christ's word). Without any tangible proof that his son was healed, he took Jesus at His word **and started off** for home.

Leaving Cana in the Galilean hill country, the official went **down** toward Capernaum, on the north shore of the Sea of Galilee (about seven hundred feet below sea level). On the way, **his slaves met him,** already having left the town to find him and tell him the good news **that his son was living** (i.e., that he had recovered, not merely that he had not yet died). Overjoyed, the man **inquired of them the hour when he began to get better.** The servants replied, **"Yesterday at the seventh hour the fever left him."** The **seventh hour** would have been early afternoon, sometime between 1 and 3 P.M. in the broadest reckoning. By the time he left Cana and arrived in the vicinity of Capernaum, it was after midnight (**yesterday**). It is possible that Jesus' word to him relieved his anxiety about his son, allowing him to remain in Cana, perhaps to hear and see more from the Lord and understand His message. That would have been critical, because it led him to fully believe in Jesus when his servants reported the complete healing of his son, confirming the Lord's claims (v. 53).

It was the time of his son's recovery that verified to **the father** that a miracle had taken place, because he **knew that** his son's healing had happened **at that** very **hour in which Jesus** had **said to him,** **"Your son lives."** When he heard the news, the royal official **himself believed,** along with each member of **his whole household** (cf. Acts 11:14; 16:15, 31–34; 18:8; 1 Cor. 1:16; 16:15).

John concluded this account with the footnote, **This is again a second sign that Jesus performed when He had come out of Judea into Galilee.** This act of healing was the second of the eight major signs that John records as proof that Jesus was the Messiah. It was also the second sign (the first having taken place at the wedding at Cana [2:1–11]) He had performed in Galilee. That it was not Jesus' second miracle overall is made clear from 2:23. In this instance, the stunning verification of Jesus' power lifted the royal official all the way from sign-seeking unbelief to genuine saving faith.

The Persecuted Jesus
(John 5:1–16)

14

After these things there was a feast of the Jews, and Jesus went up to Jerusalem. Now there is in Jerusalem by the sheep gate a pool, which is called in Hebrew Bethesda, having five porticoes. In these lay a multitude of those who were sick, blind, lame, and withered, [waiting for the moving of the waters; for an angel of the Lord went down at certain seasons into the pool and stirred up the water; whoever then first, after the stirring up of the water, stepped in was made well from whatever disease with which he was afflicted.] A man was there who had been ill for thirty-eight years. When Jesus saw him lying there, and knew that he had already been a long time in that condition, He said to him, "Do you wish to get well?" The sick man answered Him, "Sir, I have no man to put me into the pool when the water is stirred up, but while I am coming, another steps down before me." Jesus said to him, "Get up, pick up your pallet and walk." Immediately the man became well, and picked up his pallet and began to walk. Now it was the Sabbath on that day. So the Jews were saying to the man who was cured, "It is the Sabbath, and it is not permissible for you to carry your pallet." But he answered them, "He who made me well was the one who said to me, 'Pick

up your pallet and walk.'" They asked him, "Who is the man who said to you, 'Pick up your pallet and walk'?" But the man who was healed did not know who it was, for Jesus had slipped away while there was a crowd in that place. Afterward Jesus found him in the temple and said to him, "Behold, you have become well; do not sin anymore, so that nothing worse happens to you." The man went away, and told the Jews that it was Jesus who had made him well. For this reason the Jews were persecuting Jesus, because He was doing these things on the Sabbath. (5:1–16)

The earthly ministry of the Lord Jesus Christ created an unprecedented sensation in Israel. For three and a half years He performed miraculous works unlike anything ever seen before (John 15:24; cf. Matt. 9:33; Mark 2:12). Those signs authenticated Him as the Son of God and Messiah (Matt. 11:2–5). In His compassion and grace, Jesus frequently chose to do miracles that alleviated people's suffering. He healed the sick—practically banishing disease from Israel for the duration of His ministry—raised the dead, cast out demons, and fed large crowds of hungry people.

The Lord also taught concerning the kingdom of God with boldness, confidence, and authority. Unlike the scribes, who primarily quoted other human authorities, Jesus spoke with the divine power of the Son of God (cf. Matt. 5:21–22, 27–28, 31–32, 33–34, 38–39, 43–44). As a result, "the crowds were amazed at His teaching; for He was teaching them as one having authority, and not as their scribes" (Matt. 7:28–29), and "all the people were hanging on to every word He said" (Luke 19:48). Even His enemies acknowledged, "Never has a man spoken the way this man speaks" (7:46).

Excited by His astonishing miracles and powerful preaching, people flocked to Jesus. Matthew 4:25 reports that "large crowds followed Him from Galilee and the Decapolis and Jerusalem and Judea and from beyond the Jordan." After the Sermon on the Mount, "when Jesus came down from the mountain, large crowds followed Him" (Matt. 8:1). On another occasion, "large crowds gathered to Him, so He got into a boat and sat down, and the whole crowd was standing on the beach" listening to His preaching (Matt. 13:2). Across the Jordan in the predominantly Gentile region of Perea, "large crowds followed Him, and He healed them there" (Matt. 19:2; cf. 20:29; John 6:2, 5). Luke records a time when "so many thousands of people had gathered together [to hear Jesus] that they were stepping on one another" (Luke 12:1).

But the overwhelming popularity that Jesus experienced was not as beneficial as it appeared. The crowds who flocked to Him primarily consisted of curiosity seekers. They were not devoted to Him as Lord and

Messiah, but followed Him for the excitement, healings, and free food He provided (cf. 6:26). At one point, they were so enthusiastic about what they perceived as Jesus' supernatural social welfare program that they tried to make Him king (6:15). But because they were not generally committed to Him or His gospel of the kingdom, Jesus did not commit Himself to them (2:24; 6:26, 64).

Ultimately, the fickle crowds rejected Jesus (6:66), following the example of their religious leaders. Those leaders, especially the Pharisees (the most influential religious sect of Judaism), mounted an unrelenting campaign of lies against Jesus, falsely accusing Him of being a demon-possessed Samaritan (8:48) of illegitimate birth (8:41). As noted earlier, they even attributed His miraculous signs to the power of Satan (Matt. 9:34; 10:25; 12:24; Mark 3:22; Luke 11:15). The nation's ultimate rejection came at Jesus' trial before Pilate when, urged on by the religious leaders, the crowd screamed, "Crucify Him! . . . His blood shall be on us and on our children!" (Matt. 27:23, 25). At His death, Jesus had only a handful of identifiable true disciples—120 in Jerusalem (Acts 1:15) and another 500, probably in Galilee (1 Cor. 15:6; cf. Matt. 28:7, 16).

As chronicles of His ministry, the gospels record the rising tide of opposition that Jesus faced (e.g., Matt. 9:27–34; 11:20–30; 12:1–14, 22ff.; 13:54–58; 15:1–20; 16:1–4, 21; 21:15–16, 23–27; 22:15–46; 28:11–15; Luke 4:16–31; 11:14–23; 13:10–17; John 3:32; 7:30–52; 8:12–20, 31–59; 9:13–41; 10:19–39; 11:45–53). Summing up Israel's rejection of Jesus, John observed, "He came to His own, and those who were His own did not receive Him" (1:11). The Jewish people were hostile to Him because of both their hypocritical legalism and their misconceptions concerning His mission (they looked for a political-military messiah who would free them from the yoke of Rome). After His death, they continued to reject Him because of the offense of the cross (1 Cor. 1:23; Gal. 5:11).

Chapters 5 through 7 of John's gospel note the beginning of the nation's shift in attitude toward Jesus from reservation (cf. 3:26; 4:1–3) to outright rejection (summed up in 7:52). Chapters 5 and 7 describe the opposition that He faced in Judea; chapter 6 records the opposition in Galilee. The first sixteen verses of chapter 5, which chronicle the controversy generated by Jesus' healing of a sick man on the Sabbath, signal the beginning of that hostility. It would intensify in chapter 6 when many of Jesus' followers, unwilling to accept His teaching that He was the bread of life, abandoned Him (6:66). Finally, chapter 7 records the hardening of official opposition, as the religious authorities sought unsuccessfully to arrest Him (7:30–42).

The outbreak of hostility toward Christ was triggered by an incident at a pool in Jerusalem known as Bethesda. Jesus' cleansing of the temple had stirred up antagonism (2:13–22), which only grew as His ministry gained popularity (4:1–3). His rejection of self-righteous Jews and His violation of the Jewish traditional regulations concerning the Sabbath fanned the flames of resentment into open opposition.

The passage may be divided into two parts: the miracle performed, and the Master persecuted.

THE MIRACLE PERFORMED

After these things there was a feast of the Jews, and Jesus went up to Jerusalem. Now there is in Jerusalem by the sheep gate a pool, which is called in Hebrew Bethesda, having five porticoes. In these lay a multitude of those who were sick, blind, lame, and withered, [waiting for the moving of the waters; for an angel of the Lord went down at certain seasons into the pool and stirred up the water; whoever then first, after the stirring up of the water, stepped in was made well from whatever disease with which he was afflicted.] A man was there who had been ill for thirty-eight years. When Jesus saw him lying there, and knew that he had already been a long time in that condition, He said to him, "Do you wish to get well?" The sick man answered Him, "Sir, I have no man to put me into the pool when the water is stirred up, but while I am coming, another steps down before me." Jesus said to him, "Get up, pick up your pallet and walk." Immediately the man became well, and picked up his pallet and began to walk. (5:1–9a)

The phrase **after these things** indicates that this incident took place at an unspecified time after Christ's ministry in Galilee had ended. John recorded only one event from that period, the healing of the royal official's son (4:43–54), but the Synoptic Gospels relate many more events (e.g., Jesus' rejection at Nazareth [Luke 4:16–31]; His extended preaching tour [Matt. 4:23–24]; and several healings, including a demon-possessed man [Mark 1:21–28], Peter's mother-in-law [Matt. 8:14–17], a leper [Luke 5:12–16], and a paralytic [Mark 2:1–12]). In fact, Luke 4:14–9:50 is all related to His Galilean ministry, as is Mark 1:14–9:50.

John refers to **a feast of the Jews** six times in his gospel (cf. 2:13; 6:4; 7:2; 10:22; 11:55); this is the only one he failed to identify specifically. Since **Jesus went up to Jerusalem** for this feast, it likely was one of the three major feasts held in that city (Passover, Tabernacles, Pentecost [Weeks]) that all Jewish males were required to attend (Deut. 16:16; cf. Ex. 23:17; 34:23). Perhaps John did not name this particular feast because Jesus' actions on this occasion are not related to its particulars.

The apostle likely mentioned it merely to explain why Jesus was in Jerusalem.

For his readers who were unfamiliar with the city, John explained that **there is in Jerusalem by the sheep gate a pool, which is called in Hebrew Bethesda, having five porticoes** (porches). Some see the apostle's use of the present tense verb **is** as evidence that John wrote his gospel before the destruction of Jerusalem in A.D. 70. The use of the present tense, however, is not conclusive evidence for an early date of writing. The pool evidently escaped destruction when the Romans sacked Jerusalem, since a fourth-century pilgrim to the city reported seeing it. Thus, it would still have been in existence even if John wrote after A.D. 70. John was probably writing here in the "historical present," using a present tense verb to refer to a past event; doing so would have been consistent with his writing style elsewhere (c.f. 4:5, 7; 11:38; 12:22; 13:6; 18:3; 20:1, 2, 6, 18, 26; 21:13, where the verbs translated "came" are actually in the present tense). (For a discussion of the date of writing of this gospel, see the introduction.)

The NASB italicizes the word **gate** since the noun modified by the adjective *probatikos* ("of or pertaining to **sheep**") is not expressed in the text. The reference is most likely to the sheep gate mentioned in Nehemiah 3:1, 32; 12:39, located near the northeast corner of the city's wall not far from the temple. **Bethesda** is the Greek transliteration of a **Hebrew** or Aramaic word variously understood to mean "house of outpourings" or "house of mercy." In the covered **porticoes** near the pool, where they would receive some protection from the elements, **lay a multitude of those who were sick,** including the **blind, lame, and withered** (paralyzed). The **pool** was apparently fed by an intermittent spring (cf. v. 7), and people imagined that its waters had healing powers (ancient sources indicate that the water in the pool had a reddish tint from the minerals in it).

The earliest and most reliable Greek manuscripts omit the last phrase of verse 3 and all of verse 4. Others include the passage, but mark it as spurious. Despite its brevity, the omitted section contains more than half a dozen words or phrases foreign to John's writings—including three not found anywhere else in the New Testament. These facts, along with the absence of any specific mention of angels in the rest of the passage, indicate that the section was not part of John's original account. In the years after John wrote his gospel, scribes apparently added this material as a marginal note to present the popular explanation for the stirring of the water (v. 7). (The early church father Tertullian referred to the superstition of the angel stirring the water in the late second or early third century.) Later manuscripts incorporated the scribal glosses into the text itself.

Among those gathered at the pool hoping for a miracle was a man **who had been ill for thirty-eight years.** The exact nature of his illness is not stated, but he was either paralyzed or too weak to move freely on his own. Having been incurably ill for nearly four decades, this man provided Jesus with an opportunity to display His divine power.

Jesus saw this man **lying** near the pool, **knew** (supernaturally) **that he had already been a long time in that condition,** and **said to him, "Do you wish to get well?"** The Lord's question seems strange; obviously the man wanted to be cured, or he would not have been at the pool in the first place. But Jesus never engaged in flippant, idle conversation. His question served several purposes: it secured the man's full attention, focused on his need, offered him healing, and communicated to him the depth of Christ's love and concern.

But the man failed to grasp the weight of Jesus' offer. Instead of asking Jesus for healing, the man responded by expressing his belief in the healing powers of the pool. Thus **the sick man answered Him, "Sir, I have no man to put me into the pool when the water is stirred up, but while I am coming, another steps down before me."** Whether or not he believed that an angel stirred the water (cf. the discussion of vv. 3*b*, 4 above), he did believe that when the water was stirred (maybe by a surge from the source) only the first person into the pool would be healed. Since he could not move rapidly enough on his own, and had no one to help him, he never managed to get there first.

The possibility that Jesus might heal him never entered his mind; in fact, he did not even know who Jesus was (v. 13). His only concern was finding a way to be the first one into the pool when the water began stirring. Maybe he thought that Jesus could help him by waiting there with him and carrying him into the water when the time was right. But he certainly never considered that, in a moment, Jesus could miraculously make him completely well. No doubt years of failing to make it first into the water had left him embittered and hopeless. Thus, "v. 7 reads less as an apt and subtle response to Jesus' question than as the crotchety grumblings of an old and not very perceptive man who thinks he is answering a stupid question" (D. A. Carson, *The Gospel According to John,* The Pillar New Testament Commentary [Grand Rapids: Eerdmans, 1991], 243). Like many people, his expectations of what Jesus could do for him were limited to what he believed was possible.

But Jesus gave the crippled man far more than he could have ever expected, commanding him authoritatively, **"Get up, pick up your pallet and walk"** (cf. Mark 2:11). Three imperative verbs express the completeness of the healing: the man was to stand, carry the straw mat he was lying on, and walk away. Just as Jesus spoke and the world was created (Gen. 1:3, 6, 9, 11, 14, 20, 24, 26; cf. John 1:3; Col. 1:16; Heb. 1:2), so also His words had the power to create a new body (cf. Matt. 8:16; 9:6; Mark 2:11; Luke 6:10; 13:12). Unlike many alleged modern healings, Jesus' healings were complete and instantaneous, with or without faith. This one proves the point, since the man exhibited no faith in Jesus at all. Yet he was healed instantly and wholly. John records that he **immediately . . . became well, and picked up his pallet and began to walk.**

One of the cruelest lies of contemporary "faith healers" is that the people they fail to heal are guilty of sinful unbelief, a lack of faith, or a "negative confession." In contrast, those whom Jesus healed did not always manifest faith beforehand (cf. Matt. 8:14–15; 9:32–33; 12:10–13, 22; Mark 7:32–35; 8:22–25; Luke 14:1–4; 22:50–51; John 9:1–7), and this man is a prime example.

This incident perfectly illustrates God's sovereign grace in action (cf. v. 21). Out of all the sick people at the pool, Jesus chose to heal this man. There was nothing about him that made him more deserving than the others, nor did he seek out Jesus; Jesus approached him. The Lord did not choose him because He foresaw that he had the faith to believe for a healing; he never did express belief that Jesus could heal him. So it is in salvation. Out of the spiritually dead multitude of Adam's fallen race, God chose and redeemed His elect—not because of anything they did to deserve it, or because of their foreseen faith, but because of His sovereign choice (6:37; Rom. 8:29–30; 9:16; Eph. 1:4–5; 2:4–5; 2 Thess. 2:13; Titus 3:5). Even the faith to believe was a sovereign gift (Eph. 2:8–9).

THE MASTER PERSECUTED

Now it was the Sabbath on that day. So the Jews were saying to the man who was cured, "It is the Sabbath, and it is not permissible for you to carry your pallet." But he answered them, "He who made me well was the one who said to me, 'Pick up your pallet and walk.'" They asked him, "Who is the man who said to you, 'Pick up your pallet and walk'?" But the man who was healed did not know who it was, for Jesus had slipped away while there was a crowd in that place. Afterward Jesus found him in the temple and said to him, "Behold, you have become well; do not sin anymore, so that nothing worse happens to you." The man went away, and told the Jews that it was Jesus who had made him well. For this reason the Jews were persecuting Jesus, because He was doing these things on the Sabbath. (5:9*b*–16)

John's seemingly incidental note that the healing took place on the **Sabbath** is in reality the key to this incident. It sets the stage for the open hostility that the Jewish authorities manifested toward Christ. The fury of their opposition, fueled at this pool, would only escalate throughout the remainder of His earthly ministry, finally culminating in His death.

Jesus' refusal to observe the legalistic and man-made Sabbath regulations of rabbinic tradition was a major point of contention between Him and Israel's religious establishment (cf. Matt. 12:1–14; Mark 2:23–3:6; Luke 6:1–11; 13:10–17; 14:1–6; John 7:21–23; 9:14–16). In fact, the Lord deliberately chose to heal this man on the Sabbath to confront superficial and bankrupt Jewish legalism. The man's condition was not life threatening, and he was constantly at the pool. Jesus could have easily chosen another day to heal him. But the Lord not only wanted to show mercy to this man; He also wanted to call the nation to repentance by confronting the self-righteous and unbiblical stipulations that led to their illusion of spiritual life. They had become experts at substituting their traditions for God's commands (Matt. 15:9).

Observing the Sabbath regulations was central to the legalistic Judaism of Jesus' day. Gerald L. Borchert observes,

> The Sabbath had become a pervading theme in Jewish life. . . . So significant was the Sabbath that a major section of the Mishna was devoted to Sabbath rules. Sabbath obedience became in fact an eschatological issue because it was thought at least minimally that the coming of the Messiah was linked to the perfect keeping of one Sabbath. The actions of Jesus were thus regarded by Sabbath-oriented Jews as being diametrically opposed to the expectations of the rabbis who probably would have categorized Jesus as an antinomian libertarian. He did not seem to be concerned for the precious rules of the rabbis.
>
> Not only in John, but also in the Synoptics is Jesus portrayed as seemingly unconcerned for the rabbinic traditions about the Sabbath. . . . The rules of the rabbis were a misunderstanding of God's design for the Sabbath. The Sabbath was not the means to God's approval, as the rabbis seem to have suggested. The Sabbath was not merely a rule for humans, but *a gift to humans* (cf. Mark 2:27). It was to be used to honor God and to benefit his people. More importantly, Jesus was Lord of the Sabbath (cf. Mark 2:28). If, therefore, anyone would have a right to act on Sabbath, it was Jesus. (*John 1–11*, The New American Commentary [Nashville: Broadman & Holman, 2002], 228–29. Italics in original.)

The Old Testament prohibited working on the Sabbath (Ex. 31:12–14; 35:2), but did not specify exactly what kind of work was forbidden. It seems, however, that one's customary employment was in view. The Israelites were not to participate in their normal, week-long occupations on the Sabbath day.

But rabbinic tradition went far beyond that, listing thirty-nine forbidden categories of work—including carrying goods. The rabbinic prohibition against carrying loads on the Sabbath was ostensibly based on such passages as Nehemiah 13:15–18 and Jeremiah 17:21–22. Those passages, however, were aimed at individuals who conducted their ordinary business, their livelihood or occupation, on the Sabbath. Thus they did not apply to the healed man, since he did not make his living by carrying his mat.

Nevertheless, it was for his violation of rabbinic (but not biblical) law that **the Jews** (the religious authorities) confronted **the man who was cured. "It is the Sabbath,"** they declared to him indignantly, **"and it is not permissible for you to carry your pallet."** Instead of rejoicing that he was healed, they castigated him for breaking their trivial rules. They were far more concerned with legalistic regulations than with the man's well-being (cf. Matt. 23:4)—an attitude for which the Lord sharply rebuked them (Matt. 23:13ff.). The false religion of Judaism, like all false systems, cannot change the inside, so it is left to manipulate life on the outside.

Caught in the act of violating traditional Sabbath regulations, the man attempted to defend himself by shifting the responsibility to Jesus. He replied, **"He who made me well was the one who said to me, 'Pick up your pallet and walk.'"** His fear of the authorities is in marked contrast to the formerly blind man in John 9, who boldly confronted them (John 9:17, 24–33). As Leon Morris wryly observes, "The man was not the stuff of which heroes are made (*The Gospel According to John,* The New International Commentary on the New Testament [Grand Rapids: Eerdmans, 1979], 306).

Not to be put off, the authorities immediately **asked him, "Who is the man who said to you, 'Pick up your pallet and walk'?"** What man, they demanded, would have the audacity to call for such a Sabbath violation and flaunt the authority of the rabbis? Who would dare to violate the "traditions of the elders" (Mark 7:3), which they equated with the inviolable law of God? Such impudence needed to be dealt with at once. Once again, they proved themselves to be far more concerned with the minutiae of the law than with the weightier matters—such as the mercy that had been shown to this needy individual (cf. Matt. 23:23).

To their disappointment, **the man who was healed did not know who it was** who had commanded him. The stranger had approached him, healed him, and left without giving him His name. Nor could the man point Him out to the authorities, **for Jesus had slipped away while there was a crowd in that place** (cf. 8:59; 10:39; 12:36). But Jesus did not abandon this man. Later, He **found him in the temple and said to him, "Behold, you have become well; do not sin anymore,**

so that nothing worse happens to you." Our Lord's sobering warning reflects an important biblical truth. Although Scripture is clear that illness is not always an immediate result of personal sin (9:1–3), it also teaches that some sicknesses are directly related to deliberate disobedience. For example, after committing adultery and murder, David cried out, "When I kept silent about my sin, my body wasted away through my groaning all day long. For day and night Your hand was heavy upon me; my vitality was drained away as with the fever heat of summer" (Ps. 32:3–4; cf. Ps. 38:1–8). Along these same lines, Moses warned Israel:

> If you are not careful to observe all the words of this law which are written in this book, to fear this honored and awesome name, the Lord your God, then the Lord will bring extraordinary plagues on you and your descendants, even severe and lasting plagues, and miserable and chronic sicknesses. He will bring back on you all the diseases of Egypt of which you were afraid, and they will cling to you. Also every sickness and every plague which, not written in the book of this law, the Lord will bring on you until you are destroyed. (Deut. 28:58–61; cf. Lev. 26:14–16)

Even in the church age, Paul wrote to the Corinthians, "For this reason [because of your sin] many among you are weak and sick, and a number sleep [are dead]" (1 Cor. 11:30).

The most natural understanding of the Lord's warning, then, is that the man's illness was the result of specific personal sin on his part. If the man persisted in unrepentant sin, Jesus warned, he would suffer a fate infinitely **worse** than thirty-eight years of a debilitating disease— namely, eternal punishment in hell.

The man's response suggests that he failed to heed Jesus' warning, since he promptly **went away, and told the Jews that it was Jesus who had made him well.** It is astonishing that he would accept this healing after nearly four decades of terrible distress and then walk away from Jesus and show his loyalty to the Jews who hated Him. This has to be one of the great acts of ingratitude and obstinate unbelief in Scripture. He did not intend to praise or worship Jesus for healing him. Since **the Jews** had already manifested open hostility toward Jesus (vv. 10–12), it would have been incredibly naïve to think they would now react positively. He further aided their hostility by identifying Jesus. More likely, the man's actions were a further attempt to defend himself for breaking the Sabbath regulations; he could now answer the authorities' question of verse 12 by naming Jesus (cf. the discussion of vv. 11–13 above).

The Jews also ignored the miracle, as they always did, so the result was predictable: **the Jews were** continually (as the tense of the verb makes clear) **persecuting Jesus, because He was doing these**

things on the Sabbath. Not only was He guilty (in their minds) of violating the Sabbath Himself, but even worse, He had incited another to do so. So began their open opposition toward Jesus—persecution that would eventually result in His death.

The die was cast. Jesus had not only confronted Jewish legalism at its very core by disregarding their Sabbath rules, but had also challenged them with His true identity as the Son of God, in whom "all the fullness of Deity dwells in bodily form" (Col. 2:9). As impossible as it is to imagine, the Jews' opposition to their own Messiah would harden and intensify until they finally were able to satisfy their wicked hearts when they "crucified the Lord of glory" (1 Cor. 2:8).

The Most Startling Claim Ever Made

15

(John 5:17–24)

But He answered them, "My Father is working until now, and I Myself am working." For this reason therefore the Jews were seeking all the more to kill Him, because He not only was breaking the Sabbath, but also was calling God His own Father, making Himself equal with God. Therefore Jesus answered and was saying to them, "Truly, truly, I say to you, the Son can do nothing of Himself, unless it is something He sees the Father doing; for whatever the Father does, these things the Son also does in like manner. For the Father loves the Son, and shows Him all things that He Himself is doing; and the Father will show Him greater works than these, so that you will marvel. For just as the Father raises the dead and gives them life, even so the Son also gives life to whom He wishes. For not even the Father judges anyone, but He has given all judgment to the Son, so that all will honor the Son even as they honor the Father. He who does not honor the Son does not honor the Father who sent Him. Truly, truly, I say to you, he who hears My word, and believes Him who sent Me, has eternal life, and does not come into judgment, but has passed out of death into life." (5:17–24)

Throughout the centuries, scholars and skeptics have given many different answers to the query, "Who is Jesus Christ?" His life is the most influential ever lived, and its impact continues to escalate. Still, Jesus' true identity is still hotly debated by modern historians and theologians. Countless opinions have appeared as unbelievers have attempted to explain away the truth about Him.

The Jewish leaders of Jesus' day, motivated by their own bitter jealousy, accused Him of being a Samaritan (8:48) who was demon-possessed (7:20; 8:52), insane (10:20), and of illegitimate birth (8:41). Although they could not deny Jesus' astonishing power, they discounted it as being of satanic origin (Matt. 12:24). Their successors similarly reviled Jesus as "a transgressor in Israel, who practised magic, scorned the words of the wise, [and] led the people astray" (F. F. Bruce, *New Testament History* [Garden City, N.Y.: Anchor, 1972], 165).

The theological skeptics and liberals of the eighteenth and nineteenth centuries were intent on denying Jesus' deity. They viewed Him as the quintessential strictly human moral teacher, in whom the spark of divinity inherent in all people burned most brightly. In their minds, Jesus' sacrificial life provided mankind with a model that all should follow, but not with a means by which men might be saved. Thus, He was "an example for faith, not the object of faith" (J. Gresham Machen, *Christianity and Liberalism* [Reprint; Grand Rapids: Eerdmans, 1974], 85).

To twentieth-century existentialists, such as the highly influential Rudolf Bultmann, the Jesus of history was all but unknowable. That did not bother Bultmann, however, since he believed that the "Christ of faith" invented by the church could still provide the basis for a genuine religious experience. Neoorthodox theologians, such as Karl Barth, were not willing to so completely ignore the factual significance of Jesus' life or His deity. Yet they were not willing to accept and believe the biblical record of Christ in a truly historical sense.

Other conceptions of Jesus range from the crusading sociopolitical revolutionary of liberation theology, to the cynical Jewish sage of the Jesus Seminar, to the countercultural hero of the rock musicals *Godspell* and *Jesus Christ Superstar.* But all such fanciful and blasphemous viewpoints are far removed from the God-man revealed in holy Scripture. They say more about the obstinate unbelief and perverted imaginations of the people who created them than about Jesus' true identity.

Ironically, in all the debate over Him, Jesus' own self-testimony is seldom considered reasonably. Did He, as historic Christianity has always maintained, claim to be God incarnate in human flesh? Or, as skeptics argue, did His followers later invent those claims and attribute them to Him? All this unbelieving pseudo scholarship ignores the biblical account of His life and ministry, which leaves no legitimate doubt about who Jesus declared Himself to be, and who He was.

Jesus frequently spoke of His unique, otherworldly origin, of having preexisted in heaven before coming into this world. To the hostile Jews He declared, "You are from below, I am from above; you are of this world, I am not of this world" (8:23). "What then," He asked, "if you see the Son of Man ascending to where He was before?" (6:62). In His High Priestly Prayer Jesus spoke of the glory which He had with the Father before the world existed (17:5). In John 16:28 He told His disciples, "I came forth from the Father and have come into the world; I am leaving the world again and going to the Father."

Jesus assumed the prerogatives of deity. He claimed to have control over people's eternal destinies (8:24; cf. Luke 12:8–9; John 5:22, 27–29), to have authority over the divinely ordained institution of the Sabbath (Matt. 12:8; Mark 2:28; Luke 6:5), to have the power to answer prayer (John 14:13–14; cf. Acts 7:59; 9:10–17), and to have the right to receive worship, faith, and obedience due to God alone (Matt. 21:16; John 14:1; cf. John 5:23). He also assumed the right to forgive sins (Mark 2:5–11)—something that, as His shocked opponents correctly understood, only God can do (v. 7).

Jesus also called God's angels (Gen. 28:12; Luke 12:8–9; 15:10; John 1:51) His angels (Matt. 13:41; 24:30–31); God's elect (Luke 18:7; Rom. 8:33) His elect (Matt. 24:30–31); and God's kingdom (Matt. 12:28; 19:24; 21:31; Mark 1:15; Luke 4:43; John 3:3) His kingdom (Matt. 13:41; 16:28; cf. Luke 1:33; 2 Tim. 4:1).

When a Samaritan woman said to Him, "I know that Messiah is coming (He who is called Christ); when that One comes, He will declare all things to us" (4:25) Jesus replied, "I who speak to you am He" (v. 26). In His High Priestly Prayer to the Father, He referred to Himself as "Jesus Christ whom You have sent" (17:3); "Christ" is the Greek equivalent of the Hebrew word translated "Messiah." When asked at His trial by the high priest, "Are You the Christ, the Son of the Blessed One?" (Mark 14:61) Jesus replied simply, "I am" (v. 62). He also accepted, without correction or amendment, the testimonies of Peter (Matt. 16:16–17), Martha (John 11:27), and others (e.g., Matt. 9:27; 20:30–31) that He was the Messiah .

The Lord's favorite description of Himself was "Son of Man" (cf. Matt. 8:20; Mark 2:28; Luke 6:22; John 9:35–37, etc.). Although that title seems to stress His humanity, it also speaks of His deity. Jesus' use of the term derives from Daniel 7:13–14, where the Son of Man is on equal terms with God the Father, the Ancient of Days.

The Jews viewed themselves collectively as sons of God by creation. Jesus, however, claimed to be God's Son by nature. "All things have been handed over to Me by My Father," Jesus affirmed, "and no one knows the Son except the Father; nor does anyone know the Father except the Son, and anyone to whom the Son wills to reveal Him" (Matt. 11:27). In John 5:25–26 He said, "Truly, truly, I say to you, an hour is coming and now is, when the dead will hear the voice of the Son of God, and those who hear will live. For just as the Father has life in Himself, even so He gave to the Son also to have life in Himself." After receiving word that Lazarus was ill Jesus said to the disciples, "This sickness is not to end in death, but for the glory of God, so that the Son of God may be glorified by it" (11:4). When asked at His trial, "Are You the Son of God, then?" Jesus replied, "Yes, I am" (Luke 22:70; cf. Mark 14:61–62). Instead of rejecting the title, the Lord embraced it without apology or embarrassment (Matt. 4:3, 6; 8:29; Mark 3:11–12; Luke 4:41; John 1:49–50; 11:27).

The hostile Jewish authorities clearly understood that Jesus' use of the title Son of God was a claim to deity. Otherwise, they would not have accused Him of blasphemy (cf. 10:36). In fact, it was Jesus' claim to be the Son of God that led the Jews to demand His death: "The Jews answered [Pilate], 'We have a law, and by that law He ought to die because He made Himself out to be the Son of God'" (19:7). Even while He was on the cross, some mocked Him, sneering, "He trusts in God; let God rescue Him now, if He delights in Him; for He said, 'I am the Son of God'" (Matt. 27:43).

Jesus further outraged the unbelieving Jews by taking for Himself the covenant name of God, "I am" (Yahweh). That name was so sacred to the Jews that they refused to even pronounce it, lest they take it in vain and suffer judgment (cf. Ex. 20:7). In John 8:24 Jesus warned that those who refuse to believe He is Yahweh will perish eternally: "Therefore I said to you that you will die in your sins; for unless you believe that I am He, you will die in your sins." (The word "He" is not in the original Greek.) Later in that chapter "Jesus said to [His hearers], 'Truly, truly, I say to you, before Abraham was born, I am'" (v. 58). Unlike many modern deniers of His deity, the Jews knew exactly what He was claiming, as their subsequent attempt to stone Him for blasphemy makes clear (v. 59). In John 13:19 Jesus told His disciples that when what He predicted came to pass, they would believe that He is Yahweh. Even His enemies, coming to arrest Him in Gethsemane, were overwhelmed by His divine power and fell to the ground when Jesus said "I am" (18:5–8).

All of the above lines of evidence converge on one inescapable point: Jesus Christ claimed absolute equality with God. Thus He could say, "I and the Father are one" (10:30); "He who sees Me sees the One who sent Me" (12:45); and "He who has seen Me has seen the Father" (14:9). Those who would deny that Jesus claimed to be God must deny the historical accuracy and truthfulness of the gospel records and thereby establish themselves as superior sources of truth. They are saying they know more about what was true two thousand years ago than the inspired eyewitnesses. Such skepticism is unwarranted, however, since the New Testament is by far the most well-attested document of the ancient world (cf. F. F. Bruce, *The New Testament Documents: Are They Reliable?* (Downers Grove, Ill.: InterVarsity, 1973). Skeptics are also hard-pressed to explain why Jesus' monotheistic Jewish followers would have embraced His deity so early in church history apart from His own claims. William Lane Craig notes,

> Within twenty years of the crucifixion a full-blown Christology pro-claiming Jesus as God incarnate existed. How does one explain this worship by monotheistic Jews of one of their countrymen as God incarnate, apart from the claims of Jesus Himself? . . . If Jesus never made any such claims, then the belief of the earliest Christians in this regard becomes inexplicable. (*Apologetics: An Introduction* [Chicago: Moody, 1984], 160)

This section affirming our Lord's deity flows directly from the confrontation that arose when Jesus healed a crippled man on the Sab-bath (vv. 1–16). The Lord did not violate the Old Testament Sabbath regu-lations, but rather the rabbinic additions to those regulations. Yet He did not defend Himself by pointing out the distinction between God's Law and man's extraneous tradition. Instead, He responded in a far more radical way—He maintained that He was equal with God and thus had the right to do whatever He wanted on the Sabbath. The result is one of the most profound Christological discourses in all of Scripture. In verses 17–24 Jesus makes five unmistakable claims to full equality with God: He is equal with the Father in His person, in His works, in His sovereign power, in His judgment, and in the honor due Him.

JESUS IS EQUAL TO GOD IN HIS PERSON

But He answered them, "My Father is working until now, and I Myself am working." For this reason therefore the Jews were seeking all the more to kill Him, because He not only was break-ing the Sabbath, but also was calling God His own Father, making Himself equal with God. (5:17–18)

As noted in the previous chapter of this volume, the Sabbath obser-vance was at the heart of Jewish worship in Jesus' day. The Lord's reply to those who challenged Him for violating it (5:16), **"My Father is working until now, and I Myself am working,"** implies that the Sabbath was not instituted for God's benefit but for man's (Mark 2:27). In other words, the Sabbath restriction on working did not apply to God; He was not required to rest on every seventh day. It is true that at the end of creation week, He "rested on the seventh day from all His work which He had done" (Gen. 2:2). That, however, was not because He was tired or received some benefit, for "the Everlasting God, the Lord, the Creator of the ends of the earth does not become weary or tired" (Isa. 40:28). Instead, it was to set a divine example for man to rest one day out of each week (Ex. 20:9–11). (For a discussion of the New Testament believer's relationship to the Old Testament Sabbath, see John MacArthur, *Colossians and Philemon*, The MacArthur New Testament Commentary (Chicago: Moody, 1992), 118–19.)

The significance of the seventh day is underscored by the three references to it in Genesis 2:1–3. According to verse 3, God "sanctified" ("set apart"; "separated") that day to distinguish it from the first six, none of which are so designated. Three verbs in the passage, each of them associated with the work of God, reveal why He uniquely set apart the seventh day.

"Completed" (v. 1) stresses that the entire work of God in creation was finished by the end of the sixth day. In contrast to the theory of evolution (whether atheistic or theistic), the Bible denies that the creative process is still ongoing.

Since His work of creation was completed, God "rested" (vv. 2–3). As noted above, that does not imply any weariness on His part (Isa. 40:28); the verb merely indicates that by the seventh day God had ceased to do the work of creation (cf. Ex. 20:11).

Finally, God "blessed" the seventh day (v. 3); that is, He set it aside as a memorial. Every Saturday of every week serves as a reminder that God created the entire universe in six days, and then rested from His creative activity.

But as even the rabbis themselves acknowledged, God's Sabbath rest (cf. Heb. 4:9–10) from His creative work does not obviate His unceasing providential work of sustaining the universe (Heb. 1:3). Jesus' statement that He worked on the Sabbath just like the Father was nothing less than a claim to full deity and equality with God, that "the Son of Man is Lord of the Sabbath" (Matt. 12:8). His words also served as a subtle rebuke to the Jewish legalistic system, under which He had been indicted for doing good and showing mercy on the Sabbath. After all, God Himself does good and shows mercy on the Sabbath. Jesus, therefore, maintained that it is right to do good on the Sabbath, since God does. Ironically, even the unbelieving Jews performed acts of mercy on the Sabbath (cf. 7:23; Luke 14:5)—the very thing for which they hypocritically rebuked Jesus.

The hostile **Jews** instantly grasped the import of Jesus' words and as a result **were seeking** (the tense of the verb indicates continuous action) **all the more to kill Him** (cf. v. 16). He was **not only breaking the Sabbath, but** even worse in their minds, Jesus **also was calling God His own Father, making Himself equal with God** (cf. 10:30–33). In contrast to the Jews' collective reference to God as "our Father," Jesus called God **His own Father.** The clear implication, which His opponents readily understood, was that He was claiming to be fully **equal with God** in nature (cf. 1:1; 8:58; 20:28; Phil. 2:6). In response, they intensified their efforts to take His life (cf. 7:1, 19, 25; 8:37, 40, 59; 11:53), not just for exposing their self-styled legalism, but now with justification (in their minds), because He was asserting His deity.

JESUS IS EQUAL TO GOD IN HIS WORKS

Therefore Jesus answered and was saying to them, "Truly, truly, I say to you, the Son can do nothing of Himself, unless it is something He sees the Father doing; for whatever the Father does, these things the Son also does in like manner. For the Father loves the Son, and shows Him all things that He Himself is doing; and the Father will show Him greater works than these, so that you will marvel." (5:19–20)

For a mere man to claim to be God was, to the Jews, an outrageous act of blasphemy. Therefore if they had misunderstood Him, Jesus surely would have immediately and vehemently denied making such a claim (cf. Acts 14:11–15; Rev. 19:10; 22:8–9). But instead, He became even more forceful and emphatic, introducing His next statement with the solemn affirmation, **truly, truly, I say to you** (cf. the discussion of 3:3 in chapter 8 of this volume). In the strongest possible terms, the Lord assured His hearers that what He said to them was true. He further defended His healing on the Sabbath by tying His activities directly to those of the Father. **"The Son can do nothing of Himself,"** Jesus declared, **"unless it is something He sees the Father doing."** He always acted in perfect harmony with and subordination to the Father's will. Thus, His works paralleled those of the Father in both their nature and extent, **for whatever the Father does, these things the Son also does in like manner.** Obviously, only someone who is equal to the Father could do everything that He does. Christ's statement, then, was a clear declaration of His own divinity.

The perfect harmony that characterizes the joint working of the Father and the Son stems from the absolute unity of essence that they share (cf. 17:21). Because they are one in being, one eternal God (10:30), to see Christ act is to see God act (John 12:45; 14:9–10). By accusing Jesus of wrongdoing, the religious leaders were actually doing what they charged Jesus with doing, impugning the holy nature of God Himself.

In verse 20 Jesus described the oneness of the Father and the Son as a union of love: **the Father loves the Son** (cf. 3:35; 17:26; Matt. 3:17; 17:5; 2 Peter 1:17) **and shows Him all things that He Himself is doing.** The verb translated **loves** is not *agapaō,* the love of will and choice, but *phileō,* the love of deep feelings; the warmth of affection that a father feels for his son. This is the only time in the New Testament that it is used to refer to the Father's love for the Son. The present tense of the verb indicates an eternally uninterrupted and all-knowing love that leaves no room for ignorance, making it impossible for Jesus to have been unaware of God's will, whether about the Sabbath, or about anything else.

Jesus continued by declaring that **the Father** would **show Him** still **greater works.** His healing of the crippled man had amazed the crowds. But in obedience to the Father, Jesus predicted that He would perform deeds that were even more spectacular—including raising the dead (v. 21) and judging all people (v. 22). As a result, His listeners would **marvel.**

JESUS IS EQUAL TO GOD IN HIS POWER AND SOVEREIGNTY

"For just as the Father raises the dead and gives them life, even so the Son also gives life to whom He wishes." (5:21)

By asserting His equality with God, Jesus claimed that He had the parallel power with God to raise the dead **just as the Father raises the dead and gives them life.** The Bible teaches that only God has the power to give life to the dead (Deut. 32:39; 1 Sam. 2:6; 2 Kings 5:7; Acts 26:8; 2 Cor. 1:9; Heb. 11:19), and the Old Testament records several instances where He did so (1 Kings 17:17–24; 2 Kings 4:32–37; 13:20–21). Because His power is the same as the Father, Jesus Christ is able to raise the physically dead (11:25–44; Matt. 9:18–25; Luke 7:11–15; cf. John 6:39–40, 44). Moreover, He has the power to give spiritual **life** to the spiritually dead. "Whoever drinks of the water that I will give him," Jesus promised, "shall never thirst; but the water that I will give him will become in him a well of water springing up to eternal life" (4:14). In John 6 He admonished His hearers, "Do not work for the food which perishes, but for the food which endures to eternal life, which the Son of Man will give to you," because He is "the bread of God . . . which comes down out of heaven, and gives life to the world" (vv. 27, 33; cf. vv. 35, 48, 54; 1:4; 10:28; 11:25; 14:6; 17:2).

Unlike Elijah (1 Kings 17:22) and Elisha (2 Kings 4:34–35), Jesus did not merely act as God's representative when He raised the dead, but as God Himself. **The Son** Himself **gives** resurrection and spiritual **life to whom He wishes.** As God is the source of life, so Jesus Christ is the source of life. As God chooses when He gives life, so does the Son choose, in perfect agreement with the Father, a truth illustrated by the salvation of sinners. All whom the Father chose before the foundation of the world to give to the Son will come to him, and He will not reject any of them (6:37). Even Jesus' truly human prayer in Gethsemane, "My Father, if it is possible, let this cup pass from Me; yet not as I will, but as You will" (Matt. 26:39), yields to the perfect concord between the persons of the Godhead.

JESUS IS EQUAL TO GOD IN HIS JUDGMENT

"For not even the Father judges anyone, but He has given all judgment to the Son," (5:22)

Jesus' authority to grant spiritual life to whomever He chooses is consistent with His authority to judge all men on the last day (cf. 3:18–19; 12:48). Since God is the "judge of all the earth" (Gen. 18:25; cf. 1 Sam. 2:10; 1 Chron. 16:33; Pss. 82:8; 94:2; 96:13; 98:9), the fact that the **Father judges** no one, but **has given all judgment to the Son** further attests to Christ's deity. Because their wills are in perfect harmony, all judgment can be given to Christ in the assurance that His judgment will be, in fact, the very same as the Father's judgment. Although judgment was not the primary purpose of Christ's first coming to earth (3:17; 12:47), it remains the inescapable final result of rejecting the salvation He offers (3:18).

In the future, "the Lord Jesus will be revealed from heaven with His mighty angels in flaming fire, dealing out retribution to those who do not know God and to those who do not obey the gospel of our Lord Jesus" (2 Thess. 1:7–8), because God "has fixed a day in which He will judge the world in righteousness through a Man whom He has appointed, having furnished proof to all men by raising Him from the dead" (Acts 17:31). On that final, terrible day of judgment, those who have rejected Jesus will hear Him say, "I never knew you; depart from Me, you who practice lawlessness" (Matt. 7:23).

JESUS IS EQUAL TO GOD IN HIS HONOR

"so that all will honor the Son even as they honor the Father. He who does not honor the Son does not honor the Father who sent Him. Truly, truly, I say to you, he who hears My word, and believes Him who sent Me, has eternal life, and does not come into judgment, but has passed out of death into life." (5:23–24)

The Father's purpose in entrusting all His works and judgment to Jesus is **so that all will honor the Son even as they honor the Father.** It is only fitting that those equal in nature (vv. 17–18), works (vv. 19–20), power and sovereignty (v. 21), and judgment (v. 22) would be accorded equal honor. The Father's honor is not diminished by the honor paid to Christ; on the contrary, it is enhanced.

Although the unbelieving Jews thought they were truly worshiping God while rejecting His Son (cf. 16:2), such was not the case, for **he who does not honor the Son does not honor the Father who sent Him.** This was an astounding claim on Jesus' part, as D. A. Carson notes:

> In a theistic universe, such a statement belongs to one who is himself to be addressed as God (cf. 20:28), or to stark insanity. The one who utters such things is to be dismissed with pity or scorn, or worshipped as Lord. If with much current scholarship we retreat to seeing in such material less the claims of the Son than the beliefs and witness of the Evangelist and his church, the same options confront us. Either John is supremely deluded and must be dismissed as a fool, or his witness is true and Jesus is to be ascribed the honours due God alone. There is no rational middle ground. (*The Gospel According to John,* The Pillar New Testament Commentary (Grand Rapids: Eerdmans, 1991), 255).

When He was asked, "What shall we do, so that we may work the works of God?" Jesus answered, "This is the work of God, that you believe in Him whom He has sent" (6:28–29). "He who hates Me," He warned, "hates My Father also" (15:23). Those who refuse to honor the Son while claiming to honor the Father are actually self-deceived. John Heading writes,

> It is not up to a man to decide that he will honour the One or the Other; it is either both or neither. In religious circles, it is too easy for unbelief to contemplate God but not the Son. Knowledge of One implies knowledge of the Other (John 8:19); hatred of One implies hatred of the Other (15:23); denial of the One implies denial of the Other (1 John 2:23). (*What the Bible Teaches: John* [Kilmarnock, Scotland: John Ritchie, 1988], 93)

That the Father and the Son are to be afforded equal honor force-fully asserts Christ's deity and equality with God, who declared through the prophet Isaiah, "I will not give My glory to another" (Isa. 42:8; 48:11). Yet, the Father has commanded that **all will honor the Son.** In Philippians 2:9–11 Paul wrote,

> For this reason also, God highly exalted Him, and bestowed on Him the name which is above every name, so that at the name of Jesus every knee will bow, of those who are in heaven and on earth and under the earth, and that every tongue will confess that Jesus Christ is Lord, to the glory of God the Father.

Willingly or unwillingly, everyone will eventually obey the Father's command to honor Jesus Christ.

Jesus closed this section of His discourse by reaffirming His authority to give eternal life to whomever He desires. The Lord underscored the statement's monumental significance by introducing it with the solemn formula *amēn, amēn* (**truly, truly**). He identified those who receive eternal life as those who hear His **word** (or message) and believe the Father **who sent** Him. As always in the Scriptures, divine sovereignty in salvation is not apart from human responsibility to repent and believe the gospel. The blessed promise to those who believe is that they do not **come into judgment, but** have **passed out of death into life.** As Paul wrote to the Romans, "There is now no condemnation for those who are in Christ Jesus" (Rom. 8:1).

The claims of Jesus Christ confront everyone, forcing all to make a decision either for or against Him. There is no neutral ground, for as Jesus said, "He who is not with Me is against Me; and he who does not gather with Me, scatters" (Luke 11:23). Those who accept Him for who He is, God incarnate in human flesh, will be saved from their sins through Him (Matt. 1:21; 1 Tim. 1:15; Heb. 7:25). But those who believe Him to be anything other than who He truly is will one day face His judgment (John 3:18; 9:39; 12:47–48; 16:8–9; Acts 10:38–42; 17:31; 2 Tim. 4:1).

The Two Resurrections (John 5:25–29)

16

"Truly, truly, I say to you, an hour is coming and now is, when the dead will hear the voice of the Son of God, and those who hear will live. For just as the Father has life in Himself, even so He gave to the Son also to have life in Himself; and He gave Him authority to execute judgment, because He is the Son of Man. Do not marvel at this; for an hour is coming, in which all who are in the tombs will hear His voice, and will come forth; those who did the good deeds to a resurrection of life, those who committed the evil deeds to a resurrection of judgment." (5:25–29)

To the age-old question, "If a man dies, will he live again?" (Job 14:14), the Bible answers emphatically, "Yes." All people, both believers and unbelievers, will one day be raised from the dead. Everyone will live forever, consciously and individually.

For the believer, there are two aspects to that resurrection—spiritual and physical. Spiritually, Christians are resurrected when God imparts salvation to their previously dead souls. Although they were dead in their sins (Eph. 2:1), they now enjoy new life in Christ (v. 5; cf. Rom. 6:4).

Physically, believers are confident that, even though their earthly bodies will eventually wear out, they will one day receive resurrection bodies that will endure forever. They will be given these new bodies when "the Lord Jesus Christ ... will transform the body of [their] humble state into conformity with the body of His glory, by the exertion of the power that He has even to subject all things to Himself" (Phil. 3:20–21). As a result, believers will be prepared to enjoy resurrection life in the Millennium in sinless perfection, as well as be fitted for eternal existence in the new heavens and the new earth (cf. Rev. 21–22).

The Bible teaches that unbelievers will also experience a physical resurrection. But, because they never experienced spiritual resurrection, they will be raised to face final sentencing before the Great White Throne. In keeping with their condemnation, their eternal resurrection bodies will be suited for their eternal punishment in the lake of fire (Rev. 20:11–15).

The truth of resurrection is repeated throughout the Scriptures, beginning in the book of Genesis. As he was about to sacrifice his son Isaac, "Abraham said to his young men, 'Stay here with the donkey, and I and the lad will go over there; and we will worship and return to you'" (Gen. 22:5). Confident that both he and Isaac would return from the sacrifice, Abraham was willing to kill his son because he knew "that God is able to raise people even from the dead" (Heb. 11:17–19), and would do so, if it was necessary to keep His word.

Abraham's faith is mirrored by other Old Testament saints. Answering his own question, "If a man dies, will he live again?" Job affirmed, "All the days of my struggle I will wait until my change comes" (Job 14:14). Later, he amplified his belief in the resurrection of the body:

> As for me, I know that my Redeemer lives,
> And at the last He will take His stand on the earth.
> Even after my skin is destroyed,
> Yet from my flesh I shall see God;
> Whom I myself shall behold,
> And whom my eyes will see and not another. (Job 19:25–27)

Daniel similarly noted that "those who sleep in the dust of the ground will awake, these to everlasting life, but the others to disgrace and everlasting contempt" (Dan. 12:2). And God Himself, through the prophet Hosea, asked rhetorically, "Shall I ransom them from the power of Sheol? Shall I redeem them from death? O Death, where are your thorns? O Sheol, where is your sting?" (Hos. 13:14; cf. 1 Cor. 15:55). New Testament passages such as Matthew 22:29–32, John 11:24, Acts 24:15, and Hebrews 11:35 also allude to the Old Testament teaching on the resurrection.

Building on that foundation, the New Testament gives further insight into the truth of literal, bodily resurrection. In Luke 14:14 the Lord spoke of "the resurrection of the righteous," while in John 6:39 He declared, "This is the will of Him who sent Me, that of all that He has given Me I lose nothing, but raise it up on the last day" (cf. vv. 40, 44, 54). Before raising Lazarus from the dead, Jesus proclaimed, "I am the resurrection and the life; he who believes in Me will live even if he dies" (11:25).

The apostles also preached the resurrection. Acts 4:2 records that the Jewish authorities were "greatly disturbed because they were teaching the people and proclaiming in Jesus the resurrection from the dead." Paul boldly announced the doctrine of the resurrection to the skeptical Greek philosophers in Athens (Acts 17:18, 32). While standing before the Sanhedrin, he "began crying out in the Council, 'Brethren, I am a Pharisee, a son of Pharisees; I am on trial for the hope and resurrection of the dead!'" (Acts 23:6; cf. 24:21).

The epistles continue to expand the biblical teaching regarding the resurrection of the body. Paul devoted an entire chapter, 1 Corinthians 15, to defending that vital doctrine. In verse 21 he wrote, "For since by a man came death, by a man also came the resurrection of the dead." In his second inspired letter to the Corinthians, Paul reminded them, "We know that if the earthly tent which is our house is torn down, we have a building from God, a house not made with hands, eternal in the heavens" (2 Cor. 5:1). To the Philippians, as noted earlier, he declared that Jesus Christ "will transform the body of our humble state into conformity with the body of His glory" (Phil. 3:21; cf. v. 11). At the Rapture, "the Lord Himself will descend from heaven with a shout, with the voice of the archangel and with the trumpet of God, and the dead in Christ will rise first" (1 Thess. 4:16). The apostle John also had the future resurrection of believers in mind when he wrote, "Beloved, now we are children of God, and it has not appeared as yet what we will be. We know that when He appears, we will be like Him, because we will see Him just as He is" (1 John 3:2).

In the previous section (vv. 17–24), Jesus startled and outraged His opponents by claiming to be God, and thus exempt from their man-made Sabbath restrictions. His claim, in large part, was built on two key realities: that He had the authority to give life, and that He had the authority to judge (vv. 21–22). In verse 24, He showed how those divine prerogatives affect sinners: those who believe in Him receive eternal life, while those who reject Him will be judged. Verses 25–29 further illustrate those truths, presenting both the spiritual resurrection of believers and the physical resurrection that awaits everyone.

SPIRITUAL RESURRECTION

"Truly, truly, I say to you, an hour is coming and now is, when the dead will hear the voice of the Son of God, and those who hear

will live. For just as the Father has life in Himself, even so He gave to the Son also to have life in Himself;" (5:25–26)

The discussions of both the spiritual and physical resurrections may be divided into three subpoints: the persons resurrected, the power that resurrected them, and the purpose for their resurrection.

THE PERSONS

"Truly, truly, I say to you, an hour is coming and now is, when the dead will hear the voice of the Son of God, and those who hear will live." (5:25)

The solemn phrase *amēn, amēn* (**truly, truly**) introduces an emphatic, unarguable declaration by Jesus. He began with the seemingly paradoxical statement **an hour is coming and now is.** The **hour** of the believers' resurrection **now is** in the sense that when they "were dead in [their] trespasses and sins . . . [God] made [them] alive together with Christ, . . . and raised [them] up with Him" (Eph. 2:1, 5–6; cf. Col. 2:13). Yet the **hour** is still **coming** in the sense that the resurrection of their physical bodies is yet future (1 Cor. 15:35–54; Phil. 3:20–21).

The already/not yet sense of the phrase may also be understood in another way. While Christ was present, He offered spiritual life to all who would heed His words (6:37; Matt. 7:24–27; cf. John 14:6). Yet the full expression of the new era He inaugurated would not come until the day of Pentecost (14:17). Both during Christ's earthly ministry (e.g., 4:39–42, 53), and in the fullness of the Spirit's ministry after Pentecost, **the** spiritually **dead** who responded to **the voice of the Son of God** would **live** in the Spirit (cf. Rom. 8:1–11).

The New Testament frequently describes unbelievers as those who are spiritually **dead.** Paul charged the Romans to "present yourselves to God as those alive from the dead" (Rom. 6:13). He reminded the Ephesians that in their unregenerate state they were "dead in [their] trespasses and sins" (Eph. 2:1, 5; cf. Matt. 8:22). Later in that epistle the apostle expressed the gospel invitation, "For this reason it says, 'Awake, sleeper, and arise from the dead, and Christ will shine on you'" (Eph. 5:14). To the Colossians he wrote, "When you were dead in your transgressions and the uncircumcision of your flesh, He made you alive together with Him, having forgiven us all our transgressions" (Col. 2:13). The apostle John also described salvation as having "passed out of death into life" (1 John 3:14).

To be spiritually dead is to be insensible to the things of God and totally unable to respond to Him (cf. 1 Cor. 2:14; 2 Cor. 4:3–4). Paul vividly described it as walking "according to the course of this world, according to the prince of the power of the air, of the spirit that is now working in the sons of disobedience . . . [living] in the lusts of our flesh, indulging the desires of the flesh and of the mind, and [being] by nature children of wrath" (Eph. 2:2–3). Spiritual death, according to the nineteenth-century Scottish commentator John Eadie,

> implies insensibility. The dead, which are as insusceptible as their kindred clay, can be neither wooed nor won back to existence. The beauties of holiness do not attract man in his spiritual insensibility, nor do the miseries of hell deter him. God's love, Christ's sufferings, earnest conjurations by all that is tender and by all that is terrible, do not affect him. . . . It implies inability. The corpse cannot raise itself from the tomb and come back to the scenes and society of the living world. . . . Inability characterizes fallen man. (*A Commentary on the Greek Text of the Epistle of Paul to the Ephesians* [Reprint; Grand Rapids: Baker, 1979], 120–21)

That Christ came to give eternal life to the spiritually dead is a central theme in John's gospel (1:4; 3:15–16, 36; 4:14; 5:39–40; 6:27, 33, 35, 40, 47–48, 51, 54; 8:12; 10:10, 28; 11:25; 14:6; 17:2–3; 20:31).

THE POWER

"For just as the Father has life in Himself, even so He gave to the Son also to have life in Himself;" (5:26)

The Son can give life (v. 21) because, like the **Father, He has life in Himself.** No one can give to others what he himself lacks; thus no sinful human being can generate for himself eternal life, nor impart it to anyone else. God alone possesses it, and He grants it through His Son to whomever He wills.

Those who deny the deity of Christ twist Jesus' statement that the Father **gave** life to the Son into an admission of His own creatureliness and inferiority to the Father. Such is not the case, however. John had already stated in the prologue to his gospel that the Son possessed life in Himself from all eternity (1:4). Again, it must be affirmed that when He became a man, our Lord voluntarily gave up the independent use of His divine attributes (Phil. 2:6–7; cf. John 5:19, 30; 8:28). But the Father granted Him the authority to give life (both physical and spiritual) even during the self-limiting condescension of His earthly ministry.

THE PURPOSE

"those who hear will live." (5:25b)

Those who experience spiritual resurrection will receive abundant (10:10), everlasting life. The Lord was not, of course, teaching that everyone who listens to a gospel presentation will be saved (cf. Rom. 10:9–10). It is only **those who hear** in the sense of true faith and obedience to the gospel who **will live.** In other words, those who have savingly heard will respond in repentance and belief. "My sheep hear My voice," Jesus declared, "and I know them, and they follow Me" (10:27). To Pilate He affirmed, "Everyone who is of the truth hears My voice" (18:37). In the Lord's letter to the churches in Revelation, each ends with the exhortation, "He who has an ear, let him hear what the Spirit says to the churches" (2:7, 11, 17, 29; 3:6, 13, 22). That statement identifies believers as those who have both the spiritual faculty and duty to respond to divine revelation. In contrast, the lost do not savingly hear Christ's voice; they do not understand or obey it (8:43, 47; 12:47; 14:24), and hence will not live spiritually.

THE PHYSICAL RESURRECTION

"and He gave Him authority to execute judgment, because He is the Son of Man. Do not marvel at this; for an hour is coming, in which all who are in the tombs will hear His voice, and will come forth; those who did the good deeds to a resurrection of life, those who committed the evil deeds to a resurrection of judgment." (5:27–29)

As with the authority to give life, the Father also **gave** the incarnate and submissive Son the **authority to execute judgment.** Christ received that authority **because He is the Son of Man.** As God in human flesh, a man "who has been tempted in all things as we are, yet without sin" (Heb. 4:15), Jesus is uniquely qualified to be mankind's judge. The phrase **Son of Man,** Jesus' favorite designation of Himself, derives from Daniel's messianic description of the Son of Man as the one who "was given dominion, glory and a kingdom, that all the peoples, nations and men of every language might serve Him. His dominion is an everlasting dominion which will not pass away; and His kingdom is one which will not be destroyed" (Dan. 7:14). Since He is the God-man who entered fully into human life, experience, and temptation (Heb. 2:14–18; 4:14–16), Jesus can be the ultimate judge of all mankind.

THE PERSONS

"Do not marvel at this; for an hour is coming, in which all who are in the tombs" (5:28*a*)

The unbelieving Jews were astonished and outraged at Jesus' bold claim to be the giver of spiritual life and the ultimate judge of all men. But the Lord was about to make another shocking claim. Rebuking them for their unbelief—that they would **marvel at** His teachings— Jesus continued by revealing another truth that astounded them: that He would one day raise the dead from their graves. As He did with the spiritual resurrection (v. 25), Jesus said that the **hour** of bodily resurrection is **coming.** But unlike the spiritual resurrection, He did not say that there is a present aspect of that reality. The resurrection of **all who are in the tombs** is still future. At that time, the souls of the righteous dead, now in heaven with the Lord (2 Cor. 5:6–8), and of the wicked dead, now in torment in Hades (Luke 16:22–23), will be given resurrected bodies fit for eternity.

Some argue from this text that the resurrection of both the righteous and unrighteous takes place at the same time. But while Jesus spoke here of the resurrection in general, He did not describe one general resurrection. On the contrary, in verse 29 He clearly distinguished between the resurrection of life and the resurrection of judgment. He made that same distinction in Luke 14:14, where He spoke of the resurrection of the righteous, implying that it is a distinct event. Revelation 20:4–6 also mentions two resurrections: the first consists of the righteous dead before the Millennium, and the second of the unrighteous dead for the Great White Throne judgment at the end of the Millennium. (For a detailed exposition of Revelation 20:4–6, see *Revelation 12–22,* The MacArthur New Testament Commentary [Chicago: Moody, 2000], 236ff.; Robert L. Thomas, *Revelation 8–22: An Exegetical Commentary* [Chicago: Moody, 1995], 412ff.)

The Bible teaches that the dead are raised in a specific sequence, not all at once:

> For as in Adam all die, so also in Christ all will be made alive. But each in his own order: Christ the first fruits, after that those who are Christ's at His coming, then comes the end, when He hands over the kingdom to the God and Father, when He has abolished all rule and all authority and power. (1 Cor. 15:22–24)

The adjective *tagma* ("order" or "turn") stresses that the dead are raised at different times: "Christ the first fruits," "those who are Christ's at

His coming," and the rest at "the end"—the consummation of all things when the wicked (the only ones not already mentioned) will be resurrected. The adjectives *epeita* ("after that") and *eita* ("then") almost always describe chronological (as opposed to logical) sequences of events.

Those who belong to Christ will be raised in connection with His coming. The believers of the church age (from Pentecost to the Rapture) will be raised at the Rapture (1 Thess. 4:16), and the Old Testament saints, along with those saved during the Tribulation, at the end of the Tribulation (Rev. 20:4; cf. Dan. 12:2). Although Scripture does not explicitly mention them, believers who die during the Millennium will presumably receive their resurrection bodies immediately.

THE POWER

"will hear His voice, and will come forth;" (5:28b–29a)

Jesus did not delineate the order of the resurrection in this passage because He was not concerned here with chronology, but with revealing His divine power. This time the phrase **hear His voice** does not describe the effectual hearing of faith as in verse 25, but refers to the sovereign command of Christ. At His charge, the bodies of everyone who ever lived will come back to life. It is no wonder, then, that the apostle Paul longed to "know Him and the power of His resurrection" (Phil. 3:10).

THE PURPOSE

"those who did the good deeds to a resurrection of life, those who committed the evil deeds to a resurrection of judgment." (5:29b)

The final resurrection will usher believers into the glories and joys of eternal **life,** and bring unbelievers to the endless suffering of eternal **judgment.** By characterizing believers as **those who did the good deeds** and unbelievers as **those who committed the evil deeds** Jesus was not teaching that salvation is by works. Throughout His ministry, Jesus clearly taught that salvation "is the work of God, that [people] believe in Him whom He has sent" (6:29; cf. Isa. 64:6; Rom. 4:2–4; 9:11; Gal. 2:16; Eph. 2:8–9; 2 Tim. 1:9; Titus 3:5). Good works are simply the evidence of salvation; Jesus called them "fruit" in Luke 6:43–45. Those who believe in the Son will as a result do **good deeds** (3:21; Eph. 2:10; James 2:14–20), while those who reject the Son will be characterized by **evil deeds** (3:18–19).

While works do not save, they do provide the basis for divine judgment. Scripture teaches that God judges people based on their deeds (Ps. 62:12; Isa. 3:10–11; Jer. 17:10; 32:19; Matt. 16:27; Gal. 6:7–9; Rev. 20:12; 22:12), because those deeds manifest the condition of the heart. Thus Jesus said, "The mouth speaks out of that which fills the heart" (Matt. 12:34). Later in Matthew's gospel He taught that "the things that proceed out of the mouth come from the heart, and those defile the man. For out of the heart come evil thoughts, murders, adulteries, fornications, thefts, false witness, slanders" (15:18–19). In Luke 6:45 Jesus told His hearers, "The good man out of the good treasure of his heart brings forth what is good; and the evil man out of the evil treasure brings forth what is evil." The apostle Paul also taught that people's actions reflect their inner nature. To the Romans he wrote,

> [God] will render to each person according to his deeds: to those who by perseverance in doing good seek for glory and honor and immortality, eternal life; but to those who are selfishly ambitious and do not obey the truth, but obey unrighteousness, wrath and indignation. There will be tribulation and distress for every soul of man who does evil, of the Jew first and also of the Greek, but glory and honor and peace to everyone who does good, to the Jew first and also to the Greek. (Rom. 2:6–10)

A few chapters later, Paul made it clear that those who attain to the resurrection of the righteous do not do so by their own merits, but by means of their union with Jesus Christ through faith:

> Do you not know that all of us who have been baptized into Christ Jesus have been baptized into His death? Therefore we have been buried with Him through baptism into death, so that as Christ was raised from the dead through the glory of the Father, so we too might walk in newness of life. For if we have become united with Him in the likeness of His death, certainly we shall also be in the likeness of His resurrection. (Rom. 6:3–5)

Thus good deeds reveal the presence or absence of salvation, but do not produce it. They are its effect, not its cause.

The importance of the doctrine of the resurrection cannot be overstated: without it, there is no Christian faith. Writing to the Corinthians, who were wavering on the doctrine of the resurrection, Paul made it clear that

> if the dead are not raised, not even Christ has been raised; and if Christ has not been raised, your faith is worthless; you are still in your sins. Then those also who have fallen asleep in Christ have perished. If we

have hoped in Christ in this life only, we are of all men most to be pitied. (1 Cor. 15:16–19)

The apostle's great hope, as it is of all believers, was to "attain to the resurrection from the dead" (Phil. 3:11), a reference to the resurrection of the righteous. He understood the truth that "blessed and holy is the one who has a part in the first resurrection; over these the second death has no power, but they will be priests of God and of Christ and will reign with Him for a thousand years" (Rev. 20:6). And he knew that such a resurrection was attainable only through faith in Jesus Christ (cf. Rom. 6:4–5).

Concluding his magnificent chapter on the resurrection, Paul wrote, "Therefore, my beloved brethren, be steadfast, immovable, always abounding in the work of the Lord, knowing that your toil is not in vain in the Lord" (1 Cor. 15:58). The doctrine of the resurrection provides hope for the future that energizes the Christian's life and service to God in the present.

Witnesses to the Deity of Christ (John 5:30–47)

17

"I can do nothing on My own initiative. As I hear, I judge; and My judgment is just, because I do not seek My own will, but the will of Him who sent Me. If I alone testify about Myself, My testimony is not true. There is another who testifies of Me, and I know that the testimony which He gives about Me is true. You have sent to John, and he has testified to the truth. But the testimony which I receive is not from man, but I say these things so that you may be saved. He was the lamp that was burning and was shining and you were willing to rejoice for a while in his light. But the testimony which I have is greater than the testimony of John; for the works which the Father has given Me to accomplish—the very works that I do—testify about Me, that the Father has sent Me. And the Father who sent Me, He has testified of Me. You have neither heard His voice at any time nor seen His form. You do not have His word abiding in you, for you do not believe Him whom He sent. You search the Scriptures because you think that in them you have eternal life; it is these that testify about Me; and you are unwilling to come to Me so that you may have life. I do not receive glory from men; but I know you, that you do not have the love of God in yourselves. I have come in My Father's name, and

you do not receive Me; if another comes in his own name, you will receive him. How can you believe, when you receive glory from one another and you do not seek the glory that is from the one and only God? Do not think that I will accuse you before the Father; the one who accuses you is Moses, in whom you have set your hope. For if you believed Moses, you would believe Me, for he wrote about Me. But if you do not believe his writings, how will you believe My words?" (5:30–47)

A singularly tragic theme in Scripture is that of God's unrequited love for wayward Israel. His people, whom He graciously chose for Himself (Deut. 7:7–8), repeatedly proved unthankful and unfaithful to Him in return. After God delivered them from Egypt, cared for them in the wilderness, and brought them into the Promised Land, "the people served the Lord all the days of Joshua, and all the days of the elders who survived Joshua, who had seen all the great work of the Lord which He had done for Israel" (Judg. 2:7).

But all too soon spiritual apostasy and rank idolatry began to manifest itself. After Joshua and his contemporaries died

> there arose another generation after them who did not know the Lord, nor yet the work which He had done for Israel. Then the sons of Israel did evil in the sight of the Lord and served the Baals, and they forsook the Lord, the God of their fathers, who had brought them out of the land of Egypt, and followed other gods from among the gods of the peoples who were around them, and bowed themselves down to them; thus they provoked the Lord to anger. . . . They did not listen to their judges, for they played the harlot after other gods and bowed themselves down to them. They turned aside quickly from the way in which their fathers had walked in obeying the commandments of the Lord; they did not do as their fathers. (Judg. 2:10–12, 17; cf. 8:33; Ps. 106:34–39)

As the centuries passed, the spiritual climate in Israel only worsened. Times of genuine repentance and spiritual refreshment were few and far between. Writing seven hundred years after Joshua, the prophet Isaiah pictured Israel's apostasy in a parable:

> Let me sing now for my well-beloved
> A song of my beloved concerning His vineyard.
> My well-beloved had a vineyard on a fertile hill.
> He dug it all around, removed its stones,
> And planted it with the choicest vine.
> And He built a tower in the middle of it
> And also hewed out a wine vat in it;

Then He expected it to produce good grapes,
But it produced only worthless ones.
"And now, O inhabitants of Jerusalem and men of Judah,
Judge between Me and My vineyard.
What more was there to do for My vineyard that I have not done in it?
Why, when I expected it to produce good grapes did it produce worth-
    less ones?
So now let Me tell you what I am going to do to My vineyard:
I will remove its hedge and it will be consumed;
I will break down its wall and it will become trampled ground.
I will lay it waste;
It will not be pruned or hoed,
But briars and thorns will come up.
I will also charge the clouds to rain no rain on it."
For the vineyard of the Lord of hosts is the house of Israel
And the men of Judah His delightful plant.
Thus He looked for justice, but behold, bloodshed;
For righteousness, but behold, a cry of distress. (Isa. 5:1–7)

Through the prophet Jeremiah, God gave a similar indictment: "Surely, as a woman treacherously departs from her lover, so you have dealt treacherously with Me, O house of Israel," declares the Lord" (Jer. 3:20; cf. 5:11–12). Instead of serving the Lord wholeheartedly, the nation "profaned the sanctuary of the Lord" (Mal. 2:11) and served other gods instead.

The Hebrew Scriptures frequently depict Israel as a harlot, who left her husband, the Lord, and committed adultery with idols. In fact, the Old Testament uses the term "harlot" to refer to spiritual adultery more frequently than to physical adultery. For instance, in Ezekiel 6:9, God said of Israel, "I have been hurt by their adulterous hearts which turned away from Me, and by their eyes which played the harlot after their idols" (cf. 20:30). Later in Ezekiel's prophecy, two graphic and riveting chapters are devoted to Israel's unfaithfulness (16, 23), with the nation depicted as an unfaithful wife who became a "bold-faced harlot" (16:30), forsaking the Lord to commit adultery with other nations and their idols.

But Israel's spiritual adultery and apostasy never caused God to stop loving His people or forsake His unconditional promises to them. Despite their blasphemous worship of a golden calf after the Exodus, the Lord "did not forsake them in the wilderness" (Neh. 9:19). Despite their repeated idolatry throughout the period of the judges, God eventually "could bear the misery of Israel no longer" (Judg. 10:16) and delivered them from their oppressors. And despite their stubborn rebelliousness during the divided kingdom, God patiently withheld the judgment His wayward people deserved; He "was gracious to them and had compassion on them and turned to them because of His covenant with Abraham, Isaac, and Jacob, and would not destroy them or cast them from His presence until now" (2 Kings 13:23).

Even though Israel "acted arrogantly and did not listen to [God's] commandments but sinned against [His] ordinances,... and ... turned a stubborn shoulder and stiffened their neck, and would not listen," God, "in [His] great compassion ... did not make an end of them or forsake them, for [He is] a gracious and compassionate God" (Neh. 9:29, 31). "Many times," the psalmist wrote, "[God] would deliver [Israel]; they, however, were rebellious in their counsel, and so sank down in their iniquity. Nevertheless He looked upon their distress when He heard their cry; and He remembered His covenant for their sake, and relented according to the greatness of His lovingkindness" (Ps. 106:43–45). To His people's fearful cry, "The Lord has forsaken me, and the Lord has forgotten me" (Isa. 49:14), God replied comfortingly, "Can a woman forget her nursing child and have no compassion on the son of her womb? Even these may forget, but I will not forget you. Behold, I have inscribed you on the palms of My hands" (vv. 15–16).

Perhaps the most vivid and unforgettable illustration of God's faithfulness is found in the marriage of the prophet Hosea to his unfaithful wife Gomer. Through the retelling of his own heartbreak, Hosea unfolded the poignant story of God's continuing love for His people, despite the fact that "they [had] played the harlot, departing from their God" (4:12; cf. 1:2; 3:1; 5:3–4; 6:10; 9:1).

In two dramatic passages in Jeremiah, God made it unmistakably clear that He will never abandon Israel:

> Thus says the Lord,
> Who gives the sun for light by day
> And the fixed order of the moon and the stars for light by night,
> Who stirs up the sea so that its waves roar;
> The Lord of hosts is His name: "If this fixed order departs
> From before Me," declares the Lord,
> "Then the offspring of Israel also will cease
> From being a nation before Me forever."
> Thus says the Lord,
> "If the heavens above can be measured
> And the foundations of the earth searched out below,
> Then I will also cast off all the offspring of Israel
> For all that they have done," declares the Lord. (31:35–37)

> Thus says the Lord, "If you can break My covenant for the day and My covenant for the night, so that day and night will not be at their appointed time, then My covenant may also be broken with David My servant so that he will not have a son to reign on his throne, and with the Levitical priests, My ministers. As the host of heaven cannot be

counted and the sand of the sea cannot be measured, so I will multiply the descendants of David My servant and the Levites who minister to Me.... Thus says the Lord, "If My covenant for day and night stand not, and the fixed patterns of heaven and earth I have not established, then I would reject the descendants of Jacob and David My servant, not taking from his descendants rulers over the descendants of Abraham, Isaac and Jacob. But I will restore their fortunes and will have mercy on them." (33:20–22, 25–26)

In the New Testament the apostle Paul echoed those Old Testament promises, stating definitively, "I say then, God has not rejected His people, has He? May it never be! ... God has not rejected His people whom He foreknew.... For I do not want you, brethren, to be uninformed of this mystery ... that a partial hardening has happened to Israel until the fullness of the Gentiles has come in; and so all Israel will be saved" (Rom. 11:1–2, 25–26).

The parable of the landowner pictured Israel's ultimate act of apostasy, the rejection of the Son of God, the Lord Jesus Christ:

There was a landowner who planted a vineyard and put a wall around it and dug a wine press in it, and built a tower, and rented it out to vine-growers and went on a journey. When the harvest time approached, he sent his slaves to the vine-growers to receive his produce. The vine-growers took his slaves and beat one, and killed another, and stoned a third. Again he sent another group of slaves larger than the first; and they did the same thing to them. But afterward he sent his son to them, saying, "They will respect my son." But when the vine-growers saw the son, they said among themselves, "This is the heir; come, let us kill him and seize his inheritance." They took him, and threw him out of the vineyard and killed him. (Matt. 21:33–39)

Yet even that did not cause God to abandon Israel. The church has always included a handful of individual Jewish believers. Moreover, the day is coming when the entire nation will be saved (Rom. 11:26), when God declares, "they will look on Me whom they have pierced; and they will mourn for Him, as one mourns for an only son, and they will weep bitterly over Him like the bitter weeping over a firstborn" (Zech. 12:10), and "a fountain will be opened for the house of David and for the inhabitants of Jerusalem, for sin and for impurity.... They will call on My name, and I will answer them; I will say, 'They are My people,' and they will say, 'The Lord is my God'" (13:1,9).

Even during the darkest days of Israel's apostasy there was always a remnant of true believers (cf. 1 Kings 19:14, 18), and that was the case during Christ's earthly ministry too. Here and there, like scattered outposts of light in the darkness, were those who believed in Him and were saved. John has already introduced some of them: the disciples (1:35–51; 2:11), a few Samaritans (4:29, 39–42), and a royal official and his household (4:53). Most of the Jewish people, however, did not savingly hear Christ's word (5:24–25), and therefore remained dead in their sin. Inevitably, for many, especially the religious leaders, spiritual deafness and blindness expressed itself in active hostility to the relentless confrontation of our Lord's ministry. And not to be for Him was, de facto, to be opposed. As He Himself declared, "He who is not with Me is against Me; and he who does not gather with Me, scatters" (Luke 11:23).

From verse 17 to the end of the chapter, Jesus defended Himself for healing a lame man on the Sabbath (5:1–16), an act which the Jewish authorities considered a blatant violation of Sabbath law (5:16). Jesus, however, did not break any biblical regulations, but rather the rabbinic traditions that had developed around them. Yet the Lord did not defend Himself by noting that distinction. Instead, He asserted His equality with the Father, and thus His right to work on the Sabbath just as the Father did (v. 17). Shocked by what they considered a blasphemous claim to deity, the Jews felt justified in redoubling their efforts to kill Jesus (v. 18). Jesus responded by strengthening His claims to equality with God by doing equal works, equally giving life, receiving equal honor, and equally executing final judgment on all (vv. 19–29).

Verse 30 summarizes the Son's claim to be equal with the Father. Contrary to His opponents' accusations, He did not act on His **own initiative,** but rather always and only in complete conjunction with the Father (cf. v. 19). Therefore by accusing Him of wrongdoing, the Jewish leaders were simultaneously accusing the Father as well. Since the immediate context involves the Son's activity as judge (vv. 27–29), the Lord used that as an illustration and a warning, declaring, **"As I hear, I judge; and My judgment is just, because I do not seek My own will, but the will of Him who sent Me."** Since Jesus always acts in perfect harmony with the **will of** the Father **who sent** Him, His **judgment** is always **just.** And it will be justly executed on those who reject and oppose Him.

When the Lord said, **"If I alone testify about Myself, My testimony is not true,"** He did not mean to imply that His self-witness is unreliable (cf. 8:14). His point was that His Jewish opponents claimed His own self-testimony was not sufficient. The issue was not whether that testimony was true in itself, but whether His opponents would believe Him. So He offered more testimony as evidence.

In verses 33–47 Jesus called on additional confirmation from four unimpeachable sources to corroborate His claims: the forerunner's witness, the finished works, the Father's word, and the faithful writings.

THE FORERUNNER'S WITNESS

"You have sent to John, and he has testified to the truth. But the testimony which I receive is not from man, but I say these things so that you may be saved. He was the lamp that was burning and was shining and you were willing to rejoice for a while in his light." (5:33–35)

The purpose of John the Baptist's ministry was to prepare the nation for the Messiah (1:23), and to identify Him when He came (1:31). Therefore "John testified about Him and cried out, saying, 'This was He of whom I said, "He who comes after me has a higher rank than I, for He existed before me""" (1:15), and,

> "Behold, the Lamb of God who takes away the sin of the world! This is He on behalf of whom I said, 'After me comes a Man who has a higher rank than I, for He existed before me.' I did not recognize Him, but so that He might be manifested to Israel, I came baptizing in water." John testified saying, "I have seen the Spirit descending as a dove out of heaven, and He remained upon Him. I did not recognize Him, but He who sent me to baptize in water said to me, 'He upon whom you see the Spirit descending and remaining upon Him, this is the One who baptizes in the Holy Spirit.' I myself have seen, and have testified that this is the Son of God." (1:29–34)

The Jewish authorities had **sent** a delegation **to John, and he had testified to the truth:**

> This is the testimony of John, when the Jews sent to him priests and Levites from Jerusalem to ask him, "Who are you?" And he confessed and did not deny, but confessed, "I am not the Christ." They asked him, "What then? Are you Elijah?" And he said, "I am not." "Are you the Prophet?" And he answered, "No." Then they said to him, "Who are you, so that we may give an answer to those who sent us? What do you say about yourself?" He said, "I am a voice of one crying in the wilderness, 'Make straight the way of the Lord,' as Isaiah the prophet said." . . . They asked him, and said to him, "Why then are you baptizing, if you are not the Christ, nor Elijah, nor the Prophet?" John answered them saying, "I baptize in water, but among you stands One whom you do not know. It is He who comes after me, the thong of whose sandal I am not worthy to untie." (1:19–23, 25–27)

John's testimony supported Jesus' claims to be the Messiah. Since he was generally regarded by the people as a prophet of God (Matt. 21:26; Luke 20:6)—the first one in four centuries—his testimony carried considerable weight. The authorities acknowledged John's importance by sending a delegation to hear him. But just like their fathers had rejected the prophets God sent to them (cf. 2 Kings 17:13–14; 2 Chron. 24:19; Jer. 7:25–26; 25:4; 29:19; 44:4–5), they rejected John's witness.

Jesus, of course, did not depend on human testimony to establish His claim to deity, either in the eyes of others, or in His own mind. There certainly was no deficiency in the testimony of the Father (v. 37) that needed to be supplied by human testimony. The **testimony** from His works (v. 36) and from His Father (v. 37) was of far greater significance than that **from** any **man.** Thus, He cited the testimony of John the Baptist not to make up any lack, but to confirm by the mouth of one already recognized as God's true prophet that same truth concerning Himself. He did so for the sake of His hearers—**that** they might **be saved** on account of John's faithful witness (cf. 1:35–37).

Having highlighted John's testimony to Him, Jesus in turn gave testimony to John (cf. Matt. 11:7–14). His words were both a tribute to the Baptist, and a rebuke to the Jewish leaders for rejecting his witness. John **was** (the past tense verb forms may indicate that he had by this time been imprisoned or executed) **the lamp that was burning and was shining.** His **burning** inner zeal made him a **shining** light in a dark world. Unlike Jesus, who is the Light (*phōs;* the essence of light) of the world (8:12; cf. 1:4–9; 9:5; 12:35–36, 46), John was a **lamp** (*luchnos;* a small, portable oil lamp). He was not the source of the light, but a reflector of it (cf. 1:6–8). Just as a lamp lights the way for people, so John lit the way to Jesus (1:31).

The Lord ended His tribute to John with a rebuke of the Jewish leaders, noting that they **were willing to rejoice** only **for a while in his light.** Like moths to a lamp, the people flocked excitedly to hear John who, as noted above, was the first prophet in nearly four hundred years. Their excitement peaked when he proclaimed the imminent arrival of the long-awaited Messiah (Mark 1:7–8). But his stern call for personal repentance (Matt. 3:1–2), his stinging denunciation of the nation's hypocrisy (Matt. 3:7; Luke 3:7), and his shocking practice of baptizing Jews (the Jews baptized Gentile proselytes, but regarded fellow Jews as already part of God's kingdom people, and hence not in need of baptism) alienated many of the people. Eventually, John's fearless condemnation of Herod Antipas's unlawful marriage (Mark 6:17–18) led to his arrest and execution. The thrill seekers may have rejoiced temporarily in John's ministry, but they missed its purpose—to point out Jesus as the Messiah. They were superficially drawn to John (cf. those similarly drawn to Jesus in 2:23–25), but they lacked genuine repentance. Ultimately, they turned away from the light of truth that John reflected, because they loved the evil deeds of darkness (3:19).

THE FINISHED WORKS

"But the testimony which I have is greater than the testimony of John; for the works which the Father has given Me to accomplish—the very works that I do—testify about Me, that the Father has sent Me." (5:36)

John the Baptist's testimony carried considerable weight; after all, he was the greatest man who had ever lived up to his time (Luke 7:28). **But the testimony which** Jesus was about to introduce was far **greater than the testimony of John.** More convincing than the greatest prophet's testimony to Christ were **the very works that** He did (cf. Acts 2:22). For instance, Jesus' miracles prompted Nicodemus to confess, "Rabbi, we know that You have come from God as a teacher; for no one can do these signs that You do unless God is with him" (3:2). John 7:31 records that "many of the crowd believed in Him; and they were saying, 'When the Christ comes, He will not perform more signs than those which this man has, will He?'" Even Jesus' bitter enemies "the chief priests and the Pharisees convened a council, and were saying, 'What are we doing? For this man is performing many signs'" (11:47). As He did here, the Lord Himself repeatedly pointed to His miraculous works as confirmation of His claim to be the Son of God and the Messiah (cf. 10:25, 37–38; 14:11; Matt. 11:3–5). The gospels record at least three dozen of those miracles, and Jesus performed countless others that Scripture does not record (20:30).

That Christ did only **the works which the Father** had **given** Him **to accomplish** in no way implies that He is inferior to the Father (1:1; 5:18; 10:30; cf. Phil. 2:6; Col. 2:9). As noted in the discussion of 5:26 in chapter 16 of this volume, Jesus voluntarily gave up the independent use of His divine attributes during the Incarnation. That self-emptying included submission to the Father's will and the Spirit's power. Throughout His earthly ministry, Jesus was conscious of carrying out the mission that the Father had given Him in the energy of the Spirit (Luke 4:14). In John 4:34 He told the disciples, "My food is to do the will of Him who sent Me and to accomplish His work," while in 14:31 He added, "I do exactly as the Father commanded Me." In His High Priestly Prayer to the Father Jesus declared triumphantly, "I glorified You on the earth, having accomplished the work which You have given Me to do" (17:4).

Because Jesus' works were in perfect harmony with the will of His Father, they testified **that the Father sent** Him. Not only were His works supernatural; they were also in keeping with God's exact wishes. Yet, despite Jesus' incredible works—unmatched by anyone else (15:24) and unexplainable outside of God's power—there were many who still rejected Him (cf. 1:11).

THE FATHER'S WORD

"There is another who testifies of Me, and I know that the testimony which He gives about Me is true. . . . And the Father who sent Me, He has testified of Me. You have neither heard His voice at any time nor seen His form. You do not have His word abiding in you, for you do not believe Him whom He sent." (5:32, 37–38)

In addition to the witness of John the Baptist and the evidence of Jesus' works, **there is another who testifies** that He is the Son of God and the Messiah. Moreover, the testimony **He gives about** Jesus **is** infallibly **true.** That **the Father who sent** Jesus **has testified of** Him is of infinitely greater importance than any human testimony. The gospels record two specific instances in which the Father gave verbal testimony to the Son: at His baptism and at His transfiguration, when "a voice out of the heavens said, 'This is My beloved Son, in whom I am well-pleased'" (Matt. 3:17; 17:5; cf. 2 Peter 1:17).

Jesus' statement, **You have neither heard His voice at any time nor seen His form,** was a further rebuke to the unbelieving Jews. No one can see God in the full glory of His infinitely holy essence (Ex. 33:20; John 1:18; 1 Tim. 6:16; 1 John 4:12). However there were times, throughout Israel's history, when God audibly or visibly interacted with His people. For example, He spoke to Moses (Ex. 33:11; Num. 12:8), the Israelites of the exodus (Deut. 4:12, 15; 5:5), and the prophets (Heb. 1:1). He also appeared, in some physical manifestation of His presence, to Jacob (Gen. 32:30), Gideon (Judg. 6:22), Manoah (Judg. 13:20), and others (Gen. 16:13; Ex. 24:9–11; Isa. 6:5). Yet the unbelieving Jews of Jesus' day, who had both the Old Testament Scriptures and the full revelation of God in Jesus Christ (1:18; 14:9; cf. Col. 2:9; Heb. 1:3), did **not have** God's **word abiding in** them, **for** they did **not believe Him whom** God **sent.** They refused to listen to Jesus, God's final revelation to mankind (Heb. 1:2). And, in so doing, they displayed their total ignorance of God, since those who reject Jesus cannot know the Father (cf. 5:23; 8:19; 14:6; 15:23).

On the other hand, those who love the Son have the internal witness of God in their hearts as to who Jesus is. To the Romans Paul wrote, "The Spirit Himself testifies with our spirit that we are children of God" (Rom. 8:16; cf. 1 Cor. 2:6–15). In his first epistle John also wrote of this internal witness:

> If we receive the testimony of men, the testimony of God is greater; for the testimony of God is this, that He has testified concerning His Son. The one who believes in the Son of God has the testimony in himself; the one who does not believe God has made Him a liar, because he has not believed in the testimony that God has given concerning His Son. (1 John 5:9–10)

THE FAITHFUL WRITINGS

"You search the Scriptures because you think that in them you have eternal life; it is these that testify about Me; and you are unwilling to come to Me so that you may have life. I do not receive glory from men; but I know you, that you do not have the love of God in yourselves. I have come in My Father's name, and you do not receive Me; if another comes in his own name, you will receive him. How can you believe, when you receive glory from one another and you do not seek the glory that is from the one and only God? Do not think that I will accuse you before the Father; the one who accuses you is Moses, in whom you have set your hope. For if you believed Moses, you would believe Me, for he wrote about Me. But if you do not believe his writings, how will you believe My words?" (5:39–47)

Merely knowing the facts of Scripture, without fully embracing them in the heart (Josh. 1:8; Pss. 1:2; 119:11, 15, 97) and acting on them, will not bring the blessings of salvation. In the words of Aelfric, a tenth-century English theologian, "Happy is he, then, who reads the Scriptures, if he convert the words into actions."

Though the Greek verb translated **you search** could be either imperative or indicative in form, it is best understood in the latter sense. Jesus was not commanding them to **search the Scriptures,** but noting that they were already doing so in a desperate and futile search for the key to **eternal life** (cf. Matt. 19:16; Luke 10:25). Ironically, with all their fastidious effort they utterly failed to grasp that **it is** those very Scriptures **that testify about** Jesus (1:45; Luke 24:27, 44; Rev. 19:10). The Pharisees in particular were fanatical in their preoccupation with Scripture, studying every line, every word, and even the letters in an empty effort to understand the truth.

The Bible cannot be properly understood apart from the Holy Spirit's illumination or a transformed mind. The Jews' zeal for the Scripture was commendable (cf. Rom. 10:2), but because they were **unwilling to come to** Jesus (cf. 1:11; 3:19), the sole source of **eternal life** (14:6; Acts 4:12), it did not result in salvation. Clinging to their superficial system of self-righteousness by works, in their stubborn unbelief, they became ignorant of "God's righteousness and [sought] to establish their own" (Rom. 10:3). But self-righteousness cannot save anyone, since "all our righteous deeds are like a filthy garment" (Isa. 64:6) and because "whoever keeps the whole law and yet stumbles in one point, he has become guilty of all" (James 2:10). Thus, salvation comes not from "having a righteousness of [one's] own derived from the Law, but that which is through faith in Christ, the righteousness which comes from God on the basis of faith" (Phil. 3:9; cf. Rom. 3:20–30).

The religious leaders refused to acknowledge their utter unrighteousness and inability to do anything about it, and to cry out for God's mercy and grace revealed through the Lord Jesus. They clung tightly to their deception about what was required to enter God's kingdom of salvation. Furthermore, because Jesus did not conform to their messianic expectations, the Jewish leaders turned their backs on Him. The Lord understood their hearts perfectly; His declaration, **I do not receive glory from men** is yet another illustration of His omniscient knowledge of men's thoughts and motives (cf. 2:25; 21:17). He did not want public praise and hypocritical honor from those who privately repudiated Him (cf. Matt. 22:16). The Lord knew that any respect from them was worthless because they did **not have the love of God** in themselves. Quoting Isaiah's prophecy, Jesus expressed God's utter loathing for such counterfeit spirituality: "This people honors me with their lips, but their heart is far away from me. But in vain do they worship me, teaching as doctrines the precepts of men" (Matt. 15:8–9).

That Jesus came in the **Father's name, and** they still did **not receive** Him further exposed His hearers' hardness of heart. Ironically, as the Lord pointed out, **if another** came **in his own name,** they were perfectly willing to **receive him.** Over the centuries there have been many false messiahs (as many as sixty-four according to some Jewish historians [Leon Morris, *The Gospel According to John,* The New International Commentary on the New Testament (Grand Rapids: Eerdmans, 1979), 333 n. 122]). The first-century Jewish historian Josephus noted an increase in false messiahs in the years leading up to the Jewish revolt against Rome (A.D. 66–70). Sixty years later another messianic pretender, Simon Bar Kochba, appeared. Even Rabbi Akiba, the most esteemed rabbi of the time, believed Bar Kochba to be the messiah—until his revolt was crushed by the Romans with catastrophic results for the Jewish people. False messiahs will proliferate as the second coming draws near (Matt. 24:23–24), culminating in the ultimate false messiah, the Antichrist (2 Thess. 2:3–12).

Jesus' pensive question, **"How can you believe, when you receive glory from one another and you do not seek the glory that is from the one and only God?"** offers a crucial reason for their rejection of Him. Jesus said in effect, "How can I be glorified as your Lord, when you are seeking glory?" The question is a rhetorical one; obviously, those engaged in seeking **glory from one another** do not humble themselves in order to **believe** in the glorious Lord Jesus— which is the only way to **seek the glory that is from the one and only God.** Paul further explained this in his words to the Corinthians:

> in whose case the god of this world has blinded the minds of the unbe-
> lieving so that they might not see the light of the gospel of the glory of
> Christ, who is the image of God. . . . For God, who said, "Light shall shine
> out of darkness," is the One who has shone in our hearts to give the
> Light of the knowledge of the glory of God in the face of Christ. (2 Cor.
> 4:4–6)

The glory that is from God shines in the face of Jesus Christ. This is the
"gospel of the glory of Christ."

Not to seek that honor and glory that comes from God in Jesus
Christ is culpable ignorance that will be severely judged. But Jesus will
not need to **accuse** them **before the Father;** someone else will do that.
The Lord stunned them by identifying that accuser as **Moses**—the very
one **in whom** they had **set** their **hope.** It is difficult to imagine how pro-
foundly shocked and outraged the Jewish leaders must have been by
Jesus' statement. In their minds, it was utterly incomprehensible to think
that Moses—whom they proudly affirmed as their leader and teacher
(9:28; cf. Matt. 23:2)—would one day accuse them before God. But had
they truly **believed Moses,** they **would** also **believe** Jesus, **for he
wrote about** Him. Jesus probably did not have one particular passage
(such as Deut. 18:15) in mind, but rather the entire Pentateuch that, along
with the rest of the Old Testament, points unmistakably to Him (cf. Luke
24:27).

Jesus' opponents ignored the clear evidence from the Old Testament that He was the Messiah. But at a deeper level, they also misunderstood the purpose of the Mosaic law. They saw keeping it as a means to
salvation, but that was never its intent. The law was given to reveal man's
sinfulness and utter inability to save himself. As Paul wrote in Galatians
3:24, "The Law has become our tutor to lead us to Christ, so that we may
be justified by faith." It could never save, since any violation puts people
under damnation's curse (Gal. 3:10; cf. Rom. 3:19–20).

It should come as no surprise that those who did **not believe**
Moses' **writings** would not **believe** Christ's **words** either. If they rejected
the truths taught by Moses, whom they revered, they could hardly be
expected to accept the teaching of Jesus, whom they reviled. Leon Morris writes,

> If these people, who professed to be Moses' disciples, who honored
> Moses' writings as sacred Scripture, who gave an almost superstitious
> reverence to the letter of the law, if these men did not really believe the
> things that Moses had written, and which were the constant objects of
> their study, then how could they possibly believe . . . the spoken words
> of Jesus? (*Gospel According to John,* 334–35)

The sobering reality is that those who reject Moses' teaching about Jesus will face eternal judgment—a truth taught in the story of the rich man and Lazarus. Desperate to spare his brothers the torment he was enduring, the rich man pleaded with Abraham,

> "I beg you, father, that you send [Lazarus] to my father's house—for I have five brothers—in order that he may warn them, so that they will not also come to this place of torment." But Abraham said, "They have Moses and the Prophets; let them hear them." But he said, "No, father Abraham, but if someone goes to them from the dead, they will repent!" But he said to him, "If they do not listen to Moses and the Prophets, they will not be persuaded even if someone rises from the dead." (Luke 16:27–31)

The Jewish religious teachers and authorities would express their ultimate rejection of both Moses and Jesus when they used their perverted understanding of the law to justify His execution: "The Jews answered [Pilate], 'We have a law, and by that law He ought to die because He made Himself out to be the Son of God'" (John 19:7). They rejected the fourfold testimony of John the Baptist, Jesus' works, the Father, and the Scriptures to Christ's deity. As a result, in the most heinous act of apostasy in history, they crucified their own Messiah (Acts 2:23).

A Miraculous Meal
(John 6:1–15)

18

After these things Jesus went away to the other side of the Sea of Galilee (or Tiberias). A large crowd followed Him, because they saw the signs which He was performing on those who were sick. Then Jesus went up on the mountain, and there He sat down with His disciples. Now the Passover, the feast of the Jews, was near. Therefore Jesus, lifting up His eyes and seeing that a large crowd was coming to Him, said to Philip, "Where are we to buy bread, so that these may eat?" This He was saying to test him, for He Himself knew what He was intending to do. Philip answered Him, "Two hundred denarii worth of bread is not sufficient for them, for everyone to receive a little." One of His disciples, Andrew, Simon Peter's brother, said to Him, "There is a lad here who has five barley loaves and two fish, but what are these for so many people?" Jesus said, "Have the people sit down." Now there was much grass in the place. So the men sat down, in number about five thousand. Jesus then took the loaves, and having given thanks, He distributed to those who were seated; likewise also of the fish as much as they wanted. When they were filled, He said to His disciples, "Gather up the leftover fragments so that nothing will be lost." So they gathered them up, and filled twelve

baskets with fragments from the five barley loaves which were left over by those who had eaten. Therefore when the people saw the sign which He had performed, they said, "This is truly the Prophet who is to come into the world." So Jesus, perceiving that they were intending to come and take Him by force to make Him king, withdrew again to the mountain by Himself alone. (6:1–15)

The New Testament offers numerous lines of evidence for the deity of Jesus Christ, not the least of which is His many miracles (cf. Acts 2:22). In a unique and powerful way, His miraculous works demonstrate His divine glory (John 2:11). The Lord Himself used them to support His remarkable claims: "The works which the Father has given Me to accomplish—the very works that I do—testify about Me, that the Father has sent Me" (5:36). In response to the exasperated demand of His critics, "How long will You keep us in suspense? If You are the Christ, tell us plainly" (10:24), Jesus answered, "I told you, and you do not believe; the works that I do in My Father's name, these testify of Me" (v. 25). The Lord also rebuked Chorazin, Bethsaida, and Capernaum because, in spite of the numerous miracles He had performed in those cities, they stubbornly refused to repent (Matt. 11:20–24).

When John the Baptist sent his disciples to ask Jesus, "Are You the Expected One, or do we look for someone else?" (Luke 7:20), Jesus replied by pointing them to His miraculous works:

> At that very time He cured many people of diseases and afflictions and evil spirits; and He gave sight to many who were blind. And He answered and said to them, "Go and report to John what you have seen and heard: the blind receive sight, the lame walk, the lepers are cleansed, and the deaf hear, the dead are raised up, the poor have the gospel preached to them." (vv. 21–22)

And when Jesus' own disciples failed to grasp the truth of His union with the Father He told them, "Believe Me that I am in the Father and the Father is in Me; otherwise believe because of the works themselves" (John 14:11).

Throughout His ministry, Jesus could have thrilled the watching crowds with spectacular displays of His divine power, such as lifting up the temple and suspending it in midair, or flying through the sky at supersonic speeds. But instead, He chose to display divine compassion by doing miracles that delivered people in need. He healed the sick (Matt. 4:23–24; 8:2–3, 5–13, 14–16; 9:2–7, 20–22, 27–30, 35; 12:9–13, 15; 14:14; 15:30; 19:2; 20:30–34; 21:14; Mark 6:5; 7:31–35; Luke 5:15; 6:17–19; 9:11; 14:1–4; 17:11–14; 22:51; John 4:46–53; 5:1–9; 6:2; 9:1–7), raised the dead

(Matt. 9:23–25; Luke 7:11–15; John 11:43), and cast out demons (Matt. 4:24; 8:16, 28–33; 9:32–33; 12:22; 15:21–28; 17:14–18; Mark 1:39; Luke 11:14; 13:32). Even the Lord's creative miracles were not sensational magic tricks. As noted in chapter 6 of this volume, by creating wine at the wedding at Cana (John 2:1–11) Jesus met a necessity for the guests and saved the bride and groom from a socially embarrassing situation. The miraculous feeding of the five thousand was a large act of compassion on behalf of people who would have gone hungry.

Although they could not deny His miracles, the religious authorities in Judea vehemently rejected Jesus' claims (5:16–47). But that rejection did not deter Him, or cause Him to soften His message. Nonetheless, the Lord left Judea because the Jewish leaders sought to kill Him before His appointed time (5:18; cf. 7:1, 30; 8:20). Chapter 6, then, finds Him in Galilee, the northern part of Israel. This chapter is similar in structure to chapter 5; both record a miracle by Jesus, leading to a discourse on His deity. And each recounts the response of the people, which on both occasions was an outright rejection of His message.

The feeding of the five thousand is the fourth sign that John recorded to prove that Jesus is the Messiah and Son of God (cf. 2:11; 4:54; 5:1–17). It is the only miracle (apart from Christ's resurrection) recorded by John that also appears in the Synoptic Gospels (Matt. 14:13–20; Mark 6:30–44; Luke 9:10–17)—a fact that emphasizes its importance, since most of what John wrote supplements the other gospels, providing material they did not include. Although all of Jesus' miracles were astonishing, the feeding of the five thousand demonstrated His creative power more clearly and impressively than any other miracle. In fact, in terms of the number of people affected, it was the largest of His miracles (exceeding His later feeding of four thousand, recorded in Matt. 15:32–39; Mark 8:1–9). The feeding of the five thousand also sets the stage for the Lord's discourse on the bread of life that follows (vv. 22ff.).

The narrative unfolds in four scenes: the fickle crowd, the faithless disciples, the fulfilling dinner, and the false coronation.

The Fickle Crowd

After these things Jesus went away to the other side of the Sea of Galilee (or Tiberias). A large crowd followed Him, because they saw the signs which He was performing on those who were sick. Then Jesus went up on the mountain, and there He sat down with His disciples. Now the Passover, the feast of the Jews, was near. (6:1–4)

The phrase *meta tauta* (**after these things** [cf. 5:1]) does not necessarily mean that the events recorded in chapter 6 immediately followed the events recorded in chapter 5. It simply indicates that what happened in chapter 6 occurred subsequent to the events in the previous chapter. Evidently, there was a significant time gap between chapters 5 and 6. According to verse 4, the events of chapter 6 took place shortly before Passover. If the unnamed feast of 5:1 was the Feast of Tabernacles, about six months would have elapsed between the two chapters; if it was Passover, the gap would have been a year. During that interval, Jesus continued ministering in Galilee—as the events recorded in Matthew 5:1–8:1; 8:5–13, 18, 23–34; 9:18–11:30; 12:15–14:12; Mark 3:7–6:30; and Luke 6:12–9:10 make clear. The spread of His fame over that six- to twelve-month time period helps explain the enormous size of the crowd that had gathered on this occasion.

The feeding of the five thousand took place on the **other side of the Sea of Galilee (or Tiberias).** Since the largest area of Galilee lies to the west of the lake, the **other side** would indicate the area east of the lake, more remote and less populous. The **Sea of Galilee** is also known in Scripture as the Sea of Chinnereth (Num. 34:11; Josh. 13:27), the Sea of Chinneroth (Josh. 12:3), and the Lake of Gennesaret (Luke 5:1). By the time John wrote his gospel, it had become commonly known as the Sea of Tiberias (cf. 21:1). It was named for the city of Tiberias, located on the lake's western shore, which was founded by Herod Antipas and named in honor of Emperor Tiberius (cf. Luke 3:1).

The Synoptic Gospels suggest two reasons that Jesus and the disciples withdrew to the eastern side of the lake. First, the Twelve had just returned from a preaching mission (Mark 6:7–13, 30), and Jesus, too, had been heavily involved in exhausting ministry while they were gone (Matt. 11:1). The Lord knew the disciples needed a time of rest and instruction, a sort of debriefing after the completion of their mission (Mark 6:31–32). Matthew 14:13 reveals that news of John the Baptist's death provided an additional reason for their withdrawal: "Now when Jesus heard about John [that he had been executed by Herod; 14:1–12], He withdrew from there in a boat to a secluded place by Himself."

Jesus and His disciples were not to find the peaceful seclusion they sought, however. According to Mark 6:32, they crossed the Sea of Galilee by boat, but **a large crowd** from the surrounding cities (Matt. 14:13) **followed** them on foot along the shore (Mark 6:33). By the time they reached their destination, a mass of people was already waiting for them (Matt. 14:14), with more on the way. The crowd was not motivated by faith, repentance, or genuine love for Him. On the contrary, they followed the Lord **because they saw the signs which He was performing on those who were sick** (cf. 2:1–11; 4:46–54; Matt. 8:2–4, 5–13, 14–17,

28–34; 9:1–8, 18–26, 27–33; 12:9–13; Mark 1:21–28). They were thrill seekers who failed to grasp the true significance of Jesus' miraculous signs (cf. v. 26)—which pointed unmistakably to Him as the Son of God and the Messiah. As such, they were the Galilean counterparts of the Judean false believers described in 2:23–25. They flocked to see His works, but ultimately refused to accept His words (cf. v. 66). They sought the benefits of His power in their physical lives, but not in their spiritual lives.

After arriving at the eastern shore of the lake, **Jesus went up on the mountain, and there He sat down with His disciples.** Despite the gathering crowd, the Lord wanted some time alone with the Twelve. Mountains provided the setting for many of the important scenes in Christ's life and ministry, including part of His temptation by the Devil (Matt. 4:8); the Sermon on the Mount (Matt. 5:1; 8:1); the choosing of the Twelve (Mark 3:13); the exercise of His healing ministry (Matt. 15:29–30); the transfiguration (Matt. 17:1); the Olivet Discourse (Matt. 24:3); His meeting with the disciples after the resurrection (Matt. 28:16); and His ascension (Acts 1:12). This particular **mountain** was probably located in the region known today as the Golan Heights, the site of a major battle between Israeli and Syrian forces during the Six-Day War of 1967.

As noted above, the fact that **the Passover, the feast of the Jews, was near** places this incident several months after the events of chapter 5. It also suggests that the enormous crowd may have consisted, at least in part, of pilgrims preparing to travel together to Jerusalem for the **feast.** Moreover, it was at **Passover,** which commemorates the nation's deliverance from Egypt, that the Jews' nationalistic feelings reached their peak. That may help explain the crowd's zealous attempt to make Jesus king (v. 15).

THE FAITHLESS DISCIPLES

Therefore Jesus, lifting up His eyes and seeing that a large crowd was coming to Him, said to Philip, "Where are we to buy bread, so that these may eat?" This He was saying to test him, for He Himself knew what He was intending to do. Philip answered Him, "Two hundred denarii worth of bread is not sufficient for them, for everyone to receive a little." One of His disciples, Andrew, Simon Peter's brother, said to Him, "There is a lad here who has five barley loaves and two fish, but what are these for so many people?" (6:5–9)

After spending some time on the mountain with the Twelve, Jesus saw that a **large crowd was coming to Him.** The Synoptics record that

He "healed their sick" (Matt. 14:14) and "began speaking to them about
the kingdom of God" (Luke 9:11). Mark says that Jesus was moved with
"compassion for them because they were like sheep without a shepherd"
(Mark 6:34; cf. Num. 27:17; 1 Kings 22:17; Matt. 9:36). The Lord knew the
crowd's superficial motive for following Him (v. 26), but His abundant
mercy was such that He met their needs anyway.

Late in the day (Mark 6:35) or as the day was ending (Luke 9:12)
and it "was evening, the disciples came to Him and said, 'This place is
desolate and the hour is already late; so send the crowds away, that they
may go into the villages and buy food for themselves'" (Matt. 14:15).
Jesus, however, had a different solution in mind. He **said to Philip,
"Where are we to buy bread, so that these may eat?"** Why the Lord
singled out Philip is not revealed. It may be that he was the administrator
of the Twelve, the one responsible for arranging meals and taking care of
logistical details. The question was intended to articulate the impossibility of anyplace where such bread could be secured.

Jesus was not trying to discover what Philip was thinking, since
He already knew that (cf. 2:25; 21:17). Nor did He need Philip's input to
help Him formulate a plan. He knew that Philip knew of no place to get
bread and had no plan to provide it. The Lord's purpose in questioning
Philip (and by extension the rest of the disciples; cf. Luke 9:12) was **to
test him, for He Himself knew what He was intending to do**—and
it had nothing to do with buying bread. As He does with all His people,
the Lord posed the dilemma as a way of testing the disciples to strength-
en their faith. James wrote, "Consider it all joy, my brethren, when you
encounter various trials, knowing that the testing of your faith produces
endurance. And let endurance have its perfect result, so that you may be
perfect and complete, lacking in nothing" (James 1:2–4). The apostle
Peter similarly stated, "In this you greatly rejoice, even though now for a
little while, if necessary, you have been distressed by various trials, so that
the proof of your faith, being more precious than gold which is perishable, even though tested by fire, may be found to result in praise and
glory and honor at the revelation of Jesus Christ" (1 Peter 1:6–7).

Philip's faith (along with the rest of the Twelve's) was found lacking, and he exclaimed hopelessly, **"Two hundred denarii worth of
bread is not sufficient for them, for everyone to receive a little."**
To Philip it seemed pointless to discuss where they might get bread,
since they clearly did not have enough money to buy it if they could find
it. A denarius equaled one day's pay for a common laborer (Matt. 20:2),
so **two hundred denarii** would be approximately eight months' wages
for an average worker. Philip's response stressed the impossibility of the
situation in his eyes, and revealed the insufficiency of his faith. He had
already seen Christ perform many miracles, including turning water into

wine (2:1–11). He would have also been familiar with the various Old Testament accounts of God's miraculous provision of food (Ex. 16; Num. 11:31–32; 1 Kings 17:9–16; 2 Kings 4:1–7). Yet, "rather than focusing on Jesus, Philip's mental computer began to work like a cash register, and all he could think about was the total cash that would be needed to provide just a little bread for each person" (Gerald L. Borchert, *John 1–11,* The New American Commentary [Nashville: Broadman & Holman, 2002], 253).

Andrew, unlike Philip, at least tried to find a solution (although he may have been merely trying to corroborate Philip's pessimism). He reported to Jesus that his search had led him to one little boy with **five barley loaves and two fish.** Mark 6:38 records that Jesus commanded the disciples to go find out how much food the crowd had. Apparently Andrew was reporting the results of that search. Or, perhaps, the search took place after his report and further confirmed the dismal reality of the situation. In any case, Andrew's faith, too, collapsed as he considered the enormity of the logistical problem. After recounting what he found, he added skeptically, **"But what are these for so many people?"** Andrew's response showed that he, like Philip and the rest of the Twelve, failed the test of faith. No one responded by affirming the power of Jesus to provide.

The Fulfilling Dinner

Jesus said, "Have the people sit down." Now there was much grass in the place. So the men sat down, in number about five thousand. Jesus then took the loaves, and having given thanks, He distributed to those who were seated; likewise also of the fish as much as they wanted. When they were filled, He said to His disciples, "Gather up the leftover fragments so that nothing will be lost." So they gathered them up, and filled twelve baskets with fragments from the five barley loaves which were left over by those who had eaten. (6:10–13)

With the disciples at a standstill, Jesus took charge of the situation. Instead of reprimanding them for their weak faith, He put them to work, instructing them to **have the people sit down.** Their faith may have failed, but their obedience did not, and despite their doubts they followed the Lord's instructions. John's personal recollection that **there was much grass in the place** is the type of detail an eyewitness would recall. It further confirms that the feeding of the five thousand took place in the spring (Passover [v. 4] was in March or April), before the grass withered under the scorching summer sun. Mark adds that the disciples seated the people in groups of fifty and one hundred (Mark 6:40), no doubt to make it easier to distribute the food. All four gospels record that there were **five thousand** men present, not counting women and children (Matt. 14:21). Allowing for a reasonable number of women and children, the total number of people was probably somewhere between fifteen and twenty thousand.

Simply, and without fanfare, **Jesus then took the loaves, and having given thanks, He distributed to those who were seated; likewise also of the fish.** The Lord did not create a vast amount of food all at once, but continually "broke the loaves and ... kept giving them to the disciples to set before them; and ... divided up the two fish among them all" (Mark 6:41). The astonished crowd seated on the grassy hillside that evening witnessed the Creator God at work.

Matthew, Mark, and Luke record that the Lord **distributed** the food to the crowd through the disciples. Jesus, of course, did not need to use them; He could just as easily have distributed the food to the crowd by supernatural means. God, however, often works through weak, fallible humans. He used Moses, who was "very humble, more than any man who was on the face of the earth" (Num. 12:3), to deliver His people from bondage in Egypt; He used Gideon, the youngest child in the least important family in Manasseh (Judg. 6:15), to deliver Israel from the Midianites; and He used David, an unknown shepherd boy, to kill the mighty warrior Goliath and deliver Israel from the Philistines. "God," Paul reminded the proud, arrogant Corinthians, "has chosen the foolish things of the world to shame the wise, and God has chosen the weak things of the world to shame the things which are strong" (1 Cor. 1:27).

The Lord does nothing by half measures. Instead of the little taste of which Philip dubiously spoke (v. 7), everyone ate **as much as they wanted,** so that **they were filled.** After that Jesus commanded the **disciples, "Gather up the leftover fragments so that nothing will be lost."** God's abundant provision was no excuse for wasting resources (cf. Prov. 25:16). The disciples **gathered** the leftover food, **and filled twelve baskets** (of the type used to carry food or produce) **with fragments from the five barley loaves which were left over by those who had eaten.** In an amazing display of God's abundant grace, the leftovers far exceeded the original **five barley loaves.** Some think that the twelve baskets symbolize God's provision for the twelve tribes of Israel. A simpler explanation is that there were twelve baskets because there were twelve apostles gathering the leftovers. Christ not only provided enough food to satisfy the hungry crowd, but also to provide the next day's meal for the disciples.

THE FALSE CORONATION

Therefore when the people saw the sign which He had performed, they said, "This is truly the Prophet who is to come into the world." So Jesus, perceiving that they were intending to come and take Him by force to make Him king, withdrew again to the mountain by Himself alone. (6:14–15)

Astonished by the **sign which** Jesus **had performed,** the people **said, "This is truly the Prophet who is to come into the world."** The reference is to the messianic prophecy given by Moses in Deuteronomy 18:15–19 (cf. Acts 3:20–22). No doubt Jesus' miraculous provision of food reminded the crowd of Moses and the manna God provided for Israel in the wilderness. The feeding of the huge crowd was a true creative miracle—not, as some skeptics argue, a story of how Jesus manipulated the crowd into sharing their lunches with each other. If that were all that happened, the crowd would hardly have viewed it as a miraculous sign pointing to Jesus as the Christ. The people correctly realized that the miracle was supernatural and proved Jesus was the Messiah, though they drew wrong conclusions as to what that identification meant.

The crowd's statement, made immediately after Jesus had healed their sick and filled their stomachs, revealed what the people were really looking for in a messiah. They wanted an earthly deliverer, one who would meet all their physical needs—and food and health were at the top of the list—as well as freeing them from the hated yoke of Roman oppression. Thus **they were intending to come and take Him by force to make Him king.** With Him as their provider, they would never want for food, and would have the potential to be healed of every illness. They could march to Jerusalem, overthrow the Romans, and establish the ultimate social welfare state. Jesus, however, refused to be forcibly made king on their selfish (and unrepentant) terms. Therefore, He sent the disciples away by boat (Matt. 14:22; Mark 6:45), dispersed the crowd (Matt. 14:23; Mark 6:45–46), and **withdrew again to the mountain by Himself alone.**

Jesus does not acquiesce to whims or fancies. He comes to no man on that man's terms. People cannot manipulate Him for their own selfish ends. Some modern evangelists, in an attempt to be "seeker-friendly," present Jesus to unbelievers as a quick fix for felt needs like health, wealth, and self-esteem—superficially marketing Him as providing everything unbelievers want. But that turns the gospel message upside down. People do not come to Christ on their terms, so that He can heal their broken relationships, make them successful in life, and help them feel good about themselves. Instead, they must come to Him on His terms. Jesus graciously loves believers and grants them a rich legacy of joy (John 15:11), peace (John 14:27), and comfort (2 Cor. 1:3–7). But at the same time, He calls sinners to mourn over their sin (Matt. 5:4), repent (Matt. 4:17), and acknowledge Him as the sovereign Lord (Rom. 10:9; cf. Phil. 2:9–11), to whom they owe complete obedience (John 14:15, 21; 1 John 5:3). Even today, He continues to withdraw from those who seek Him for their own self-serving ends, just as He did from the crowd that sought to make Him king on their terms. And, as becomes clear later in chapter 6, He drives others away with the hard demands of the gospel (v. 66).

Characteristics of True and False Disciples
(John 6:16–29)

19

Now when evening came, His disciples went down to the sea, and after getting into a boat, they started to cross the sea to Capernaum. It had already become dark, and Jesus had not yet come to them. The sea began to be stirred up because a strong wind was blowing. Then, when they had rowed about three or four miles, they saw Jesus walking on the sea and drawing near to the boat; and they were frightened. But He said to them, "It is I; do not be afraid." So they were willing to receive Him into the boat, and immediately the boat was at the land to which they were going. The next day the crowd that stood on the other side of the sea saw that there was no other small boat there, except one, and that Jesus had not entered with His disciples into the boat, but that His disciples had gone away alone. There came other small boats from Tiberias near to the place where they ate the bread after the Lord had given thanks. So when the crowd saw that Jesus was not there, nor His disciples, they themselves got into the small boats, and came to Capernaum seeking Jesus. When they found Him on the other side of the sea, they said to Him, "Rabbi, when did You get here?" Jesus answered them and said, "Truly, truly, I say to you, you seek Me, not because you saw

signs, but because you ate of the loaves and were filled. Do not work for the food which perishes, but for the food which endures to eternal life, which the Son of Man will give to you, for on Him the Father, God, has set His seal." Therefore they said to Him, "What shall we do, so that we may work the works of God?" Jesus answered and said to them, "This is the work of God, that you believe in Him whom He has sent." (6:16–29)

One of Hawaii's most famous landmarks is Diamond Head, an extinct volcano on the island of Oahu. Early Western explorers gave it that name not because of its shape, but because of the shining rocks they saw embedded in its slopes. Observing those rocks from a distance, the excited sailors imagined that they had discovered diamonds. But, to their disappointment, closer examination revealed that the "diamonds" were actually just worthless calcite crystals.

In a similar sense, there are many who look from a distance like they are Christ's disciples, but closer investigation shows them to be something other than what they claim. Such people shine outwardly like brilliant diamonds, but inside they are nothing more than worthless rock. The New Testament describes them as tares among the wheat (Matt. 13:25–30); bad fish that are thrown away (13:48); goats condemned to eternal punishment (25:33, 41); those left standing outside when the head of the house shuts the door (Luke 13:25–27); foolish virgins shut out of the wedding feast (Matt. 25:1–12); and useless slaves who bury their master's talent in the ground (25:24–30). They are apostates who eventually leave the fellowship of believers (1 John 2:19), manifest an evil, unbelieving heart by abandoning the living God (Heb. 3:12), continue to sin willfully after receiving the knowledge of the truth (Heb. 10:26), and fall away from the truth to everlasting destruction (v. 39). Although they may even think they are on their way to heaven, they are actually on the broad path leading to hell (Matt. 7:13–14).

In light of the serious danger of being deceived, the Bible stresses the cost of being a genuine disciple of Jesus Christ. When a would-be follower said to Him, "Lord, permit me first to go and bury my father" (Matt. 8:21)—a figure of speech meaning, "Wait until I receive my inheritance"—Jesus replied, "Follow Me, and allow the [spiritually] dead to bury their own dead" (v. 22). When another told Him, "I will follow You, Lord; but first permit me to say good-bye to those at home" (Luke 9:61), Jesus replied, "No one, after putting his hand to the plow and looking back, is fit for the kingdom of God" (v. 62). Luke 14:27–35 records the Lord's sobering warning to count carefully the cost of following Him:

> Whoever does not carry his own cross and come after Me cannot be My disciple. For which one of you, when he wants to build a tower, does not first sit down and calculate the cost to see if he has enough to complete it? Otherwise, when he has laid a foundation and is not able to finish, all who observe it begin to ridicule him, saying, "This man began to build and was not able to finish." Or what king, when he sets out to meet another king in battle, will not first sit down and consider whether he is strong enough with ten thousand men to encounter the one coming against him with twenty thousand? Or else, while the other is still far away, he sends a delegation and asks for terms of peace. So then, none of you can be My disciple who does not give up all his own possessions. Therefore, salt is good; but if even salt has become tasteless, with what will it be seasoned? It is useless either for the soil or for the manure pile; it is thrown out. He who has ears to hear, let him hear.

To be His disciple, Jesus warned, means to love Him above all else—even one's own family:

> Do not think that I came to bring peace on the earth; I did not come to bring peace, but a sword. For I came to set a man against his father, and a daughter against her mother, and a daughter-in-law against her mother-in-law; and a man's enemies will be the members of his household. He who loves father or mother more than Me is not worthy of Me; and he who loves son or daughter more than Me is not worthy of Me. (Matt. 10:34–37; cf. 19:29)

It also means to love Him more than life. In Luke 9:23–24 Jesus "was saying to them all, 'If anyone wishes to come after Me, he must deny himself, and take up his cross daily and follow Me. For whoever wishes to save his life will lose it, but whoever loses his life for My sake, he is the one who will save it'" (cf. Matt. 10:38–39; Luke 14:27; 17:33; John 12:25; 1 Cor. 15:31). Jesus was not speaking about the general trials of life when He referenced the cross on this occasion. Nor was He referring to Calvary, since He had not yet suffered there. His hearers understood His point perfectly—the cross meant death. Only true disciples are willing to submit to Christ's lordship in everything—even if it means persecution and execution. No price is too high for the gift of eternal life.

In contrast, false disciples fall apart when the going gets tough. When "affliction or persecution arises because of the word," or "the worry of the world and the deceitfulness of wealth choke the word" (Matt. 13:21–22), they show their true colors. As we will see later in chapter 6, after hearing the Lord teach that He is the Bread of Life, "many of His disciples, when they heard this said, 'This is a difficult statement; who can listen to it?' ... As a result of this many of His disciples withdrew and were not walking with Him anymore" (John 6:60, 66). Such false disciples do not come to Christ to bow before Him as Lord and Savior; rather they come seeking their own personal gain. When their selfish desires do not materialize, they forsake Him altogether.

This chapter shows that not all "disciples" are true believers (v. 66), but all believers are "disciples"—devoted followers of Jesus Christ. It should be noted that "disciples" are not a special class of Christians who are actively pursuing sanctification, as opposed to "believers," who have merely believed in Christ and been justified. The Bible makes it clear that all Christians are true disciples ("disciple" becomes a synonym for "believer" throughout the book of Acts; e.g., 6:1–2, 7; 9:1, 19, 26, 36, 38; 11:26, 29; 13:52; 15:10; 18:23, 27; 19:9, 30; 20:1; 21:4, 16), and that all true Christians pursue sanctification (1 Cor. 1:30; Eph. 2:10; James 2:14–26; cf. 1 Cor. 6:11). (For a further discussion of this issue, see my book *The Gospel According to Jesus* [Rev. ed., Grand Rapids: Zondervan, 1994].)

Verses 16–29 comprise two passages that set the stage for Jesus' discourse on the Bread of Life. They also portray the stark contrast between true and false disciples. The first account describes Jesus walking on the water to the Twelve, who were caught in a storm on the Sea of Galilee. It illustrates the response that true disciples have toward Christ. The second story, in which the crowd that Jesus had just fed (6:1–15) sought Him for another free meal, reveals how false disciples respond to the Lord. For both groups Jesus performed a supernatural sign. Yet the subsequent responses in each case were entirely different.

THE RESPONSE OF TRUE DISCIPLES

Now when evening came, His disciples went down to the sea, and after getting into a boat, they started to cross the sea to Capernaum. It had already become dark, and Jesus had not yet come to them. The sea began to be stirred up because a strong wind was blowing. Then, when they had rowed about three or four miles, they saw Jesus walking on the sea and drawing near to the boat; and they were frightened. But He said to them, "It is I; do not be afraid." So they were willing to receive Him into the boat, and immediately the boat was at the land to which they were going. (6:16–21)

Jesus' walking on the water (cf. the accounts of this miracle in Matt. 14:24–33; Mark 6:47–52) is the fifth (cf. John 2:11; 4:54; 5:1–17; 6:1–15) miraculous sign John recorded in his gospel (20:30–31). In keeping with John's purpose, it demonstrates Christ's deity by revealing His power over the laws of nature. And, in contrast to the false disciples of vv. 22–29, it exposes the reverent response of Jesus' true followers.

THE SUPERNATURAL SIGN

Now when evening came, His disciples went down to the sea, and after getting into a boat, they started to cross the sea to Capernaum. It had already become dark, and Jesus had not yet come to them. The sea began to be stirred up because a strong wind was blowing. Then, when they had rowed about three or four miles, they saw Jesus walking on the sea and drawing near to the boat; and they were frightened. (6:16–19)

When He dismissed the crowd (thus thwarting their attempt to make Him king by force; 6:14–15), Jesus also sent the disciples away (Matt. 14:22). They were no doubt excited by the crowd's response. It must have seemed that their Master was finally getting the honor He was due. Jesus had taught them to pray for God's kingdom to come (Matt. 6:10), and it might have looked like that prayer was about to be answered. Knowing their hearts and not wanting them to be swept up in the crowd's superficial enthusiasm, the Lord removed the disciples from the situation. They probably did not fully understand why Jesus sent them away, but they obeyed Him nonetheless.

According to Mark 6:45, their initial destination was Bethsaida, not far from where the thousands were fed. Apparently, they were planning to meet Jesus there before crossing the lake to the western shore (Matt. 14:34; Mark 6:53). **When evening came, the disciples went down to the sea, and after getting into a boat, they started to cross the sea to Capernaum. Evening** here refers to the second evening (cf. Ex. 12:6 where "at twilight" lit. reads "between the two evenings"), from sunset to dark. They waited at Bethsaida until **it had already become dark.** Then, since **Jesus had not yet come to them,** the disciples reluctantly returned to their boat and took their voyage to Capernaum, on the northwest shore.

The Sea of Galilee lies nearly 700 feet below sea level in the Jordan Rift, while the surrounding hills rise abruptly to about 2,000 feet above sea level. The sharp drop of nearly 3,000 feet from the tops of the hills to the surface of the lake creates ideal conditions for the sudden, violent storms for which the Sea of Galilee is notorious (cf. Matt. 8:23–27). The cooler air rushes down the slopes and strikes the surface of the lake with great force, churning the water into whitecaps and creating dangerous conditions for small boats.

As they sailed across the lake toward Capernaum, the disciples found themselves caught in one of those sudden squalls. John recalled that **the sea began to be stirred up because a strong wind was blowing.** The wind was so powerful that it blew the disciples' little boat off course, pushing it "a long distance from the land" (Matt. 14:24) toward "the middle of the sea" (Mark 6:47). Despite being "battered by the waves" (Matt. 14:24), the disciples continued "straining at the oars" (Mark 6:48), desperately trying to reach the safety of the western shore. (Even if their boat had been equipped with a sail, it would have done the disciples little good, since they were heading into the wind [Matt. 14:24].) But their progress was painfully slow. The disciples had left for Capernaum sometime between 6:00 and 9:00 P.M. (John 6:16), and according to Matthew 14:25 and Mark 6:48 it was now the fourth watch of the night (3:00 to 6:00 A.M.). During those long, dark, exhausting, stressful hours, they **had rowed** only **about three or four miles.**

Meanwhile, Jesus was alone on the mountain praying (6:15; Matt. 14:23; Mark 6:46). Ever the faithful Shepherd (John 10:11–14), however, He had not forgotten the disciples. In His infinite wisdom, He planned to help them according to His perfect timing. Divine sovereignty, omnipotence, and omniscience are never in a hurry. Of course, the disciples could never have imagined what form that help would take.

Suddenly, through the darkness, swirling wind, stinging spray, and raging waves, **they saw Jesus walking on the sea and drawing near to the boat.** They had struggled for hours, making little headway. He, however, was walking effortlessly into the teeth of the gale. In fact, Jesus was moving so rapidly that it looked to the disciples as if He would pass right by them (Mark 6:48). Because of the darkness, and the wind-whipped mist and spray, the disciples did not recognize the mysterious figure who came walking toward their boat.

Many (perhaps as many as seven) of the disciples were fishermen by trade, and were used to being on the lake at night and in rough weather (cf. 21:3; Luke 5:5). Though no doubt concerned (cf. Matt. 8:23–27; Mark 4:36–41; Luke 8:22–25), because the waves threatened to swamp their boat (Mark 4:37; Luke 8:23), they were familiar with these types of storms. But they were certainly not accustomed to seeing human figures walking on the water. Not surprisingly, **they were frightened,** and cried out in terror, "It is a ghost!" (Matt. 14:26; Mark 6:49).

Some unbelieving skeptics have suggested that Jesus was actually walking along the shore, and that the terrified disciples mistakenly thought He was walking on the water. But the disciples' boat was much too far from the land (Matt. 14:24 literally reads "many stadia"; a stadion was about an eighth of a mile) for them to have seen through the stormy darkness a person walking on the shore. The idea that these experienced fishermen thought someone walking on the shore was walking on the water is merely a desperate attempt to deny what the gospels clearly portray as supernatural. Like all His miracles, the Lord's walking on the water was not a frivolous magic trick. By suspending the law of gravity, He gave His disciples dramatic, visible proof that He is the Creator and controller of the physical universe (1:3; Col. 1:16; Heb. 1:2).

THE SUBSEQUENT RESPONSE

But He said to them, "It is I; do not be afraid." So they were willing to receive Him into the boat, and immediately the boat was at the land to which they were going. (6:20–21)

As noted above, and as would be expected, the Twelve responded to Jesus' miraculous appearance with sheer terror. There was no natural explanation for what they had seen. Adding to their fear, the disciples did not initially recognize Jesus as He approached. But the Lord calmed His panic-stricken disciples, telling them, "Take courage [Matt. 14:27; Mark 6:50]; **it is I; do not be afraid.**" Recognizing Jesus at last, the disciples **were willing** and glad **to receive Him into the boat.**

The Twelve, like all true disciples of Jesus Christ, longed for His presence. They had been reluctant to leave when He dismissed them along with the crowd (the verb translated "He made" in Matt. 14:22 and Mark 6:45 literally means "to compel," or "to force" people to do something they do not want to do; cf. its use in Luke 14:23; Acts 26:11; 28:19; 2 Cor. 12:11; Gal. 2:3, 14; 6:12). They no doubt were disappointed when Jesus did not meet them before they started their voyage across the lake (vv. 16–17). Now, to their astonishment and relief, He had returned to them in a most unexpected way, and they were overjoyed.

Bold and impetuous as ever, Peter could not wait for the Lord to get in the boat. He was so eager to be near Jesus that he leaped overboard to get to Him sooner:

> Peter said to Him, "Lord, if it is You, command me to come to You on the water." And He said, "Come!" And Peter got out of the boat, and walked on the water and came toward Jesus. But seeing the wind, he became frightened, and beginning to sink, he cried out, "Lord, save me!" Immediately Jesus stretched out His hand and took hold of him, and said to him, "You of little faith, why did you doubt?" (Matt. 14:28–31)

The story of Christ's walking on the water actually includes not one miracle, but four. Not only did Jesus walk on the water, but so also did Peter (at least for a few moments). Matthew and Mark record a third miracle. When Jesus (along with a soaking wet and thoroughly chastened Peter) got into the boat, the wind immediately stopped (Matt. 14:32; Mark 6:51). Finally, John records a fourth miracle: after Jesus got on board and calmed the storm, **immediately the boat was at the land to which they were going.** Miraculously, the boat instantly traversed the remaining distance to the western shore.

Utterly astonished (cf. Mark 4:41), "those who were in the boat worshiped Him, saying, 'You are certainly God's Son!'" (Matt. 14:33). The only appropriate response to Jesus Christ is to fall before Him in worship, as did the wise men at His birth (Matt. 2:11), a Canaanite woman (15:25), a blind man whom Jesus healed (John 9:38), the women who came to the tomb after the resurrection (Matt. 28:9), Thomas (John 20:28), and the rest of the eleven disciples (Matt. 28:17; Luke 24:52). Although they were amazed by Jesus' miracle, the Twelve responded as all true followers of Jesus Christ do—with adoration and worship.

THE RESPONSE OF FALSE DISCIPLES

The next day the crowd that stood on the other side of the sea saw that there was no other small boat there, except one, and that Jesus had not entered with His disciples into the boat, but that His disciples had gone away alone. There came other small boats from Tiberias near to the place where they ate the bread after the Lord had given thanks. So when the crowd saw that Jesus was not there, nor His disciples, they themselves got into the small boats, and came to Capernaum seeking Jesus. When they found Him on the other side of the sea, they said to Him, "Rabbi, when did You get here?" Jesus answered them and said, "Truly, truly, I say to you, you seek Me, not because you saw signs, but because you ate of the loaves and were filled. Do not work for the food which perishes, but for the food which endures to eternal life, which the Son of Man will give to you, for on Him the Father, God, has set His seal." Therefore they said to Him, "What shall we do, so that we may work the works of God?" Jesus answered and said to them, "This is the work of God, that you believe in Him whom He has sent." (6:22–29)

John's account continues by contrasting the response of the Twelve with the response of the crowd which Jesus had just fed. They too had witnessed His divine creative power. But, instead of responding with heartfelt worship, they responded with selfishness and greed.

THE SUPERNATURAL SIGN

The next day the crowd that stood on the other side of the sea saw that there was no other small boat there, except one, and that Jesus had not entered with His disciples into the boat, but that His disciples had gone away alone. There came other small boats from Tiberias near to the place where they ate the bread after the Lord had given thanks. So when the crowd saw that Jesus was not there, nor His disciples, they themselves got into the small boats, and came to Capernaum seeking Jesus. (6:22–24)

With Jesus and the disciples having crossed the lake to the western shore during the night, the scene **the next day** shifted back to the east side of the lake. At least part of the **crowd that** had witnessed Jesus' healings (v. 2) and been miraculously fed (vv. 3–13) **stood** the following morning **on the other** (eastern) **side of the sea.** They had spent the night there (Matt. 14:22; Mark 6:45), and in the morning they were looking for Him, hoping for another free meal (v. 26), and perhaps still intending to make Him king by force so He could be a permanent source of miraculous provision (v. 15).

Gradually, it dawned on them that something strange had happened. They remembered **that there** had been **no other small boat there** the previous day, **except** the **one** the disciples had used. They also knew **that Jesus had not entered with His disciples into the boat, but that His disciples had gone away alone.** The mystery, then, was where was Jesus, if He had not left with the disciples? The crowd, of course, could not know what had really happened; they had not witnessed Him walking on the water.

Verse 23 is a parenthesis, explaining where the **small boats** that transported the crowd back to Capernaum came from. **Tiberias** was an important city on the western shore of the Sea of Galilee (see the discussion of 6:1 in chapter 18 of this volume). Why the flotilla came **to the place where** the thousands **ate the bread after the Lord had given thanks** is not clear. Perhaps the owners of the boats had heard of the miraculous feeding and had come to investigate. Or they may have come to pick up their friends and loved ones, or to act as water taxis, seeking to cash in on the large numbers of people in need of transportation. Or they may have been forced to seek shelter from the same storm in which the disciples had been caught the night before.

After searching unsuccessfully for Him, **the crowd** finally realized **that Jesus was not there, nor His disciples.** Accordingly, **they themselves got into the small boats, and came to Capernaum seeking Jesus. Capernaum,** Jesus' adopted home town (Matt. 4:13), was the logical place to look for Him. Some of the people may also have overheard the Lord telling the disciples to sail there (Matt. 14:22).

Though the crowd sought Jesus (v. 24), they did so for the wrong reasons. They followed Him for what they could get; they were not interested in either worshiping or obeying Him. The previous evening they had experienced His miraculous power and provision (of healing and feeding); they had all witnessed and personally benefited from that supernatural sign. But instead of responding with humble worship (like the Twelve), they wanted more from Him. They had no other interest in Jesus. They wanted Him to serve them. The superficial crowd is always an easy target for the false promise of personal prosperity.

THE SUBSEQUENT RESPONSE

When they found Him on the other side of the sea, they said to Him, "Rabbi, when did You get here?" Jesus answered them and said, "Truly, truly, I say to you, you seek Me, not because you saw signs, but because you ate of the loaves and were filled. Do not work for the food which perishes, but for the food which endures to eternal life, which the Son of Man will give to you, for on Him the Father, God, has set His seal." Therefore they said to Him, "What shall we do, so that we may work the works of God?" Jesus answered and said to them, "This is the work of God, that you believe in Him whom He has sent." (6:25–29)

When they finally **found** Jesus in Capernaum, the people **said to Him** in amazement, **"Rabbi, when did You get here?"** As noted above, they knew He had not left in the disciples' boat. Nor could He have walked (on land) to Capernaum without them having seen Him. Although they had found Him, the mystery of how Jesus came to Capernaum still remained.

Jesus purposely did not answer their question. Just the day before they had tried to make Him king by force after He miraculously fed them; telling them of another, even more spectacular miracle would only have fueled their misguided messianic fervor. Besides, the Lord did not commit Himself to thrill-seeking false disciples (2:24; cf. Ps. 25:14; Prov. 3:32; Matt. 13:11). He ignored their irrelevant and superficial question and addressed the deeper issue of their sinful motives.

As it does throughout John's gospel (e.g., 1:51; 3:3, 5; 5:24; 6:47, 53; 8:51, 58; 13:21), the solemn affirmation *amēn, amēn* (**truly, truly**) introduces an important truth to which Jesus wanted His hearers to pay careful attention. The Lord's rebuke, "**you seek Me, not because you saw**

signs, but because you ate of the loaves and were filled," laid bare their selfish, materialistic hearts. So blinded were they by their superficial desire for food and miracles that they missed the true spiritual significance of Jesus' person and mission. "They were moved not by full hearts, but by full bellies" (Leon Morris, *The Gospel According to John,* The New International Commentary on the New Testament [Grand Rapids: Eerdmans, 1979], 358). Though they had witnessed the miraculous **signs** Jesus had performed (v. 14), they failed to grasp the spiritual implications of those miracles. Amazingly, after the feeding of the crowd, even the Twelve "had not gained any insight from the incident of the loaves, but their heart was hardened" (Mark 6:52). They had failed to comprehend the full reality that God was in their midst, until He walked on water. Then they said, "You are certainly God's Son!" (Matt. 14:33). When the Lord earlier calmed another storm on that same lake, they only asked the question, "What kind of a man is this?" (Matt. 8:27). Thus our Lord called them "men of little faith" (Matt. 8:26).

Jesus rebuked the crowd for their crass materialism. Instead of working **for the food which perishes,** the physical food they sought, Jesus exhorted them to pursue **the food which endures to eternal life** (Jesus Himself, the Bread of Life; vv. 35, 54). While He was certainly aware of their need for physical nourishment (cf. vv. 10–12), He was much more interested in their spiritual well-being. As He earlier had distinguished physical water from the "water springing up to eternal life" (4:14), Jesus here pointed His hearers away from literal food to Himself as the Bread of Life (vv. 33, 35, 48, 51). Rather than focusing on the decaying outer man (2 Cor. 4:16), they needed to seek the spiritual nourishment **which** only **the Son of Man** can **give.** After all, to gain the whole material world but forfeit one's eternal soul profits nothing (Matt. 16:26; Luke 12:16–21). As the one **on** whom **the Father, God, has set His seal** of approval, Jesus has the authority to dispense the spiritual food that comes from God and satisfies the hunger for righteousness (Matt. 5:6).

In response to Jesus' command in verse 27 to pursue the spiritual, nonperishing food of eternal life, the people **said to Him, "What shall we do, so that we may work the works of God?"** They filtered Jesus' words through their own warped minds and thought He was saying they needed to do some works to earn eternal life. What was that work they should do, they wondered. Similarly, the rich young ruler asked Him, "Teacher, what good thing shall I do that I may obtain eternal life?" (Matt. 19:16), and in Luke 10:25 "a lawyer stood up and put Him to the test, saying, 'Teacher, what shall I do to inherit eternal life?'" It was a familiar matter for the Jews to pursue eternal life through their religion, so the question was common.

True salvation, of course, is not by works (Titus 3:5). Thus, Jesus answered their question by noting that the only **work** acceptable to God is to **believe in Him whom He has sent.** Salvation is by grace alone (Eph. 2:8–9) through faith alone (Rom 3:28) in Christ alone (Acts 4:12), "because by the works of the Law no flesh will be justified in His sight" (Rom. 3:20; Gal. 2:16). Salvation is the gift of God (John 4:10; Rom. 5:15; 6:23; Eph. 2:8). Jesus called faith a **work,** since

> on the one hand, a person cannot earn acceptability with God by working for it. On the other hand, acceptability with God cannot be on the basis of "belief" in a mere theological formulation about God. . . . Acceptability with God is a relationship God gives ([Rom.] 6:27), there-fore, and both believing and obeying are parallel ways one acknowl-edges dependence on God. (Gerald L. Borchert, *John 1–11*, The New American Commentary [Nashville: Broadman & Holman, 2002], 263)

Thus, salvation does not come from human effort, achievement, or moral works, but from a faith that inevitably produces good works (Eph. 2:10; cf. Matt. 3:10; 7:16–20; 12:33; 13:23; Luke 6:43–46; Eph. 5:8–9; Col. 1:10). A "faith" that does not produce fruit is dead, meaning that it is not really biblical faith at all (James 2:14–26).

The rest of John chapter 6 develops Jesus' teaching regarding the food which endures to eternal life. Pointing to Himself as the Bread of Life, Jesus offered Himself to His listeners as their eternal deliverer. The crowd, however, was ultimately not interested. They had been intrigued by His earlier healings, and they had been temporarily satisfied by His miraculous meal. But their initially enthusiastic response to those super-natural signs (v. 15) quickly faded when their superficial expectations went unmet. Unlike the Twelve, who responded to Jesus' power with praise, the crowd responded first with curiosity, but unwilling to aban-don their false righteousness and repent, they were left finally with rejec-tion. Although they followed Christ for a little while, even sailing across the Sea of Galilee to find Him, they eventually demonstrated that they were not true followers at all.

The Bread of Life— Part 1: Jesus, the True Bread from Heaven

20

(John 6:30–50)

So they said to Him, "What then do You do for a sign, so that we may see, and believe You? What work do You perform? Our fathers ate the manna in the wilderness; as it is written, 'He gave them bread out of heaven to eat.'" Jesus then said to them, "Truly, truly, I say to you, it is not Moses who has given you the bread out of heaven, but it is My Father who gives you the true bread out of heaven. For the bread of God is that which comes down out of heaven, and gives life to the world." Then they said to Him, "Lord, always give us this bread." Jesus said to them, "I am the bread of life; he who comes to Me will not hunger, and he who believes in Me will never thirst. But I said to you that you have seen Me, and yet do not believe. All that the Father gives Me will come to Me, and the one who comes to Me I will certainly not cast out. For I have come down from heaven, not to do My own will, but the will of Him who sent Me. This is the will of Him who sent Me, that of all that He has given Me I lose nothing, but raise it up on the last day. For this is the will of My Father, that everyone who beholds the Son and believes in Him will have eternal life, and I Myself will raise him up on the last day." Therefore the Jews were grumbling about Him, because He said, "I am the

**bread that came down out of heaven." They were saying, "Is not
this Jesus, the son of Joseph, whose father and mother we know?
How does He now say, 'I have come down out of heaven'?" Jesus
answered and said to them, "Do not grumble among yourselves.
No one can come to Me unless the Father who sent Me draws him;
and I will raise him up on the last day. It is written in the
prophets, 'And they shall all be taught of God.' Everyone who has
heard and learned from the Father, comes to Me. Not that anyone
has seen the Father, except the One who is from God; He has seen
the Father. Truly, truly, I say to you, he who believes has eternal
life. I am the bread of life. Your fathers ate the manna in the
wilderness, and they died. This is the bread which comes down
out of heaven, so that one may eat of it and not die."** (6:30–50)

The annals of church history are full of many notable preachers,
men whom God has called to evangelize the lost and edify the
redeemed. Beginning with Peter's sermon at Pentecost (Acts 2:14–40),
the powerful preaching of the apostles (5:42; 14:7, 15, 21; 15:35; 16:10)
and their contemporaries (7:1–56; 8:4, 12, 35, 40; 11:20; 15:35) fueled the
spread of Christianity throughout the Roman Empire. In the centuries
that followed, gifted orators such as Basil, John Chrysostom ("golden-
mouthed"), and Augustine took up that same torch of explanation and
exhortation. A thousand years later, when the light of the gospel was
shrouded in confusion, the Reformation was sparked by the bold witness
of Martin Luther, John Calvin, John Knox, and others. The seventeenth-
century Puritan movement was likewise fueled by clear biblical preaching, as men such as Richard Baxter, John Owen, and John Bunyan
faithfully expounded God's Word. The Great Awakening of eighteenth-
century America was energized in much the same way—through the
passionate sermons of godly leaders like Jonathan Edwards, George
Whitefield, and John Wesley. The nineteenth and twentieth centuries
also saw many gifted preachers, including eloquent Christian statesmen
like Charles Spurgeon and D. Martyn Lloyd-Jones.

But the most noble and powerful preacher who ever lived was
the Lord Jesus Christ. At the conclusion of the Sermon on the Mount, "the
crowds were amazed at His teaching; for He was teaching them as one
having authority, and not as their scribes" (Matt. 7:28–29). Luke 4:22
records that "all were speaking well of Him, and wondering at the gracious words which were falling from His lips." Even His enemies were
awed by the power of Jesus' words. Explaining why they had failed to
arrest Him as ordered (John 7:32), officers of the temple police force
reported to the chief priests and Pharisees, "Never has a man spoken the
way this man speaks" (v. 46).

Preaching was central to Christ's mission. In His hometown synagogue at Nazareth He declared,

> "The spirit of the Lord is upon me, because He anointed me to preach the gospel to the poor. He has sent me to proclaim release to the captives, and recovery of sight to the blind, to set free those who are oppressed, to proclaim the favorable year of the Lord." And He closed the book, gave it back to the attendant and sat down; and the eyes of all in the synagogue were fixed on Him. And He began to say to them, "Today this Scripture has been fulfilled in your hearing." (Luke 4:18–21)

At the outset of His earthly ministry, "Jesus began to preach and say, 'Repent, for the kingdom of heaven is at hand'" (Matt. 4:17). Matthew 11:1 records that "when Jesus had finished giving instructions to His twelve disciples, He departed from there to teach and preach in their cities." Later in that same chapter Jesus pointed to His preaching ministry as proof that He was the Messiah: "Jesus answered and said to [the disciples of John the Baptist], 'Go and report to John what you hear and see: the blind receive sight and the lame walk, the lepers are cleansed and the deaf hear, the dead are raised up, and the poor have the gospel preached to them'" (vv. 4–5). After a successful evening of ministering in Capernaum,

> In the early morning, while it was still dark, Jesus got up, left the house, and went away to a secluded place, and was praying there. Simon and his companions searched for Him; they found Him, and said to Him, "Everyone is looking for You." He said to them, "Let us go somewhere else to the towns nearby, so that I may preach there also; for that is what I came for." And He went into their synagogues throughout all Galilee, preaching and casting out the demons. (Mark 1:35–39)

Luke 8:1 describes Jesus' habitual practice of "going around from one city and village to another, proclaiming and preaching the kingdom of God." The Lord faithfully preached the gospel to the very end of His earthly ministry: "On one of the days [during Passion Week] while He was teaching the people in the temple and preaching the gospel, the chief priests and the scribes with the elders confronted Him" (Luke 20:1).

The gospels record several of Jesus' sermons, including the Sermon on the Mount (Matt. 5–7), the commissioning of the twelve apostles (Matt. 10), the kingdom parables (Matt. 13), the childlikeness of the believer (Matt. 18), the Olivet Discourse (Matt. 24–25), the teaching on the Son's equality with the Father (John 5:19–47), and the Upper Room Discourse (John 14–17). John 6:22–59 records another of Jesus' most famous and beloved sermons, in which He presents Himself as the Bread of Life. Verses 22–29, along with the story of the miraculous feeding of the five thousand (vv. 1–21), set the stage for the Bread of Life Discourse, while verses 60–71 describe its aftermath.

John's approach in his gospel was to record Jesus' miracles briefly, matter-of-factly, and without fanfare, explanation, or defense. For example, the apostle describes the astonishing miracle of the feeding of the five thousand in simple, straightforward, unpretentious words: "Jesus then took the loaves, and having given thanks, He distributed to those who were seated; likewise also of the fish as much as they wanted" (6:11). John described Jesus' equally astounding miracle of walking on the water in similarly modest terms: "Then, when they had rowed about three or four miles, they saw Jesus walking on the sea and drawing near to the boat; and they were frightened" (v. 19).

It is almost as though the apostle hurries through the accounts of Christ's miracles to get to His words. While His miracles reveal His divine power, it is Christ's words that correctly define who He is. Jesus is no mere wonder worker; He is the Son of God and the Messiah. His miracles authenticate Him and His message as coming from God. But signs and wonders alone are not enough for salvation (cf. 12:37; 15:24; Matt. 11:20–24; Luke 16:31; Acts 6:8–14; 14:3–6; Rom. 1:18–32), because "faith comes from hearing, and hearing by the word of Christ" (Rom. 10:17). The crowd that Jesus miraculously fed was a perfect illustration. Though the people never questioned Jesus' power and enjoyed personally its benefits, they were indifferent or hostile to His gospel preaching.

The first section (vv. 30–50) of this magnificent sermon that Jesus preached in the synagogue at Capernaum (6:59) will be discussed under three headings: the contrast, the confusion, and the complaint.

THE CONTRAST

So they said to Him, "What then do You do for a sign, so that we may see, and believe You? What work do You perform? Our fathers ate the manna in the wilderness; as it is written, 'He gave them bread out of heaven to eat.'" Jesus then said to them, "Truly, truly, I say to you, it is not Moses who has given you the bread out of heaven, but it is My Father who gives you the true bread out of heaven. For the bread of God is that which comes down out of heaven, and gives life to the world." (6:30–33)

Incredibly, despite the miracles they had witnessed (6:2), including their massive meal the day before, the crowd **said to** Jesus, **"What then do You do for a sign, so that we may see, and believe You?**

What work do You perform?" They were brazenly demanding Jesus' credentials, in response to His claim in verse 29 to be the One sent from God. The people's foolish demand demonstrated their thickheaded and self-centered curiosity, graphically illustrating the spiritual blindness that engulfs the unredeemed. John Calvin observed, "This wicked question clearly shows the truth of what is said elsewhere: 'A wicked and adulterous generation asks for a miraculous sign' (Matthew 12:39)" (Alister McGrath and J. I. Packer, eds., *John*, The Crossway Classic Commentaries [Wheaton, Ill.: Crossway, 1994], 156). Jesus' miraculous feeding of the huge crowd just the day before was ample proof of His deity.

Unbelief, however, is never satisfied, no matter how much evidence is given. Luke 16:31 says that those who reject the truth of God's Word "will not be persuaded even if someone rises from the dead." At the crucifixion the unbelieving Jewish leaders said mockingly, "Let this Christ, the King of Israel, now come down from the cross, so that we may see and believe!" (Mark 15:32). Yet when Jesus rose from the dead—a far greater miracle than merely coming down from the cross—they still refused to believe in Him. Rather than admit the truth, they desperately attempted to cover up the reality of His resurrection (Matt. 28:11–15; Acts 4:1–3).

Jesus had exhorted the crowd to believe (6:29), but instead they demanded another sign (cf. 2:18; Matt. 12:38; 16:1; Luke 11:16; 1 Cor. 1:22). Specifically, they wanted a repeat performance of the miraculous feeding they had just experienced, as is indicated by their statement, **"Our fathers ate the manna in the wilderness; as it is written** (cf. Ex. 16:4, 15; Neh. 9:15; Pss. 78:24; 105:40), **'He gave them bread out of heaven to eat'"** (cf. v. 26). Rather than worshiping Jesus as Messiah and Savior, they wanted Him to continually give **them bread out of heaven to eat** with their mouths, not their hearts, like Moses had done by providing **manna in the wilderness** for the entire nation for forty years. That, in fact, was what contemporary Jewish thought expected the Messiah to do when He came (Colin Kruse, *The Gospel According to John*, The Tyndale New Testament Commentaries [Grand Rapids: Eerdmans, 2003], 168–69; Leon Morris, *The Gospel According to John*, The New International Commentary on the New Testament [Grand Rapids: Eerdmans, 1979], 363). Thus, the crowd challenged Jesus to prove He was the Messiah by providing them with an unending (cf. v. 34) supply of food.

Jesus, however, had no intention of gratifying the people's materialistic whims. For Him to have done so would have been to assume the very role of political and social Messiah that He had just rejected (6:14–15). Using the phrase *amēn, amēn* (**truly, truly**) to underscore the significance of what He was about to say, Jesus rebuked the people for their fourfold misunderstanding of the manna in the wilderness.

First, it was **not Moses who** gave them **the bread out of heaven, but** God the **Father.** In Exodus 16:4 "the Lord said to Moses, 'Behold, I will rain bread from heaven for you'" (cf. v. 15; Deut. 8:3, 16; Neh. 9:20; Pss. 78:24–25; 105:40). Moses merely relayed God's instructions about gathering the manna to the Israelites (Ex. 16:15–30).

Second, the manna was not the true bread from heaven. Jesus told them, **"My Father** now **gives you the true bread out of heaven."** The present tense of *didōmi* (**gives**) indicates that the true bread was not the manna of the past, but what the Father was currently giving. Further, *alēthinos* (**true**) means "genuine," or "real." The manna, though it was truly bread supplied by God, was merely a type that foreshadowed the ultimate, **true bread . . . which comes down out of heaven** (vv. 38, 50–51, 58; 3:13; cf. 1:9, 14; 8:42)—the Lord Jesus Christ.

Third, the manna gave physical life, but **the bread of God** (the phrase is synonymous with "the bread of heaven" in v. 32, as "kingdom of God" and "kingdom of heaven" are synonymous in the gospels) **which comes down out of heaven . . . gives** spiritual **life.** As it does throughout John's gospel, *zōē* (**life**) refers not to the physical and temporal life which the manna sustained, but to the spiritual and eternal life that comes only through Jesus Christ (cf. 1:4; 5:29, 40; 6:53; 10:10; 14:6; 20:31).

Finally, unlike the manna, which was given only to Israel, the true bread from heaven is for **the world.** God offers salvation through Jesus Christ to all who believe (vv. 40, 47; 3:15–16, 18, 36; 5:24; 11:25–26; 20:31), regardless of their national, racial, or ethnic background (1:29; 3:17; 4:39–42; 10:16; Matt. 12:18–21; Luke 2:25–32; Acts 8:5–8, 14–17, 25; 11:18; 13:46–48; 14:27; 15:3, 7, 14–17; 26:23; 28:28; Rom. 1:5, 16; 10:11–13; 1 Cor. 12:13; Gal. 3:8, 28; Eph. 3:4–6; 1 John 2:1–2; 4:14).

So Jesus was the true bread sent by God from heaven, and thus infinitely superior to Moses (cf. Heb. 3:3). The crowd's desire for more proof exposed both their evil motives and their ignorance of the Old Testament Scriptures and the words of the Son of God.

The Confusion

Then they said to Him, "Lord, always give us this bread." Jesus said to them, "I am the bread of life; he who comes to Me will not hunger, and he who believes in Me will never thirst. But I said to you that you have seen Me, and yet do not believe. All that the Father gives Me will come to Me, and the one who comes to Me I will certainly not cast out. For I have come down from heaven, not to do My own will, but the will of Him who sent Me. This is the will of Him who sent Me, that of all that He has given Me I lose

nothing, but raise it up on the last day. For this is the will of My Father, that everyone who beholds the Son and believes in Him will have eternal life, and I Myself will raise him up on the last day." (6:34–40)

The crowd's second request (cf. vv. 30–31) again reveals their spiritual blindness. Completely missing Jesus' point in verses 32 and 33, **they** eagerly **said to Him, "Lord, always give us this** (physical) **bread."** Their continuing desire to use Jesus for their physical needs is evident from this demand and a clear indication of their superficial interest. It still marks the shallow, temporary followers of Jesus who fill churches looking for their needs and desires to be met. There are always churches that accommodate them. Today they are often the places that draw the largest crowds, but have the lowest percentage of true believers. Having first insisted that He prove Himself, they now insisted that He give them what they wanted. *Kurios* (**Lord**) would be better understood as their way to say, "Sir" (as it is in 4:11, 15, 19, 49; 5:7; 12:21; 20:15; Matt. 13:27; 21:30; 27:63; Luke 13:8), since it is clear from verse 36 that the crowd did not truly believe in Jesus. They were still focused on having their physical needs met (cf. 4:15), as with the provision of manna (Ex. 16:35). In their obtuseness, they exhibited the fact that "a natural man does not accept the things of the Spirit of God, for they are foolishness to him; and he cannot understand them, because they are spiritually appraised" (1 Cor. 2:14).

Their dullness and lack of understanding prompted Jesus to declare unambiguously **to them, "I am the bread of life."** The Lord had not been referring to actual bread, as they mistakenly thought, but to Himself; He is the very bread He earlier promised to give (v. 27). No bread, not even manna, or the fish and bread Jesus had just created the evening before (6:1–13), could permanently cure physical hunger. Thus, when the Lord declared that those who come to Him will never again **hunger** or **thirst,** He had to be speaking not of the body, but of the soul. Here, as in Matthew 5:6, the human need to know God is expressed metaphorically as hungering and thirsting (cf. Pss. 42:1–2; 63:1).

Two simple verbs in verse 35 define man's part in the salvation process: **comes** and **believes.** To come to Christ is to forsake the old life of sin and rebellion and submit to Him as Lord. Though John does not use the term "repentance" in his gospel, the concept is clearly implied in the idea of coming to Christ (cf. 1 Thess. 1:9). As Charles Spurgeon put it, "You and your sins must separate, or you and your God will never come together" ("Rightly Dividing the Word of Truth," in *The Metropolitan Tabernacle Pulpit,* vol. 21 [Pasadena, Tex.: Pilgrim, 1980], 88). To believe in Christ is to trust completely in Him as the Messiah and Son of God, and to acknowledge that salvation comes solely through faith in Him (14:6; Acts 4:12). Repentance and faith are two sides of the same coin; to repent is to turn from sin, and to believe is to turn to the Savior. They are inseparable.

This is the first of seven highly significant statements in John's gospel where "I am" is joined with metaphors expressing Christ's work as Savior. In addition to the bread of life, Jesus also used "I am" to describe Himself as "the Light of the world" (8:12), "the door of the sheep" (10:7, 9), "the good shepherd" (10:11, 14), "the resurrection and the life" (11:25), "the way, and the truth, and the life" (14:6), and "the true vine" (15:1, 5). Jesus also used *egō eimi* ("I am") in an absolute, unqualified sense (4:26; 8:24, 28, 58; 13:19; 18:5–8) to appropriate for Himself the Old Testament name of God (Ex. 3:14).

Having declared that He was the Bread of Life, Jesus rebuked His hearers for their unbelief (note the similar rebuke of the Judeans in 5:38–40), adding the indictment, **"But I said to you that you have seen Me, and yet do not believe."** The specific rebuke to which Jesus was referring (when He **said** this to them in the past) is not known, but clearly their unbelief was in the face of His self-revelation, so their rejection was inexcusable. *Alla* (**but**) indicates a sharp contrast between the crowd's actual response and the one Jesus desired (cf. Matt. 23:37). Although they had **seen** Him, they failed to grasp the significance of His miracles, and missed the point of His teaching. As was the case with their forefathers in the wilderness, "The word they heard did not profit them, because it was not united by faith in those who heard" (Heb. 4:2). The miracles they had seen merely whetted their appetite for more miracles; they were intrigued by what Jesus could do to ease the difficulties of life, but they were not willing to **believe** in Him as their Messiah and Lord.

In spite of the crowd's response, Jesus was not discouraged. His confidence in the success of His mission was firmly rooted in the omnipotent sovereignty of God. He knew that **all** those whom **the Father gives** to Him (cf. v. 39; 10:29; 17:2, 6, 9, 24) **will come to** Him. The neuter singular form of *pas* (**all**) views those whom God gives to Jesus as a collective body, those chosen in Him before the foundation of the world (Eph. 1:4). This profound reality teaches us that all who are saved are a love gift from the Father to the Son. The whole history of redemption is the gathering of this redeemed body—or the calling of a bride for the Son as a love gift from the Father. The Son views every soul given by the Father to Him as an expression of the Father's irresistible love, so that all whom He gives **will come** to Christ.

From the standpoint of human responsibility, "God is now declaring to men that all people everywhere should repent" (Acts 17:30; cf. Matt. 3:2; 4:17; Mark 6:12), and "whoever will call on the name of the Lord will be saved" (Rom. 10:13; cf. John 3:15–16). Yet salvation does not depend on the human will. The redeemed are those "who were born, not ... of the will of man, but of God" (John 1:13). Salvation "does not depend on the man who wills or the man who runs, but on God who has mercy" (Rom. 9:16). Both repentance (Acts 11:18; 2 Tim. 2:25) and faith (Eph. 2:8–9; Phil. 1:29; cf. Acts 16:14) are granted by God. Otherwise no one would ever come to Him, since "there is none who seeks for God" (Rom. 3:11; cf. 8:7–8; 1 Cor. 2:14; 2 Cor. 4:4; Eph. 2:1–3).

That God is absolutely sovereign in salvation is foundational to the Christian faith. Those errant theological systems (i.e., Pelagianism, semi-Pelagianism, and Arminianism) that make salvation dependent on man's will in effect dethrone God, and are contrary to the clear statements of Scripture:

> No one can come to Me unless the Father who sent Me draws him; and I will raise him up on the last day. (v. 44)

> And He was saying, "For this reason I have said to you, that no one can come to Me unless it has been granted him from the Father." (v. 65)

> For many are called, but few are chosen. (Matt. 22:14)

> Unless the Lord had shortened those days, no life would have been saved; but for the sake of the elect, whom He chose, He shortened the days. (Mark 13:20)

> When the Gentiles heard this, they began rejoicing and glorifying the word of the Lord; and as many as had been appointed to eternal life believed. (Acts 13:48)

> And we know that God causes all things to work together for good to those who love God, to those who are called according to His purpose. For those whom He foreknew, He also predestined to become conformed to the image of His Son, so that He would be the firstborn among many brethren; and these whom He predestined, He also called; and these whom He called, He also justified; and these whom He justified, He also glorified. (Rom. 8:28–30)

> Just as He chose us in Him before the foundation of the world, that we would be holy and blameless before Him. (Eph. 1:4)

> So, as those who have been chosen of God, holy and beloved, put on a heart of compassion, kindness, humility, gentleness and patience. (Col. 3:12)

> Knowing, brethren beloved by God, His choice of you. (1 Thess. 1:4)

But we should always give thanks to God for you, brethren beloved by the Lord, because God has chosen you from the beginning for salvation through sanctification by the Spirit and faith in the truth. (2 Thess. 2:13)

Who has saved us and called us with a holy calling, not according to our works, but according to His own purpose and grace which was granted us in Christ Jesus from all eternity. (2 Tim. 1:9)

For this reason I endure all things for the sake of those who are chosen, so that they also may obtain the salvation which is in Christ Jesus and with it eternal glory. (2 Tim. 2:10)

Paul, a bond-servant of God and an apostle of Jesus Christ, for the faith of those chosen of God and the knowledge of the truth which is according to godliness. (Titus 1:1)

Listen, my beloved brethren: did not God choose the poor of this world to be rich in faith and heirs of the kingdom which He promised to those who love Him? (James 2:5)

Peter, an apostle of Jesus Christ, To those who reside as aliens, scattered throughout Pontus, Galatia, Cappadocia, Asia, and Bithynia, who are chosen according to the foreknowledge of God the Father. (1 Peter 1:1–2)

But you are a chosen race, a royal priesthood, a holy nation, a people for God's own possession, so that you may proclaim the excellencies of Him who has called you out of darkness into His marvelous light. (1 Peter 2:9)

The unbelief of spiritually dead (Eph. 2:1) sinners cannot thwart the saving work of God. Having chosen them in eternity past, He graciously and irresistibly calls them to Himself.

Lest any seeking souls should fear that they might not be among the elect, Jesus described the one whom the Father gave to the Son as none other than **the one who comes to Me.** From God's view, we are given by His sovereign power to the Son. From our view, we come to Christ. And, of course, our Lord would never reject one who comes as a love gift from the Father. So Jesus added, **I will certainly not cast** that one **out.** The strong double negative *ou mē* states emphatically that Christ will not reject anyone who sincerely and submissively comes to Him. True saving faith can never be exercised in vain, but only at the prompting of the Father (v. 44).

Here again is the incomprehensible (to the human mind) interplay between divine sovereignty and human responsibility: only those given to the Son by the Father will come to Him, yet all who are "thirsty [may] come" and anyone "who wishes [may] take the water of life without cost" (Rev. 22:17). Though they seem impossible to harmonize, there is no conflict between those two truths in the infinite mind of God (Deut. 29:29). (God's sovereignty in salvation does not negate the believer's responsibility to evangelize the lost—Matt. 24:14; 26:13; 28:19; Mark 13:10; cf. Acts 8:25, 40; 14:7, 15, 21; 16:10; Rom. 1:15; 15:19–20; 1 Cor. 1:17; 9:16, 18; 15:1; 2 Cor. 10:16; 11:7; Gal. 1:8–9, 11; 2:2; Phil. 4:15; 1 Peter 1:12).

Certainly, the Son would never reject any part of the Father's gift to Him. Such disunity within the Trinity is utterly inconceivable, as Jesus' next statement, **"I have come down from heaven, not to do My own will, but the will of Him who sent Me,"** made clear. The Lord came to earth for one purpose: to perfectly obey **the will of** the Father who sent Him. To the disciples Jesus declared, "My food is to do the will of Him who sent Me and to accomplish His work" (4:34). Later He added, "I can do nothing on My own initiative . . . because I do not seek My own will, but the will of Him who sent Me" (5:30; cf. Matt. 26:39). "So that the world may know that I love the Father," He affirmed in 14:31, "I do exactly as the Father commanded Me." In His High Priestly Prayer Jesus said to the Father, "I glorified You on the earth, having accomplished the work which You have given Me to do" (17:4).

The reality that Jesus came to do **the will of** the Father **who sent** Him (vv. 39–40) guarantees the salvation of the elect and their eternal security. It is the Father's will **that of all that He has given** to the Son, the Son should **lose nothing, but raise it up on the last day.** As in verse 37, the neuter form of the pronoun *pas* (**all**) views the elect as a collective unit. No part of that group, which the Father assigned to Christ in eternity past and gives to Him in time, will be lost; the fourfold promise that the Son will **raise it up** intact **on the last day** (40, 44, 54) constitutes an ironclad guarantee of eternal salvation to all true believers. Jesus reiterated that truth in the strongest terms when He declared in John 10:27–30,

> My sheep hear My voice, and I know them, and they follow Me; and I give eternal life to them, and they will never perish; and no one will snatch them out of My hand. My Father, who has given them to Me, is greater than all; and no one is able to snatch them out of the Father's hand.

In His High Priestly Prayer He said to the Father, "While I was with them, I was keeping them in Your name which You have given Me; and I guarded them and not one of them perished but the son of perdition [Judas Iscariot, who was not one of those given to Christ by the Father; cf. 6:64, 70–71], so that the Scripture would be fulfilled" (17:12).

The rest of the New Testament echoes the Lord's teaching regarding the perseverance and protection of the saints. The apostle Paul wrote in Romans 8:29–30,

> For those whom He foreknew, He also predestined to become conformed to the image of His Son, so that He would be the firstborn among many brethren; and these whom He predestined, He also called; and these whom He called, He also justified; and these whom He justified, He also glorified.

The repeated phrase "He also" links the entire salvation process from eternity past to eternity future in an unbreakable chain. All whom God foreknew will be predestined, called, justified, and glorified; no one will be lost along the way (cf. 8:31–39). In Philippians 1:6 Paul expressed his confidence that "He who began a good work in [believers] will perfect it until the day of Christ Jesus." To the Colossians he wrote, "For you have died and your life is hidden with Christ in God. When Christ, who is our life, is revealed, then you also will be revealed with Him in glory" (Col. 3:3–4). All who are united with Christ in His death will return with Him in glory (cf. Rev. 19:14). In his first epistle Peter wrote that those who are

> chosen according to the foreknowledge of God the Father, by the sanctifying work of the Spirit, to obey Jesus Christ and be sprinkled with His blood . . . [will] obtain an inheritance which is imperishable and undefiled and will not fade away, reserved in heaven for [them], [because they] are protected by the power of God through faith for a salvation ready to be revealed in the last time. (1 Peter 1:1–2, 4–5)

In the introduction to his epistle Jude described believers as "those who are the called . . . kept for Jesus Christ" (Jude 1). He concluded his letter with the marvelous benediction, "Now to Him who is able to keep you from stumbling, and to make you stand in the presence of His glory blameless with great joy, to the only God our Savior, through Jesus Christ our Lord, be glory, majesty, dominion and authority, before all time and now and forever. Amen" (vv. 24–25).

The blessing of eternal security or the preservation and perseverance of believers is never apart from personal repentance and faith, so our Lord affirms that heaven belongs to **everyone who beholds the Son and believes in Him.** It is they who **will have eternal life** (vv. 47, 54; 3:15–16, 36; 5:24; 10:28), which by its very nature can never end (3:16; 10:28; Matt. 25:46). That fact further reinforces the protection and security of believers taught in verses 37–39. The **eternal life** that comes through Jesus, the Bread of Life, should be sought with far more zeal than the physical bread the crowd selfishly sought.

THE COMPLAINT

Therefore the Jews were grumbling about Him, because He said, "I am the bread that came down out of heaven." They were saying, "Is not this Jesus, the son of Joseph, whose father and mother we know? How does He now say, 'I have come down out of heaven'?" Jesus answered and said to them, "Do not grumble among yourselves. No one can come to Me unless the Father who sent Me draws him; and I will raise him up on the last day. It is written in the prophets, 'And they shall all be taught of God.' Everyone who has heard and learned from the Father, comes to Me. Not that anyone has seen the Father, except the One who is from God; He has seen the Father. Truly, truly, I say to you, he who believes has eternal life. I am the bread of life. Your fathers ate the manna in the wilderness, and they died. This is the bread which comes down out of heaven, so that one may eat of it and not die." (6:41–50)

Because their unbelief kept them from understanding, **the Jews** (this term has a negative connotation here as it frequently does in John's gospel [cf. 1:19; 2:18–20; 5:10, 15–16, 18; 7:1; 8:48, 52, 57; 9:18, 22; 10:24, 31, 33; 19:7, 12, 14, 20, 21, 38; 20:19]) **were grumbling about** Jesus (as their ancestors had grumbled against God; Ex. 16:2, 8–9; Num. 11:4–6). Specifically, they were disturbed by two things He had said. The first was His claim to be the source of eternal life (v. 35). The verb translated **grumbling** (*gogguzō*) is an onomatopoetic word that both means and sounds like muttered complaints and whispers of displeasure. They were also outraged at His declaration that He came **down out of heaven.** They thought of Him merely on the human level, as a fellow Galilean, **the son of Joseph, whose father and mother** they knew (cf. 4:44; 7:27; Matt. 13:55–57). They also knew that He came from the despised town of Nazareth (cf. 1:46). And so, like the Jews in Judea (5:18), these Galileans hardened their hearts against their Messiah, who called for repentance and faith as a prerequisite to entering His kingdom (Matt. 4:17) and who outrageously, in their view, claimed equality with God.

Those who continually reject the truth may find that God will judicially harden their hearts. For those who refused to believe His teaching, Jesus made the truth more obscure by means of parables. To

His disciples' question, "Why do You speak to them in parables?" (Matt. 13:10) the Lord replied,

> To you it has been granted to know the mysteries of the kingdom of heaven, but to them it has not been granted. For whoever has, to him more shall be given, and he will have an abundance; but whoever does not have, even what he has shall be taken away from him. Therefore I speak to them in parables; because while seeing they do not see, and while hearing they do not hear, nor do they understand. In their case the prophecy of Isaiah is being fulfilled, which says, "You will keep on hearing, but will not understand; you will keep on seeing, but will not perceive; for the heart of this people has become dull, with their ears they scarcely hear, and they have closed their eyes, otherwise they would see with their eyes, hear with their ears, and understand with their heart and return, and I would heal them." (vv. 11–15; cf. Isa. 6:10)

John 12:37–40 says of those who rejected Jesus after witnessing His miracles,

> But though He had performed so many signs before them, yet they were not believing in Him. This was to fulfill the word of Isaiah the prophet which he spoke: "Lord, who has believed our report? And to whom has the arm of the Lord been revealed?" For this reason they could not believe, for Isaiah said again, "He has blinded their eyes and He hardened their heart, so that they would not see with their eyes and perceive with their heart, and be converted and I heal them."

In the end times, those who will "not receive the love of the truth so as to be saved" (2 Thess. 2:10) will find that "God will send upon them a deluding influence so that they will believe what is false" (v. 11). At the present time, there is a partial hardening of Israel (Rom. 11:25), leading to the salvation of the Gentiles (v. 11). But one day, during the future time of tribulation, God will remove Israel's blindness, and all the believing remnant of the Jewish people will be saved (v. 26; cf. Zech. 12:10–13:1).

Rather than answer their confusion, Jesus commanded the Jews, **"Do not grumble among yourselves."** He called for them to stop the mumbling complaints that reflected their rebellious and hard hearts. He had said and done enough, if they had been open and willing. Thus, there was no point in responding to their muttering discontent and disrespect with a detailed defense. They had willfully hardened their hearts, and would have only rejected the truth of His heavenly origin had He elaborated on it.

Then Jesus uttered some very solemn words: **"No one can come to Me unless the Father who sent Me draws him,"** emphasizing man's helplessness and utter inability to respond to Him apart from God's sovereign call. Unbelievers are unable to come to Jesus on their own initiative (cf. the discussion of verse 37 above). If God did not irresistibly draw sinners to Christ, **no one** would ever **come** to Him.

To explain how lost sinners supposedly have the power to accept or reject the gospel of their own free will, some theologians introduce the concept of prevenient grace. Millard J. Erickson explains,

> As generally understood, prevenient grace is grace that is given by God to all men indiscriminately. It is seen in God's sending the sunshine and the rain upon all. It is also the basis of all the goodness found in men everywhere. Beyond that, it is universally given to counteract the effect of sin. . . . Since God has given this grace to all, everyone is capable of accepting the offer of salvation; consequently, there is no need for any special application of God's grace to particular individuals. (*Christian Theology* [Grand Rapids: Baker, 1985], 3:920)

But the Bible indicates that fallen man is unable, of his own volition, to come to Jesus Christ. Unregenerate people are dead in sin (Eph. 2:1; Col. 2:13), slaves to unrighteousness (John 8:34; Rom. 6:6, 17, 20), alienated from God (Col. 1:21), and hostile to Him (Rom. 5:10; 8:7). They are spiritually blind (2 Cor. 4:4) captives (2 Tim. 2:26) trapped in Satan's kingdom (Col. 1:13), powerless to change their sinful natures (Jer. 13:23; Rom. 5:6), unable to please God (Rom. 8:8), and incapable of understanding spiritual truth (1 Cor. 2:14; cf. John 14:17). Although the human will is involved in coming to Christ (since no one is saved apart from believing the gospel—Mark 1:15; Acts 15:7; Rom. 1:16; 10:9–15; Eph. 1:13), sinners cannot come to Him of their own free will. (Moreover, a comparison of verse 44 with verse 37 shows that God's drawing cannot apply to all unregenerate people, as proponents of prevenient grace argue, because verse 37 limits it to the redeemed whom God has given to Christ.) God irresistibly, efficaciously draws to Christ only those whom He chose for salvation in eternity past (Eph. 1:4–5, 11).

Once again, Jesus repeated the wonderful promise that all whom the Father chooses will be drawn, will come, will be received, and He **will raise** them **on the last day** (vv. 39–40, 54). Everyone who comes to Christ will be kept by Him; there is no possibility that even one elect person given to Him by the Father will be lost (see the discussion of v. 39 above).

In verse 45 the Lord paraphrased Isaiah 54:13 to emphasize that His teaching was consistent with the Old Testament. What was **written in the prophets, "And they shall all be taught of God,"** restates the truth of verse 44 in different terms. Those who come to saving faith do so because they are supernaturally instructed by God. Drawing and teaching are merely different aspects of God's sovereign call to salvation; it is through the truth of His Word that God draws people to embrace His Son (Rom. 10:14, 17; cf. 1 Peter 1:23–25). As a result, **everyone who has heard and learned from the Father, comes to** Christ. Jesus' statement was also a subtle rebuke of His Jewish opponents, who prided themselves on their knowledge of Scripture. But had they truly understood the Old Testament, they would have eagerly embraced Him (5:39).

As the only way to God (John 14:6), Jesus hastened to add that no one **has seen the Father** (1:18; 5:37; Ex. 33:20; 1 Tim. 6:16) **except the One who is from God.** Because He was eternally in heaven one with the Father, and then sent to earth by the Father, the Son can speak authoritatively about the Father (cf. Heb. 1:2). No one else can rightly make such a claim. Thus, only the Son is qualified to speak firsthand about the expectations of the Father and the truth of salvation.

Jesus' solemn statement, **"Truly, truly, I say to you, he who believes has eternal life"** (cf. v. 40; 3:15–16, 36; 5:24) sums up the importance of trusting God's self-revelation in Christ. Those who believe in Jesus not only have the hope of eternal life in the future, but also enjoy the possession of that life even now, as the present tense of *pisteuō* (**believes**) indicates.

The Lord concluded this portion of His sermon by restating the truth that He is **the bread of life** (cf. v. 35). He then contrasted Himself as the true bread of heaven (cf. v. 33) with the **manna** (cf. v. 31) that the Hebrew **fathers ate . . . in the wilderness.** Although it was miraculously provided by God to sustain the Israelites' physical life, **the manna** could not impart eternal life, since the **fathers** who **ate the manna . . . died** (Heb. 3:17; cf. Jude 5). Jesus, however, is the true **bread which comes down out of heaven** (vv. 33, 35), **so that one may eat of it and not die. Eat** refers metaphorically to believing savingly in Jesus, which alone rescues sinners from eternal death (cf. 3:16; 11:26). Appropriating Jesus as the Bread of Life is the theme of the next section of this sermon.

The Bread of Life—
Part 2: Appropriating
the Bread of Life
(John 6:51–59)

21

"I am the living bread that came down out of heaven; if anyone
eats of this bread, he will live forever; and the bread also which I
will give for the life of the world is My flesh." Then the Jews
began to argue with one another, saying, "How can this man give
us His flesh to eat?" So Jesus said to them, "Truly, truly, I say to
you, unless you eat the flesh of the Son of Man and drink His
blood, you have no life in yourselves. He who eats My flesh and
drinks My blood has eternal life, and I will raise him up on the
last day. For My flesh is true food, and My blood is true drink. He
who eats My flesh and drinks My blood abides in Me, and I in
him. As the living Father sent Me, and I live because of the Father,
so he who eats Me, he also will live because of Me. This is the
bread which came down out of heaven; not as the fathers ate and
died; he who eats this bread will live forever." These things He
said in the synagogue as He taught in Capernaum. (6:51–59)

We live in a spiritually hungry world desperate for meaning and
hope in life. From the beginning, human beings were created to serve
God and fellowship with Him (cf. Gen. 1:26; 3:8). He was to be both their
focus and their fulfillment. But by rejecting Him, men and women have

been left with an aching void deep in their souls. In their misguided attempts to fill that emptiness they, like Israel of old, have forsaken the Lord, "the fountain of living waters, to hew for themselves cisterns, broken cisterns that can hold no water" (Jer. 2:13). Yet, fallen men do not find the exhilarating freedom they seek by casting God aside. Instead, they discover only the horrifying meaninglessness of a godless life. Christian apologist William Lane Craig explains:

> "Who am I?" man asks. "Why am I here? Where am I going?" Since the Enlightenment, when he threw off the shackles of religion, man has tried to answer these questions without reference to God. But the answers that came back were not exhilarating, but dark and terrible. "You are the accidental by-product of nature," he is told, "a result of matter plus time plus chance. There is no reason for your existence. All you face is death."
>
> Modern man thought that when he had got rid of God, he had freed himself from all that repressed and stifled him. Instead, he discovered that in killing God, he had also killed himself.
>
> For if there is no God, then man's life becomes absurd. . . .
>
> [Apart from God] mankind is a doomed race in a dying universe. Because the human race will eventually cease to exist, it makes no ultimate difference whether it ever did exist. Mankind is thus no more significant than a swarm of mosquitos or a barnyard of pigs, for their end is all the same. The same blind cosmic process that coughed them up in the first place will eventually swallow them again. (*Apologetics: An Introduction* [Chicago: Moody, 1984], 39, 41)

Of course, the hopelessness of life without God is not a recent discovery. Long before modern rationalism led to nihilistic despair, the great church father Augustine cried out to the Lord, "You made us for yourself and our hearts find no peace until they rest in you" (*Confessions,* I.1). And centuries before Augustine, the wisest man who ever lived also recognized the vanity of life apart from God. Despite his wisdom, Solomon sought happiness and satisfaction apart from the Lord. In Ecclesiastes 2, he summarized his futile pursuits, including the chase for pleasure (vv. 1–3, 8c), productivity (vv. 4–6), possessions (vv. 7–8), political power (vv. 9–10), and even wisdom itself (vv. 12–14). Yet, at the end of it all, he realized that it was all meaningless (vv. 11, 15–23). Only in God could true purpose and meaning be found, "for who can eat and who can have enjoyment without Him?" (v. 25; cf. 12:13–14).

Throughout the rest of Ecclesiastes, Solomon warned against following the path of human wisdom that proved so empty. The key term in the book is "vanity" (sometimes translated "futility" in the NASB), which appears some three dozen times. The term expresses the futility of life "under the sun" (a phrase used almost as often) apart from God. Solomon's point was that pursuing earthly goals as ends in themselves (without seeing them as a means to glorify and serve God) leads only to emptiness and hopeless despair (1:2–3, 8–11, 14; 2:12–23; 3:9; 4:2–3; 5:10–11, 16; 6:7, 12; 7:1; 9:2–3; 12:8).

Into this fallen world of disappointment, despondency, and desperation came the Lord Jesus Christ. He is the Bread of Life, the only One who can satisfy the deepest longings of the human soul. Only through Him (Acts 4:12) can sinners obtain forgiveness (Matt. 26:28; Acts 5:30–31; 10:43; Eph. 4:32), be restored to a right relationship with God (John 14:6; 1 Peter 3:18), and receive eternal life (John 3:15–16, 36; 5:24; 17:2; 1 John 5:11–12).

In the first section of His sermon on the Bread of Life, Jesus presented Himself as spiritual food for the famished soul (6:30–50). In the concluding section (vv. 51–59), He urged the people to appropriate Him personally by faith. The passage includes Jesus' pronouncement, the Jews' perplexity, and Jesus' promises.

THE PRONOUNCEMENT

"I am the living bread that came down out of heaven; if anyone eats of this bread, he will live forever; and the bread also which I will give for the life of the world is My flesh." (6:51)

For the fifth time in this discourse (cf. vv. 33, 35, 48, 50), Jesus claimed to be **the living bread that came down out of heaven.** He then added the promise that **if anyone eats of this bread, he will live forever.** Here, as in verses 35 and 40, human responsibility to believe in Christ is in view (God's sovereignty in salvation is taught in vv. 37, 39, 44, 65).

Ever the master teacher, Jesus used the simple, everyday routine of eating to communicate profound spiritual truth. The analogy of eating suggests five parallels to appropriating spiritual truth.

First, just as food is useless unless it is eaten, so also spiritual truth does no good if it is not internalized. Merely knowing the truth, without acting on it, both profits nothing (Heb. 4:2) and does not allow one to remain neutral (Luke 11:23). In fact, it will result in a more severe judgment (Luke 12:47–48; Heb. 10:29).

Second, eating is prompted by hunger; those who are full are not interested in food. In the same way, sinners who are satiated with their sin have no hunger for spiritual things (cf. Luke 5:31–32; 6:21). When God awakens them to their lost condition, however, the hunger for forgiveness, deliverance, peace, love, hope, and joy drives them to the Bread of Life.

Third, the food people eat becomes part of them through the operation of the body's digestive system. So it is spiritually. People may admire Christ, be impressed with His teaching, and even bemoan His death on the cross as a great tragedy. But not until they appropriate Him by faith do they become one with Him (17:21; 1 Cor. 6:17; 2 Cor. 4:10; Gal. 2:20; Eph. 3:17).

Fourth, eating involves trust. No one knowingly eats tainted or spoiled food; the very act of eating implies faith that the food is edible (cf. Mark 7:15). Thus, the metaphor of eating the Bread of Life implies believing in Jesus.

Finally, eating is personal. No one can eat a meal for another; there is no such thing as eating by proxy. Nor is there salvation by proxy. In Psalm 49:7 the psalmist wrote, "No man can by any means redeem his brother or give to God a ransom for him." Sinners must appropriate the Bread of Life as individuals to receive salvation and **live forever** (vv. 50, 58; 3:16; 8:51; 11:26; Rom. 8:13).

The Lord further defined **the bread** of life as that **which** He would voluntarily (10:18) **give for the life of the world:** His **flesh** (cf. 1:14). The concept of Jesus giving Himself sacrificially for sinners is a repeated New Testament theme (e.g., Matt. 20:28; Gal. 1:4; 2:20; Eph. 5:2, 25; 1 Tim. 2:6; Titus 2:14). The Lord referred prophetically here to His death on the cross (2 Cor. 5:21; Gal. 3:13; 1 Peter 2:24), one of many such predictions recorded in the gospels (John 2:19–22; 12:24; Matt. 12:40; 16:21; 17:22; 20:18; Mark 8:31; 9:31; 10:33–34; Luke 9:22, 44; 18:31–33; 24:6–7). It is Jesus' offering of His **flesh** that is the price of redemption. Had He merely come and proclaimed God's standards, it would have left the human race in a hopeless predicament. Since no one can keep those standards, there would have been no way for sinners to have a relationship with God. But to make reconciliation between sinful man and holy God possible, "Christ also died for sins once for all, the just for the unjust, so that He might bring us to God" (1 Peter 3:18; cf. 2:24; Isa. 53:4–6; Rom. 3:21–26; 2 Cor. 5:21).

Since "the wages of sin is death" (Rom. 6:23) and "without shedding of blood there is no forgiveness" (Heb. 9:22), Christ became the final sacrifice for sin, "the Lamb of God who takes away the sin of the world!" (John 1:29). His death, for all who believed and would believe, God accepted as the full payment for sin (Rom. 3:25–26; 4:25; Heb. 2:17; 1 John 2:2; 4:10), so that complete pardon was provided for the sins of all the penitent faithful (Acts 10:43; 13:38–39; Eph. 1:7; Col. 1:14; 2:13–14; 1 John 1:9; 2:12).

The death of Christ was a real, genuine, actual satisfaction of divine justice. It was a true payment and atonement in full—actually, not potentially, paid to God by Christ on behalf of all who would ever believe, because they were chosen and redeemed by the power of God.

The death of Christ was definite, particular, specific, and actual on behalf of God's chosen people, limited in extent by His sovereign purposes, but unlimited in effect for all for whom it was rendered.

Redemption is the work of God. Christ died to accomplish it, not merely to make it possible and then finally accomplished when the sinner believes. The Bible does not teach that Jesus died for everyone potentially, but no one actually. On the contrary, Christ procured salvation for all whom God would call and justify; He actually paid the penalty in full for all who would ever believe. Sinners do not limit the atonement by their lack of faith; God does by His sovereign design.

Christ offered His **flesh** as a sacrifice not merely for Israel, but for the **world** (cf. 1:29; 4:42; 1 John 4:14). He died for people from all races, cultures, ethnic groups, and social strata (cf. Gal. 3:28; Col. 3:11). Thus God said in Isaiah 45:22, "Turn to Me and be saved, all the ends of the earth," and Jesus commissioned the church to "make disciples of all the nations" (Matt. 28:19). The Lord also declared, "As Moses lifted up the serpent in the wilderness, even so must the Son of Man be lifted up; so that whoever believes will in Him have eternal life" (John 3:14–15), and "I, if I am lifted up from the earth, will draw all men to Myself" (12:32). He is the only Savior for the world of lost sinners.

THE PERPLEXITY

Then the Jews began to argue with one another, saying, "How can this man give us His flesh to eat?" (6:52)

The Lord was obviously not talking about cannibalism when He spoke of eating His flesh. Rather, He was giving a physical illustration of a spiritual truth. Once again, however, **the** antagonistic **Jews** completely missed the significance of Jesus' statement. As a result, they **began to argue with one another. Argue** translates a form of the verb *machomai*, which means "to fight," or "to quarrel" (cf. Acts 7:26; 2 Tim. 2:24; James 4:2), indicating that it was a heated dispute. The discussion centered on the question, **"How can this man give us His flesh to eat?"** Blinded by the ignorance of their own unbelief, they were unable to understand the spiritual significance of which Jesus spoke (cf. v. 42; 3:4, 9; 4:11–12; 9:16; 12:34).

It should be noted that the Roman Catholic Church appeals to this passage as a proof of the doctrine of transubstantiation—the false teaching that the body and blood of Christ are literally present in the bread and wine of the Mass. Catholic theologian Ludwig Ott writes, "The body and the blood of Christ together with His soul and His divinity and therefore the whole Christ are truly present in the Eucharist" (*Fundamentals of Catholic Dogma* [St. Louis: B. Herder, 1954], 382). It is a false foundation for a false doctrine, however, to suggest that Jesus was referring to the Eucharist (Communion or the Lord's Table) here, since He used the word *sarx* (**flesh**). A different word, *sōma* ("body"), appears in the passages referring to Communion (Matt. 26:26; Mark 14:22; Luke 22:19; 1 Cor. 10:16; 11:24, 27). Two additional considerations reinforce the fact that this passage does not refer to Communion: First, the Lord's Table had not yet been instituted; therefore, the Jews would not have understood what Jesus was talking about if He were speaking of Communion. Second, Jesus said that anyone who partakes of His flesh has eternal life. If that was a reference to the Lord's Table, it would mean that eternal life could be gained through taking Communion. That is clearly foreign to Scripture, however, which teaches that Communion is for those who are already believers (1 Cor. 11:27–32) and that salvation is by faith alone (Eph. 2:8–9). (For further arguments against a sacramental interpretation of eating Christ's flesh and drinking His blood, see D. A. Carson, *The Gospel According to John,* The Pillar New Testament Commentary [Grand Rapids: Eerdmans, 1991], 296–98; for a critique of the Roman Catholic doctrine of the Mass, see James G. McCarthy, *The Gospel According to Rome* [Eugene, Ore.: Harvest House, 1995], chaps. 6–7.)

Both the Roman Catholic Church and Jesus' Jewish opponents missed His point. As noted in the discussion of verse 51 above, the Lord was not speaking literally, but metaphorically to the people—encouraging them to appropriate Him by faith.

THE PROMISES

So Jesus said to them, "Truly, truly, I say to you, unless you eat the flesh of the Son of Man and drink His blood, you have no life in yourselves. He who eats My flesh and drinks My blood has eternal life, and I will raise him up on the last day. For My flesh is true food, and My blood is true drink. He who eats My flesh and drinks My blood abides in Me, and I in him. As the living Father sent Me, and I live because of the Father, so he who eats Me, he also will live because of Me. This is the bread which came down out of heaven; not as the fathers ate and died; he who eats this bread will live forever." These things He said in the synagogue as He taught in Capernaum. (6:53–59)

Although confronted with their willful unbelief, Jesus did not tone down, soften, or even clarify His words. Instead, He made His teaching even harder for them to swallow by adding the shocking concept of drinking His **blood.** To drink blood or eat meat with the blood still in it was strictly prohibited by the Old Testament law:

> And any man from the house of Israel, or from the aliens who sojourn among them, who eats any blood, I will set My face against that person who eats blood and will cut him off from among his people. For the life of the flesh is in the blood, and I have given it to you on the altar to make atonement for your souls; for it is the blood by reason of the life that makes atonement. Therefore I said to the sons of Israel, "No person among you may eat blood, nor may any alien who sojourns among you eat blood." So when any man from the sons of Israel, or from the aliens who sojourn among them, in hunting catches a beast or a bird which may be eaten, he shall pour out its blood and cover it with earth. For as for the life of all flesh, its blood is identified with its life. Therefore I said to the sons of Israel, "You are not to eat the blood of any flesh, for the life of all flesh is its blood; whoever eats it shall be cut off." (Lev. 17:10–14; cf. 7:26–27; Gen. 9:4; Deut. 12:16, 23–24; 15:23; Acts 15:29)

Jesus, of course, was not speaking of literally drinking the fluid in His veins any more than He was of literally eating His flesh. Both metaphors refer to the necessity of accepting Jesus' sacrificial death. The New Testament frequently uses the term **blood** as a graphic metonym speaking of Christ's death on the cross as the final sacrifice for sin (Matt. 26:28; Acts 20:28; Rom. 3:25; 5:9; 1 Cor. 11:25; Eph. 1:7; 2:13; Col. 1:20; Heb. 9:12, 14; 10:19, 29; 13:12; 1 Peter 1:2, 19; 1 John 1:7; Rev. 1:5; 5:9; 7:14; 12:11). His sacrifice was the one to which all of the Old Testament sacrifices pointed.

But the concept of a crucified Messiah was a major stumbling block for Israel. In response to the Lord's declaration, "And I, if I am lifted up from the earth, will draw all men to Myself" (John 12:32), "the crowd then answered Him, 'We have heard out of the Law that the Christ is to remain forever; and how can You say, "The Son of Man must be lifted up?" ' " (v. 34). On the road to Emmaus, the resurrected Christ rebuked two of His disciples for their hesitancy to accept the necessity of His death: "O foolish men and slow of heart to believe in all that the prophets have spoken! Was it not necessary for the Christ to suffer these things and to enter into His glory?" (Luke 24:25–26). "We preach Christ crucified," the apostle Paul wrote to the Corinthians, "to Jews a stumbling block" (1 Cor. 1:23), and in Galatians 5:11 he referred to the "the stumbling block of the cross." Thus, the major thrust of Paul's evangelistic message to the Jews at Thessalonica involved "explaining and giving evidence that the Christ had to suffer and rise again from the dead, and saying, 'This Jesus whom I am proclaiming to you is the Christ' " (Acts 17:3).

It should be noted that the verbs translated **eat** and **drink** are aorists, not present tense verbs. That suggests a one-time appropriation of Christ at salvation, not the continual eating and drinking of His body and blood portrayed by the Roman Catholic Mass (see the discussion of v. 52 above).

In verses 53–56 Jesus made four promises to those who eat His flesh and drink His blood. The first one is expressed negatively; those who reject Jesus **have no life in** themselves. Conversely, then, those who appropriate Him by faith do have such **life.** They are guaranteed abundant spiritual life, even now, by the Lord Himself (5:24; 10:10).

The second promise is that the one who **eats** His **flesh and drinks** His **blood has eternal life.** The abundant life that believers experience in the present will not end with death, but will expand into completeness and last forever. That this verse does not describe a ritualistic act is obvious when it is compared with verse 40. The results in the two verses are the same: eternal life and resurrection. But in verse 40, those results come from beholding and believing in the Son, while in verse 54 they come from eating His flesh and drinking His blood. It follows, then, that the eating and drinking of verse 54 are parallel to the beholding and believing of verse 40.

The third promise, that Christ **will raise up on the last day** all who eat His flesh and drink His blood, is repeated here for the fourth time in this passage (vv. 39, 40, 44). The resurrection to everlasting life is the believer's great hope (Acts 23:6; 24:15; cf. Titus 2:13; 1 Peter 1:3); apart from it, the Christian gospel is meaningless. To the Corinthians, some of whom were questioning the reality of the resurrection, Paul wrote,

> Now if Christ is preached, that He has been raised from the dead, how do some among you say that there is no resurrection of the dead? But if there is no resurrection of the dead, not even Christ has been raised; and if Christ has not been raised, then our preaching is vain, your faith also is vain. Moreover we are even found to be false witnesses of God, because we testified against God that He raised Christ, whom He did not raise, if in fact the dead are not raised. For if the dead are not raised, not even Christ has been raised; and if Christ has not been raised, your faith is worthless; you are still in your sins. Then those also who have fallen asleep in Christ have perished. If we have hoped in Christ in this life only, we are of all men most to be pitied. (1 Cor. 15:12–19)

Jesus introduced the fourth and final promise by declaring that His **flesh is true food, and** His **blood is true drink**—the sustenance that provides the very life of God to the believer. In light of that, the Lord declared, **"He who eats My flesh and drinks My blood abides in Me, and I in him."** The promise here is that of union with Christ. In John 14:20

Jesus promised His disciples, "In that day you will know that I am in My Father, and you in Me, and I in you." In 15:5 the Lord declared, "I am the vine, you are the branches; he who abides in Me and I in him, he bears much fruit, for apart from Me you can do nothing." "If anyone is in Christ," Paul wrote, "he is a new creature; the old things passed away; behold, new things have come" (2 Cor. 5:17). Later in that same epistle the apostle exhorted the Corinthians, "Test yourselves to see if you are in the faith; examine yourselves! Or do you not recognize this about yourselves, that Jesus Christ is in you—unless indeed you fail the test?" (2 Cor. 13:5). To the Galatians he wrote, "I have been crucified with Christ; and it is no longer I who live, but Christ lives in me; and the life which I now live in the flesh I live by faith in the Son of God, who loved me and gave Himself up for me" (Gal. 2:20). "Christ in you," he reminded the Colossians, is "the hope of glory" (Col. 1:27). In his first epistle the apostle John wrote, "We know that the Son of God has come, and has given us understanding so that we may know Him who is true; and we are in Him who is true, in His Son Jesus Christ. This is the true God and eternal life" (1 John 5:20; cf. 2:24; 3:24; 4:13; John 17:21; Rom. 6:3–8; 8:10; 1 Cor. 1:30; 6:17; Eph. 3:17; Col. 2:10).

In verse 57 Jesus declared the source of His authority to make such promises: **"the living Father sent Me, and I live because of the Father, so he who eats Me, he also will live because of Me."** Jesus had earlier stated, "As the Father has life in Himself, even so He gave to the Son also to have life in Himself" (5:26). Therefore, those who believe in Jesus **will live because of** Him. Jesus has life in Himself; and believers also have life in Him.

The Lord concluded this magnificent teaching by repeating the thought of verses 49 and 50. The invitation is as clear today as it was that memorable day **in the synagogue . . . in Capernaum.** The one who pursues material things will die as surely as the rebellious Israelites died in the wilderness. But **he who eats the bread which came down out of heaven . . . will live forever.**

The Bread of Life— Part 3: Responding to the Bread of Life (John 6:60–71)

22

Therefore many of His disciples, when they heard this said, "This is a difficult statement; who can listen to it?" But Jesus, conscious that His disciples grumbled at this, said to them, "Does this cause you to stumble? What then if you see the Son of Man ascending to where He was before? It is the Spirit who gives life; the flesh profits nothing; the words that I have spoken to you are spirit and are life. But there are some of you who do not believe." For Jesus knew from the beginning who they were who did not believe, and who it was that would betray Him. And He was saying, "For this reason I have said to you, that no one can come to Me unless it has been granted him from the Father." As a result of this many of His disciples withdrew and were not walking with Him anymore. So Jesus said to the twelve, "You do not want to go away also, do you?" Simon Peter answered Him, "Lord, to whom shall we go? You have words of eternal life. We have believed and have come to know that You are the Holy One of God." Jesus answered them, "Did I Myself not choose you, the twelve, and yet one of you is a devil?" Now He meant Judas the son of Simon Iscariot, for he, one of the twelve, was going to betray Him. (6:60–71)

Gospel preaching that fails to convey God's Word accurately, and to command obedience, falls short of the biblical standard. Both John the Baptist (Matt. 3:2) and Jesus (4:17) charged their audiences to act on the truth they were given, exhorting them to "repent, for the kingdom of heaven is at hand," and then demonstrate the fruit of true repentance (3:8). As a result of John's confrontive preaching

> the crowds were questioning him, saying, "Then what shall we do?" And he would answer and say to them, "The man who has two tunics is to share with him who has none; and he who has food is to do likewise." And some tax collectors also came to be baptized, and they said to him, "Teacher, what shall we do?" And he said to them, "Collect no more than what you have been ordered to." Some soldiers were questioning him, saying, "And what about us, what shall we do?" And he said to them, "Do not take money from anyone by force, or accuse anyone falsely, and be content with your wages." (Luke 3:10–14)

Peter's sermon on the day of Pentecost also compelled a response:

> Now when they heard this, they were pierced to the heart, and said to Peter and the rest of the apostles, "Brethren, what shall we do?" Peter said to them, "Repent, and each of you be baptized in the name of Jesus Christ for the forgiveness of your sins; and you will receive the gift of the Holy Spirit." (Acts 2:37–38)

Generally speaking, those who hear the powerful preaching of the Word will respond in one of three ways (cf. Matt. 13:3–9, 18–23). Some will scoff and react with outright rejection. Such were the scribes and Pharisees who responded to Jesus by consistently opposing His teaching and scorning His person. Their rejection culminated in Matthew 12:24 when, after seeing Jesus' miracles, they attributed them to Satan: "But when the Pharisees heard this [the crowd wondering if Jesus was the Messiah; v. 23], they said, 'This man casts out demons only by Beelzebul the ruler of the demons.'" They deliberately chose to dismiss the overwhelming evidence regarding who Jesus truly was.

Some will respond with a temporary or shallow faith. These false disciples are the curiosity seekers who are superficially attracted to Christ. But when He makes demands on them, or there is a cost to be paid for following Him, they disappear, desiring neither to let go of the world, nor to deny themselves (cf. Luke 9:23–25). John 2:23–25 discusses such people:

> Now when He was in Jerusalem at the Passover, during the feast, many believed in His name, observing His signs which He was doing. But Jesus, on His part, was not entrusting Himself to them, for He knew all

men, and because He did not need anyone to testify concerning man, for He Himself knew what was in man.

In his first epistle, John further described them as those who "went out from us, but they were not really of us; for if they had been of us, they would have remained with us; but they went out, so that it would be shown that they all are not of us" (1 John 2:19). Their numbers include men like Demas (2 Tim. 4:10), Simon the magician (Acts 8:18–21), and, above all, Judas Iscariot (Acts 1:25).

Finally, some will respond with true faith. This small nucleus of true disciples is the "little flock" to whom the Father has gladly chosen to give the kingdom (Luke 12:32), having drawn them to His Son (John 6:37, 44). They believe savingly in Jesus as the Son of God and Messiah.

Jesus' sermon on the Bread of Life, along with the response to it, is the thematic climax of the Lord's entire Galilean ministry. The crowd's reaction was typical, not only of the Jews of Jesus' day, but also of all people who are confronted with the truth. Those who heard His message exhibited each of the three responses noted above. Some rejected Jesus before the sermon was even finished, interrupting it and "grumbling about Him, because He said, 'I am the bread that came down out of heaven'" and "saying, 'Is not this Jesus, the son of Joseph, whose father and mother we know? How does He now say, "I have come down out of heaven"?'" (vv. 41–42).

Sadly, that response typified most of the Galileans. Although Jesus had taught in their cities and villages (Matt. 4:23) and performed many miracles in their midst (John 2:1–11; 4:46–54; 6:4–13; Matt. 8:2–4, 5–13, 14–17, 28–34; 9:1–8, 18–26; 12:9–14; 14:34–36; Mark 8:22–26; Luke 7:11–17), they still refused to believe in Him. Their willful rejection was inexcusable, and Jesus sternly rebuked two Galilean towns, Chorazin and Bethsaida, for their hardness of heart:

> Then He began to denounce the cities in which most of His miracles were done, because they did not repent. "Woe to you, Chorazin! Woe to you, Bethsaida! For if the miracles had occurred in Tyre and Sidon which occurred in you, they would have repented long ago in sackcloth and ashes. Nevertheless I say to you, it will be more tolerable for Tyre and Sidon in the day of judgment than for you. And you, Capernaum, will not be exalted to heaven, will you? You will descend to Hades; for if the miracles had occurred in Sodom which occurred in you, it would have remained to this day. Nevertheless I say to you that it will be more tolerable for the land of Sodom in the day of judgment, than for you." (Matt. 11:20–24)

As Jesus concluded His words, the outright rejecters left, leaving only those who claimed to be His disciples—some of whom possessed genuine faith and some of whom did not. Verses 60–71 describe the reactions of those two groups (the false disciples and the true disciples) to the Bread of Life Discourse.

THE REACTION OF THE FALSE DISCIPLES

Therefore many of His disciples, when they heard this said, "This is a difficult statement; who can listen to it?" But Jesus, conscious that His disciples grumbled at this, said to them, "Does this cause you to stumble? What then if you see the Son of Man ascending to where He was before? It is the Spirit who gives life; the flesh profits nothing; the words that I have spoken to you are spirit and are life. But there are some of you who do not believe." For Jesus knew from the beginning who they were who did not believe, and who it was that would betray Him. And He was saying, "For this reason I have said to you, that no one can come to Me unless it has been granted him from the Father." As a result of this many of His disciples withdrew and were not walking with Him anymore. (6:60–66)

That the people introduced here are called **disciples** does not imply that they were true followers of Christ. The term *mathētēs* ("disciple") refers to someone who attaches himself to a teacher as a student or learner, but does not imply anything about the disciple's sincerity or devotion. In addition to the disciples of Jesus, the New Testament also notes disciples of John the Baptist (Matt. 9:14), the Pharisees (22:15–16), Paul (Acts 9:25), and Moses (John 9:28).

While large crowds followed Jesus (cf. Matt. 4:25; 8:1; 19:2; Mark 4:1; Luke 12:1), especially early in His ministry, most of them were fascinated by the sensational miracles He performed—especially healing their diseases and, on at least two occasions, feeding them. But they were thrill seekers, not truth seekers.

The **disciples** introduced in verse 60 were no different. They were superficially attracted to Jesus by the miracles they had seen (v. 2), the meal they had eaten (vv. 3–13), and the hope that He would deliver them from the Romans (vv. 14–15). They were not ready to accept Him as the Son of God and the Messiah, but they had not yet chosen to abandon Jesus. That was about to change, however. By demanding that He be acknowledged as the Bread of Life (vv. 33, 35, 48, 50, 51) and insisting that eternal life is found only in fully committing to Him (vv. 51, 53–58), Jesus required more than they were willing to give. Consequently, they chose to turn their backs on Him and salvation.

Unable to swallow Jesus' teaching any longer, these **disciples, when they heard** His words, **said, "This is a difficult statement; who can listen to it?"** It finally dawned on them that following Jesus meant far more than merely hanging around Him, hoping to see and experience the physical benefits of His power. The adjective *sklēros* (**difficult**) literally means "rough," "withered," or "stiff." Figuratively, it describes something harsh, unpleasant, or hard to accept (cf. Matt. 25:24; Acts 26:14; Jude 15). Here it and the parallel statement **who can listen to it?** describe Jesus' **statement** not as incomprehensible, but as unacceptable. They rejected His words as objectionable and offensive. Like those who dismissed Jesus' teaching outright, they were scandalized by His claim to have come down from heaven (vv. 33, 38, 41–42, 50–51), His contention that He was the only answer to mankind's spiritual need (vv. 33, 35, 40), and His call for them to eat His flesh and drink His blood (51–57). In reality, however, what shut them out of the kingdom was not Jesus' teaching being unacceptable, but rather their being unbelieving and unaccepting.

Their reaction is typical of false disciples: as long as they perceived Jesus to be a source of healing, free food, and deliverance from enemy oppression, the self-serving disciples flocked to Him. But when He demanded that they acknowledge their spiritual bankruptcy, confess their sin, and commit themselves to Him as the only source of salvation, they became offended and left. Like countless other false disciples throughout the history of the church, they followed Jesus for what they thought they could get from Him. True disciples, on the other hand, come to Christ poor in spirit (Matt. 5:3), mourning over their sin (5:4), and hungering and thirsting for the righteousness that only He can supply (5:6). Our Lord left nothing to doubt when He identified the elements of true discipleship:

> If anyone wishes to come after Me, he must deny himself, and take up his cross daily and follow Me. For whoever wishes to save his life will lose it, but whoever loses his life for My sake, he is the one who will save it. For what is a man profited if he gains the whole world, and loses or forfeits himself? (Luke 9:23–25; cf. Matt. 10:34–39)

False disciples do not follow Christ because of who He is, but because of what they want from Him. They have no problem viewing Him as a baby in the manger at Christmas; a social reformer with a broad message of love and tolerance; the ideal human everyone should emulate; or a source of health, wealth, and worldly happiness. But they are unwilling to embrace the biblical Jesus—the God-man who fearlessly rebuked sinners and warned them of eternal hell, and that salvation from that hell comes only through believing His words (John 5:24). Those who resist or reject Jesus' teaching fail the test of true discipleship that He Himself laid down in John 8:31: "So Jesus was saying to those Jews who had believed Him, 'If you continue in My word, then you are truly disciples of Mine'" (cf. 15:8). Continued obedience to the words of Jesus Christ always marks true disciples (cf. 1 John 2:3–5).

Since **Jesus** understood the heart of every person (2:25; cf. Matt. 12:25; Luke 5:22), He was **conscious that His disciples grumbled** (cf. John 6:41; Ex. 16:2) **at** His teaching, so He **said to them, "Does this cause you to stumble?" Stumble** translates a form of the verb *skandalizō*, which can mean either "to take offense" (e.g., Matt. 13:57; 15:12) or "to give up believing" (e.g., 13:21; 24:10). Both meanings are appropriate here; the false disciples took offense at Jesus' teaching, and that caused them to abandon their superficial faith in Him.

Knowing that central in their rejection was His claim to have come down from heaven, Jesus asked, **"What then if you see the Son of Man ascending to where He was before?"** His implication seems to be, "If you saw Me go up into heaven, would that not convince you of My heavenly origin?" (The reference to His ascension also rules out any crassly literal interpretation of eating His flesh and drinking His blood, since Jesus would ascend bodily into heaven [cf. Acts 1:3–11].) It should be noted that some commentators see Jesus' reference to **ascending** as an implied reference to His crucifixion (3:14; 12:32, 34), which led to His resurrection, and then His ascension. According to that view, the Lord was making a crucial point: If the false disciples were scandalized by His teaching, how much more would they be offended by His execution (cf. 1 Cor. 1:23)? In any case, Jesus left the question open-ended, because how His hearers responded to Him would determine how they would answer it.

As He did in 3:6, Jesus contrasted **the Spirit who gives life** with **the flesh** that **profits nothing.** Spiritual life comes only when the Holy Spirit imparts Christ's life to the believer (Gal. 2:20; Col. 3:3–4). It does not come through "the will of the flesh" (1:13), which as R. V. G. Tasker notes, "signifies the outward to the exclusion of the inward, the visible apart from the invisible, the material unrelated to the spiritual, and the human dissociated from the divine" (*The Gospel According to St. John,* The Tyndale New Testament Commentaries [Grand Rapids: Eerdmans, 1975], 96). The Lord exhorted those who took issue with eating His flesh (v. 52) to focus instead on partaking of His Spirit (vv. 53–58).

Of course, no one can do that apart from hearing and obeying **the words that** Jesus has **spoken,** which, He declared, **are spirit and**

are life. It is Jesus' words that reveal who He really is. As noted earlier, accepting or rejecting those words separates true and false disciples. True disciples continue in His Word (8:31), which abides in them (15:7; cf. Jer. 15:16; Col. 3:16; 1 John 2:14); false disciples ultimately reject His word (8:37, 43, 47). To embrace Jesus' words is to receive Him, for they reveal His person. Thus the Bible teaches that salvation comes through the agency of the Word of God:

> Now the parable is this: the seed is the word of God.... The seed in the good soil, these are the ones who have heard the word in an honest and good heart, and hold it fast, and bear fruit with perseverance. (Luke 8:11, 15)

> But He answered and said to them, "My mother and My brothers are these who hear the word of God and do it." (Luke 8:21)

> In the exercise of His will He brought us forth by the word of truth, so that we would be a kind of first fruits among His creatures. (James 1:18)

> Therefore, putting aside all filthiness and all that remains of wickedness, in humility receive the word implanted, which is able to save your souls. (James 1:21)

> For you have been born again not of seed which is perishable but imperishable, that is, through the living and enduring word of God. (1 Peter 1:23)

Jesus then said, **"But there are some of you who do not believe."** As always with those who reject God's offer of salvation, the issue was not a lack of information, but a lack of faith. The Lord held these false disciples personally responsible for rejecting Him, not because they could not understand, but because they would not believe.

While the Lord was certainly saddened by the false disciples' unbelief, it did not take Him by surprise; **Jesus knew from the beginning who they were who did not believe.** He even knew all along **who it was that would betray Him**—Judas Iscariot, the supreme example of an unbelieving false disciple (see the discussion of vv. 70–71 below). Jesus' parting words to the false disciples, **"For this reason I have said to you, that no one can come to Me unless it has been granted him from the Father,"** reinforced His earlier teaching that God is absolutely sovereign in salvation (vv. 37, 39, 44–45). Verses 64 and 65 maintain the tension between divine sovereignty and human responsibility found throughout Scripture. On the one hand, unbelievers are condemned for their unbelief (v. 64); on the other hand, they are lost because the Father did not draw them (v. 65).

Sadly, but predictably, **as a result of this many of His disciples withdrew and were not walking with Him anymore.** Abandoning any further pretense of being His followers, they deserted Him and joined the scoffers who had rejected Jesus outright. *Ek toutou* (**as a result of this**) could also be translated "from this time." Both translations are correct. The false disciples permanently abandoned Jesus after this point **as a result** of His teaching in the sermon in general (especially vv. 48–58), and His condemnation of their unbelief in particular (v. 64). "What they wanted, he would not give; what he offered, they would not receive" (F. F. Bruce, *The Gospel of John* [Grand Rapids: Eerdmans, 1983], 164).

The Reaction of the True Disciples

So Jesus said to the twelve, "You do not want to go away also, do you?" Simon Peter answered Him, "Lord, to whom shall we go? You have words of eternal life. We have believed and have come to know that You are the Holy One of God." Jesus answered them, "Did I Myself not choose you, the twelve, and yet one of you is a devil?" Now He meant Judas the son of Simon Iscariot, for he, one of the twelve, was going to betray Him. (6:67–71)

This is the first occurrence in John's gospel of the term **the twelve,** which commonly designates the apostles in the Synoptic Gospels (e.g., Matt. 10:2; 20:17; Mark 4:10; 9:35; Luke 8:1; 18:31). John did not record the call of the Twelve and, except for verses 70 and 71, used the term elsewhere only in 20:24. It may be that the Twelve were all who remained after the temporary disciples left. Or Jesus may have spoken to them later in private. In the Greek text, the Lord's question expects a negative answer, hence the NASB translation, **"You do not want to go away also, do you?"** Jesus used the defection of the false disciples to contrast the faith of the Twelve.

As on so many other occasions, **Simon Peter** acted as the spokesman for the Twelve (cf. 13:36–37; Matt. 14:28; 15:15; 16:16, 22; 17:4; 18:21; 19:27; 26:33, 35; Mark 11:21; Luke 5:8; 8:45; 12:41). His declaration, **"Lord, to whom shall we go? You have words of eternal life. We have believed and have come to know that You are the Holy One of God,"** is reminiscent of his confession of Jesus as the Messiah in Caesarea Philippi (Matt. 16:16; cf. 14:33). While the crowd was only willing to accept Jesus as a kind of second Moses whom they hoped would supply their material needs, the Twelve saw Him for who He really is. There was no other teacher to whom they could turn, Peter said, for it was Christ alone who has the **words of eternal life** (cf. v. 63).

Yet, not even all of the Twelve had truly believed in and come to know Jesus, as the Lord was quick to point out. They must have been shocked when Jesus declared that there was a traitor in their ranks: **"Did I Myself not choose you, the twelve, and yet one of you is a devil?"** He is not here referring to election to salvation, but rather selection to apostleship. He chose twelve men, one of whom was to slander Him in the most unthinkable way. After Judas had been dismissed from the Upper Room the night of the Last Supper, then the Lord spoke to the remaining eleven as being chosen for salvation. As He said to them, "You did not choose Me but I chose you, and appointed you that you would go and bear fruit, and that your fruit would remain, so that whatever you ask of the Father in My name He may give to you" (15:16). His sovereign choice of them, both to salvation and apostleship, ruled out any pretentiousness or self-importance they may have otherwise felt.

The **devil** in their midst, of course, was **Judas the son of Simon Iscariot. Iscariot** derives from a Hebrew phrase meaning "man of Kerioth." The reference was probably to the Judean village of Kerioth (Josh. 15:25), though there was also a Moabite town of the same name (Jer. 48:24, 41; Amos 2:2). Despite Judas Iscariot's spiritual privilege, **one of the twelve,** the Lord knew that he **was** ultimately **going to betray Him.** (As the most notorious traitor in history, Judas is always introduced in the gospels as the betrayer of Jesus [cf. 12:4; 13:2; 18:2; Matt. 10:4; Mark 3:19; Luke 6:16].) *Diabolos* (**devil**) means "slanderer" (cf. 1 Tim. 3:11; 2 Tim. 3:3; Titus 2:3, where the plural form of the noun is rendered "malicious gossips"), or "false accuser." It would accurately reflect the Lord's intent here to render the phrase, "One of you is *the* devil." Satan, the supreme adversary of God, used Judas as his tool in opposing the work of God (13:2, 27). As in the incident involving Peter's presumptuous rebuke of Jesus (Matt. 16:23), the Lord identified Satan as the source behind Judas.

That does not exonerate or excuse Judas for his heinous act. The New Testament places the responsibility for Jesus' betrayal squarely at Judas Iscariot's feet. In the chilling words of Jesus, "The Son of Man is to go, just as it is written of Him; but woe to that man by whom the Son of Man is betrayed! It would have been good for that man if he had not been born" (Matt. 26:24).

Peter's affirmation in verses 68 and 69 expressed two key marks of true disciples: faith (**we have believed**)—which marks their spiritual birth—and faithfulness (**Lord, to whom shall we go?**)—which marks their character. The perfect tense of the verbs translated **have believed** and **have come to know** conveys the idea of an act completed in the past, but with ongoing results. The initial faith of true disciples results in continued commitment and loyalty to Christ. Unlike the false disciples who had made a final decision to abandon Jesus, the Twelve (except for Judas) had made a permanent pledge to follow Him. In this way, John contrasted the stark difference between those who are fickle and those who are faithful.

Following the Divine Timetable
(John 7:1–13)

23

After these things Jesus was walking in Galilee, for He was unwilling to walk in Judea because the Jews were seeking to kill Him. Now the feast of the Jews, the Feast of Booths, was near. Therefore His brothers said to Him, "Leave here and go into Judea, so that Your disciples also may see Your works which You are doing. For no one does anything in secret when he himself seeks to be known publicly. If You do these things, show Yourself to the world." For not even His brothers were believing in Him. So Jesus said to them, "My time is not yet here, but your time is always opportune. The world cannot hate you, but it hates Me because I testify of it, that its deeds are evil. Go up to the feast yourselves; I do not go up to this feast because My time has not yet fully come." Having said these things to them, He stayed in Galilee. But when His brothers had gone up to the feast, then He Himself also went up, not publicly, but as if, in secret. So the Jews were seeking Him at the feast and were saying, "Where is He?" There was much grumbling among the crowds concerning Him; some were saying, "He is a good man"; others were saying, "No, on the contrary, He leads the people astray." Yet no one was speaking openly of Him for fear of the Jews. (7:1–13)

From the unbelieving world's point of view, history is an unexplained succession of seemingly random events—a meaningless chain of causes and effects. In contrast, the Bible portrays history as the very opposite, the purposeful and perfect outworking of God's eternal plan. As the "ruler over all the kingdoms of the nations" (2 Chron. 20:6; cf. 1 Chron. 29:11–12; Ps. 47:2, 8) and the "blessed and only Sovereign, the King of kings and Lord of lords" (1 Tim. 6:15; cf. Rev. 17:14; 19:16), God is in complete control of every situation, working all things together for His glory and the good of His children (cf. Rom. 8:28; 11:36).

Nebuchadnezzar, the arrogant ruler of the Babylonian Empire, learned the truth about God's sovereignty in a most humiliating manner. Though he was warned in a dream that "the Most High is ruler over the realm of mankind and bestows it on whomever He wishes" (Dan. 4:25; cf. v. 17; 2:21), Nebuchadnezzar nevertheless "reflected and said, 'Is this not Babylon the great, which I myself have built as a royal residence by the might of my power and for the glory of my majesty?'" (v. 30). God's judgment on Nebuchadnezzar's prideful boast was swift and devastating:

> While the word was in the king's mouth, a voice came from heaven, saying, "King Nebuchadnezzar, to you it is declared: sovereignty has been removed from you, and you will be driven away from mankind, and your dwelling place will be with the beasts of the field. You will be given grass to eat like cattle, and seven periods of time will pass over you until you recognize that the Most High is ruler over the realm of mankind and bestows it on whomever He wishes." Immediately the word concerning Nebuchadnezzar was fulfilled; and he was driven away from mankind and began eating grass like cattle, and his body was drenched with the dew of heaven until his hair had grown like eagles' feathers and his nails like birds' claws. (vv. 31–33)

After living like an animal for seven years, a humbled Nebuchadnezzar reflected on the lessons he had so painfully learned:

> At the end of that period, I, Nebuchadnezzar, raised my eyes toward heaven and my reason returned to me, and I blessed the Most High and praised and honored Him who lives forever; for His dominion is an everlasting dominion, and His kingdom endures from generation to generation. All the inhabitants of the earth are accounted as nothing, but He does according to His will in the host of heaven and among the inhabitants of earth; and no one can ward off His hand or say to Him, "What have You done?" (vv. 34–35)

Years earlier Sennacherib, ruler of the feared Assyrian Empire, had also needed to learn that same lesson. His nation's conquests, of which it so proudly boasted (cf. Isa. 10:12–14), were not a result of its own military strength, but of God's sovereign design:

> Have you not heard?
> Long ago I did it,
> From ancient times I planned it.
> Now I have brought it to pass,
> That you should turn fortified cities into ruinous heaps.
> Therefore their inhabitants were short of strength,
> They were dismayed and put to shame;
> They were as the vegetation of the field and as the green herb,
> As grass on the housetops is scorched before it is grown up.
> But I know your sitting down
> And your going out and your coming in
> And your raging against Me. (Isa. 37:26–28)

But Sennacherib's attempt to conquer Jerusalem, God's holy city, failed disastrously; his army was destroyed (Isa. 37:36), and he was later murdered by his own sons (v. 38). Moreover, when Assyria's allotted time in God's program had ended, the nation was judged and destroyed (Isa. 10:12–19; 30:31–33; 31:8–9; Ezek. 31:3–17; Nah. 1:1–3:19)—just as Babylon, Medo-Persia, Greece, and Rome were each destroyed after her (Dan. 2:31–45; 7:1–23). Throughout the millennia since, nations have risen to prominence, had their moment in the sun, and faded from the scene— all in keeping with their "appointed times," which God has determined (Acts 17:26).

God's sovereignty and providence extend beyond nations and governments to include all people and events. Everything happens according to His divine schedule. At the pinnacle of that schedule are the birth, death, resurrection, and return of Jesus Christ—history's most significant events. Jesus was born "when the fullness of the time came, [and] God sent forth His Son, born of a woman, born under the Law" (Gal. 4:4). His death also took place according to God's perfect timing. Paul notes that "at the right time Christ died for the ungodly" (Rom. 5:6), having given "Himself as a ransom for all, the testimony given at the proper time" (1 Tim. 2:6). The Lord will likewise return at the precise moment chosen by God; Paul reminded Timothy of "the appearing of our Lord Jesus Christ, which He will bring about at the proper time" (1 Tim. 6:14–15; cf. Mark 13:33; Acts 1:6–7).

Throughout His earthly ministry, Jesus was always conscious of doing the Father's will according to His divine timetable—a truth that is in the first thirteen verses of chapter 7 (cf. v. 6). Chapters 7 and 8 usher in a new, more volatile section of John's gospel, as the smoldering resentment that Jesus encountered in chapters 1–6 finally burst into a blazing inferno of hatred. Chapter 8 even ends with an unsuccessful attempt on Jesus' life:"Therefore they picked up stones to throw at Him, but Jesus hid Himself and went out of the temple" (8:59). The hatred Jesus faced would reach its peak in 11:45–57, when the Jewish authorities made their final decision to kill Him—a plot that culminated in His crucifixion.

As chapter 7 opens, Jesus was still in Galilee, but preparing to return to Jerusalem at the time predetermined in God's plan. The section obviously divides into two elements: the wrong time and the right time.

THE WRONG TIME

After these things Jesus was walking in Galilee, for He was unwilling to walk in Judea because the Jews were seeking to kill Him. Now the feast of the Jews, the Feast of Booths, was near. Therefore His brothers said to Him, "Leave here and go into Judea, so that Your disciples also may see Your works which You are doing. For no one does anything in secret when he himself seeks to be known publicly. If You do these things, show Yourself to the world." For not even His brothers were believing in Him. So Jesus said to them, "My time is not yet here, but your time is always opportune. The world cannot hate you, but it hates Me because I testify of it, that its deeds are evil. Go up to the feast yourselves; I do not go up to this feast because My time has not yet fully come." Having said these things to them, He stayed in Galilee. (7:1–9)

These verses recount Jesus' decision to remain in Galilee until the timing was right to go to Jerusalem, His brothers' request that He leave before the appointed time, and His response to their request.

THE REMAINING

After these things Jesus was walking in Galilee, for He was unwilling to walk in Judea because the Jews were seeking to kill Him. (7:1)

The phrase **after these things** refers to the events described in chapter 6, which took place around the time of Passover in April (6:4). Since chapter 7 opens at the time of the Feast of Tabernacles in October (7:2), there is a gap of about six months between chapters 6 and 7. John records nothing about that interval, except that Jesus spent it **walking** (traveling and ministering) **in Galilee.** The apostle's purpose in composing his gospel was not to write an exhaustive biography of Jesus Christ, but to present Him as the Son of God and Messiah (20:21). The other gospel writers note that during those six months, Jesus traveled the length of Galilee, from Tyre and Sidon, northwest of Galilee (Matt. 15:21–28) to Decapolis, in the southeast (Mark 7:31–37). During that time He performed miracles, including healing (Matt. 15:29–31; Mark 8:22–26), casting out demons (Matt. 15:21–28; 17:14–18), and feeding the four thousand (Matt. 15:32–38).

Most of the six months, however, was spent discipling the Twelve. The Lord taught them extensively (Matt. 16:13–27; 17:19–23; 18:1–35), including telling them for the first time of His impending rejection, crucifixion, and resurrection (Matt. 16:21; cf. 17:22–23). He also revealed to the inner circle (Peter, James, and John) a glimpse of His divine glory (Matt. 17:1–8).

That Jesus spent only two days with the large crowd (perhaps 20,000 people) mentioned in chapter 6 but six months predominantly involved with the Twelve is highly significant. It shows that the primary focus of the Lord's ministry was not on mass meetings, but on discipleship. He devoted His time and effort to the small core group of men who would carry on His ministry after He was gone. The Christian church is in large measure the legacy of those eleven men (plus Matthias [Acts 1:26] and Paul [1 Cor. 9:1]), who faithfully discipled their followers who discipled others and so on, down through the centuries to our own day.

Discipleship must also be a priority for the church. The Lord did not commission the church to attract large crowds, but to go and make disciples (Matt. 28:19). Likewise, Paul charged the young pastor Timothy, "The things which you have heard from me in the presence of many witnesses, entrust these to faithful men who will be able to teach others also" (2 Tim. 2:2). The measure of any church's success is not the size of its congregation, but the depth of its discipleship.

In addition to discipling the Twelve, Jesus also remained in Galilee and **was unwilling to walk in Judea because the Jews were** constantly **seeking to kill Him.** Feelings of hostility toward the Lord, at least in **Judea,** had already reached the point where the Jewish leaders wanted Him dead (cf. 5:18). Jesus was therefore **unwilling to walk** (that is, to conduct His life and ministry) openly there, because the time was not yet right in God's plan for the events leading to His death. He was not, of course, unwilling to die; that was why He came into the world (John 12:27; cf. Matt. 20:28). As John Calvin wrote, "Although Christ avoided dangers, he did not turn aside a hair's breadth from the course of his duty" (*John,* The Crossway Classic Commentaries, Alister McGrath and J. I. Packer, eds. [Wheaton,

Ill.: Crossway, 1994], 180). Until His hour came, Jesus would not put God to the test (Matt. 4:5–7).

THE REQUEST

Now the feast of the Jews, the Feast of Booths, was near. There-fore His brothers said to Him, "Leave here and go into Judea, so that Your disciples also may see Your works which You are doing. For no one does anything in secret when he himself seeks to be known publicly. If You do these things, show Yourself to the world." For not even His brothers were believing in Him. (7:2–5)

The **Feast of Booths,** also called the Feast of Tabernacles or Ingathering, lasted for seven days during the Jewish month Tishri (Sept.–Oct.) with a special festival assembly on the eighth day (Lev. 23:33–36; Neh. 8:18). During the feast, the people built and lived in shel-ters made of branches (Lev. 23:42), as their ancestors had done after leaving Egypt (v. 43). City dwellers built their booths on the roofs of their houses, and in the streets and squares (Neh. 8:14–17). According to the first-century Jewish historian Josephus, the Feast of Tabernacles was the most popular of the three major Jewish feasts. It was marked by celebra-tions and parties, and featured water-drawing and lamp-lighting rites (cf. John 7:37–38; 8:12). In the millennial kingdom, the Feast of Tabernacles will again be celebrated, in honor of Messiah's dwelling with His people, and the ingathering of the nations into His kingdom (Zech. 14:16–19).

Since that feast **was near,** and was one of the three that all Jew-ish males were required to attend (Deut. 16:16; cf. Ex. 23:14–17; 34:22–24), Jesus' **brothers** assumed He would soon **leave** Galilee **and go into Judea** to celebrate it. Jesus' brothers were His half brothers, the children of both Mary and Joseph. Matthew 13:55 lists their names—James, Joseph, Simon, and Judas (or Jude). Although they did not believe in Him at this time (see the discussion of v. 5 below), they would later come to believe in Him (Acts 1:14). Two of His brothers, James and Jude, penned the epistles that bear their names, and James became the head of the Jerusalem church (Acts 12:17; 15:13; 21:18; cf. Gal. 1:19; 2:9).

Jesus' brothers challenged Him to perform His miracles openly, on the grand stage that Jerusalem would provide during the Feast of Tabernacles. Then, they reasoned, His **disciples** from both Galilee and Judea would **see** the **works which** He was **doing**—works which demon-strated that He was in fact the Messiah. Further, some of the disciples who had recently abandoned Him (6:66) might be won back. The Lord's brothers were not, as some mistakenly think, zealous for Him to show His glory. On the contrary, they did not even believe in Him yet (v. 5).

Their comments appear to have had a dual motivation. First, they may have wanted to see Jesus perform miracles, so they could decide for themselves whether or not His works were genuine. Second, they were probably expecting a political Messiah, like the crowd Jesus fed (6:14–15). Thus, in their minds, the acid test of Jesus' messiahship would be at Jerusalem (the political center of Israel), and not in Galilee. If the ruling authorities at Jerusalem signed off on Jesus, His brothers would also accept Him as the Messiah.

Their next statement to Him, **"For no one does anything in secret when he himself seeks to be known publicly,"** would have made perfect sense if Jesus were the political Messiah they sought. For Him to remain relatively secluded in Galilee seemed inconsistent with His messianic claims. But like the crowd that wanted to make Him king (6:14–15), Jesus' brothers completely misunderstood His mission, as He would soon point out. Their final challenge, **"If You do these things, show Yourself to the world,"** reveals their doubt and unbelief. The word **if** foreshadows the mocking unbelief that Jesus faced on the cross (Matt. 27:40), and is reminiscent of Satan's challenge (4:3, 6) during Christ's temptation.

The apostle John's footnote, **For not even His brothers were believing in Him,** explains why they spoke to Him the way they did. Earlier in His ministry, their unbelief had led them to think He had lost His mind (cf. Mark 3:21, 31–34). Nothing the Lord had done since then had penetrated their hard hearts. It would take His resurrection from the dead to finally persuade them that He was the Son of God (Acts 1:14).

THE RESPONSE

So Jesus said to them, "My time is not yet here, but your time is always opportune. The world cannot hate you, but it hates Me because I testify of it, that its deeds are evil. Go up to the feast yourselves; I do not go up to this feast because My time has not yet fully come." Having said these things to them, He stayed in Galilee. (7:6–9)

In reply to His brothers' misguided attempt to force His hand, **Jesus said to them, "My time is not yet here."** He would not allow His brothers' skepticism to dictate His actions. His course of action was determined by the sovereign Father who orchestrated everything in His time.

The Lord had responded similarly to His mother at the wedding in Cana:"My hour has not yet come" (cf. the exposition of 2:4 in chapter 6 of this volume). There Christ also rejected pressure from His family to reveal Himself prematurely. But He would not manifest Himself before the right time, the moment chosen by the Father.

In its fullest sense, the divine time would not come until the next great feast, Passover, the following spring. Though He would minister in Judea for most of the intervening months (cf. Luke 9:51–19:11), the Lord would not enter Jerusalem publicly and openly declare Himself to be the Messiah until then (Matt. 21:1–11; cf. Luke 19:37–40). And just as He had predicted (Matt. 16:21; 17:22–23; 20:17–19; 26:2), that final manifestation would lead to His death.

In contrast, His brothers' **time** was **always opportune.** As part of the unbelieving world (v. 7), they were not concerned with operating on God's timetable. They knew nothing of His plans and purposes, and were indifferent to His providence. Any time would do for them to go to the feast. Leon Morris observed, "In this respect the brothers joined with the world. Since the world (and the brothers) have cut themselves off from the divinely appointed 'time' all times are alike to them" (*The Gospel According to John,* The New International Commentary on the New Testament [Grand Rapids: Eerdmans, 1979], 398).

Unlike Jesus, they would face no hostility at Jerusalem from the Jewish authorities. **The world** could not **hate** them, since they were part of it, and it loves its own (15:19). But the world, as Jesus reminded His brothers, **"hates Me because I testify of** (or against) **it, that its deeds are evil"** (cf. 2:14–16; 3:19–20; 5:30–47; 12:48; 15:22–25). Since it is controlled by Satan (1 John 5:19), the activities and priorities of the world are inherently sinful. When believers **testify** against the world and confront its wickedness, like Jesus did, they arouse its antagonism and hatred (cf. 15:18–19; 17:14; Matt. 10:22; 24:9; Luke 6:22; 1 John 3:13; 2 Tim. 3:12; James 4:4).

Because the time was not yet right, Jesus refused His brothers' request, telling them, **"Go up to the feast yourselves."** The Lord, for the reasons already noted, chose not to go with them in what would have probably been a large caravan of people (cf. Luke 2:44). Such a public journey would have risked another attempt to make Him king by force (as in 6:14–15), or perhaps have triggered a premature triumphal entry. Either might have sparked a confrontation with the Jewish authorities, resulting in Jesus' death before the proper time, which was to be precisely at Passover.

The Greek manuscripts are about evenly divided between the reading *ouk* (**not**) and *oupō* ("not yet"; cf. the NIV). *Ouk* is most likely the correct reading, since it is unlikely that anyone would replace *oupō* with *ouk*, thereby introducing a seeming contradiction into the text (cf. v. 10). On the other hand, there is an obvious reason for scribes to have replaced *ouk* with *oupō*, since doing so removes the apparent contradiction with verse 10. In either case, however, the Lord's meaning is clear. He was not saying that He would not attend the feast at all, but that He would not go with his brothers in the manner they expected. Nor would He allow the Jewish leaders to take His life **because** His **time** had **not yet fully come.** When Jesus did lay down His life, six months later, it would be at the very moment God had predetermined (cf. v. 30; 8:20). Thus, **having said these things to** His brothers, **He stayed in Galilee** for a little while.

THE RIGHT TIME

But when His brothers had gone up to the feast, then He Himself also went up, not publicly, but as if, in secret. So the Jews were seeking Him at the feast and were saying, "Where is He?" There was much grumbling among the crowds concerning Him; some were saying, "He is a good man"; others were saying, "No, on the contrary, He leads the people astray." Yet no one was speaking openly of Him for fear of the Jews. (7:10–13)

By delaying His departure until after **His brothers had gone up to the feast** Jesus was able to go to Jerusalem **not publicly, but as if, in secret.** The Lord's caution was in marked contrast to the course of action His brothers had urged Him to take and, to them, inconsistent with Him being the Messiah. According to verse 14, Jesus did not arrive in Jerusalem until the middle of the feast. By the time He left Galilee most people would have already arrived in Jerusalem, and the roads would have been relatively deserted. The Lord also traveled through Samaria (New Testament scholars believe the journey through Samaria described in Luke 9:51–56 took place at this time), which few Jews were willing to do. Doing so allowed Jesus to avoid any unnecessary publicity and fanfare—attention that could have led to a premature confrontation with the Jewish leaders.

Meanwhile, events in Jerusalem confirmed the wisdom of the Lord's caution. John notes that **the Jews were seeking Him at the feast and were saying, "Where is He?"** The phrase **the Jews** does not refer to the common people who made up the crowds (v. 11), but to the Jewish leaders who were **seeking** to kill Him (5:18).

The leaders were not the only ones discussing Jesus in His absence; **there was much grumbling** and disagreement **among the**

crowds of worshipers **concerning Him.** On the one hand, **some were saying, "He is a good man,"** while **others were saying, "No, on the contrary, He leads the people astray."** Actually, both views of Jesus were incorrect. He was not merely **a good man,** since good men do not claim to be God (5:18; cf. 8:24, 28, 58; 10:33). Nor was **He** one who **leads the people astray,** because deceivers do not perform the supernatural and authenticating miracles that Jesus did (10:25, 37–38; 14:10–11; cf. 3:2; 5:36).

Sadly, it was this second view of Jesus—that He was a deceiver—that eventually prevailed among the majority of the Jewish people. The second-century apologist Justin Martyr wrote that the Jews "dared to call Him a magician, and a deceiver of the people" (*Dialogue of Justin with Trypho, a Jew,* 69, cf. 108). **Yet no one,** whether they thought He was good or a deceiver, **was speaking openly of Him for fear of the Jews** (cf. 9:22; 12:42; 19:38; 20:19). Though it was clear that the authorities rejected Jesus, the Sanhedrin had not yet rendered a formal judgment regarding Him. Thus, the people were careful to guard their words, speaking neither for Him or against Him until they knew what the official response to Jesus would be. In any case, the crowds certainly did not want to publicly contradict their religious leaders. The consequences for doing so were severe and could include excommunication from the synagogue (9:22; cf. 16:2). That dreaded punishment cut a person off from all of Jewish life.

As this account in John's gospel illustrates, Jesus followed God's timetable perfectly. He always performed God's will exactly as the Father wished. Those who are true followers of Christ also have the ability to follow God's revealed will—because they have been given both His Word and His Spirit. His Word informs believers as to what His will is (Ps. 40:8), and His Spirit empowers them to obey that will with gladness (143:10; cf. 119:111).

Unbelievers do not have the capacity to understand God's Word (1 Cor. 2:14) or the ability to obey His Spirit (Rom. 8:5–9). Nonetheless, for those who have not yet come to Him, the time is right to do so, "for He says, 'At the acceptable time I listened to you, and on the day of salvation I helped you.' Behold, now is 'The acceptable time,' behold, now is 'the day of salvation'" (2 Cor. 6:2).

Verifying the Claims of Christ (John 7:14–24)

24

But when it was now the midst of the feast Jesus went up into the temple, and began to teach. The Jews then were astonished, saying, "How has this man become learned, having never been educated?" So Jesus answered them and said, "My teaching is not Mine, but His who sent Me. If anyone is willing to do His will, he will know of the teaching, whether it is of God or whether I speak from Myself. He who speaks from himself seeks his own glory; but He who is seeking the glory of the One who sent Him, He is true, and there is no unrighteousness in Him. Did not Moses give you the Law, and yet none of you carries out the Law? Why do you seek to kill Me?" The crowd answered, "You have a demon! Who seeks to kill You?" Jesus answered them, "I did one deed, and you all marvel. For this reason Moses has given you circumcision (not because it is from Moses, but from the fathers), and on the Sabbath you circumcise a man. If a man receives circumcision on the Sabbath so that the Law of Moses will not be broken, are you angry with Me because I made an entire man well on the Sabbath? Do not judge according to appearance, but judge with righteous judgment." (7:14–24)

The most startling assertion Jesus made was His claim to be God (cf. chap. 15 of this volume). But He made many other statements that shocked those who heard Him. For example, He claimed

—to have come down from heaven (John 3:13; 6:38, 62; 8:23)

—to have been sent into the world by the Father (Matt. 10:40; Mark 9:37; Luke 10:16; John 3:17; 4:34; 5:23–24, 30, 36–38; 6:29, 39, 44, 46, 57; 7:16, 18, 28–29, 33; 8:16, 18, 26, 29, 42; 9:4; 10:36; 11:42; 12:44–45, 49; 13:20; 14:24; 15:21; 16:5; 17:3, 8, 18, 21, 23, 25; 20:21)

—to be the Savior of the world (Matt. 20:28; Luke 9:56; 19:10; John 3:17; 12:47; cf. 1:29; 4:42; Matt. 1:21; 1 John 4:14)

—to be the determiner of people's eternal destinies (Matt. 16:27; 25:31–46; John 5:22, 27, 30; cf. Luke 12:8–9; John 8:24)

—to be the source of eternal life (Mark 10:29–30; John 3:16; 4:14; 5:39–40; 6:27, 40, 47, 54; 10:28; 11:25; 14:6; 17:2)

—to be the only way to God (John 14:6; cf. Acts 4:12)

—to have the right to be honored on an equal basis with the Father (John 5:23; cf. Matt. 21:15–16)

—to be one with the Father (John 10:30; cf. 1:1; 12:45; 14:9; 17:21)

—to have the power to raise the dead (John 5:28–29; 6:39–40, 44, 54) and even rise from the dead Himself (Matt. 16:21; 17:9, 22–23; 20:17–19; 26:32; 27:63; Luke 24:6–7; John 2:19–22)

—to be the One to whom the Old Testament Scriptures pointed (John 5:39, 46; cf. Matt. 5:17; Luke 24:27, 44)

—to be the supreme judge who will one day return in glory (Matt. 16:27; 24:30; cf. Acts 1:11; 2 Thess. 1:7)

—to be without sin (John 8:46; cf. 2 Cor. 5:21; Heb. 4:15; 1 Peter 2:22)

—to have all authority in heaven and on earth (Matt. 11:27; 28:18; John 17:2; cf. John 3:35; 13:3; 1 Cor. 15:27; Heb. 1:2)

—to have the authority to forgive sins (Matt. 9:6)

—to have authority over the Sabbath (Matt. 12:8)

—to have the authority to answer prayer (John 14:13–14)

—to have the authority to authorize prayer in His name (John 15:16; 16:23–24, 26)

—to be greater than the temple (Matt. 12:6), Jonah (12:41), Solomon (12:42), Jacob (John 4:12–14), and Abraham (8:51–58)

—to be the Bread of Life, the only source of spiritual sustenance (John 6:33, 35, 48, 51; cf. chaps. 20–22 of this volume)

—to be the Light of the World (John 3:19; 8:12; 9:5; 12:35–36, 46; cf. 1:4–5, 7–9)

—to be the resurrection and the life (John 11:25)

—to be the Messiah (Matt. 16:20; 26:63–64; John 4:25–26; cf. 1:41)

—to be the Son of God (Matt. 11:27; 27:43; Luke 22:70; John 3:18; 5:19–20, 25–26; 6:40; 10:36; 11:4; 19:7) who would be seated at the right hand of God in glory (Matt. 22:44; 26:64; Luke 22:69; cf. Acts 2:33–34; 5:31; 7:55–56; Rom. 8:34; Eph. 1:20; Col. 3:1; Heb. 1:3; 8:1; 10:12; 12:2; 1 Peter 3:22)

There are only three possible explanations for the amazing claims Jesus made. Either He was a deranged madman, a diabolical deceiver, or exactly who He claimed to be. He could not possibly have been merely a good moral teacher, for such people do not make the kind of claims Jesus made. As C. S. Lewis notes,

> A man who was merely a man and said the sort of things Jesus said would not be a great moral teacher. He would either be a lunatic—on a level with the man who says he is a poached egg—or else he would be the Devil of Hell. You must make your choice. Either this man was, and is, the Son of God: or else a madman or something worse. You can shut Him up for a fool, you can spit at Him and kill Him as a demon; or you can fall at His feet and call Him Lord and God. But let us not come with any patronising nonsense about His being a great human teacher. He has not left that open to us. He did not intend to. (*Mere Christianity* [New York: Macmillan, 1971], 56)

Jesus' claims polarized those who heard them. On the one hand, some believed Him. For example, John the Baptist proclaimed Him to be "the Lamb of God who takes away the sin of the world!" (1:29). Philip said of Him, "We have found Him of whom Moses in the Law and also the Prophets wrote—Jesus of Nazareth, the son of Joseph" (1:45). Nathanael said to Him, "Rabbi, You are the Son of God; You are the King of Israel" (1:49). Many in the Samaritan village of Sychar believed Him (4:39, 41), affirming, "[We] know that this One is indeed the Savior of the world" (v. 42). Even a Gentile royal official believed in Him along with his whole household (4:53). Speaking for the Twelve, Peter said to Jesus, "We have believed and have come to know that You are the Holy One of God" (6:69; cf. 1:49; Matt. 14:33; 16:16). Others, including Thomas (John 20:28), Zaccheus (Luke 19:8–9), Martha (John 11:27), a formerly blind man (9:35–38), Nicodemus (7:50–51; 19:39), and Joseph of Arimathea (19:38), also believed in Him.

The majority, however, rejected Jesus' claims. "He was in the world, and the world was made through Him," John wrote in the prologue to his gospel, "and the world did not know Him. He came to His own, and those who were His own did not receive Him" (1:10–11). To Nicodemus (prior to Nicodemus's conversion) Jesus declared, "Truly, truly, I say to you, we speak of what we know and testify of what we have seen, and you do not accept our testimony. If I told you earthly things and you do not believe, how will you believe if I tell you heavenly things?" (3:11–12). John the Baptist said of Christ, "What He has seen and heard, of that He testifies; and no one receives His testimony" (3:32). To His Jewish opponents Jesus said, "You do not have His word abiding in you, for you do not believe Him whom He sent. . . . I have come in My Father's name, and you do not receive Me; if another comes in his own name, you will receive him" (5:38, 43). Christ rebuked His hearers in the Capernaum synagogue for their unbelief: "You have seen Me, and yet do not believe" (6:36). In Matthew 23:37 the Lord lamented, "Jerusalem, Jerusalem, who kills the prophets and stones those who are sent to her! How often I wanted to gather your children together, the way a hen gathers her chicks under her wings, and you were unwilling." Even at His trial, as His earthly ministry came to a close, the Sanhedrin demanded, "'If You are the Christ, tell us.' But He said to them, 'If I tell you, you will not believe'" (Luke 22:67).

At the end of chapter 6, Jesus said to His followers, "'But there are some of you who do not believe.' For Jesus knew from the beginning who they were who did not believe, and who it was that would betray Him" (6:64; cf. v. 66). Then, chapter 7 opens with the tragic report that "not even His brothers were believing in Him" (v. 5). Jesus was not deterred by the unbelief He encountered, but instead relentlessly continued to confront unbelievers with His claims and promises. As a result, the hostility of His hardened enemies steadily increased, until it culminated in His crucifixion.

The first thirteen verses of chapter 7 recount the Lord's refusal to go openly to the Feast of Tabernacles and declare Himself to be the Messiah, despite the urgings of His brothers. After the crowds had left for Jerusalem, however, Jesus went up to the city privately (v. 10) in **the midst of the feast;** that is, the halfway point (the participle *mesousēs* [**midst**] is from the verb *mesoō,* which literally means "to be in the middle," or "to be half over"). On this occasion the escalating hostility became vocal as the crowd accused Him of being demonized.

Jerusalem would have been teeming with pilgrims from all over Israel and the Jewish settlements outside of the land. Fearlessly, **Jesus went up into the temple** (the customary location for rabbis to teach) **and began to teach.** His unexpected public appearance caught the Jewish authorities off guard, and thwarted any plans they might have made to seize Him quietly when He arrived in Jerusalem (cf. v. 11). Many still had a favorable view of Jesus (v. 12), which made it difficult for the authorities to arrest Him in public. (Their spur-of-the-moment attempt to do so in verse 32 proved utterly unsuccessful when His words stopped the temple police from arresting Him [vv. 44–46].)

Despite the mounting opposition He faced, Jesus fearlessly proclaimed the uncensored truth about His identity and mission. The ensuing dialog in verses 15–24 provides five features to lead doubters and skeptics to believe His astounding claims: His source of knowledge, His surety, His selflessness, His sentence, and His signs, all of which proved Him to be the Son of God.

HIS SOURCE OF KNOWLEDGE

The Jews then were astonished, saying, "How has this man become learned, having never been educated?" So Jesus answered them and said, "My teaching is not Mine, but His who sent Me. (7:15–16)

As they listened to Jesus' unequalled teaching, **the Jews,** as so many had been, **were astonished.** His mastery of Scripture surely amazed them, as it had earlier to those who heard the Sermon on the Mount (Matt. 7:28–29), those in His hometown of Nazareth (13:54), and those in Capernaum (Mark 1:22). His preaching would even astound the temple police sent to arrest Him (vv. 45–46).

It was most likely the indignant and hostile Jewish authorities, who continually felt threatened by Jesus, who led the attack on Him by questioning His credentials. They exclaimed, **"How has this man become learned, having never been educated?"** (Later, they would be similarly stunned by the powerful preaching of the "uneducated and untrained" Peter and John [Acts 4:13].) Their point was not that Jesus demonstrated ignorance, but that He had received no formal training in the prescribed rabbinic schools. In today's terms, He had not been to seminary or been ordained by any formal ecclesiastical body. Since they could not refute Jesus' teaching, they questioned His credentials—challenging His authority to teach because He lacked an authorized education and legitimate right to teach. The implication was that His words should be disregarded as merely the opinion of a self-styled intruder who had no true connection to the established and authoritative fraternity of teachers.

The Lord's reply was direct and devastating. He **answered them and said, "My teaching is not Mine, but His who sent Me."** It was true that His knowledge was not derived from any human institution and His teaching opposed that of the teachers in Judaism. But that did not mean that it was merely His own personal opinion, as the authorities implied; in fact, it came directly from God the Father **who sent** Him. (Jesus was always conscious of having been sent by the Father; cf. vv. 28–29, 33; 3:17; 4:34; 5:24, 30, 36, 37; 6:38–39, 44, 57; 8:16, 18, 26, 29, 42; 9:4; 11:42; 12:44–45, 49; 13:20; 14:24; 15:21; 16:5; 17:8, 18, 21, 23, 25; 20:21; Matt. 10:40; Mark 9:37; Luke 4:18; 10:16.) "When you lift up the Son of Man," Jesus declared in John 8:28, "then you will know that I am He, and I do nothing on My own initiative, but I speak these things as the Father taught Me." And in 12:49–50 He added, "For I did not speak on My own initiative, but the Father Himself who sent Me has given Me a commandment as to what to say and what to speak. I know that His commandment is eternal life;

therefore the things I speak, I speak just as the Father has told Me" (cf. 8:26, 38, 40; 14:10, 24; 17:8, 14). That Jesus' teaching was directly and immediately from God was also an indictment of the Jewish leaders. By disagreeing with Him, they revealed that their teaching was not from God (8:47).

Since only Jesus has perfect knowledge of the Father (Matt. 11:27; cf. John 10:15), only He could speak directly from Him. The Lord's **teaching,** being directly from God, was thus radically different from that of the rabbis, who generally drew their teaching from other rabbis as their source of authority. Matthew records that at the conclusion of the Sermon on the Mount, "the crowds were amazed at His teaching; for He was teaching them as one having authority, and not as their scribes" (Matt. 7:28–29). Jesus was also different from the Old Testament prophets, even though they, like Him, were sent from God and proclaimed His truth. But whereas they said, "Thus says the Lord" (e.g., Isa. 7:7; Jer. 2:2; Ezek. 2:4; Amos 1:3; Obad. 1:1; Mic. 2:3; Nah. 1:12; Hag. 1:2; Zech. 1:3; Mal. 1:4), Jesus authoritatively declared, "I say to you" (e.g., John 5:24; 6:32, 53; 8:51, 58; Matt. 5:18, 20, 22, 28, 32, 34, 39, 44; 6:2, 5; 8:11; 10:15; 11:22, 24; 17:12; 19:9; 21:43; 23:36; Mark 10:15; 11:24; Luke 13:35; 18:17, 29–30).

HIS SURETY

If anyone is willing to do His will, he will know of the teaching, whether it is of God or whether I speak from Myself. (7:17)

Throughout His ministry, Jesus was often asked to perform additional and unnecessary signs to prove His authenticity, as if it were open to honest question (cf. Matt. 16:1; John 2:18). Yet, He consistently denied such requests, because He knew that they came from hard-hearted unbelievers. No matter how many miracles He performed, the Lord understood that such people would refuse to believe.

Nonetheless, Jesus promised the person who honestly seeks the truth revealed by God, the one who is **willing to do** God's **will,** that **he will know** the truth about Christ's **teaching, whether it is of God or whether** it is not. The Lord's challenge to the crowd was simple: If they would humble themselves before God's Word (wherein His will is revealed) to know and obey it, they would come to a sure realization that His teaching was true. That challenge still stands two millennia later. The assurance promised in this verse is available to all genuine believers. Such confidence comes through the Holy Spirit, who confirms the truth about Christ to the willing heart (1 John 2:20, 27), both internally, through His testimony (1 Cor. 2:10–15; cf. Rom. 8:16), and externally, through manifestations that demonstrate the truth of the gospel (John 3:2; 5:36; 10:38; Acts 2:22).

Jesus' challenge was bold, but it was not without precedent. Similar promises are given throughout the Old Testament. In the book of Deuteronomy, God promised Israel, "You will seek the Lord your God, and you will find Him if you search for Him with all your heart and all your soul" (Deut. 4:29). David counseled Solomon, "As for you, my son Solomon, know the God of your father, and serve Him with a whole heart and a willing mind; for the Lord searches all hearts, and understands every intent of the thoughts. If you seek Him, He will let you find Him; but if you forsake Him, He will reject you forever" (1 Chron. 28:9). In Psalm 119:2 the psalmist wrote, "How blessed are those who observe His testimonies, who seek Him with all their heart." "You will seek Me and find Me," God said through the prophet Jeremiah, "when you search for Me with all your heart" (Jer. 29:13).

The personification of wisdom in Proverbs 1:20–33 illustrates the clear-cut challenge Jesus made in this verse—one no false messiah would dare make. Those who heed wisdom's call, who are willing to do God's will, will receive further knowledge:

> Wisdom shouts in the street,
> She lifts her voice in the square;
> At the head of the noisy streets she cries out;
> At the entrance of the gates in the city she utters her sayings:
> "How long, O naive ones, will you love being simple-minded?
> And scoffers delight themselves in scoffing
> And fools hate knowledge?
> Turn to my reproof,
> Behold, I will pour out my spirit on you;
> I will make my words known to you." (vv. 20–23)

But verses 24–33 reveal the fate of those who harden their hearts and are unwilling to turn to God:

> Because I called and you refused,
> I stretched out my hand and no one paid attention;
> And you neglected all my counsel
> And did not want my reproof;
> I will also laugh at your calamity;
> I will mock when your dread comes,
> When your dread comes like a storm
> And your calamity comes like a whirlwind,
> When distress and anguish come upon you.
> Then they will call on me, but I will not answer;

They will seek me diligently but they will not find me,
Because they hated knowledge
And did not choose the fear of the Lord.
They would not accept my counsel,
They spurned all my reproof.
So they shall eat of the fruit of their own way
And be satiated with their own devices.
For the waywardness of the naive will kill them,
And the complacency of fools will destroy them.
But he who listens to me shall live securely
And will be at ease from the dread of evil.

Accepting or rejecting the claims of Jesus Christ is never a purely intellectual decision; there are inescapable moral and spiritual implications that are also involved. Those who willingly seek and obey the truth will find it and will be set free from their slavery to ignorance and sin (John 8:32). But those who reject the truth prove themselves to be children of their "father the devil, [who] want to do the desires of [their] father. He was a murderer from the beginning, and does not stand in the truth because there is no truth in him" (v. 44). Unless they repent, they will share his fate.

HIS SELFLESSNESS

"He who speaks from himself seeks his own glory; but He who is seeking the glory of the One who sent Him, He is true, and there is no unrighteousness in Him." (7:18)

There are at least two characteristics of every false teacher and would-be messiah. First, he **speaks from himself;** that is, on his own authority, not God's (cf. Jer. 14:14; 23:16, 21, 26, 32; 27:15; 28:15; 29:9, 31; Neh. 6:10–12; Ezek. 13:2, 6). And second, he **seeks his own glory,** not God's. False prophets invariably proclaim their own musings to attract followers and secure personal gain. Their goal is not to feed the flock, but to fleece it. The prophet Micah graphically depicted the greedy false prophets of his day: "Thus says the Lord concerning the prophets who lead my people astray; when they have something to bite with their teeth, they cry, 'Peace,' but against him who puts nothing in their mouths they declare holy war" (Mic. 3:5). In verse 11 he denounced them as "prophets [who] divine for money." Isaiah called them greedy dogs who are never satisfied (Isa. 56:11). And Ezekiel warned, "Thus says the Lord God, 'Woe, shepherds of Israel who have been feeding themselves! Should not the shepherds feed the flock? You eat the fat and clothe yourselves with the wool, you slaughter the fat sheep without feeding the flock'" (Ezek. 34:2–3). The apostle Paul characterized false teachers as "slaves, not of our Lord Christ but of their own appetites" (Rom. 16:18), "whose god is their appetite" (Phil. 3:19), "who suppose that godliness is a means of gain" (1 Tim. 6:5), and who are guilty of "teaching things they should not teach for the sake of sordid gain" (Titus 1:11). Peter warned that they greedily exploit people (2 Peter 2:3; cf. Acts 8:18–19), because they have "a heart trained in greed, . . . having followed the way of Balaam, the son of Beor, who loved the wages of unrighteousness" (2 Peter 2:14–15; cf. Jude 11).

Instead of seeking to honor God, false teachers seek honor for themselves. Jesus castigated the scribes and Pharisees as those who "do all their deeds to be noticed by men; for they broaden their phylacteries and lengthen the tassels of their garments. They love the place of honor at banquets and the chief seats in the synagogues, and respectful greetings in the market places, and being called Rabbi by men" (Matt. 23:5–7), and "for appearance's sake offer long prayers" (Luke 20:47). False teachers are "those who desire to make a good showing in the flesh" (Gal. 6:12) and "boast according to the flesh" (2 Cor. 11:18). Like Diotrephes, they love the place of prominence (3 John 9). But those whose goal is to "be honored by men. . . . have their reward in full" (Matt. 6:2; cf. vv. 5, 16).

Jesus, however, never sought His own glory (cf. 5:41; 8:50), since He "did not come to be served, but to serve, and to give His life a ransom for many" (Matt. 20:28), for He is "gentle and humble in heart" (Matt. 11:29; cf. 2 Cor. 10:1). "Although He existed in the form of God," Paul wrote, Jesus "did not regard equality with God a thing to be grasped, but emptied Himself, taking the form of a bond-servant, and being made in the likeness of men. Being found in appearance as a man, He humbled Himself by becoming obedient to the point of death, even death on a cross" (Phil. 2:6–8; cf. 2 Cor. 5:21; 1 Peter 2:24). False teachers are materialistic, but "the Son of Man ha[d] nowhere to lay His head" (Luke 9:58); false teachers are self-seeking and demanding, but Jesus "got up from supper, and laid aside His garments; and taking a towel, He girded Himself. Then He poured water into the basin, and began to wash the disciples' feet and to wipe them with the towel with which He was girded" (John 13:4–5)—thus performing a menial task normally reserved for the lowliest slaves.

That Jesus came **seeking the glory of the One who sent Him,** instead of glorifying Himself, verified His claim to be the **true** Messiah, **and** showed that **there** was **no unrighteousness in Him** (cf. 8:46; 2 Cor. 5:21; Heb. 4:15; 7:26; 1 Peter 2:22). It is not surprising that the Jewish leaders rejected the One who sought God's glory, since they were those who "receive[d] glory from one another and . . . [did] not seek the glory that is from the one and only God" (5:44).

His Sentence

"Did not Moses give you the Law, and yet none of you carries out the Law? Why do you seek to kill Me?" The crowd answered, "You have a demon! Who seeks to kill You?" (7:19–20)

Aware of the Jewish authorities' venomous hatred and desire to kill Him (cf. 5:18; 7:1), Jesus pronounced judgment directly on the people with the rhetorical question, **"Did not Moses give you the Law"**—to which they would, of course, have answered emphatically, "Yes" (cf. Rom. 2:17–20) —**"yet none of you carries out the Law?"** That was the most accurate statement the Lord could make as to the truth of human sinfulness. No one can keep the Law; that is the reality in every human life. Though the Jews revered the Law of Moses, and sought to keep it and acquire their salvation by their careful efforts at obeying and honoring the Law, not one person has ever entered the kingdom by means of obeying the Law. That is the unmistakable teaching of the New Testament. Consider the following New Testament Scriptures that draw on the same teaching in the Old Testament:

> What then? Are we better than they? Not at all; for we have already charged that both Jews and Greeks are all under sin; as it is written, "There is none righteous, not even one; there is none who understands, there is none who seeks for God; all have turned aside, together they have become useless; there is none who does good, there is not even one. Their throat is an open grave, with their tongues they keep deceiving, the poison of asps is under their lips; whose mouth is full of cursing and bitterness; their feet are swift to shed blood, destruction and misery are in their paths, and the path of peace they have not known. There is no fear of God before their eyes." Now we know that whatever the Law says, it speaks to those who are under the Law, so that every mouth may be closed and all the world may become accountable to God; because by the works of the Law no flesh will be justified in His sight; for through the Law comes the knowledge of sin. (Rom. 3:9–20)

> For as many as are of the works of the Law are under a curse; for it is written, "Cursed is everyone who does not abide by all things written in the book of the Law, to perform them." Now that no one is justified by the Law before God is evident; for, "The righteous man shall live by faith." . . . Is the Law then contrary to the promises of God? May it never be! For if a law had been given which was able to impart life, then righteousness would indeed have been based on law. But the Scripture has shut up everyone under sin, so that the promise by faith in Jesus Christ might be given to those who believe. But before faith came, we were kept in custody under the law, being shut up to the faith which was later to be revealed. Therefore the Law has become our tutor to lead us to Christ, so that we may be justified by faith. (Gal. 3:10–11, 21–24)

> And I testify again to every man who receives circumcision, that he is under obligation to keep the whole Law. You have been severed from Christ, you who are seeking to be justified by law; you have fallen from grace. For we through the Spirit, by faith, are waiting for the hope of righteousness. For in Christ Jesus neither circumcision nor uncircumcision means anything, but faith working through love. (Gal. 5:3–6)

The Law of Moses was made to reveal sin, not to save. The Jews had perverted it to be the means of salvation, and refused to be indicted by it and driven to the mercy of God in the Messiah Jesus. No matter how they studied and endeavored to apply the Law, it was clear they failed. They refused to allow the Law to do its intended work of convicting them and humbling them and driving them to repentance and faith in Jesus. He was the end of the Law (Rom. 10:4). But they were so far from understanding the Law's purpose that they rejected the only One who could deliver them from the Law's condemnation and sought to kill Him.

Our Lord's sentence on them came in His question, **Why do you seek to kill Me?** They prided themselves on being disciples of Moses (9:28; cf. 5:45; Matt. 23:2), yet their treatment of Jesus was an outrage before the God who gave the Law and sent His Son to deliver them from its curse (cf. Matt. 23:2–4; Rom. 2:23–24). Specifically, they were seeking to murder the Lord, proving themselves to be blasphemous and unworthy descendants not only of Moses, but also of Abraham (8:40). They were blind to the truth of their own Scriptures, as Jesus indicated on several occasions (cf. John 5:39; Luke 16:29; 24:27).

The **crowd** affirmed the accuracy of the indictment by showing their graceless hearts. They **answered** with ignorant incredulity, **"You have a demon!** (cf. 8:48, 52; 10:20) **Who seeks to kill You?"** They resented His allegation, and accused Him of being possessed by an evil spirit and thus irrationally paranoid. Although the common people did not share the murderous intentions of their leaders at this time, they would ultimately reject Jesus with equal enthusiasm when manipulated by them—screaming out for His crucifixion (Mark 15:11). The sentence of guilt for violating the Law is confirmed by their hatred of the Son of God, who fulfilled the Law blamelessly (Matt. 3:17; Heb. 7:26).

His Signs

Jesus answered them, "I did one deed, and you all marvel. For this reason Moses has given you circumcision (not because it is from Moses, but from the fathers), and on the Sabbath you circumcise a man. If a man receives circumcision on the Sabbath

so that the Law of Moses will not be broken, are you angry with Me because I made an entire man well on the Sabbath? Do not judge according to appearance, but judge with righteous judgment." (7:21–24)

Ignoring the crowd's insulting remark, Jesus went on to say, **"I did one deed, and you all marvel."** As verses 22 and 23 make clear, Jesus was referring to His healing of the sick man at the pool of Bethesda (5:2–9). That miracle alone offered sufficient proof that He was who He claimed to be (cf. 3:2; 5:36; 7:31; 9:16, 30–33). But instead of responding to it with belief, the Jewish authorities reacted by plotting to kill Jesus (5:16, 18). John 12:37 records the tragic truth that "though He had performed so many signs before them, yet they were not believing in Him." Those who saw the signs but refused to believe merely compounded their guilt. "If I had not done among them the works which no one else did," Jesus declared, "they would not have sin; but now they have both seen and hated Me and My Father as well" (15:24).

In His earlier dialogue with the Jewish leaders, Jesus had defended His right to heal the sick man on the Sabbath because of His absolute equality with the Father (5:16ff.). Now He defended that healing by pointing out their misinterpretation of the Sabbath regulations. The Lord began by reminding them that **Moses** (so they believed) had **given** them **circumcision.** Actually, as Jesus' parenthetical remark indicates, circumcision predated **Moses.** It was instituted during the time of **the fathers,** the patriarchal period (Gen. 17:10–14), and later included in the Mosaic law. Every male Jewish child was circumcised when he was eight days old (Gen. 17:12; Lev. 12:3; Luke 1:59; 2:21). If the eighth day happened to fall **on the Sabbath** the Jews would **circumcise** the baby anyway— despite the injunction in the Law against working on the Sabbath (Ex. 20:10). Thus, circumcision took precedence over the Law of Moses.

Now the absurdity of the Jews' accusation against Jesus became clear. **"If a man receives circumcision on the Sabbath so that the Law of Moses will not be broken,"** Jesus asked, why **"are you angry with Me because I made an entire man well on the Sabbath?"** His argument from the lesser to the greater was irrefutable. If they themselves broke the Sabbath law to circumcise children, how could they object to Him making **an entire man well on the Sabbath?** If they did not object to the ceremonial cleansing of one part of the body on the Sabbath, how could they object to His healing the entire body on the Sabbath? In this way, Jesus not only exposed their rank hypocrisy (cf. Matt. 12:11–12; Luke 13:10–16), but He also demonstrated that it was permissible to do good on the Sabbath.

The Lord's concluding exhortation, **"Do not judge according to**

appearance, but judge with righteous judgment," was both an indictment of their utter lack of moral and theological discernment and a plea
for it. The harsh, censorious judgment of self-righteous legalism is always
unacceptable to God (Matt. 7:1), but so is superficial judgment **according to appearance** (cf. 1 Sam. 16:7). In the context, Jesus was urging His
hearers to abandon their misconceptions regarding Him and **judge** His
claims **with righteous judgment.** Those who do so will find Him to be
exactly who He claimed to be, just as He promised they would (John 7:17).

Reactions to the Claims of Christ (John 7:25–36)

25

So some of the people of Jerusalem were saying, "Is this not the man whom they are seeking to kill? Look, He is speaking publicly, and they are saying nothing to Him. The rulers do not really know that this is the Christ, do they? However, we know where this man is from; but whenever the Christ may come, no one knows where He is from." Then Jesus cried out in the temple, teaching and saying, "You both know Me and know where I am from; and I have not come of Myself, but He who sent Me is true, whom you do not know. I know Him, because I am from Him, and He sent Me." So they were seeking to seize Him; and no man laid his hand on Him, because His hour had not yet come. But many of the crowd believed in Him; and they were saying, "When the Christ comes, He will not perform more signs than those which this man has, will He?" The Pharisees heard the crowd muttering these things about Him, and the chief priests and the Pharisees sent officers to seize Him. Therefore Jesus said, "For a little while longer I am with you, then I go to Him who sent Me. You will seek Me, and will not find Me; and where I am, you cannot come." The Jews then said to one another, "Where does this man intend to go that we will not find Him? He is not intending to go to the Dispersion

**among the Greeks, and teach the Greeks, is He? What is this state-
ment that He said, 'You will seek Me, and will not find Me; and
where I am, you cannot come'?"** (7:25–36)

When the Lord came to Jerusalem for the Feast of Tabernacles
(7:2), only about six months remained before He would again come to
Jerusalem for His crucifixion (at Passover the following spring). From
this point forward, now more than ever, Jesus would walk in the looming
shadow of the cross.

As the Feast of Tabernacles approached, Jesus' brothers had
urged Him to make a grand entry into the city and thus openly declare
Himself to be the Messiah (vv. 3–5). But Jesus declined, choosing instead
to go privately to the feast (v. 10), arriving halfway through it (v. 14). When
He entered Jerusalem, He immediately went to the temple and began to
teach (v. 14), where both His unexpected appearance and unprecedented authority (vv. 45–46) caused a stir. The Jewish leaders responded
with predictable hostility (vv. 15–19), even attempting to have Him arrested
(v. 32). The people, on the other hand, were deeply divided over Jesus—
some violently opposed Him (v. 30), while others enthusiastically believed in Him (v. 31).

Over the next six months, as He ministered primarily in the towns
and villages of Judea, opposing the devilish Judaism that dominated the
people at its core, the hostility exhibited on this day would only intensify.
As John stated at the outset of his gospel, Christ "came to His own, and
those who were His own did not receive Him" (1:11). The reality of this
conflict manifested itself at the beginning of His ministry. After the Lord
cleansed the temple, the outraged "Jews then said to Him, 'What sign do
You show us as your authority for doing these things?' Jesus answered
them, 'Destroy this temple, and in three days I will raise it up.' The Jews
then said, 'It took forty-six years to build this temple, and will You raise it
up in three days?'" (2:18–20). Later, when Jesus realized that the hostile
"Pharisees had heard that [He] was making and baptizing more disciples than John, . . . He left Judea and went away again into Galilee" (4:1,
3). After He healed a sick man, "the Jews were persecuting Jesus,
because He was doing these things on the Sabbath" (5:16). And when
the Lord defended Himself by asserting His equality with the Father, "The
Jews were seeking all the more to kill Him, because He not only was
breaking the Sabbath, but also was calling God His own Father, making
Himself equal with God" (v. 18). The crowd in the Capernaum synagogue
demanded of Him, "What then do You do for a sign, so that we may see,
and believe You? What work do You perform?" (6:30)—an astonishing
demonstration of unbelief since Jesus had miraculously fed thousands
of people just the day before (vv. 1–13). Reacting to His claim to be the

Bread of Life, "Many of His disciples, when they heard this said, 'This is a difficult statement; who can listen to it?'" (v. 60), prompting Jesus to note sadly, "There are some of you who do not believe" (v. 64). The tragic result was that even many who claimed to be His followers "withdrew and were not walking with Him anymore" (v. 66).

John began this chapter with the somber note that "Jesus was walking in Galilee, for He was unwilling to walk in Judea because the Jews were seeking to kill Him" (v. 1). It records the Lord's dialogue with His unbelieving brothers (vv. 3–8), during which He observed, "The world . . . hates Me because I testify of it, that its deeds are evil" (v. 7). The chapter goes on to reveal the deep controversy that surrounded Him, dividing the crowds in Jerusalem (v. 12) even before Jesus arrived in the city. But whether it was from the Jewish leaders, the Jerusalem crowds, or the Lord's own brothers, the hostility Jesus faced all stemmed from the same source: unbelief.

Despite the opposition, Jesus never mitigated or moderated His claim to have been sent from God (cf. vv. 16–18; cf. 5:30; 6:38–39, 44). This section again records how the crowds responded to Him. It reveals their dense confusion, divided conviction, and derisive contempt.

Dense Confusion

So some of the people of Jerusalem were saying, "Is this not the man whom they are seeking to kill? Look, He is speaking publicly, and they are saying nothing to Him. The rulers do not really know that this is the Christ, do they? However, we know where this man is from; but whenever the Christ may come, no one knows where He is from." Then Jesus cried out in the temple, teaching and saying, "You both know Me and know where I am from; and I have not come of Myself, but He who sent Me is true, whom you do not know. I know Him, because I am from Him, and He sent Me." (7:25–29)

Unlike the pilgrims visiting the city (v. 20), **some of the people of Jerusalem** were well aware of their leaders' murderous intentions toward Jesus. (The Greek grammar of the question, **"Is this not the man whom they are seeking to kill?"** expects an affirmative answer.) Yet those same leaders had listened in paralyzed silence as Jesus openly condemned their hypocrisy (vv. 19, 21–24). Perhaps the authorities feared debating Him in public, knowing they would come out on the losing end (cf. vv. 15–18). Or they may have been awed by His commanding presence, remembering how He boldly cleansed the temple (2:14–16).

They may have also been concerned that seizing Jesus in public might spark a riot (for which the Romans would have held them accountable; cf. 11:48), since many in the crowd still had a favorable impression of Him (cf. v. 12).

Astonished, both by their rulers' speechlessness and by the Lord's fearlessness, the Jerusalem residents exclaimed, **"Look, He is speaking publicly, and they are saying nothing to Him."** (The term *parrēsia* [**publicly**] can also mean "boldly," or "confidently.") In contrast to the leaders' silence, Jesus' authoritative proclamation captivated the people.

Isaiah 50:7–9, one of the four Servant songs (messianic soliloquies) in Isaiah's prophecy, pictures the bold confidence that Christ possessed. In that song Messiah says,

> For the Lord God helps Me,
> Therefore, I am not disgraced;
> Therefore, I have set My face like flint,
> And I know that I will not be ashamed.
> He who vindicates Me is near;
> Who will contend with Me?
> Let us stand up to each other;
> Who has a case against Me?
> Let him draw near to Me.
> Behold, the Lord God helps Me;
> Who is he who condemns Me?
> Behold, they will all wear out like a garment;
> The moth will eat them.

Like Jesus, the Spirit-filled early church also displayed supernatural boldness. Acts 4:31 records that "when they had prayed, the place where they had gathered together was shaken, and they were all filled with the Holy Spirit and began to speak the word of God with boldness." The Sanhedrin was amazed at the bold confidence of Peter and John (Acts 4:13). Immediately after his conversion Paul spoke "boldly in the name of Jesus," both in Damascus (Acts 9:27) and in Jerusalem (v. 28). Acts 13:46 records that "Paul and Barnabas spoke out boldly and said, 'It was necessary that the word of God be spoken to you first; since you repudiate it and judge yourselves unworthy of eternal life, behold, we are turning to the Gentiles.'" The two missionaries "spent a long time [in Iconium] speaking boldly with reliance upon the Lord" (Acts 14:3). Acts 18:26 notes that Apollos "began to speak out boldly in the synagogue." When he arrived in Ephesus, Paul "entered the synagogue and continued speaking out boldly for three months, reasoning and persuading them about the kingdom of God" (Acts 19:8). Imprisoned in Rome, Paul nevertheless was "preaching the kingdom of God and teaching concerning the Lord Jesus Christ with all openness [*parrēsia*], unhindered" (Acts 28:31). He later asked the Ephesians, "Pray on my behalf, that utterance may be given to me in the opening of my mouth, to make known with boldness the mystery of the gospel, for which I am an ambassador in chains; that in proclaiming it I may speak boldly, as I ought to speak" (Eph. 6:19–20). To the Philippians he expressed that same desire: "[It is] my earnest expectation and hope, that I will not be put to shame in anything, but that with all boldness, Christ will even now, as always, be exalted in my body, whether by life or by death" (Phil. 1:20). In his first letter to them, he reminded the Thessalonians, "After we had already suffered and been mistreated in Philippi, as you know, we had the boldness in our God to speak to you the gospel of God amid much opposition" (1 Thess. 2:2). Not only was Paul bold in person (cf. 2 Cor. 3:12), but also in his letters to the churches (cf. Rom. 15:15; 2 Cor. 10:1).

The people were shocked to find that the **rulers** said **nothing** in response to Jesus, despite being publicly humiliated by Him. Some were so surprised that they began to voice the unthinkable: **"The rulers do not really know that this is the Christ, do they?"** Perhaps the leaders had received further information about Jesus, and decided (privately) that He was the Messiah. Perhaps that could explain their failure to arrest Him. But the idea seemed so farfetched that it was immediately rejected. (This time the Greek construction indicates that the question expected a negative answer.)

Verse 27 explains why some of the crowd rejected the possibility that Jesus might be the Messiah. **"We know where this man is from,"** they reasoned; **"but whenever the Christ may come, no one knows where He is from."** Their argument was a combination of misinformation and popular legend. Despite their confident assertion, they really did not **know where** Jesus was **from;** they thought He was from Nazareth (cf. 1:45–46; 6:42; Matt. 21:11) where He had been raised (Luke 4:16). Apparently, they did not know that He had actually been born in Bethlehem (Matt. 2:1).

Their statement that **"whenever the Christ may come, no one knows where He is from"** expressed a popular belief. Based on a misinterpretation of such passages as Isaiah 53:8, "Who will declare His generation?" (NKJV) and Malachi 3:1, "The Lord, whom you seek, will suddenly come to His temple," this tradition held that the Messiah would be unknown until He suddenly appeared to redeem Israel. The author of the apocryphal book of 4 Esdras wrote, "He said to me, 'Just as no one can explore or know what is in the depths of the sea, so no one on earth can see my Son or those who are with him, except in the time of his day'" (4 Esdras 13:52 RSV; cf. 7:28; 13:32). Trypho, the Jewish opponent of the second-century Christian apologist Justin Martyr, said to Justin, "But Christ—if He has indeed been born, and exists anywhere—is unknown, and does not even know Himself, and has no power until Elias come to anoint Him, and make Him manifest to all" (*Dialogue with Trypho* 8). Since they knew Jesus' background (cf. Matt. 13:55–56), they assumed that meant He could not be the Messiah.

This popular belief, however, ran completely contrary to the Old Testament, which clearly predicted that the Messiah would be born in Bethlehem (Mic. 5:2; cf. Matt. 2:4–6)—a point that others in the crowd later acknowledged (John 7:42). Although the misconception was obviously false, Jesus did not take the time to show how it contradicted the Old Testament. Nor did He protest that although He had been raised in Nazareth, He had been born in Bethlehem. Instead, He responded by directly confronting their hard-hearted unbelief. The fact that **Jesus cried out,** meaning that He yelled so as to be heard by all, stressed the critical nature of what He was about to say (cf. v. 37; 1:15; 12:44).

A comparison of the Lord's words, **"You both know Me and know where I am from"** with His declaration in 8:19, "You know neither Me nor My Father," reveals that His comment here was intended as irony. Jesus certainly would not contradict Himself, nor would He affirm that His opponents knew Him, but not the Father (cf. 5:23; 8:19; 15:23; 16:3). And He would hardly have said that those who regarded Him as an impostor and a charlatan actually knew Him. In fact, Jesus was asserting that they did not know Him, saying in effect, "So you think you know Me and where I am from, do you?" This was another of their false assumptions of spiritual knowledge.

There was ample evidence that Jesus was not the self-appointed false prophet and pseudo-Messiah the leaders accused Him of being. In reality, as He declared, **"I have not come of Myself, but He who sent Me is true."** He had **not come** on His own, but rather had been **sent** by the **true** God. But to the unbelieving crowd, and more shockingly to the religious leaders, Jesus said, **"you do not know** [the God you profess]" (cf. John 8:41–47).

That statement was a devastating indictment and a stunning rebuke, especially to the scribes and Pharisees. As Israel's religious elite, they had devoted their entire lives to the study of the Old Testament. They prided themselves on their knowledge of God. To them, as Paul noted, "belong[ed] the adoption as sons, and the glory and the covenants and the giving of the Law and the temple service and the promises" (Rom. 9:4; cf. 2:17–20).

Yet despite all those privileges, they were woefully ignorant of the very God they so proudly professed to know. Like the sons of Eli, they were "worthless men; they did not know the Lord" (1 Sam. 2:12). They were like those of whom Jeremiah wrote, "The priests did not say, 'Where is the Lord?' And those who handle the law did not know Me" (Jer. 2:8; cf. 8:8–9). Through the prophet Hosea God lamented, "My people are destroyed for lack of knowledge" (Hos. 4:6), while Paul wrote that "they have a zeal for God, but not in accordance with knowledge" (Rom. 10:2). Sadly, their preoccupation with the minutiae of self-righteous legalism, along with their devotion to the rabbinic traditions, had blinded them to the true knowledge of God (cf. Matt. 12:7; 23:23; Mark 7:10–13). They were "blind guides of the blind" (Matt. 15:14; cf. 23:16, 24), who made their followers twice the sons of hell that they themselves were (23:15). Not surprisingly, Jesus frequently denounced them as unbelieving hypocrites (cf. Matt. 15:7; 22:18; 23:13–15, 23, 25, 27, 29; Luke 12:56) and even children of Satan (John 8:44).

On the other hand, Jesus truly did **know Him,** sharing the same eternal essence and omniscience **because,** as He declared, **"I am from Him, and He sent Me."** As noted in the exposition of 7:16 in the previous chapter of this volume, the fact that Jesus was sent by the Father is foundational to the gospel.

DIVIDED CONVICTION

So they were seeking to seize Him; and no man laid his hand on Him, because His hour had not yet come. But many of the crowd believed in Him; and they were saying, "When the Christ comes, He will not perform more signs than those which this man has, will He?" The Pharisees heard the crowd muttering these things about Him, and the chief priests and the Pharisees sent officers to seize Him. (7:30–32)

Infuriated by what they considered blasphemy, **His enemies were seeking to seize Him.** This was evidently a spontaneous effort by some in the crowd, as opposed to the official attempt to arrest Him described in verse 32. Why they failed, humanly speaking, to **seize** Jesus is not stated, but it was likely because many in the crowd were protective of Him (v. 31).

John quickly gave the divine aspect when he stated that the reason **no man laid his hand on Him** was **because His hour had not yet come.** As noted in chapter 23 of this volume, Jesus always operated according to God's sovereign timetable. Nothing, including impulsive mob violence, could precipitate His death before the appointed **hour.** As always, redemptive history at that moment was perfectly on schedule; God's sovereign purpose would not be thwarted (cf. Job 23:13; Ps. 33:10–11; Prov. 19:21; 21:30; Isa. 14:24, 27; 46:10; Eph. 1:11).

The sovereign timing of Christ's death—that it would take place at the exact hour chosen by God—is a repeated theme in this gospel. In 8:20, as in this passage, His enemies were prevented from seizing Him "because His hour had not yet come." As the time for His death drew near, Jesus told His disciples, "The hour has come for the Son of Man to be glorified" (12:23; cf. 13:1) and prayed, "Now My soul has become troubled; and what shall I say, 'Father, save Me from this hour'? But for this purpose I came to this hour" (12:27; cf. 17:1). Jesus Christ would die at the appointed time (cf. 1 Cor. 5:7) and in the appointed manner (as laid out in the Old Testament [Matt. 26:24; Luke 24:25–26]), not during the Feast of Tabernacles at the hands of an unruly mob.

Jesus' exalted claims forced people to decide about Him, and the result was division. That was exactly what Jesus had said He would bring. In Matthew 10:34–36 He cautioned,

> Do not think that I came to bring peace on the earth; I did not come to bring peace, but a sword. For I came to set a man against his father, and a daughter against her mother, and a daughter-in-law against her mother-in-law; and a man's enemies will be the members of his household. (cf. Luke 12:49–53)

So it was on this occasion. Some angrily rejected Jesus, and wanted to seize Him (v. 30). **But** on the other hand, **many of the crowd believed in Him.** Their rhetorical (the question in the Greek text expects a negative answer) question, **"When the Christ comes, He will not perform more signs than those which this man has, will He?"** explains what convinced them of Jesus' authenticity. They were familiar with Old Testament prophecy, which foretold that the Messiah would perform miracles (e.g., Isa. 29:18; 35:5–6; cf. Matt. 11:2–5); and they could not imagine that **the Christ** (Messiah) would **perform more signs than those** that Jesus had performed (John 2:23; 3:2; 6:2). The pilgrims from Galilee would have remembered the wedding where Jesus made wine out of water (2:1–11) and the miraculous meal where thousands were fed (6:1–13). And the Judeans would have known about the sick man Jesus healed at the pool of Bethesda (5:1–9). In addition, all would have been aware of the multitude of other miracles that Jesus performed (cf. 2:23; 3:2; 6:2).

When **the Pharisees heard the crowd muttering these things about** Jesus, they became alarmed. They did not even want people to speak of Jesus (v. 13); yet here some were quietly suggesting that He might be the Messiah. The Pharisees were so distressed by the popularity of Jesus that they joined forces with their archrivals the Sadducees. Though the two groups historically were at opposite ends of the theological spectrum, the mutual hatred they felt for Jesus drove them together (cf. v. 45; 11:47,57; 18:3; Matt. 21:45–46; 27:62).

After consulting with each other (possibly in a formal meeting of the Sanhedrin), **the chief priests** (Sadducees who were former high priests and members of important priestly families) **and the Pharisees sent officers to seize** Jesus. **The officers** (temple guards) were a kind of police force consisting of Levites, who were responsible for maintaining order in the busy temple grounds (especially at feast times), though the Sanhedrin could also employ them elsewhere in matters not affecting Roman policy.

This section strikingly illustrates the nation's division over Jesus. While some were prone to hail Him as the Messiah and would do so at the start of Passion Week (Luke 19:37–39), others sought desperately to silence Him. And the leaders, who should have been the first to recognize His authenticity, led the effort to have Him eliminated.

DERISIVE CONTEMPT

Therefore Jesus said, "For a little while longer I am with you, then I go to Him who sent Me. You will seek Me, and will not find Me; and where I am, you cannot come." The Jews then said to one another, "Where does this man intend to go that we will not find Him? He is not intending to go to the Dispersion among the Greeks, and teach the Greeks, is He? What is this statement that He said, 'You will seek Me, and will not find Me; and where I am, you cannot come'?" (7:33–36)

As will become evident later in the narrative (vv. 45–46), the officers of the temple guard could not fulfill their assignment and failed to arrest the Lord. **Therefore Jesus** continued to boldly proclaim the truth about Himself, declaring, **"For a little while longer I am with you, then I go to Him who sent Me."** In a few months, at Passover the following spring, Jesus would be crucified. He would then rise from the dead and ascend **to** the Father **who sent** Him.

Jesus continued by solemnly warning His hearers, **"You will seek Me, and will not find Me; and where I am, you cannot come."** Those who reject Jesus will never come to where He was going when He ascended and currently rests at His Father's right hand in heaven, because they will die in their sins (8:21). (Jesus would later tell His disciples that they would not be able to follow Him to heaven immediately [13:33], but would do so later [v. 36].)

Instead of heeding the Lord's warning, **the** unbelieving **Jews** merely ridiculed Him. **"Where does this man intend to go that we will not find Him?"** they scoffed. **"He is not intending to go to the Dispersion among the Greeks, and teach the Greeks, is He?"** They found the idea that the Messiah would minister to Gentiles to be preposterous. The **Greeks** they scornfully referred to were probably Gentile proselytes to Judaism. (Ironically, it was because of Israel's spiritual blindness in rejecting her Messiah that the gospel would indeed reach the Gentiles who had no interest in Judaism [cf. Rom. 11:7–11].) Mockingly, they offered Jesus' **statement, "You will seek Me, and will not find Me; and where I am, you cannot come,"** as support for their derisive suggestion.

Tragically, these scoffers missed Jesus' point completely. Like Isaiah, who wrote, "Seek the Lord while He may be found; call upon Him while He is near" (Isa. 55:6), Jesus was warning His opponents not to delay conversion until it is too late. As Paul wrote to the Corinthians, "Behold, now is 'the acceptable time,' behold, now is 'the day of salvation'" (2 Cor. 6:2); and the writer of Hebrews pleaded, "Today if you hear His voice, do not harden your hearts" (Heb. 4:7; cf. 3:15). Jesus Himself promised, "I am the bread of life; He who comes to Me will not hunger, and he who believes in Me will never thirst. . . . All that the Father gives Me will come to Me, and the one who comes to Me I will certainly not cast out" (John 6:35, 37).

Answering Life's Ultimate Question (John 7:37–52)

26

Now on the last day, the great day of the feast, Jesus stood and cried out, saying, "If anyone is thirsty, let him come to Me and drink. He who believes in Me, as the Scripture said, 'From his innermost being will flow rivers of living water.'" But this He spoke of the Spirit, whom those who believed in Him were to receive; for the Spirit was not yet given, because Jesus was not yet glorified. Some of the people therefore, when they heard these words, were saying, "This certainly is the Prophet." Others were saying, "This is the Christ." Still others were saying, "Surely the Christ is not going to come from Galilee, is He? Has not the Scripture said that the Christ comes from the descendants of David, and from Bethlehem, the village where David was?" So a division occurred in the crowd because of Him. Some of them wanted to seize Him, but no one laid hands on Him. The officers then came to the chief priests and Pharisees, and they said to them, "Why did you not bring Him?" The officers answered, "Never has a man spoken the way this man speaks." The Pharisees then answered them, "You have not also been led astray, have you? No one of the rulers or Pharisees has believed in Him, has he? But this crowd which does not know the Law is accursed." Nicodemus (he who

came to Him before, being one of them) said to them, "Our Law does not judge a man unless it first hears from him and knows what he is doing, does it?" They answered him, "You are not also from Galilee, are you? Search, and see that no prophet arises out of Galilee." (7:37–52)

The ultimate question that everyone must eventually face, the most crucial issue determining one's eternal destiny, is, "What shall I do with Jesus Christ?"

Ironically, that very question was posed by the man who sentenced the Lord to death. The Jewish authorities had arrested Jesus and, after a mock trial of their own, brought Him before Pilate, the Roman governor of Judea. Their reason for involving the hated Romans was simple: they wanted Jesus dead and the occupying Romans had not given them the right to enforce capital punishment (18:31). Therefore they needed the Roman authority to approve the murder.

After examining Jesus, Pilate declared, "I find no guilt in this man" (Luke 23:4) and sought to release Him (John 19:12). The governor's desire to do so only intensified when his "wife sent him a message, saying, 'Have nothing to do with that righteous Man; for last night I suffered greatly in a dream because of Him'" (Matt. 27:19). Since it was customary at Passover for Pilate "to release for them any one prisoner whom they requested" (Mark 15:6), the governor offered the mob a choice between Jesus and the "notorious prisoner" (Matt. 27:16) Barabbas. He assumed they would ask for Jesus to be released, but "the chief priests and the elders persuaded the crowds to ask for Barabbas and to put Jesus to death" (Matt. 27:20). It was then that a frustrated Pilate asked the momentous question, "What shall I do with Jesus who is called Christ?" (Matt. 27:22).

The frenzied crowd, stirred up by the chief priests (Mark 15:11), "cried out all together, saying, 'Away with this man, and release for us Barabbas!'" (Luke 23:18). But "Pilate, wanting to release Jesus, addressed them again" (Luke 23:20) and said, "Why, what evil has He done?" (Mark 15:14). Having officially pronounced Jesus innocent (three times; Luke 23:22), Pilate should have released Him. But instead, when he realized "that he was accomplishing nothing, but rather that a riot was starting, he took water and washed his hands in front of the crowd, saying, 'I am innocent of this Man's blood; see to that yourselves'" (Matt. 27:24). He capitulated, because the people "were insistent, with loud voices asking that [Jesus] be crucified" (Luke 23:23), and because the Jewish leaders threatened to report him again to the emperor as an inept leader: "If you release this Man, you are no friend of Caesar; everyone who makes himself out to be a king opposes Caesar" (John 19:12). So "wishing to satisfy the crowd" (Mark 15:15), "Pilate pronounced sentence that their demand be granted" (Luke 23:24), and "handed Him over to them to be crucified" (John 19:16).

Pilate failed to correctly answer his own question regarding Jesus. Although he feared that Jesus might have supernatural powers (19:7–9), he did not acknowledge Him to be the Son of God. By sentencing the innocent Savior to death, Pilate ultimately condemned himself.

The crowd that demanded Jesus' execution also brought judgment on themselves. For generations the people of Israel had longed for their Messiah. But when He finally came, they rejected His message and used their Roman overlords to execute Him (cf. Acts 2:22–23). In their blind rage, they accepted responsibility for Jesus' execution, even pronouncing on themselves the fearful curse, "His blood shall be on us and on our children!" (Matt. 27:25). Unless they later repented and believed, they were eternally damned.

Over the centuries, countless millions of people have likewise made the wrong choice concerning Jesus Christ. Like Pilate, the Jewish leaders, and the crowd, they have rejected Him as the only Savior of the world. But there is only one correct response to Him: "Confess with your mouth Jesus as Lord, and believe in your heart that God raised Him from the dead" (Rom. 10:9); acknowledge that "there is salvation in no one else; for there is no other name under heaven that has been given among men by which we must be saved" (Acts 4:12; cf. John 14:6); confess your sins (1 John 1:9) to the "Son of Man [who] has authority on earth to forgive sins" (Matt. 9:6); and bow in submission to Him as the sovereign Lord (Phil. 2:10–11). Those who do so "will be saved" (Rom. 10:9; cf. 5:1; 8:1; 1 Thess. 5:9; 2 Tim. 2:10; 3:15; Heb. 2:10; 5:9). But those who fail to do so will face eternal judgment (Ps. 2:12; Luke 13:3, 5; John 3:36; Rom. 1:18; 2:12; Gal. 3:10; Eph. 5:6; 2 Thess. 2:10; Heb. 10:29).

Israel was given many opportunities to respond rightly to Him. Verses 37–52 describe an incident typical of Israel's rejection, occurring about six months before His crucifixion. The setting was Jerusalem, on the last day of the Feast of Tabernacles (7:2, 37). With authority and precision, Jesus posed the question of His identity in the form of an invitation to believe in Him. The reactions of the people separated them into four groups: the convinced, the contrary, the confused, and the contemplative. Those responses encompass the universal pattern of reactions to Jesus Christ from the first century to the present day.

THE INVITATION

Now on the last day, the great day of the feast, Jesus stood and cried out, saying, "If anyone is thirsty, let him come to Me and

drink. He who believes in Me, as the Scripture said, 'From his innermost being will flow rivers of living water.'" But this He spoke of the Spirit, whom those who believed in Him were to receive; for the Spirit was not yet given, because Jesus was not yet glorified. (7:37–39)

This was neither Jesus' first public invitation to believe in Him (cf. 3:12–18; 5:24, 38–47; 6:29, 35–36, 40, 47), nor was it the first time He had pictured salvation as living water (4:10–14; 6:35). (The Lord also had earlier used a similar metaphor, describing Himself as the Bread of Life [6:30–59].) Drawing upon imagery from Isaiah's prophecy (12:3; 55:1), Jesus' reference to salvation as living water would have been familiar to His hearers. In the relatively dry land of Israel, thirst was an apt picture of one's need for salvation.

Jesus gave His invitation **on the last day, the great day of the feast** of Tabernacles. Whether this was the seventh day or the eighth day, on which a special festival assembly was held (Lev. 23:36), is not clear. In either case, it was a different day from the one on which the events of vv. 14–36 took place (cf. v. 14). As He had done earlier (v. 28), Jesus **cried out** in a loud voice, calling all to hear and heed His invitation. That the Lord **stood** to deliver His message (rabbis normally sat when they taught; cf. Matt. 5:1; 13:2; 26:55; Luke 4:20; 5:3), further emphasized its importance.

By using water to illustrate the truth about Himself, Jesus capitalized on a very prominent ceremony that was happening at the feast. The major feature of the Feast of Tabernacles was the booths (shelters) which the people prepared (Lev. 23:42; Neh. 8:14). But on each of its seven days there was also an important water ritual. That ceremony was not prescribed in the Old Testament, but had become a tradition in the centuries just before Jesus' time. It commemorated God's miraculous provision of water during Israel's wilderness wandering (Ex. 17:6; Num. 20:8–11; Deut. 8:15; Neh. 9:15; Pss. 105:41; 114:8; Isa. 48:21), and anticipated the blessings of the messianic age (cf. Isa. 30:25; 35:6–7; 43:19–20; 44:3–4; 49:10; Ezek. 47:1–9; Joel 3:18; Zech. 14:8). It was also a symbolic prayer for rain.

Each day of the feast the high priest drew water from the pool of Siloam and carried it in a procession back to the temple. At the Water Gate (on the south side of the inner court of the temple), three blasts were sounded on a shofar (a trumpet made out of a rams' horn) to mark the joy of the occasion. Isaiah 12:3 ("Therefore you will joyously draw water from the springs of salvation.") was also recited. At the temple the priests marched around the altar while the temple choir sang the Hallel (Pss. 113–118). The water was then poured out as an offering to God.

It was against the backdrop of that ceremony that Jesus spoke His stunning words, **"If anyone is thirsty, let him come to Me and drink."** If He gave this invitation on the seventh day of the feast, it would have coincided with the finale of the water ceremony. (On the seventh day, the priests marched around the altar seven times before pouring out the water.) Our Lord was inviting thirsty souls to come to Him for spiritual, eternal, life-giving water, instead of the physical, temporal water of the ceremony. If it was the eighth day (when there was no ceremony), it may not have been as dramatic an announcement, but the people could still make the connection with the water drawing ceremony each day. In either case, Jesus shifted the focus from the need of the parched mouths in the wilderness to the spiritual need of the thirsty soul for the water of life.

Three key words summarize Jesus' gospel invitation. First, the **thirsty** ones are those who recognize their spiritual thirst (cf. Isa. 55:1; Matt. 5:6). Next, if they are to find relief, such individuals must **come** to Jesus, the only source of living water. But not all who acknowledge their need and approach Him have their thirst quenched. The rich young ruler, though he eagerly "ran up to Him and knelt before Him, and asked Him, 'Good Teacher, what shall I do to inherit eternal life?'" (Mark 10:17), in the end "went away grieving" (v. 22) with his thirst still unquenched. Having approached Christ, he was unwilling to take the critical third step and **drink;** that is, appropriate Him by faith.

Only those who do will receive the living water in Christ; all others prove themselves to be false disciples (6:53), whose repentance is insincere and incomplete. The "repentance that leads to life" (Acts 11:18) and results in the "forgiveness of sins" (Luke 24:47) involves far more than mere remorse. Those who manifest genuine repentance acknowledge the deep thirst of their personal guilt before holy God, realizing that they can do nothing on their own to avert His judgment that they deserve. Thus they rely on the sacrifice of Jesus Christ (as payment for their sins), affirming Him to be the only Savior (John 14:6; Acts 4:12), and the Lord of their lives (Rom. 10:9–10). In this way, they drink the living water that He provides, which becomes in them "a well of water springing up to eternal life" (John 4:14). In the words of Horatio Bonar's hymn, "I Heard the Voice of Jesus Say,"

> I heard the voice of Jesus say,
> "Behold, I freely give
> The living water; thirsty one
> Stoop down and drink and live."
> I came to Jesus and I drank
> Of that life-giving stream;
> My thirst was quenched, my soul revived,
> And now I live in Him.

But God did not intend for believers to be ponds in which the living water of salvation stagnates. Instead, Jesus declared, **"He who believes in Me, as the Scripture said, 'From his innermost being will flow rivers of living water.'"** The Lord's words were not a direct quote of a specific Old Testament text, but reflect such passages as Proverbs 11:25, Ezekiel 47:1–9, and Zechariah 13:1. Believers are to be channels through which the **rivers of living water** are sent to others. Leon Morris writes, "The believer is not self-centered. As he receives the gift of God, so he passes it on to others. Or to put the same thought in another way, when a man believes he becomes a servant of God, and God uses him to be the means of bringing the blessing to others" (*The Gospel According to John*, The New International Commentary on the New Testament [Grand Rapids: Eerdmans, 1979], 426). By evangelizing the lost (which is the primary emphasis here) and edifying the saints (1 Cor. 12:4–11; 1 Peter 4:10–11), believers allow the spiritual life within them to spill over and impact those around them.

As the apostle John's inspired footnote indicates, Jesus **spoke of the Spirit,** through whom eternal life is imparted to those who believe (3:5–8; 6:63; Rom. 8:9; 1 Cor. 6:11; 1 Peter 1:1–2). The Spirit also empowers them to bring the living water of salvation to other thirsty souls (cf. Acts 4:31; Rom. 15:18–19; Eph. 4:11). When the Lord spoke, the promise that **those who believed in Him were to receive** the Holy Spirit was still future, **for the Spirit was not yet given, because Jesus was not yet glorified.**

This comment needs an explanation so that there is no misunderstanding of the Spirit's work. Our Lord is not saying that the Holy Spirit was not present or active at that time, or in past redemptive history. He was saying that there was to come for believers a giving of the Spirit by which unique power would be provided for ministry and evangelism.

The words of Jesus in John 14:17 are helpful in this matter: "the Spirit of truth . . . you know Him because He abides with you and will be in you." Clearly in that Upper Room dinner with the apostles, Jesus promised a future coming of the Holy Spirit (14:16, 20, 26; 15:26–27; 16:13–14). But the comment in 14:17 that "He abides with you" affirms the obvious fact that no one in any era of redemptive history could be saved or sanctified, empowered for service and witness, or guided in understanding Scripture and praying in the will of God apart from the Spirit's presence.

There are Old Testament references to the Spirit's ministry, such as the following:

> Then the Lord said, "My Spirit shall not strive with man forever, because he also is flesh; nevertheless his days shall be one hundred and twenty years." (Gen. 6:3)

> Do not cast me away from Your presence
> And do not take Your Holy Spirit from me. (Ps. 51:11)
>
> Where can I go from Your Spirit?
> Or where can I flee from Your presence?
> If I ascend to heaven, You are there;
> If I make my bed in Sheol, behold, You are there.
> If I take the wings of the dawn,
> If I dwell in the remotest part of the sea,
> Even there Your hand will lead me,
> And Your right hand will lay hold of me.
> If I say, "Surely the darkness will overwhelm me,
> And the light around me will be night,"
> Even the darkness is not dark to You,
> And the night is as bright as the day.
> Darkness and light are alike to You. (Ps. 139:7–12)
>
> Teach me to do Your will,
> For You are my God;
> Let Your good Spirit lead me on level ground. (Ps. 143:10)
>
> I will put My Spirit within you and cause you to walk in My statutes, and you will be careful to observe My ordinances. (Ezek. 36:27)

Prior to Pentecost the Spirit was the author of repentance (cf. John 16:8–11) and the power behind regeneration (John 3:4–5). He also illuminated believers in the face of persecution (Mark 13:11; Luke 12:11). Still, after Pentecost the Spirit was given to believers in a new fullness that became normative for all believers since (Rom. 8:9; 1 Cor. 12:13).

That Jesus **was not yet glorified** (cf. 12:16; 17:4–5) refers to His ascension to heavenly glory (Acts 1:9–11), at which point the Father sent the Holy Spirit. This sending of the Spirit after Christ's return to heaven made possible the "greater works" believers do (John 14:12).

Those who responded to Christ's invitation received the living water of salvation He offered that very day. But the **Spirit** would not be **given** in fullness until several months later, on the Day of Pentecost, following Jesus' death, resurrection, and ascension (16:7; Acts 1:4–5, 8; 2:1–4). Since the close of the transitional period in the book of Acts, however, all Christians receive the Holy Spirit at the moment of salvation.

THE RESPONSES

Some of the people therefore, when they heard these words, were saying, "This certainly is the Prophet." Others were saying,

"This is the Christ." Still others were saying, "Surely the Christ is not going to come from Galilee, is He? Has not the Scripture said that the Christ comes from the descendants of David, and from Bethlehem, the village where David was?" So a division occurred in the crowd because of Him. Some of them wanted to seize Him, but no one laid hands on Him. The officers then came to the chief priests and Pharisees, and they said to them, "Why did you not bring Him?" The officers answered, "Never has a man spoken the way this man speaks." The Pharisees then answered them, "You have not also been led astray, have you? No one of the rulers or Pharisees has believed in Him, has he? But this crowd which does not know the Law is accursed." Nicodemus (he who came to Him before, being one of them) said to them, "Our Law does not judge a man unless it first hears from him and knows what he is doing, does it?" They answered him, "You are not also from Galilee, are you? Search, and see that no prophet arises out of Galilee." (7:40–52)

As noted above, how people respond to Jesus Christ separates them into four groups—the convinced, the contrary, the confused, and the contemplative—all of which are represented in this passage.

THE CONVINCED

Some of the people therefore, when they heard these words, were saying, "This certainly is the Prophet." Others were saying, "This is the Christ." (7:40–41a)

When some of the people . . . heard Jesus' gracious words of invitation in verses 37–39, they became convinced that He was the Prophet of whom Moses wrote (Deut. 18:15–18). As noted in the discussion of 1:21 in chapter 4 of this volume, some identified the Prophet as the Messiah (the correct interpretation; cf. Acts 3:22–23; 7:37). Others viewed Him as a forerunner of the Messiah. At the very least, these individuals viewed Jesus as a great prophet (cf. Matt. 21:11, 46; Mark 6:15; Luke 7:16; 24:19; John 4:19; 6:14; 9:17). Thus, while their knowledge may not have been complete, they were at least convinced that He was sent from God.

Others had a clearer understanding of who Jesus was and were saying of Him, "This is the Christ." They earlier had been intimidated into silence by fear of the Jewish authorities (7:13; cf. 9:22; 12:42; 19:38; 20:19). But now, having become convinced of Jesus' identity, they boldly proclaimed it. These individuals were part of the believing remnant of Israel (2 Kings 19:30–31; Isa. 10:20–22; 28:5; 37:31–32; 46:3; Jer. 23:3; 31:7; 50:20; Mic. 2:12; 5:7–8; Rom. 9:27; 11:1–5); members of the "little flock" (Luke 12:32); those who entered through the narrow gate that leads to eternal life (Matt. 7:13–14); thirsty people who had accepted Christ's invitation and come to Him, drinking of the living water that He provides.

THE CONTRARY

Still others were saying, "Surely the Christ is not going to come from Galilee, is He? Has not the Scripture said that the Christ comes from the descendants of David, and from Bethlehem, the village where David was?" So a division occurred in the crowd because of Him. Some of them wanted to seize Him, but no one laid hands on Him. (7:41b–44)

Not all in the crowd were convinced of Jesus' authenticity, however. While some were ready to accept Him as the great prophet Moses promised, or even the Messiah, **still others** remained skeptical. **"Surely the Christ is not going to come from Galilee, is He?"** they scornfully asked. The question expects a negative answer; the idea that the Messiah could come from the boondocks of Galilee seemed ludicrous to the sophisticated Judeans (cf. v. 52; 1:46). Besides, they insisted, **"Has not the Scripture said that the Christ comes from the descendants of David, and from Bethlehem, the village where David was?"** To their credit, both of those points were valid. The Old Testament **Scripture** reveals that **the Christ comes from the descendants of David** (2 Sam. 7:12; Pss. 89:3–4; 132:10–11; Isa. 11:1, 10; Jer. 23:5; 33:15; cf. Matt. 22:42), and that the Messiah would come **from Bethlehem** (Mic. 5:2; cf. Matt. 2:3–6).

Secure in their smug unbelief, however, the scoffers failed to examine the situation fully. Had they done so, they would have discovered that Jesus met both of those qualifications. He was a descendant of David (Matt. 1:1; Luke 1:32; 3:23, 31; cf. Matt. 1:20; Luke 1:27; 2:4), and had been born in Bethlehem (Matt. 2:1; Luke 2:4–7, 11, 15). They hastily assumed that since Jesus had grown up in Nazareth (Matt. 2:21–23; Luke 2:39, 51; 4:16; cf. Matt. 21:11; 26:71; Luke 18:37; John 1:45), He must have been born there. They had no interest in investigating His messianic credentials.

Obviously, as a result of the differing opinions regarding Jesus, **a division occurred in the crowd** (cf. 9:16; 10:19). This incident illustrates the truth that Jesus divides people. In Luke 12:51–53 He warned,

Do you suppose that I came to grant peace on earth? I tell you, no, but rather division; for from now on five members in one household will be divided, three against two and two against three. They will be divided, father against son and son against father, mother against daughter and daughter against mother, mother-in-law against daughter-in-law and daughter-in-law against mother-in-law.

He divides believers from unbelievers (3:18, 36; 1 John 5:10); those who walk in the light from those who walk in darkness (John 8:12; 12:35, 46; Eph. 5:8; 1 Thess. 5:5; 1 Peter 2:9; 1 John 2:9); the sheep from the goats (Matt. 25:32–33; cf. John 10:26); and the children of God from the children of the devil (1 John 3:10; cf. v. 8; John 8:44). Everyone is either for Him or against Him; there is no middle ground (Matt. 12:30).

For the third time since Jesus arrived in Jerusalem (cf. vv. 30, 32), an unsuccessful attempt was made **to seize Him.** As was the case with the earlier attempt by some of the crowd (v. 30), **no one laid hands on Him,** because the time was not right in God's plan (see the discussion of v. 30 in chapter 25 of this volume).

THE CONFUSED

The officers then came to the chief priests and Pharisees, and they said to them, "Why did you not bring Him?" The officers answered, "Never has a man spoken the way this man speaks." The Pharisees then answered them, "You have not also been led astray, have you? No one of the rulers or Pharisees has believed in Him, has he? But this crowd which does not know the Law is accursed." (7:45–49)

Unlike those in the crowd who either believed in or rejected Christ, **the officers** of the temple police were confused by Him. They had been sent several days earlier (cf. vv. 14, 32, 37) by **the chief priests and Pharisees** to arrest Jesus (v. 32). When they returned empty-handed, their superiors demanded of **them, "Why did you not bring Him?"** Interestingly, the **officers** did not claim that the crowd prevented them from arresting Jesus, though that may in fact have been the case (cf. vv. 31, 40–41, 43). Instead, they expressed bewilderment and amazement, declaring, **"Never has a man spoken the way this man speaks"** (cf. Matt. 7:28; Mark 1:22; 12:17; Luke 4:32; 20:26). They were religiously trained Levites, and Jesus' words left them stunned. While they did not accept Him as the Messiah, neither did they openly reject Him. They did not know what to do with Him. Caught between the power and grace of His message and the hatred of their leaders, they were paralyzed into inactivity.

Infuriated by the **officers'** failure to arrest Jesus, **the Pharisees then answered them, "You have not also been led astray, have you?"** That scathing rebuke, though phrased in the form of a question, chided the **officers** not for their lack of professionalism (as members of the temple police), but for their alleged lack of spiritual discernment (as Levites). It accused them of naively being duped by a religious charlatan, and it condescendingly placed them on the same level as the uneducated crowd (see v. 49). In contrast, the Pharisees self-righteously maintained, **"No one of the rulers or Pharisees has believed in Him, has he?"** The arrogant implication was that if Jesus were really the Messiah, the religious experts would have been the first to recognize Him.

The Pharisees continued by deriding the common people as **"this crowd which does not know the Law."** (The **Law** was a reference both to the Old Testament and, especially, the rabbinic traditions.) The Pharisees viewed themselves as the spiritual elite; men who were above the possibility of being wrong about religious matters. In their minds, only those who were gullible, uneducated, and simple-minded could be deceived by Jesus' claims. Such people were **accursed,** according to the Pharisaic perspective, for their ignorance of God's law.

In ridiculing the crowd, the Pharisees implicitly appealed to the officers' pride and desire for prestige. The officers had a crucial decision to make. They could either reject Jesus and be applauded by the apostate religious establishment, or believe in Him and be castigated with the redeemed. John does not record what choice the officers ultimately made.

THE CONTEMPLATIVE

Nicodemus (he who came to Him before, being one of them) said to them, "Our Law does not judge a man unless it first hears from him and knows what he is doing, does it?" They answered him, "You are not also from Galilee, are you? Search, and see that no prophet arises out of Galilee." (7:50–52)

The Pharisees' claim that the religious rulers had unanimously rejected Jesus was, in fact, not true (cf. 12:42). The prominent rabbi **Nicodemus** (the same one **who came to** Jesus earlier [3:1–2]), perhaps the preeminent teacher in all of Israel (cf. 3:10) was the most notable exception. He was probably not a disciple of Jesus at this point (though he would later become one; [19:39]), but his mind was open to the Lord's claims. Nicodemus did not openly defend Jesus, but he did raise a procedural point in His favor, reminding his colleagues, **"Our Law does**

not judge a man unless it first hears from him and knows what he is doing, does it?" Even the despised Romans did not condemn people without a hearing (Acts 25:16).

But his fellow members of the Sanhedrin, their minds already closed against Jesus, were in no mood to be fair. Instead, they turned on Nicodemus savagely. **"You are not also from Galilee, are you?"** they taunted him. To identify Nicodemus with the despised, unsophisticated Galileans was the most demeaning insult they could make.

Then they mockingly invited him to **"search, and see that no prophet arises out of Galilee,"** conveniently overlooking the fact that Jonah (who was from a city near Nazareth in the tribal region of Zebulun; 2 Kings 14:25; cf. Josh. 19:10) was from Galilee. (Some scholars believe that Nahum and Hosea, and possibly other prophets, may also have been from Galilee.) They implied that he was ignorant of the most basic theological truths. But the statement actually exposed their own lack of knowledge, since some prophets had come from Galilee and Jesus was originally from Bethlehem. Nonetheless, their minds were already made up regarding Him. Thus they saw no need to seek the truth.

Despite their derision, Nicodemus continued to pursue the truth (cf. 7:17), and eventually found it in Christ. Sadly, the same cannot be said of many of his colleagues, members of the Sanhedrin who would ultimately kill their own Messiah.

Jesus Confronts Hypocrisy
(John 7:53–8:11)

27

Everyone went to his home. But Jesus went to the Mount of Olives. Early in the morning He came again into the temple, and all the people were coming to Him; and He sat down and began to teach them. The scribes and the Pharisees brought a woman caught in adultery, and having set her in the center of the court, they said to Him, "Teacher, this woman has been caught in adultery, in the very act. Now in the Law Moses commanded us to stone such women; what then do You say?" They were saying this, testing Him, so that they might have grounds for accusing Him. But Jesus stooped down and with His finger wrote on the ground. But when they persisted in asking Him, He straightened up, and said to them, "He who is without sin among you, let him be the first to throw a stone at her." Again He stooped down and wrote on the ground. When they heard it, they began to go out one by one, beginning with the older ones, and He was left alone, and the woman, where she was, in the center of the court. Straightening up, Jesus said to her, "Woman, where are they? Did no one condemn you?" She said, "No one, Lord." And Jesus said, "I do not condemn you, either. Go. From now on sin no more." (7:53–8:11)

Although it is often cited and taught, this familiar passage may not have actually been an original part of John's gospel. Along with Mark 16:9–20, it is one of the longest and most famous New Testament texts whose authenticity is questioned. To determine whether or not it was in the original inspired manuscript, two lines of evidence must be considered: the internal evidence (of the passage itself), and the external testimony (of the Greek text, early versions, and church fathers).

The passage contains several internal indicators that cast doubt on its authenticity. Its placement here disrupts the flow of thought in this section. In 7:37–52 Jesus referred to one of the rituals associated with the Feast of Tabernacles, the water pouring ceremony (see the exposition of those verses in chapter 26 of this volume). In 8:12 the Lord alluded to the second great ritual associated with the feast, the lamp lighting ceremony (see the exposition of 8:12–21 in chapter 28 of this volume). Jesus' claim to be the Light of the World in 8:12 follows logically after His claim to be the source of living water in 7:37–52. (The word "again" in verse 12 also implies a continuity between 7:37–52 and 8:12–21.) That claim to be the Light of the World may also be an allusion to Isaiah 9:1–2 (cf. Matt. 4:12–16), and thus an indirect reply to the Pharisees' contemptuous remark in verse 52 that "no prophet arises out of Galilee." Interposing the story of the woman taken in adultery obscures the Lord's rebuttal of the Pharisees' false claim (cf. Philip Comfort, "The Pericope of the Adulteress," *The Bible Translator* 40 [January 1989], 145–47).

Since the story does not seem to fit here, some manuscripts insert it in different locations. While the majority place it after John 7:52, some locate it after 7:36, 7:44, 21:25, or even after Luke 21:38. As James R. White notes, "Such moving about by a body of text is plain evidence of its later origin and the attempt on the part of scribes to find a place where it 'fits'" (*The King James Only Controversy* [Minneapolis: Bethany House 1995], 262). D. A. Carson adds, "The diversity of placement confirms the inauthenticity of the verses" (*The Gospel According to John,* The Pillar New Testament Commentary [Grand Rapids: Eerdmans, 1991], 333).

The vocabulary and style of the story offer further evidence that John did not write it (Carson, *John,* 334; Leon Morris, *The Gospel According to John,* The New International Commentary on the New Testament [Grand Rapids: Eerdmans, 1979], 883 n. 3; B. F. Westcott, *The Gospel According to St. John* [Reprint; Grand Rapids: Eerdmans, 1978], 142). For example, the scribes and Pharisees (8:3), paired so frequently in the Synoptic Gospels (Matt. 5:20; 12:38; 15:1; 23:2, 13–15, 23, 25, 27, 29; Mark 2:16; 7:1, 5; Luke 5:21, 30; 6:7; 11:53; 15:2) do not appear together anywhere else in John's gospel. The passage also suggests that Jesus spent the night on the Mount of Olives (8:1–2). Yet the Synoptic Gospels record that happening only during Passion Week (Luke 21:37; cf. 22:39), which was still about six months away. (It is, of course, possible that Jesus spent nights on the Mount of Olives during earlier visits to Jerusalem and the Synoptic Gospels did not record it.) And though the Synoptic Gospels refer to the Mount of Olives (Matt. 21:1; 24:3; 26:30; Mark 11:1; 13:3; 14:26; Luke 19:29,37; 21:37; 22:39), John does not (outside of this passage).

The external evidence also casts doubt on the authenticity of these verses. The earliest and most reliable manuscripts, from a variety of textual traditions, omit it. Others that do include it mark it to indicate that there were questions regarding its authenticity. Many of the most significant early versions (translations of the Scriptures into other languages) also omit this section. None of the early Greek church fathers—even those who dealt with the text of John verse by verse—commented on this passage. The first to do so was Euthymius Zigabenus in the twelfth century, and even he acknowledged that the accurate manuscripts did not contain it.

Some (most notably Augustine) have speculated that overly zealous scribes may have excised this passage from the manuscripts because they feared it was too lenient on adultery. But there is no other known instance of scribes making such an extensive textual deletion on moral grounds (Bruce M. Metzger, *A Textual Commentary on the Greek New Testament* [New York: United Bible Societies, 1975], 221). If that was the reason this section was deleted, why would the scribes have deleted 7:53–8:2? Those three verses have nothing to do with adultery, and would have connected well with 8:12. And why cut this passage, but leave in the text of John's gospel the account of the Samaritan woman? She too was guilty of sexual immorality (4:17–18), and Jesus' rebuke of her was even milder and less direct than His rebuke of the adulterous woman (cf. 8:11).

This passage, then, was most likely not part of the original text of John's gospel. Yet it "is beyond doubt an authentic fragment of apostolic tradition" (Westcott, *John*, 125) that describes an actual historical event from Christ's life. It contains no teaching that contradicts the rest of Scripture. The picture it paints of the wise, loving, forgiving Savior is consistent with the Bible's portrait of Jesus Christ. Nor is it the kind of story the early church would have made up about Him. "No ascetically minded monk [most of the scribes who copied the early manuscripts were monks] would have invented a narrative which closes with what seems to be only a mild rebuke on Jesus' part" (Bruce M. Metzger, *The Text of the New Testament* [New York: Oxford, 1982], 223).

The story was most likely history, a piece of oral tradition that circulated in parts of the Western church. (Most of the limited early support for its authenticity comes from Western manuscripts and versions, and from Western church fathers such as Jerome, Ambrose, and Augustine.)

Eventually, it was written down and found its way into the later manuscripts. Because it is not possible to be absolutely certain that this story
was added later, its exposition is included in this commentary.

This passage is not primarily the story of an adulteress, or of the
hypocritical religious leaders who cynically used her to attack Jesus. The
central figure of this gripping drama of immorality, hypocrisy, and forgiveness, as in all of John's gospel, is the Lord Jesus Christ. From it a fourfold
picture of Him emerges. The passage reveals His humility, His wisdom,
His indictment, and His forgiveness.

His Humility

**Everyone went to his home. But Jesus went to the Mount of
Olives. Early in the morning He came again into the temple, and
all the people were coming to Him; and He sat down and began to
teach them.** (7:53–8:2)

Since this incident has disputable authenticity, it is obviously
impossible to know for certain where it might fit into the chronology of
Christ's life. Because these three introductory verses closely parallel Luke
21:37–38, the event may have taken place during Passion Week. Jesus
was evidently in Jerusalem, since when **everyone** else **went to his
home,** He **went to the Mount of Olives** to spend the night. Whether
the Lord slept out on the mountainside, or stayed at the home of Mary,
Martha, and Lazarus in Bethany (on the eastern slope of the Mount of
Olives), is unknown.

That Jesus, the Creator of all things, had no place of His own to
stay strikingly illustrates the humiliation and condescension of the Incarnation—when He "emptied Himself, taking the form of a bond-servant,
and being made in the likeness of men. Being found in appearance as a
man, He humbled Himself by becoming obedient to the point of death,
even death on a cross" (Phil. 2:7–8). At His birth His mother "wrapped
Him in cloths, and laid Him in a manger, because there was no room for
them in the inn" (Luke 2:7). During His ministry He said to a would-be
follower, "The foxes have holes and the birds of the air have nests, but the
Son of Man has nowhere to lay His head" (Matt. 8:20). Jesus Christ, God in
human flesh, was not given the reception even the most minor human
dignitary would have received (cf. 1:11).

The text notes that, simply and without fanfare, **early the** next
morning He came again into the temple to teach. No angelic herald
announced Jesus' arrival, nor did He perform any sensational miracles to
draw a crowd. But such was the power of His teaching (cf. 7:46; Matt.

7:28–29; Luke 4:22) that **all the people were coming to Him** (cf. Mark 2:13; Luke 21:38). In His humility, the Lord used no gimmicks to market or promote Himself, but offered His teaching freely to all who would listen. In typical rabbinical style, **He** simply **sat down** somewhere in the temple complex **and began to teach** the people.

Throughout Jesus' ministry He exhibited this kind of humility. This is in stark contrast to His second coming, which will be marked by His exaltation and glory. When He returns, He will come "with power and great glory" (Matt. 24:30; cf. 16:27; Mark 8:38; Luke 9:26), "on the clouds of heaven" (Matt. 26:64), and "every eye will see Him" (Rev. 1:7). "He will sit on His glorious throne" (Matt. 25:31; cf. 19:28), and He will rule the nations with majesty and power (cf. Rev. 19:15).

His Wisdom

The scribes and the Pharisees brought a woman caught in adultery, and having set her in the center of the court, they said to Him, "Teacher, this woman has been caught in adultery, in the very act. Now in the Law Moses commanded us to stone such women; what then do You say?" They were saying this, testing Him, so that they might have grounds for accusing Him. But Jesus stooped down and with His finger wrote on the ground. But when they persisted in asking Him, He straightened up, and said to them, "He who is without sin among you, let him be the first to throw a stone at her." Again He stooped down and wrote on the ground. (8:3–8)

Suddenly, the Lord's teaching was interrupted by **scribes and the Pharisees.** As noted above, those two groups appear together frequently in the Synoptic Gospels, but nowhere else in John's gospel (John does not mention the scribes). The **scribes** (sometimes called lawyers) were the experts in interpreting the Law. They were usually, but not always, **Pharisees,** who along with the Sadducees, Zealots, and Essenes were one of the four major religious sects in first-century Judaism. The Pharisees were noted chiefly for their strict adherence to the Mosaic Law and their oral traditions. Though few in number (about 6,000 at the time of Herod the Great according to the first-century Jewish historian Josephus), they were the dominant religious influence among the Jewish people.

With the exception of Nicodemus (3:1ff.; 7:50–51; 19:39–40), the Pharisees are always hostile to Jesus in John's gospel (4:1; 7:32, 45–52; 8:13; 9:13–16, 40–41; 11:46–53, 57; 12:19, 42; 18:3). (Later, some would come to believe in Him [cf. Acts 15:5]—most notably the zealous Pharisee [Acts 23:6; Gal. 1:14] Saul of Tarsus.) The Pharisees viewed Jesus' popularity with alarm. They feared both losing their influence with the people, and retaliation by the Romans if Jesus' followers started a revolt (John 11:47–48; cf. 6:15). (For more information on the Pharisees, see the exposition of 3:1 in chapter 8 of this volume.)

Bringing with them **a woman caught in adultery,** the scribes and Pharisees barged into the crowd of people listening to Jesus and **set her in the center of the court.** Addressing Him with mock politeness as **"Teacher"** (or "Rabbi") they exclaimed, **"This woman has been caught in adultery, in the very act."** Then they demanded a ruling from Him: **"Now in the Law Moses commanded us to stone such women; what then do You say?"** The last clause is emphatic in the Greek, and could be translated "You . . . what do you say?" or "What's your opinion on this?"

The seventh commandment forbids adultery (Ex. 20:14; Deut. 5:18), and Leviticus 20:10 prescribes the death penalty for those who commit it: "If there is a man who commits adultery with another man's wife, one who commits adultery with his friend's wife, the adulterer and the adulteress shall surely be put to death." Jesus Himself upheld the Old Testament condemnation of adultery (Matt. 5:27; 19:18). In fact, He made the prohibition stronger, condemning not only the physical act, but also the lustful attitude that conceives it (Matt. 5:28).

From a purely legal standpoint, then, these men were correct in saying that the woman deserved to die. But the circumstances suggest that they had something else in mind. By its very nature, adultery is a sin that involves two people—yet the Pharisees were accusing only the woman. The obvious question was: Where was the man? Those who had apprehended the woman had certainly seen him too, since she had been seized **in the very act.** Why had they not also arrested him and brought him before Jesus, since the Law demanded that both guilty parties be executed (Lev. 20:10)? And if justice was all they sought, why bring the woman to Jesus at all? Why not try her in their own courts, where such cases would normally be heard? Jesus was not a judge (cf. Luke 12:13–14) or a member of the Sanhedrin. Nor was there any legal difficulty that would necessitate consulting a rabbi; it was an open-and-shut case.

The Pharisees' motive was obvious: they were merely using the woman in an attempt to trap Jesus. There was something far more important to them than seeing justice done; **they were testing Him, so that they might have grounds for accusing Him.** As was so often the case, they were trying to force Jesus to say something that they could use to destroy Him (cf. Matt. 12:10; 16:1; 19:3; 22:34–40; Mark 8:11; Luke 10:25; 11:53–54; 20:20–40).

The woman's accusers thought they had the Lord between a proverbial rock and hard place. If He objected to stoning her, He would be guilty of opposing the Mosaic Law, and thus discredit His claim to be the Messiah. On the other hand, if He agreed with her accusers that she should be stoned, His reputation for compassion toward sinners (cf. Matt. 9:11; Luke 7:34; 15:2; 19:7) would be destroyed. Further, the Jewish leaders could then report Him to the Romans as having instigated an execution in defiance of Roman authority (cf. John 18:31).

The challenge brought by the scribes and Pharisees also raised a deeper issue—namely, how divine justice and mercy are to be harmonized. God is holy (Lev. 11:44–45; 19:2; 1 Sam. 2:2; Ps. 99:9; 1 Peter 1:15–16), and His "Law is holy, and the commandment is holy and righteous and good" (Rom. 7:12). The Law knows nothing of forgiveness (Rom. 3:20; 8:3; Gal. 2:16; 3:11; James 2:10). It declares, "The soul who sins will die" (Ezek. 18:4) because "all who have sinned under the Law will be judged by the Law" (Rom. 2:12), "for the Law brings about wrath" (4:15). How then does God forgive sinners without violating His holy law?

The answer is, through the Lord Jesus Christ. His sacrificial death fully satisfied the demands of God's justice; as Paul wrote to the Romans: "For what the Law could not do, weak as it was through the flesh, God did: sending His own Son in the likeness of sinful flesh and as an offering for sin, He condemned sin in the flesh" (Rom. 8:3). Those who put their faith in Him are "justified as a gift by His grace through the redemption which is in Christ Jesus; whom God displayed publicly as a propitiation in His blood through faith" (Rom. 3:24–25), because "He Himself bore our sins in His body on the cross, so that we might die to sin and live to righteousness; for by His wounds you were healed" (1 Peter 2:24; cf. 3:18; Isa. 53:4–6, 10; Matt. 20:28; John 10:11; Rom. 4:25; 5:8–10; 1 Cor. 15:3; 2 Cor. 5:14–15, 21; Gal. 1:4; 2:20; 3:13; Eph. 1:7; 5:2; 1 Tim. 2:5–6; Titus 2:14; Heb. 9:28; 10:11–12; 1 John 2:2; 3:16; 4:9–10; Rev. 1:5; 5:9).

In Jesus Christ divine justice and mercy harmonize. Because His sacrificial death paid the penalty for the sins of all who believe in Him, God can "be just and the justifier of the one who has faith in Jesus" (Rom. 3:26); in Him "lovingkindness and truth have met together; righteousness and peace have kissed each other" (Ps. 85:10). God poured out His wrath against sin on Jesus so He can pour out His grace and mercy on those who believe. And Jesus was the lamb "slain from the foundation of the world" (Rev. 13:8 NKJV), not only in the prophetic sense, but also in the sense of application. All through redemptive history, all who were forgiven and given eternal life had the future sacrifice of the Son of God applied to their sins.

The dramatic scene in the temple courtyard had reached its climax. The woman, her sin publicly exposed, was humiliated, terrified, and about to be stoned. The scribes and Pharisees were jubilant, thinking they had caught Jesus in an impossible dilemma. The crowd was hushed, watching intently to see how Jesus would react. But He, for the moment, surprisingly did nothing.

Seemingly oblivious to what was going on, **Jesus stooped down and with His finger wrote on the ground.** Because the text does not say what He wrote, some speculate that the Lord was acting out Jeremiah 17:13: "Those who depart from Me shall be written in the earth, because they have forsaken the Lord, the fountain of living waters" (NKJV). Others suggest that He wrote the words He would say in verse 7, or part of the Law (such as the prohibition against being a malicious witness in Ex. 23:1). Perhaps the most popular view is that He listed the sins of the woman's accusers. What Jesus wrote is obviously not essential to the story, however, since it was not recorded; all of those suggestions are speculation.

The scribes and Pharisees were no doubt puzzled by Jesus' silence. Perhaps they thought He did not know how to reply, so, thinking they finally had impaled Him on the horns of a dilemma, the scribes and Pharisees **persisted in asking Him.** Always the master of the moment, Jesus remained silent, allowing them to reveal unmistakably their hatred and hypocrisy as they insistently pressed their attack.

At last, He **straightened up,** no doubt gave His opponents a piercing glance, **and said to them, "He who is without sin among you, let him be the first to throw a stone at her."** After making that startling and unexpected statement, He calmly **stooped down** once more **and wrote on the ground,** and said nothing.

The Lord's reply was simple, yet profound. It upheld the Law, since He did not deny the woman's guilt, and broadened the Law's power by exposing the sins of the accusers. It also avoided the charge of instigating an execution in violation of Roman authority, since the Lord put the responsibility back on the accusers. And it mercifully spared the woman from being stoned for her sin.

Jesus knew that according to the Law, the witnesses to a capital offense were to be the first to throw stones at the guilty person (Deut. 13:9; 17:7). Obviously, they could not have been participants in the crime, or they too would have been executed. Jesus was not making sinless perfection a requirement for carrying out the Law (or else no one could have done so). It may be, then, that the woman's accusers were themselves guilty of adultery (if not the physical act, certainly the lust of the heart [Matt. 5:28]).

Jesus' masterful answer neither minimized the woman's guilt, nor denied the Law's sanctity. But it cut the ground out from under the scribes and Pharisees by revealing that they were unfit to be her judges and executioners. They were guilty of the hypocrisy that the apostle Paul condemned in Romans 2:1:"Therefore you have no excuse, everyone of you who passes judgment, for in that which you judge another, you condemn yourself; for you who judge practice the same things" (cf. Matt. 7:1–5).

HIS INDICTMENT

When they heard it, they began to go out one by one, beginning with the older ones, (8:9a)

Having **heard** the Lord's devastating reply, the stunned scribes and Pharisees **began to go out one by one.** Some manuscripts add, "being convicted by their conscience," which is certainly implied. That the accusers exited **beginning with the older ones** provides an interesting insight into human nature. It may be that they were the first to realize that they had suffered a humiliating defeat, and that it was pointless to continue. But they may also have been more keenly aware of their sins and the impossibility of meeting Jesus' challenge. The older ones also had more sin to remember.

Ironically, those who came to put Jesus to shame left ashamed; those who came to condemn the woman went away condemned. Unfortunately, their indictment and sense of guilt did not lead them to repentance and faith in Christ. Like many who hear and feel the convicting truth of the law, they hardened their hearts and turned away from Him, not even open to gospel forgiveness.

HIS FORGIVENESS

and He was left alone, and the woman, where she was, in the center of the court. Straightening up, Jesus said to her, "Woman, where are they? Did no one condemn you?" She said, "No one, Lord." And Jesus said, "I do not condemn you, either. Go. From now on sin no more." (8:9b–11)

After the departure of the scribes and Pharisees, Jesus **was left alone** with **the woman,** who remained standing **where she was, in the center of the court.** The text does not say whether the crowd that had been listening to Jesus' teaching (v. 2) had also left. Whether they were still there or not, the focus of the narrative is on the Lord and the woman.

For the first time, someone addressed the woman. **Straighten-**

ing up from His posture of stooping to write, **Jesus said to her, "Woman, where are they? Did no one condemn you?"** The term **woman** was a polite, respectful form of address (cf. Matt. 15:28; Luke 13:12; 22:57), one with which Jesus addressed His mother (John 2:4; 19:26), the Samaritan woman at the well (4:21), and Mary Magdalene (20:13, 15). With her accusers gone, there was **no one** left to **condemn** her. Exercising His divine prerogative to forgive sin (Matt. 9:6; cf. John 3:17; 12:47), **Jesus said, "I do not condemn you, either. Go. From now on sin no more."**

Forgiveness does not imply license to sin. Jesus did not condemn her, but He did command her to abandon her sinful lifestyle. Gerald L. Borchert writes,

> Jesus' verdict, "neither do I condemn," however, was not rendered as a simple acquittal or a noncondemnation. The verdict was in fact a strict charge for her to live from this point on (*apo tou nun*) very differently —to sin no more (*mēketi hamartane*). The liberating work of Jesus did not mean the excusing of sin. Encountering Jesus always has demanded the transformation of life, the turning away from sin. . . . Sin was not treated lightly by Jesus, but sinners were offered the opportunity to start life anew. (*John 1–11,* The New American Commentary [Nashville: Broadman & Holman, 2002], 376)

As Paul wrote in Romans 6:1–2, "What shall we say then? Are we to continue in sin so that grace may increase? May it never be! How shall we who died to sin still live in it?"

This story is far more than a battleground for textual critics. It paints a marvelous picture of the Lord Jesus Christ, whose gracious humility, infinite wisdom, convicting speech, and tender forgiveness are its central themes. All Christians should be grateful to God for sovereignly preserving it.

Jesus: The Light of the World
(John 8:12–21)

28

Then Jesus again spoke to them, saying, "I am the Light of the world; he who follows Me will not walk in the darkness, but will have the Light of life." So the Pharisees said to Him, "You are testifying about Yourself; Your testimony is not true." Jesus answered and said to them, "Even if I testify about Myself, My testimony is true, for I know where I came from and where I am going; but you do not know where I come from or where I am going. You judge according to the flesh; I am not judging anyone. But even if I do judge, My judgment is true; for I am not alone in it, but I and the Father who sent Me. Even in your law it has been written that the testimony of two men is true. I am He who testifies about Myself, and the Father who sent Me testifies about Me." So they were saying to Him, "Where is Your Father?" Jesus answered, "You know neither Me nor My Father; if you knew Me, you would know My Father also." These words He spoke in the treasury, as He taught in the temple; and no one seized Him, because His hour had not yet come. Then He said again to them, "I go away, and you will seek Me, and will die in your sin; where I am going, you cannot come." (8:12–21)

We live in a dark world—a world eclipsed by the long shadow of sin. In desperation, the lost people around us search frantically for truth, without the facility to find it. Because of their spiritual blindness, they only stumble deeper into sin's hopeless gloom—finding themselves utterly trapped in the snares of immorality, idolatry, and all "the unfruitful deeds of darkness" (Eph. 5:11).

The Bible describes sinners as "those who leave the paths of uprightness to walk in the ways of darkness" (Prov. 2:13); consequently, "The way of the wicked is like darkness; they do not know over what they stumble" (4:19). Yet those who foolishly "substitute darkness for light and light for darkness" (Isa. 5:20) are without excuse, "for even though they knew God, they did not honor Him as God or give thanks, but they became futile in their speculations, and their foolish heart was darkened" (Rom. 1:21); they are "darkened in their understanding, excluded from the life of God because of the ignorance that is in them, because of the hardness of their heart" (Eph. 4:18). As a result of that ignorance, "the fool walks in darkness" (Eccl. 2:14), and "he who walks in the darkness does not know where he goes" (John 12:35).

Into this sin-darkened world came Jesus Christ as "the Light [that] shines in the darkness" (1:5); "the true Light which, coming into the world, enlightens every man" (v. 9). When He was an infant, Simeon called Him "a light of revelation to the Gentiles, and the glory of Your people Israel" (Luke 2:32), while Matthew records that His ministry in Galilee was "to fulfill what was spoken through Isaiah the prophet: 'The land of Zebulun and the land of Naphtali, by the way of the sea, beyond the Jordan, Galilee of the Gentiles—the people who were sitting in darkness saw a great light, and those who were sitting in the land and shadow of death, upon them a light dawned'" (Matt. 4:14–16). Jesus Christ is, as He declared, the Light of the world (v. 12; cf. 3:19–21; 9:5; 12:35–36, 46).

One would think that sinners, hopelessly lost in the darkness, would flock to the Light. Yet in a strange paradox, people love the very darkness that ensares them. Like a dying man who cherishes his deadly disease, they cherish the sin that produces spiritual and eternal death. In 3:19 Jesus explained, "This is the judgment, that the Light has come into the world, and men loved the darkness rather than the Light, for their deeds were evil."

But those who through repentance and faith in Jesus Christ "turn from darkness to light and from the dominion of Satan to God . . . receive forgiveness of sins and an inheritance among those who have been sanctified by faith in [God]" (Acts 26:18). They are "rescued . . . from the domain of darkness, and transferred . . . to the kingdom of His beloved Son" (Col. 1:13), becoming "sons of light and sons of day," no longer "of night nor of darkness" (1 Thess. 5:5). Because God "has called [them] out of darkness into His marvelous light" (1 Peter 2:9), those who "were formerly darkness ... now ... are Light in the Lord" (Eph. 5:8).

In 7:37–38 Jesus presented Himself as the source of living water (see the discussion of those verses in chapter 26 of this volume). Here Jesus made another astounding claim about Himself—that He is the Light of the World. As before, His words generated severe opposition, especially from the Jewish religious leaders.

These verses may be discussed under five headings: the area in which the conflict took place, the Lord's assertion, the leaders' accusation, the Lord's answer to that accusation, and His announcement of their impending judgment.

THE AREA

These words He spoke in the treasury, as He taught in the temple; and no one seized Him, because His hour had not yet come. (8:20)

The setting for the Lord's confrontation with the religious leaders was the temple **treasury.** The reference was not to a building, but to the thirteen trumpet-shaped receptacles or treasure boxes located in the section in the temple complex called the Court of the Women (the second outermost court). It was so named because it was as far into the temple area as women were normally permitted to go. Each treasure box was marked to designate how the money put in it would ostensibly be used (for the temple tax and various offerings). It was at this site that Jesus would later observe a poor widow making her cent offering (Mark 12:41–44; Luke 21:1–4).

Since the Court of the Women was a busy public location, it was ideal for Jesus to teach there. The Sanhedrin met in a nearby hall, almost within earshot of the Lord's voice, yet **no one seized Him, because His hour had not yet come.** Jesus was always under the sovereign control of His Father and the divine schedule, so that His enemies were powerless to harm Him before the appointed time (cf. the discussion of this point in chapters 23 and 25 of this volume).

THE ASSERTION

Then Jesus again spoke to them, saying, "I am the Light of the world; he who follows Me will not walk in the darkness, but will have the Light of life." (8:12)

As noted in the previous chapter of this volume, the word **again** appears to link this passage with 7:37–52, rather than 7:53–8:11, likely not in the original. More important, this is the second of seven **"I am"** statements in John's gospel that reveal different facets of Christ's nature as God and His work as Savior (cf. the discussion of 6:35 in chapter 20 of this volume). John had already used the metaphor of light to describe Jesus (1:4, 8–9; cf. Rev. 21:23), and it was one rich in Old Testament allusions (cf. Ex. 13:21–22; 14:19–20; Neh. 9:12, 19; Pss. 27:1; 36:9; 43:3; 44:3; 104:2; 119:105, 130; Prov. 6:23; Isa. 60:19–20; Ezek. 1:4, 13, 26–28; Mic. 7:8; Hab. 3:3–4; Zech. 14:5b–7).

By claiming to be **the Light of the world** Jesus was clearly claiming to be God (cf. Ps. 27:1; Isa. 60:19; 1 John 1:5) and to be Israel's Messiah, sent by God as the "light to the nations" (Isa. 42:6; cf. 49:6; Mal. 4:2).

Jesus Christ alone brings the light of salvation to a sin-cursed world. To the darkness of falsehood He is the light of truth; to the darkness of ignorance He is the light of wisdom; to the darkness of sin He is the light of holiness; to the darkness of sorrow He is the light of joy; and to the darkness of death He is the light of life.

The analogy of light, as with Jesus' earlier use of the metaphor of living water (7:37–39), was particularly relevant to the Feast of Tabernacles. The daily water-pouring ceremony had its nightly counterpart in a lamp-lighting ceremony. In the very Court of the Women where Jesus was speaking, four huge candelabra were lit, pushing light up into the night sky like a searchlight. So brilliant was their light that one ancient Jewish source declared, "There was not a courtyard in Jerusalem that did not reflect [their] light" (cited in F. F. Bruce, *The Gospel of John* [Grand Rapids: Eerdmans, 1983], 206 n. 1). They served as a reminder of the pillar of fire by which God had guided Israel in the wilderness (Ex. 13:21–22). The people—even the most dignified leaders—danced exuberantly around the candelabra through the night, holding blazing torches in their hands and singing songs of praise. It was against the backdrop of that ceremony that Jesus made the stunning announcement that He is the true Light of the world.

But unlike the temporary and stationary candelabra, Jesus is a light that never goes out and a light to be followed. Just as Israel followed the pillar of fire in the wilderness (Ex. 40:36–38), so Jesus called men to follow Him (John 1:43; 10:4, 27; 12:26; 21:19, 22; Matt. 4:19; 8:22; 9:9; 10:38; 16:24; 19:21). The one **who follows** Him, Jesus promised, **will not walk in the darkness** of sin, the world, and Satan, **but will have the Light** that produces spiritual **life** (cf. 1:4; Pss. 27:1; 36:9; Isa. 49:6; Acts 13:47; 2 Cor. 4:4–6; Eph. 5:14; 1 John 1:7). Having been illumined by Jesus, believers reflect His light in the dark world (Matt. 5:14; Eph. 5:8; Phil. 2:15;

1 Thess. 5:5); "They, having kindled their torches at His bright flame, show to the world something of His light" (Leon Morris, *The Gospel According to John,* The New International Commentary on the New Testament [Grand Rapids: Eerdmans, 1979], 438).

Akoloutheō (**follows**) is sometimes used in a general sense to speak of the crowds who followed Jesus (e.g., 6:2; Matt. 4:25; 8:1; 12:15; Mark 2:15; 3:7; Luke 7:9; 9:11). But it can also refer, more specifically, to following Him as a true disciple (e.g., 1:43; 10:4, 27; 12:26; Matt. 4:20, 22; 9:9; 10:38; 16:24; 19:27; Mark 9:38). In that context, it has the connotation of complete submission to Jesus as Lord. God does not accept a half-hearted following of Christ—of receiving Him as Savior, but not following Him as Lord. The person who comes to Jesus comes to Him on His terms, or he does not come at all—a truth Jesus illustrated in Matthew 8:18–22:

> Now when Jesus saw a crowd around Him, He gave orders to depart to the other side of the sea. Then a scribe came and said to Him, "Teacher, I will follow You wherever You go." Jesus said to him, "The foxes have holes and the birds of the air have nests, but the Son of Man has nowhere to lay His head." Another of the disciples said to Him, "Lord, permit me first to go and bury my father." But Jesus said to him, "Follow Me, and allow the dead to bury their own dead."

An even more striking illustration of that principle is found in Jesus' dialogue with the rich young ruler:

> A ruler questioned Him, saying, "Good Teacher, what shall I do to inherit eternal life?" And Jesus said to him, "Why do you call Me good? No one is good except God alone. You know the commandments, 'Do not commit adultery, do not murder, do not steal, do not bear false witness, honor your father and mother.'" And he said, "All these things I have kept from my youth." When Jesus heard this, He said to him, "One thing you still lack; sell all that you possess and distribute it to the poor, and you shall have treasure in heaven; and come, follow Me." But when he had heard these things, he became very sad, for he was extremely rich. And Jesus looked at him and said, "How hard it is for those who are wealthy to enter the kingdom of God! For it is easier for a camel to go through the eye of a needle than for a rich man to enter the kingdom of God." They who heard it said, "Then who can be saved?" But He said, "The things that are impossible with people are possible with God." (Luke 18:18–27)

In a shocking contradiction of contemporary evangelistic principles, Jesus actually turned away an eager prospect. But the Lord was not interested in making salvation artificially easy for people, but genuine. He wanted their absolute allegiance, obedience, and submission. In Luke 9:23–24 He said, "If anyone wishes to come after Me, he must deny himself, and take up his cross daily and follow Me. For whoever wishes to save his life will lose it, but whoever loses his life for My sake, he is the one who will save it." (For a discussion of the biblical view of the lordship of Christ, see John MacArthur, *The Gospel According to Jesus,* rev. ed. [Grand Rapids: Zondervan, 1994], and *The Gospel According to the Apostles* [Nashville: Thomas Nelson, 1993.)

Following Christ is not burdensome, as walking in the light illustrates. It is far easier than stumbling around in the dark (cf. Jer. 13:16).

THE ACCUSATION

So the Pharisees said to Him, "You are testifying about Yourself; Your testimony is not true." (8:13)

Not unexpectedly, **the Pharisees** reacted negatively to Jesus' claim. In what was likely a mocking reference to the Lord's own words in 5:31 ("If I alone testify about Myself, My testimony is not true."), they **said to Him, "You are testifying about Yourself; Your testimony is not true."** According to the Old Testament Law, every fact in a legal matter had to be established by the testimony of more than one witness (Num. 35:30; Deut. 17:6; 19:15; cf. Matt. 18:16; 2 Cor. 13:1; 1 Tim. 5:19; Heb. 10:28). In typical fashion, the Pharisees refused to consider the possibility that Jesus' claim might be true. Instead, they arbitrarily dismissed it on a legal technicality.

In reality, of course, there were others who could testify to the truthfulness of Jesus' claims (e.g., John the Baptist [1:7–8, 19–27, 34, 36; 3:26; 5:33], the Twelve [1:49; 6:69; Matt. 14:33; 16:16], the Samaritan woman [John 4:39], Martha [11:27], those who witnessed His raising of Lazarus [12:17], Jesus' works [5:36; 10:25], the Scriptures [5:39], and, above all, the Father [see the discussion of vv. 17–18 below]). Thus, there is no contradiction between Jesus' statements here and in 5:31; He was not, as the Pharisees alleged, the only witness who could verify His claims.

The Pharisees' skeptical response illustrates just how obtuse unbelief is; it is never convinced no matter how compelling the evidence. Jesus performed miracles unparalleled in human history (15:24). Yet "though He had performed so many signs before them, . . . they were not believing in Him" (12:37; cf. Matt. 11:20–24). Nonetheless, to those who honestly seek the truth Jesus promised, "If anyone is willing to do [the Father's] will, he will know of the teaching, whether it is of God or whether I speak from Myself" (John 7:17).

THE ANSWER

Jesus answered and said to them, "Even if I testify about Myself, My testimony is true, for I know where I came from and where I am going; but you do not know where I come from or where I am going. You judge according to the flesh; I am not judging anyone. But even if I do judge, My judgment is true; for I am not alone in it, but I and the Father who sent Me. Even in your law it has been written that the testimony of two men is true. I am He who testifies about Myself, and the Father who sent Me testifies about Me." So they were saying to Him, "Where is Your Father?" Jesus answered, "You know neither Me nor My Father; if you knew Me, you would know My Father also." (8:14–19)

In response to the Pharisees' issue of single testimony, **Jesus answered and said to them, "Even if I testify about Myself, My testimony is true."** Obviously, the testimony of one person may be true, even if not corroborated by anyone else. The demand for two or three witnesses was a means for establishing the truth in a court of law. What Jesus said was the truth in utter perfection, since God is true (Rom. 3:4; Titus 1:2; Heb. 6:18). Still, He gave His enemies three evidences to support His self-testimony as the truth, each related to His deity—the very thing that scandalized them the most.

First, Jesus supported His claim by referring to His divine origin and destiny, while the Pharisees were ignorant of both. Therefore He was qualified to testify about Himself, but they were not. **"For I know where I came from and where I am going,"** He told them, **"but you do not know where I come from or where I am going."** The Lord was always conscious of His heavenly origin and destiny; in 16:28 He said: "I came forth from the Father and have come into the world; I am leaving the world again and going to the Father" (cf. 3:11–13; 5:36–37; 6:38; 7:28–29, 33; 8:42; 10:36; 13:3; 14:28; 16:5; 17:5, 8, 13, 18). His self-knowledge and divine omniscience (cf. 2:25; 16:30; 21:17) thoroughly confirmed His testimony.

His opponents, on the other hand, had no such knowledge; they did not know either where He came from or where He was going. Like the crowd (7:27), they thought that they knew, but were terribly mistaken. In fact, they were unaware of His earthly birthplace (7:41–42, 52), let alone His heavenly origin.

Jesus further exposed their ignorance when He declared to them, **"You judge according to the flesh;"** according to earthly standards; as sinful men in a fallen world. They not only understood nothing of His heavenly origin, but even what they thought they knew about Him was incorrect. Thus, their judgment of Him was limited, superficial, and wrong. Proud, arrogant, and self-righteous, they had failed to heed Jesus' earlier admonition, "Do not judge according to appearance, but judge with righteous judgment" (7:24). Like the pagans of whom Paul wrote in 1 Corinthians 1:21 they, too, "through [their] wisdom did not come to know God." To the Jews Jesus was "a stumbling block" (1 Cor. 1:3; cf. 2:14). They were the opposite of the apostle Paul, who wrote to these same Corinthians, "Therefore from now on we recognize no one according to the flesh; even though we have known Christ according to the flesh, yet now we know Him in this way no longer" (2 Cor. 5:16). Because believers have spiritual understanding, we see Christ for who He truly is, and even see all other people as spiritual and eternal souls.

There are two ways of understanding Jesus' statement, **"I am not judging anyone."** He may have meant that He did not judge according to the flesh (superficially, externally) like the Pharisees did (cf. D. A. Carson, *The Gospel According to John,* The Pillar New Testament Commentary [Grand Rapids: Eerdmans, 1991], 339). Or the Lord may have meant that He did not judge anyone yet, since "God did not send the Son into the world to judge the world, but that the world might be saved through Him" (3:17; cf. 12:47; Luke 9:56). In the future, however, Jesus will judge, "For not even the Father judges anyone, but He has given all judgment to the Son" (5:22; cf. v. 27; 9:39; Matt. 16:27; 25:31–46; Acts 10:42; 17:31; Rom. 2:16; 2 Tim. 4:1).

The second support for the credibility of Jesus' testimony is based on His divine nature shared with the Father. **"But even if I do judge,"** the Lord went on to say, **"My judgment is true; for I am not alone in it, but I and the Father who sent Me."** By insisting that He was one with the Father in judgment, Jesus was claiming essential equality with Him. In 5:17 He made a similar claim: "My Father is working until now, and I Myself am working." Enraged, "the Jews were seeking all the more to kill Him, because He not only was breaking the Sabbath, but also was calling God His own Father, making Himself equal with God" (v. 18). Jesus' testimony was true because He was of the same nature as the one true, living God (10:30).

As a final vindication that His self-witness was true, Jesus rebutted the Pharisees' false allegation that He was His only witness (v. 13). **In the law** to which they had appealed and which was binding on them **it has been written that the testimony of two men is true** (Deut. 17:6; 19:15). Reinforcing the very claim that most outraged His enemies, the Lord then provided those two witnesses, declaring, **"I am He who testifies about Myself, and the Father who sent Me testifies about Me."** In perfect agreement, the Father and the Son bear witness to the truth of Jesus' claims (cf. v. 29 and the discussion of 5:31–32, 37–38 in chapter 17 of this volume). He called on God as witness to the validity of

His claim, since "if Jesus really stands in the relationship to God in which He says He does, then no mere man is in a position to bear witness. No human witness can authenticate a divine relationship" (Morris, *The Gospel According to John*, 443).

Predictably, even that did not satisfy the Pharisees. Thinking in purely human terms (cf. 3:4; 6:42, 52), **they were saying to Him, "Where is Your Father?"** Were they asking to see Joseph, who likely had died by this time, to prove Jesus had an earthly father? In light of verse 41, were they intending to insult Him as illegitimate? In any case, they rejected Him. Jesus' reply was simple and devastating: **"You know neither Me nor My Father; if you knew Me, you would know My Father also."** The very fact that they thought like they did proves that they did not know the Father. In Matthew 11:27 Jesus said, "All things have been handed over to Me by My Father; and no one knows the Son except the Father; nor does anyone know the Father except the Son, and anyone to whom the Son wills to reveal Him." Those who reject the Son give incontrovertible proof that they do not know the eternal Father (cf. 1:18; 14:6–9). Although they prided themselves on knowing Him, the Pharisees—blinded by their own hard-heartedness—were actually ignorant of spiritual reality (Matt. 15:14; 23:16, 24).

THE ANNOUNCEMENT

Then He said again to them, "I go away, and you will seek Me, and will die in your sin; where I am going, you cannot come." (8:21)

In 7:33–34 Jesus had warned the crowd, "For a little while longer I am with you, then I go to Him who sent Me. You will seek Me, and will not find Me; and where I am, you cannot come." Here He said again that He would **go away** (a reference to His impending death, resurrection, and ascension to the Father). But this time the Lord added the warning that those who reject Him **will die in** their **sin** and not be with Him in the Father's presence in the glory of heaven. Later in this dialogue He would repeat that warning in even stronger terms (v. 24). The reality of this sobering truth, which is repeated throughout Scripture, is that those who reject Christ will suffer the consequences of their sin—eternal separation from God. By refusing the Light of the world, they doom themselves to the eternal darkness of hell (Matt. 8:12; 22:13; 25:30).

How to Die in Your Sins
(John 8:22–30)

29

So the Jews were saying, "Surely He will not kill Himself, will He, since He says, 'Where I am going, you cannot come'?" And He was saying to them, "You are from below, I am from above; you are of this world, I am not of this world. Therefore I said to you that you will die in your sins; for unless you believe that I am He, you will die in your sins." So they were saying to Him, "Who are You?" Jesus said to them, "What have I been saying to you from the beginning? I have many things to speak and to judge concerning you, but He who sent Me is true; and the things which I heard from Him, these I speak to the world." They did not realize that He had been speaking to them about the Father. So Jesus said, "When you lift up the Son of Man, then you will know that I am He, and I do nothing on My own initiative, but I speak these things as the Father taught Me. And He who sent Me is with Me; He has not left Me alone, for I always do the things that are pleasing to Him." As He spoke these things, many came to believe in Him. (8:22–30)

Life in a fallen world is full of missed opportunities and personal regrets—the painful and sometimes devastating consequences of poor, sinful choices. The original missed opportunity, the one from which all the rest flow, came in the Garden of Eden. By eating the fruit that God had forbidden, Adam (and Eve) directly violated the Lord's command. Adam's sin cost him (and the entire human race) the privilege of continuing in uninterrupted fellowship with God (Gen. 3:6–8). As a result, "the Lord God sent him out from the garden of Eden, to cultivate the ground from which he was taken. So He drove the man out; and at the east of the garden of Eden He stationed the cherubim and the flaming sword which turned every direction to guard the way to the tree of life" (vv. 23–24).

Moses and Aaron also experienced the painful consequences of a sinful choice. Their disobedience at Meribah cost them the opportunity to enter the Promised Land:

> And the Lord spoke to Moses, saying, "Take the rod; and you and your brother Aaron assemble the congregation and speak to the rock before their eyes, that it may yield its water. You shall thus bring forth water for them out of the rock and let the congregation and their beasts drink." So Moses took the rod from before the Lord, just as He had commanded him; and Moses and Aaron gathered the assembly before the rock. And he said to them, "Listen now, you rebels; shall we bring forth water for you out of this rock?" Then Moses lifted up his hand and struck the rock twice with his rod; and water came forth abundantly, and the congregation and their beasts drank. But the Lord said to Moses and Aaron, "Because you have not believed Me, to treat Me as holy in the sight of the sons of Israel, therefore you shall not bring this assembly into the land which I have given them." (Num. 20:7–12)

Solomon, too, faced the consequences that poor decisions bring. Though he was Israel's wisest and wealthiest king, he forfeited the opportunity to fully enjoy the blessings God had granted him, "for when Solomon was old, his wives turned his heart away after other gods; and his heart was not wholly devoted to the Lord his God, as the heart of David his father had been" (1 Kings 11:4). As a result, life for Solomon became nothing but vanity (Eccl. 1:2).

Judas Iscariot had the priceless opportunity of being one of the twelve men closest to the Lord Jesus Christ during His earthly ministry. Yet he threw away that privilege for a mere "thirty pieces of silver" (Matt. 26:15) and betrayed Jesus (26:47–50). By never repenting of his horrific treachery, Judas damned his soul forever (Acts 1:25; cf. Matt. 26:24).

Judas was the most notorious example of one who saw Jesus' works, heard His words, observed His sinless life, and yet rejected Him. But he was certainly not the only one. By the time the dialogue recorded in this passage took place, all in Israel were well aware of Jesus' ministry. For the past three years He had performed countless miracles. He had virtually banished disease from Israel, miraculously fed thousands of people, authoritatively cast out demons, and instantly calmed a raging storm on the Sea of Galilee (and later even walked across it). Those amazing and unprecedented (15:24; cf. 9:32; Matt. 9:33; Mark 2:12) miracles clearly demonstrated that Jesus was the Son of God (John 10:25; cf. v. 38; 3:2; 5:36; 7:31; 14:11; Acts 2:22)—as did the Lord's astonishing claims (John 4:25–26; 5:18) and profound teaching (cf. Matt. 7:28–29; 13:54; Luke 4:32; 19:48; John 7:46).

In light of the overwhelming evidence, unbelief in Jesus is inexcusable. Those who hear the gospel and reject it will be eternally punished—with no one to blame but themselves. (It should be noted that even those who have not heard the gospel are still culpable for rejecting the truth that they have been given. Such truth includes aspects of the existence and character of God, as revealed through both the created order [Rom. 1:18–21] and the conscience [Rom. 2:14–15].) Thus all who reject Jesus Christ are fully responsible for choosing to die in their sins (John 3:19).

This passage reveals four ways people can ensure such a tragic and eternal death: by being self-righteous, worldly, unbelieving, or willfully ignorant.

Be Self-righteous

So the Jews were saying, "Surely He will not kill Himself, will He, since He says, 'Where I am going, you cannot come'?" (8:22)

In 8:21 Jesus had warned the self-righteous religious leaders that their unwillingness to believe in Him meant they would die in their sins. Unforgiven, unredeemed, and unprepared to meet God, they had accumulated a lifetime of culpability that would result in an eternity of punishment. The Lord repeated what He had said earlier to the crowd (7:33–34), that He was going to a place where those who refuse to believe in Him can never come. In response to that earlier declaration, His enemies had speculated that He might be planning to leave Israel for the Diaspora (7:35). Here, however, they offered a more sinister suggestion.

Faced with Jesus' startling pronouncement in verse 21, the response of **the Jews** (the leaders in particular are in view here) was to turn His sobering warning into a venomous joke. **"Surely He will not kill Himself, will He?"** they asked sarcastically. Ironically, those who were plotting to take His life asked if He intended to commit suicide. They understood that when He said, **"Where I am going, you cannot come,"** Jesus was speaking of His death. The Jews abhorred suicide, and believed that those who killed themselves went to the blackest part of hell. Reflecting this conventional belief, the first-century Jewish historian Josephus wrote, "The souls of those whose hands have acted madly against themselves are received by the darkest place in Hades" (*The Wars of the Jews,* iii. viii. 5). Since they assumed that they were going to heaven, the Jews mockingly suggested that Jesus must be speaking of killing Himself, in which case He would go to hell.

Smugly confident in their self-righteousness, they were not just deaf to Jesus' words, but they mockingly, blasphemously twisted their meaning. It is true that Jesus, though not committing suicide, would give up His life voluntarily. In John 10:17–18 He said,

> "For this reason the Father loves Me, because I lay down My life so that I may take it again. No one has taken it away from Me, but I lay it down on My own initiative. I have authority to lay it down, and I have authority to take it up again. This commandment I received from My Father" (cf. 6:51; Matt. 20:28).

But He would not die by His own hand, but rather at the hands of those very men who now mocked Him (Acts 2:23). And the place to which He was referring—where He would go but they could not follow—was not hell, but heaven.

Self-righteousness is a deadly deception, and utterly contrary to genuine salvation. The Judaism of Jesus' day was an intricate legalistic system of salvation by human achievement. The people based their hope of salvation on performing good works, observing ceremonies and rituals, and, above all, keeping the Law (at least outwardly). As the apostle Paul wrote, "Not knowing about God's righteousness and seeking to establish their own, they did not subject themselves to the righteousness of God" (Rom. 10:3). Tragically, they failed to understand what Paul, who had been raised a zealous Pharisee (Acts 23:6; Gal. 1:13–14), later came to understand that "by the works of the Law no flesh will be justified in [God's] sight" (Rom. 3:20), because to break the Law in one place, one time, is to be guilty of all (James 2:10).

The truth that salvation cannot be attained through self-righteousness should have come as no surprise to anyone familiar with the Old Testament. In Psalm 14:2–3 David wrote, "The Lord has looked down from heaven upon the sons of men to see if there are any who understand, who seek after God. They have all turned aside, together they have become corrupt; there is no one who does good, not even one." "All the ways of a man are clean in his own sight," Solomon noted, "but the Lord weighs the motives" (Prov. 16:2), while in 20:9 he added, "Who can say, 'I have cleansed my heart, I am pure from my sin'?" Proverbs 30:12 warns,

"There is a kind who is pure in his own eyes, yet is not washed from his filthiness." "I will declare your [false, external] righteousness and your deeds," God declared to wayward Israel, "but they will not profit you" (Isa. 57:12). A few chapters later Isaiah expressed the utter inability of sinners to save themselves: "We have sinned . . . and we need to be saved. But we are all like an unclean thing, and all our righteousnesses are like filthy rags" (Isa. 64:5–6 NKJV).

The New Testament also teaches that no one can be saved by self-righteousness. In Matthew 5:20 Jesus told His hearers, "Unless your righteousness surpasses that of the scribes and Pharisees, you will not enter the kingdom of heaven." External compliance to the Law will save no one; salvation comes only from Christ's righteousness imputed to those who believe (2 Cor. 5:21). That genuine righteousness far surpasses the outward, legalistic righteousness of the scribes and Pharisees. Though the latter impresses men, it does not result in salvation (Matt. 6:1; cf. Rom. 3:20). The Lord scathingly denounced the Pharisees as those who "outwardly appear righteous to men, but inwardly . . . are full of hypocrisy and lawlessness" (Matt. 23:28; cf. vv. 23, 25).

In Matthew 9:11 the Pharisees demanded of Jesus' disciples, "Why is your Teacher eating with the tax collectors and sinners?" They did not approve of His interaction with the riffraff of Jewish society. The Lord's devastating reply was, "It is not those who are healthy who need a physician, but those who are sick. But go and learn what this means: 'I desire compassion, and not sacrifice,' for I did not come to call the righteous, but sinners" (vv. 12–13; cf. Luke 15:7). Jesus denounced the Pharisees as "those who justify [themselves] in the sight of men, but God knows [their] hearts; for that which is highly esteemed among men is detestable in the sight of God'" (Luke 16:15). Later in Luke's gospel Jesus

> told this parable to some people who trusted in themselves that they were righteous, and viewed others with contempt: "Two men went up into the temple to pray, one a Pharisee and the other a tax collector. The Pharisee stood and was praying this to himself: 'God, I thank You that I am not like other people: swindlers, unjust, adulterers, or even like this tax collector. I fast twice a week; I pay tithes of all that I get.' But the tax collector, standing some distance away, was even unwilling to lift up his eyes to heaven, but was beating his breast, saying, 'God, be merciful to me, the sinner!' I tell you, this man went to his house justified rather than the other; for everyone who exalts himself will be humbled, but he who humbles himself will be exalted." (Luke 18:9–14)

To the Philippians Paul wrote that salvation comes "not [from] having a righteousness of [one's] own derived from the Law, but that which is through faith in Christ, the righteousness which comes from God on the basis of faith" (Phil. 3:9; cf. Gal. 2:16–21). In Titus 3:5 he added, "He saved us, not on the basis of deeds which we have done in righteousness, but according to His mercy, by the washing of regeneration and renewing by the Holy Spirit." The Jews should have known from the Scriptures the truth that Paul wrote to the churches of Galatia:

> Even so Abraham believed God, and it was reckoned to him as righteousness. Therefore, be sure that it is those who are of faith who are sons of Abraham. The Scripture, foreseeing that God would justify the Gentiles by faith, preached the gospel beforehand to Abraham, saying, "All the nations will be blessed in you." So then those who are of faith are blessed with Abraham, the believer. For as many as are of the works of the Law are under a curse; for it is written, "Cursed is everyone who does not abide by all things written in the book of the Law, to perform them." Now that no one is justified by the Law before God is evident; for, "The righteous man shall live by faith." However, the Law is not of faith; on the contrary, "He who practices them shall live by them." Christ redeemed us from the curse of the Law, having become a curse for us—for it is written, "Cursed is everyone who hangs on a tree"—in order that in Christ Jesus the blessing of Abraham might come to the Gentiles, so that we would receive the promise of the Spirit through faith. (Gal. 3:6–14)

The scribes and Pharisees were the epitome of self-righteous human achievers. Those who follow their example and trust in good works, morality, and religious activities to save them; who refuse to admit their inability to contribute anything to saving themselves and cry out, "God, be merciful to me, the sinner!" (Luke 18:13), will likewise die in their sins. The self-righteous will never see heaven.

Be Worldly

And He was saying to them, "You are from below, I am from above; you are of this world, I am not of this world." (8:23)

Jesus refused to acknowledge the Jews' mocking suggestion that He was going to commit suicide and thus condemn Himself to hell (cf. 1 Peter 2:23). Instead, He elaborated on His warning in verse 21 that they would die in their sin and not go where He was going (heaven). The Lord pointed out that their origin, like their destiny, was altogether different than His. They were from a completely different realm; they were **from below;** that is, they were part **of this world.**

Kosmos (**world**) is an important New Testament term. It refers in this context to the invisible spiritual system of evil that opposes the kingdom of God, comprises "every lofty thing raised up against the knowledge of God" (2 Cor. 10:5), and is controlled by Satan (John 12:31; 14:30; 16:11; 1 John 5:19). The world does not recognize Jesus' true identity (1:10), or that of believers (1 John 3:1). It is also ignorant of the Holy Spirit whom Jesus sent (14:17). Those engulfed in the world "[love] the darkness rather than the Light, for their deeds [are] evil" (John 3:19). As a result, they are utterly blind to spiritual truth (2 Cor. 4:4; cf. Matt. 13:11; John 12:39–40; Rom. 8:5; 1 Cor. 2:14)—having filled themselves with hatred toward Jesus (and His followers; John 15:18–19; 17:14; 1 John 3:13) for confronting their sin (John 7:7; 15:18). Because it hates God, the world rejoices in the death of His Son (16:20; cf. Matt. 21:37–39).

Materialism, humanism, immorality, pride, and selfishness—"the lust of the flesh and the lust of the eyes and the boastful pride of life" (1 John 2:16)—are the world's hallmarks. It is utterly opposed to divine truth, righteousness, virtue, and holiness. Its opinions are wrong; its aims are selfish; its pleasures are sinful; its influences are demoralizing; its politics are corrupt; its honors are empty; its smiles are phony; its love is false and fickle.

The source of the Jews' antagonism and hostility to Christ was hell itself; they were, as Jesus would forcefully declare in verse 44, children of the devil, walking "according to the course of this world, according to the prince of the power of the air, of the spirit that is now working in the sons of disobedience" (Eph. 2:2). Their "friendship with [the Greek word could also be translated "affection for" or "love for"] the world" marked their "hostility toward God," because "whoever wishes to be a friend of the world makes himself an enemy of God" (James 4:4). "If anyone loves the world," John added, "the love of the Father is not in him" (1 John 2:15).

In sharp contrast to His opponents, Jesus is **from above** (heaven) and thus **not** a part **of this world** system. As noted in the discussion of 8:14 in chapter 28 of this volume, the Lord was always conscious of His heavenly origin (3:11–13; 5:36–37; 6:33, 38, 50–51, 58; 7:28–29, 33; 8:42; 10:36; 13:3; 14:28; 16:5, 28; 17:5, 8, 13, 18; 18:36; cf. 1 Cor. 15:47; Eph. 4:10).

Though once "without God in the world" (Eph. 2:12), believers are no longer part of the world system (cf. Col. 1:13; 1 John 4:5–6). "If you were of the world," Jesus said to His disciples, "the world would love its own; but because you are not of the world, but I chose you out of the world, because of this the world hates you" (John 15:19). They "are not of the world, even as [Jesus is] not of the world" (17:14, 16). When they were redeemed, they "escaped the corruption that is in the world by lust" (2 Peter 1:4). On the other hand, to be "worldly-minded" is to be "devoid of the Spirit" (Jude 19) and thus die in your sins and be consigned to hell.

BE UNBELIEVING

"Therefore I said to you that you will die in your sins; for unless you believe that I am He, you will die in your sins." (8:24)

Here Jesus went beyond the self-righteousness and worldliness that damns to the ultimate issue—unbelief. Repeating His warning from verse 21, Jesus declared that those who reject Him **will die in** their **sins** because they refuse to **believe that I am He.** The Lord's use of the absolute, unqualified phrase **I am** (the pronoun **He** does not appear in the Greek text) is nothing less than a direct claim to full deity. When Moses asked God His name He replied, "I AM WHO I AM" (Ex. 3:14). In the Septuagint (the Greek translation of the Old Testament), that is the same phrase (*egō eimi*) Jesus used here (the Septuagint similarly uses *egō eimi* of God in Deut. 32:39; Isa. 41:4; 43:10, 25; 45:18; 46:4). Jesus was applying to Himself the tetragrammaton (YHWH, often transliterated as Yahweh)—the name of God that was so sacred that the Jews refused to pronounce it. Unlike many modern cult groups (such as the Jehovah's Witnesses), the Jews of Jesus' day understood perfectly that He was claiming to be God. In fact, they were so shocked by His use of that name, in reference to Himself (cf. vv. 28, 58), that they attempted to stone Him for blasphemy (v. 59).

Unmistakably, the Lord Himself says that those who reject Him cannot be saved, but will **die in** their **sins.** To be a Christian one must believe the full biblical revelation about Jesus: that He is the eternal second person of the Trinity, that He entered space and time as God incarnate, that He was born of a virgin, that He lived a sinless life, that His death on the cross is the only sufficient, substitionary sacrifice for the sins of all who would ever believe in Him, that He rose from the dead and ascended to the Father in heaven, that He now intercedes for His own redeemed people, and that He will one day return in glory. To reject those truths about Him is to "be led astray from the simplicity and purity of devotion to Christ" (2 Cor. 11:3), to worship "another Jesus" (v. 4), to be cursed by God (Gal. 1:8–9), and ultimately to hear the Lord say, "I never knew you; depart from Me, you who practice lawlessness" (Matt. 7:23).

The word **unless** introduces the only hope of escape from God's wrath and judgment on sin. R. C. H. Lenski notes,

> The sins of these men will destroy them by robbing them of life eternal only if they refuse to believe in Jesus. The "if" clause [in the KJV] is pure gospel, extending its blessed invitation anew. Yet it is again combined with the warning about dying in sins. This note of warning with its terrifying threat persists because these Jews had chosen the course of unbelief. Yet the "if" opens the door of life in the wall of sin. (*The*

Interpretation of St. John's Gospel [Reprint; Peabody, Mass.: Hendrickson, 1998], 614)

Persistent unwillingness to believe the truth about Jesus Christ, by its very nature, precludes the possibility of forgiveness, since salvation comes only through faith in Him (3:15–16, 36; 6:40, 47; Acts 16:31; Rom. 10:9–10; Gal. 3:26; 1 John 5:10–13). Those who continue in unbelief, refusing to embrace in faith all that Jesus is and has done, will die in their sins and be lost forever (cf. 3:18, 36; Heb. 2:3). And apart from the knowledge of the gospel of Jesus Christ, no one can be saved. Therefore believers are commanded to go to the world and preach Christ to everyone (Mark 16:15–16; Luke 24:47; Acts 1:8).

BE WILLFULLY IGNORANT

So they were saying to Him, "Who are You?" Jesus said to them, "What have I been saying to you from the beginning? I have many things to speak and to judge concerning you, but He who sent Me is true; and the things which I heard from Him, these I speak to the world." They did not realize that He had been speaking to them about the Father. So Jesus said, "When you lift up the Son of Man, then you will know that I am He, and I do nothing on My own initiative, but I speak these things as the Father taught Me. And He who sent Me is with Me; He has not left Me alone, for I always do the things that are pleasing to Him." As He spoke these things, many came to believe in Him. (8:25–30)

The jailer holding them captive in unbelief was their own obstinate ignorance. The Jews' incredulous question, **"Who are You?"** was amazing in light of all the miraculous signs Jesus had performed (5:36; cf. Matt. 11:4–5) and the repeated claims He had already made (cf. 5:17ff.; 6:35ff.; 7:28–38; 8:12). There may have been an undercurrent of more mockery in the question; they may have been, in effect, sarcastically asking a rhetorical question: "Who are You to tell us we are going to die in our sins?" But the query in any case reflects their stubborn, willful ignorance (cf. Matt. 15:14; 23:16–26). The overwhelming evidence made it patently obvious who Jesus was, so He merely replied that He was who He had been claiming to be **from the beginning** of His ministry. He had nothing more to say to the willful ignorance of hard-hearted unbelief.

Nonetheless, Jesus did have **many things to speak and to judge concerning** them. They had been given more than enough revelation to be held responsible; their ignorance was inexcusable. His judgment of them would be in perfect harmony with the Father's will, for it was the Father **who sent** Him, and Jesus spoke only **the things which** He **heard from Him** (cf. vv. 28, 40; 3:32, 34; 5:30; 7:16; 8:16; 15:15; 17:8).

Incredibly, despite the fact that Jesus had spoken so clearly to them, **they** still **did not realize that He had been speaking to them about the Father.** Such was the deceptive power of their willful unbelief. They had no ears to hear.

There was coming a day, however, when the truth of His claims would be confirmed, so as to become undeniable. Therefore **Jesus said, "When you lift up the Son of Man** (a reference to His crucifixion and implying His resurrection; cf. 3:14; 12:32–33), **then you will know that I am He, and I do nothing on My own initiative, but I speak these things as the Father taught Me"** (cf. 3:34; 5:19, 30; 6:38). Christ's death and resurrection vindicated every claim ever made for Jesus by the prophets and apostles, and erased all doubt to any open mind as to His deity. That great and glorious work proved that He truly spoke the **things** that **the Father taught** Him, that the Father was one **with** Him and could **not** leave Him **alone,** and that He **always** did **the things that are pleasing to** the Father, for He could do nothing else in His divine perfection (Heb. 7:26).

Some of the Jews who rejected Jesus would later realize that they had been terribly mistaken about Him. On the day of Pentecost alone, about 3,000 Jews would come to receive Him as the Messiah (Acts 2:36–37, 41, 47). Even on this occasion, six months before the cross, His words were so powerful that **as He spoke these things, many came to believe in Him,** at least outwardly (cf. the exposition of 8:31–36 in chapter 30 of this volume). But the majority, in spite of the evidence, refused to believe—choosing instead to remain self-righteous, worldly, unbelieving, and willfully ignorant to the end. As a result, they condemned themselves to ultimately die in their sins and never see heaven, but suffer eternal wrath.

The Truth Will Make You Free (John 8:31–36)

30

So Jesus was saying to those Jews who had believed Him, "If you continue in My word, then you are truly disciples of Mine; and you will know the truth, and the truth will make you free." They answered Him, "We are Abraham's descendants and have never yet been enslaved to anyone; how is it that You say, 'You will become free'?" Jesus answered them, "Truly, truly, I say to you, everyone who commits sin is the slave of sin. The slave does not remain in the house forever; the son does remain forever. So if the Son makes you free, you will be free indeed." (8:31–36)

Throughout history people have always sought to know the truth about reality, about what is right and wrong, and about what is meaningful and purposeful in life. As a result, endless philosophies, worldviews, and religious systems have arisen over the centuries, each purporting to teach absolute truth, and each in turn canceling out the "absolute" truths of those that came before it.

The belief that mankind, on his own, could formulate the perfect philosophical system—one that would fully explain all of reality—reached its peak during the Enlightenment. Human reason, it was thought, would eventually discover the answers to all of life's questions, and thereby solve all of society's problems. The assumption was that, through intellectual achievements and the growing body of scientific knowledge, humanity would eventually bring about a utopia. Hence, there was no need for religion, which had kept people in stifling darkness for centuries. There was no interest in divine revelation or salvation, since man believed he could save himself from his problems.

But the optimism of the Enlightenment has faded to black in recent times. The unimaginable slaughter of two world wars, the unfathomable evil of the Holocaust, and the terrifying reality of nuclear war quickly shattered the unrealistic idealism of the eighteenth and nineteenth centuries. In its place, skepticism and pessimism began to take hold, as feelings of uncertainty (about life and even reality) became more and more widespread. Increasingly, the very concept of truth itself came under fire, especially the possibility of knowing absolute truth. Sinners want to do evil and feel no guilt, so the lack of absolutes accommodates the desperately wicked human heart (Jer. 17:9). As Francis Schaeffer put it, all of Western culture—including philosophy, art, music, literature, education, and modern theology—in rejecting Scripture plunged beneath the line of despair (see especially his books *The God Who Is There* and *Escape from Reason*). People imagined that by denying the existence of absolute truth and by throwing off the shackles of biblical morality they would finally be set free. Instead, they found themselves only more empty and enslaved to destructive passions.

The skepticism of the twentieth century culminated with the rise of postmodernism, a worldview that is still in vogue today. In contrast to the modernists, whose rationalistic optimism flowed out of the Enlightenment, postmodernists reject the notion that ultimate truth is knowable or even exists. Rather, they contend that the "truths" people believe are merely societal norms created by the culture in which they live. Thus there are no timeless truths, but only ephemeral preferences. Whatever works for people is true for them; pragmatism and relativism reign supreme. (Ironically, the only thing postmodernists are absolutely certain of is that nothing is absolutely certain. As a result, they are forced to defend an illogical position—namely that it is a universal, comprehensive truth that there are no universal, comprehensive truths.)

Because postmodernists want to sin freely (primarily, it seems, in the sexual area), they need to view all truth as culturally determined, and argue that no morality or law is supreme. The noblest virtue therefore is tolerance of other views. Such is especially true in the area of morals, where imposing one's values on someone else is seen as an egregious offense. That makes biblical Christianity the most intolerable belief. By rejecting the possibility of absolute truth, postmodernism commits eternal suicide by simultaneously rejecting the only path to true freedom—the absolutely, universally, and exclusively true message of the gospel. Even the contemporary church no longer believes in the gospel as the only way to heaven; 85 percent of American "Christians" believe there are other ways to heaven. Ninety-one percent of Roman Catholics agree (*Newsweek,* August 2005). Obviously, this postmodern tolerance redefines the gospel and missions in a disastrous way, and denigrates doctrine and dogmatism as unloving, thus destroying the foundational truths necessary for salvation.

In contrast to the transient speculations of men, the Bible teaches timeless truth—truth that is absolute for all people in all cultures in all ages—about God and man, good and evil, life and death, and especially the way of salvation (John 14:6; Acts 4:12). Biblical Christianity thus rejects both the antisupernatural bias of modernism, and the skepticism and relativism of postmodernism.

While the world clings to its own uncertain wisdom, which Scripture describes as "earthly, natural, demonic" (James 3:15), believers have been given in Scripture the rock solid truth of God Himself. It declares that God is the "God of truth" (Ps. 31:5; Isa. 65:16); Jesus is "full of . . . truth" (John 1:14; cf. v. 17; Eph. 4:21) and "the way, and the truth, and the life" (John 14:6); and the Holy Spirit is the "Spirit of truth" (John 14:17; 15:26; 16:13; 1 John 5:6). The Bible is the "word of truth" (2 Tim. 2:15); as Jesus prayed to the Father, "Sanctify them in the truth; Your word is truth" (John 17:17; cf. 2 Sam. 7:28; Ps. 119:43, 142, 151, 160). Like God Himself, His truth is eternal (Ps. 117:2) and unchanging (Ps. 119:89).

Salvation comes from "faith in the truth" (2 Thess. 2:13; cf. 1 Tim. 2:4; 2 Tim. 2:25), thus the redeemed are "those who believe and know the truth" (1 Tim. 4:3). In contrast, unbelievers are those who are "deprived of the truth" (1 Tim. 6:5); "have gone astray from the truth" (2 Tim. 2:18); are "always learning and never able to come to the knowledge of the truth" (2 Tim. 3:7); "oppose the truth" (v. 8); and "turn away their ears from the truth" (2 Tim. 4:4; cf. Titus 1:14).

Believers, on the other hand, are to worship God in truth (John 4:23–24), be committed to the truth (Pr. 23:23), obey the truth (1 Peter 1:22; cf. Rom. 2:8; Gal. 5:7), love the truth (cf. 2 Thess. 2:10), speak the truth in love (Eph. 4:15), and walk in the truth (Pss. 26:3; 86:11; 2 John 4; 3 John 3–4). In fact, truth is central to the existence and mission of the church, which is to be "the pillar and support of the truth" (1 Tim. 3:15). Paul's repeated command to Timothy, "O Timothy, guard what has been entrusted to you. . . . Guard, through the Holy Spirit who dwells in us, the treasure which has been entrusted to you" (1 Tim. 6:20; 2 Tim. 1:14), reflects the church's responsibility to protect the precious truths of Scripture.

The truth that brings spiritual freedom is the theme of this brief but powerful passage. The dialogue it records took place in the waning months of the Lord's earthly ministry. Jesus had repeatedly presented His claim to be the Son of God and Messiah, and had performed countless miracles to verify that claim (cf. 10:25, 37–38; 14:11; 15:24). Yet the people and the leaders had rejected Him. Their growing hostility had resulted in increasing opposition, culminating in a plot to murder Him (cf. 5:18; 7:1, 19, 25)—a plot that would come to fruition at the cross, now less than six months away.

But not everyone was hostile to Jesus. Verse 30 notes that "as He spoke these things, many came to believe in Him" (cf. 4:39, 41, 50, 53; 7:31). Their belief, as will soon become evident, was not saving faith, but was merely the first step toward it. Thus the Lord's goal in this section was to point them to full saving faith in Him—the type of faith that would truly set them free from sin, death, Satan, and hell. To that end, He began by explaining the pathway to freedom—the necessary steps that lead to the freedom of genuine salvation. Then He exposed the pretense of freedom—the false notions that deceived these Jews into thinking that they were already genuinely saved. Finally, He extended the promise of freedom—the absolute guarantee of true freedom for all who come to genuine saving faith.

THE PATHWAY TO FREEDOM

So Jesus was saying to those Jews who had believed Him, "If you continue in My word, then you are truly disciples of Mine; and you will know the truth, and the truth will make you free." (8:31–32)

Through His response to those who professed faith in Him, the Lord delineated the program that brings true spiritual freedom: believing in Him, continuing in His Word, knowing the truth, and being made free.

BELIEVING IN CHRIST

So Jesus was saying to those Jews who had believed Him, (8:31*a*)

"This section of discourse," writes Leon Morris, "is addressed to those who believe, and yet do not believe. Clearly they were inclined to think that what Jesus said was true. But they were not prepared to yield him the far-reaching allegiance that real trust in him implies" (*The Gospel According to John,* The New International Commentary on the New Testament [Grand Rapids: Eerdmans, 1979], 454). Morris goes on to caution, "This is a most dangerous spiritual state. To recognize that truth is in Jesus and to do nothing about it means that in effect one ranges oneself with the enemies of the Lord" (Ibid., 454).

Belief is the initial point of contact with Christ. But the Bible warns that not all faith is saving faith. Jesus would later describe these same **Jews who had believed** as those who were still slaves of sin (v. 34). They did not really love Jesus (v. 42), but were actually children of the devil (vv. 38, 41, 44) who refused to believe in Him (vv. 45–46), blasphemed Him (vv. 48, 52), and sought to kill Him (vv. 37, 40, 59). Earlier in his gospel John observed,

> Now when He was in Jerusalem at the Passover, during the feast, many believed in His name, observing His signs which He was doing. But Jesus, on His part, was not entrusting Himself to them, for He knew all men, and because He did not need anyone to testify concerning man, for He Himself knew what was in man. (2:23–25)

In chapter 6, many of those who excitedly wanted to crown Jesus king (vv. 14–15) soon "withdrew and were not walking with Him anymore" (v. 66; cf. v. 60). John 12:42 records the encouraging news that "many even of the rulers believed in Him." Their belief stopped short of saving faith, however, since "because of the Pharisees they were not confessing Him, for fear that they would be put out of the synagogue" (cf. Rom. 10:9–10). In the parable of the sower, Jesus described "those on the rocky soil" as "those who, when they hear, receive the word with joy; and these have no firm root; they believe for a while, and in time of temptation fall away" (Luke 8:13).

The apostle Paul similarly warned against believing in vain (1 Cor. 15:2) and exhorted his readers, "Test yourselves to see if you are in the faith; examine yourselves!" (2 Cor. 13:5). In Hebrews 10:38 God declared, "My righteous one shall live by faith; and if he shrinks back, My soul has no pleasure in him," thus making a clear distinction between "those who shrink back to destruction" because their faith is not genuine and "those who have [genuine] faith to the preserving of the soul" (v. 39). James 2:17 notes that "faith, if it has no works, is dead, being by itself" (cf. v. 20). Mere assent to the facts does not equal saving faith, since even the demons have that kind of faith (v. 19). But genuine faith manifests itself in a person's changed life (v. 18), as well as an enduring love for and devotion to Christ. Speaking of such perseverance, the apostle John wrote, "They went out from us but they were not really of us; for if they had been of us, they would have remained with us; but they went out, so that it would be shown that they all are not of us" (1 John 2:19).

Saving faith consists of three elements, commonly referred to by theologians with the Latin terms *notitia, assensus,* and *fiducia. Notitia* (knowledge) is the intellectual component of faith. It involves an understanding of the basic biblical facts regarding salvation. *Assensus* (assent) goes one step beyond *notitia* and confidently affirms those facts to be true. *Fiducia* (trust) acts on them by personally appropriating Jesus Christ as the only hope for salvation.

The classic biblical definition of faith in Hebrews 11 embraces all three of those elements: *notitia* ("by faith we understand"; v. 3); *assensus* ("faith is the assurance of things hoped for"; v. 1), and *fiducia* ("[faith is] the conviction of things not seen"; v. 1). In saving faith the entire person—the intellect (knowledge), the emotions (assent), and the will (trust)—embraces Jesus Christ as Savior and Lord. The writer of Hebrews goes on in the remainder of chapter 11 to give examples of those whose saving faith never wavered despite suffering, persecution, and death. The pattern of their lives reinforces the truth that genuine saving faith involves trust and commitment, not merely knowledge and assent. (For a further discussion of the nature of saving faith, see my books *The Gospel According to Jesus,* rev. ed. [Grand Rapids: Zondervan, 1994], *The Gospel According to the Apostles* [Nashville: Thomas Nelson, 1993, 2000], and *Hard to Believe* [Nashville: Thomas Nelson, 2004].)

CONTINUING IN THE WORD

"If you continue in My word, then you are truly disciples of Mine" (8:31*b*)

Those whose faith is the real, saving trust; those who **are truly** (actually, in reality) **disciples** of Jesus Christ will **continue** (remain, abide) **in** both faith and obedience to His **word.** The present tense of the verb *eimi* (**are**) suggests that Jesus was not telling them the requirements for becoming a disciple; He did not say, "If you continue in My word you *will become* My genuine disciples." Instead, He declared that the nature of true discipleship consists of continued obedience to His Word. Scripture repeatedly affirms that only those who obey Christ are truly His disciples:

> "For whoever does the will of My Father who is in heaven, he is My brother and sister and mother." (Matt. 12:50)

> "If you love Me, you will keep My commandments." (John 14:15)

> "He who has My commandments and keeps them is the one who loves Me; and he who loves Me will be loved by My Father, and I will love him and will disclose Myself to him. . . . If anyone loves Me, he will keep My

word; and My Father will love him, and We will come to him and make Our abode with him. He who does not love Me does not keep My words; and the word which you hear is not Mine, but the Father's who sent Me." (John 14:21, 23–24)

"If you keep My commandments, you will abide in My love; just as I have kept My Father's commandments and abide in His love." (John 15:10)

"You are My friends if you do what I command you." (John 15:14)

The one who says, "I have come to know Him," and does not keep His commandments, is a liar, and the truth is not in him; but whoever keeps His word, in him the love of God has truly been perfected. By this we know that we are in Him: the one who says he abides in Him ought himself to walk in the same manner as He walked. (1 John 2:4–6)

The one who keeps His commandments abides in Him, and He in him. (1 John 3:24)

For this is the love of God, that we keep His commandments. (1 John 5:3)

Such passages make it clear that there can be no dichotomy between truly accepting Christ as Savior and also obeying Him as Lord. "Surrender to Jesus' lordship is not an addendum to the biblical terms of salvation; the summons to submission is at the heart of the gospel invitation throughout Scripture" (*The Gospel According to the Apostles*, 23). It is not possible to be saved without confessing Christ as Lord, and giving willing obedience to His lordship.

Disciples translates the plural form of the noun *mathētēs*. The word primarily refers to a learner, one who adheres to the teaching of a spiritual leader (cf. Matt. 11:29). The New Testament mentions disciples of John the Baptist (Matt. 9:14; 11:2; 14:12; John 3:25), the Pharisees (Matt. 22:15–16; Mark 2:18), Moses (John 9:28), and Paul (Acts 9:24–25), in addition to those of Jesus. All Christians are disciples ("disciples" is used as a synonym for "believers" in Acts 6:1–2, 7; 9:1, 19, 38; 11:26; 13:52; 14:20–22, 28; 15:10; 18:23, 27; 19:9; 20:1; 21:4, 16); however, not all disciples are Christians (John 6:66; 1 John 2:19; cf. Matt. 13:20–21; John 15:2; 2 John 9).

True disciples are Word oriented. They recognize that it is "the word of His grace, which is able to build [them] up" (Acts 20:32). They understand the importance of being "doers of the word, and not merely hearers who delude themselves" (James 1:22). True believers are "like newborn babies, long[ing] for the pure milk of the word, so that by it [they] may grow in respect to salvation" (1 Peter 2:2). They possess the desire that the psalmist had when he wrote,"O how I love your law!" (Ps. 119:97),"With all my heart I will observe your precepts" (v. 69),"Your law is my delight," (v. 77), and, "The law of Your mouth is better to me than thousands of gold and silver pieces" (v. 72).

KNOWING THE TRUTH

"and you will know the truth," (8:32*a*)

The inevitable blessing of believing in Jesus and continuing to obey His Word is to **know the truth.** "Grace and truth were realized through Jesus Christ" (1:17), He is "the way, and the truth, and the life" (14:6), and "truth is in Jesus" (Eph. 4:21). In a postmodern world, where the hope of discovering absolute truth has been largely abandoned, such knowledge is revolutionary. Like Pilate, who asked the cynical question, "What is truth?" (18:38), modern skeptics are left with nothing but their own ignorance and despair—the fruit of their futile search for truth apart from God.

The truth comes not only from knowing the revelation of Scripture concerning Christ, but also from being taught by the Holy Spirit, the "Spirit of truth" (14:17; 15:26; 16:13; 1 John 5:6). The apostle John referred to the Spirit's teaching of believers in 1 John 2:27 when he wrote, "As for you, the anointing which you received from Him abides in you, and you have no need for anyone to teach you; but as His anointing teaches you about all things, and is true and is not a lie, and just as it has taught you, you abide in Him."

Scripture is the revelation of divine truth. In it Jesus Christ, truth incarnate, is revealed, and through it the Holy Spirit teaches the truth to believers. Thus Jesus prayed, "Sanctify them in the truth; Your word is truth" (John 17:17; cf. Ps. 119:142, 151, 160). The all-sufficient Scripture is "inspired by God and profitable for teaching, for reproof, for correction, for training in righteousness; so that the man of God may be adequate, equipped for every good work" (2 Tim. 3:16–17). And not just "the man of God," the preacher, but all who are taught by him.

BEING MADE FREE

"and the truth will make you free." (8:32*b*)

The reality of believing in Jesus, obeying His Word, and knowing the truth brings spiritual freedom. Such freedom is multifaceted, and includes freedom from the bondage of falsehood, Satan (John 17:15;

2 Cor. 4:4; 1 John 5:18), condemnation (Rom. 8:1), judgment (John 3:18; 5:24), spiritual ignorance (8:12), spiritual death (8:51), and, most significantly in this context (v. 34), sin (Rom. 6:18, 22).

It was to liberate lost sinners that Jesus came into the world (Luke 19:10). In the synagogue in His hometown of Nazareth, the Lord applied the following words from Isaiah to His ministry: "The Spirit of the Lord is upon Me, because He anointed Me to preach the gospel to the poor. He has sent Me to proclaim release to the captives, and recovery of sight to the blind, to set free those who are oppressed" (Luke 4:18). Those who are set free in Christ must heed Paul's admonition to the Galatians: "It was for freedom that Christ set us free; therefore keep standing firm and do not be subject again to a yoke of slavery" (Gal. 5:1).

THE PRETENSE OF FREEDOM

They answered Him, "We are Abraham's descendants and have never yet been enslaved to anyone; how is it that You say, 'You will become free'?" Jesus answered them, "Truly, truly, I say to you, everyone who commits sin is the slave of sin." (8:33–34)

Indignantly rejecting Jesus' offer of freedom, the Jews insisted that they were already free. **They answered Him, "We are Abraham's descendants and have never yet been enslaved to anyone; how is it that You say, 'You will become free'?"** Since they had been enslaved by Egypt, Assyria, Babylon, Medo-Persia, Greece, Syria, and finally Rome, they must have been referring to spiritual, not political freedom. Secure in their identity as **Abraham's descendants,** they were confident that though in pagan bondage, nationally they were spiritually free.

But the freedom to which Jesus referred does not derive from racial and religious identity (cf. vv. 39–44). "For he is not a Jew who is one outwardly," Paul wrote, "nor is circumcision that which is outward in the flesh. But he is a Jew who is one inwardly; and circumcision is that which is of the heart, by the Spirit, not by the letter; and his praise is not from men, but from God" (Rom. 2:28–29; cf. Luke 3:8; Rev. 2:9).

The Lord's reply to their assertion was simple and devastating: **"Truly, truly, I say to you, everyone who commits sin is the slave of sin."** As it does throughout John's gospel (cf. 1:51; 3:3, 5, 11; 5:19, 24–25; 6:26, 32, 47, 53; 8:52, 58; 10:1, 7; 12:24; 13:16, 20–21, 38; 14:12; 16:20, 23; 21:18), the solemn phrase *amēn, amēn* (**truly, truly**) introduces a statement of great importance. The present tense of the participle translated **commits** views sin as a life principle, innate fallenness and essential wickedness, not merely as individual acts. Despite their proud, self-righteous pretense of freedom, the Jews were in reality slaves to sin, since "by what a man is overcome, by this he is enslaved" (2 Peter 2:19). To be a **slave** is to be totally under the control of another and unable to free one's self. Sin, like a cruel taskmaster, controls every aspect of an unbeliever's life, enslaving that person "to various lusts and pleasures" (Titus 3:3) "in the bondage of iniquity" (Acts 8:23). While these Jews thought their religion and relationship to Abraham united them to God, Jesus pointed out that they had no relationship to God. As slaves to sin, and deceived about it, they desperately needed to be set free from their spiritual bondage.

The only way for sinners to be released from sin's grip and penalty is to be united by faith with Jesus Christ, who in His death and resurrection provides deliverance (Rom. 6:1–7). Having then died to sin in Christ (Rom. 6:2; cf. 7:4; Gal. 2:19–20; 1 Peter 2:24), it will no longer be their master (Rom. 6:14, 18, 20, 22; cf. 8:2). Instead, they will become free to be servants of God and righteousness (Rom. 6:22; 1 Peter 2:16).

THE PROMISE OF FREEDOM

"The slave does not remain in the house forever; the son does remain forever. So if the Son makes you free, you will be free indeed." (8:35–36)

The Lord used the analogy of slavery again in these two verses, but for different purposes. His statement that **the slave does not remain in the house forever,** but **the son does remain forever** was a warning. The **son** has permanent rights in the household; the **slave** does not. Even though the Jews were Abraham's descendants (and thus part of God's chosen nation), they were like slaves, not sons, and in danger of eternally forfeiting the privileges they had received. In Matthew 8:11–12 the Lord warned, "I say to you that many will come from east and west, and recline at the table with Abraham, Isaac and Jacob in the kingdom of heaven; but the sons of the kingdom will be cast out into the outer darkness; in that place there will be weeping and gnashing of teeth." It is only those who receive Jesus Christ as the Son of God (whether descended from Abraham or not) who are truly sons of God (1:12; Rom. 8:14; Gal. 3:26; 4:6; 1 John 3:1–2).

In verse 36 Jesus reiterated His promise of verse 32, declaring that those whom **the Son makes free, will be free indeed.** As the Son who rules over God's house (Heb. 3:6), Jesus has the authority to release those who put their faith in Him from their bondage to sin and make them sons of God. Through Him they are "set . . . free from the law of sin and of death" (Rom. 8:2). And not only does He release them, but He also adopts them into God's household (1:12; Rom. 8:15; Gal. 4:5; Eph. 1:5), taking them from a position of slavery to one of sonship (cf. Rom. 8:17). As Charles Wesley's magnificent hymn "And Can It Be" so wonderfully summarizes:

> Long my imprisoned spirit lay
> Fast bound in sin and nature's night;
> Thine eye diffused a quick'ning ray,
> I woke, the dungeon flamed with light;
> My chains fell off, my heart was free;
> I rose, went forth and followed Thee.

Children of Abraham, or Satan?
(John 8:37–47)

31

"I know that you are Abraham's descendants; yet you seek to kill Me, because My word has no place in you. I speak the things which I have seen with My Father; therefore you also do the things which you heard from your father." They answered and said to Him, "Abraham is our father." Jesus said to them, "If you are Abraham's children, do the deeds of Abraham. But as it is, you are seeking to kill Me, a man who has told you the truth, which I heard from God; this Abraham did not do. You are doing the deeds of your father." They said to Him, "We were not born of fornication; we have one Father: God." Jesus said to them, "If God were your Father, you would love Me, for I proceeded forth and have come from God, for I have not even come on My own initiative, but He sent Me. Why do you not understand what I am saying? It is because you cannot hear My word. You are of your father the devil, and you want to do the desires of your father. He was a murderer from the beginning, and does not stand in the truth because there is no truth in him. Whenever he speaks a lie, he speaks from his own nature, for he is a liar and the father of lies. But because I speak the truth, you do not believe Me. Which one of you convicts Me of sin? If I speak truth, why do you not

believe Me? He who is of God hears the words of God; for this reason you do not hear them, because you are not of God." (8:37–47)

In a world filled with trouble and turmoil, and with the inevitable reality of death and the afterlife, people long for security. They seek comfort, stability, a positive outlook for the future, a sense of purpose, and hope after death. Also, whether they are conscious of it or not, they yearn to ease the crushing burden of sin that dominates life. The Word of God gives ample instruction on the folly of seeking security in the wrong things. A general consideration of this matter will set the stage for our text and the true and only security.

Some look to wealth and possessions to provide security and eliminate anxiety. But "riches are not forever" (Prov. 27:24); thus Proverbs 23:4–5 counsels, "Do not weary yourself to gain wealth, cease from your consideration of it. When you set your eyes on it, it is gone. For wealth certainly makes itself wings like an eagle that flies toward the heavens." In Matthew 6:19–21 Jesus said,

> Do not store up for yourselves treasures on earth, where moth and rust destroy, and where thieves break in and steal. But store up for yourselves treasures in heaven, where neither moth nor rust destroys, and where thieves do not break in or steal; for where your treasure is, there your heart will be also.

In Luke 12:15 He cautioned, "Beware, and be on your guard against every form of greed; for not even when one has an abundance does his life consist of his possessions." Then in verses 16–21 the Lord told a parable illustrating the folly of those who try to find security in riches:

> "The land of a rich man was very productive. And he began reasoning to himself, saying, 'What shall I do, since I have no place to store my crops?' Then he said, 'This is what I will do: I will tear down my barns and build larger ones, and there I will store all my grain and my goods. And I will say to my soul, "Soul, you have many goods laid up for many years to come; take your ease, eat, drink and be merry." But God said to him, 'You fool! This very night your soul is required of you; and now who will own what you have prepared?' So is the man who stores up treasure for himself, and is not rich toward God." (cf. 16:25; Job 21:13; Ps. 52:7)

To Timothy Paul wrote, "Instruct those who are rich in this present world not to be conceited or to fix their hope on the uncertainty of riches, but on God, who richly supplies us with all things to enjoy" (1 Tim. 6:17).

Since "riches do not profit in the day of wrath" (Prov. 11:4; cf. Ezek. 7:19; Zeph. 1:18), "he who trusts in his riches will fall" (Prov. 11:28; cf. James 1:11). And, of course, material wealth has no connection with, nor can it make any contribution to, eternity.

Others, who are equally shortsighted, look for security in personal power. Job asked, "Why do the wicked still live, continue on, also become very powerful?" (Job 21:7). But such power is fleeting, providing only a false hope of stability. As David noted: "I have seen the wicked in great power, and spreading himself like a native green tree. Yet he passed away, and behold, he was no more; indeed I sought him, but he could not be found" (Ps. 37:35–36 NKJV). The gruesome death of Herod Agrippa demonstrates just how vulnerable and insecure even the most powerful people can be:

> On an appointed day Herod, having put on his royal apparel, took his seat on the rostrum and began delivering an address to them. The people kept crying out, "The voice of a god and not of a man!" And immediately an angel of the Lord struck him because he did not give God the glory, and he was eaten by worms and died. (Acts 12:21–23)

Those who think they can quiet the angst of their hearts by finding security in their social standing and prestige will likewise be disappointed. The scribes and Pharisees "love[d] the place of honor at banquets and the chief seats in the synagogues" (Matt. 23:6) as well as "the respectful greetings in the market places" (Luke 11:43; cf. 20:46). They ignored Solomon's wise counsel, "Do not claim honor in the presence of the king, and do not stand in the place of great men; for it is better that it be said to you, 'Come up here,' than for you to be placed lower in the presence of the prince, whom your eyes have seen" (Prov. 25:6–7; cf. Luke 14:7–11). Despite their impressive religious image, the Pharisees of Jesus' day were in reality sons of hell (Matt. 23:15).

There are also those who narcissistically seek security in their physical appearance and looks, not realizing that "charm is deceitful and beauty is vain" (Prov. 31:30; cf. 11:22). Saul, for instance, was "a choice and handsome man, and there was not a more handsome person than he among the sons of Israel" (1 Sam. 9:2). Yet, as a king, he was an utter failure, ultimately committing suicide after being defeated in battle (1 Sam. 31:1–6). David's son Absalom was also very striking. Second Samuel 14:25–26 records that

> in all Israel was no one as handsome as Absalom, so highly praised; from the sole of his foot to the crown of his head there was no defect in him. When he cut the hair of his head (and it was at the end of every year that he cut it, for it was heavy on him so he cut it), he weighed the hair of his head at 200 shekels by the king's weight.

But in spite of his handsome appearance, Absalom too suffered a shameful death, caught helplessly in the branches of a tree by the very hair he so vainly prized (2 Sam. 18:9–14). As both Saul and Absalom illustrate, one's physical appearance cannot provide lasting security, since "our outer man is decaying" (2 Cor. 4:16) and, more important, "God sees not as man sees, for man looks at the outward appearance, but the Lord looks at the heart" (1 Sam. 16:7).

If anyone could have put his heart to rest and found peace in earthly things it would have been Solomon. As Ecclesiastes records, he tried everything: human wisdom (1:12–18), hedonism (2:1–3, 10), achievements (2:4–11), entertainment (2:8a), sex (2:8b), work (2:18–23), and wealth (2:8; 4:8; 5:10). But, after experiencing it all, his conclusion was that such pursuits were nothing more than "vanity and striving after wind" (1:14). In the end, Solomon realized that security comes only from being rightly related to God: "The conclusion, when all has been heard, is: fear God and keep His commandments, because this applies to every person" (12:13).

As Solomon discovered, any attempt to ground one's security and hope in temporal, earthly things rather than God is doomed to failure. Only through His salvation in Jesus Christ can true, eternal safety be found. Those who put their faith in the Savior have nothing to fear from "death, nor life, nor angels, nor principalities, nor things present, nor things to come, nor powers, nor height, nor depth, nor any other created thing, [for nothing] will be able to separate [them] from the love of God, which is in Christ Jesus [their] Lord" (Rom. 8:38–39).

Satan, of course, recognizes the innate human longing for security, and knows that only the gospel provides for it. Therefore he offers in its place the ultimate source of counterfeit hope: false religion. False religion is his deadly strategy (cf. 2 Cor. 4:3–4; 11:13–15), because it deceives people into thinking they are right with God when in reality they are not. That artificial sense of security lies to and numbs their consciences, blinding them to their desperate need for the truth of the gospel.

In this section, which continues the dialogue that began in verse 31, the Lord confronted the false security that the Jews looked for in their self-righteous legalism. As He did so, the Jewish leaders whom He addressed grew increasingly hostile toward Him. In fact, their hatred was so intense that they were already planning to murder Him (vv. 37, 40; 5:16–18; 7:1, 19, 25). But, instead of backing down or softening His message, the Lord became even more direct and forceful in His condemnation, to the point that He openly identified His enemies as children of the devil (v. 44; cf. vv. 38, 41).

Jesus demolished the Jews' false security for eternal life with God by refuting each of the three claims on which they based it: their claim to be Abraham's physical children, their claim to be Abraham's spiritual children, and their claim to be God's children.

THEIR CLAIM TO BE ABRAHAM'S PHYSICAL CHILDREN

"I know that you are Abraham's descendants; yet you seek to kill Me, because My word has no place in you. I speak the things which I have seen with My Father; therefore you also do the things which you heard from your father." (8:37–38)

Jesus acknowledged the validity of the Jews' claim, made in verse 33, to be **Abraham's** physical **descendants** (cf. Luke 13:16; 19:9; Acts 3:25; 7:2; 13:26; Rom. 11:1; 2 Cor. 11:22). He also knew that they based their security largely on that fact, believing that they were guaranteed entrance into God's kingdom simply because they were Abraham's offspring. The second-century Christian apologist Justin Martyr said to his Jewish opponent: "They [the Jewish teachers] beguile themselves and you, supposing that the everlasting kingdom will be assuredly given to those of the dispersion who are of Abraham after the flesh, although they be sinners, and faithless, and disobedient towards God" (*Dialogue with Trypho,* 140).

But the New Testament shatters that false hope of security:

> But if you bear the name "Jew" and rely upon the Law and boast in God, and know His will and approve the things that are essential, being instructed out of the Law . . . you who boast in the Law, through your breaking the Law, do you dishonor God? For "The name of God is blasphemed among the Gentiles because of you," just as it is written. For indeed circumcision is of value if you practice the Law; but if you are a transgressor of the Law, your circumcision has become uncircumcision. So if the uncircumcised man keeps the requirements of the Law, will not his uncircumcision be regarded as circumcision? And he who is physically uncircumcised, if he keeps the Law, will he not judge you who though having the letter of the Law and circumcision are a transgressor of the Law? For he is not a Jew who is one outwardly, nor is circumcision that which is outward in the flesh. But he is a Jew who is one inwardly; and circumcision is that which is of the heart, by the Spirit, not by the letter; and his praise is not from men, but from God. (Rom. 2:17–18, 23–29)

Ethnic descent from Abraham and physical circumcision count for nothing apart from the "circumcision . . . which is of the heart" (cf. Deut. 10:16; 30:6; Jer. 4:4; Col. 2:11); the cleansing of sin that is wrought "by the

Spirit"in salvation. Apart from that all the promised blessings and advantages of the Jewish people, of which there are many (cf. Rom. 3:1–2; 9:4–5), ultimately mean nothing.

In Romans 9:6 Paul noted that "they are not all Israel who are descended from Israel." No one was ever saved merely by having Abraham as an ancestor. It is only the believing remnant (comprised of those Jews who come to true faith in Jesus Christ) who will be saved, as Paul pointed out in verse 27: "Isaiah cries out concerning Israel, 'Though the number of the sons of Israel be like the sand of the sea, it is the remnant that will be saved'" (cf. 11:5; Isa. 10:22). To the Galatians he wrote, "Even so Abraham believed God, and it was reckoned to him as righteousness. Therefore, be sure that it is those who are of faith who are sons of Abraham. . . . So then those who are of faith are blessed with Abraham, the believer" (Gal. 3:6–7, 9).

The actions of Jesus' opponents, however, showed they were not among the believing remnant. "Your father Abraham rejoiced to see My day," Jesus told them, "and he saw it and was glad" (v. 56; cf. Heb. 11:13). Abraham looked forward to the coming of the Messiah, who would be the ultimate fulfillment of God's promises to him. **Yet** the Jews sought to **kill** Jesus—the very Messiah for whom Abraham had hoped. And unlike Abraham, who believed God's word (Gen. 15:6), Jesus' **word** had **no place in** them; they rejected His teaching (cf. vv. 31, 43, 45, 47; Matt. 13:19; 1 Cor. 2:14). The term *chōreō* (**has no place**) can mean "to advance," "to make progress," or "to go forward." Though they heard Jesus' word they did not heed it, and hence it never bore fruit in them. It penetrated their hardened hearts no deeper than the seed that fell beside the road in the parable of the sower (Matt. 13:4, 19). In contrast, "the word of God . . . performs its work in [those] who believe" (1 Thess. 2:13).

The Lord continued by explaining the logical implication of their hard-heartedness: **"I speak the things which I have seen with My Father; therefore you also do the things which you heard from your father."** Jesus spoke to them of heavenly realities, of the divine truth that He alone could reveal because He heard it from the **Father** (cf. v. 26; 3:11, 31–32, 34; 6:46; 12:49; 14:10, 24; 15:15; 17:8). But they rejected Jesus' words and instead did **the things which** they **heard from** their **father.** In the same way that Jesus' conduct proved His Father was God, the conduct of Jesus' enemies proved that their father was not God—but was actually the devil (cf. v. 44).

Thus they did not truly know Him, nor did they understand the words that He spoke. And because they did not know Him, they did not know His Father either. As He had earlier told them, "You know neither Me nor My Father; if you knew Me, you would know My Father also" (8:19).

THEIR CLAIM TO BE ABRAHAM'S SPIRITUAL CHILDREN

They answered and said to Him, "Abraham is our father." Jesus said to them, "If you are Abraham's children, do the deeds of Abraham. But as it is, you are seeking to kill Me, a man who has told you the truth, which I heard from God; this Abraham did not do. You are doing the deeds of your father." (8:39–41a)

The Jews' reply, **"Abraham is our father,"** indicates that once again they failed to grasp the import of Jesus' words. They bitterly insisted that they were also Abraham's spiritual children; that is, that they were following his pattern of faith in God. Our Lord's response indicates this because He calls for them to demonstrate the righteousness that marked Abraham. Jesus' challenge, **If you are Abraham's children, do the deeds of Abraham,** pointed out the vast discrepancy between their actions and those of their patriarch.

Abraham was a man of extraordinary faith. Genesis 15:6 records that he "believed in the Lord; and He reckoned it to him as righteousness." The New Testament repeatedly emphasizes Abraham's faith; in fact, Paul devotes an entire chapter (Rom. 4) to show that Abraham was saved by faith, and not by works (v. 2), circumcision (vv. 10–12), or the Law (vv. 13–16). To the Galatians he wrote,

> Even so Abraham believed God, and it was reckoned to him as righteousness. Therefore, be sure that it is those who are of faith who are sons of Abraham. The Scripture, foreseeing that God would justify the Gentiles by faith, preached the gospel beforehand to Abraham, saying, "All the nations will be blessed in you." So then those who are of faith are blessed with Abraham, the believer. For as many as are of the works of the Law are under a curse; for it is written, "Cursed is everyone who does not abide by all things written in the book of the law, to perform them." Now that no one is justified by the Law before God is evident; for, "The righteous man shall live by faith." However, the Law is not of faith; on the contrary, "He who practices them shall live by them." Christ redeemed us from the curse of the Law, having become a curse for us —for it is written, "Cursed is everyone who hangs on a tree"—in order that in Christ Jesus the blessing of Abraham might come to the Gentiles, so that we would receive the promise of the Spirit through faith. (Gal. 3:6–14)

The writer of Hebrews also praised Abraham's faith, setting it forth as an example to be followed (Heb. 11:8–12, 17–19).

In contrast to Abraham, however, Jesus' opponents were self-righteously trying to earn favor with God by their own good works. They did not follow Abraham's example, since it is "those who are of faith [who] are blessed with Abraham, the believer" (Gal. 3:9). Salvation is not based on legalistic effort, religious affiliation, or ethnic background (cf. Phil. 3:1–7). Rather, it comes solely through faith in Jesus Christ. He alone is "the way, and the truth, and the life; no one comes to the Father but through [Him]" (John 14:6); "there is salvation in no one else; for there is no other name under heaven that has been given among men by which we must be saved" (Acts 4:12); and, "there is one God, and one mediator also between God and men, the man Christ Jesus" (1 Tim. 2:5).

Had they truly been Abraham's children, Jesus' opponents would have done the same kind of deeds that Abraham did. God's testimony concerning him was that "Abraham obeyed Me and kept My charge, My commandments, My statutes and My laws" (Gen. 26:5; cf. 22:18). But Jesus' opponents were **seeking to kill** Him (cf. v. 37), **a man who told** them **the truth, which** He **heard from God.** Such murderous intentions were far removed from Abraham's obedience. Their disobedience and rejection of God the Son proved conclusively that they were not Abraham's spiritual children since, needless to say, **this Abraham did not do.**

The contrast between Jesus' opponents and Abraham was sharply drawn: Abraham was not a murderer, yet they sought to murder Jesus; Abraham obeyed and loved the truth, while they vehemently rejected it; Abraham welcomed God (Gen. 18:1ff.), but they rejected Him (Heb. 1:1–2). No wonder Jesus said to them again, **"You are doing the deeds of your father."** The clear implication, as in verse 38, was that their father was neither Abraham nor God, but Satan (v. 44).

Their Claim to Be God's Children

They said to Him, "We were not born of fornication; we have one Father: God." Jesus said to them, "If God were your Father, you would love Me, for I proceeded forth and have come from God, for I have not even come on My own initiative, but He sent Me. Why do you not understand what I am saying? It is because you cannot hear My word. You are of your father the devil, and you want to do the desires of your father. He was a murderer from the beginning, and does not stand in the truth because there is no truth in him. Whenever he speaks a lie, he speaks from his own nature, for he is a liar and the father of lies. But because I speak the truth, you do not believe Me. Which one of you convicts Me of sin? If I speak truth, why do you not believe Me? He who is of

God hears the words of God; for this reason you do not hear them, because you are not of God." (8:41b–47)

Infuriated by Jesus' continued insistence that they were not Abraham's spiritual children, the Jews lashed out at Him with a vicious insult. Their mocking statement, **"We were not born of fornication,"** was undoubtedly a disparaging reference to the controversy surrounding Jesus' birth. In other words, they were implying that His birth, unlike theirs, was illegitimate (cf. v. 48).

The Jewish leaders went on to insist, **"We have one Father: God."** No doubt they had in mind such Old Testament passages as Exodus 4:22: "Thus says the Lord, 'Israel is My son, My firstborn'" and Jeremiah 31:9: "I am a father to Israel, and Ephraim is My firstborn" (cf. 3:19; Deut. 32:6; 1 Chron. 29:10). It was true that God was the Father of all Israel in a national sense. But, spiritually speaking, He was the Father only of those who had truly come to saving faith (cf. the discussion of v. 37 above).

Perhaps at this point Jesus' opponents began to grasp what He was implying and would soon say—that they were children of Satan (vv. 38, 41). In response, they maintained that their religion was pure, untainted by idolatrous false religion. Hence they could not be Satan's children, because he was the spiritual father of the heathen. Thus, they asserted with confidence, they must be children of God.

But their proud boast was palpably false; as **Jesus said to them, "If God were your Father** (and the implication is that He was not), **you would love Me, for I proceeded forth and have come from God, for I have not even come on My own initiative, but He sent Me."** Those who profess love for God yet reject the One who **proceeded forth and** came **from** Him cannot be true children of God. By refusing to embrace Jesus, the Jewish leaders completely undermined their claim that God was their Father. As Jesus had said to them earlier, "He who does not honor the Son does not honor the Father who sent Him" (5:23); later He would warn them, "He who hates Me hates My Father also" (15:23). True children of God are inherently characterized by a love for His Son.

The Lord then asked the rhetorical question, **"Why do you not understand what I am saying?"** The obvious answer, as Jesus went on to point out, was **because** they could not **hear** His **word.** As noted earlier in the exposition of verse 38, their inability to **hear** and **understand** Him proved that they were not God's children. Instead, it demonstrated that they were truly **of** their **father the devil.** What He had implied in verses 38 and 41 Jesus now bluntly stated: physically, his opponents were children of Abraham, but spiritually and morally they were children of Satan (cf. Matt. 13:38; Acts 13:10; 1 John 3:12). It was therefore not surprising that they wanted **to do the** evil **desires of** their **father.** In the same way that physical children naturally take after their earthly fathers, these individuals bore a spiritual resemblance to Satan himself. As the familiar adage puts it, "Like father, like son."

Two evil **desires** in particular characterize Satan: murder and lying. **He was,** Jesus said, **a murderer from the beginning.** The reference is to the fall, when Satan's temptation of Adam and Eve brought about their spiritual death and that of the entire human race (Gen. 2:17; Rom. 5:12; 1 Cor. 15:21–22). The reference may also encompass the first murder in human history, that of Abel by Cain (Gen. 4:1–8). Ever since the fall, Satan's hatred for mankind has driven him to prowl "around like a roaring lion, seeking someone to devour" (1 Peter 5:8). He cares nothing for even the most evil men, those most devoted to his service. They are merely pawns whom he attempts to use in his war against God. Their attempt to murder Him proved who Jesus' enemies' true spiritual father was.

Satan is not only a murderer, but also a liar. He **does not stand in the truth because there is no truth in him. Whenever he speaks a lie, he speaks from his own nature, for he is a liar and the father of lies.** His convincing lie to Eve, "You surely will not die!" (Gen. 3:4; cf. 2 Cor. 11:3), led to the spiritual ruin of the human race. To this day he continues to deceive people (2 Cor. 4:4), cleverly "disguis[ing] himself as an angel of light" (2 Cor. 11:14; cf. Rev. 12:9; 20:2–3, 10). By rejecting the truth incarnate (1:17; 14:6; Eph. 4:21), the Jewish leaders unarguably marked themselves as children of Satan. **"Because I speak the truth,"** Jesus declared, **"you do not believe Me."** As children of the father of lies they were unable and unwilling to receive the truth.

These unbelieving Jews were not, of course, the only members of Satan's spiritual family; in his first epistle John wrote that any "one who practices sin is of the devil" (1 John 3:8). And unless the Lord opens his or her heart to respond to the truth (John 6:44; Acts 16:14; 2 Cor. 3:14–16), no unbeliever will listen to it. Instead, "wanting to have their ears tickled, they will accumulate for themselves teachers in accordance to their own desires, and will turn away their ears from the truth and will turn aside to myths" (2 Tim. 4:3–4). Having been duped by Satan's schemes (2 Cor. 2:11; 4:4; Eph. 6:11), and having participated in his work, all unrepentant sinners will share in their father's condemnation (1 Tim. 3:6).

As the Lord concluded this section, He challenged His opponents with two more rhetorical questions. The first, **"Which one of you convicts Me of sin?"** is a bold affirmation of what theologians refer to as Christ's impeccability; that is, His utter holiness and separation from sin. Second Corinthians 5:21 says that He "knew no sin"; Hebrews 4:15 that He "has been tempted in all things as we are, yet without sin";

Hebrews 7:26 describes Him as "holy, innocent, undefiled, separated from sinners"; and 1 Peter 2:22 affirms that He "committed no sin." Only the perfectly holy One, in intimate communion with the Father, could dare to issue such a challenge. Though His enemies wrongly believed Him to be guilty of sin, they could not prove Him guilty of anything. At His trial before Annas Jesus issued a similar challenge: "If I have spoken wrongly, testify of the wrong; but if rightly, why do you strike Me?" (18:23). There, as here, the challenge went unanswered.

The Lord's second rhetorical question pressed the point relentlessly: **"If I speak truth, why do you not believe Me?"** If He was not guilty of sin, He must have been speaking the truth. What grounds, therefore, did they have for rejecting Him?

When His stunned opponents offered no reply, Jesus answered His own question: **"He who is of God hears the words of God; for this reason you do not hear them, because you are not of God."** The syllogism is clear; the Lord's logic irrefutable: **He who is of God** hears the words of God; they did **not hear them;** therefore they were **not of God.**

Like John the Baptist before Him (Luke 3:8), Jesus demolished the false hope of security that the Jews sought in being Abraham's descendants. Though they claimed to be children of Abraham (both in lineage and in faith), Jesus made it clear to them that, spiritually speaking, they were actually children of Satan. Unless they repented, they were doomed to share the Devil's punishment in hell. The same is also true today for all who base their hope on anything other than the person and work of Jesus Christ.

Jesus Confronts His Enemies
(John 8:48–59)

32

The Jews answered and said to Him, "Do we not say rightly that You are a Samaritan and have a demon?" Jesus answered, "I do not have a demon; but I honor My Father, and you dishonor Me. But I do not seek My glory; there is One who seeks and judges. Truly, truly, I say to you, if anyone keeps My word he will never see death." The Jews said to Him, "Now we know that You have a demon. Abraham died, and the prophets also; and You say, 'If anyone keeps My word, he will never taste of death.' Surely You are not greater than our father Abraham, who died? The prophets died too; whom do You make Yourself out to be?" Jesus answered, "If I glorify Myself, My glory is nothing; it is My Father who glorifies Me, of whom you say, 'He is our God'; and you have not come to know Him, but I know Him; and if I say that I do not know Him, I will be a liar like you, but I do know Him and keep His word. Your father Abraham rejoiced to see My day, and he saw it and was glad." So the Jews said to Him, "You are not yet fifty years old, and have You seen Abraham?" Jesus said to them, "Truly, truly, I say to you, before Abraham was born, I am." Therefore they picked up stones to throw at Him, but Jesus hid Himself and went out of the temple. (8:48–59)

Ever since his initial rebellion (cf. Isa. 14:12–14; Ezek. 28:12–16; Luke 10:18), Satan has tirelessly waged war against God and His servants. The conflict, which began in the angelic realm (Dan. 10:13,20; Eph. 6:12; Rev. 12:4,7–9), was brought to earth when Satan tempted Adam and Eve in the Garden of Eden (Gen. 3:1–19). Since then, the Devil has done everything within his extensive, though limited, power to hinder God's purposes and obscure God's message. Though God's complete and total victory is absolutely certain (1 Cor. 15:24–25; Rev. 20:10), in the present the spiritual battle continues to rage (2 Cor. 4:3–4; Eph. 6:12–18).

As the cosmic war of the ages has played out on the stage of human history, men of God have consistently confronted the satanic enemies of divine truth—men like Moses, who demanded that Pharaoh let God's people go (Ex. 5:1; 6:27); Micaiah, who boldly rebuked the evil king Ahab (1 Kings 22:6–28); Elijah, who challenged prophets of Baal (1 Kings 18:19–40); John the Baptist, who reproved the corrupt Pharisees and Sadducees (Matt. 3:7–10); Stephen, who confronted the Sanhedrin and paid for it with his life (Acts 7:51–53); Peter and John, who denounced the sorcerer Simon (Acts 8:9–24); and Paul and Barnabas, who condemned the false prophet Bar-Jesus (Acts 13:9–11).

But above all the human heroes of the faith, the Lord Jesus Christ confronted the armies of hell. John wrote in 1 John 3:8 that "the Son of God appeared for this purpose, to destroy the works of the devil" (cf. Gen. 3:15; Mark 1:24; Col. 2:15; Heb. 2:14). Jesus Himself warned that His mission would bring conflict. "Do not think that I came to bring peace on the earth," He warned; "I did not come to bring peace, but a sword" (Matt. 10:34).

The Synoptic Gospels are replete with confrontations between Christ and Satan's forces, both demonic (e.g., Matt. 8:31; 17:14–18; Mark 7:25–30; Luke 4:33–35, 41; 9:42; 11:14; 13:32) and human. On the human level, the Jewish religious establishment (which primarily consisted of self-righteous false teachers) received His harshest attacks. As apostate hypocrites, the Jewish leaders were actually the enemies of the God they claimed to serve—and Jesus was quick to expose their true spiritual condition.

When the scribes and Pharisees insisted that He perform a sign for them (Matt. 12:38; cf. 16:1–4), Jesus "answered and said to them, 'An evil and adulterous generation craves for a sign; and yet no sign will be given to it but the sign of Jonah the prophet'" (Matt. 12:39). When they demanded to know why His disciples did not keep the tradition of the elders (Matt. 15:1–2), Jesus denounced them as hypocrites (v. 7), whose hearts were far from God (v. 8), whose worship was vain (v. 9), and whose teaching was false (v. 9). When they challenged His teaching on divorce (Matt. 19:3), Jesus rebuked them for being hard-hearted adulterers (vv. 8–9). When the Sadducees allowed greedy merchants to corrupt God's holy temple, Jesus physically removed them (Matt. 21:12–13). When the religious leaders grumbled at His eating with tax collectors and sinners (Luke 5:30), Jesus sarcastically condemned their arrogant self-righteousness (vv. 31–32). When they expressed surprise that the Lord did not ceremonially wash before eating (Luke 11:37–38), He accused them of being outwardly righteous but inwardly wicked (vv. 39–40). When a synagogue official became indignant because Jesus healed on the Sabbath (Luke 13:14), the Lord exposed him as a hypocrite, more concerned about the well-being of animals than people (vv. 15–16; cf. 14:1–6). And to "some people who trusted in themselves that they were righteous, and viewed others with contempt" (Luke 18:9), Jesus told a parable contrasting the arrogant self-righteousness of a Pharisee with the humble penitence of a tax collector (vv. 10–14). The Lord's point was that "everyone who exalts himself will be humbled, but he who humbles himself will be exalted" (v. 14), and it was the tax collector—not the Pharisee—who was justified by God (v. 14).

The Lord's judgment and condemnation of the false religious leaders reached its peak during Passion Week. In Matthew 23, Jesus pronounced sevenfold retribution on them as sons of hell (v. 15), whose false teaching excluded others from God's kingdom (v. 13), who swore oaths that they did not keep (v. 16), who were diligent in tithing, but ignored the more important aspects of the Law (vv. 23–24), who outwardly observed the Law, but inwardly were filled with wickedness (v. 25), who appeared to be righteous, but in reality were defiled (vv. 27–28), and who piously distanced themselves from their ancestors' murder of the prophets (vv. 29–30), while at the same time plotting to murder the Messiah.

This gospel also portrays Jesus as actively confronting the servants of the enemy; in particular, as in the Synoptics, Israel's apostate leadership. His cleansing of the temple (the incident John records in 2:13–17 took place at the outset of Jesus' public ministry, in contrast to the one in the Synoptics, which took place near its end) outraged the Jewish authorities, who demanded a sign to prove His authority (v. 18). When the religious leaders persecuted Him for healing a man on the Sabbath (5:16), Jesus boldly asserted His deity and equality with the Father (5:17–23). After He healed a man born blind, Jesus declared, "For judgment I came into this world, so that those who do not see may see, and that those who see may become blind" (9:39). Offended, some of the Pharisees protested, "We are not blind too, are we?" (v. 40), to which the Lord replied, "If you were blind, you would have no sin; but since you say, 'We see,' your sin remains" (v. 41). Cornering Jesus in the temple, the exasperated "Jews . . . were saying to Him, 'How long will You keep us in suspense? If You are the Christ, tell us plainly'" (10:24). In response He rebuked them for their stubborn unbelief in the face of overwhelming evidence (v. 25) and declared that they did not believe because they were not of His sheep (v. 26).

Verses 48–59 of chapter 8 record another skirmish in the ongoing battle between the Lord and the hostile Jewish religious leaders. The passage marks the culmination of a dialogue between Jesus and those leaders that began back in verse 12. As the discussion went on, the leaders became increasingly agitated and abusive. To Jesus' declaration in verses 31 and 32 that spiritual freedom comes only from being His disciples, they indignantly "answered Him, 'We are Abraham's descendants and have never yet been enslaved to anyone; how is it that You say, "You will become free"?'" (v. 33). When He hinted that God was not their father (vv. 38, 41) they scornfully "said to Him, 'We were not born of fornication; we have one Father: God'" (v. 41). Jesus' indictment of them reached its height in verse 44, where He openly declared them to be children of Satan. Like their father, they were liars, murderers, and enemies of God.

This concluding portion of the dialogue may be discussed under four headings: the dishonor, the doubting, the defiance, and the disappearance.

THE DISHONOR

The Jews answered and said to Him, "Do we not say rightly that You are a Samaritan and have a demon?" Jesus answered, "I do not have a demon; but I honor My Father, and you dishonor Me. But I do not seek My glory; there is One who seeks and judges. Truly, truly, I say to you, if anyone keeps My word he will never see death." (8:48–51)

Outraged by Jesus' pronouncement that they were children of Satan (v. 44), the **Jews** lashed out **and said to Him, "Do we not say rightly that You are a Samaritan and have a demon?"** They probably called Jesus a Samaritan in part because He, like the Samaritans, questioned their claim to be the true children of Abraham. They may have also been repeating their insult from verse 41, where they questioned the legitimacy of Jesus' birth as a full-blooded Jew. (For more on both of those points, see the exposition of 8:37–47 in the previous chapter of this volume.)

In either case, the Jews were obviously unable to counter the content of Jesus' keen wisdom. Therefore they resorted to an *ad hominem* attack, calling Jesus names rather than refuting His arguments. In this case, they mockingly denounced Him as a **Samaritan,** which was the most cutting insult one Jew could hurl at another. Jesus' words (in vv. 37–47) had clearly hit a nerve. But instead of responding with repentance, these Jews ridiculed Him.

The Jews despised the Samaritans as physical and spiritual half-breeds. To review, the Samaritans were the descendants of Jews who had remained in the northern kingdom after its fall and intermarried with pagans transplanted there by the Assyrians (2 Kings 17:23–24). When the Samaritans offered to help rebuild the temple after the exile, the Jews refused and the Samaritans were insulted (Ezra 4:1–3). The bitter rivalry between the two groups only intensified throughout the intertestamental period. By Jesus' day the mutual animosity was so great that the Jews avoided dealing with the Samaritans altogether (John 4:9), and some refused even to travel through Samaria. Some of the Samaritans reciprocated by denying any hospitality to the Jews who did travel through their region (Luke 9:51–53). Jesus, however, was no respecter of racial barriers. He first revealed Himself as Messiah to a Samaritan woman (John 4:25–26), and also used a Samaritan to illustrate a good neighbor (Luke 10:33–35). (For a further discussion of the Samaritans, see the exposition of 4:9 in chapter 11 of this volume.)

By calling Jesus a Samaritan, the Jewish leaders were in effect labeling Him a false teacher (because He obviously did not agree with their interpretation of the Law), and a traitor to Israel (since He allegedly sided with Israel's bitter enemies the Samaritans). In their blindness, they were confident that He must be an enemy of God.

In their anger, the Jews took their blasphemous accusations one step further by claiming that Jesus was also possessed by **a demon**—the same slanderous charge they had earlier hurled at John the Baptist (Matt. 11:18). This was not the first time they had made that outrageous allegation about Him. In Mark 3:22, "The scribes who came down from Jerusalem were saying, 'He is possessed by Beelzebul' (Satan), and 'He casts out the demons by the ruler of the demons'" (cf. 3:30; Matt. 10:25). John 7:20 records that "the crowd answered [Jesus], 'You have a demon! Who seeks to kill You?'" Later in John's gospel, the charge would be made again: "Many of [the Jews] were saying, 'He has a demon and is insane. Why do you listen to Him?'" (10:20). To say someone was demon-possessed was tantamount to saying that he was insane, since demon-possessed people often acted irrationally (e.g., Luke 8:27, 29, 35; 9:38–39). In a clear demonstration of their spiritual blindness, they processed all Jesus said and did into the conclusion that a demon had driven Him mad. It is this kind of decision, in the face of full revelation, that is described in Hebrews 6:4–8:

> For in the case of those who have once been enlightened and have tasted of the heavenly gift and have been made partakers of the Holy Spirit, and have tasted the good word of God and the powers of the age

to come, and then have fallen away, it is impossible to renew them again to repentance, since they again crucify to themselves the Son of God and put Him to open shame. For ground that drinks the rain which often falls on it and brings forth vegetation useful to those for whose sake it is also tilled, receives a blessing from God; but if it yields thorns and thistles, it is worthless and close to being cursed, and it ends up being burned.

But Jesus did not reply in kind to their malicious charges; "while being reviled, He did not revile in return" (1 Peter 2:23; cf. Prov. 15:1). Instead, He calmly **answered, "I do not have a demon."** In fact, the opposite was true. **"I honor My Father"** (cf. v. 29; 4:34; 5:19, 30; 6:38; 14:31; 15:10; 17:4; Matt. 3:17; 17:5), He told them. Obviously, then, He could not have been demon-possessed, since no demon-possessed person could possibly honor God.

Ironically, by their **dishonor** of Jesus, the Jews were dishonoring the very God whom they claimed as their Father. Earlier Jesus had told them, "If God were your Father, you would love Me, for I proceeded forth and have come from God, for I have not even come on My own initiative, but He sent Me" (v. 42). "He who does not honor the Son," Jesus warned, "does not honor the Father who sent Him" (5:23; cf. 15:23; 1 John 2:23). Thus, it is only those who honor the Son whom the Father honors in return (12:26; cf. 1 Cor. 12:3).

Unlike His opponents, who exalted themselves (5:44; cf. 7:18; 12:43; Matt. 23:5; Luke 16:15), Jesus did **not seek** His own **glory.** Had that been His desire, He could have remained in heaven and continued in the divine glory that had been His from all eternity (John 17:5, 24). Christ, however, did not come to earth seeking His own accolades, but "to seek and to save that which was lost" (Luke 19:10); to "bear the sins of many" (Heb. 9:28; cf. Isa. 53:11–12); and to "save His people from their sins" (Matt. 1:21). The omnipotent Creator (John 1:3; Col. 1:16; Heb. 1:2) and sustainer (Col. 1:17; Heb. 1:3) of the universe

> Left His Father's throne above,
> So free, so infinite His grace;
> Emptied Himself of all but love,
> And bled for Adam's helpless race.
> (Charles Wesley, "And Can It Be That I Should Gain")

Though Jesus did not seek His own glory, **there is One who seeks** honor for the Son—the Father. Unlike sinful men, He **judges** rightly, and has determined that His Son is worthy of glory. Both at Christ's baptism (Matt. 3:17) and at His transfiguration (Matt. 17:5) the Father said of the Son, "This is My beloved Son, in whom I am well-pleased."

Because the Son obediently humbled Himself even to the point of death on the cross,

> God highly exalted Him, and bestowed on Him the name which is above every name, so that at the name of Jesus every knee will bow, of those who are in heaven and on earth and under the earth, and that every tongue will confess that Jesus Christ is Lord, to the glory of God the Father. (Phil. 2:9–11)

In an Old Testament counterpart to that passage, the psalmist described the Father's glorifying of the Son:

> But as for Me, I have installed My King
> Upon Zion, My holy mountain.
> I will surely tell of the decree of the Lord:
> He said to Me, "You are My Son,
> Today I have begotten You.
> Ask of Me, and I will surely give the nations as Your inheritance,
> And the very ends of the earth as Your possession.
> You shall break them with a rod of iron,
> You shall shatter them like earthenware."
> Now therefore, O kings, show discernment;
> Take warning, O judges of the earth.
> Worship the Lord with reverence
> And rejoice with trembling.
> Do homage to the Son, that He not become angry, and you perish in the way,
> For His wrath may soon be kindled.
> How blessed are all who take refuge in Him! (Ps. 2:6–12)

Along those same lines, Psalm 110:1 says, "The Lord says to my Lord: 'Sit at My right hand until I make Your enemies a footstool for Your feet.'" And in Isaiah 52:13 the Father declared of the Son, "Behold, My servant will prosper, He will be high and lifted up and greatly exalted." After His death and resurrection, Christ ascended to the place of supreme honor at the Father's right hand (Matt. 26:64; Acts 2:33–35; 5:31; 7:55–56; Rom. 8:34; Eph. 1:20; Col. 3:1; Heb. 1:3; 8:1; 10:12; 12:2; 1 Peter 3:21–22).

To those who honor and glorify Him by obedience to His call to salvation, Jesus promised, **"Truly, truly, I say to you, if anyone keeps My word he will never see death."** *Amēn, amēn* **(truly, truly)**, as it always does in John's gospel (cf. vv. 34, 58; 1:51; 3:3, 5, 11; 5:19, 24–25; 6:26, 32, 47, 53; 10:1, 7; 12:24; 13:16, 20–21, 38; 14:12; 16:20, 23; 21:18), introduces a statement of major significance. The one who **keeps** His **word** (i.e., obeys it; cf. v. 55; 14:15, 21, 23–24; 15:10, 20; Matt. 5:19) is a true child of

God (John 1:12), in His kingdom (3:3–5), and is His true disciple (8:31), who will never experience eternal separation from God (Rev. 2:11; 20:6; cf. 20:14; 21:8). To Nicodemus Jesus declared, "For God so loved the world, that He gave His only begotten Son, that whoever believes in Him shall not perish, but have eternal life" (John 3:16). In 5:24 He reiterated that truth: "Truly, truly, I say to you, he who hears My word, and believes Him who sent Me, has eternal life, and does not come into judgment, but has passed out of death into life." Jesus is "the bread which comes down out of heaven, so that one may eat of it and not die" (6:50). Comforting Martha after the death of her brother Lazarus, the Lord declared, "I am the resurrection and the life; he who believes in Me will live even if he dies, and everyone who lives and believes in Me will never die" (11:25–26).

Jesus' statement here is merely another way of expressing the truth that eternal life results from humbly and obediently believing in His Word and following Him (Matt. 19:29; 25:46; John 3:15–16, 36; 4:14; 5:24; 6:27, 40, 47, 54, 63, 68; 10:10, 28; 17:2–3; Rom. 5:21; 6:23; 1 Tim. 1:16; 1 John 5:11–12). Even to these who scornfully rejected His gospel and dishonored Him, Jesus still graciously offered eternal life—another offer that intensified the severity of their eternal judgment if they rejected it (Luke 12:47–48).

THE DOUBTING

The Jews said to Him, "Now we know that You have a demon. Abraham died, and the prophets also; and You say, 'If anyone keeps My word, he will never taste of death.' Surely You are not greater than our father Abraham, who died? The prophets died too; whom do You make Yourself out to be?" Jesus answered, "If I glorify Myself, My glory is nothing; it is My Father who glorifies Me, of whom you say, 'He is our God'; and you have not come to know Him, but I know Him; and if I say that I do not know Him, I will be a liar like you, but I do know Him and keep His word. Your father Abraham rejoiced to see My day, and he saw it and was glad." So the Jews said to Him, "You are not yet fifty years old, and have You seen Abraham?" Jesus said to them, "Truly, truly, I say to you, before Abraham was born, I am." (8:52–58)

Hearing Jesus' words in a strictly literal and earthly sense, the incredulous **Jews** retorted, **"Now we know that You have a demon. Abraham died, and the prophets also; and You say, 'If anyone keeps My word, he will never taste of death.' Surely You are not**

greater than our father Abraham, who died? The prophets died too; whom do You make Yourself out to be?" Neither the revered patriarch **Abraham** nor any of **the prophets** had the power to defeat death, since they had all **died.** Flinging Jesus' own words back at Him, **If anyone keeps My word, he will never taste of death,** the Jewish leaders indignantly demanded, **"Surely You are not greater than our father Abraham or the prophets** who **died; whom do You make Yourself out to be?"** Or, "Just who do You think You are?" The tone of their questioning is obviously abusive; they were sure that only a demon-possessed person could make such an outlandish claim.

Calmly and patiently, Jesus repeated the truth He had stated in verses 49 and 50: **"If I glorify Myself, My glory is nothing; it is My Father who glorifies Me."** He was not seeking His own glory, but was secure in the knowledge that the **Father . . . glorifies** Him. Jesus' claims were not those of a demoniac or a maniac, because the glory He possesses was not evil or satanic, but divine. It was His by His eternal relation to His Father (17:24)—the very One **of whom** the Jewish leaders said, **"He is our God."** For them to piously claim to know God while blaspheming and rejecting His Son was ludicrous. Therefore Jesus, pointing out the obvious again, plainly told them, **You have not come to know Him.** Despite their outward pretense, they did not know God; they were children of Satan (v. 44). Their delusion was that they were God's children and that Jesus was in league with the Devil (cf. Matt. 12:24).

Despite the fierce opposition of His opponents and the impending outcome, Jesus steadfastly refused to back down or deny that He knew the Father. **"I know Him,"** He affirmed, **"and if I say that I do not know Him, I will be a liar like you, but I do know Him and keep His word."** They were liars because they claimed to know God when they actually did not; Jesus would have been a liar if He had denied knowing God, whom He did know in a profound and eternal oneness (cf. 1:18; 7:29; 10:15; Matt. 11:27). The Lord maintained the truth of His divine knowledge of His Father as one in nature with Him, though it became the issue for which they sought to murder Him (cf. John 19:6–7).

In contrast to their rejection of Him, the Lord told them, **"Your father Abraham rejoiced to see My day, and he saw it and was glad."** Hebrews 11:13 records that Abraham saw and welcomed Christ's day. He saw in his son Isaac the beginning of God's fulfillment of His covenant with him (Gen. 12:1–3; 15:1–21; 17:1–8), which would culminate in the coming of the Messiah. Once again (cf. vv. 39–40), Jesus contrasted His opponents' behavior with that of their patriarch, proving that they were not Abraham's spiritual children. They wanted to murder the very One in whose coming Abraham rejoiced (cf. v. 37).

Stubbornly persisting in their misunderstanding of Jesus' words, the **Jews said to Him, "You are not yet fifty years old, and have You seen Abraham?"** Abraham had lived more than two millennia earlier; Jesus could not possibly have seen him. They also twisted His words; the Lord had not said that He had seen Abraham, but that Abraham had (prophetically) seen Him. It should be noted that the Jews' statement that Jesus was **not yet fifty years old** does not specify Jesus' exact age, but rather places an upper limit on it. The Lord would have been only in His early thirties, since He was about thirty when He began His ministry (Luke 3:23).

Jesus' climactic reply, **"Truly, truly, I say to you, before Abraham was born, I am,"** was nothing less than a claim to full deity. The Lord once again took for Himself the sacred name of God (see the discussion of 8:24 in chapter 29 of this volume). Obviously, as the eternal God (John 1:1–2), He existed before Abraham's time. Homer Kent explains, "By using the timeless 'I am' rather than 'I was,' Jesus conveyed not only the idea of existence prior to Abraham, but timelessness—the very nature of God himself (Exod. 3:14)" (*Light in the Darkness* [Grand Rapids: Baker, 1974], 128–29).

THE DEFIANCE

Therefore they picked up stones to throw at Him, (8:59*a*)

The Jewish leaders understood Jesus' claim perfectly. In response, their hatred flamed into violence. Infuriated by what they perceived as blasphemy (cf. 10:33), they took the law into their own hands and **picked up stones to throw at Him** (cf. Lev. 24:16).

Here is the grip of unbelief so powerful that in the face of irrefutable evidence they were unwilling to accept that as God in human flesh, Jesus was incapable of committing blasphemy; rather all of His claims, no matter how astonishing, were absolutely true. How ironic that the Jewish religious leaders, seemingly so passionate for God's honor that they were ready to cast stones at a blasphemer, were, in fact, accusing God Himself of blaspheming God.

THE DISAPPEARANCE

but Jesus hid Himself and went out of the temple. (8:59*b*)

Significantly, the Lord did not protest that He had been misunderstood. Clearly, He was claiming to be God. Since His hour to die had not yet come (John 7:30; 8:20; 13:1), **Jesus** would not allow Himself to be killed, but supernaturally **hid Himself and went out of the temple** (cf. Luke 4:30). (John's brief and straightforward description of this miraculous escape is reminiscent of how he records other supernatural events in his gospel—cf. John 6:11, 19.) Thus ends this tragic dialogue between Jesus and the doomed Jewish religious leaders.

As on this occasion, so it always is that there are only two possible responses to Jesus' claims. One is to accept them as true, and bow before Him in humble, repentant faith, confessing Him as Savior and Lord. The other response, illustrated by Jesus' opponents in this passage, is that of hardened, bitter rejection. The tragic, fearful result of that response will be eternal damnation in hell. As Jesus soberly warned, "Therefore I said to you that you will die in your sins; for unless you believe that I am He, you will die in your sins" (8:24).

Jesus Opens Blind Eyes
(John 9:1–12)

33

As He passed by, He saw a man blind from birth. And His disciples asked Him, "Rabbi, who sinned, this man or his parents, that he would be born blind?" Jesus answered, "It was neither that this man sinned, nor his parents; but it was so that the works of God might be displayed in him. We must work the works of Him who sent Me as long as it is day; night is coming when no one can work. While I am in the world, I am the Light of the world." When He had said this, He spat on the ground, and made clay of the spittle, and applied the clay to his eyes, and said to him, "Go, wash in the pool of Siloam" (which is translated, Sent). So he went away and washed, and came back seeing. Therefore the neighbors, and those who previously saw him as a beggar, were saying, "Is not this the one who used to sit and beg?" Others were saying, "This is he," still others were saying, "No, but he is like him." He kept saying, "I am the one." So they were saying to him, "How then were your eyes opened?" He answered, "The man who is called Jesus made clay, and anointed my eyes, and said to me, 'Go to Siloam and wash'; so I went away and washed, and I received sight." They said to him, "Where is He?" He said, "I do not know." (9:1–12)

Sickness is a universal effect of the fall, as a result of which sin, death, and decay exist in this imperfect world. It afflicts all human beings, periodically reminding each of them that they "are but dust" (Ps. 103:14), and that one day "to dust [they] shall return" (Gen. 3:19). No matter how careful or health conscious people try to be, sickness is ultimately inevitable.

Throughout history massive outbreaks of disease have destroyed the lives of millions. In the fourteenth century, the infamous Black Death (bubonic plague) killed an estimated one-third to one-half of Europe's population. In the nineteenth century, twice as many Civil War soldiers died of disease as were killed in combat. And in the twentieth century, the influenza epidemic of 1918–19 claimed 30 to 50 million lives—dwarfing the number of those who died in the First World War. Even today, with many diseases no longer a threat, the AIDS virus continues to kill thousands, as do injuries, cancer, and heart problems. Those who dedicate their lives to researching and treating diseases are held in the highest regard among their peers. And rightly so, since they provide society's frontline defense against ubiquitous physical illness.

Despite all of the sophisticated technologies that they utilize, modern medical professionals are limited in the amount of healing they can ultimately offer. The scientific advances of recent times are certainly impressive, but they can only do so much in delaying death. God, on the other hand, is not at all limited in His ability to heal. As with all of life, He is perfectly sovereign over illness and health (cf. Deut. 32:39). He has the power to do "whatever He pleases" (Ps. 115:3) and, at certain historical times, He has chosen to heal in supernatural ways.

Though rare and confined to limited times, examples of God's miraculous healing are recorded in the Old Testament. God healed Naaman of leprosy (2 Kings 5:1–14), Hezekiah of a terminal illness (2 Kings 20:1–11), the Israelites of poisonous snake bites (Num. 21:6–9), Sarah, Leah, and Rachel of infertility (Gen. 21:1–2; 29:31; 30:22), and Job of a debilitating infirmity (Job 42:10). In addition, three dead individuals were restored to life: the widow's son at Zarephath (1 Kings 17:17–24), the Shunammite woman's son (2 Kings 4:18–37), and a man whose body was thrown into Elisha's grave (2 Kings 13:21).

In the New Testament, the book of Acts also records examples of divine healings. Through the apostles, and to authenticate them as messengers of the truth of God (cf. 2 Cor. 12:12), God healed lame men both in Jerusalem (Acts 3:6) and at Lystra (14:8–10), the sick on whom Peter's shadow fell (5:15–16), many paralyzed individuals at Samaria (8:7), those who touched Paul's handkerchiefs or aprons (19:11–12), and the father of Publius on the island of Malta (28:8–9). In addition, Dorcas (9:36–43) and Eutychus (20:9–12) were restored to life. Beyond the apostolic ministry in the record of Acts, miracles are absent from Scripture until the events of the Lord's return prophesied in Revelation.

By far the greatest manifestation of miraculous healing in history occurred during the earthly ministry of the Lord Jesus Christ. Nothing even remotely close to the miraculous display through Him has ever occurred, and rightly so. It has been said that He virtually banished disease from Palestine during that time in an explosion of miraculous healings (cf. Matt. 4:23–25; 8:16; 9:35; 12:15; 14:35–36; 15:30; Luke 6:17–19; 7:21; 9:11; John 21:25) for several vital reasons and purposes: they fulfilled messianic prophecy (Matt. 8:17), authenticated His messianic ministry (11:2–5; cf. John 20:30–31; Acts 2:22), glorified God (John 9:3; 11:4), and, most significantly, demonstrated His deity (Mark 2:7, 10).

There were at least six major characteristics of Jesus' healing ministry. First, Jesus healed with only a word or touch (Matt. 8:5–13, 15; 9:6, 20–22; 14:35–36; 20:34; Mark 5:24–29; Luke 13:10–13; John 5:1–9).

Second, Jesus healed instantly (Matt. 8:3, 13, 15; 9:6–7, 28–30; 15:28, 30–31; 17:18; 20:34; Mark 3:1–5; 5:29; 7:33–35; Luke 13:10–13; 17:14; John 4:53; 5:9); unlike some of the alleged healings of modern faith healers, none of His healings were progressive or gradual. Thus, there was no question that they were genuine miracles, not natural recoveries over time.

Third, Jesus healed completely. For example, after He healed Peter's mother-in-law "she immediately got up and waited on them" (Luke 4:39). When Jesus healed a certain paralytic, the man also "got up and immediately picked up the pallet and went out in the sight of everyone" (Mark 2:12; cf. John 5:9). As an immediate result of Jesus' healings the blind saw, the lame walked, the lepers were cleansed, and the deaf heard—all having been completely restored to physical wholeness (3:2; 7:31; 9:16; 11:47; Acts 2:22).

Fourth, Jesus healed everyone who came to Him. Unlike contemporary false faith healers, He did not leave disappointed, unhealed people in His wake. Luke 4:40 records that "while the sun was setting, all those who had any who were sick with various diseases brought them to Him; and laying His hands on each one of them, He was healing them" (cf. 9:11).

Fifth, Jesus healed organic, physical diseases and infirmities— not invisible ailments such as lower back pain, heart palpitations, and headaches. He restored and replaced crippled legs (Matt. 11:5), withered hands (12:10–13), bent spines (Luke 13:10–13), blind eyes (Matt. 9:28–30), and deaf ears (Mark 7:32–37). No infirmity was beyond His power, so that He healed "every kind of disease and every kind of sickness among the people" (Matt. 4:23).

Finally, unlike modern fakes, Jesus raised dead people (Mark 5:22–24, 35–43; Luke 7:11–16; John 11:43–44; cf. Matt. 11:5).

Jesus' healing of the blind man in this passage cannot be explained by anything other than His miraculous, divine power. (Since during His incarnation Jesus voluntarily gave up the independent exercise of His divine attributes, the Bible says that His power was granted Him by the authority of the Father [Matt. 12:28; Luke 5:17; 11:20; John 5:19; Acts 2:22; 10:38], and delivered to Him by the Holy Spirit [Luke 4:14; Matt. 12:22–32].) It could not have been a natural recovery of sight, since the man was blind from birth (9:1) and saw immediately (v. 7). Nor could it have been a result of medical treatment, since the cure for blindness was far beyond the limited medical knowledge of the time.

The flow of the account falls into four elements: the problem, the purpose, the power, and the perplexity.

THE PROBLEM

As He passed by, He saw a man blind from birth. (9:1)

Some connect the phrase **as He passed by** with the previous narrative, and place this healing immediately after Jesus left the temple (8:59). The wording, however, is general enough that the precise time and location of the healing cannot be determined. Since Jesus sent the blind man to wash at the pool of Siloam (v. 7), the incident must have taken place in Jerusalem. The temple was a prime location for beggars (cf. Matt. 21:14; Acts 3:1–10), since people coming there to worship would be more likely to give them alms. The temple was also a place where large crowds gathered. Possibly, then, the Lord encountered this man near the temple grounds.

Blindness was an all too common occurrence in the ancient world (cf. Lev. 19:14; 21:18; Deut. 27:18; 28:29; 2 Sam. 5:6, 8; Job 29:15); and the uncared-for blind were reduced to begging (cf. Mark 10:46). As Isaiah 42:7 predicted that the Messiah would do, Jesus gave sight to the blind on several occasions (Matt. 9:27–28; 11:5; 12:22; 15:30–31; 20:30–34; 21:14; Mark 8:22–25; Luke 4:18).

The text does not say how the disciples knew that this man had been **blind from birth** (v. 2). Presumably he was a familiar enough figure that his background was common knowledge. Or the blind man himself may have told them. In either case, this is the only recorded instance in the gospels of Jesus healing someone who is said to have had a congenital condition.

THE PURPOSE

And His disciples asked Him, "Rabbi, who sinned, this man or his parents, that he would be born blind?" Jesus answered, "It was neither that this man sinned, nor his parents; but it was so that the works of God might be displayed in him. We must work the works of Him who sent Me as long as it is day; night is coming when no one can work. While I am in the world, I am the Light of the world." (9:2–5)

The blind man's condition created a theological dilemma in the minds of the **disciples.** The question they posed, **"Rabbi, who sinned, this man or his parents, that he would be born blind?"** assumed the popular Jewish doctrine that anyone's physical suffering is the direct result of personal sin. Therefore they saw only two possible explanations for his condition: either the sins of **this man** or those of **his parents** had caused his blindness.

But the man, having been born blind, could not have been responsible for his condition unless he had somehow sinned before he was born. Perhaps the disciples considered that a possibility, since the view that children could sin while still in the womb was widespread in contemporary Judaism. In addition, some Hellenistic Jews, influenced by Greek philosophy, argued for the soul's preexistence. Therefore, they believed people could be punished in this life for sins they committed in a previous existence. (The Bible, of course, rejects such views.) On the other hand, if the man's parents were responsible, it hardly seems fair that their child should be punished for their sin.

The disciples' reasoning, although not completely illogical, was based on a false premise. Certainly, it is true that suffering in general is ultimately a result of sin in general. And it is also true that a specific illness can sometimes be the direct consequence of a specific sin. Miriam, for example, was stricken with leprosy for rebelling against Moses' authority (Num. 12:10). Jesus had earlier warned the man He healed at the pool of Bethesda, "Behold, you have become well; do not sin anymore, so that nothing worse happens to you" (John 5:14). The apostle Paul likewise told the Corinthians, who were partaking of the Lord's supper in an unworthy manner, "Many among you are weak and sick, and a number sleep" (1 Cor. 11:30).

Tragically, there are also times when children are forced to suffer the natural consequences of their parents' sinful choices. For example, the eyes of babies born to women who have gonorrhea can become infected when they pass through the birth canal. If the babies' eyes are not treated medically after birth, blindness can result. A baby's health can also be negatively affected by the mothers' smoking, excessive drinking, or substance abuse during pregnancy.

The disciples may also have been thinking of certain Old Testament passages in which God seems to promise punishment on children for the sins of their parents. In Exodus 20:5 God said to Israel, "I, the Lord your God, am a jealous God, visiting the iniquity of the fathers on the children, on the third and the fourth generations of those who hate Me." Exodus 34:7 repeats the warning that God "will by no means leave the guilty unpunished, visiting the iniquity of fathers on the children and on the grandchildren to the third and fourth generations" (cf. Num. 14:18; Deut. 5:9).

Such passages, however, must be understood in a national or societal sense. The point is that the corrupting effect of a wicked generation seeps into subsequent generations. This is axiomatic, an obvious reality. The idea that a child will be punished for the sins of his own parents is a concept foreign to Scripture. Deuteronomy 24:16 commands, "Fathers shall not be put to death for their sons, nor shall sons be put to death for their fathers; everyone shall be put to death for his own sin" (cf. 2 Chron. 25:4). Through Jeremiah God declared, "In those days they will not say again, 'The fathers have eaten sour grapes, and the children's teeth are set on edge.' But everyone will die for his own iniquity; each man who eats the sour grapes, his teeth will be set on edge" (Jer. 31:29–30). Ezekiel 18:20 adds, "The person who sins will die. The son will not bear the punishment for the father's iniquity, nor will the father bear the punishment for the son's iniquity; the righteousness of the righteous will be upon himself, and the wickedness of the wicked will be upon himself."

Subsequent generations ("to the third and fourth" [Ex. 34:7]) of children, however, have suffered the consequences of a previous generation's disobedience. The Hebrew children of the Exodus, for example, suffered through forty years of wilderness wandering because of the sins of their parents' generation. Centuries later, when the northern and southern kingdoms were carried off into captivity, generations of children suffered for the sins of their elders.

Jesus' reply, **"It was neither that this man sinned, nor his parents; but it was so that the works of God might be displayed in him,"** exposed the error in the disciples' thinking. There is not always a direct link between suffering and personal sin. When Job's would-be counselors rested their case for his suffering on this wrong assumption, they caused him needless misery (cf. Job 13:1–13; 16:1–4) and ultimately received a rebuke from God (42:7). On another occasion, Jesus taught that neither those Galileans whom Pilate slaughtered in the temple nor those killed when the tower in Siloam fell on them (Luke 13:1–5) suffered those deadly effects because they were particularly vile sinners—as His audience had smugly assumed. Instead, the Lord used those two incidents to warn His hearers that all sinners, including them, face death, and when it comes would perish unless they repented and trusted in Him.

The truth was that like Job (Job 1, 2), the blind man was afflicted **so that the works of God might be displayed in him.** But as F. F. Bruce notes,

> This does not mean that God deliberately caused the child to be born blind in order that, after many years, his glory should be displayed in the removal of the blindness; to think so would again be an aspersion on the character of God. It does mean that God overruled the disaster of the child's blindness so that, when the child grew to manhood, he might, by recovering his sight, see the glory of God in the face of Christ, and others, seeing this work of God, might turn to the true Light of the World. (*The Gospel of John* [Grand Rapids: Eerdmans, 1994], 209)

God sovereignly chose to use this man's affliction for His own glory.

Having addressed their misunderstanding and introduced the matter of doing God's work, Jesus affirmed it as the priority, saying to the disciples, **"We must work the works of Him who sent Me."** Their focus was backward, on analyzing how the blind man came to be in his condition; the Lord's concern was forward, on putting God's power on display for the man's benefit. As noted in the discussion of 4:4 in chapter 11 of this volume, John frequently used the verb *dei* (**must**) to describe Jesus' active fulfillment of the mission given Him by the Father (cf. 3:14; 10:16; 12:34; 20:9). Here the plural pronoun **we** includes the disciples, who also were empowered to do **the works of** the Father **who sent** Jesus.

The phrase **as long as it is day** conveys a sense of urgency (cf. 7:33; 11:9–10; 12:35; 13:33). It refers to the brief time (only a few months remained until the crucifixion) that Jesus would still be physically present with the disciples. After that, He said, **"Night is coming when no one can work"**—a reference to His being taken away from the disciples in death. They would then be overtaken by the darkness (cf. 12:35) and unable to **work** (cf. 20:19; Matt. 26:56) until the coming of the Holy Spirit on the day of Pentecost once again empowered them to minister.

But **while** Jesus was still **in the world,** He was **the Light of the world.** The Lord, of course, did not cease to be the **Light of the world** after His death, since He carried on His ministry through the disciples (Matt. 28:18–20). Yet that Light shone most clearly and brightly during His earthly ministry. What Jesus told the disciples applies to all believers.

They are to serve God with a sense of urgency, "making the most of [their] time, because the days are evil" (Eph. 5:16; cf. Col. 4:5). The noble Puritan pastor Richard Baxter captured that sense of urgency when he wrote, "I preached as never sure to preach again, and as a dying man to dying men" (cited in I. D. E. Thomas, *A Puritan Golden Treasury* [Edinburgh: Banner of Truth, 1977], 223).

THE POWER

When He had said this, He spat on the ground, and made clay of the spittle, and applied the clay to his eyes, and said to him, "Go, wash in the pool of Siloam" (which is translated, Sent). So he went away and washed, and came back seeing. (9:6–7)

The One who is the spiritual Light of the World would also provide physical light for this man who had lived his entire life in darkness. The healing is thus a living parable, illustrating Jesus' ministry as the Light shining in a spiritually darkened world (cf. 1:5).

Having finished His dialogue with the disciples, the Lord **spat on the ground, and made clay of the spittle, and applied the clay to** the blind man's **eyes, and said to him, "Go, wash in the pool of Siloam."** Jesus had earlier used His saliva in the healing of a deaf and mute man (Mark 7:33) and a blind man (8:23), but only here did He make **clay of the spittle.** Why He did so is not stated. Some of the early church fathers interpreted Jesus' actions in light of Genesis 2:7. In that case, making the clay would symbolize the Lord's creating a new, functioning pair of eyes to replace those which had never seen. But as Leon Morris notes, "Jesus performed His miracles with a sovereign hand and He cannot be limited by rules of procedure. He cured how He willed" (*The Gospel According to John,* The New International Commentary on the New Testament [Grand Rapids: Eerdmans, 1979], 480).

The **pool of Siloam,** which has recently been rediscovered (for a report on this find, see "The Pool of Siloam Revealed," www.bibleplaces. com/poolofsiloam.htm), was located near the southeast corner of the city wall. Water flowed to it from the Gihon spring, located in the Kidron valley. Fearing a siege by the Assyrians (2 Chron. 32:4), Hezekiah had constructed a tunnel from the Gihon spring to the pool of Siloam (2 Kings 20:20) to ensure a continual supply of water. It was from the pool of Siloam that the high priest drew water during the Feast of Tabernacles (cf. the discussion of 7:37 in chapter 26 of this volume).

John's parenthetical note calls attention to the significance of the name **Siloam,** which transliterates a Hebrew word that means **Sent.**

The name probably originated because of the water sent into the pool (via Hezekiah's tunnel) from the Gihon spring. But, as its use in the Feast of Tabernacles suggests, the name also symbolized the blessings God sent to Israel. Here it symbolizes God's ultimate blessing to the nation: Jesus the Messiah, the One sent from God (5:24, 30, 36–37; 6:38–39, 44, 57; 7:16, 28–29, 33; 8:16, 18, 26, 29, 42; 11:42; 12:44–45, 49; 13:20; 14:24; 15:21; 16:5; 17:8, 18, 21, 23, 25; 20:21; Matt. 10:40; Mark 9:37; Luke 4:18; 9:48; 10:16). Sadly, just as their ancestors "rejected the gently flowing waters of Shiloah [Siloam]" (Isa. 8:6), so also did the people reject Jesus, the true Siloam, the One sent by God to save lost sinners (Luke 19:10).

As Jesus instructed, the blind man obediently **went away and washed** in the pool, **and came back seeing.** His response to the Lord's command symbolizes the obedience that marks genuine saving faith (Rom. 1:5; 15:18; 16:26; Heb. 5:9)—which he would shortly manifest (see the discussion of vv. 35–38 in chapter 35 of this volume).

THE PERPLEXITY

Therefore the neighbors, and those who previously saw him as a beggar, were saying, "Is not this the one who used to sit and beg?" Others were saying, "This is he," still others were saying, "No, but he is like him." He kept saying, "I am the one." So they were saying to him, "How then were your eyes opened?" He answered, "The man who is called Jesus made clay, and anointed my eyes, and said to me, 'Go to Siloam and wash'; so I went away and washed, and I received sight." They said to him, "Where is He?" He said, "I do not know." (9:8–12)

The healing of the blind man understandably caused a sensation among his **neighbors** and all who had previously known **him as a beggar.** The transformation was so shocking that some **were saying** in confusion, **"Is not this the one who used to sit and beg?"** Others confidently asserted, **"This is he,"** but **still others,** unable to believe that a miracle had taken place (cf. v. 32), **were saying, "No, but he is like him."** They found it easier to believe in a case of mistaken identity than in a miraculous healing. The Pharisees would later repeat their speculation that this was not the same man (v. 18). The discussion was cut short by the formerly blind man himself, who emphatically asserted, **"I am the one."**

At least some were convinced that this was indeed the man who had been blind, and **they were saying to him, "How then were your eyes opened?"** In response, with no attempt to explain how, he succinctly summarized what had happened: **"The man who is called Jesus made clay, and anointed my eyes, and said to me, 'Go to Siloam and wash'; so I went away and washed, and I received sight."** Wanting to meet the One who performed such an incredible miracle, the crowd **said to him, "Where is He?"** But the man did **not know** where Jesus was and, having never seen Him, could not have identified Him in any case. The Lord had disappeared from the narrative after verse 7, leaving only the formerly blind man on center stage. Not until verse 35 does Jesus reappear.

This account of Jesus' healing of a blind man beautifully illustrates the salvation process. Blinded by sin (12:40; 2 Cor. 4:4), lost sinners have no capacity to recognize the Savior or find Him on their own (Rom. 3:11; 8:7). The blind man would not have been healed had Jesus not sought him and revealed Himself to him. So it is in salvation; if God did not reach out to spiritually blind sinners, no one would be saved (Rom. 5:6; cf. John 6:44, 65). And just as the blind man was healed only when he obeyed Jesus' command and washed in the pool of Siloam, so also are sinners saved only when they humbly and obediently embrace the truth of the gospel (Rom. 1:5; 15:18; 16:26; Heb. 5:9; cf. 2 Thess. 1:8; 1 Peter 4:17).

Unbelief Investigates a Miracle
(John 9:13–34)

34

They brought to the Pharisees the man who was formerly blind. Now it was a Sabbath on the day when Jesus made the clay and opened his eyes. Then the Pharisees also were asking him again how he received his sight. And he said to them, "He applied clay to my eyes, and I washed, and I see." Therefore some of the Pharisees were saying, "This man is not from God, because He does not keep the Sabbath." But others were saying, "How can a man who is a sinner perform such signs?" And there was a division among them. So they said to the blind man again, "What do you say about Him, since He opened your eyes?" And he said, "He is a prophet." The Jews then did not believe it of him, that he had been blind and had received sight, until they called the parents of the very one who had received his sight, and questioned them, saying, "Is this your son, who you say was born blind? Then how does he now see?" His parents answered them and said, "We know that this is our son, and that he was born blind; but how he now sees, we do not know; or who opened his eyes, we do not know. Ask him; he is of age, he will speak for himself." His parents said this because they were afraid of the Jews; for the Jews had already agreed that if anyone confessed Him to be Christ, he

_397_

**was to be put out of the synagogue. For this reason his parents
said, "He is of age; ask him." So a second time they called the man
who had been blind, and said to him, "Give glory to God; we
know that this man is a sinner." He then answered, "Whether He
is a sinner, I do not know; one thing I do know, that though I was
blind, now I see." So they said to him, "What did He do to you?
How did He open your eyes?" He answered them, "I told you
already and you did not listen; why do you want to hear it again?
You do not want to become His disciples too, do you?" They
reviled him and said, "You are His disciple, but we are disciples
of Moses. We know that God has spoken to Moses, but as for this
man, we do not know where He is from." The man answered and
said to them, "Well, here is an amazing thing, that you do not
know where He is from, and yet He opened my eyes. We know
that God does not hear sinners; but if anyone is God-fearing and
does His will, He hears him. Since the beginning of time it has
never been heard that anyone opened the eyes of a person born
blind. If this man were not from God, He could do nothing." They
answered him, "You were born entirely in sins, and are you
teaching us?" So they put him out.** (9:13–34)

As God's chosen people (Ex. 19:5; Deut. 4:37; 7:6–8; 10:15; 26:18;
32:9; Amos 3:2), the nation of Israel inherited His unique and gracious
promises (Deut. 15:6; Rom. 9:4; Eph. 2:12)—the basic earthly promise of
the land (cf. Gen. 50:24; Ex. 12:25; Deut. 6:3; 12:20; 19:8; 27:3; Josh. 23:5),
and the heavenly pledge of salvation through the promised Messiah
(Gen. 3:15; 49:10; Deut. 18:18; Isa. 7:14; 9:6; 11:1–2; 52:13–53:12; Jer. 23:5–6;
Mic. 5:2; John 4:22; Gal. 3:16).

Tragically, Israel missed out on both of those promises. Although
they lived in the Promised Land, the Israelites never possessed all of the
territory God had promised them. Nor were they able to remain in the
land permanently, since due to their idolatry and sin, they were eventually
conquered by the Assyrians and Babylonians, and carried away into
exile. Though a remnant returned in the days of Ezra and Nehemiah, they
soon fell under the rule of the Greeks, Syrians, and Romans. And only a
few decades (A.D. 70 and following) after rejecting Jesus, they were both
massacred and driven from their land for a second time, not to return to
form an independent nation again for nearly two thousand years.

Israel's disobedience, which prevented her from fully experiencing all of God's promised blessings, was triggered by persistent unbelief.
That unbelief began even before the nation entered the Promised Land.
Not long after the Israelites left Egypt, God "said to Moses, 'How long will
this people spurn Me? And how long will they not believe in Me, despite

all the signs which I have performed in their midst?'" (Num. 14:11). Because of their stubborn lack of faith, God prevented the entire generation of Israelite adults (except Caleb and Joshua; Num. 14:30, 38; 26:65) from entering Canaan. As the writer of Hebrews explains: "And to whom did He swear that they would not enter His rest, but to those who were disobedient? So we see that they were not able to enter because of unbelief" (Heb. 3:18–19). Jude added, "The Lord, after saving a people out of the land of Egypt, subsequently destroyed those who did not believe" (Jude 5; cf. Num. 14:26–30; Deut. 1:32, 34–35; 9:23). In Psalm 78 the psalmist lamented the unbelief of that generation:

> Then they spoke against God;
> They said, "Can God prepare a table in the wilderness?
> Behold, He struck the rock so that waters gushed out,
> And streams were overflowing;
> Can He give bread also?
> Will He provide meat for His people?"
> Therefore the Lord heard and was full of wrath;
> And a fire was kindled against Jacob
> And anger also mounted against Israel,
> Because they did not believe in God
> And did not trust in His salvation. (vv. 19–22; cf. v. 32; 106:24)

Even Moses and Aaron succumbed to temptation and were barred from entering the Promised Land (Num. 20:12).

Unfortunately, succeeding generations failed to learn from their ancestors' unbelief. Second Kings 17:14 explains that the northern kingdom (Israel) was destroyed by the Assyrians because "they did not listen, but stiffened their neck like their fathers, who did not believe in the Lord their God." Later the southern kingdom (Judah) also turned away from the Lord in unbelief and was taken into captivity by Babylon. Using the metaphor of an olive tree to symbolize the richness of God's covenant blessings, Paul wrote that the Israelites "were broken off for their unbelief" (Rom. 11:20).

The gospel of John, which emphasizes belief in Christ, also documents Israel's refusal to believe (John 1:11). They truly were, as the Lord characterized them, an "unbelieving generation" (Mark 9:19). Jesus said to Nicodemus, "If I told you earthly things and you do not believe, how will you believe if I tell you heavenly things?" (3:12), and cautioned, "He who does not believe has been judged already, because he has not believed in the name of the only begotten Son of God" (v. 18). Responding to the feeble, sign-based curiosity of a Galilean nobleman, Jesus rebuked him (and others like him). "Unless you people see signs and wonders," He said, "you simply will not believe" (4:48). The Lord told the

hostile Jewish religious leaders, "You do not have [God's] word abiding
in you, for you do not believe Him whom He sent. . . . How can you
believe, when you receive glory from one another and you do not seek
the glory that is from the one and only God?" (5:38, 44; cf. 7:48). To the
crowd in Capernaum, eagerly seeking another miraculous feeding, Jesus
said, "But I said to you that you have seen Me, and yet do not believe"
(6:36). Unbelief even characterized some who had claimed to be His followers (v. 64). John records that "not even His brothers were believing in
Him" (7:5). Nonetheless, Jesus continued to speak the truth boldly, confronting His opponents with irrefutable logic and undeniable evidence.
Challenging a hostile crowd in Jerusalem, He bluntly asked, "If I speak
truth, why do you not believe Me?" (8:46). And when the Jewish leaders
accosted Him in the temple and demanded, "How long will You keep us
in suspense? If You are the Christ, tell us plainly" (10:24), Jesus replied, "I
told you, and you do not believe; the works that I do in My Father's name,
these testify of Me. But you do not believe because you are not of My
sheep" (10:25–26). The sad reality is that "though [Jesus] had performed
so many signs before [the people], yet they were not believing in Him"
(12:37; cf. 16:9). Like their ancestors in the wilderness, most of the Jews of
Jesus' day failed to believe. (It should be noted, however, that in the
future, prior to Christ's return to earth and His millennial kingdom, the
rebels of Israel will be purged and the nation of Israel will finally come to
believe in Him as the Messiah. At that time, the Jews will fully experience
all of God's promised blessings, including full possession of the renewed
Promised Land, and eternal salvation through their promised Savior
[Rom. 11:25–26; cf. Isa. 45:11–17; Ezek. 20:36–44; Hos. 14:1–9; Amos
9:11–15; Zech. 12–14.) They will live with all the saints forever in the new
heavens and new earth spoken of by Isaiah (65:17; 66:22) and John (Rev.
21:1–22:5).

Jesus' amazing healing of a man who had been blind from birth
was not enough to soften the hardened hearts of the Pharisees. Verses
13–34 expose the character of their stubborn unbelief and record the
first overt break between Jesus' followers and the Jewish religious establishment. The blind man is the first person known to have been put out
of the synagogue because of loyalty to Christ (cf. 16:2).

Four characteristics of willful unbelief emerge from this passage:
unbelief is inconsistent, intractable, irrational, and insolent.

UNBELIEF IS INCONSISTENT

**They brought to the Pharisees the man who was formerly blind.
Now it was a Sabbath on the day when Jesus made the clay and**

opened his eyes. Then the Pharisees also were asking him again how he received his sight. And he said to them, "He applied clay to my eyes, and I washed, and I see." Therefore some of the Pharisees were saying, "This man is not from God, because He does not keep the Sabbath." But others were saying, "How can a man who is a sinner perform such signs?" And there was a division among them. (9:13–16)

Unable to comprehend the startling healing of the formerly blind man (vv. 8–12), some who knew about it **brought** him **to the Pharisees.** It was only natural to seek an explanation from the religious authorities regarding this unprecedented (v. 32) incident. They probably did not bring him to the Pharisees on the day of the healing, however, because **it was a Sabbath on the day when Jesus made the clay and opened** the blind man's **eyes.** The fastidious Pharisees would not likely have held such an inquiry on the Sabbath.

Beyond seeking an explanation, those who brought the man to the Pharisees may have wanted to see how their leaders would react to this blatant violation of the Sabbath restrictions. Whether or not this was a formal inquiry is not clear, though the fact that the Pharisees put the man out of the synagogue (v. 34) suggests that they met in some official capacity. Perhaps the Sanhedrin delegated them to investigate the incident. Whatever the technical nature of the enclave, it had an official effect.

Like those who escorted the man (v. 10), the **Pharisees also were asking him again how he received his sight.** He repeated all he knew, what the Lord had done, and his own action, stating succinctly, Jesus **"applied clay to my eyes, and I washed, and I see."**

The immediate and predictable reaction of **some of the Pharisees,** who **were saying, "This man** Jesus **is not from God, because He does not keep the Sabbath,"** reveals the biased approach that controlled their investigation. In their eyes, Jesus had broken the Sabbath, not because He had violated any of the divine Sabbath regulations revealed in Scripture, but because He had ignored the restrictions and extrabiblical applications of the rabbis. For example, the Lord had made mud from His saliva and some dust, which supposedly violated the prohibition against kneading on the Sabbath. The rabbinic regulations also forbade giving medical treatment on the Sabbath unless a person's life was in immediate danger, which was obviously not the case with the blind man. Additionally, some rabbis taught that it was not permitted to anoint the eyes with medicine (saliva was thought to have medicinal qualities) on the Sabbath, though opinion was divided on that issue.

This was not the first time Jesus had deliberately violated traditional Sabbath regulations. In Matthew 12:1–8 He defended His disciples for picking grain on the Sabbath, in violation of rabbinic law. Then shortly afterward He healed a man with a withered hand on the Sabbath (Matt. 12:9–13; cf. Luke 13:10–16; 14:1–6). Earlier in John's gospel, Jesus had healed a man at the pool of Bethesda on the Sabbath, so enraging the Jewish authorities that they sought to kill Him (5:9–18).

Why did He deliberately provoke the leaders by violating their Sabbath regulations? First and foremost, because it displayed His divine authority as Lord of the Sabbath (Luke 6:5). But He also did it to demonstrate that such extrabiblical standards were an unnecessary and oppressive burden on the people. By making the seventh day a wearisome one governed by dozens of trivial, hairsplitting rules, the Jewish leaders had perverted God's design for this weekly day of rest and thanks to God; after all, as Jesus pointed out, "The Sabbath was made for man, and not man for the Sabbath" (Mark 2:27). The religious leaders prided themselves on keeping the minutiae of the legalistic Sabbath rules, while at the same time ignoring far more important issues such as showing mercy (cf. Matt. 12:11–12; Mark 3:4; Luke 13:15–16). No wonder Jesus excoriated them for "[tying] up heavy burdens and lay[ing] them on men's shoulders, [while] they themselves are unwilling to move them with so much as a finger" (Matt. 23:4). They corrupted the Sabbath, turning it from a day of glorifying God into a means of legalistic self-glorification.

Blinded by their own self-righteous system, it seemed obvious to this first group of Pharisees that Jesus could not be from God. Those who are from God, they reasoned, keep the Sabbath; Jesus did not observe the Sabbath regulations; therefore He could not be from God (cf. Deut. 13:1–5). But **others were** not so easily convinced. **"How can a man who is a sinner perform such signs?"** they wondered, countering the first group's reasoning with a syllogism of their own: Only those who are from God can open blind eyes; Jesus opened blind eyes; therefore Jesus is from God. As a result **there was a division among them,** just as there earlier had been among the crowd (7:40–43).

Unbelief Is Intractable

So they said to the blind man again, "What do you say about Him, since He opened your eyes?" And he said, "He is a prophet." The Jews then did not believe it of him, that he had been blind and had received sight, until they called the parents of the very one who had received his sight, and questioned them, saying, "Is this your son, who you say was born blind? Then how does he now see?" His parents answered them and said, "We know that this is our son, and that he was born blind; but how he now sees, we do

not know; or who opened his eyes, we do not know. Ask him; he is of age, he will speak for himself." His parents said this because they were afraid of the Jews; for the Jews had already agreed that if anyone confessed Him to be Christ, he was to be put out of the synagogue. For this reason his parents said, "He is of age; ask him." So a second time they called the man who had been blind, and said to him, "Give glory to God; we know that this man is a sinner." (9:17–24)

That Jesus had performed the miracle was incontestable; it was literally staring the Pharisees in the face in the person of the seeing man. Obstinately unwilling to accept the evidence, however, they remained willfully unconvinced of the truth. They were like those whom God Himself described as "a perverse generation, children in whom is no faith" (Deut. 32:20 NKJV).

Continuing their interrogation, the Pharisees **said to the blind man again, "What do you say about Him, since** (as you claim; cf. v. 18) **He opened your eyes?"** That the high-handed Pharisees would ask the opinion of a lowly beggar reflects either their scorn and mockery of the man, or their confusion and division (v. 16). The man's bold and emphatic reply, **"He is a prophet"** (cf. 4:19; 6:14; 7:40) shows that he grasped the reality that the spiritually blind Pharisees refused to see— that Jesus was sent from God. His words reflect a growing understanding on his part as to the true identity of "the man who is called Jesus" (v. 11). As one commentator notes, "The man's eyes are opening wider: he is beginning to see still more clearly, while the eyes of his judges are becoming clouded over with blinding, theological mist" (D. A. Carson, *The Gospel According to John,* The Pillar New Testament Commentary [Grand Rapids: Eerdmans, 1991], 368). His knowledge of Jesus, however, was not yet complete (cf. vv. 35–38).

Despite the evidence and the man's clear and unequivocal testimony, **the Jews did not believe it of him, that he had been blind and had received sight.** Like those in verse 9 who "were saying, 'No, but he is like him,'" the **Jews** (a title John often used to denote those hostile to Jesus, especially among the religious elite; cf. 2:18, 20; 5:16, 18; 6:41, 52; 7:1, 15, 35; 8:22, 48, 52, 57–59; 10:24, 31, 33; 19:38; 20:19) decided that perhaps this was merely a case of mistaken identity. Therefore they **called the parents of the very one who had received his sight.** Although others might be mistaken about this man's identity, his parents would know if this was their son.

When the man's parents arrived, the Pharisees **questioned them,** evidently with their son not present (v. 24). They presented three related questions: **Is this your son? was** he **born blind?** and if so, **how**

does he now see? For a reason that will soon become apparent (v. 22), the man's parents answered cautiously. They identified him as their **son,** and affirmed that he had in fact been **born blind.** But though their son had undoubtedly told them about his miracle, they carefully evaded the last question, instead telling the Pharisees, **"How he now sees, we do not know; or who opened his eyes, we do not know."** Then, in an effort to avoid any further interrogation and reprisal, they suggested that the Pharisees **ask** their son for an explanation, since **he** was **of** a responsible **age** and could **speak for himself.**

John's parenthetical note gives the reason for their hesitancy to get involved in the matter. **His parents,** John explained, **said this because they were afraid of the Jews; for the Jews had already agreed that if anyone confessed Him to be Christ, he was to be put out of the synagogue. For this reason his parents said, "He is of age; ask him."** Contrary to what they told the Pharisees, the man's parents evidently did know that Jesus had healed their son. Had they not known that, there would have been no reason for them to be **afraid** that **the Jews** might **put** them **out of the synagogue** because of Jesus. The term *apsosunagōgas*, unknown to secular writers, meant to be excommunicated or put under a ban and a curse, a banishment that meant being cut off from the religious and social life of Israel; it was therefore a dreaded punishment (cf. 12:42; 16:2).

With the son positively identified and the Pharisees left with no legitimate excuse for denying that a genuine miracle had taken place, they were still unwilling to believe the claims of Jesus. They wanted the healed man to join them in that unbelief, so **they called the man who had been blind, and said to him, "Give glory to God; we know that this man** Jesus **is a sinner."** Demanding that he not give credit to Jesus for his healing, they insisted instead that he give the credit to God. Their exhortation to the blind man, **Give glory to God,** can also be understood as a charge to stop lying by saying that Jesus healed him and tell the truth, in the same manner as Joshua's charge to Achan, "My son, I implore you, give glory to the Lord, the God of Israel, and give praise to Him; and tell me now what you have done. Do not hide it from me" (Josh. 7:19). Such a confession on the man's part would equal agreement with the leaders' conviction that Jesus was a **sinner** and not at all empowered by God (cf. John 8:52).

UNBELIEF IS IRRATIONAL

He then answered, "Whether He is a sinner, I do not know; one thing I do know, that though I was blind, now I see." So they said

to him, **"What did He do to you? How did He open your eyes?"** He answered them, **"I told you already and you did not listen; why do you want to hear it again? You do not want to become His disciples too, do you?"** They reviled him and said, **"You are His disciple, but we are disciples of Moses. We know that God has spoken to Moses, but as for this man, we do not know where He is from."** The man answered and said to them, **"Well, here is an amazing thing, that you do not know where He is from, and yet He opened my eyes."** (9:25–30)

Undaunted by the Pharisees' pronouncement about Jesus, the formerly blind man **answered, "Whether He is a sinner, I do not know."** He left that determination to the theological "experts." But he stubbornly clung to the undeniable reality of his sight, declaring, **"One thing I do know, that though I was blind, now I see."** He ignored their biased dilemma and declared the uncomplicated truth—Jesus had definitely healed him.

Stopped dead in their tracks by the incontestable testimony of the man, and left with no way to advance their lame argument, the Pharisees began to go over the same ground they had previously covered. They had already asked the question, **"What did He do to you? How did He open your eyes?"** in verse 15. Perhaps they hoped that this time around the man would contradict what he had said earlier, or say something else that they could use against Jesus.

Understandably exasperated by the Pharisees' repeated questioning and obvious bias, the healed man **answered them, "I told you already and you did not listen; why do you want to hear it again?"** He saw no point in rehashing his testimony, since they obviously did not believe him anyway. Comprehending their animosity toward Jesus, he asked them sarcastically whether their repeated questions about Jesus implied that they wanted to be clear on the truth, so as **to become His disciples.**

His bold rebuke and biting wit struck a nerve. Incensed at his insolence, the Pharisees exploded in rage, **reviled him and said, "You are His disciple, but we are disciples of Moses."** Pulling themselves up by their self-righteous bootstraps and reacting to the man's mockery, they retreated to the safety of their supposed loyalty to Moses. If an uneducated beggar like him wanted to follow an outcast sinner like Jesus, that was his choice; they would follow Moses. After all, as they heatedly told him, **"God has spoken to Moses, but as for this man** (they could not even bring themselves to name Jesus), **we do not know where He is from."** They saw Jesus as a deranged (see the discussion of 8:48 in chapter 32 of this volume) and untrained (7:15) blasphemer (19:7) from an insignificant family in the despised village of Nazareth (cf. 1:46).

The beggar's rejoinder was devastating: **"Well, here is an amazing thing, that you do not know where He is from, and yet He opened my eyes."** Jesus was able to do what only God's power can do, to heal congenital blindness and create new, seeing eyes, yet the religious authorities claimed to be totally ignorant of His origin. Such was the irrational folly that resulted from their stubborn rejection of the facts. It has been this way ever since among those who know the gospel truth and cling to their sin and unbelief.

UNBELIEF IS INSOLENT

"We know that God does not hear sinners; but if anyone is God-fearing and does His will, He hears him. Since the beginning of time it has never been heard that anyone opened the eyes of a person born blind. If this man were not from God, He could do nothing." They answered him, "You were born entirely in sins, and are you teaching us?" So they put him out. (9:31–34)

This humble beggar now proceeded to give a theological lecture to the haughty, insolent religious leaders of his nation. He responded to the Pharisees' syllogism (cf. the discussion of v. 16 above) with one of his own. His major premise was that **God does not hear sinners** (Job 27:9; Ps. 66:18; Isa. 1:15), **but if anyone is God-fearing and does His will, He hears him** (Ps. 34:15; Prov. 15:8, 29; 1 Peter 3:12). His minor premise was that God obviously heard Jesus, since He gave Him the power to do something unheard of **since the beginning of time:** to open **the eyes of a person born blind.** His irrefutable conclusion was that **"if this man were not from God, He could do nothing"** like this.

Unable to reply to the man's irresistible logic, and outraged that he would presume to lecture them, the Pharisees resorted to heaping personal abuse on him. **"You were born entirely in sins,** they sneered, **and are you teaching us?"** With sarcasm and scorn, they retaliated with an ad hominem attack, implying that for him to have been blind from birth he (or possibly his parents; cf. v. 2) must have been guilty of gross iniquity. Ironically, through their disparaging words, they admitted the fact that this man who now saw had indeed been born blind—a point they had earlier denied (v. 18). Then **they put him out** of the synagogue—extending to him the excommunication that his parents had narrowly avoided.

As this passage illustrates, when unbelieving skeptics investigate the miracles of Christ, or any other supernatural event recorded in the Bible, there can be only one outcome. Unless the Holy Spirit opens their blind eyes, they will deny the veracity of such accounts no matter what the evidence. The Pharisees in this passage were presented with living proof of Jesus' divine power. And yet, shrouded in unbelief, they attempted both to deny the undeniable and to refute the irrefutable. As a former Pharisee (the apostle Paul) would later explain, "A natural man does not accept the things of the Spirit of God, for they are foolishness to him; and he cannot understand them, because they are spiritually appraised" (1 Cor. 2:14; cf. John 6:44).

Spiritual Sight or Spiritual Blindness? (John 9:35–41)

35

Jesus heard that they had put him out, and finding him, He said, "Do you believe in the Son of Man?" He answered, "Who is He, Lord, that I may believe in Him?" Jesus said to him, "You have both seen Him, and He is the one who is talking with you." And he said, "Lord, I believe." And he worshiped Him. And Jesus said, "For judgment I came into this world, so that those who do not see may see, and that those who see may become blind." Those of the Pharisees who were with Him heard these things and said to Him, "We are not blind too, are we?" Jesus said to them, "If you were blind, you would have no sin; but since you say, 'We see,' your sin remains." (9:35–41)

Christ's miraculous healing of the man born blind was an astounding display of His divine power, and a life-changing event for the formerly blind man. But physical sight was not all the Lord was planning to give this undeserving beggar. Jesus was yet to do something even more amazing—grant him spiritual sight.

Throughout Scripture blindness is used metaphorically to represent fallen man's inability to comprehend divine truth. Isaiah referred to "the people who are blind, even though they have eyes" (Isa. 43:8), while

Jeremiah described the "foolish and senseless people, who have eyes but do not see" (Jer. 5:21). Isaiah also portrayed the corrupt spiritual leaders of Israel as "watchmen [who] are blind, all of [whom] know nothing" (56:10). Centuries later, Jesus would similarly denounce the Pharisees as "blind guides" and "blind men" (Matt. 15:14; 23:16–17, 19, 24, 26). Like their leaders, even with the Scriptures the people of Jesus' day also lacked spiritual understanding.

After His resurrection and ascension, Christ sent the apostle Paul to the Gentiles "to open their eyes so that they may turn from darkness to light" (Acts 26:18), which was necessary because they too were "darkened in their understanding" (Eph. 4:18). In Revelation, the risen Christ also warned of spiritual blindness even in the church. He rebuked the lukewarm congregation at Laodicea with these words: "You say, 'I am rich, and have become wealthy, and have need of nothing,' and you do not know that you are wretched and miserable and poor and blind and naked" (Rev. 3:17). So neither very religious Jews, nor pagan nations, nor those who are only professing Christians are exempt from this blindness.

As if the sinful blindness of those who love "the darkness rather than the Light" (John 3:19) were not bad enough, "the god of this world has blinded the minds of the unbelieving so that they might not see the light of the gospel of the glory of Christ, who is the image of God" (2 Cor. 4:4). Those who willfully continue to walk naturally in darkness may also find that God judicially blinds them, giving them over to the darkness they love (cf. Rom. 1:21–25). Therefore, in further judgment, the Lord spoke to the crowds in parables

> because while seeing they do not see, and while hearing they do not hear, nor do they understand. In their case the prophecy of Isaiah is being fulfilled, which says, "You will keep on hearing, but will not understand; you will keep on seeing, but will not perceive; for the heart of this people has become dull, with their ears they scarcely hear, and they have closed their eyes, otherwise they would see with their eyes, hear with their ears, and understand with their heart and return, and I would heal them." (Matt. 13:13–15; cf. Isa. 6:9–10; 29:9–10; John 12:40; Acts 28:26–27; Rom. 11:8)

Writing of those who worship idols, Isaiah said, "They do not know, nor do they understand, for He has smeared over their eyes so that they cannot see and their hearts so that they cannot comprehend" (Isa. 44:18). Those who persistently refused to believe in Jesus eventually "could not believe, for Isaiah said again, 'He has blinded their eyes and he hardened their heart, so that they would not see with their eyes and perceive with their heart, and be converted and I heal them'" (John 12:39–40). Paul wrote of unbelieving Israel, "God gave them a spirit of stupor, eyes to see not and ears to hear not, down to this very day" (Rom. 11:8).

As spiritually blind sinners, the unsaved are confined to the darkness, unable to see the light of divine truth. They "walk in the ways of darkness" (Prov. 2:13; cf. 4:19; Eccl. 2:14); "substitute darkness for light and light for darkness" (Isa. 5:20); grope along with no sense of direction (cf. Acts 17:27), since the one who "walks in the darkness does not know where he goes" (John 12:35; 1 John 2:11); "participate in the unfruitful deeds of darkness" (Eph. 5:11); belong to "the domain of darkness" (Col. 1:13); and do not have fellowship with God, who is Light (1 John 1:6; cf. 2:9).

The only cure for spiritual blindness is saving faith in the Lord Jesus Christ. The Old Testament predicted that the Messiah would bring spiritual sight to His people (cf. Isa. 42:7). "The people who walk in darkness," Isaiah wrote, "will see a great light; those who live in a dark land, the light will shine on them. . . . Out of their gloom and darkness the eyes of the blind will see" (Isa. 9:2; 29:18). In Isaiah 49:6 God said of the Messiah, "It is too small a thing that You should be My Servant to raise up the tribes of Jacob and to restore the preserved ones of Israel; I will also make You a light of the nations so that My salvation may reach to the end of the earth."

Zacharias, the father of John the Baptist, said that Messiah would "shine upon those who sit in darkness and the shadow of death, to guide our feet into the way of peace" (Luke 1:79). Jesus applied the words of Isaiah's prophecy to Himself: "The Spirit of the Lord is upon Me, because He anointed Me to preach the gospel to the poor. He has sent Me to proclaim release to the captives, and recovery of sight to the blind" (Luke 4:18). Matthew also quoted Isaiah's prophecy concerning Messiah's ministry: "The people who were sitting in darkness saw a great light, and those who were sitting in the land and shadow of death, upon them a light dawned" (Matt. 4:16). Jesus said of Himself, "I am the Light of the world; he who follows Me will not walk in the darkness, but will have the Light of life" (John 8:12), and, "I have come as Light into the world, so that everyone who believes in Me will not remain in darkness" (12:46).

At salvation God "rescued us from the domain of darkness, and transferred us to the kingdom of His beloved Son" (Col. 1:13). Believers "were formerly darkness, but now . . . are Light in the Lord" (Eph. 5:8; cf. 2 Cor. 4:6). We "are not in darkness . . . [but] are all sons of light and sons of day" (1 Thess. 5:4–5), because God "has called [us] out of darkness into His marvelous light" (1 Peter 2:9).

This passage, which concludes the story of the blind man whom Jesus healed, reveals the characteristics of both spiritual sight (on the part of the man) and spiritual blindness (on the part of the Pharisees).

SPIRITUAL SIGHT

Jesus heard that they had put him out, and finding him, He said, "Do you believe in the Son of Man?" He answered, "Who is He, Lord, that I may believe in Him?" Jesus said to him, "You have both seen Him, and He is the one who is talking with you." And he said, "Lord, I believe." And he worshiped Him. (9:35–38)

John's account of this incident reveals four characteristics of spiritual sight: it requires divine initiative, responds in faith, recognizes Christ, and results in worship.

SPIRITUAL SIGHT REQUIRES DIVINE INITIATIVE

Jesus heard that they had put him out, and finding him, He said, "Do you believe in the Son of Man?" (9:35)

After healing the blind man (9:1–7), Jesus had disappeared from the narrative. The man was then questioned (first by his astonished neighbors [vv. 8–12] and then by the hostile Pharisees [vv. 13–34]), abandoned by his parents (vv. 21–22; cf. Ps. 27:10), and finally excommunicated from the synagogue (v. 34). When **Jesus heard that they had put him out** of the synagogue, He went to find him. Just as He did in granting him his physical sight, the Lord took the initiative in opening his spiritual eyes. Rejected by the religious leaders, he was sought by the Redeemer.

If God did not take the initiative in salvation, no one would be saved, since sinners cannot seek Him on their own. Romans 3:10–12 sums up the sinner's total inability: "There is none righteous, not even one; there is none who understands, there is none who seeks for God; all have turned aside, together they have become useless; there is none who does good, there is not even one." "No one can come to Me," Jesus said, "unless the Father who sent Me draws him; and I will raise him up on the last day" (John 6:44, cf. v. 65). "You did not choose Me," Jesus told the disciples, "but I chose you" (15:16). Just as the physically blind are incapable of restoring their own sight, so also the spiritually dead and blind cannot live or see by their own will or power. Salvation depends on God's initiative, power, and sovereign grace (cf. 1:12–13). (For a discussion of God's sovereignty in salvation, see the exposition of 6:37 in chapter 20 of this volume.)

After **finding him,** Jesus asked the formerly blind man the crucial question, **"Do you believe in the Son of Man?"** By using the personal pronoun **you** in addition to the verb, Jesus emphasized the man's need to respond; the question could be translated, "You . . . do you believe in the Son of Man?" not just as a miracle worker with power from God, but as Messiah. In this way, the man was confronted with his need to place his trust for forgiveness and salvation in Christ as his Lord and Savior. The title Son of Man (cf. 1:51; 3:13; 6:27, 62; 8:28) is messianic and drawn from Daniel 7:13–14, which prophesies His coming and everlasting kingdom. (For a further discussion of the title **Son of Man,** see the exposition of 1:51 in chapter 5 of this volume.)

SPIRITUAL SIGHT RESPONDS IN FAITH

He answered, "Who is He, Lord, that I may believe in Him?" (9:36)

The man's reply revealed a heart divinely prepared to **believe in** Jesus. He already viewed Him as a prophet (v. 17), who had been sent from God (v. 33), and had experienced His supernatural power in the miraculous healing. Not yet fully aware of who the Messiah was, but convinced Jesus was a messenger from God who did know, he trusted Him implicitly to direct him to the One in whom he was to **believe.** His trust illustrates the truth that though divinely initiated, salvation is never apart from a faith response. At the outset of His public ministry Jesus declared it necessary for lost sinners to "repent and believe in the gospel" (Mark 1:15). In the prologue to his gospel John wrote, "But as many as received Him, to them He gave the right to become children of God, even to those who believe in His name" (1:12). The most familiar verse in the New Testament promises "that whoever believes in [Jesus] shall not perish, but have eternal life" (John 3:16; cf. vv. 15, 36; 5:24). "For this is the will of My Father," Jesus said, "that everyone who beholds the Son and believes in Him will have eternal life, and I Myself will raise him up on the last day" (6:40). Later in that same discourse He solemnly affirmed, "Truly, truly, I say to you, he who believes has eternal life" (6:47). The apostle John wrote his gospel "so that [people] may believe that Jesus is the Christ, the Son of God; and that believing [they] may have life in His name" (20:31). Peter told Cornelius and the other Gentiles, "Through [Jesus'] name everyone who believes in Him receives forgiveness of sins" (Acts 10:43). When the Philippian jailor asked Paul and Silas, "'Sirs, what must I do to be saved?' They said, 'Believe in the Lord Jesus, and you will be saved, you and your household'" (Acts 16:30–31). Writing to the Romans, Paul explained that the gospel is "the power of God for salvation to everyone who believes" (Rom. 1:16). Later in that same epistle he wrote, "If you confess with your mouth Jesus as Lord, and believe in your heart that

God raised Him from the dead, you will be saved; for with the heart a person believes, resulting in righteousness, and with the mouth he confesses, resulting in salvation" (Rom. 10:9–10). Paul also told Timothy that
Jesus Christ had showed him mercy so that He "might demonstrate His
perfect patience as an example for those who would believe in Him for
eternal life" (1 Tim. 1:16).

Acts 13:48 sums up the interplay of divine sovereignty and
human responsibility in salvation: "When the Gentiles heard this, they
began rejoicing and glorifying the word of the Lord; and as many as had
been appointed to eternal life believed." In other words, God sovereignly
chose those who would be empowered, awakened, and enabled to
respond in faith (cf. Eph. 2:8–9).

SPIRITUAL SIGHT RECOGNIZES CHRIST

**Jesus said to him, "You have both seen Him, and He is the one
who is talking with you." And he said, "Lord, I believe."** (9:37–38a)

When the Samaritan woman had referred to the coming Messiah,
"Jesus said to her, 'I who speak to you am He'" (4:26). Here in response to
the healed man's request for the Son of Man's identity, **Jesus said to
him, "You have both seen Him, and He is the one who is talking
with you."** The Lord presented Himself as the object of saving faith, just
as He had earlier done at Capernaum: "This is the work of God, that you
believe in Him whom He has sent" (6:29). It is the one "who believes in
the Son [who] has eternal life" (3:36; cf. vv. 15–16, 18; 6:35, 40; 7:38; 8:24;
11:25–26; 12:36, 46; 17:20; 20:31).

Unhesitatingly, the man **said, "Lord, I believe."** The Spirit of
God had opened his heart to the truth (cf. 3:5–8), revealing to him Jesus'
true identity (cf. Matt. 16:16–17). He exemplified the principle Jesus enu-
merated in 7:17: "If anyone is willing to do His will, he will know of the
teaching, whether it is of God or whether I speak from Myself." Jesus
never turns away those whom the Father gives Him; as He Himself said,
"the one who comes to Me I will certainly not cast out" (6:37).

SPIRITUAL SIGHT RESULTS IN WORSHIP

And he worshiped Him. (9:38b)

As the last vestiges of spiritual darkness were dispelled, the eyes
of the man's heart were opened, and he saw clearly who Jesus is. The

inevitable result of such a revelation is always worship (Matt. 14:33; Luke 24:45, 52; Phil. 2:10). Preaching on this passage, Charles Spurgeon summed up the joy and delight the man must have felt at that moment:

> Then, further, *he acted as a believer:* for "he worshipped him." This proves how his faith had grown. I should like to ask you who are the people of God when you are happiest. . . . My happiest moments are when I am worshipping God, really adoring the Lord Jesus Christ. . . . It is the nearest approach to what it will be in heaven, where, day without night, they offer perpetual adoration unto him that sitteth upon the throne, and unto the Lamb. Hence, what a memorable moment it was for this man when he worshipped Christ! Now, if Christ was not God, that man was all idolater, a man-worshipper. . . . If Christ was not God, we are not Christians; we are deceived dupes, we are idolaters, as bad as the heathen whom we now pity. It is making a man into a God if Christ be not God. But, blessed be his holy name, he is God; and we feel that it is the supreme delight of our being to worship him. We cannot veil our face with our wings, for we have none; but we do veil them with his own robe of righteousness whenever we approach him. We cannot cover our feet with our wings, as the angels do; but we do take his blood and his righteousness both as a covering for our feet, and as wings with which we fly up to him; and though as yet we have no crowns to cast at his dear feet, yet, if we have any honor, any good repute, any grace, anything that is comely, anything that is honest, we lay it all at his feet, and cry, "Not unto us, O Lord, not unto us, but unto thy name give glory, for thy mercy, and for thy truth's sake." ("A Pressed Man Yielding to Christ," in *The Metropolitan Tabernacle Pulpit* Vol. 46 (Pasadena, Tex.: Pilgrim Publications, 1977), 46:142. Italics in original.)

SPIRITUAL BLINDNESS

And Jesus said, "For judgment I came into this world, so that those who do not see may see, and that those who see may become blind." Those of the Pharisees who were with Him heard these things and said to Him, "We are not blind too, are we?" Jesus said to them, "If you were blind, you would have no sin; but since you say, 'We see,' your sin remains." (9:39–41)

By way of contrast, four features of spiritual blindness may also be recognized in this passage, illustrated by the Pharisees in the final verses of the chapter: it receives judgment, refuses to admit its blindness, rejects spiritual sight, and results in doom.

SPIRITUAL BLINDNESS RECEIVES JUDGMENT

And Jesus said, "For judgment I came into this world, so that those who do not see may see, and that those who see may become blind." (9:39)

Jesus' words, **"For judgment I came into this world,"** appear at first glance to contradict the truth that "God did not send the Son into the world to judge the world, but that the world might be saved through Him" (3:17). They also seem to oppose the unambiguous revelation of 5:22 and 27: "For not even the Father judges anyone, but He has given all judgment to the Son ... and He gave Him authority to execute judgment, because He is the Son of Man." But far from being contradictory, those two truths are complementary; they are two sides of the same reality. To reject Jesus' peace is to receive His punishment; to reject His grace is to receive His justice; to reject His mercy is to receive His wrath; to reject His love is to receive His anger; to reject His forgiveness is to receive His judgment. While Jesus came to save, not to condemn (cf. 12:47; Luke 19:10), those who reject His gospel condemn themselves, and subject themselves to **judgment** (John 3:18, 36). Spiritual sight comes only to **those** who acknowledge that they **do not see,** who confess their spiritual blindness and their need for the Light of the World. On the other hand, **those who** think they **see** on their own apart from Christ delude themselves, and will remain **blind.** They will not come to the Light, because they love the darkness and do not want their evil deeds to be exposed (3:19).

This was precisely the issue in the synagogue at Nazareth, where Jesus offered the gospel's salvation only to those who were aware of their sin—the penitent spiritually poor, imprisoned, blind, and oppressed (Luke 4:18). The hearers, like most in Israel, did not see themselves as such and reacted by trying to murder Jesus (Luke 4:29). Their response was self-condemning.

As noted earlier, the danger faced by those who think they see is that their rejection and unbelief is irreversible, and they **may become** permanently **blind.** The sobering truth is that those who willfully reject the light of salvation in Christ may find themselves fixed in their condition by God (cf. 12:39–40; Isa. 6:10; Matt. 13:13–15; Acts 28:26–27; Rom. 11:8–10). Scripture records not only that Pharaoh hardened his heart against God (Ex. 8:15, 32; 9:34; 1 Sam. 6:6), but also that, as a result, God hardened Pharaoh's heart (Ex. 4:21; 7:3; 9:12; 10:1, 20, 27; 11:10; 14:4, 8). Some of the Pharisees reached that same point when they rejected the full light of God's revelation in Christ and attributed His divine power to Satan (Matt. 12:24–32).

SPIRITUAL BLINDNESS REFUSES TO ADMIT ITS CONDITION

Those of the Pharisees who were with Him heard these things and said to Him, "We are not blind too, are we?" (9:40)

Evidently Jesus was not alone when He found the blind man; some of the **Pharisees . . . were** still **with Him.** Having **heard** the **things** Jesus said in verse 39, they indignantly **said to Him, "We are not blind too, are we?"** The form of their question in the Greek expects a negative answer. Surely Jesus could not be suggesting that they were spiritually **blind** like the common people who did not know the Law (7:49)? After all, they were the elite, self-proclaimed experts in the Law and devout disciples of Moses (9:28). As the recognized religious leaders of Israel, they were confident that they did not lack spiritual perception. But the reality was that they were blind to spiritual truth, even though they did not know it. And by refusing to admit their blindness, they confirmed the darkened condition of their hearts and increased their hatred for the only One who could save them from Satan and their damning sin.

SPIRITUAL BLINDNESS REJECTS SPIRITUAL SIGHT

Jesus said to them, "If you were blind, you would have no sin;" (9:41*a*)

The Lord's answer must have surprised the Pharisees, who no doubt expected a more direct answer to their question. But Jesus' point was that **if** the Pharisees would confess that they **were** spiritually **blind** (thereby admitting their need for Christ, the true Light) they **would have no sin,** because it would be forgiven (Ps. 32:5; Prov. 28:13; 1 John 1:9).

As John Calvin explained,

> He is *blind* who, aware of his own blindness, seeks a remedy to cure his disease. In this way the meaning will be, "If you would acknowledge your disease, it would not be altogether incurable; but now because you think that you are in perfect health, you continue in a desperate state." When he says that *they who are blind have no sin,* this does not excuse ignorance, as if it were harmless, and were placed beyond the reach of condemnation. He only means that the disease may easily be cured, when it is truly felt; because, when a *blind* man is desirous to obtain deliverance, God is ready to assist him; but they who, insensible to their diseases, despise the grace of God, are incurable. (*Commentary on the Gospel According to John,* translated by William Pringle [Grand Rapids: Baker, 2003], 393. Italics in original.)

Unfortunately, the Pharisees were like those of whom Solomon said, "Do you see a man wise in his own eyes? There is more hope for a fool than for him" (Prov. 26:12; cf. 12:15; Isa. 5:21). Many, by stubbornly refusing to admit their blindness, doomed themselves to darkness forever.

SPIRITUAL BLINDNESS RESULTS IN DOOM

"but since you say, 'We see,' your sin remains." (9:41b)

Since the Pharisees were unwilling to acknowledge their blindness, but claimed to **see,** they remained culpable and unforgiven for all their **sin.** They could not plead ignorance or lack of opportunity. In particular, the **sin** in view here, and the one that always damns, is that of unbelief. Jesus' pronouncement that their **sin remains** (cf. Matt. 12:32; Heb. 6:4–6; 10:29–31) carries with it a sense of finality. It may be that at this point He permanently confirmed them in their willful spiritual blindness, as He did with some other Pharisees in Matthew 15:13–14. On that occasion, when He was told by His disciples that some Pharisees were offended by His words, Jesus had replied, "Every plant which My heavenly Father did not plant shall be uprooted. Let them alone; they are blind guides of the blind. And if a blind man guides a blind man, both will fall into a pit." Those three shocking words, "Let them alone," reveal that God will sometimes judge directly unrepentant sinners by abandoning them (and even hardening them) in their unbelief (cf. Hos. 4:17; Rom. 1:18, 24, 26, 28).

As the King of kings and Lord of lords (Rev. 19:16), Jesus Christ is the determiner of human destiny. Simeon said prophetically of Him, "Behold, this Child is appointed for the fall and rise of many in Israel" (Luke 2:34). The Lord Himself said of His ministry,

> Do you suppose that I came to grant peace on earth? I tell you, no, but rather division; for from now on five members in one household will be divided, three against two and two against three. They will be divided, father against son and son against father, mother against daughter and daughter against mother, mother-in-law against daughter-in-law and daughter-in-law against mother-in-law. (Luke 12:51–53)

Those who, like the blind beggar, acknowledge their spiritual blindness and turn to the Light "will not walk in the darkness, but will have the Light of life" (John 8:12). But those who, like the Pharisees, persist in loving the darkness rather than the Light (3:19) will continue to wander aimlessly in the gloom (12:35; 1 John 2:11), bereft of any spiritual vision (Matt.

6:23). The first group is destined to spend eternity in the glorious light of heaven (Rev. 22:5); the latter will be condemned to the horrifying darkness of eternal hell (Matt. 8:12; 22:13; 25:30).

The Good Shepherd
(John 10:1–21)

36

"Truly, truly, I say to you, he who does not enter by the door into the fold of the sheep, but climbs up some other way, he is a thief and a robber. But he who enters by the door is a shepherd of the sheep. To him the doorkeeper opens, and the sheep hear his voice, and he calls his own sheep by name and leads them out. When he puts forth all his own, he goes ahead of them, and the sheep follow him because they know his voice. A stranger they simply will not follow, but will flee from him, because they do not know the voice of strangers." This figure of speech Jesus spoke to them, but they did not understand what those things were which He had been saying to them. So Jesus said to them again, "Truly, truly, I say to you, I am the door of the sheep. All who came before Me are thieves and robbers, but the sheep did not hear them. I am the door; if anyone enters through Me, he will be saved, and will go in and out and find pasture. The thief comes only to steal and kill and destroy; I came that they may have life, and have it abundantly. I am the good shepherd; the good shepherd lays down His life for the sheep. He who is a hired hand, and not a shepherd, who is not the owner of the sheep, sees the wolf coming, and leaves the sheep and flees, and the wolf snatches

them and scatters them. He flees because he is a hired hand and is not concerned about the sheep. I am the good shepherd, and I know My own and My own know Me, even as the Father knows Me and I know the Father; and I lay down My life for the sheep. I have other sheep, which are not of this fold; I must bring them also, and they will hear My voice; and they will become one flock with one shepherd. For this reason the Father loves Me, because I lay down My life so that I may take it again. No one has taken it away from Me, but I lay it down on My own initiative. I have authority to lay it down, and I have authority to take it up again. This commandment I received from My Father." A division occurred again among the Jews because of these words. Many of them were saying, "He has a demon and is insane. Why do you listen to Him?" Others were saying, "These are not the sayings of one demon-possessed. A demon cannot open the eyes of the blind, can he?" (10:1–21)

The Bible refers to Jesus Christ by many titles. He is called the Amen (Rev. 3:14; cf. 2 Cor. 1:20), the Alpha and the Omega (Rev. 22:13), the Advocate (1 John 2:1), the Apostle (Heb. 3:1), the Author and Perfecter of faith (Heb. 12:2), the Author of salvation (Heb. 2:10), the Beginning (source, origin) of the creation of God (Rev. 3:14), the Branch (Jer. 23:5), the Bread of Life (John 6:35), the Cornerstone (Eph. 2:20), the Consolation of Israel (Luke 2:25), the Counselor (Isa. 9:6), the Deliverer (Rom. 11:26), the Door of the sheep (John 10:7), Eternal Father (Isa. 9:6), the Faithful witness (Rev. 1:5), the First and the Last (Rev. 1:17), the Firstborn (Preeminent One) of the dead (Rev. 1:5) and over all creation (Col. 1:15), the Forerunner (Heb. 6:20), the Great High Priest (Heb. 4:14), God blessed forever (Rom. 9:5), the Guardian of souls (1 Peter 2:25), the Head of the church (Col. 1:18), the Holy One of God (John 6:69), I AM (John 8:58), Immanuel (Isa. 7:14), the King of Israel (John 1:49; cf. Zech. 9:9), King of kings and Lord of lords (1 Tim. 6:15), the last Adam (1 Cor. 15:45), the Lamb of God (John 1:29), the Light of the World (John 8:12), the Lion of the tribe of Judah (Rev. 5:5), Lord (John 13:13), the Lord of Glory (1 Cor. 2:8), the Mediator (1 Tim. 2:5), the Messenger of the covenant (Mal. 3:1), the Messiah (John 1:41; 4:25–26), the Mighty God (Isa. 9:6), the Morning Star (Rev. 22:16), the Only Begotten (Unique One) from the Father (John 1:14), our Passover (1 Cor. 5:7), the Prince of life (Acts 3:15), the Prince of Peace (Isa. 9:6), the Resurrection and the Life (John 11:25), the Righteous One (Acts 7:52), the Rock (1 Cor. 10:4), the Root and Descendant of David (Rev. 22:16), the Root of Jesse (Isa. 11:10), the Ruler in Israel (Mic. 5:2; Matt. 2:6), the Ruler of the kings of the earth (Rev. 1:5), Savior (Luke 2:11; Titus 1:4), the Servant (Isa. 42:1), Shiloh (Gen. 49:10), the Son of the Blessed One (Mark 14:61), the Son of David (Matt. 12:23; 21:9), the Son of God (Luke 1:35), the Son of Man (John 5:27); the Son of the Most High (Luke 1:32), the Sun of Righteousness (Mal. 4:2), the Sunrise from on high (Luke 1:78), the True God (1 John 5:20), the True Vine (John 15:1), the Way, the Truth, and the Life (John 14:6), the Word (John 1:1, 14), the Word of God (Rev. 19:13), and the Word of Life (1 John 1:1).

But perhaps His most endearing and intimate title is that of Shepherd. Centuries before the Messiah came, the Old Testament had predicted that He would shepherd His people. In Ezekiel 34:23 God said, "Then I will set over them one shepherd, My servant David [a reference to the Messiah, David's descendant], and he will feed them; he will feed them himself and be their shepherd" (cf. 37:24). Micah prophesied that the Messiah would "arise and shepherd His flock in the strength of the Lord, in the majesty of the name of the Lord His God" (Mic. 5:4). Predicting Messiah's death, Zechariah 13:7 says, "'Awake, O sword, against My Shepherd, and against the man, My Associate,' declares the Lord of hosts. 'Strike the Shepherd that the sheep may be scattered; and I will turn My hand against the little ones.'"

The New Testament also depicts Christ as Shepherd. When asked by Herod where the Messiah would be born, the chief priests and scribes quoted Micah 5:2: "And you, Bethlehem, land of Judah, are by no means least among the leaders of Judah; for out of you shall come forth a ruler who will shepherd my people Israel" (Matt. 2:6). Predicting that the disciples would desert Him when He was arrested, Jesus quoted Zechariah 13:7: "You will all fall away because of Me this night, for it is written, 'I will strike down the Shepherd, and the sheep of the flock shall be scattered'" (Matt. 26:31). The apostle Peter described Jesus as the Shepherd of believers' souls (1 Peter 2:25), and later as the Chief Shepherd of the church (5:4). The writer of Hebrews closed his epistle with the benediction, "Now the God of peace, who brought up from the dead the great Shepherd of the sheep through the blood of the eternal covenant, even Jesus our Lord, equip you in every good thing to do His will, working in us that which is pleasing in His sight, through Jesus Christ, to whom be the glory forever and ever. Amen" (Heb. 13:20–21). Even beyond this life, Jesus will continue to shepherd His people for all eternity in heaven; "the Lamb in the center of the throne will be their shepherd, and will guide them to springs of the water of life; and God will wipe every tear from their eyes" (Rev. 7:17).

Nowhere in all of Scripture is Jesus Christ more clearly portrayed as the Shepherd of His people than in the tenth chapter of John's gospel. This discourse in which He presents Himself as the Good Shepherd flows directly from the events of the preceding chapter; there is no time gap or break in thought between chapters 9 and 10 (cf. 10:21). The Lord continued to speak to the same people—His disciples, the formerly blind beggar, the hostile Pharisees, and the others in the ever-present crowd.

This opening section of chapter 10 presents four distinctives of the Good Shepherd's pastoral work. It is a shepherding ministry marked by contrast to false shepherds, by concern for the flock, by compliance to the Father, and by controversy in a fallen world.

A Ministry Marked by Contrast to False Shepherds

"Truly, truly, I say to you, he who does not enter by the door into the fold of the sheep, but climbs up some other way, he is a thief and a robber. But he who enters by the door is a shepherd of the sheep. To him the doorkeeper opens, and the sheep hear his voice, and he calls his own sheep by name and leads them out. When he puts forth all his own, he goes ahead of them, and the sheep follow him because they know his voice. A stranger they simply will not follow, but will flee from him, because they do not know the voice of strangers." This figure of speech Jesus spoke to them, but they did not understand what those things were which He had been saying to them. So Jesus said to them again, "Truly, truly, I say to you, I am the door of the sheep. All who came before Me are thieves and robbers, but the sheep did not hear them. I am the door; if anyone enters through Me, he will be saved, and will go in and out and find pasture. The thief comes only to steal and kill and destroy; I came that they may have life, and have it abundantly." (10:1–10)

Throughout Israel's history, shepherding had always been a familiar part of everyday agrarian life. And the people all knew that sheep are the most helpless, defenseless, straying, and dirty of animals. They require constant oversight, leading, rescue, and cleaning or they will die. Being a shepherd was good training for leading people. In fact, the patriarchs Abraham, Isaac, and Jacob had been shepherds (Gen. 13:1–11; 26:12–14; 46:32; 47:3), as were Israel's greatest leaders: Moses (Ex. 3:1) and David (1 Sam. 16:11; 17:28, 34; 2 Sam. 7:8). It is not surprising, then, that the Old Testament writers frequently used shepherding imagery, depicting Israel as God's flock (Pss. 74:1; 77:20; 78:52; 79:13; 80:1; 95:7; 100:3; Ezek. 34:12–16), God as her Shepherd (Gen. 48:15; 49:24; Pss. 23:1; 28:9; 80:1; Isa. 40:11; Jer. 23:3; Ezek. 34:11–12; Mic. 7:14), and her leaders as God's undershepherds (Num. 27:16–17; 2 Sam. 5:2; 1 Chron. 17:6; Ps. 78:70–72; Jer. 3:15; 23:4). The New Testament writers also used that same familiar terminology to describe the church (Acts 20:28–29; 1 Peter 5:2–3).

But while the metaphor of a shepherd suggests tender care, it can also depict harsh, abusive, autocratic rule. As will be seen in the discussion of verse 1 below, the Bible refers to false spiritual leaders, as well as true ones, as shepherds. In verses 1–10 Jesus contrasted Himself with Israel's false shepherds by using two images: He is the true Shepherd of the sheep, and He is the only door to the sheepfold.

JESUS IS THE TRUE SHEPHERD OF THE SHEEP

"Truly, truly, I say to you, he who does not enter by the door into the fold of the sheep, but climbs up some other way, he is a thief and a robber. But he who enters by the door is a shepherd of the sheep. To him the doorkeeper opens, and the sheep hear his voice, and he calls his own sheep by name and leads them out. When he puts forth all his own, he goes ahead of them, and the sheep follow him because they know his voice. A stranger they simply will not follow, but will flee from him, because they do not know the voice of strangers." This figure of speech Jesus spoke to them, but they did not understand what those things were which He had been saying to them. (10:1–6)

As noted earlier in this volume (cf. the discussion of 8:34 in chapter 30), the phrase *amēn, amēn* (**truly, truly**) introduces a statement of notable importance. Jesus began this discourse by identifying Himself as the true Shepherd, in sharp contrast to all false shepherds. Each village in the sheepherding regions of Palestine had a **fold** where **sheep** were kept at night. The shepherds would graze their flocks in the surrounding countryside during the day, and then lead them back to the communal sheepfold in the evening. There the shepherds would stop each sheep at the entrance with their rods and carefully inspect it before allowing it to enter the fold (cf. Ezek. 20:37–38). Once in the fold, the sheep were in the care of the **doorkeeper** (a hired undershepherd; v. 12), who would keep watch over them during the night. He would give only the shepherds access to the sheepfold; therefore anyone **who** could **not enter by the door into the fold of the sheep, but** climbed **up some other way,** was **a thief and a robber.** Since the doorkeeper obviously would not let strangers in, would-be rustlers had to climb the wall of the sheepfold to get at the sheep. Only the one **who** entered **by the door** was **a shepherd of the sheep.**

Each of those common elements of everyday life had a symbolic meaning in the Lord's metaphor. Though some argue that the **sheepfold** represents the church or heaven, the context (cf. v. 16) indicates that it represents Israel. In addition, it is hard to see how thieves could break into either the church or heaven and steal sheep (cf. vv. 27–29). The **door** is Jesus Himself (vv. 7, 9), who alone has the authority to lead out of Israel's fold His own elect sheep. The thieves and robbers represent the self-appointed (cf. Matt. 23:2) Jewish religious leaders, who, doing the work of the devil, not God, climbed the walls of the sheepfold to spiritually fleece and slaughter the people.

Those leaders were the latest in a long line of false shepherds in Israel. Isaiah pictured such hypocrites in graphic terms as "mute dogs unable to bark, dreamers lying down, who love to slumber; . . . dogs [who] are greedy, [and] are not satisfied . . . shepherds who have no understanding; they have all turned to their own way, each one to his unjust gain, to the last one" (Isa. 56:10–11). "The shepherds have become stupid," wrote Jeremiah, "and have not sought the Lord; therefore they have not prospered, and all their flock is scattered" (Jer. 10:21). In 12:10 the Lord said through Jeremiah, "Many shepherds have ruined My vineyard, they have trampled down My field; they have made My pleasant field a desolate wilderness." "My people have become lost sheep," God lamented in 50:6. "Their shepherds have led them astray. They have made them turn aside on the mountains; they have gone along from mountain to hill and have forgotten their resting place."

But Israel's false shepherds would not escape God's judgment. In Jeremiah 23:1–2 God warned,

> "Woe to the shepherds who are destroying and scattering the sheep of My pasture!" declares the Lord. Therefore thus says the Lord God of Israel concerning the shepherds who are tending My people: 'You have scattered My flock and driven them away, and have not attended to them; behold, I am about to attend to you for the evil of your deeds,' declares the Lord."

In a devastating indictment of the false shepherds, and what may have been in our Lord's mind and prompted His teaching, God declared through Ezekiel,

> "Son of man, prophesy against the shepherds of Israel. Prophesy and say to those shepherds, 'Thus says the Lord God, "Woe, shepherds of Israel who have been feeding themselves! Should not the shepherds feed the flock? You eat the fat and clothe yourselves with the wool, you slaughter the fat sheep without feeding the flock. Those who are sickly you have not strengthened, the diseased you have not healed, the broken you have not bound up, the scattered you have not brought back,

nor have you sought for the lost; but with force and with severity you have dominated them. They were scattered for lack of a shepherd, and they became food for every beast of the field and were scattered. My flock wandered through all the mountains and on every high hill; My flock was scattered over all the surface of the earth, and there was no one to search or seek for them."" Therefore, you shepherds, hear the word of the Lord: "As I live," declares the Lord God, "surely because My flock has become a prey, My flock has even become food for all the beasts of the field for lack of a shepherd, and My shepherds did not search for My flock, but rather the shepherds fed themselves and did not feed My flock; therefore, you shepherds, hear the word of the Lord: 'Thus says the Lord God, "Behold, I am against the shepherds, and I will demand My sheep from them and make them cease from feeding sheep. So the shepherds will not feed themselves anymore, but I will deliver My flock from their mouth, so that they will not be food for them.""" (Ezek. 34:2–10)

Lying prophets, often posing as true shepherds, also threatened the early church (as they still do today). Jesus cautioned, "Beware of the false prophets, who come to you in sheep's clothing, but inwardly are ravenous wolves" (Matt. 7:15). Paul warned the elders of the Ephesian church, "I know that after my departure savage wolves will come in among you, not sparing the flock" (Acts 20:29). Peter wrote, "False prophets also arose among the people, just as there will also be false teachers among you, who will secretly introduce destructive heresies, even denying the Master who bought them, bringing swift destruction upon themselves" (2 Peter 2:1). In his first epistle John cautioned, "Beloved, do not believe every spirit, but test the spirits to see whether they are from God, because many false prophets have gone out into the world" (1 John 4:1). (For a further discussion of false teachers in the church, see *2 Peter and Jude,* The MacArthur New Testament Commentary [Chicago: Moody, 2005], especially chapters 5–7, 11–13.)

Scripture also predicts the coming of the ultimate false shepherd, the final Antichrist. Zechariah 11:16–17 reveals that as part of His divine judgment on Israel (and the world), God is

going to raise up a shepherd in the land who will not care for the perishing, seek the scattered, heal the broken, or sustain the one standing, but will devour the flesh of the fat sheep and tear off their hoofs. Woe to the worthless shepherd who leaves the flock! A sword will be on his arm and on his right eye! His arm will be totally withered and his right eye will be blind. (cf. Dan. 11:36–45; 2 Thess. 2:3–10; Rev. 13:3–10)

Continuing with the figure of speech, Christ said that His **sheep hear** His **voice** when He calls them out of Israel and into His messianic fold. His imagery pictures the human response to the effectual, divine call to salvation (John 6:44, 65; 17:6, 9, 24; 18:9; Rom. 1:7; 8:28–30; 9:24; 1 Cor.1:2, 23–24; Gal. 1:6, 15; Eph. 4:1, 4; Col. 3:15; 1 Thess. 4:7; 2 Thess. 2:13–14; 1 Tim. 6:12; 2 Tim. 1:9; 1 Peter 1:15; 2:9, 21; 5:10; 2 Peter 1:3; Jude 1). Jesus **calls his own sheep by name,** because they are His. Their names were "written from the foundation of the world in the book of life of the Lamb who has been slain" (Rev. 13:8; cf. 3:5; 17:8; 20:12, 15; 21:27; Phil. 4:3), and they have been given to Him by the Father (John 6:37).

After calling His sheep, Christ **leads them out** of the fold, **puts** them **forth** to pasture, **goes ahead of them, and the sheep follow him.** In the Near East the shepherd went ahead of his flock, alert to any potential dangers, making sure the trail was safe and passable, and leading the sheep to feed in the green pastures he had already scouted. So it is in salvation. Jesus savingly calls His sheep and leads them out of the fold where they were kept, taking them to the "green pastures" and "quiet waters" of God's truth and blessing (Ps. 23:2).

The reason **the sheep follow** the Shepherd is **because they know his voice.** Actual sheep recognize the voice of their own shepherd, and will not respond to that of another. Philip Keller writes,

> The relationship which rapidly develops between a shepherd and the sheep under his care is to a definite degree dependent upon the use of the shepherd's voice. Sheep quickly become accustomed to their owner's particular voice. They are acquainted with its unique tone. They know its peculiar sounds and inflections. They can distinguish it from that of any other person.
>
> If a stranger should come among them, they would not recognize nor respond to his voice in the same way they would to that of the shepherd. Even if the visitor should use the same words and phrases as that of their rightful owner they would not react in the same way. It is a case of becoming actually conditioned to the familiar nuances and personal accent of their shepherd's call. (*A Shepherd Looks at the Good Shepherd and His Sheep* [Grand Rapids: Zondervan, 1979], 39–40)

On the other hand, **a stranger they simply will not follow, but will flee from him, because they do not know the voice of strangers.** True believers will not abandon Christ, the Good Shepherd, to follow false shepherds. True believers recognize the truth revealed by God (8:31–32, 47, 51–52) and reject error. John expressed that truth in his first epistle:

> Beloved, do not believe every spirit, but test the spirits to see whether they are from God, because many false prophets have gone out into the world. By this you know the Spirit of God: every spirit that confess-

es that Jesus Christ has come in the flesh is from God; and every spirit that does not confess Jesus is not from God; this is the spirit of the antichrist, of which you have heard that it is coming, and now it is already in the world. You are from God, little children, and have overcome them; because greater is He who is in you than he who is in the world. They are from the world; therefore they speak as from the world, and the world listens to them. We are from God; he who knows God listens to us; he who is not from God does not listen to us. By this we know the spirit of truth and the spirit of error. (1 John 4:1–6)

No one who is genuinely saved will finally and completely turn away from Jesus Christ. Jesus' warning that "false Christs and false prophets will arise and will show great signs and wonders, so as to mislead, if possible, even the elect" (Matt. 24:24) clearly implies that such deception is impossible. Those who abandon their profession of faith in the truth prove that neither their faith nor their salvation was ever genuine. "They went out from us," John wrote, "but they were not really of us; for if they had been of us, they would have remained with us; but they went out, so that it would be shown that they all are not of us" (1 John 2:19). John, then, contrasts such departure from the truth, the voice of the Shepherd, with faithfulness to His voice. He writes of the true sheep,

> But you have an anointing from the Holy One, and you all know. I have not written to you because you do not know the truth, but because you do know it, and because no lie is of the truth. Who is the liar but the one who denies that Jesus is the Christ? This is the antichrist, the one who denies the Father and the Son. Whoever denies the Son does not have the Father; the one who confesses the Son has the Father also. As for you, let that abide in you which you heard from the beginning. If what you heard from the beginning abides in you, you also will abide in the Son and in the Father. (1 John 2:20–24)

Those who are Christ's do not leave Him to follow those who deny the truth.

The apostle John concluded this first metaphor with a footnote: **This figure of speech Jesus spoke to them, but they did not understand what those things were which He had been saying to them.** The Greek word translated **figure of speech** (*paroimia*) describes veiled, enigmatic language that conceals a symbolic meaning. Though the **figure of speech** was presented plainly enough to the religious leaders, they failed to grasp its significance. So ingrained was their belief that as Abraham's descendants they were part of God's flock that they completely missed Jesus' indictment of them when He stated that He was the true Shepherd and they were false shepherds to whom the sheep would not listen. Like His parables (Matt. 13:10–16), this **figure of speech** served a twofold purpose: It revealed spiritual truth to His followers, and concealed it from those who rejected Him.

JESUS IS THE ONLY DOOR TO THE FOLD

So Jesus said to them again, "Truly, truly, I say to you, I am the door of the sheep. All who came before Me are thieves and robbers, but the sheep did not hear them. I am the door; if anyone enters through Me, he will be saved, and will go in and out and find pasture. The thief comes only to steal and kill and destroy; I came that they may have life, and have it abundantly." (10:7–10)

Here Jesus changed the metaphor slightly. In the first figure of speech, He was the Shepherd; here He is the Door to the sheepfold. This is the third of seven statements in John's gospel where "I AM" is followed by a predicate nominative (v. 11; 6:35; 8:12; 11:25; 14:6; 15:1,5).

Since the religious leaders had failed to understand His first figure of speech, **Jesus said to them again, "Truly, truly, I say to you, I am the door of the sheep."** Sometimes the shepherd slept in the opening of the sheepfold to guard the sheep. No one could enter or leave except through him. In Jesus' metaphor He is the **door** through which the **sheep** enter the safety of God's fold and go out to the rich pasture of His blessing. It is through Him that lost sinners can approach the Father and appropriate the salvation He provides; Jesus alone is "the way, and the truth, and the life; no one comes to the Father but through [Him]" (14:6; cf. Acts 4:12; 1 Cor. 1:30; 3:11; 1 Tim. 2:5). Only Jesus is the true source of the knowledge of God and salvation, and the basis for spiritual security.

The Lord's assertion, **"All who came before Me are thieves and robbers,"** does not, of course, include Israel's true spiritual leaders (such as Moses, Joshua, David, Solomon, Ezra, Nehemiah, Isaiah, Jeremiah, Ezekiel, and Daniel, among many others). Jesus was referring to Israel's false shepherds—her wicked kings, corrupt priests, false prophets, and pseudo-messiahs. However, **the** true **sheep did not hear them;** they did not heed them and were not led astray by them (see the discussion of vv. 4 and 5 above).

Then Jesus reiterated the vital truth of verse 7: **"I am the door;"** and He added the promise, **"If anyone enters through Me, he will be saved"** from sin and hell. Christ's sheep will experience God's love, forgiveness, and salvation; they will **go in and out** freely, always having access to God's blessing and protection, and never fearing any harm or danger. They will find satisfying **pasture** as the Lord feeds them (cf. Ps.

23:1–3; Ezek. 34:15) on His Word (cf. Acts 20:32). In utter contrast to the thieving false shepherds who, like their father the devil (8:44) came **only to steal and kill and destroy** the sheep, Jesus **came that they may have** spiritual and eternal **life** (cf. John 5:21; 6:33, 51–53, 57; Rom. 6:4; Gal. 2:20; Eph. 2:1, 5; Col. 2:13), **and have it abundantly.** *Perissos* (**abundantly**) describes something that goes far beyond what is necessary. The matchless gift of eternal life exceeds all expectation (cf. John 4:10 with 7:38; see also Rom. 8:32; 2 Cor. 9:15).

A Ministry Marked by Concern for the Flock

"I am the good shepherd; the good shepherd lays down His life for the sheep. He who is a hired hand, and not a shepherd, who is not the owner of the sheep, sees the wolf coming, and leaves the sheep and flees, and the wolf snatches them and scatters them. He flees because he is a hired hand and is not concerned about the sheep. I am the good shepherd, and I know My own and My own know Me, even as the Father knows Me and I know the Father; and I lay down My life for the sheep. I have other sheep, which are not of this fold; I must bring them also, and they will hear My voice; and they will become one flock with one shepherd." (10:11–16)

This section reveals three blessings the Good Shepherd gives to His sheep because He is genuinely concerned for them (cf. v. 13): He dies for them, loves them, and unites them.

THE GOOD SHEPHERD DIES FOR HIS SHEEP

"I am the good shepherd; the good shepherd lays down His life for the sheep. He who is a hired hand, and not a shepherd, who is not the owner of the sheep, sees the wolf coming, and leaves the sheep and flees, and the wolf snatches them and scatters them. He flees because he is a hired hand and is not concerned about the sheep." (10:11–13)

Jesus' identification of Himself as **the good shepherd** points back to the true shepherd described in verses 2 to 5. It is the fourth "I AM" statement in John's gospel (see the discussion of v. 7 above). The Greek text literally reads, "the shepherd, the good one," setting Christ the Good Shepherd apart from all other shepherds. *Kalos* (**good**) refers to His noble character (cf. 1 Tim. 3:7; 4:6; 2 Tim. 2:3; 1 Peter 4:10); He is the perfect, authentic Shepherd; in a class by Himself; preeminent above all others.

Being a faithful shepherd entailed a willingness to lay one's life on the line to protect the sheep. Robbers and wild animals such as wolves, lions, and bears were a constant danger (cf. 1 Sam. 17:34; Isa. 31:4; Amos 3:12). But Jesus, **the good shepherd,** went far beyond merely being willing to risk or actually risking His life for His sheep; He actually laid **down His life for** them (cf. v. 15; 6:51; 11:50–51; 18:14). The phrase **lays down His life** is unique to John's writings and always refers to a voluntary, sacrificial death (vv. 15, 17–18; 13:37–38; 15:13; 1 John 3:16). Jesus gave His life for His sheep, because they were chosen to become part of His flock. The preposition *huper* (**for**) is frequently used in the New Testament to refer to Christ's substitutionary atonement for the elect (cf. v. 15; 6:51; 11:50–51; 18:14; Luke 22:19; Rom. 5:6, 8; 8:32; 1 Cor. 11:24; 15:3; 2 Cor. 5:14–15, 21; Gal. 1:4; 2:20; 3:13; Eph. 5:2, 25; 1 Thess. 5:9–10; 1 Tim. 2:6; Titus 2:14; Heb. 2:9; 1 Peter 2:21; 3:18; 1 John 3:16). His death was an actual atonement to provide propitiation for the sins of all who would believe, as they were called and regenerated by the Spirit, because they were chosen by the Father.

Opposite the Good Shepherd, who gives His life for the sheep, is **he who is a hired hand** (like the doorkeeper of v. 3), **and not a shepherd, who is not the owner of the sheep,** who **sees the wolf coming** (cf. Matt. 7:15; Acts 20:29), **and leaves the sheep and flees, and the wolf snatches them and scatters them** (cf. Matt. 9:36; Mark 6:34). The **hired hand** symbolizes the Jewish religious leaders and, by extension, all false shepherds. They are always mercenaries, doing ministry not for love of the souls of men or even love for the truth, but for money (Titus 1:10–11; 1 Peter 5:2; 2 Peter 2:3). Therefore they flee at the first sign of threat to their well-being, because they are **not concerned about the sheep.** Their overriding priority is self-preservation, and the last thing they care to do is to sacrifice themselves for anyone.

THE GOOD SHEPHERD LOVES HIS SHEEP

"I am the good shepherd, and I know My own and My own know Me, even as the Father knows Me and I know the Father; and I lay down My life for the sheep." (10:14–15)

It is because the Lord loves His own that He gave His life for them. The word **know** is used here to denote that love relationship. In Genesis 4:1, 17, 25; 19:8; 24:16; and 1 Samuel 1:19 the term **know** describes the intimate love relationship between husband and wife (the

NASB translates the Hebrew verb "to know" in those verses "had relations with"). In Amos 3:2 God said of Israel, "You only have I known of all the families of the earth" (NKJV), speaking not as if He were unaware of any other nations, but of His unique love relationship with His people. Matthew 1:25 literally reads that Joseph "was not knowing [Mary]" until after the birth of Jesus. On the day of judgment, Jesus will send unbelievers away from Him because He does not know them; that is, He has no love relationship with them (Matt. 7:23). In these verses, **know** has that same connotation of a relationship of love. The simple truth here is that Jesus in love knows His own, they in love know Him, the Father in love knows Jesus, and He in love knows the Father. Believers are caught up in the deep and intimate affection that is shared between God the Father and the Lord Jesus Christ (cf. 14:21, 23; 15:10; 17:25–26).

THE GOOD SHEPHERD UNITES HIS SHEEP

"I have other sheep, which are not of this fold; I must bring them also, and they will hear My voice; and they will become one flock with one shepherd." (10:16)

The **other sheep** in view here are Gentiles, who **are not of** Israel's **fold.** They, too, **will hear** Jesus' **voice** calling them to salvation (cf. Isa. 42:6; 49:6; Rom. 1:16), and redeemed Jews and Gentiles **will become one flock with one shepherd.** To suggest that Jews and Gentiles would be united in one flock was a revolutionary concept. The Jews despised Gentiles, and they returned the animosity. Even Jewish believers were so programmed to prejudice that they were slow to accept Gentiles as equal members in the church (cf. Acts 10:9–16, 28; 11:1–18; 15:1–29). But as Caiaphas unwittingly prophesied,

> "It is expedient for you that one man die for the people, and that the whole nation not perish." Now he did not say this on his own initiative, but being high priest that year, he prophesied that Jesus was going to die for the nation, and not for the nation only, but in order that He might also gather together into one the children of God who are scattered abroad. (John 11:50–52)

To the Ephesians Paul wrote,

> Therefore remember that formerly you, the Gentiles in the flesh, who are called "Uncircumcision" by the so-called "Circumcision," which is performed in the flesh by human hands—remember that you were at that time separate from Christ, excluded from the commonwealth of

Israel, and strangers to the covenants of promise, having no hope and without God in the world. But now in Christ Jesus you who formerly were far off have been brought near by the blood of Christ. For He Himself is our peace, who made both groups into one and broke down the barrier of the dividing wall, by abolishing in His flesh the enmity, which is the Law of commandments contained in ordinances, so that in Himself He might make the two into one new man, thus establishing peace, and might reconcile them both in one body to God through the cross, by it having put to death the enmity. (Eph. 2:11–16)

True unity between Jews and Gentiles defines the church because both are sheep who belong to the same Shepherd.

A Ministry Marked by Compliance to the Father

"For this reason the Father loves Me, because I lay down My life so that I may take it again. No one has taken it away from Me, but I lay it down on My own initiative. I have authority to lay it down, and I have authority to take it up again. This commandment I received from My Father." (10:17–18)

Two attitudes define the relationship of the incarnate Christ to the Father: love and obedience. The two are inseparably linked, since it is impossible to love God without obeying Him (John 15:9; 1 John 2:3–5; 5:3). The **Father loves** the Son **because** He laid **down** His **life** for the sheep, all of whom the Father had chosen in eternity past and given to the Son in time; the Son demonstrated His love to the Father "by becoming obedient to the point of death, even death on a cross" (Phil. 2:8). He did so voluntarily; **no one** took His life **away from** Him, **but** He laid it **down on** His **own initiative.** At His trial Jesus told Pilate, who would order His execution, "You would have no authority over Me, unless it had been given you from above" (John 19:11; cf. Matt. 26:53–54). The Lord's twice-repeated declaration that He would **take** His life **up again** points forward to His resurrection—the ultimate demonstration of His messiahship and deity (Rom. 1:4). As with everything He did, Christ exercised His authority to lay down His life and take it up again in voluntary compliance with and loving obedience to the **commandment** He **received from** the **Father.** By the power of His resurrection, He would raise all His flock to eternal glory (John 6:39–40, 44).

A Ministry Marked by Controversy in a Fallen World

A division occurred again among the Jews because of these words. Many of them were saying, "He has a demon and is insane. Why do you listen to Him?" Others were saying, "These are not the sayings of one demon-possessed. A demon cannot open the eyes of the blind, can he?" (10:19–21)

As was always the case, Jesus' teaching created heated controversy among those who heard Him, and **a division occurred again among the Jews because of these words** (cf. 7:12, 43; 9:16). **Many of them were** reiterating the familiar accusations, **saying, "He has a demon and is insane. Why do you listen to Him?"** (7:20; 8:48, 52; cf. Matt. 9:34; 10:25; 12:24). Instead of even considering what Jesus was saying, **many** arbitrarily dismissed His words—responding with ridicule rather than repentance and faith in their own Messiah. Having already rejected Jesus (and His claim to be from God), they held their ground stubbornly and attributed His ministry to demons. Such a blasphemous and deluded conclusion is damning.

Others, however, not so blindly biased, were able to conclude the obvious—what the lucid, majestic sense and clarity of Christ's words indicated: **"These are not the sayings of one demon-possessed."** Then, reaching the same conclusion as the blind man whom Jesus had healed (9:30–33) they added, **"A demon cannot open the eyes of the blind, can he?"** Like the blind man, they realized that Jesus' miraculous power was undeniable proof that He truly was sanctioned by and sent from God (cf. 7:31).

Rejecting the Claims of Christ (John 10:22–42)

37

At that time the Feast of the Dedication took place at Jerusalem; it was winter, and Jesus was walking in the temple in the portico of Solomon. The Jews then gathered around Him, and were saying to Him, "How long will You keep us in suspense? If You are the Christ, tell us plainly." Jesus answered them, "I told you, and you do not believe; the works that I do in My Father's name, these testify of Me. But you do not believe because you are not of My sheep. My sheep hear My voice, and I know them, and they follow Me; and I give eternal life to them, and they will never perish; and no one will snatch them out of My hand. My Father, who has given them to Me, is greater than all; and no one is able to snatch them out of the Father's hand. I and the Father are one." The Jews picked up stones again to stone Him. Jesus answered them, "I showed you many good works from the Father; for which of them are you stoning Me?" The Jews answered Him, "For a good work we do not stone You, but for blasphemy; and because You, being a man, make Yourself out to be God." Jesus answered them, "Has it not been written in your Law, 'I said, you are gods'? If he called them gods, to whom the word of God came (and the Scripture cannot be broken), do you say of Him, whom the Father

sanctified and sent into the world, 'You are blaspheming,' because I said, 'I am the Son of God'? If I do not do the works of My Father, do not believe Me; but if I do them, though you do not believe Me, believe the works, so that you may know and understand that the Father is in Me, and I in the Father." Therefore they were seeking again to seize Him, and He eluded their grasp. And He went away again beyond the Jordan to the place where John was first baptizing, and He was staying there. Many came to Him and were saying, "While John performed no sign, yet everything John said about this man was true." Many believed in Him there. (10:22–42)

This passage marks the end of John's presentation of Christ's public ministry. For more than three years, Jesus had traveled the length and breadth of Israel, preaching the gospel, calling for repentance, confronting hypocritical false religion, instructing His disciples, and performing countless signs and wonders, which confirmed that He was the Messiah. Through both His words and His works, Jesus had clearly demonstrated His deity and equality with God.

But tragically the nation of Israel, led by her religious leaders, rejected the Messiah—just as the Old Testament predicted would happen (cf. Ps. 22:6–8; Isa. 49:7; 50:6; 53:3). At the end of His life, Jesus had a mere handful of genuine followers; the Bible mentions 120 in Jerusalem (Acts 1:15), and several hundred more, probably in Galilee (1 Cor. 15:6; cf. Matt. 28:7, 16). Instead of embracing Him as their long-awaited Redeemer King, the people of Israel "nailed [Him] to a cross by the hands of godless men and put Him to death" (Acts 2:23). As noted in previous chapters of this volume, the nation's rejection of Jesus is a frequent theme in John's gospel (cf. 1:10–11; 3:32; 4:1–3; 5:16–18; 6:41–43, 66; 7:1, 20, 26–27, 30–52; 8:13–59; 9:16, 24, 29, 40–41; 10:20; 11:46–57; 12:37–40).

In keeping with that theme, in the concluding section of chapter 10 John punctuates the long presentation of our Lord's public ministry (which began in 1:35) with yet another confrontation between Jesus and the Jewish religious leaders. The dialogue between them unfolds in five scenes: the confrontation, the claim, the charge, the challenge, and the consequences.

The Confrontation

At that time the Feast of the Dedication took place at Jerusalem; it was winter, and Jesus was walking in the temple in the portico of

Solomon. The Jews then gathered around Him, and were saying to Him, "How long will You keep us in suspense? If You are the Christ, tell us plainly." (10:22-24)

John's note that it was now the **time** of **the Feast of the Dedication** sets the stage for the next episode. There is a gap of approximately two months between verse 21 (which is still set at the time of the Feast of Tabernacles [7:2, 10, 37]) and verse 22. Some commentators think that Jesus left Jerusalem during that two-month period, since verse 22 calls attention to **Jerusalem** again as the setting for this dialogue. Others believe the Lord remained in the vicinity of Jerusalem, since verse 22 does not say that He went up to Jerusalem—the usual wording for going to the city from another region (cf. 2:13; 5:1; 11:55; Matt. 20:17-18; Luke 2:22; 19:28; Acts 11:2; 15:2; 21:12, 15; 24:11; 25:1, 9; Gal. 1:17-18). Both views are only speculative, since the gospels do not say where Jesus was during those two months.

Known today as Hanukkah, or the Feast of Lights (because of the lamps and candles lit in Jewish homes as part of the celebration), **the Feast of the Dedication** was celebrated on the twenty-fifth day of the Jewish month Chislev (Nov.–Dec.). It was not one of the feasts prescribed in the Old Testament, but originated during the intertestamental period. The feast commemorated the Israelites' victory over the infamous Syrian king Antiochus Epiphanes (175–164 B.C.). A devotee of Greek culture, Antiochus, in a decree given by him in 167 B.C., sought to impose it on his subjects (a process known as Hellenization). Antiochus captured Jerusalem and desecrated the temple (170 B.C.) by sacrificing a pig on the altar, setting up a pagan altar in its place, and erecting a statue of Zeus in the most holy place. As he attempted to systematically stamp out Judaism, Antiochus brutally oppressed the Jews, who clung tenaciously to their religion. Under his despotic direction, the Jews were required to offer sacrifices to pagan gods; they were not allowed to own or read the Old Testament Scriptures, and copies of it were destroyed; and they were forbidden to perform such mandatory religious practices as observing the Sabbath and circumcising children. Antiochus was the first pagan king to persecute the Jews for their religion (cf. Dan. 8:9–14, 23–25; 11:21–35).

Antiochus' savage persecution caused the pious Jews to rise in revolt, led by a priest named Mattathias and his sons. After three years of guerilla warfare the Jews, under the brilliant military leadership of Judas Maccabeus (the son of Mattathias), were able to retake Jerusalem. On 25 Chislev 164 B.C., they liberated the temple, rededicated it, and established the Feast of Dedication. The apocryphal book of 2 Maccabees recounts an historical version of the story:

Now Maccabeus and his followers, the Lord leading them on, recovered the temple and the city; and they tore down the altars which had been built in the public square by the foreigners, and also destroyed the sacred precincts. They purified the sanctuary, and made another altar of sacrifice; then, striking fire out of flint, they offered sacrifices, after a lapse of two years, and they burned incense and lighted lamps and set out the bread of the Presence. And when they had done this, they fell prostrate and besought the Lord that they might never again fall into such misfortunes, but that, if they should ever sin, they might be disciplined by him with forbearance and not be handed over to blasphemous and barbarous nations. It happened that on the same day on which the sanctuary had been profaned by the foreigners, the purification of the sanctuary took place, that is, on the twenty-fifth day of the same month, which was Chislev. And they celebrated it for eight days with rejoicing, in the manner of the feast of booths, remembering how not long before, during the feast of booths, they had been wandering in the mountains and caves like wild animals. Therefore bearing ivy-wreathed wands and beautiful branches and also fronds of palm, they offered hymns of thanksgiving to him who had given success to the purifying of his own holy place. They decreed by public ordinance and vote that the whole nation of the Jews should observe these days every year. (10:1–8)

The Feast of Dedication, which celebrated the successful revolt, took place in **winter,** which may explain why **Jesus,** who **was walking in the temple,** was specifically **in the portico of Solomon.** It was probably cold, and may have been raining, since winter is the rainy season in Palestine. The **portico of Solomon** would have provided a measure of protection from the elements; it was a roofed colonnade supported by pillars, located on the east side of the temple area and overlooking the Kidron Valley below. Many people frequented the site, especially in inclement weather. Some walked there to meditate, and rabbis sometimes taught their students there. Later, the early Christians would gather in the portico of Solomon to proclaim the gospel (Acts 3:11; 5:12).

Some see in John's reference to **winter** a metaphor for the Jews' spiritual state—that it described not only the season of the year, but also Israel's spiritual coldness. "The thoughtful reader of the Gospel understands that time and temperature notations in John are reflections of the spiritual condition of the persons in the stories (cf. 3:2; 13:30; 18:18; 20:1, 19; 21:3–4)" (Gerald L. Borchert, *John 1–11,* The New American Commentary [Nashville: Broadman & Holman, 2002], 337–38).

The hostile **Jews** accosted the Lord (the verb weakly translated **gathered around** literally means "to surround," or "to encircle" [cf. Luke 21:20; Acts 14:20; Heb. 11:30]) and demanded of Him, **"How long will**

You keep us in suspense? If You are the Christ, tell us plainly." By asking Jesus if He was the Messiah, the Jewish leaders were certainly asking the right question; indeed, it is the most significant question anyone can ask (cf. Matt. 16:15–16). But given the revelation they had seen and heard, and their hostility to Jesus over the course of that revelation, their motive was suspect. Far from being an honest request for information, their inquiry was actually just another attempt to trap Jesus with a view to getting rid of Him. Because He was the greatest threat to their power and prestige, they were desperately looking for a way to discredit Him and dispose of Him altogether. They were unsettled by the miraculous signs He performed (11:47); tired of the divisions He caused (Luke 12:51–53), even within their own ranks (cf. 9:16); fearful of the revolt He might spark against Rome, which would jeopardize their privileged political status (11:48); angered by His public rebuke of their hypocrisy (e.g., Matt. 23:1–36); and, most of all, outraged by His unapologetic claim to be God (5:18; 10:33; 19:7). The Jewish authorities' strategy was to make Him declare publicly (the verb translated **plainly** can also be translated "publicly," or "openly" [7:4, 13, 26; 11:54; 18:20]) that He was the Messiah, so that they would have a pretext for arresting Him.

THE CLAIM

Jesus answered them, "I told you, and you do not believe; the works that I do in My Father's name, these testify of Me. But you do not believe because you are not of My sheep. My sheep hear My voice, and I know them, and they follow Me; and I give eternal life to them, and they will never perish; and no one will snatch them out of My hand. My Father, who has given them to Me, is greater than all; and no one is able to snatch them out of the Father's hand. I and the Father are one." The Jews picked up stones again to stone Him. (10:25–31)

But Jesus already *had* **told** them plainly who He was (cf. 5:17ff.; 8:12, 24, 58); in fact, He had spent the last three years doing so. Not only that, **the works that** He did **in** the **Father's name** also demonstrated that He was the Messiah; the Son of God; God in human flesh (cf. vv. 32, 38; 3:2; 5:36; 7:31; 11:47; 14:11; Acts 2:22). The Lord's twice-repeated declaration, **you do not believe,** indicates that the problem was not due to any ambiguity in the revelation of the truth, but rather to their spiritual blindness. They lacked understanding, not because they lacked information, but because they lacked repentance and faith. Their unbelief was not due to insufficient exposure to the truth, but to their hatred of the truth and love of sin and lies (John 3:19–21). Anyone who willingly seeks the truth will find it (7:17), but Jesus refused to commit Himself to those who willfully rejected the truth. Had He again given them the plain answer they were demanding, they would not have believed Him anyway (cf. 8:43; Matt. 26:63–65; Luke 22:66–67).

From the perspective of human responsibility, the hostile Jews did not believe because they had deliberately rejected the truth. But from the standpoint of divine sovereignty, they did **not believe because** they were **not of** the Lord's **sheep,** which were given Him by the Father (v. 29; 6:37; 17:2, 6, 9). A full understanding of exactly how those two realities, human responsibility and divine sovereignty, work together lies beyond human comprehension; but there is no difficulty with them in the infinite mind of God. Significantly, the Bible does not attempt to harmonize them, nor does it apologize for the logical tension between them. For example, speaking of Judas Iscariot's treachery, Jesus said in Luke 22:22, "The Son of Man is going [to be betrayed] as it has been determined." In other words, Judas's betrayal of Christ was in accord with God's eternal purpose. But then Jesus added, "Woe to that man by whom He is betrayed!" That Judas's betrayal was part of God's plan did not relieve him of the responsibility for his crime. In Acts 2:23 Peter said that Jesus was "delivered over [to the cross] by the predetermined plan and foreknowledge of God." Yet he also charged Israel with responsibility for having "nailed [Jesus] to a cross by the hands of godless men and put Him to death." God's sovereignty never excuses human sin. (For a more complete discussion of the interplay of divine sovereignty and human responsibility, see the exposition of 6:35–40 in chapter 20 of this volume.)

Repeating what He said in His discourse on the Good Shepherd (see the exposition of vv. 3–5 in the previous chapter of this volume), Jesus said, **"My sheep hear My voice, and I know them, and they follow Me."** The elect will heed Christ's call to salvation and continue in faith and obedience to eternal glory (cf. Rom. 8:29–30).

The Lord continued by articulating the wonderful truth that those who are His sheep need never fear being lost. **"I give eternal life to them,"** Jesus declared, **"and they will never perish; and no one will snatch them out of My hand. My Father, who has given them to Me, is greater than all; and no one is able to snatch them out of the Father's hand."** Nowhere in Scripture is there a stronger affirmation of the absolute eternal security of all true Christians. Jesus plainly taught that the security of the believer in salvation does not depend on human effort, but is grounded in the gracious, sovereign election, promise, and power of God.

Christ's words reveal seven realities that bind every true Christian forever to God. First, believers are His **sheep,** and it is the duty of the

Good Shepherd to protect His flock. "This is the will of Him who sent Me," Jesus said, "that of all that He has given Me I lose nothing, but raise it up on the last day" (6:39). To insist that a true Christian can somehow be lost is to deny the truth of that statement. It is also to defame the character of the Lord Jesus Christ—making Him out to be an incompetent shepherd, unable to hold on to those entrusted to Him by the Father.

Second, Christ's sheep hear only His **voice** and **follow** only Him. Since they will not listen to or follow a stranger (10:5), they could not possibly wander away from Him and be eternally lost.

Third, Christ's sheep have **eternal life.** To speak of eternal life ending is a contradiction in terms.

Fourth, Christ **gives** eternal life to His sheep. Since they did nothing to earn it, they can do nothing to lose it.

Fifth, Christ promised that His sheep **will never perish.** Were even one to do so, it would make Him a liar.

Sixth, no one—not false shepherds (the thieves and robbers of v. 1), or false prophets (symbolized by the wolf of v. 12), nor even the Devil himself—is powerful enough to **snatch** Christ's sheep **out of** His **hand.**

Finally, Christ's sheep are held not only in His hand, but also in the hand of the Father, who **is greater than all; and** thus **no one is able to snatch them out of** His **hand** either. Infinitely secure, the believer's "life is hidden with Christ in God" (Col. 3:3).

The Father and the Son jointly guarantee the eternal security of believers because, as Jesus declared, **"I and the Father are one"** (the Greek word **one** is neuter, not masculine; it speaks of "one substance," not "one person"). Thus their unity of purpose and action in safeguarding believers is undergirded by their unity of nature and essence. The whole matter of security is summarized in our Lord's own words in John 6:39–40:

> This is the will of Him who sent Me, that of all that He has given Me I lose nothing, but raise it up on the last day. For this is the will of My Father, that everyone who beholds the Son and believes in Him will have eternal life, and I Myself will raise him up on the last day.

Incensed by what they accurately and unmistakably perceived as another blasphemous claim to deity by Jesus, **the Jews,** self-righteously exploding in a fit of passion, **picked up stones again to stone Him**—the fourth time in John's gospel that they had attempted to kill Him (5:16–18; 7:1; 8:59). Though the Romans had withheld the right of capital punishment from the Jews (18:31), this angry lynch mob was ready to take matters into its own hands.

The Charge

Jesus answered them, "I showed you many good works from the Father; for which of them are you stoning Me?" The Jews answered Him, "For a good work we do not stone You, but for blasphemy; and because You, being a man, make Yourself out to be God." (10:32–33)

Showing majestic calm in the face of His opponents' murderous rage, Jesus asked them pointedly, **"I showed you many good** (the adjective *kalos* means "noble," "excellent," or "beautiful") **works from the Father; for which of them are you stoning Me?"** The Lord did not soften or withdraw His claim to be equal with God. Instead, He forced them to face and deal with His miraculous good works done at the direction of **the Father** (cf. 5:19–23). Those works offered visible, tangible, and inescapable proof of His oneness with God (cf. 5:36), and thus proved that He was not a blasphemer, as, in fact, His opponents were. The Lord's question also put the Jewish leaders in the awkward position of opposing the very public and popular good things He had done in healing the sick, feeding the hungry, liberating the demon-possessed, and even raising the dead (cf. Luke 7:14–15; 8:52–56; John 11).

But the enraged **Jews** were not deterred by any miracles. Unlike the formerly blind man, who had drawn the proper conclusion from Jesus' miraculous deeds (cf. 9:33), the angry mob simply brushed His works aside. They **answered Him, "For a good work we do not stone You, but for blasphemy; and because You, being a man, make Yourself out to be God."** As noted above, the signs Jesus' performed demonstrated His oneness with the Father, and proved that He was not guilty of **blasphemy.** But the Lord's appeal to His mighty works was lost on those in the crowd. Their minds were made up, and their love of sin held them captive to Satan, death, and judgment.

In contrast to those who deny that Christ ever actually claimed to be God, the hostile Jews understood perfectly that He was saying exactly that. But they refused to consider the possibility that His claim might be true. In their minds, Jesus was guilty of the ultimate act of blasphemy because, as they told Him, **"You, being a man, make Yourself out to be God."** As was the case with Jesus' earlier claims to deity, their ultimate reaction was a plot to kill Him (5:16–18; 8:58–59). Ironically, their charge of blasphemy was the reverse of the truth. Far from being a mere man who was arrogantly promoting himself as God, Jesus was in fact almighty God who had selflessly humbled Himself in becoming a man to die for the world (1:14; cf. Phil. 2:5–11).

THE CHALLENGE

Jesus answered them, "Has it not been written in your Law, 'I said, you are gods'? If he called them gods, to whom the word of God came (and the Scripture cannot be broken), do you say of Him, whom the Father sanctified and sent into the world, 'You are blaspheming,' because I said, 'I am the Son of God'? If I do not do the works of My Father, do not believe Me; but if I do them, though you do not believe Me, believe the works, so that you may know and understand that the Father is in Me, and I in the Father." (10:34–38)

It is important to note that **Jesus,** having been charged with blasphemy because His opponents knew exactly what He was claiming, did not claim that they had misunderstood Him. His refusal to do so makes it clear that His declaration, "I and the Father are one" (v. 30), was in fact what they knew it to be, a claim to be God.

Jesus knew how seriously they took the very word **God,** so He addressed that one matter by quoting a passage from the Old Testament: **"Has it not been written in your Law, 'I said, you are gods'? If he called them gods, to whom the word of God came (and the Scripture cannot be broken), do you say of Him, whom the Father sanctified and sent into the world, 'You are blaspheming,' because I said, 'I am the Son of God'?** The very **Law** (a reference here to the entire Old Testament, not just the Pentateuch) that the Jews prized so highly used the term **gods** to refer to others than God Himself. The reference is to Psalm 82:6, where God rebuked Israel's unjust judges, calling them **gods** (in a far lesser sense) because they ruled as His representatives and spokesmen (cf. Ex. 4:16; 7:1). The Jewish leaders could not dispute the fact that those judges were called **gods,** because the **Scripture cannot be broken**—a clear and unambiguous declaration of the absolute authority and inerrancy of the Bible. Scripture can never be nullified or set aside (see the discussion of Matt. 5:17–19 in *Matthew 1–7,* The MacArthur New Testament Commentary [Chicago: Moody, 1985], 249–273), though the Jews often tried (cf. Mark 7:13).

Since God called the unjust judges **gods,** Jesus' argument ran, how could His opponents **say of Him, whom the Father sanctified and sent into the world, "You are blaspheming," because He said, "I am the Son of God?"** If mere men, who were evil, could in some sense be called gods, how could it be inappropriate for Jesus, the One **whom the Father sanctified and sent into the world,** to call Himself the **Son of God** (cf. 5:19–27)? The point is not to add to the evidence of His deity; it is simply a rebuke on the level of their overreaction to the use of the word **God** in reference to Jesus. He had proven that He was entitled to that title in the full divine sense, as He would affirm again in vv. 37–38. They were merely those **to whom the word of God came;** Jesus was the Incarnate Word of God (1:1, 14). As one commentator further explains,

> This passage is sometimes misinterpreted as though Jesus was simply classing himself with men in general. He appeals to the psalm that speaks of men as "gods," so runs the reasoning, and thus justifies his speaking of himself as Son of God. He is "god" in the same sense as others. But this is not taking seriously enough what Jesus actually says. He is arguing from the less to the greater. If the word *god* could be used of people who were no more than judges, how much more could it be used of one with greater dignity, greater importance and significance than any mere judge, one "whom the Father sanctified and sent into the world"? He is not placing himself on a level with men, but setting himself apart from them. (Leon Morris, *Reflections on the Gospel of John* [Peabody, Mass.: Hendrickson, 2000], 396)

The Lord's appeal to the Old Testament was a challenge again for the Jewish leaders to abandon their biased conclusions about Him and consider the objective evidence. In that same vein Jesus continued by saying, **"If I do not do the works of My Father, do not believe Me; but if I do them, though you do not believe Me, believe the works, so that you may know and understand that the Father is in Me, and I in the Father."** As He had so many other times before, with annoying patience (cf. vv. 25, 32; 5:19–20, 36; 14:10–11) the Lord appealed to His **works** as proof of His indivisible union with the **Father** (v. 30). But incredibly, the religious leaders of Israel were so spiritually blind that they could not recognize God's works. **If** Jesus did **not do the works of** the **Father,** they would have been right in refusing to **believe** Him. On the other hand, because He did **do them,** they should have put aside their reluctance to **believe** His words, and chosen instead to **believe** the clear testimony of His **works.** As supposed men of God, they should have been willing to follow the evidence to its logical conclusion.

THE CONSEQUENCES

Therefore they were seeking again to seize Him, and He eluded their grasp. And He went away again beyond the Jordan to the place where John was first baptizing, and He was staying there. Many came to Him and were saying, "While John performed no sign, yet everything John said about this man was true." Many believed in Him there. (10:39–42)

Not unexpectedly, the Lord's challenge to His opponents fell on deaf ears. Instead of considering the evidence, the Jewish leaders responded as they had before by **seeking again to seize Him.** It may be that they were planning to haul Him out of the temple before stoning Him (cf. Acts 21:30–32), but more likely they meant to arrest Him and hold Him for trial before the Sanhedrin. No matter what they intended, His hour still had not come (7:30; 8:20), so Jesus **eluded their grasp.** He left Jerusalem, not to return until three or four months later to raise Lazarus from the dead (John 11:1ff.) and enter Jerusalem in triumph (12:12ff.).

But as always, there were some who believed and embraced Him (cf. vv. 19–21; 7:12, 43; 9:16; 11:45). After leaving Jerusalem, the Lord **went away again beyond the Jordan to the place where John was first baptizing** (Bethany beyond the Jordan; see the exposition of 1:28 in chapter 4 of this volume). While He **was staying there many came to Him and were saying, "While John performed no sign, yet everything John said about this man was true."** The people there remembered Him and **came to Him** as they had earlier flocked to John the Baptist. While **John performed no sign,** that is to say did no miracles, he was nonetheless the preeminent witness to Jesus; as the people noted, **"Everything John said about** Him **was true."** Not surprisingly, **many believed in Him there.**

So Jesus' public ministry closed with one last rejection by the very leaders who should have hailed Him as the Messiah. Their rejection foreshadowed His final rejection a few months later, when the people, under their influence (Matt. 27:20), "cried out, 'Away with Him, away with Him, crucify Him!'" (John 19:15).

Even today, there are many who, like the hostile Jewish nation, allow their preconceived ideas about religion and their love for sin to blind them to the saving truth about Jesus Christ. Nonetheless those who are drawn to Him in repentance and faith will come to know the truth of who He is (7:17). To them will be given "the right to become children of God, even to those who believe in His name" (1:12).

The Resurrection and the Life— Part One: Sickness for the Glory of God (John 11:1–16)

38

Now a certain man was sick, Lazarus of Bethany, the village of Mary and her sister Martha. It was the Mary who anointed the Lord with ointment, and wiped His feet with her hair, whose brother Lazarus was sick. So the sisters sent word to Him, saying, "Lord, behold, he whom You love is sick." But when Jesus heard this, He said, "This sickness is not to end in death, but for the glory of God, so that the Son of God may be glorified by it." Now Jesus loved Martha and her sister and Lazarus. So when He heard that he was sick, He then stayed two days longer in the place where He was. Then after this He said to the disciples, "Let us go to Judea again." The disciples said to Him, "Rabbi, the Jews were just now seeking to stone You, and are You going there again?" Jesus answered, "Are there not twelve hours in the day? If anyone walks in the day, he does not stumble, because he sees the light of this world. But if anyone walks in the night, he stumbles, because the light is not in him." This He said, and after that He said to them, "Our friend Lazarus has fallen asleep; but I go, so that I may awaken him out of sleep." The disciples then said to Him, "Lord, if he has fallen asleep, he will recover." Now Jesus had spoken of his death, but they thought that He was speaking of

literal sleep. So Jesus then said to them plainly, "Lazarus is dead, and I am glad for your sakes that I was not there, so that you may believe; but let us go to him." Therefore Thomas, who is called Didymus, said to his fellow disciples, "Let us also go, so that we may die with Him." (11:1–16)

The most important theme in the universe is the glory of God. It is the underlying reason for all of God's works, from the creation of the world, to the redemption of fallen sinners, to the judgment of unbelievers, to the manifestation of His greatness for all eternity in heaven.

Because God's glory is intrinsic to His nature the Bible refers to Him as the God of glory (Ps. 29:3; Acts 7:2), the Glory of Israel (1 Sam. 15:29), the King of glory (Ps. 24:7–10), and the high and exalted One (Isa. 57:15; cf. 33:5). God the Father is called the Father of glory (Eph. 1:17; cf. 2 Peter 1:17); Jesus Christ, the Lord of glory (1 Cor. 2:8); and the Holy Spirit, the Spirit of glory (1 Peter 4:14). God's intrinsic glory is uniquely His, and He will not share it with anyone else (Isa. 42:8; 48:11).

The Word of God consistently extols the greatness of His glory. In Psalm 57:11 David exclaimed, "Be exalted above the heavens, O God; let Your glory be above all the earth" (cf. 108:5). Echoing his father's thought Solomon wrote, "Blessed be His glorious name forever; And may the whole earth be filled with His glory" (Ps. 72:19). Psalm 113:4 further describes God's glory as being "above the heavens"; Psalm 138:5 proclaims, "Great is the glory of the Lord"; and Psalm 148:13 adds, "His glory is above earth and heaven."

God's glory is revealed in an infinite number of ways, one of which is in His creation. In Psalm 19:1 David wrote, "The heavens are telling of the glory of God; and their expanse is declaring the work of His hands." Isaiah 6:3 declares, "The whole earth is full of His glory"; it is the display case in which "His invisible attributes, His eternal power and divine nature, [are] clearly seen" (Rom. 1:20). Everything God created gives Him glory—except fallen angels and fallen men. And even they, in a negative sense, bring Him glory, since He displays His holiness by judging them (cf. Ex. 14:4, 17–18).

God's glory is also seen in redemption. He saved sinners "to make known the riches of His glory upon vessels of mercy, which He prepared beforehand for glory" (Rom. 9:23). In 2 Corinthians 4:4 Paul called the message of salvation "the gospel of the glory of Christ," and noted that the saving "grace which is spreading to more and more people [will] cause the giving of thanks to abound to the glory of God" (v. 15). To the Ephesians Paul wrote, "[God] predestined us to adoption as sons through Jesus Christ to Himself, according to the kind intention of His will, to the praise of the glory of His grace, which He freely bestowed on us in the Beloved"

(Eph. 1:5–6; cf. vv. 12, 14, 18). Salvation transforms believers, filling them "with the fruit of righteousness which comes through Jesus Christ, to the glory and praise of God" (Phil. 1:11; cf. John 15:8).

At various times in redemptive history, God visibly manifested His glory to His people. Moses, overwhelmed with the responsibility of leading Israel, cried out to God,

> "I pray You, show me Your glory!" And [the Lord] said, "I Myself will make all My goodness pass before you, and will proclaim the name of the Lord before you; and I will be gracious to whom I will be gracious, and will show compassion on whom I will show compassion." But He said, "You cannot see My face, for no man can see Me and live!" Then the Lord said, "Behold, there is a place by Me, and you shall stand there on the rock; and it will come about, while My glory is passing by, that I will put you in the cleft of the rock and cover you with My hand until I have passed by. Then I will take My hand away and you shall see My back, but My face shall not be seen." (Ex. 33:18–23)

Throughout their wilderness wanderings, the glory of God appeared repeatedly to the people of Israel, primarily in the form of either a cloud or a fiery pillar (Ex. 13:21–22; 16:10; 24:16–17; Lev. 9:23–24; Num. 14:10; 16:19, 42). A visible manifestation of God's glory also appeared at the dedication ceremonies of both the tabernacle (Ex. 40:34–35) and Solomon's temple (1 Kings 8:10–11).

To prepare him for his prophetic ministry, God also gave Isaiah an overwhelming vision of His majestic, glorious holiness:

> In the year of King Uzziah's death I saw the Lord sitting on a throne, lofty and exalted, with the train of His robe filling the temple. Seraphim stood above Him, each having six wings: with two he covered his face, and with two he covered his feet, and with two he flew. And one called out to another and said, "Holy, Holy, Holy, is the Lord of hosts, the whole earth is full of His glory." And the foundations of the thresholds trembled at the voice of him who called out, while the temple was filling with smoke. Then I said, "Woe is me, for I am ruined! Because I am a man of unclean lips, and I live among a people of unclean lips; for my eyes have seen the King, the Lord of hosts." (Isa. 6:1–5)

But the most gracious and complete manifestation of God's glory came in the person of the Lord Jesus Christ, "the Word [who] became flesh, and dwelt among us, and we saw His glory, glory as of the only begotten from the Father, full of grace and truth" (John 1:14). Explaining the significance of the Lord's first miracle, John wrote, "This beginning of

His signs Jesus did in Cana of Galilee, and manifested His glory, and His disciples believed in Him" (2:11). Although Jesus' divine glory was veiled in human flesh, on one occasion He did unveil His true majesty to three of His disciples: "Jesus took with Him Peter and James and John his brother, and led them up on a high mountain by themselves. And He was transfigured before them; and His face shone like the sun, and His garments became as white as light" (Matt. 17:1–2; cf. 2 Peter 1:16–18).

Chapter 11 records the last and most powerful of the seven miraculous signs in the gospel of John (cf. 2:1–11; 4:46–54; 5:1–17; 6:1–14; 6:15–21; 9:1–41), the resurrection of Lazarus four days after he died. The miracle's primary purpose, however, was not to restore him to life, or to comfort his grieving sisters. Jesus raised Lazarus from the dead, first and foremost, so that He and the Father would be glorified (vv. 4, 40).

The glory of Jesus Christ blazes in this passage against a dark backdrop of rejection and hatred on the part of the Jewish leaders. As noted in the previous chapter of this volume, the Lord's confrontation with the Jewish authorities in Solomon's portico (10:22–39) marked the end of John's record of His public ministry; chapters 11 and 12 form a bridge between Christ's public ministry and His passion, recorded in chapters 13–21. After the confrontation, Jesus withdrew across the Jordan River (10:40) to the region of Perea, where He remained and ministered for a few months before returning to Jerusalem for Passion Week. It was in the midst of that Perean ministry that He returned briefly to the vicinity of Jerusalem to raise Lazarus from the dead. Yet, in spite of the undeniable miracle Jesus would perform, the Jewish authorities' hatred for Him only intensified (11:46–53). Therefore, after raising Lazarus, the Lord would once again leave the area surrounding Jerusalem (v. 54), not to return until His triumphal entry.

The resurrection of Lazarus evidenced Christ's glory in three ways: it pointed unmistakably to His deity (11:25–27); it strengthened the faith of the disciples (11:15); and it led directly to the cross (11:53). As the account unfolds in chapter 11, it may be divided into four sections: the preparation for the miracle (11:1–16); the arrival of Jesus (11:17–36); the miracle itself (11:37–44); and the aftermath (11:45–57).

The first section provides the background for the miracle by introducing three sets of characters: the critical man, the concerned sisters, and the cautious disciples.

THE CRITICAL MAN

Now a certain man was sick, Lazarus of Bethany, the village of Mary and her sister Martha. It was the Mary who anointed the

Lord with ointment, and wiped His feet with her hair, whose brother Lazarus was sick. (11:1–2)

The unembellished introduction of him only as **a certain man** who **was sick** emphasizes that **Lazarus** is not the primary focus of the story. As noted above, the main emphasis is that Jesus and the Father would be glorified through his resurrection. **Lazarus** is a shortened form of the Hebrew name Eleazar, which means "God has helped," or "helped by God"—a fitting name in light of this story. Since the name was a common one, John further identified him by the village where he lived, **Bethany.** This was not the Bethany beyond the Jordan where John the Baptist had ministered (see the exposition of 1:28 in chapter 4 of this volume) and where Jesus was currently ministering (see the discussion of 10:40 in the previous chapter of this volume). This was the **Bethany** in Judea (v. 18).

John further identified Bethany as **the village of Mary and her sister Martha.** The apostle, giving no further details, evidently expected his readers to be familiar with the two sisters (who are referred to in Luke's gospel [Luke 10:38–42]). Thus, he could write that **it was the Mary who anointed the Lord with ointment, and wiped His feet with her hair, whose brother Lazarus was sick;** even though he would not relate that story of that anointing until chapter 12, his readers already knew of it from the Synoptic Gospels (Matt. 26:6–13; Mark 14:3–9).

Through the resurrection of Lazarus Jesus and the Father would receive glory, the disciples' faith would be strengthened, and the final straw would be dropped that prompted the hostile Jewish leaders to bring about Jesus' execution.

The Concerned Sisters

So the sisters sent word to Him, saying, "Lord, behold, he whom You love is sick." But when Jesus heard this, He said, "This sickness is not to end in death, but for the glory of God, so that the Son of God may be glorified by it." Now Jesus loved Martha and her sister and Lazarus. So when He heard that he was sick, He then stayed two days longer in the place where He was. (11:3–6)

Understandably, **the sisters** were deeply concerned about their brother's condition. They sent **word to** Jesus, **saying, "Lord, behold, he whom You love is sick."** The nature of Lazarus's illness is not specified, but his death was imminent. Mary and Martha believed that Jesus was willing to heal their brother because of His deep **love** for Lazarus; and they were equally confident that He had the power to do so (vv. 21, 32).

Since Jesus was across the Jordan (10:40), a messenger from Bethany would have needed at least a day to reach Him. (Of course, the Lord in His omniscience already knew about Lazarus's serious illness [cf. vv. 11, 13–14]). Due to the severity of his condition, Lazarus may have even died before the messenger reached Jesus, since he had already been dead for four days when Jesus arrived in Bethany (vv. 17, 39). (The messenger's journey to Jesus would have accounted for one day, the Lord then delayed two days (v. 6) before taking one more day to travel to Lazarus' home. That brings the total number of days to four.)

The sisters' message is beautiful in its tender simplicity. They did not spell out the details of Lazarus's condition, nor did they specifically ask the Lord to do anything. (They realized that it would be extremely dangerous for Him to travel anywhere near Jerusalem at this time; cf. v. 8.) They also did not attempt to manipulate Jesus by reminding Him of Lazarus's affection for Him. They merely appealed to the Lord's **love** (*phileō;* the love of friendship and affection) for their brother and humbly and trustingly brought the need to His attention (cf. Pss. 37:5; 46:1; 55:22; 1 Peter 5:7).

When Jesus heard the message, **He said, "This sickness is not to end in death."** The Lord obviously did not mean that Lazarus was not going to die, but rather that death would not be the ultimate outcome. Like the blind man (9:3), his illness, death, and resurrection were all **for the glory of God.** Contrary to the teaching of some, Christ's response indicates that sickness and even death may sometimes be God's will for His people (cf. 21:19; Ex. 4:11; Job 1, 2). In this case, Lazarus's circumstances would bring **glory** to **God** because through them the **Son** of God would be **glorified** (cf. 12:23, 28).

John's note that **Jesus loved Martha and her sister and Lazarus** makes explicit what is implied throughout the story. The Lord was close to this family, having undoubtedly spent much time in their home during His visits to nearby Jerusalem (cf. Matt. 21:17; Mark 11:11–12; and the discussion of 8:1 in chapter 27 of this volume). John interjected the thought here to show that the Lord's subsequent action did not reflect a lack of love and compassion on His part.

The Lord's close relationship with Lazarus, Mary, and Martha makes what happened next seem all the more puzzling. Instead of rushing back to Bethany in response to the sisters' message, **when** Jesus **heard that** Lazarus **was sick, He then stayed two days longer in the place where He was.** The Lord did not delay to allow Lazarus to die since, as noted above, he had probably died before the messenger reached Jesus. The delay did serve several purposes: it strengthened the sisters' faith in the Lord by forcing them to trust Him; it made it clear that Lazarus was truly dead (cf. the discussion of v. 17 in chapter 39 of this volume) and hence that Jesus' raising of him was indeed a miracle; and, as always, Jesus operated according to God's timetable, not man's.

THE CAUTIOUS DISCIPLES

Then after this He said to the disciples, "Let us go to Judea again." The disciples said to Him, "Rabbi, the Jews were just now seeking to stone You, and are You going there again?" Jesus answered, "Are there not twelve hours in the day? If anyone walks in the day, he does not stumble, because he sees the light of this world. But if anyone walks in the night, he stumbles, because the light is not in him." This He said, and after that He said to them, "Our friend Lazarus has fallen asleep; but I go, so that I may awaken him out of sleep." The disciples then said to Him, "Lord, if he has fallen asleep, he will recover." Now Jesus had spoken of his death, but they thought that He was speaking of literal sleep. So Jesus then said to them plainly, "Lazarus is dead, and I am glad for your sakes that I was not there, so that you may believe; but let us go to him." Therefore Thomas, who is called Didymus, said to his fellow disciples, "Let us also go, so that we may die with Him." (11:7–16)

After the two-day delay was over, Jesus **said to the disciples, "Let us go to Judea again."** Astonished and appalled, **the disciples** protested, **"Rabbi, the Jews were just now seeking to stone You** (8:59; cf. 10:31), **and are You going there again?"** Why, they reasoned, leave a fruitful ministry (10:41–42) for a life-threatening journey to the vicinity of Jerusalem? The situation did not seem to require the Lord's immediate attention or presence; He Himself had said that Lazarus was not going to die (v. 4). And if Jesus did need to heal Lazarus, why not do it from a distance like He had done before (cf. 4:46–53)?

The Lord replied with a proverbial saying meant to allay the disciples' fears: **"Are there not twelve hours in the day? If anyone walks in the day, he does not stumble, because he sees the light of this world. But if anyone walks in the night, he stumbles, because the light is not in him."** The Jews divided the daylight period into **twelve hours,** which unlike modern hours varied in length at different seasons of the year. The **twelve hours in the day** symbolize the duration of the Lord's earthly ministry as allotted by the Father. Just as no one can lengthen or shorten a day, so the disciples' concern could not extend the time allotted to Jesus, nor could the Jews' hostility shorten it. The one who **walks in the day** need not fear that he might **stumble;** thus Jesus was perfectly safe for the prescribed time of His life (7:30; 8:20). The **night,** signifying the end of His earthly ministry (cf. 12:35), would come at the precise time set by God's eternal plan, and only then would the Lord **stumble** in death (cf. the discussion of 9:4 in chapter 33 of this volume).

The phrase **this He said, and after that He said to them** suggests that Jesus paused to allow the truth of what He had said in verses 9 and 10 to sink in. Then He explained to the disciples why He needed to return to Judea: **"Our friend Lazarus has fallen asleep; but I go, so that I may awaken him out of sleep." Sleep** is used throughout the Bible as a euphemism for death, particularly that of believers (cf. the repeated use of the phrase "slept with his fathers" in 1 and 2 Kings and 2 Chron.; 1 Kings 2:10; 11:43; Ps. 13:3; Dan. 12:2; Matt. 9:24; 27:52; Acts 7:60; 13:36; 1 Cor. 11:30; 15:6, 18, 20, 51; 1 Thess. 4:13–15; 5:10; 2 Peter 3:4); for Jesus, therefore, to say that He would **awaken him out of sleep** was to speak metaphorically of raising Lazarus from the dead.

Relieved to hear that Lazarus was on the road to recovery (or so they thought), **the disciples then said to Him, "Lord, if he has fallen asleep, he will recover."** "Why not just let him rest?" they reasoned. They saw no need for their Master to risk His life by returning to Judea. But their reasoning was based on a misunderstanding of Jesus' words; He **had spoken of** Lazarus's **death, but they thought that He was speaking of literal sleep.** The disciples' mistake flowed from their misunderstanding of Jesus' words in verse 4; they still believed that Lazarus' condition was improving, and would continue to do so with adequate rest.

At that point Jesus ended their confusion, and **said to them plainly, "Lazarus is dead."** Here is an unmistakable indication of the Lord's omniscience, since the messenger had merely said that Lazarus was sick (v. 3), and there was no way for Jesus to have heard that Lazarus had already died.

Jesus' next statement, **"I am glad for your sakes that I was not there, so that you may believe,"** does not mean that He rejoiced in the death of His dear friend (cf. vv. 33, 35, 38). The Lord's point was that Lazarus' resurrection from the dead would do far more to strengthen the disciples' faith than a healing alone would have done. Jesus' time on earth was rapidly nearing its end, and with the cross looming ever nearer, the disciples needed a powerful support for their faith.

Seeing that Jesus was determined to return to Judea, **Thomas, who is called Didymus** (**Thomas** [Hebrew] and **Didymus** [Greek] both mean "twin"), **said** resignedly **to his fellow disciples, "Let us also go, so that we may die with Him." Thomas** is known to history as "Doubting Thomas" (cf. John 20:24–28), but there was much more to him, as his words here reflect love, devotion, and courage, in spite of his pessimism. His negativity led him to believe he would die if they went to Jerusalem. On the other hand, his love for Jesus was so strong that he was willing to **die with** Him.

Thomas was sincere in his intentions. Yet at the crucial moment in Gethsemane (just a short time away) his faith, like that of the rest of the disciples, would be found wanting. When Jesus was arrested in the garden, "all the disciples left Him and fled" (Matt. 26:56). Here, however, Thomas was an example of courage and strength to the wavering disciples. Following his bold lead, despite their doubts (vv. 8, 12), they all went to Bethany with Jesus.

The Resurrection and the Life— Part Two: The Arrival of the Savior

(John 11:17–36)

39

So when Jesus came, He found that he had already been in the tomb four days. Now Bethany was near Jerusalem, about two miles off; and many of the Jews had come to Martha and Mary, to console them concerning their brother. Martha therefore, when she heard that Jesus was coming, went to meet Him, but Mary stayed at the house. Martha then said to Jesus, "Lord, if You had been here, my brother would not have died. Even now I know that whatever You ask of God, God will give You." Jesus said to her, "Your brother will rise again." Martha said to Him, "I know that he will rise again in the resurrection on the last day." Jesus said to her, "I am the resurrection and the life; he who believes in Me will live even if he dies, and everyone who lives and believes in Me will never die. Do you believe this?" She said to Him, "Yes, Lord; I have believed that You are the Christ, the Son of God, even He who comes into the world." When she had said this, she went away and called Mary her sister, saying secretly, "The Teacher is here and is calling for you." And when she heard it, she got up quickly and was coming to Him. Now Jesus had not yet come into the village, but was still in the place where Martha met Him. Then the Jews who were with her in the house, and consoling her,

**when they saw that Mary got up quickly and went out, they fol-
lowed her, supposing that she was going to the tomb to weep
there. Therefore, when Mary came where Jesus was, she saw
Him, and fell at His feet, saying to Him, "Lord, if You had been
here, my brother would not have died." When Jesus therefore
saw her weeping, and the Jews who came with her also weeping,
He was deeply moved in spirit and was troubled, and said,
"Where have you laid him?" They said to Him, "Lord, come and
see." Jesus wept. So the Jews were saying, "See how He loved
him!"** (11:17–36)

One of the most unsettling aspects of death is that man has no
control over it. Just as "no man has authority to restrain the wind," so also
no man has "authority over the day of death" (Eccl. 8:8). When that day
comes man "is torn from the security of his tent, and they march him
before the king of terrors"—a poetic reference to death (Job 18:14).

The sobering reality that this life could end at any moment only
underscores its brevity. As Job lamented, "Man, who is born of woman, is
short-lived and full of turmoil. Like a flower he comes forth and withers.
He also flees like a shadow and does not remain" (Job 14:1–2). "As for the
days of our life," wrote Moses, "they contain seventy years, or if due to
strength, eighty years, yet their pride is but labor and sorrow; for soon it is
gone and we fly away" (Ps. 90:10).

The truth expressed in the flippant statement, "You can't take it
with you!" indicates that everything done in this life (apart from serving
God) is ultimately meaningless. For Solomon, that realization reduced all
he had accomplished to vanity:

> Thus I hated all the fruit of my labor for which I had labored under the
> sun, for I must leave it to the man who will come after me. And who
> knows whether he will be a wise man or a fool? Yet he will have con-
> trol over all the fruit of my labor for which I have labored by acting
> wisely under the sun. This too is vanity. (Eccl. 2:18–19)

Job exclaimed, "Naked I came from my mother's womb, and naked I shall
return there" (Job 1:21). Paul wrote, "For we have brought nothing into
the world, so we cannot take anything out of it either" (1 Tim. 6:7). To a
greedy man consumed with his earthly possessions, God declared, "You
fool! This very night your soul is required of you; and now who will own
what you have prepared?" (Luke 12:20). As has been wryly noted, there
are no pockets in shrouds, and no one ever saw a hearse pulling a trailer.
Tragically, people spend their entire lives accumulating possessions,
which death snatches from them in an instant.

But the wonderful truth is that death does not have to be the end of all man's hopes and dreams. For believers, it can be faced with joyous anticipation instead of anxious fear, because Jesus Christ has conquered death. As He promised His followers, "I am the resurrection and the life; he who believes in Me will live even if he dies, and everyone who lives and believes in Me will never die" (11:25–26) and, "Because I live, you will live also" (14:19; cf. 1 Cor. 15:20–23). Death marks the beginning of true life in glorified perfection and perfect fellowship with Christ for those who put their faith in the Lord. He will raise them up on the last day (6:39–40, 44), and they will live forever in His presence.

Christ's raising of Lazarus vividly demonstrated His power over death (cf. Luke 7:11–15; 8:52–56). The miracle formed a bridge between His public ministry to the nation and His private ministry to the disciples, preparing them for His departure. Thus it both strengthened the disciples' faith (cf. v. 15) and also provided indisputable evidence to Israel that Jesus was who He claimed to be. Furthermore, the miracle gave credence to Jesus' repeated claims that He would one day rise from the dead Himself (cf. 2:19; Mark 8:31; 9:31; Luke 24:7).

As noted in the previous chapter of this volume, the eleventh chapter of John's gospel divides into four scenes. Verses 1–16 record Lazarus's illness and his sisters' message to Jesus, verses 17–36 describe Jesus' arrival in Bethany, verses 37–44 recount the miracle itself, and verses 45–57 relate its aftermath.

In this second scene in the drama Jesus, the central figure in the story, arrives at Bethany. As verses 17–36 further set the stage for the miracle, they reveal three visible demonstrations of Jesus' genuine care: His coming, His claim, and His compassion.

HIS COMING

So when Jesus came, He found that he had already been in the tomb four days. Now Bethany was near Jerusalem, about two miles off; and many of the Jews had come to Martha and Mary, to console them concerning their brother. (11:17–19)

After His journey from Perea, the region across the Jordan River (10:40), **Jesus** arrived at the outskirts of Bethany. Rabbinic writings suggest a possible reason for John's note that Lazarus **had already been in the tomb four days** (see the discussion of 11:6 in the previous chapter of this volume). The Jews believed that the soul hovered around the body for three days after death, hoping to reenter it. But on the fourth day, after noticing that the body was beginning to decompose (cf. v. 39), the soul departed. Only then would a death be considered completely irreversible. Lazarus had been dead for **four days,** and his body had already started to decompose (v. 39). The Jews therefore would have recognized that only a divine miracle could restore him to life.

John's explanation that **Bethany was near Jerusalem** (**about two miles** east of the city on the road to Jericho) serves a twofold purpose. It highlights the risk Jesus took by coming so near to **Jerusalem,** which was a hotbed of murderous opposition to Him. And it also implies that **many of the Jews** who **had come to Martha and Mary** came from Jerusalem. That so **many Jews** from the capital came to **console them concerning their brother** suggests that the family was prominent, and probably wealthy (cf. 12:1–3). From the human perspective, the mourners were there to comfort the sisters in their loss. But from God's perspective, they were there to witness Jesus' stunning miracle. The raising of Lazarus would be done in public before numerous onlookers, many of whom were hostile to the Lord. As a result, not even Jesus' enemies would be able to deny what He had done (v. 47).

It was customary to bury the deceased on the day of their death (cf. Acts 5:5–6, 10), since the climate was warm and the Jews did not practice embalming. Men and women would walk separately in the funeral procession, after which the women alone would return from the burial site to begin the thirty-day mourning period. The first seven days of mourning were the most intense, and many of the mourners would remain with the family for that entire week. That explains why the **Jews** who came to **console** Martha and Mary were still with them four days after the burial.

His Claim

Martha therefore, when she heard that Jesus was coming, went to meet Him, but Mary stayed at the house. Martha then said to Jesus, "Lord, if You had been here, my brother would not have died. Even now I know that whatever You ask of God, God will give You." Jesus said to her, "Your brother will rise again." Martha said to Him, "I know that he will rise again in the resurrection on the last day." Jesus said to her, "I am the resurrection and the life; he who believes in Me will live even if he dies, and everyone who lives and believes in Me will never die. Do you believe this?" She said to Him, "Yes, Lord; I have believed that You are the Christ, the Son of God, even He who comes into the world." (11:20–27)

When word reached **Martha** that **Jesus was coming** into the village she **went to meet Him, but Mary stayed at the house.** The actions of the two sisters are in keeping with the picture of them in Luke 10:38–42. Martha was the bustling, active one ("distracted with all her preparations"; Luke 10:40), Mary was the quiet, contemplative one ("seated at the Lord's feet, listening to His word"; v. 39). According to Jewish custom, those who suffered the loss of a loved one remained seated while the other mourners consoled them. But Martha, in keeping with her forceful personality, left her house and went to meet Jesus as He approached.

When Martha reached Him, the disturbing thought that had been uppermost in her mind (and her sister's; v. 32) for the last few days came pouring out: **"Lord, if You had been here, my brother would not have died."** Although obviously heartbroken, she was not rebuking the Lord for failing to prevent Lazarus's death. As noted in the previous chapter of this volume, the sisters' message had arrived too late, humanly speaking, for Jesus to have returned to Bethany in time to heal him. Martha's words were simply a poignant expression of grief mingled with the faith she expressed in her next statement: **"Even now I know that whatever You ask of God, God will give You."** That confidence, however, evidently did not extend to Jesus' ability to resurrect her brother, as her later hesitation when the tomb was opened makes clear (v. 39). She seems to have had faith in the Lord's power to heal, but not in His power to raise the dead (perhaps the possibility had not even crossed her mind). Nonetheless Martha recognized that Jesus had a special relationship with God. She was therefore confident that through His prayers some good could still come out of the tragedy.

Jesus responded by assuring her, **"Your brother will rise again."** He meant that Lazarus was going to be resurrected immediately, but Martha missed the point. She assumed that Jesus, like the other mourners, was comforting her by pointing out that Lazarus would **rise again** at the end of the age. Martha, however, was already familiar with that truth, and so she replied, **"I know that he will rise again in the resurrection on the last day."** The resurrection of the body was taught in the Old Testament (e.g., Job 19:25–27; Ps. 16:10; Dan. 12:2), and affirmed by the Pharisees (though not by the Sadducees; Matt. 22:23; Acts 23:6–8). It was also, as Martha knew, the teaching of Jesus (cf. 5:21, 25–29; 6:39–40, 44, 54). Ironically, while she believed Jesus had the power to raise her brother in the distant future, she did not think that He could also do so immediately.

Challenging Martha to move beyond an abstract belief in the final resurrection to complete faith in Him, **Jesus said to her, "I am the resurrection and the life."** This is the fifth of the seven "I AM" deity claims in John's gospel (6:35; 8:12; 10:7, 9, 11, 14; 14:6; 15:1, 5). Martha's focus was on the end of the age, but time is no obstacle for the One who has the power of **resurrection** and **life** (cf. 5:21, 26). Jesus will raise the dead in the future resurrection of which Martha spoke. But He was also going to raise her brother immediately. The Lord called her to a personal trust in Him as the One who alone has power over death.

Jesus' next two statements, **"he who believes in Me will live even if he dies, and everyone who lives and believes in Me will never die,"** are not redundant. They teach separate, though related, truths. The one **who believes in** Jesus **will live even if he dies** physically because He will raise him on the last day (5:21, 25–29; 6:39–40, 44, 54). And since **everyone who lives and believes in** Him has eternal life (3:36; 5:24; 6:47, 54), they **will never die** spiritually (see the discussion of 8:51 in chapter 32 of this volume), since eternal life cannot be extinguished by physical death. As a result, all who trust in Christ can exult, "O death, where is your victory? O death, where is your sting?" (1 Cor. 15:55).

When Jesus challenged Martha, **"Do you believe this?"** He was not asking her if she believed that He was about to raise her brother. The Lord was calling her to personally believe that He alone was the source of resurrection power and eternal life. R. C. H. Lenski writes,

> To believe "this" is to believe what he says of himself and thus to believe "in him." It is one thing to hear it, to reason and to argue about it; and quite another thing to believe, embrace, trust it. To believe is to receive, hold, enjoy the reality and the power of it, with all that lies in it of joy, comfort, peace, and hope. The measure of our believing, while it is not the measure of our possessing, since the smallest faith has Jesus, the resurrection and the life, completely, is yet the measure of our enjoyment of it all. (*The Interpretation of St. John's Gospel* [Reprint; Peabody, Mass.: Hendrickson, 1998], 803)

Because of His infinite love for Martha's soul, Jesus pointed her to the only source of spiritual life and well-being—Himself.

Martha's affirmation of faith in Jesus stands with the other great confessions of His identity in the gospels (1:49; 6:69; Matt. 14:33; 16:16). It anticipates John's purpose statement for writing his gospel: "These have been written so that you may believe that Jesus is the Christ, the Son of God; and that believing you may have life in His name" (20:31). Martha emphatically (the Greek text has the personal pronoun in addition to the verb) declared three vital truths about Jesus: Like Andrew (1:41), she confessed that He was the **Christ,** or Messiah; like John the Baptist (1:34), Nathanael (1:49), and the disciples (Matt. 14:33) she affirmed that He was the **Son of God;** and finally, like the Old Testament had predicted (cf. Is. 9:6; Mic. 5:2), she referred to Him as **He who comes into the world**—the deliverer sent by God (Luke 7:19–20; cf. John 1:9; 3:31; 6:14).

HIS COMPASSION

When she had said this, she went away and called Mary her sister, saying secretly, "The Teacher is here and is calling for you." And when she heard it, she got up quickly and was coming to Him. Now Jesus had not yet come into the village, but was still in the place where Martha met Him. Then the Jews who were with her in the house, and consoling her, when they saw that Mary got up quickly and went out, they followed her, supposing that she was going to the tomb to weep there. Therefore, when Mary came where Jesus was, she saw Him, and fell at His feet, saying to Him, "Lord, if You had been here, my brother would not have died." When Jesus therefore saw her weeping, and the Jews who came with her also weeping, He was deeply moved in spirit and was troubled, and said, "Where have you laid him?" They said to Him, "Lord, come and see." Jesus wept. So the Jews were saying, "See how He loved him!" (11:28–36)

Having affirmed her faith in Jesus, Martha **went away and called Mary her sister, saying secretly, "The Teacher is here and is calling for you."** Mary was still in the house (v. 20) being comforted by the mourners. Although the text does not record it, Jesus evidently sent Martha to get her. She probably gave the message to Mary **secretly,** hoping that she also could have a private meeting with Jesus before the crowd of mourners spotted Him. Since Martha still did not realize that the Lord intended to raise her brother, she may also have been trying to keep Him away from the hostile Jews (especially the leaders) who were in attendance.

Whatever Martha's motive, her attempt at privacy failed. **When** Mary **heard** her sister's message, **she got up quickly and** went to meet Jesus. He **had not yet come into the village, but was still** on the outskirts, **in the place where Martha met Him.** But Mary's hasty departure did not escape the attention of **the Jews who were with her in the house, and consoling her** (v. 19). **When they saw that Mary got up quickly and went out, they followed her.** Assuming she was going to **weep** at the **tomb,** as was customary (cf. 2 Sam. 3:32), they felt it was their duty as her comforters to go with her. Once again, God sovereignly orchestrated the circumstances to perfectly fit His purposes, ensuring that Jesus' miracle would be witnessed by the whole group.

Mary appears to have been the more emotional of the sisters, and when she **came where Jesus was, she saw Him, and fell at His feet.** She said **to Him** what they had surely discussed, since Martha had said it earlier: **"Lord, if You had been here, my brother would not have died."** As was the case with her sister, Mary meant no reproach to Jesus (cf. the discussion of v. 21 above); her statement was simply a reflection of their grief.

The scene was understandably one of intense sorrow and pain. Not only was Mary **weeping** (a form of the verb *klaiō;* "to wail," or "to lament loudly"), but **the Jews who came with her** were **also weeping** and wailing loudly. According to Jewish custom, even the poorest family was expected to hire at least two flute players and a professional wailing woman. Since Mary, Martha, and Lazarus were a prominent family, they would likely have had even more professional mourners, in addition to the others who came to pay their respects (v. 19).

Observing the chaotic scene, Jesus **was deeply moved in spirit and was troubled. Deeply moved** is a misleading translation of the verb *embrimaomai,* which literally means to snort like a horse. Apart from its use in v. 38, it appears only three other times in the New Testament (Matt. 9:30; Mark 1:43; 14:5), where it is translated "sternly warned" or "scolding." It thus includes the connotation of anger, outrage, or indignation. Jesus appears to have been angry not only over the painful reality of sin and death, of which Lazarus was a beloved example, but perhaps also with the mourners, who were acting like the pagans who have no hope (cf. 1 Thess. 4:13). *Tarassō* (**troubled**) further emphasizes the intensity of the Lord's reaction. The term is similarly used elsewhere to describe strong emotions, such as Herod's reaction to the magi's arrival (Matt. 2:3), the disciples' terror when they saw Jesus walking on the water (14:26); Zacharias's fear when he saw the angel in the temple (Luke 1:12); the disciples' amazement at seeing Jesus after His resurrection (24:38); Jesus' reaction to His impending death (John 12:27); and His response to Judas's imminent betrayal (13:21).

Jesus then asked, **"Where have you laid him?" They said to Him, "Lord, come and see."** Whom the term **they** refers to is not defined, but it evidently refers to some in the crowd who were favorably disposed to Jesus, since they addressed Him respectfully as **Lord.**

Like the others, **Jesus wept.** But the Greek verb is not *klaiō* as in verse 33, but *dakruō,* a rare word used only here in the New Testament. In contrast to the loud wailing implied by *klaiō, dakruō* has the connotation of silently bursting into tears, unlike the typical funeral mourners. Jesus' tears were generated both by His love for Lazarus, and by His grief over the deadly and incessant effects of sin in a fallen world. Verse 35, though it is the shortest verse in the Bible, is rich with meaning. It emphasizes Jesus' humanity; He was truly "a man of sorrows and acquainted with grief" (Isa. 53:3). But while the **Jews were** correct in seeing Jesus' sorrow as evidence that **He loved** Lazarus, they were wrong to think that His tears reflected the same hopeless despair that they felt.

The stage was now set for the compassionate Savior to visibly substantiate His claim to be the resurrection and the life. In the next section He would convincingly demonstrate His power over death by restoring Lazarus to life.

The Resurrection and the Life— Part Three: The Raising of Lazarus (John 11:37–44)

40

But some of them said, "Could not this man, who opened the eyes of the blind man, have kept this man also from dying?" So Jesus, again being deeply moved within, came to the tomb. Now it was a cave, and a stone was lying against it. Jesus said, "Remove the stone." Martha, the sister of the deceased, said to Him, "Lord, by this time there will be a stench, for he has been dead four days." Jesus said to her, "Did I not say to you that if you believe, you will see the glory of God?" So they removed the stone. Then Jesus raised His eyes, and said, "Father, I thank You that You have heard Me. I knew that You always hear Me; but because of the people standing around I said it, so that they may believe that You sent Me." When He had said these things, He cried out with a loud voice, "Lazarus, come forth." The man who had died came forth, bound hand and foot with wrappings, and his face was wrapped around with a cloth. Jesus said to them, "Unbind him, and let him go." (11:37–44)

During His earthly ministry, the Lord Jesus Christ made many astonishing claims about Himself (see the list in chapter 24 of this volume). Yet He also gave powerful and convincing evidence, through the miraculous signs He performed, to support the truthfulness of those claims. When His enemies demanded to know whether or not He was the Messiah, Jesus pointed to those very signs as proof of His authenticity. He said,

> The works that I do in My Father's name, these testify of Me. . . . If I do not do the works of My Father, do not believe Me; but if I do them, though you do not believe Me, believe the works, so that you may know and understand that the Father is in Me, and I in the Father." (John 10:25, 37–38)

Earlier in John's gospel He declared, "The works which the Father has given Me to accomplish—the very works that I do—testify about Me, that the Father has sent Me" (5:36). And on the night before His death the Lord told His disciples, "The Father abiding in Me does His works. Believe Me that I am in the Father and the Father is in Me; otherwise believe because of the works themselves" (14:10–11).

By healing a paralyzed man, Jesus proved that "the Son of Man has authority on earth to forgive sins" (Matt. 9:6); by casting out demons, He demonstrated that "the kingdom of God ha[d] come upon" His hearers (Luke 11:20). When John the Baptist sent messengers to ask Him, "Are You the Expected One [the Messiah], or do we look for someone else?" Jesus replied, "Go and report to John what you have seen and heard: the blind receive sight, the lame walk, the lepers are cleansed, and the deaf hear, the dead are raised up, the poor have the gospel preached to them" (Luke 7:19, 22).

When the outraged Jewish authorities demanded to know what authority He had to cleanse the temple Jesus replied, "Destroy this temple, and in three days I will raise it up" (John 2:19). As John notes, "He was speaking of the temple of His body" (v. 21). The Lord repeatedly told His disciples that He would rise from the dead (Matt. 16:21; 17:22–23; 20:18–19; Luke 24:6–7), and—as the greatest evidence of all—His resurrection proved that He was who He claimed to be. In the words of the apostle Paul, Jesus was "declared the Son of God with power by the resurrection from the dead" (Rom. 1:4).

Just as the feeding of the five thousand illustrated Jesus' claim to be the bread of life (6:35), so also the raising of Lazarus illustrated His claim to be the resurrection and the life (11:25). This miracle is the last and most spectacular of the seven miraculous signs recorded in the gospel of John (for the others, see 2:1–11; 4:46–54; 5:1–17; 6:1–14; 6:15–21; 9:1–41). It was both a powerful encouragement to the disciples' faith, and a powerful rebuke to the unbelieving Jews for their hard-hearted rejection of Him.

The entire eleventh chapter of John's gospel revolves around

Christ's claim to be the resurrection and the life (vv. 25–26). He, not Lazarus, is the primary focus of the passage. The resurrection of Lazarus was not an end in itself (even for Lazarus, who had to die again); the goal was that Jesus and the Father would be glorified (vv. 4, 40). This passage is the third of the four sections into which the account of Lazarus's resurrection may be divided: verses 1–16 recounted his illness and his sisters' message to Jesus; verses 17–36 described Jesus' arrival in Bethany; and verses 45–57 will relate the aftermath of the miracle.

The dramatic account of the actual raising of Lazarus in verses 37–44 unfolds in five scenes: the perplexity, the problem, the promise, the prayer, and the power.

THE PERPLEXITY

But some of them said, "Could not this man, who opened the eyes of the blind man, have kept this man also from dying?" (11:37)

Throughout His ministry Jesus polarized people (cf. 7:12, 43; 9:16; 10:19), and this incident was no exception. After seeing Him weeping (v. 35), some of the mourners exclaimed, "See how He loved him!" (v. 36). Others, however, were not so sure and, picking up the attitude of the sisters, asked, **"Could not this man, who opened the eyes of the blind man, have kept this man also from dying?"** The Lord's healing of the man born blind (9:1–41), the last major miracle He had performed in the vicinity of Jerusalem, had caused such a sensation among the people that it was still fresh in their minds several months later. The mourners were probably mocking, but confused; they knew by experience that Jesus had the power to heal, as their reference to that previous incident indicates. But if Jesus truly loved Lazarus as much as He appeared to, why had He delayed? Why had He not made every effort to reach Bethany while Lazarus was still alive?

The answer is that God "works all things after the counsel of His will" (Eph. 1:11) and "does not give an account of all His doings" (Job 33:13; cf. 40:2; Deut. 29:29). Jesus delayed because His purpose was not to heal Lazarus, but to raise him from the dead and thereby bring glory to Himself and to the Father (vv. 4, 40).

THE PROBLEM

So Jesus, again being deeply moved within, came to the tomb. Now it was a cave, and a stone was lying against it. Jesus said,

"Remove the stone." Martha, the sister of the deceased, said to Him, "Lord, by this time there will be a stench, for he has been dead four days." (11:38–39)

The doubts expressed in verse 37 by some of the mourners resulted in **Jesus again being deeply moved** (*embrimaomai;* cf. the discussion of v. 33 in the previous chapter of this volume) **within** as He **came to the tomb.** The **tomb,** as was common in Israel, **was a cave** (cf. Gen. 23:19). This was apparently a natural cave (the word translated **cave** is used elsewhere to describe natural as opposed to man-made caves; Heb. 11:38; Rev. 6:15), though tombs were sometimes artificially carved out of rock (Matt. 27:60). In either case, the floor would be leveled, and shelves for the bodies cut into the walls. The tomb was located outside the village, so that the living would not become ritually defiled by contact with dead bodies (Num. 19:16; cf. Matt. 23:27; Luke 11:44). It was also sealed by a large round **stone,** which was rolled in front of the opening to keep grave robbers and animals out.

Jesus' terse command, **"Remove the stone,"** sent Martha (who by now had joined Mary and the other mourners) into a state of panic. She still did not understand that the Lord intended to raise Lazarus. Her concern was that her brother's corpse, after **four days** in the tomb, would have begun to decompose. The Jews did not embalm, but used aromatic spices to temporarily mask the odor of decay. After four days, however, the **stench** coming out of an opened grave and a rotting corpse would have overpowered the aroma of the spices.

Martha evidently assumed that Jesus wanted to take one last look at the body of His friend. She, however, was horrified at the thought of seeing (and smelling) her beloved brother's body in a state of decomposition, or of having his body viewed publicly in that condition. In her mind it was too late for Jesus to do anything for Lazarus; He had not arrived in time (v. 21). Since her brother had already **been dead four days** (the perfect tense of the participle indicates she believed that Lazarus had entered into a permanent state of death), Martha had given up all hope.

THE PROMISE

Jesus said to her, "Did I not say to you that if you believe, you will see the glory of God?" (11:40)

Martha's despair elicited a response from **Jesus** designed partly to give her hope, and partly as a gentle rebuke. The text does not record the Lord making this exact statement to Martha in their prior conversation (vv. 20–28). Therefore He may have been referring to an earlier remark that does not appear in Scripture, or this statement may have been intended as a composite of verse 4 (His words there were no doubt reported to Mary and Martha) and verses 23–26.

In either case, Jesus' reminder challenged Martha to stop being concerned about her brother's body and to start focusing on Him. The Lord promised her that if she would **believe** she would see **the glory of God** revealed. That did not, of course, make the miracle dependent on her faith. It was a sovereign act of Christ, designed to glorify Himself and the Father by putting His resurrection power on display. Consequently it would have happened no matter how Martha had responded. But though all present would see the miracle, only those who had faith in Christ would see the fullness of God's glory reflected in it. Leon Morris explains,

> For [Jesus] the "glory of God" was the one important thing. This means that the real meaning of what He would do would be accessible only to faith. All who were there, believers or not, would see the miracle. But Jesus is promising Martha a sight of the glory. The crowd would see the miracle, but only believers would perceive its real significance, the glory. (*The Gospel According to John*, The New International Commentary on the New Testament [Grand Rapids: Eerdmans, 1979], 560)

THE PRAYER

So they removed the stone. Then Jesus raised His eyes, and said, "Father, I thank You that You have heard Me. I knew that You always hear Me; but because of the people standing around I said it, so that they may believe that You sent Me." (11:41–42)

Reassured by the Lord's promise, Martha gave her consent, and some of the bystanders **removed the stone** from the entrance to the tomb. Jesus, of course, did not need their help; a stone is no obstacle for the One who has the power to raise the dead. It may be, as the church father Chrysostom thought (Morris, *John*, p. 360 n. 79), that Jesus involved the bystanders so there would be no doubt that it was really Lazarus who was raised (cf. 9:9).

Jesus was not asking the Father to raise Lazarus, but thanking Him that He had already **heard** and granted His request, just as He **always** heard Him. In contrast to the Jewish practice of His day, Jesus addressed God directly as **Father** (e.g., 12:28; 17:1, 5, 11, 21, 24–25; Matt. 11:25–26; 26:39, 42; Luke 23:34, 46). The prayer was not for Jesus' benefit, but so **the people standing around** would **believe that** He had been **sent** by the Father (cf. 4:34; 5:23–24, 30, 36–38; 6:29, 38–39, 44, 57; 7:16, 18, 28–29, 33; 8:16, 18, 26, 29, 42; 9:4; 10:36; 12:44–45, 49; 13:3, 20; 14:24; 15:21; 16:5, 27; 17:3, 8, 18, 21, 23, 25; 20:21; Matt. 10:40; Mark 9:37; Luke 4:43; 10:16). It was a public affirmation of Jesus' mission and unity with the Father, which would soon be authenticated by the raising of Lazarus.

THE POWER

When He had said these things, He cried out with a loud voice, "Lazarus, come forth." The man who had died came forth, bound hand and foot with wrappings, and his face was wrapped around with a cloth. Jesus said to them, "Unbind him, and let him go." (11:43–44)

Having concluded His prayer, Jesus called Lazarus back to life. The text emphasizes the loudness of His command; the verb *kraugazō* (**cried out**) in itself means "to shout," or "to speak with a loud voice," even without the added phrase **a loud voice.** Why Jesus **cried out with a loud voice** is not expressly stated. It may have symbolized the power it took to raise the dead. Or He may have done it to distance Himself from the whispered mutterings of sorcerers and magicians (cf. Isa. 8:19). In any case, His voice immediately captured the complete attention of everyone present.

It has often been observed that the Lord's power is so great that had He not addressed **Lazarus** by name, all the dead in all the graves would have come forth. One day in the future, that is precisely what will happen. Earlier in John's gospel Jesus said, "Do not marvel at this; for an hour is coming, in which all who are in the tombs will hear His voice, and will come forth; those who did the good deeds to a resurrection of life, those who committed the evil deeds to a resurrection of judgment" (5:28–29). Jesus' raising of Lazarus was a preview of the divine power He will display when He raises all the dead on the last day.

The actual wording of Jesus' command was succinct, terse, almost abrupt in its simplicity. The Greek text literally reads, "Lazarus! Here! Outside!" Stumbling blindly toward the familiar, beloved voice that called him, **the man who had died came forth.** In contrast to the circuslike atmosphere that marks the performances of modern "faith healers" (who in any case cannot raise the dead), there was no showmanship, theatrics, or hype. Jesus was content to let His divine power speak for itself. At His command the king of terrors (Job 18:14) yielded up his lawful captive; the grave was robbed of its victory (1 Cor. 15:55);

the door of death and Hades was unlocked by the One who alone holds the keys (Rev. 1:18).

The onlookers stared in shocked amazement as the strange apparition, **bound hand and foot with wrappings,** with **his face wrapped around with a cloth** (cf. 20:7), shuffled his way to the door of the tomb. (In keeping with Jewish burial custom, Lazarus's body was loosely wrapped in strips of cloth, which allowed him to walk awkwardly on his own.) Some of the bystanders likely fled in panic, bewildered and unnerved by the startling scene.

After the miracle, Jesus immediately gave the practical command to **unbind** Lazarus **and let him go** (note His equally practical order to give Jairus's daughter something to eat after He raised her [Mark 5:43]). "Jesus was never so carried away by the wonder of His miracles that He forgot the needs of the person" (Morris, *John*, 562).

And with that John draws a curtain on the scene. He does not describe Lazarus's tearful reunion with Martha and Mary, or the stunned reactions of the people in the crowd. Nor does he report on Lazarus's experience after resurrection. All of that would have detracted from his reasons for recounting the miracle—that the Lord Jesus Christ might be glorified (v. 4) and that the readers of John's gospel might believe that Jesus is who He claimed to be (20:31).

There is significance in Jesus' involving the bystanders in touching and unwrapping Lazarus: "The very mourners who doubted [Jesus] were agents in the completion of the miracle. In their participation the mourners in fact became part of the sign and therefore were undeniable witnesses to the power of Jesus" (Gerald L. Borchert, *John 1–11*, The New American Commentary [Nashville: Broadman & Holman, 2002], 363).

Although it was the climactic miraculous sign of Jesus' earthly ministry, the raising of Lazarus "could be only a pale anticipation of what was yet to come" (D. A. Carson, *The Gospel According to John*, The Pillar New Testament Commentary [Grand Rapids: Eerdmans, 1991], 419). Just a short time later, Jesus would Himself rise from the dead (Matt. 28:1–8; Mark 16:1–8; Luke 24:1–11; John 20:1–10; Acts 2:30–33; 1 Cor. 15:1–11). Lazarus rose with a mortal, corruptible body that would one day die again. But Jesus Christ rose as the conqueror of death who is "the first fruits of all who are asleep. . . . For as in Adam all die, so also in Christ all will be made alive" (1 Cor. 15:20–22). Because of His resurrection, all believers (including Lazarus) will one day receive glorified, incorruptible bodies. Then, Paul writes, "this perishable will have put on the imperishable, and this mortal will have put on immortality, then will come about the saying that is written, 'Death is swallowed up in victory'" (1 Cor. 15:54).

41

The Resurrection and the Life— Part Four: Reactions to the Resurrection of Lazarus
(John 11:45–57)

Therefore many of the Jews who came to Mary, and saw what He had done, believed in Him. But some of them went to the Pharisees and told them the things which Jesus had done. Therefore the chief priests and the Pharisees convened a council, and were saying, "What are we doing? For this man is performing many signs. If we let Him go on like this, all men will believe in Him, and the Romans will come and take away both our place and our nation." But one of them, Caiaphas, who was high priest that year, said to them, "You know nothing at all, nor do you take into account that it is expedient for you that one man die for the people, and that the whole nation not perish." Now he did not say this on his own initiative, but being high priest that year, he prophesied that Jesus was going to die for the nation, and not for the nation only, but in order that He might also gather together into one the children of God who are scattered abroad. So from that day on they planned together to kill Him. Therefore Jesus no longer continued to walk publicly among the Jews, but went away from there to the country near the wilderness, into a city called Ephraim; and there He stayed with the disciples. Now the Passover of the Jews was near, and many went up to Jerusalem out of

the country before the Passover to purify themselves. So they were seeking for Jesus, and were saying to one another as they stood in the temple, "What do you think; that He will not come to the feast at all?" Now the chief priests and the Pharisees had given orders that if anyone knew where He was, he was to report it, so that they might seize Him. (11:45–57)

The gospel of John has rightly been called the gospel of belief. Throughout its pages, there is a clear emphasis on genuine saving faith in the Lord Jesus Christ (e.g., 1:12; 3:15–16, 18, 36; 5:24; 6:29, 35, 40, 47; 7:38; 8:24; 11:25–26; 14:1, 12; 17:8, 20–21; 19:35). As John himself stated, his purpose for writing was "so that [his readers] may believe that Jesus is the Christ, the Son of God; and that believing [they] may have life in His name" (20:31).

In keeping with that purpose, John consistently presented the claim of Jesus Christ to be God in human flesh (e.g., 5:17–47; 8:24, 58; 10:30). The Lord's seven "I AM" statements, for instance, are nothing less than emphatic declarations of His deity and messiahship (6:35; 8:12; 10:7, 9; 10:11, 14; 11:25; 14:6; 15:1, 5). As the response of the unbelieving Jews (they wanted to stone Jesus for blasphemy) indicates, they clearly were outraged because they understood exactly who He was claiming to be (5:18; 8:59; 10:31).

To authenticate His claims, Jesus performed many miraculous signs (21:25), of which seven are featured in the gospel of John (2:1–11; 4:46–54; 5:1–18; 6:1–15; 6:16–21; 9:1–41; 11:1–57; John also highlighted a post-resurrection miracle of Jesus in 21:6–11). These seven signs culminated with the Lord's spectacular display of divine power in raising Lazarus from the dead. As has been noted in earlier chapters of this volume, while the miracle strengthened believers (11:15) and substantiated Jesus' claim to be divine, its purpose was that all who would ever know of it might give glory to Jesus and the Father (11:4, 40).

Such a radical assertion (that Jesus is God) always compels people to make a decision—they can either acknowledge His claim as true or reject it as false. Essentially, those are the only two possible responses, belief or unbelief. As John states in his gospel, "He who believes in the Son has eternal life; but he who does not obey the Son will not see life, but the wrath of God abides on him" (3:36). There is no third, neutral position toward Christ; those who claim to be indifferent are in reality opposed to Him. In the words of Jesus, "He who is not with Me is against Me; and he who does not gather with Me, scatters" (Luke 11:23).

During Jesus' ministry, some of the Jews reacted to Him with open hostility. The people of His hometown of Nazareth, for example, rejected Him and even attempted to kill Him (Matt. 13:54–58; Luke 4:16–31). Others accused Him of being demon-possessed (John 7:20;

10:20), as did the religious authorities (8:48, 52). Those same leaders also attributed His miraculous power directly to Satan (Matt. 9:34; 12:24; Luke 11:15); charged Him with violating the tradition of the elders (Matt. 15:1–9); accused Him of being a blasphemer (Luke 5:21); demeaned Him for associating with the outcasts of society (5:30; 7:36–50); and accosted Him for violating their manmade Sabbath regulations (6:1–11). They disputed His authority (Matt. 21:23; John 2:18), challenged His teachings (Matt. 22:15–33; Luke 11:53–54), and ultimately plotted successfully to take His life (Matt. 26:3–5; John 7:1).

Others, perhaps the majority of the people, reacted to Jesus with apparent indifference. They were thrill seekers (6:22–31), lukewarm followers (cf. Matt. 4:25; 8:1; 13:2; Mark 5:24; Luke 5:15), and false believers (John 2:23–25; 6:60–66; 8:30–31). But Jesus condemned such spiritual coldness and indifference (cf. Rev. 3:15–16). On one occasion, He declared the indifference of Chorazin, Bethsaida, and Capernaum— three cities that had witnessed many of His miracles—to be worse than the paganism of Tyre and Sidon, and even the immorality of Sodom (Matt. 11:20–24).

But in contrast to those unbelievers who were hostile and indifferent, there was also the "little flock" (Luke 12:32) consisting of those whose faith in Jesus Christ was genuine. Among them were the Twelve (minus Judas Iscariot), who "left everything and followed" Him (Matt. 19:27), believed in Him (John 2:11; cf. 1:35–51), and affirmed Him to be "God's Son" (Matt. 14:33; cf. 16:16; John 6:69; cf. 20:28–29); the repentant chief tax collector Zaccheus (Luke 19:1–10); some of the Samaritans in the little village of Sychar (John 4:5ff.); a royal official (and his household) whose son Jesus healed (4:53); a blind man whose sight Jesus restored (9:35–38); and many to whom He ministered across the Jordan River in Perea (10:42).

The various reactions of the Jewish people to Jesus after He raised Lazarus from the dead are typical responses. In verses 45–57 the responses of faith, hostility, and indifference are all represented. Thus we meet the many (who display faith), the murderers (who display hostility), and the multitudes (who display indifference).

THE MANY

Therefore many of the Jews who came to Mary, and saw what He had done, believed in Him. (11:45)

Why only **Mary** is mentioned is not clear. Perhaps she, being the more emotional of the two sisters (cf. vv. 31–33), required more consoling than Martha did. Or Mary may have had a wider circle of acquaintances than her sister, or been considered the more "spiritual." Whatever the reason they came to her, it was because of the raising of Lazarus that **many of the Jews who** had witnessed the miracle **believed in Him.** They not only **saw** it with their eyes, but also contemplated it with their minds, noted its significance, and drew the only right conclusion from it.

The statement that they **believed in Him** is simple but critical, since saving faith is always placed in the Lord Jesus Christ and no other, as John emphasized throughout his gospel (1:12; 2:11; 3:16, 18, 36; 4:39; 6:29, 35, 40; 7:31, 38–39; 9:35–36; 10:42; 11:25–26; 12:44, 46; 14:1, 12; cf. 1 John 3:23; 5:10, 13). Christ alone is "the way, and the truth, and the life; no one comes to the Father but through [Him]" (John 14:6), because "there is salvation in no one else; for there is no other name under heaven that has been given among men by which we must be saved" (Acts 4:12).

It is, however, also true that not everyone who believed in Jesus manifested true saving faith (cf. 2:23–25; 6:66; 8:30–31; James 2:19). Nonetheless, the faith of these individuals (in 11:45) appears to have been genuine for several reasons. First, verses 49–52 refer to Christ's death resulting in salvation for His people—a salvation that, in context, seems to include this group of Jews who believed in Him. Second, Jesus' primary reason for raising Lazarus was to glorify Himself and the Father (vv. 4, 40), and the Lord is glorified when people truly believe and are saved (2 Cor. 4:15). Third, the Jewish authorities evidently viewed these people as genuine followers of Jesus Christ (v. 48); they saw them as a legitimate threat to their hypocritical religious authority. Fourth, those who are said to believe are contrasted with the unbelievers who reported the incident to the Pharisees (v. 46); the apostle John makes a clear distinction between the two groups. Finally, though faith based solely on Jesus' miracles was not always genuine (2:23), this miracle was so powerful and convincing that it was unlikely to have produced shallow, superficial believers.

THE MURDERERS

But some of them went to the Pharisees and told them the things which Jesus had done. Therefore the chief priests and the Pharisees convened a council, and were saying, "What are we doing? For this man is performing many signs. If we let Him go on like this, all men will believe in Him, and the Romans will come and take away both our place and our nation." But one of them, Caiaphas, who was high priest that year, said to them, "You know nothing at all, nor do you take into account that it is expedient for

you that one man die for the people, and that the whole nation not perish." Now he did not say this on his own initiative, but being high priest that year, he prophesied that Jesus was going to die for the nation, and not for the nation only, but in order that He might also gather together into one the children of God who are scattered abroad. So from that day on they planned together to kill Him. Therefore Jesus no longer continued to walk publicly among the Jews, but went away from there to the country near the wilderness, into a city called Ephraim; and there He stayed with the disciples. (11:46–54)

Jesus' words and actions frequently caused division among those who heard and witnessed them (cf. vv. 36–37; 7:12, 43; 9:16; 10:19–21); as He Himself said, "Do you suppose that I came to grant peace on earth? I tell you, no, but rather division" (Luke 12:51). While many believed in Jesus, having seen the true significance of Lazarus's resurrection (v. 45), **some** did not. Instead they **went to the Pharisees** to tell them what **Jesus had done.**

Some commentators argue that these individuals **went to the Pharisees** because they were perplexed, or to try to win the Jewish leaders over. But since they are contrasted with the many who believed (v. 45), and they surely knew of the Pharisees' bitter hatred for Jesus (cf. 7:13), their intent was likely hostile. They had been unbelievers before the miracle and, incredibly, remained so afterward. Homer Kent observes,

> This response of unbelief in the face of the clearest proof is confirmation of Christ's teaching in Luke 16:31: "If they hear not Moses and the prophets, neither will they be persuaded, though one rose from the dead." The chief cause of unbelief is not inadequate information, but a heart in rebellion against the authority of God and his word. (*Light in the Darkness: Studies in the Gospel of John* [Grand Rapids: Baker, 1977], 152)

That they **told** the Pharisees **the things which Jesus had done** further confirms their hostility to Him, because "those who believed would no doubt want to stay with Jesus, whereas the skeptics would be desirous of letting the religious authorities know what had happened so that they could take the necessary action" (Merrill C. Tenney, "The Gospel of John," in Frank E. Gaebelein, ed., *The Expositor's Bible Commentary* [Grand Rapids: Zondervan, 1981], 9:121–22).

It is not surprising that they sought out the Pharisees instead of the Sadducees. As the experts in the law, as teachers and leaders of the synagogue, the Pharisees had more contact with the common people than the aristocratic Sadducees. Nonetheless, the Sadducees would soon be involved with the Pharisees in finding a way to silence Jesus (vv. 47–52). By informing the Pharisees about Jesus' actions, these unbelievers evidenced their own stubborn hard-heartedness. Their response demonstrates that no amount of evidence, even something as spectacular as the raising of a dead man, can convince some sinners to abandon their hypocrisy and sin to come to the Savior.

Alarmed by the news of the most astonishing miracle yet performed by Christ, and understanding the public effect of it, the Pharisees were galvanized into action. They did not have the authority to act on their own (since the Sadducees were the majority party and controlled the Sanhedrin), so along with some of **the chief priests** (former high priests and members of important priestly families) **the Pharisees convened** a meeting of the full **council** (the Sanhedrin). The Sanhedrin was the ruling body of Israel and had wide-ranging authority in civil and criminal, as well as religious, matters (though the Romans withheld the right of capital punishment [18:31]). (For more information on the Sanhedrin, see the exposition of 3:1 in chapter 8 of this volume.)

The Pharisees and Sadducees normally did not get along, as they had little in common. The Pharisees were devoted to the Law (both the inspired Old Testament Scriptures and their human traditions); the Sadducees accepted only the Pentateuch as authoritative. The Pharisees affirmed the resurrection of bodies and the existence of angels, both of which the Sadducees rejected (Matt. 22:23; Acts 23:8). The Pharisees were ultranationalists and chafed under the yoke of Rome; the Sadducees were compromising political opportunists. The Pharisees were primarily from the middle class of Jewish society; the Sadducees tended to be wealthy aristocrats. (For more information on the Pharisees and Sadducees, see the exposition of 3:1 in chapter 8 of this volume.) But despite their differences, their mutual hatred for Jesus drove them to take joint action against Him. What brought them together was the threat Jesus posed to their power and influence.

There was only one item on the meeting's agenda: what to do about Him. The question that opened the meeting, **"What are we doing?"** or "What are we accomplishing?" (NIV) could also be rendered "What shall we do?" (NKJV). Both meanings are appropriate; if the question is taken in the first sense, the answer was, "Not very much!" in light of the Lord's popularity (cf. 12:19). And as to what they should do, they would soon hear a sinister proposal from their leader (vv. 49–53).

The Sanhedrin's concern was that Jesus was **performing many signs,** and **if** they **let Him go on** doing them, **all men** would **believe in Him** (cf. 12:19), **and the Romans** would **come and take away both** their **place** (the temple [cf. Acts 6:13–14; 21:28]; symbolic of their authority, power, and privilege) **and** their **nation** (the Jewish people). That even

Jesus' most bitter enemies did not deny His miracles offers convincing proof of their authenticity. But despite their admission that He was **performing many signs,** they refused to believe in Him as Messiah and Lord, choosing instead to hold to their damning hypocrisy and eliminate Him. They were masters at deliberately ignoring the evidence, as they had earlier done when Jesus healed a man born blind (9:1–41). The old adage that there are none so blind as those who will not see was certainly true in their case (cf. 9:39–41).

For the Sanhedrin, Jesus threatened the status quo. Its members were not judging the situation based on objective standards of right and wrong, but by how they would be affected. If Jesus' miraculous signs ignited the fervent messianic passions of the Jewish people (cf. 6:15), the Sanhedrin could lose everything. That danger was especially grave, they knew, since the Passover was approaching and Jerusalem would be packed with huge crowds of zealous pilgrims. If the Roman governor got wind of a potential uprising, his response would be swift and harsh— Pilate had already demonstrated his capacity for ruthlessness (Luke 13:1). Rome did not tolerate insurrection (as the Jews would learn a few decades later when the Romans crushed their revolt and sacked Jerusalem); any uprising would be brutally put down. But in this as in everything else, His opponents completely misjudged Jesus; He had not come to incite a revolution (cf. 18:36; Matt. 22:21), but "to seek and to save that which was lost" (Luke 19:10). (It is not until He returns to earth at His second coming that He will vanquish all rulers, set up His earthly kingdom, and rule as King of kings and Lord of lords [Rev. 20:1–6].)

With the Sanhedrin unsure of its next move, **Caiaphas, who was high priest that year,** proposed a radical direction. Joseph Caiaphas had been appointed high priest in A.D 18 by the Roman prefect Valerius Gratus. He would continue in office until he was deposed in A.D. 36. He was the son-in-law of Annas, who had served as high priest from A.D. 6–15 and still retained a great deal of power and influence (cf. 18:22; Luke 3:2). John's note that he **was high priest that year** does not imply that John mistakenly believed that high priests served only for one year. It merely means that Caiaphas was the high priest at that time. Theoretically, a high priest served for life. By the first century, however, the office had become heavily politicized, with the Romans frequently removing those high priests who displeased them. Caiaphas's tenure as high priest was actually one of the longest in the first century, a tribute to his political acumen and his conniving and opportunistic nature.

His opening remark, **"You know nothing at all,"** was not designed to win friends or flatter his colleagues. It typified the kind of rude, boorish behavior that, according to the first-century Jewish historian Josephus, characterized the Sadducees. "The behavior of the Sadducees one toward another is in some degree wild," he wrote, "and their conduct with those who are of their own party is as barbarous as if they were strangers to them" (*The Wars of the Jews,* 2.166. It should be remembered, however, that Josephus was a Pharisee and thus hardly an unbiased observer). Caiaphas was frustrated by the indecision of the rest of the Sanhedrin; in response to their hesitancy he proposed a radical, thoroughly ruthless solution—one in keeping with his character.

His proposal was death. **"It is expedient,"** he told them, **"that one man die for the people, and that the whole nation not perish."** He presented them with a false either/or dilemma, giving them two extreme alternatives as if there were no other options. Either Jesus dies, Caiaphas argued, or the nation perishes. His outward veneer of patriotic concern masked his seething hatred and jealousy of Jesus. Such pious hypocrisy would reach its apex during Jesus' trial. Caiaphas would tear his robes in feigned shock and sorrow over Jesus' "blasphemy," while secretly being delighted that he had found a way to condemn Him (Matt. 26:64–65). Ironically, though the Sanhedrin was successful in crucifying Jesus, the nation did not escape. The **whole nation** did **perish** at the hands of the Romans in the massacre of A.D. 70 and the years that followed.

The startling footnote that Caiaphas **did not say this on his own initiative** does not mean that he was forced to act against his will; he was no puppet, and was responsible for his own wicked words. But God providentially invested those words with a meaning that he did not intend. In his capacity as **high priest** and hence technically by office God's spokesman (cf. Num. 27:21; 2 Sam. 15:27), God ordained an opposite meaning when Caiaphas **prophesied that Jesus was going to die for the nation.** He spoke cynical words of political expediency, claiming that Jesus must die to preserve the Sanhedrin's power and the nation's existence. However, Caiaphas unwittingly spoke prophetically of Christ's sacrificial death (cf. 2 Cor. 5:21; 1 Peter 2:24). God sovereignly turned his wicked, blasphemous words into truth (cf. Gen. 50:20; Ps. 76:10; Prov. 16:9; 19:21; Acts 4:27–28).

While Caiaphas thought only in terms of Israel, Jesus' death was much broader in scope. It was **not** to be **for the nation only, but in order that He might also gather together into one the children of God who are scattered abroad.** From a purely Jewish perspective, **the children of God who are scattered abroad** referred to the Jews of the Diaspora, those who lived outside of Palestine. They, too, would be gathered into the body of Christ's redeemed people (cf. Acts 2:5, 41; 11:19). But in a wider sense, it referred to the salvation of the Gentiles (cf. 10:16; 12:32; Isa. 42:6; 49:6; 56:6–8; Acts 9:15; 10:1–11:18; Rom. 1:16) and their union with the Jews in the church (1 Cor. 12:13; Gal. 3:28; Eph. 2:11–18; 3:6; Col. 3:11).

The high priest's malicious proposal to execute Jesus met with the Sanhedrin's approval, **so from that day on they planned together to kill Him.** Their decision, made well before Jesus was even arrested, rendered His later trial a total mockery. It was a mere formality, confirming a sentence that had already been passed.

In the wake of the Sanhedrin's decision to put Him to death, **Jesus no longer continued to walk publicly among the Jews, but went away from there to the country near the wilderness, into a city called Ephraim; and there He stayed with the disciples.** Whether He exercised His omniscience on this occasion, or was informed of the Sanhedrin's decision by one of its members who was sympathetic to Him (such as Nicodemus [John 7:50] or Joseph of Arimathea [Mark 15:43]), or both, Jesus became aware of the decision and took appropriate action. The Lord remained in absolute control of the circumstances, and would not allow Himself to be taken before the appointed time in God's plan (7:8, 30, 44; 8:20; 11:9–10). "To those with eyes to see he was making a theological statement: no human court could force him to the cross" (D. A. Carson, *The Gospel According to John*, The Pillar New Testament Commentary (Grand Rapids: Eerdmans, 1991), 423).

The **city called Ephraim** to which Jesus went and **stayed with the disciples** is probably to be identified with the Old Testament city of Ephron (2 Chron. 13:19). It was located about four miles northeast of Bethel on the edge of the **wilderness,** and about a dozen miles from Jerusalem. From there Jesus would make a brief visit to Samaria and Galilee (Luke 17:11–19:28) before returning to Jerusalem for the Passover at the appointed time for His passion (John 12:23).

THE MULTITUDES

Now the Passover of the Jews was near, and many went up to Jerusalem out of the country before the Passover to purify themselves. So they were seeking for Jesus, and were saying to one another as they stood in the temple, "What do you think; that He will not come to the feast at all?" Now the chief priests and the Pharisees had given orders that if anyone knew where He was, he was to report it, so that they might seize Him. (11:55–57)

This is the third and final **Passover** mentioned in John's gospel (2:13; 6:4). As required by the Law (cf. Num. 9:6), **many went up to Jerusalem out of the country before the Passover to purify themselves.** Jerusalem was crowded well before Passover began;

some estimate that more than a million people packed the city during the three major feasts (Andreas J. Köstenberger, *John*, Baker Exegetical Commentary on the New Testament [Grand Rapids: Baker, 2004], 354). It is bitterly ironic that the people zealously purified themselves "while their leaders had indelibly stained themselves as they ruthlessly plotted the death of the blameless Son of God" (Gerald L. Borchert, *John 1–11*, The New American Commentary [Nashville: Broadman & Holman, 2002], 368).

The huge crowds that gathered in Jerusalem eagerly **were seeking for Jesus, and were saying to one another as they stood in the temple, "What do you think; that He will not come to the feast at all?"** Would He dare show Himself in Jerusalem, they wondered, since **the chief priests and the Pharisees had given orders that if anyone knew where He was, he was to report it, so that they might seize Him?** They showed intense interest in Jesus, but no commitment. They were, in fact, ultimately indifferent to Him; many who eagerly anticipated Jesus' arrival and hailed Him as Messiah would soon cry out, "Away with Him, away with Him, crucify Him!" (19:15). Their fickle devotion proved that, despite their superficial concern, they were actually just as hard-hearted as their hostile leaders.

The resurrection of Lazarus, like the rest of Christ's life and ministry, forced people to a decision about Him. Many responded in faith; others were indifferent; and some were murderously hostile. As Jesus' final Passover drew near, it would not be long before those who were indifferent and those who were hostile would unite to crucify the Lord of glory (1 Cor. 2:8).

Bibliography

Barclay, William. *The Gospel of John*. Volume 1. Louisville: Westminster John Knox, 2001.

_____. *The Gospel of John*. Volume 2. Louisville: Westminster John Knox, 2001.

Borchert, Gerald L. *John 1–11*. The New American Commentary. Nashville: Broadman & Holman, 2002.

Bruce, F. F. *The Gospel of John*. Grand Rapids: Eerdmans, 1983.

Calvin, John. *John*. The Crossway Classic Commentaries. Alister McGrath and J. I. Packer, eds. Wheaton, Ill.: Crossway, 1994.

Carson, D. A. *The Gospel According to John*. The Pillar New Testament Commentary. Grand Rapids: Eerdmans, 1991.

Carson, D. A., Douglas J. Moo, and Leon Morris. *An Introduction to the New Testament*. Grand Rapids: Zondervan, 1992.

Guthrie, Donald. *New Testament Introduction*. Revised edition, Downers Grove, Ill.: InterVarsity, 1990.

Heading, John. *What the Bible Teaches: John*. Kilmarnock, Scotland: John Ritchie, 1988.

Hendriksen, William. *The Gospel According to John*. Volume 1. Grand Rapids: Baker, 1953.

_____.*The Gospel According to John.* Volume 2. Grand Rapids: Baker, 1954.

Hiebert, D. Edmond. *An Introduction to the Gospels and Acts.* Chicago: Moody, 1975.

Kent, Homer A. *Light in the Darkness: Studies in the Gospel of John.* Grand Rapids: Baker, 1974.

Köstenberger, Andreas J. *John.* Baker Exegetical Commentary on the New Testament. Grand Rapids: Baker, 2004.

Kruse, Colin. *The Gospel According to John.* The Tyndale New Testament Commentaries. Grand Rapids: Eerdmans, 2003.

Lenski, R. C. H. *The Interpretation of St. John's Gospel.* Reprint. Peabody, Mass.: Hendrickson, 1998.

MacArthur, *John.* "The Gospel According to John." In The MacArthur Bible Commentary. Nashville: Thomas Nelson, 2005.

_____.*Twelve Ordinary Men.* Nashville: W Publishing Group, 2002.

Michaels, J. Ramsey. *John.* New International Biblical Commentary. Peabody, Mass.: Hendrickson, 1989.

Morris, Leon. *The Gospel According to John.* The New International Commentary on the New Testament. Grand Rapids: Eerdmans, 1979.

Tasker, R. V. G. *The Gospel According to St. John.* The Tyndale New Testament Commentaries. Grand Rapids: Eerdmans, 1975.

Tenney, Merrill C. "The Gospel of John," in Frank E. Gaebelein, ed. *The Expositor's Bible Commentary.* Volume 9. Grand Rapids: Zondervan, 1981.

Towns, Elmer. *The Gospel of John.* Twenty-first Century Biblical Commentary Series. Chattanooga, Tenn.: AMG, 2002.

Wallace, Daniel B. "The Gospel of John: Introduction, Argument, Outline." Biblical Studies Press, www.bible.org, 1999.

Westcott, B. F. *The Gospel According to St. John.* Reprint. Grand Rapids: Eerdmans, 1978.

Indexes

Index of Greek Words and Phrases

Index of Scripture

Index of Subjects

Dana,H.E.,18
Darkness,spiritual,23–24
David,27–33,48,60,92,118,123–25,
137–38,207,224,291,309–10,
365–66,423–30,450
Davidic covenant,123–25
Day of Pentecost,266. *See also* Pente-
cost
Day of the Lord,29
Demas,267
Demons and demon-possession,1–2,
23–28,95,137,171–72,182,
379–80,435
Devil.*See* Satan
Diaspora,5
Didymus,456–57.*See also* Thomas
Dionysius of Alexandria,4
Disciples
definition of,357–58
faithless,221–23
true vs. false,227–38
Dishonor,of Jesus Christ,378–82
Divine timetable,275–84
Docetists,40
Dods,Marcus,14,129
Door and doorkeeper,Jesus as,421–36
Dorcas,388–89
Douglas,J.D.,128
Dying to sin,teachings on,341–50

Eadie,John,197
Edwards,Jonathan,240
Egerton Papyrus 2,4–5,9
Eleazar,453.*See also* Lazarus
Elect,183,253–54
Eli,17
Elijah/Elias,17,27–29,51–53,83–86,
132,154,189,209,376
Elisha,83,154,189,388
Elizabeth,29,48
Enlightenment,352
Erickson,Millard J.,253
Essenes,325–26
Eternal life,114–17,265–74. *See also*
Bread of Life
Eusebius,3–4,7,9,40–41,87–88
Euthymius Zigabenus,323
Eutychus,388–89

Eve,110,342,376
Exegesis,46
Existentialism and existentialists,182
Expected One.*See* Messiah,Jesus
Christ as

Fall of Adam,20–21,76,110,175,342,
388
False doctrines,260
False messiahs.*See* Pseudo-messiahs
False teachers,293
Feast days and Holy days
Feast of Passover.*See* Passover
Feast of Tabernacles (Booths),5,
278–81,288,300–302,
311–12,334
Feast of the Dedication (Feast of
Lights),5,438–41
Feast of Unleavened Bread,88–89
Fig tree,73
First and Last,14
Flesh,13–15,39,97–99,257–60,337–39

Gabriel,49,49
Gaebelein,Frank E.,481,488
Garden of Eden,342,376
Gideon,212
Gnostics,4,20
God-Man,38
Godspell, 182
Goliath,224
Good man,25
Gospel of John
authorship of,3–9
background and historical per-
spectives of,*vii–viii,*1–12
date and place of writing of,9
purposes of,9–10
Gospel of Thomas,4
Grace,42–43
Great Awakening,240
Great White Throne judgment,199.*See
also* Judgments
Gundry,Stanley,N.,7
Guthrie,Donald,487

Hades,343–44
Hammurabi,48

Titles in the
MacArthur New Testament Commentary Series

MOODY
PUBLISHERS

THE NAME YOU CAN TRUST.

1-800-678-6928 www.MoodyPublishers.org